Malerei: Prozess und Expansion. Von den 1950er-Jahren bis heute
Painting: Process and Expansion. From the 1950s to the Present Day

Diese Publikation erscheint anlässlich der Ausstellung *Malerei: Prozess und Expansion. Von den 1950er-Jahren bis heute*
im Museum Moderner Kunst Stiftung Ludwig Wien (9. Juli 2010 bis 3. Oktober 2010)
This catalogue has been published on the occasion of the exhibition *Painting: Process and Expansion. From the 1950s to the Present Day*
at the Museum Moderner Kunst Stiftung Ludwig Wien (July 9th 2010 – October 3rd 2010)

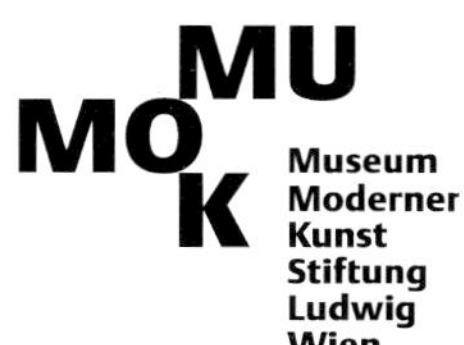

Malerei: Prozess und Expansion
Von den 1950er-Jahren bis heute

Painting: Process and Expansion
From the 1950s to the Present Day

Herausgegeben von / Edited by
Museum Moderner Kunst Stiftung Ludwig Wien
Edelbert Köb

Verlag der Buchhandlung Walther König, Köln / Cologne

Inhalt / Contents

Vorwort

Aus der Sammlung

Die Ausstellung vertieft und präzisiert zwei zentrale Aspekte der Entwicklung abstrakter Nachkriegsmalerei: Malerei als prozessuales, selbstreflexives Medium sowie die mit der Auflösung des Bildes einhergehende Expansion der Malerei in objekthafte und räumliche Bezüge. Prozessuale Malerei wird als Versuch vorgestellt, Bildgestaltung primär aus den fundamentalen Eigenschaften und Reaktionsweisen der Farben zu entwickeln und nicht aus narrativen oder kompositionellen Vorstellungen. Durch An- und Zumalen, Zuspachteln, Drippen, Spritzen, Eintauchen oder Anschütten entstehen kreativ gelenkte Selbstdarstellungen von Malerei, in denen die Konsistenz der Farbe in ihrem Verhältnis zur Schwerkraft oder zur Beschaffenheit des Bildgrundes sichtbar wird. Grundgelegt waren solche Ansätze in der gestisch-prozessualen Malerei des Informel, deren zunehmende Entleerung zur pathetisch-akademischen Attitüde aber zum Gegenbild dieser neuen, selbstreflexiven Malerei wurde.

Der zweite Teil der Ausstellung verfolgt die in den 1950er-Jahren einsetzende Erweiterung und Auflösung des klassischen Malereibegriffes. Diese Geschichte lässt sich als Eroberung des Raumes durch die Malerei sowie als deren Transformation in installative und objekthafte Szenarien nachzeichnen. Die in der Pop-Art, in der Minimal und Concept-Art sowie im Fluxus formulierte Kritik am historischen Bild- und Kompositionsbegriff führte zu einer radikalen Neubestimmung von Malerei und Bild in ihrem Verhältnis zum Raum und zum Betrachter. Der Bogen der gezeigten Werke spannt sich in beiden Themen von bereits historischen Positionen der 1960er- und 1970er-Jahre bis in die jüngste Vergangenheit und Gegenwart.

Malerei: Prozess und Expansion ist eine Ausstellung aus der Sammlung. Ihre Themen wurden aus dem Bestand der Sammlung beziehungsweise aus vorhandenen Schwerpunkten entwickelt. Daraus erklären sich die rigide Fokussierung auf den speziellen Aspekt des Prozessualen im Rahmen der klassischen Topoi von Bild und Malerei einerseits und andererseits die weite Öffnung des malerischen Spektrums in alle erdenklichen Grenzbereiche und -überschreitungen. Damit werden zwei sowohl gegensätzliche wie sich vielfach überschneidende relevante Entwicklungen der abstraktiven Malerei nach 1945 in ihren Konturen abgesteckt. Die Breite und Intensität der hier angeschnittenen Diskurse, in die zahlreiche österreichische Künstler mehrerer Generationen involviert waren und sind, beweisen die ungebrochene Dynamik und Relevanz des so oft totgesagten Mediums, das immer noch als zentrales intellektuelles Referenzfeld der heutigen diversifizierten Kunst fungiert.

Die Zahl und die Qualität der aus der Sammlung des MUMOK stammenden Werke in der Ausstellung – oder auch die relativ wenigen Leihgaben, die notwendig waren, um thematische Entwicklungslinien und Zusammenhänge aufzuzeigen – sprechen für die Kompetenz und den Weitblick der seit den Anfängen für den Sammlungsaufbau verantwortlichen Leiter des Hauses. Andererseits machen derartige Ausstellungen Versäumnisse und Lücken schmerzlich bewusst. Sie liefern aber auch Erkenntnisse und Perspektiven für die Zukunft.

Mit der Ausstellung und dem vorliegenden Katalog, der neben den ausgestellten auch alle inhaltlich zugehörigen Werke der Sammlung sowie im Anhang alle Leihgaben enthält, wird ein vorläufiges Resümee gezogen und die Basis für eine weitere Sammlungsentwicklung in diesem Bereich gelegt. Darüber hinaus hoffen wir, damit einen relevanten, sowohl historisch fundierten als auch aktuellen Beitrag zur diskursiven Malerei geleistet zu haben.

Allen großzügigen Leihgebern und den Künstlern möchte ich auf das Herzlichste für ihre Werke und ihre Kooperationsbereitschaft danken. Den Autoren des Kataloges danke ich für ihre profunden Textbeiträge, Agnes Falkner für die Betreuung dieses Buches. Tina Lipsky danke ich stellvertretend für alle engagierten Mitarbeiter des Hauses für die Organisation der Ausstellung. Vor allem aber gilt mein Dank Rainer Fuchs, der den Bereich „Expansion" umgesetzt hat und mir in allen Belangen und Phasen des Projektes ein unersetzlicher Partner gewesen ist.

Edelbert Köb
Direktor, Kurator
Museum Moderner Kunst Stiftung Ludwig Wien

Preface

From the Collection

The exhibition explores and clarifies two central aspects of the development of post-war abstract art: the idea of painting as a processual, self-reflexive medium and its expansion to include space-related and object-related forms of painting—a development that has gone hand in hand with the dissolution of the picture. Processual painting is presented as an attempt to develop images primarily from the fundamental properties and reactions of paint rather than from narrative or compositional ideas. Such practices as dabbing or daubing, slathering on paint with a palette knife, dripping, squirting, throwing or splashing paint, or even submerging the canvas in the medium gave rise to creatively guided self-representations of painting that made visible, for example, the relationship between the consistency of paint and, for example, the forces of gravity, the surface texture of the support and so on. The groundwork for such approaches was laid by the gestural, processual painting style of art informel, whose increasing degradation into an affective and academic pose ultimately made it the antithesis of this new self-reflexive type of painting.

The second part of the exhibition traces the inflation and dissolution of the classical concept of painting that started in the 1950s. This historical narrative can be read both as the conquest of space by painting, and as the transformation of painting into objects and installations. The critique of the traditional concept of the painting and of composition articulated by pop art, minimal and concept art, and Fluxus led to a radical redefinition of painting and the picture in relation to space and to the observer. The spectrum of works on show range from those that can already be deemed historical to the ultra-contemporary, spanning both the 1960s and 1970s and continuing right through to the present day.

The works included in *Painting: Process and Expansion* are drawn from our collection, and the themes of the exhibition grew out of existing emphases in the holdings. This explains the clear focus on the special aspect of the processual within the framework of the classical topoi of the picture and painting, on the one hand, and, on the other, on the way in which painting has been pushing boundaries in every conceivable transitional and transgressional direction. What the exhibition stakes out are two key developments in post-1945 abstract art—developments that at times intersect and at times are antithetical. Numerous Austrian artists spanning several generations have participated in the discourse outlined here and they continue to do so to this day. The breadth and intensity of what they have to say testify to the unbroken dynamism and relevance of painting, which having so often been declared dead, continues to thrive as the central intellectual frame of reference for contemporary art in all its many guises.

The number and quality of works in the exhibition that come from MUMOK's own collection, and hence the relatively small number of loans that were necessary to illustrate thematic developments and interrelationships, speak for the competence and far-sightedness of the directors who have been responsible for building up MUMOK's collection since its inception. And if exhibitions of this kind also make us painfully aware of various gaps and omissions, they nonetheless provide us with some useful insights and ideas for the future.

The exhibition and the catalog—which includes illustrations of all the MUMOK works featured in the exhibition as well as other thematically relevant works from the collection, and an appendix with illustrations of all the works on loan—take stock of the present state of the collection and in doing so provide a basis for further development in this area. In addition, we hope to have made a significant, historically underpinned, and at the same time up-to-date contribution to the subject of discursive painting.

I would like to thank both the generous lenders and the artists themselves who kindly agreed to make their works available to us. Thanks are also due to the authors of the insightful essays in this catalog and to Agnes Falkner for overseeing its publication. I would like to thank Tina Lipsky and indeed all the committed museum staff for organizing the exhibition. My greatest thanks, however, are reserved for Rainer Fuchs, who was in charge of the Expansion section and who has been my indispensable partner in all aspects and phases of the project.

Edelbert Köb
Director, Curator
Museum Moderner Kunst Stiftung Ludwig Wien

Prozess / Process

Edelbert Köb

Malerei über Malerei. Kuratorische Ergänzungen
Painting about Painting: A Postscript

Dieser Text zum Ausstellungteil „Malerei – Prozess"
macht den Versuch, „Leerstellen" zwischen den profunden theoretischen Katalogbeiträgen mehrerer
Autoren und der finalen Realität der Ausstellung zu
füllen. Einer ihnen immanenten Logik folgend, entwickeln und verändern sich Ausstellungen oft bis
zum Eröffnungstag, während Texte meist eine län-
gere Vorlaufzeit haben. So hat etwa der titelgebende
Begriff des Prozessualen erst durch die Ausstellung
selbst eine Präzisierung erfahren. Das Prozessuale
hat – weil ein Aspekt jeder Malerei, ausgenommen
vielleicht der die „Machart" verschleiernde Fotorealismus – bisher in übergreifenden Darstellungen
weder in der Literatur noch in Ausstellungen eine
Rolle gespielt. „Prozessuale Malerei" ist dement-
sprechend auch kein etablierter kunsthistorischer
Begriff, wie es die Termini „analytische", auch
„radikale" oder „essenzielle Malerei" sind, die sich
in den 1970er-Jahren herausgebildet haben. Hier
wird Malerei von und in der Nachfolge Robert
Rymans als rein materielle Tätigkeit aufgefasst und
das Gemälde als rein materieller Körper definiert.
In letzter Konsequenz bedeutet das den Verzicht auf
alle inneren Beziehungen des Bildes wie Komposition und Illusion sowie deren Substitution durch
Monochromie, Zufall und Serialität. Das definito-
rische Referenzfeld für den dieser Ausstellung zugrunde liegenden, weiter gefassten Begriff des Prozessualen ist diese radikale, selbstreferenzielle,
analytische Malerei. Das heißt aber lediglich, dass
das Mehr oder Weniger an Prozessualität jedes
Werkes von ihr aus gemessen wird. Einfacher gesagt:
Die explizite Reflexion des Mediums selbst und/oder

This article focuses on the Painting Process section of the exhibition and attempts to bridge the
gaps between the various theoretical essays in this
catalog and the final reality of the exhibition itself.
Exhibitions develop and change according to their
own immanent logic, often right up to their opening. Essays, on the other hand, tend to have a
longer lead time. Consequently, the concept of
process contained in the exhibition's title continued
to elude any exact definition until the exhibition
itself was complete. The processual character of
the medium—it being an inherent aspect of all
painting with the possible exception of photorealism that seeks to conceal the manner of its making—has not played a role in art-historical surveys
or in exhibitions up to now. Unlike the terms analytical, radical or essential painting, all of which
crystallized in the 1970s, processual painting has
never become an established art-historical term.
Painting, as practiced by Robert Ryman and others
like him, is defined here as a purely material
activity and the finished work of art as a purely
material object. In its most extreme manifestation,
it forgoes all internal pictorial relationships such
as composition and illusion, and replaces them
with the monochrome, chance and serialism. This
radical, self-referential, analytical type of painting
provides the frame of reference for the broader
definition of process underpinning this exhibition. But this only means that we have a frame
of reference with which to gauge the degree of
processuality manifested by each work. To put it
more simply, the pictures were selected primarily

according to the extent to which they explicitly reflected upon the medium of painting itself or revealed their own gestation process. This explains the inclusion of works that are generally classified as belonging to the informel movement (Pierre Soulages, fig. p. 77) or whose creators insist on the existence of their work's reality over and above its material existence (Helmut Federle, fig. p. 306, Andreas Eriksson, fig. p. 72)

This narrowing of the concept of painting in the Process section of the exhibition is intended to contrast with the much broader definition applied in both thematic areas of the Expansion section. These apparently dichotomous concepts are nevertheless closely interlinked and there are numerous works that resist easy categorization or classification because of their sheer complexity. In particular, this is especially true of the monochrome paintings. Those included in the Expansion section of the exhibition rather than in the monochrome part of the Process section are either serial variations (Alan Charlton, fig. p. 242), works in which the monochrome goes hand in hand with a dissolution of the traditional format (François Morellet, fig. p. 253), or works that are no longer suspended from the wall (Adrian Schiess, fig. p. 266). The diversity of things that appear equivalent or similar is particularly striking and a recurring feature of discursive painting. Even the finest nuancing and most decisive transgressions are part of a closed system of references. The exhibition attempts to reveal some of the most significant strands of these interrelationships. In addition, the catalog's contributors attempt to reconstruct the intensive dialog that all artists and all works hold with one another over time and space and via mysterious communication channels.

The exhibition was augmented in the final phase of its realization with loans embodying important developments in Austrian art. *Process and Expansion* will thus for the first time highlight the significant contribution of Austrian artists to international art discourse from the 1960s right up to the present day—in terms of both quality and quantity. That, too, is an aspect that requires further exploration.

die Offenlegung des Entstehungsprozesses waren die maßgeblichen Kriterien der Bildauswahl. Daraus erklärt sich die Einbeziehung von Werken, die dem Informel zuzuordnen sind (Pierre Soulages, Abb. S. 77) oder deren Autoren auf der Existenz einer Wirklichkeit des Gemäldes jenseits seiner materiellen Existenz bestehen (Helmut Federle, Abb. S. 306; Andreas Eriksson, Abb. S. 72).

Die hier vorgenommene Einengung des Malereibegriffes kontrastiert bewusst mit dessen offener Auslegung im Ausstellungsteil „Expansion" in beiden Themenfeldern. Trotzdem gibt es ein dichtes Netz von Bezügen zwischen den beiden polaren Werkbegriffen und zahlreiche Werke, die aufgrund ihrer Komplexität jeder vereinfachenden Kategorisierung und Zuordnung Widerstand leisten. Das gilt in besonderem Maß für die Monochromie, die in ihren seriellen Varianten (Alan Charlton, Abb. S. 242), wenn sie mit der Auflösung des Formats einhergeht (François Morellet, Abb. S. 253) oder wenn die Farbobjekte die Wand verlassen (Adrian Schiess, Abb. S. 266), nicht den Monochromien, sondern dem Ausstellungsteil „Expansion" zugeordnet ist. Die hier besonders eklatante Unterschiedlichkeit von gleichartig oder ähnlich Erscheinendem ist ein durchgehendes Phänomen diskursiver Malerei. Auch ihre feinsten Differenzierungen und entschlossensten Grenzüberschreitungen sind Teil eines geschlossenen Systems von Referenzen. Die Ausstellung versucht, einige signifikante Stränge des Beziehungsnetzes vorzuzeigen. Die Autoren des Katalogs versuchen darüber hinaus, den intensiven Dialogen nachzuspüren, die alle Künstler und Werke dieser Welt über Zeit und Raum und über geheimnisvolle Kommunikationskanäle miteinander führen.

In der letzten Phase der Realisierung wurde die Ausstellung noch mit zahlreichen Leihgaben wichtiger österreichischer Positionen ergänzt. Im Fokus von *Prozess und Expansion* werden dadurch erstmals auch der Umfang und die Qualität der heimischen Beiträge zu den hier verhandelten internationalen Diskursen augenscheinlich, und zwar von den 1960er-Jahren bis in die Gegenwart. Auch das ist ein Aspekt, der textlich zu ergänzen ist.

Sein und Schein

Das Back-to-the-roots der analytischen Malerei hatte die Spielräume für kreative Interpretationen sowohl eng gemacht als gleichzeitig auch Fakten geschaffen, die von den Nachkommenden nicht ignoriert werden konnten. Avancierte abstrakte Malerei hat heute zumindest *auch* prozessual zu sein, so sie nicht geometrisch-konstruktiv ist.

Am Beispiel der österreichischen Malerei der letzten 20 Jahre lässt sich geradezu exemplarisch verfolgen, wie sich Künstler im Spannungsfeld von neuen Konventionen und eigenem Ausdruckswillen noch positionieren können. Es ist interessant, dass gerade für die Generation der heute etwa 50-Jährigen, der ehemaligen so genannten „wilden" und figurativen Malerei angehörend, das Prozessuale irgendwann in ihrer Entwicklung zu einem neuen Ausgangs- und Angelpunkt ihrer Kunst geworden ist. So können beispielsweise Thomas Reinholds ausgestellte Bilder diesbezüglich als geradezu programmatisch bezeichnet werden: für das Zufallsprinzip, wenn er bei einem Atelierbrand auf ein Bild herabgefallene Neonröhren einfach integriert (Abb. S. 307); ein anderes Mal für die freigesetzte, rinnende Farbe und die Pinselspur als bilderzeugende Faktoren (Abb. S. 307). Was sich nach Yves Klein, Morris Louis, Hermann Nitsch und neben Bernard Frize noch ernsthaft aus der Schwerkraft der Farbe entwickeln lässt, demonstrieren auf völlig unterschiedliche Weise auch Christina Zurfluh (Abb. S. 311) und Andreas Reiter Raabe (Abb. S. 307). Gerade diese Ernsthaftigkeit ist es, gegen die sich Christian Eisenberger, Jahrgang 1978, stellt. Seiner Generation ist nämlich der Glaube an das autonome Bildwerk längst abhanden gekommen (Abb. S. 306). „Wieder einmal!", ist man, auf Niki de Saint Phalles Bild *Tir* von 1961 verweisend (Abb. S. 91), versucht zu sagen; und typisch für die zyklischen Entwicklungen der Kunst beziehungsweise deren Revivals von Revolutionen, Konventionen und Konterrevolutionen.

Andere Künstler pflegen einen offeneren Umgang mit dem Prozessualen. Schließt doch auch die ausdrückliche Demonstration des Malvorganges letztlich nicht die Illusion von Bildräumlichkeit

Appearance and Reality

The back-to-the-roots impulse of analytical painting had narrowed the scope for creative interpretations and simultaneously created precedents that could not be ignored by succeeding generations of artists. Whatever else it is, today's advanced abstract painting must *also* be processual, if it is not geometric, constructivist art.

Austrian art of the last 20 years is full of examples of artists who have succeeded in finding a place for themselves between the push and pull of new conventions and their own desire for self-expression. Interestingly, the processual began at some stage to figure as a new starting point and crux in the development of the 50-something generation of artists who had once belonged to the figurative, neo-expressive junge Wilde movement. The paintings by Thomas Reinhold included in the exhibition, for example, can be described as almost programmatic in this respect. His integration of a neon tube into a painting after it fell on the work during a fire at his studio demonstrates his adoption of the principle of chance (fig. p. 307), while another work exemplifies how dripping paint and brush marks are factors in the emergence of a picture (fig. p. 307). Christina Zurfluh (fig. p. 311) and Andreas Reiter Raabe (fig. p. 307) also show in very different ways what—after Yves Klein, Morris Louis, Hermann Nitsch and alongside Bernard Frize—can still in all earnestness be achieved by consciously subjecting paint to the forces of gravity. Christian Eisenberger, born 1978, pits himself against this very same earnestness. His generation has long since lost its belief in the autonomy of the work (fig. p. 306). Comparing this work with Niki de Saint Phalle's work *Tir* from 1961 (fig. p. 91), it is tempting to say "Here we go again!" Yet this is typical of art's cyclical trends, or what we might alternatively call its perpetual revival of conventions, revolutions and counterrevolutions.

Other artists take a more open approach to process. The explicit demonstration of the process of painting need not exclude either the illusion of space or light, or even representation, as Gerhard

Richter's fascinating *Parkstück* demonstrates (fig. p. 66). Here a photographic motif is transformed into an all-over tissue of bold, randomly applied impasto brushstrokes that structure the entire surface of the picture. The reality of painting and the appearance of representation enter into perfect symbiosis.

"Illusion, or rather appearance, semblance, is the theme of my life. Painting is exclusively concerned with appearance and in this respect differs from all other art forms. Painters see the appearance of things and repeat it, i.e. without producing the things themselves. They create only the appearance of things and if this no longer reminds us of an object, then this artificially created appearance functions only because we scrutinize it to find something that appears similar to a familiar object. But even if this act of searching and comparing is, as it were, prohibited by experience or consent, it still works in fundamentally the same way. While we no longer compare a white picture by R. Rauschenberg with a white wall, but rather with the intellectual experience of monochrome and other problems of art history, we do, however, compare it with snow, flour, toothpaste and whatever else."[1]

Gerhard Richter makes an assertion here whose incontrovertibility he himself rebuts in his own monochromes. Yet what he describes here is one of the central issues of abstract painting, and a matter of fundamental concern to Hubert Scheibl, Herbert Brandl and Walter Vopava. All three artists oscillate between the purely processual and the associative to a varying degree. To illustrate the potential range of possibilities, the exhibition displays large-format paintings by Scheibl, Brandl and Vopava alongside Richter's *Parkstück*.

Walter Vopava constructs a patchy, subtly differentiated chiaroscuro ground. He does not paint right up to the edge, but leaves the raw canvas around the picture ground visible, thus drawing attention to its materiality. The artist destroys any apparent similarities with things familiar, such as patches of cloud, by covering the painting with bold, broad brushstrokes, which rudely bring back the viewer to the reality of the painting (fig. p. 71).

oder Licht, ja, nicht einmal von Abbildlichkeit aus, wie das faszinierende *Parkstück* Gerhard Richters aus der Sammlung beweist (Abb. S. 66). Ein fotografisches Motiv wird in ein gleichmäßiges, die Bildfläche strukturierendes All-over-Geflecht aus heftigen, ungerichteten Pinselstrichen in pastoser Farbe umgesetzt. Das Sein der Malerei und der Schein des Abgebildeten gehen eine perfekte Symbiose ein.

„Illusion, besser Schein ist mein Lebensthema [...]. Die Malerei beschäftigt sich wie keine andere Kunstart ausschließlich mit dem Schein. Der Maler sieht den Schein der Dinge und wiederholt ihn, d. h. ohne die Dinge selbst herzustellen, stellt er nur ihren Schein her, und wenn das an keinen Gegenstand mehr erinnert, funktioniert dieser künstlich hergestellte Schein nur, weil er nach Ähnlichkeiten mit einem vertrauten, d. h. gegenstandsbezogenen Schein abgesucht wird. Selbst wenn Erfahrung oder Übereinkunft dieses vergleichende Absuchen quasi verbieten: man vergleicht ein weiß angestrichenes Bild von R. Rauschenberg nicht mehr mit einer weiß angestrichenen Mauer, sondern mit den intellektuellen Erfahrungen der Monochromie und anderen kunsttheoretischen Problemen – selbst dann funktioniert es fundamental noch immer in dieser Weise: wir vergleichen es doch mit Schnee, Mehl, Zahnpasta und wer weiß noch was."[1]

Gerhard Richter stellt hier eine Behauptung auf, deren Apodiktik er zwar selbst mit seinen Monochromien entkräftet, die aber tatsächlich eine zentrale Problemstellung abstrakter Malerei ist, die als Motto auch dem Werk von Hubert Scheibl, Herbert Brandl und Walter Vopava vorangesetzt werden könnte. Alle drei Künstler oszillieren in ihrer Arbeit zwischen dem rein Prozessualen und dem Assoziativen in unterschiedlichen und wechselnden Eindeutigkeiten. Zur Illustration des möglichen Spannungsbogens werden in der Ausstellung Großformate der drei Künstler mit dem *Parkstück* Richters konfrontiert.

Walter Vopava baut einen fleckigen, malerisch differenzierten Helldunkelbildgrund. Er lässt dabei die Bildränder frei, um den Malgrund, die rohe Leinwand, vorzuführen und damit auf die Materialität des Bildes zu verweisen. Ähnlichkeiten mit einem vertrauten, das heißt gegenstandsbezogenen

Schein (etwa Wolkenfetzen) macht er endgültig den Garaus, indem er das Format mit entschlossenen, breiten Bürstenzügen nachzeichnet und die suchenden Betrachter abrupt in die Realität der Malerei zurückholt (Abb. S. 71).

Auch Hubert Scheibls Bild ist eine radikal malerische Konkretisierung, die sichtbar und nachvollziehbar aus großflächigen Bewegungen, Verteilungen und Überlagerungen des Farbmaterials – hier streng horizontal und vertikal – mittels Rakeln entwickelt wird. Die solchermaßen „prozessual" generierten Farbräume eröffnen aber bewusst ein breites Assoziationsspektrum, das vom dramatisch Landschaftlichen bis zu den Licht- und Projektionswänden einer urbanen und medialen Welt reicht: Das Bildimmanente wird vom Künstler mit Erfahrungen, Erinnerungen und Erlebnissen der realen Welt in eine permanente Wechselbeziehung gesetzt (Abb. S. 308).

Von Herbert Brandl kennen wir rein prozessuale, oft auch monochrome Bilder, die aus der seriellen Wiederholung vertikaler oder horizontaler Pinselzüge aufgebaut sind und nur durch Struktur und Lichteinfall ein malerisches „Leben" entwickeln. *Ohne Titel* von 2008 (Abb. S. 305) ist gleichermaßen seriell angelegt, provoziert jedoch durch Farbwechsel, vor allem aber durch die Aufhellung in der Bildmitte und die Verdunkelung am linken unteren Bildrand die Assoziation eines dunstverhangenen Sonnenauf- oder -untergangs. In der Balance von Prozessualem und Assoziativem haben wir es hier einerseits mit einem perfekten Äquivalent zu Richters *Parkstück* zu tun, andererseits mit einem – das gilt auch für Scheibl – überzeugenden Exempel authentischer Malerei. Was die Bedeutung der Methode relativiert.

Homogene Sehfelder

Die radikalste Form des Prozessualen ist zweifellos die Monochromie. Der Spekulation verdächtigt, dient sie dem Bourgeois auch heute noch als Synonym für die solipsistischen Verirrungen der modernen Kunst. Wenig bekannt ist, dass sie bereits auf eine exakt 89-jährige Geschichte verweisen kann, deren Kenntnis wohl eine Voraussetzung für

Hubert Scheibl's picture is also a radical concretization of the act of painting, developed by using squeegees to distribute and build up layers of paint in large sweeping movements—in this case either strictly horizontal or vertical. The color spaces generated in such a processual fashion, however, consciously open up a broad spectrum of associations ranging from dramatic landscapes to the illuminated surfaces of an urban and media-dominated world. The artist sets in motion a constant interplay between the painting's immanent qualities and experiences and memories from the real world (fig. p. 308).

Herbert Brandl is known for his purely processual and frequently monochrome paintings, created by the constant repetition of vertical or horizontal brushstrokes. What brings the paintings to life is their structure and the play of light upon their surface. *Ohne Titel* from 2008 (fig. p. 305) has this kind of serial structure, but because of the change of color, and even more so the tonal lightening in the center of the work and darkening at bottom left, it inevitably makes us think of a sunrise or sunset shrouded in mist or haze. This fine balance between process and allusion on the one hand makes it a perfect match for Richter's *Parkstück*. Yet it is also a persuasive example of authentic painting, as is Scheibl's work, too; and this relativizes the importance of its underlying method.

Homogenous Fields of Vision

The monochrome represents without doubt the most radical form of processual painting. Suspected of being overly theoretical, it still serves traditionalists as a synonym for the solipsistic aberrations of modern art. What is less widely known is that it can point to a history that already stretches back exactly 89 years. Acquaintance with this history is probably a prerequisite to understanding this liminal area of painting.

Alexander Rodchenko painted his *Black on Black* series in 1918 as a reaction to Kazimir Malevich's white pictures. However, it was not until 1921 that he produced art history's first purely monochrome paintings. These programmatic works were also pioneering in that they simultaneously transcended the figure-ground composition until then regarded as an indispensable constituent of a picture. Rodchenko was also explicit in his opposition to the metaphysical tendencies of suprematism: "I reduced painting to its logical conclusion and exhibited three canvases: red, blue and yellow. I affirmed: this is the end of painting. These are the three primary colors. Every plane is a discrete plane and there will be no more representation."[2] For Rodchenko this marked the end of his involvement with painting. From then onward he devoted himself to more socially relevant work in the applied arts.

Rodchenko could not know back then that far from marking an endpoint, he was in fact opening up a new field of painting. Generations of painters would go on to develop this specialist discipline in diverging ways, albeit only starting 30 years later. This is all the more astonishing given the extremely limited room to maneuver within this specialist discipline. While on the one hand, it seems it was these same restrictions that presented the challenge, on the other hand, there was a certain logic to the fact that many of the artists who experimented with the monochrome were aiming to renew painting from the inside, by drawing on the essence of the medium, pure color and the painting process.

It was Robert Rauschenberg who in 1951 picked up the monochrome's lost thread again in his *White Paintings*, creating neutral projection screens for light, shadow and particles intended to hone the viewers' senses and powers of concentration. Yet these works represented merely a passing episode in his oeuvre. Just a little later Yves Klein discovered his dematerialized "superficie bleue" and called for the development of a spiritually aware painterly sensibility.

If it had not been so before, reference-free monochrome painting was now more or less out of the question; Rodchenko, Rauschenberg and Klein had given the monochrome an art-historical lineage. These artists had defined the parameters of the genre, which ranged from the approach

das Verständnis dieses Grenzbereichs der Malerei sein dürfte.

1918 malt Rodtschenko die Serie *Schwarz auf Schwarz* als Reaktion auf Malewitschs weiße Bilder. Die ersten „reinen" Monochromien der Kunstgeschichte schafft er aber erst 1921. Mit diesen programmatischen Werken überwindet er erstmals in der Kunstgeschichte die Figur-Grund-Komposition, ein bis dahin unabdingbares bildkonstituierendes Element der Malerei, und stellt sich auch explizit gegen die metaphysischen Tendenzen des Suprematismus: „Ich habe die Malerei zu ihrem logischen Ende gebracht und habe drei Bilder ausgestellt: ein rotes, ein blaues und ein gelbes, und dies mit der Feststellung: Alles ist zu Ende. Es sind die Grundfarben. Jede Fläche ist eine Fläche und es soll keine Darstellungen geben."[2] Persönlich schließt er damit die Malerei ab und widmet sich nur mehr gesellschaftsrelevanten, angewandten Gestaltungsaufgaben.

Rodtschenko konnte damals nicht ahnen, dass er nicht einen Endpunkt gesetzt, sondern der Malerei ein neues Feld eröffnet hatte: eine Spezialdisziplin, die Generationen von Malern ausdifferenzieren würden – wenn auch erst 30 Jahre später. Das ist umso erstaunlicher, als der Gestaltungsspielraum dieser Spezialdisziplin gar nicht enger definiert sein konnte. Es scheint, dass einerseits gerade dieser Umstand eine besondere Herausforderung darstellte; andererseits folgt es einer gewissen Logik, dass sich auf diesem Feld viele Künstler wiederfanden, die eine Erneuerung der Malerei aus dem Wesen des Mediums, der reinen Farbe und des Malprozesses, anstrebten.

1951 nimmt Robert Rauschenberg mit seinen weißen Bildern den verlorenen Faden der Monochromie erstmals wieder auf und kreiert in einem für ihn Episode bleibenden Akt neutrale Projektionsflächen für Licht, Schatten und Partikel, die die Sinne und die Konzentrationszeiten der Betrachter schärfen sollen. Wenig später entdeckt Yves Klein seine entmaterialisierte „superficie bleue" und fordert spirituell erfahrene malerische Sensibilität ein.

Referenzfreie Monochromie ist spätestens ab diesem Zeitpunkt – Rodtschenko, Rauschenberg und Klein haben eine Kunstgeschichte der Monochromie zugrunde gelegt – eigentlich nicht mehr möglich.

Diese Künstler haben die Pole zwischen „What you see is what you see" (Frank Stella) und einem über das Bild hinausreichenden spirituellen Anspruch definiert, zwischen denen Nachkommende sich zwangsläufig positionieren müssen. Rudolf Schwarzkogler in seinem als Hommage (Abb. S. 118), Brice Marden in seinem wohl gleichzeitig als Hommage und Kritik an Klein zu verstehenden Werk mit dem Titel *Tropézienne (Thinking Blue)* (Abb. S. 124). Träumte doch der junge Yves Klein am Strand von Saint-Tropez davon, die unendliche, reine Tiefe des Himmels und des Meeres in Malerei zu übersetzen, während Marden nur eine materiale Oberfläche mit Arbeitsspuren und den Bildgrund vorzeigt. Das Gleiche macht Richter: Ebenso mit Oberflächenstrukturen und Grautönen experimentierend, möchte er noch jedes letzte der Farbe innewohnende emotionale und symbolische Potenzial tilgen (Abb. S. 125).

Dagegen will Jules Olitski Farbe und Malgrund verbinden und trotzdem die Farbe ausstrahlend den Betrachter umfangen lassen (Abb. S. 123), während Joseph Marioni den Blick in die Tiefe des aus vielen rinnenden Farbschichten aufgebauten Bildes lenken möchte (Abb. S. 84). Arnulf Rainer behauptet ein Darunter, widmet aber seine ganze malerische Energie der Verdichtung und Strukturierung der deckenden Schicht (Abb. S. 116). Günter Umberg überlistet wie Yves Klein unsere Wahrnehmung, ohne aber die Entmaterialisierung der Farbe mit deren Mystifizierung gleichzusetzen (Abb. S. 310). Christian Stock ist neben Marioni und Umberg der jüngste unter den Spezialisten, die sich ausschließlich der Monochromie verschrieben haben. Er entlockt der Disziplin und dem Prozessualen noch erstaunliche Varianten, indem er durch täglichen Farbauftrag auf denselben Bildträger über Monate und Jahre hinweg die Monochromie um die Dimensionen Raum, Skulptur und Zeit erweitert (Abb. S. 308, 309, 310).

Die schon eingangs erwähnte Unterschiedlichkeit des vermeintlich Gleichartigen in der Monochromie, wie sie hier am Beispiel der Bilder einer Ausstellung skizziert wurde, ist damit noch längst nicht erschöpfend behandelt. Ist man bereit, sich in die Feinheiten dieser Disziplin zu vertiefen, die man mit einiger Berechtigung als „sophisticated" bezeichnen darf,

formulated by Frank Stella as "What you see is what you see" to a spiritual ambition that extended beyond the painting. Their successors were forced to position themselves between these two poles. Rudolf Schwarzkogler did this in a work (fig. p. 118) that can be seen as a homage to Klein, while Brice Marden's *Tropézienne (Thinking Blue)* (fig. p. 124) can be understood as both critique of and homage to the French artist. While the young Yves Klein was dreaming on the beach at Saint Tropez about how to translate the pure and infinite depth of sky and sea into art, Marden wanted only a material surface and ground that would reveal the traces of his labor. Richter did likewise in his experiments with surface structure and gray tones, although his goal was to expunge all possible emotional and symbolic possibilities from paint (fig. p. 125).

By contrast, Jules Olitski aims to bond paint and canvas, while nevertheless allowing the viewer to be enveloped in the luminous sheen of the paint (fig. p. 123). Joseph Marioni, on the other hand, seeks to draw attention to the depth of a picture made of many layers of paint allowed to run (fig. p. 84). Arnulf Rainer asserts the existence of an underlying layer, but devotes all his artistic energy to condensing and structuring the surface (fig. p. 116). Like Yves Klein, Günther Umberg plays tricks on our perception, yet without equating the dematerialization of the paint with its mystification (fig. p. 310). Alongside Marioni and Umberg, Christian Stock is the youngest of those specialists who have dedicated themselves to exploring the monochrome to the exclusion of everything else. Stock has managed to elicit an astonishing range of variations from both discipline and process. By applying a new layer of paint to the same support each day for months and even years on end, he has lent the monochrome a spatial, sculptural and chronological dimension as well (fig. p. 308, 309, 310).

As the examples discussed above all show, the monochrome may have gained a reputation for uniformity, but it is in fact extremely diverse in character. Nor is that by any means all that can be said about this discipline, which can with some justification be described as sophisticated. Up to now I have examined the works on the basis of formal criteria and the artists' expressed intentions. Those willing to explore its subtleties in greater depth, however, will soon find themselves identifying additional differences and defining characteristics. In *Grau Nr. 349/3* (fig. p. 125), for example, Gerhard Richter disproves his own assertion, quoted above, that the viewer of a monochrome work has no choice but to compulsively scan the picture in search of something recognizable. The demonstrative materiality and "artificiality" of the painting allow no such associations with anything outside the picture. All that it shows is gray oil paint and a surface that indicates that the paint was applied with a sheepskin roller. In his pursuit of entirely reference-free painting, Richter employs a simple technique—as do all his likeminded counterparts. The paint material lies like a skin, a clearly perceptible layer, on the unframed support or canvas, which either shines through in places (as in Marden's case), or can at least be glimpsed at the margins of the picture (as in Richter's, Schwarzkogler's and Stock's case). Yves Klein avoids this kind of "unmasking" of the paint as a material by painting right over the edges of the canvas to create a painted object, while Umberg tapers the edges of his support inwards at the back so that his color fields appear to float. This was an effect that Klein occasionally tried to achieve by hanging his works so that they protruded from the wall.

Analytical painters avoid conventional framing as a rule. Although this would underline their artistic character in the face of possible skepticism concerning their pictorial or artistic credentials, a frame also creates a window, which, in turn, is conducive to the illusion of space. Olitski, for example, uses a frame to increase the a priori spatial effect created by the luminosity of the paint, and the idea of an above and below is already implicit in Rainer's overpaintings.

The dividing line between the monochrome and monochrome structural and monochrome material paintings may be extremely blurred, but this does not mean that they are not distinct

lassen sich bei den beschriebenen Werken nach formalen und intentionalen Kriterien noch weitere Differenzierungen und spezifische Eigenschaften ausmachen. So widerlegt Gerhard Richter mit *Grau Nr. 349/3* (Abb. S. 125) seine weiter oben zitierte Behauptung, dass auch die Betrachter eines monochromen Werkes gar nicht anders könnten, als dieses zwanghaft nach einem vertrauten Gegenstandsbezug „abzusuchen": Die demonstrative Materialität und die „Künstlichkeit" des Bildes lassen nämlich absolut keine außerbildlichen Assoziationen zu. Es zeigt ausschließlich die Ölfarbe Grau und eine Oberfläche vor, die auf die Verwendung einer Fellrolle schließen lässt. Um das Ziel völliger Referenzlosigkeit zu erreichen, bedient sich Richter – wie alle Gleichgesinnten – eines einfachen Kunstgriffs: Das Farbmaterial liegt als Haut, als Schicht, klar wahrnehmbar auf dem ungerahmten Bildträger respektive der Leinwand, was entweder an freiliegenden Stellen der Bildfläche (wie bei Marden) oder zumindest an den Seitenflächen ersichtlich ist (bei Richter, aber auch bei Schwarzkogler und Stock). Eine derartige „Demaskierung" der Farbe als Material vermeidet Yves Klein, indem er die Farbe über die Kanten zieht und ein Farbobjekt schafft, Umberg durch die Abschrägung des Bildträgers nach innen, was seine Farbfelder schwebend erscheinen lässt. Eine Wirkung, die auch Klein bisweilen durch eine vorgesetzte Hängung zu erreichen suchte.

Eine konventionelle Rahmung von Monochromien wird in der Regel von analytischen Malern vermieden. Sie würde zwar deren eventuell angezweifelten Bild- beziehungsweise Kunstcharakter bekräftigen, schafft aber ein Sichtfenster und begünstigt dadurch die Entstehung von Illusionsräumlichkeit. So wird bei Olitski die a priori räumliche Dimension ausstrahlende Farbe durch die „Fassung" noch gesteigert, bei Rainer ist eine solche schon durch das Thema der Übermalung, eines gedachten Darunter und Darüber, angelegt.

So fließend die Übergänge von der Monochromie zu monochromen Struktur- und Materialbildern auch sind, bilden diese doch eigene Kategorien. Um als Strukturbild zu gelten, bedarf es also eines deutlichen Mehr an zusätzlicher Strukturierung, wie sie die Werke von Piero Dorazio (Abb. S. 306) oder

Josef Danner (Abb. S. 102) aufweisen. Noch weiter geht Jakob Gasteiger, wenn er pastose Farbe in mehrfach angesetzten, parallelen Kammzügen auf den Bildträger bringt (Abb. S. 98, 99). Material und Methode werden so ausdrücklich vorgeführt, dass der Bildträger erkennbar zur Auflagefläche einer körperhaften Farbschicht mutiert und sich die Einheit von Grund und Farbe der klassischen Monochromie auflöst. Nicht mehr ein – wie auch immer zu interpretierendes – homogenes Sehfeld ist das Ziel, sondern allein die Demonstration des Prozesses. Das bestätigen auch die rein prozessual durch Abkühlung von flüssigem Aluminium im Ölbad generierten Skulpturen (Abb. S. 306) oder das durch Abziehen einer auf Aluminiumpaste gedrückten Auflage entstandene Strukturbild (Abb. 306). Womit bei Gasteiger auch der Zufall als Zentralaspekt des Prozessualen ins Spiel kommt.

Der Zufall

Eine weitere radikale Form prozessualer Bildgestaltung ist deren totale Entsubjektivierung beziehungsweise die Delegation bildkonstituierender Entscheidungen an außerbildliche und außerkünstlerische Faktoren. Das bedeutet in erster Linie Kontrollverlust und Reduktion der Eigenverantwortung des Künstlers, die auf die Definition von Rahmenbedingungen respektive die Strukturierung von Abläufen reduziert wird, deren Ergebnisse in ihrer ästhetischen Ausformung nur sehr eingeschränkt vorhersehbar sind. Wenn das ästhetische Konstrukt weitgehend ein Produkt des Zufalls ist, beschränkt sich die Autorschaft des Künstlers auf die nachträgliche Selektion der Zufallsergebnisse und eventuell auf deren Präsentationsform. Das Hauptkriterium für die Auswahl der Zufallsergebnisse ist meist deren Ähnlichkeit mit bereits approbierten Formen gegenstandsloser Malerei, andernfalls sie ja als Kunstobjekte kaum identifizierbar wären. Malerei im engeren Sinn – als manuelle Realisierung einer kompositionellen und farblichen Vorstellung – ist nur noch Bezugspunkt. In letzter Konsequenz handelt es sich oft um Antimalerei, wie sie beispielsweise von der japanischen Gutai-Gruppe schon Mitte der 1950er-Jahre betrieben wurde, etwas

categories. If a work is to be classed as a structural painting, the additional structuring has to be considerable, as in the works of Piero Dorazio (fig. p. 306) or Josef Danner (fig. p. 102), for example. Jakob Gasteiger goes one stage further, using a comb to rake his impasto into parallel lines across the painting support (fig. p. 98, 99). Material and method are so clearly displayed that the support can almost be seen mutating into a platform for a rather corporeal layer of paint, thus dissolving the unity of ground and paint found in the classical monochrome. No longer is the aim to create a homogenous field of vision—however we might interpret this. Rather, the only goal is to demonstrate the process itself. Purely processual sculptures generated by cooling molten aluminum in an oil bath (fig. p. 306) or a structural picture created by pressing a support onto aluminum paste and then removing it (fig. 306) also attest to this fact. Chance as a central aspect of process is also a key factor here in Gasteiger's work.

Chance

Another radical form of processual art is total depersonalization, or rather the delegation of creative decisions to external factors—extrinsic to both painting and artist. Primarily, this means that the artist cedes responsibility and control. His or her role is reduced to setting the parameters or structuring a sequence of events, whose results are foreseeable only to a very limited extent. If the aesthetic construct is largely a product of chance, then the artist's authorship is confined to the post hoc selection of random results and, possibly, the manner in which they are presented. These random results tend to be chosen on the basis of their similarity with existing forms of abstract painting. The use of any other selection criteria would make them extremely difficult to identify as works of art. Painting in its narrower sense—that of the manual realization of a creative color composition—is no more than a point of reference. Ultimately, what it often results in is anti-painting, as practiced by the Gutai group in Japan in the mid-1950s, for example, and a little later by the

Viennese actionists. In both cases, the public destruction of paintings played an important role in defining an artistic zero point and marking a new beginning (fig. p. 308).

The external forces controlling a processual picture can be mechanical, physical or chemical in nature. They produce "picturesque" signs of wear and tear, dirt or decay which are frequently of considerable aesthetic charm. The artists directing the action can also be inspired by extremely divergent motives. Gérard Deschamps, a member of the nouveaux réalistes, set out to discover the aesthetic potential in banal everyday phenomena, such as the paint flaking off a tarpaulin that had been stored folded up and then unrolled, and which typologically counts as a ready-made (fig. p. 104). Similarly, nouveau réalisme's first manifesto stated: "Easel painting (like no other means of classical expression in painting or sculpture) has served its time. It now lives out the last seconds, still occasionally sublime, of a long monopoly. What else is proposed? The thrilling adventure of the real perceived in itself and not through the prism of conceptual or imaginative transcriptions."[3]

From 1960 onward, the idea of the autonomous artistic subject and the auratic work of art with its dream of immortality were increasingly called into question. It was a development that was reflected in both Deschamps and Dieter Roth's work. Roth undermined the first contention by collaborating with other artists and the second by limiting the lifetime of his works and planning their ultimate demise. *Schimmelgraphik*, which dates from 1969, is now in the final stage of decomposition, devoured by mold spores—the same autonomous forces of nature that created the work in the first place (fig. p. 110).

Half a century separates Karin Sander's ironic painting and the positions of Deschamps and Roth born of their skepticism towards the abstract painting of their age. The ideological militancy of their 1960s discourse has been replaced by a dialogical examination of art history, which views the postulates of modernism from a critical distance. Sander's *Mailed Painting* is a round canvas that has been slightly soiled and worn by having been

später auch von den Wiener Aktionisten. In beiden Fällen spielten Akte der Bildzerstörung eine wichtige Rolle für die Definition eines künstlerischen Nullpunkts und Neubeginns (Abb. S. 308).

Die von außerhalb gesteuerten Kräfte eines prozessualen Bildes können mechanischer, physikalischer oder chemischer Natur sein. Sie erzeugen „pittoreske" Spuren der Abnützung, der Beschädigung, der Verschmutzung oder des Verfalls, oft von hohem ästhetischem Reiz. Die Absichten der Regie führenden Künstler können dabei völlig unterschiedlicher Art sein. Bei Gérard Deschamps, Mitglied der Nouveaux Réalistes, ist es die Entdeckung ästhetischer Potenziale im banal Alltäglichen, beispielsweise in den Abblätterungen einer gefaltet gelagerten und dann aufgerollten, bemalten Plane, die typologisch eigentlich ein Readymade ist (Abb. S. 104). Sinngemäß heißt es dazu im ersten Manifest des Nouveau Réalisme: „Heute tut [die Malerei auf der Staffelei] die letzten, manchmal noch immer großzügigen Atemzüge einer langen Alleinherrschaft. Was kann man uns sonst anbieten? Das hinreißende Abenteuer des wirklichen Sehens, nicht durch die Brille leicht fasslicher oder erfundener Übersetzung."[3]

Deschamps verbindet mit Dieter Roth die um 1960 aufkommende Infragestellung des autonomen Künstlersubjekts und des auratischen Kunstwerks mit Ewigkeitsanspruch. Die erste Behauptung unterlief Roth in Gemeinschaftsarbeiten mit anderen Künstlern, die zweite durch die Beschränkung der Lebensdauer seiner Werke und deren geplanten finalen Verfall. Seine *Schimmelgraphik* von 1969 befindet sich im letzten Stadium der Selbstauflösung durch autonome Kräfte der Natur, jene Schimmelpilze, die sie zuvor generiert hatten (Abb. S. 110).

Zwischen Deschamps' und Roths aus der Skepsis gegenüber der abstrakten Malerei ihrer Zeit geborenen Setzungen und der ironischen Malerei von Karin Sander liegt bereits ein halbes Jahrhundert. Das Kämpferisch-Ideologische der 1960er-Jahre-Diskurse ist einer dialogischen Auseinandersetzung mit der Kunstgeschichte gewichen, die von kritischer Distanz zu den Postulaten der Moderne gekennzeichnet ist. Sanders *Mailed Painting*, eine durch mehrfachen Postversand leicht abgeschabte und verschmutzte, runde Leinwand, stellt auf subtile und durchaus humorige Weise den Bedeutungsanspruch des so genannten Sublimen in der reduktionistischen Malerei infrage. Ihr *Gebrauchsbild (Rampe)* (Abb. S. 308), ein den Schmutzpartikeln einer Autowerkstätte temporär ausgesetztes Rechteckformat, soll ebenso vertraute Klischees reduktionistischer Malerei evozieren wie die Schab- und Schmutzspuren des *Mailed Painting, Bonn–Berlin–Wien* (Abb. S. 308).

Das Unbewusste

Allerdings kann nicht übersehen werden, dass die zuvor beschriebenen zufallsgenerierten Werke begrifflich zwar Bilder, aber deshalb noch längst nicht Malerei sind. Malerei definiert sich über Farbmaterial, Werkzeuge und die ausführende Hand, nicht nur über den Bildträger und das Format. Eine solche Malerei im engeren Sinn wollten noch in den 1950er-Jahren beispielsweise Ellsworth Kelly, François Morellet oder Robert Rauschenberg nicht aufgeben, obwohl auch sie das autonome Künstlersubjekt infrage stellten und von tiefem Misstrauen gegen die subjektivistisch-gestische Expression ihrer Zeit erfüllt waren. Unter dem Einfluss John Cages und der Zen-Philosophie kultivierten auch sie das Prinzip des Zufalls, aber ebenso jenes der Leere, um dadurch vorerst zu einer extrem reduktionistischen Malerei zu gelangen. Andere Künstler dagegen suchten eine Erneuerung der Malerei, ohne auf den Reichtum ihrer sinnlichen Potenziale verzichten zu wollen, die sie von Pollock bis Frize entweder in der Automatisierung und Serialisierung von Malvorgängen oder in der Aktivierung und Nutzbarmachung unbewusster Prozesse fanden, wie es schon ihre Vorläufer in der Écriture automatique und im Surrealismus getan hatten.

Aus durchaus vergleichbaren Beweggründen, wenn auch aus völlig unterschiedlicher geistiger und künstlerischer, österreichischer Tradition kommend, setzt auch Max Weiler um 1963 einen radikalen Akt der Neuorientierung. In den Stapeln seiner eigenen Schmierpapiere – in ohne gestalterische Absicht entstandenen Nebenprodukten des Malprozesses – findet er das von ihm gesuchte Wesen der Malerei

sent through the post on a number of occasions. It is a subtle and tongue-in-cheek way of casting doubt on the significance claimed by the "sublime" in reductionist painting. Her *Gebrauchsbild (Rampe)* (fig. p. 308), a rectangular canvas temporarily exposed to the dirt and dust of a mechanics' garage, is intended to evoke all the usual clichés of reductionist painting in much the same way as the dirt, scratches and scrapes of *Mailed Painting, Bonn–Berlin–Wien* (fig. p. 308) do.

The Unconscious

One thing, however, is impossible to ignore: while the works of art described above, which were generated by chance, can, on the face of it, be called paintings, that is still a long way from making them painting. Painting is more than just a support and format; the paint itself, the tools used and the hand that executed it are an intrinsic part of it. Even as late as the 1950s Ellsworth Kelly, François Morellet and Robert Rauschenberg—among others—were loath to relinquish this more narrowly defined concept of painting, even though they had all called into question the autonomous artistic subject and all deeply mistrusted the subjectivism and gestural expressionism of their age. Under the influence of John Cage and Zen philosophy, they, too, cultivated not just the principle of chance, but also the principle of emptiness to arrive at what at first was an extremely reductionist form of painting. By contrast, other artists ranging from Pollock to Frize sought to bring about a renewal of painting without forgoing its wealth of sensory possibilities, discovering that potential in the automation or serialization of painting processes, or in the activation and utilization of unconscious processes, just as the proponents of automatic writing and surrealism had done before them.

Austrian artist Max Weiler may have come from a completely different intellectual and artistic tradition, but his radical act of reorientation in 1963 was inspired by very similar motives. He discovered the essence of painting in all its diversity in by-products of the painting process—in piles of scrap paper and rough workings generated without any creative intention (fig. p. 107). All he needed to do was to transpose what was on this waste paper, or rather palm-sized fragments of it, onto large formats or, better still, to painstakingly reconstruct it in as much detail as possible (fig. p. 106). The very act of doing so created a metaphor for the elementary forces of nature, for had not the cosmos itself evolved in processes comparable to those involved in painting—by liquefying, coalescing, drying and solidifying under the influence of complex forces? The paintings based on scrap paper workings (1963–1967) represented the ultimate realization of Weiler's cosmological world view. As artifacts that he had unconsciously produced, but which, like him, were part of the natural world and subject to a higher law, they were a means of reconciling painting, nature and the self.

Weiler was probably unaware of the fact that he had created, in passing as it were, a distinct variation of processual painting and in doing so had indirectly introduced the ready-made into painting. While he still regarded a painstaking implementation process as necessary before his own objets trouvés could be elevated to the status of art, Herbert Brandl and Franz West adopted a much more direct approach 50 years later. Their work is about discovery rather than invention, as is reflected by the blunt titles of their works. *Schmierage* (fig. p. 105) and *Palettentisch, Working table in Aspic* or simply *Tisch* were also readymades that arose during the work process (fig. p. 305, 310). The artistic act is thus reduced to the selection and presentation of the relics of manual work processes that came about by chance or were the result of unconscious acts. What they provide is "[t]he thrilling adventure of the real perceived in itself and not through the prism of conceptual or imaginative transcription."

The 50-year period from Weiler to Brandl brings us full circle. Yet the circle is only one of the many overlapping circles that together make up processual painting—the complexity of which we have merely touched on.

in seinem ganzen Reichtum der Erscheinungsformen (Abb. S. 107). Er braucht sie beziehungsweise handtellergroße Details daraus nur noch auf große Formate zu übertragen, besser in akribischer Detailarbeit neu zu bauen, um damit gleichzeitig Metaphern einer elementaren Natur zu erzeugen (Abb. S. 106). Bildete sich doch einmal auch der Kosmos aus den Malvorgängen vergleichbaren Prozessen von Verflüssigung, Vermischung, Trocknung und Erstarrung unter dem Einfluss komplexer Kräfte. Mit den Malereien nach den Probierblättern (1963–1967), nach von ihm unbewusst erzeugten Artefakten, die aber wie er selbst Teil einer Natur sind, die einem übergeordneten Gesetz folgt, schloss sich in Weilers kosmologischem Weltverständnis der Kreis: Malerei, Natur und Selbst werden eins.

Weiler war sich wohl kaum dessen bewusst, dass er sozusagen en passant nicht nur eine solitäre Variante prozessualer Malerei kreiert, sondern auch indirekt das Readymade in die Malerei eingeführt hatte. Während er noch einen aufwändigen Umsetzungsprozess für erforderlich hielt, um das von ihm selbst stammende Fundstück in den Status eines Kunstwerkes zu heben, gehen Herbert Brandl und Franz West 50 Jahre später ganz direkt vor. Findung statt Erfindung ist ihre Devise. *Schmierage* (Abb. S. 105) und *Palettentisch, Working table in Aspic* oder schlicht *Tisch* sind die unverblümten Titel ihrer ebenfalls im Arbeitsprozess entstandenen Readymades (Abb. S. 305, 310). Der künstlerische Akt wird auf die Selektion und Präsentation von zufällig und unbewusst entstandenen, ebenfalls von eigener Hand stammenden Relikten aus Arbeitsprozessen reduziert. Angeboten wird „das hinreißende Abenteuer des wirklichen Sehens, nicht durch die Brille leicht fasslicher oder erfundener Übersetzung".

Von Weiler bis Brandl schließt sich hier über den Zeitraum von 50 Jahren einer von vielen der sich überlagernden Kreise im Beziehungsgeflecht prozessualer Malerei. Dieses kann in seiner Komplexität nur angedeutet werden.

1   Gerhard Richter, *Text. Schriften und Interviews*, Frankfurt/M., Leipzig 1993, S. 171.
2   Alexander Rodtschenko, zit. n.: Kat. *Von der Malerei zum Design. Russische konstruktivistische Kunst der zwanziger Jahre*, Galerie Gmurzynska, Köln, 1981, S. 118.
3   Pierre Restany, „Les Nouveaux Réalistes, erstes Manifest" (1960), in: Kat. *Nouveau Réalisme*, Museum Moderner Kunst Stiftung Ludwig Wien, 2005, S. 123.

1   Gerhard Richter, *Schriften und Interviews*, Frankfurt, Leipzig, 1993, p.171. Translation is the translator's own.
2   Alexander Rodchenko, quoted in: *From Painting to Design: Russian Constructivist Art of the Twenties*, Cologne, Galerie Gmurzynska, 1981, p. 191.
3   Pierre Restany, "The Nouveaux Réalistes Declaration of Intention" (1960) in: *Theories and Documents of Contemporary Art: A Sourcebook of Artists' Writings*, (eds.) Kristine Stiles and Peter Stelz, Berkeley and Los Angeles, CA, London, 1996, p. 306–307, p. 306.

Christoph Bruckner

Der Weg ist das Ziel
Über das Prozessuale in der Malerei

The Journey Is Its Own Reward
On the Processual Aspect of Painting

Pollock und die Folgen

Jede Kunstproduktion und somit auch jede Malerei
ist in irgendeiner Art und Weise an Prozesse gebunden. Obwohl es zwar auch, wie Robert Morris 1970
spekulierte, hin und wieder zutreffen mag, dass die,
die über Kunst schreiben, fast nichts darüber wissen,
wie sie gemacht wird,[1] ist es doch vor allem der ubi-
quitäre Charakter des Prozessualen, der dazu führt,
dass der Prozessbegriff so gut wie nie zur diskursiven Unterscheidung herangezogen wird. Dabei ist
es keineswegs ein Pleonasmus, Malerei als prozessual
zu bezeichnen, da das Prozessuale ja auch *betont*
werden kann. Anders gesagt: Jede Malerei ist prozessual, aber nicht jede Malerei kann als prozessual
bezeichnet werden.

Zwar haben sich auch vor dem Zweiten Weltkrieg die malerischen Prozesse verändert, doch erst
mit Jackson Pollocks ersten Drip-Paintings waren
die Differenzen zu den davor üblichen malerischen
Prozessen größer als die Gemeinsamkeiten. Keine
Malerei ist per se prozessual, das Prozessuale zeigt
sich immer nur als *Differenz* und führt das Nicht-
prozessuale ex negativo immer mit sich.

An der von Pollock verwendeten Technik lassen
sich einige Merkmale, die dazu führen, das Prozessuale in einem malerischen Werkentwurf zu betonen, und einige allgemeine Charakteristika des Prozessualen ablesen. Pollock ließ Farbe mithilfe eines
Stocks beziehungsweise eines umgedrehten Pinsels

Pollock and His Impact

Every work of art—and therefore every painting—
involves processes in one way or another. Although,
as Robert Morris speculated in 1970, it may sometimes be the case that those who write about art
know almost nothing about how it is made,[1] it
is the ubiquitous nature of the artistic process
itself which guarantees that the notion of the
process is almost never used as a distinguishing
criterion in artistic discourse. It is by no means
tautological to describe painting as processual,
for its processual nature can also be *accentuated*.
Or to put it differently: all paintings are processual, but not every painting can be *described* as
processual.

Although painting processes did change prior
to World War II, it was not until the arrival of
Jackson Pollock's first drip paintings that the
differences between the new artistic process and
those of existing painting processes outweighed
their similarities. No painting is processual per se.
Instead, the processual appears only as *difference*
with the non-processual always forming part of
the definition ex-negativo.

If we examine the technique used by Pollock,
we can pinpoint some features that accentuate the
processual aspect of an artwork, as well as some
characteristics of the processual in general. Using
a stick or paintbrush handle, Pollock dripped

Jackson Pollock, 1950
Fotografie von / Photograph by Hans Namuth
Courtesy Center for Creative Photography
© Hans Namuth Estate

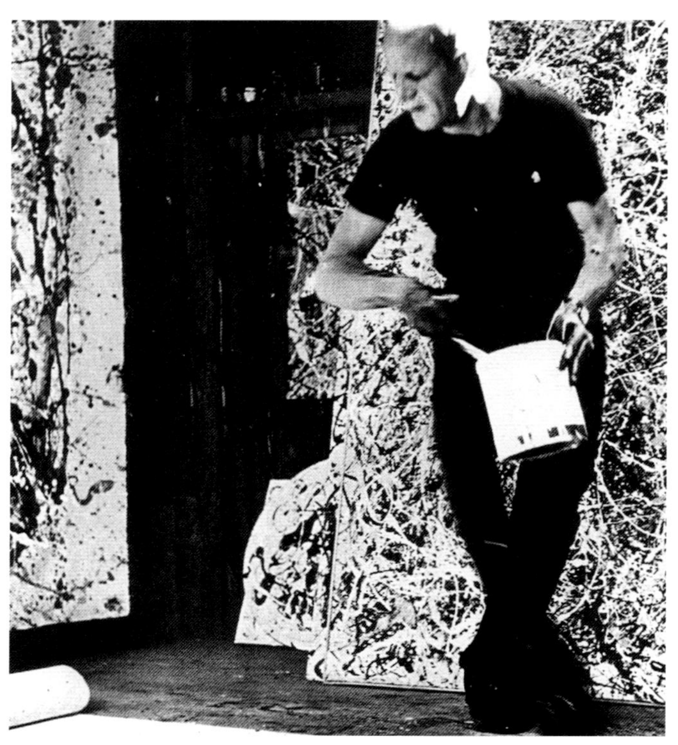
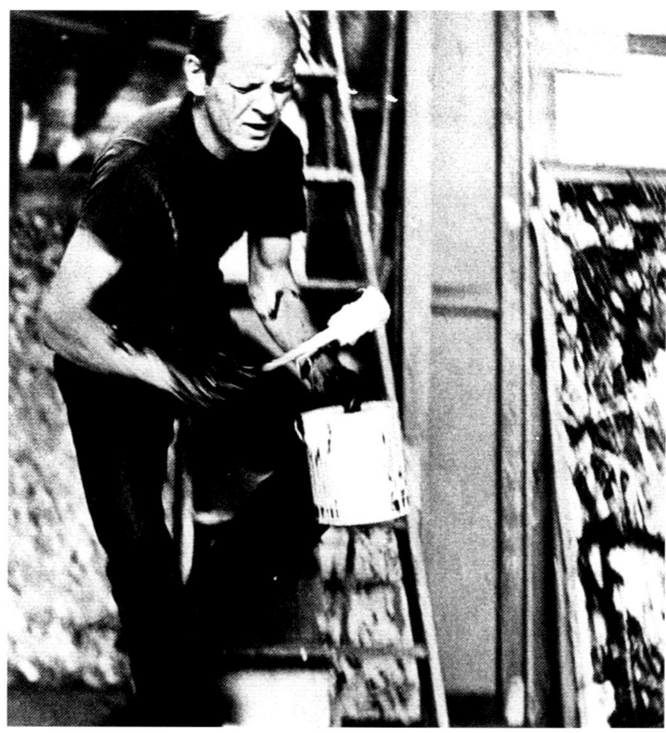
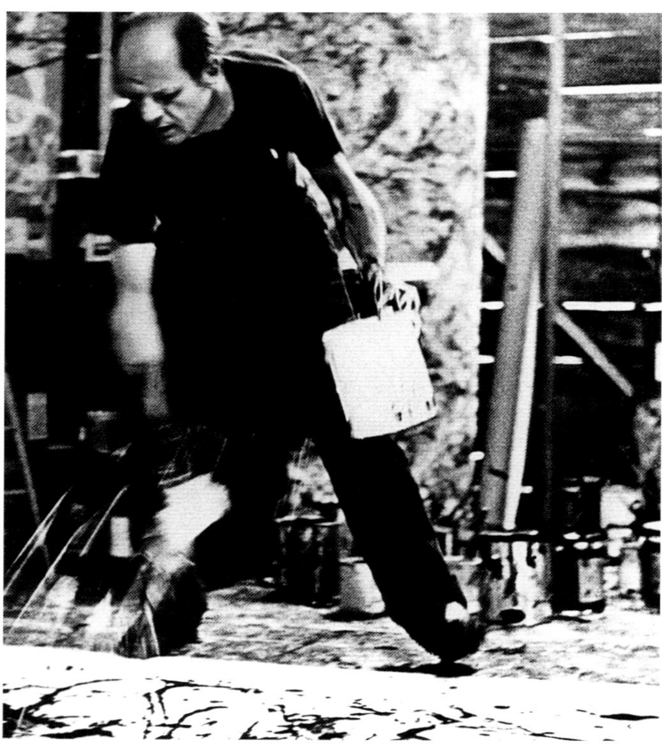
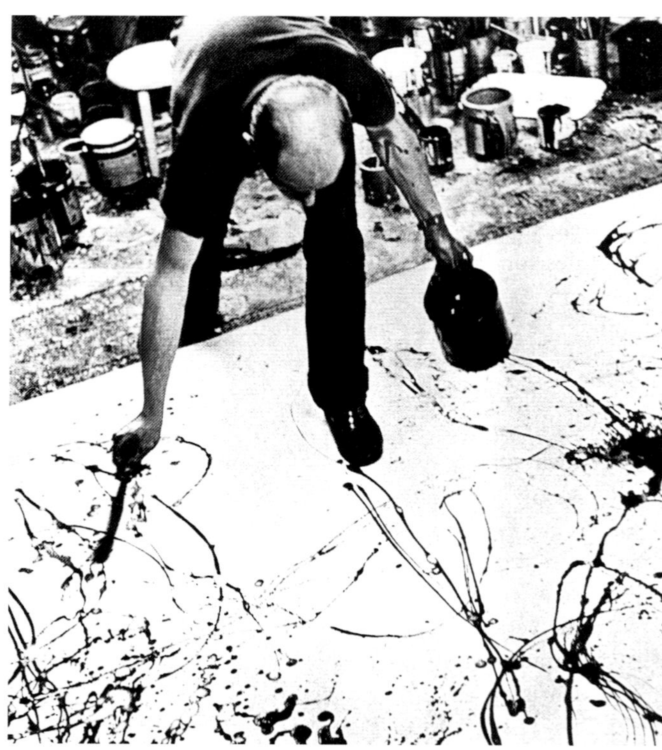

aus einer Dose auf eine auf dem Boden liegende Leinwand tropfen. Die zufälligen Elemente, die dieser filmisch und fotografisch ausführlich dokumentierte Prozess mit sich brachte, waren so groß, dass Pollock keine andere Möglichkeit sah, als den Zufall in seiner Malerei schlicht zu verleugnen.[2] Er verwendete keinen Pinsel, beziehungsweise er verweigerte sich der tradierten Funktionalität des Pinsels und ebnete so den Weg für eine Vielzahl an malerischen Positionen, die das Prozessuale dadurch betonen, dass sie andere Malwerkzeuge als den Pinsel verwenden, was natürlich nicht den Umkehrschluss zulässt, mit dem Pinsel Gemaltes könnte per se nicht prozessual sein. Nach Pollock wurde Farbe zum Beispiel mit den Händen, mit Schwämmen, Sprühpistolen oder sogar mithilfe von Gewehren aufgetragen. Außerdem veränderte Pollock die *Lage* der Leinwand. Im Anschluss an diesen Schachzug könnte man unter dem Gesichtspunkt des Prozessualen auch diverse Beispiele – etwa die Malerei von Alfons Schilling – anführen, die nicht (nur) die Lage der Leinwand, sondern überhaupt ihren dynamischen Status veränderten. Noch eines zeigt das Beispiel Pollocks: Hat ein Künstler einmal einen Prozess – er muss ihn nicht einmal selbst erfunden haben – künstlerisch besetzt, verunmöglicht er es anderen weitgehend, denselben Prozess für ihre Arbeit zu verwenden. Nichts eignet sich, abgesehen von der Verwendung eines bestimmten Materials, so sehr als Alleinstellungsmerkmal wie die Verwendung eines eigenen Prozesses. So spielt es in der Wahrnehmung des von Pollock bevorzugten Prozesses auch kaum eine Rolle, dass sich Janet Sobel einige Jahre vor Pollock desselben malerischen Prozesses bediente.[3] Die starke Bindung von malerischen Prozessen an Personen und ihre Biografien[4] mag auch ein Grund dafür sein, dass das Prozessuale in übergreifenden, nicht monografischen Darstellungen von Malerei so gut wie keine Rolle spielt.

Pollocks Beispiel machte aus den genannten Gründen zwar keine Schule, blieb aber dennoch nicht ohne Folgen, da sich Teilaspekte wie zum Beispiel die Veränderung der Lage der Leinwand auch in darauf folgenden Werkentwürfen finden. So schrieb Christopher Knight über Helen Frankenthalers bekanntestes Gemälde, *Mountains and Sea* (1952):

paint from a can onto a canvas laid out on the floor. The films and photographs of Pollock at work seem to stress the random nature of his artistic process to such an extent that he had no other choice than to plainly deny the role of chance in his painting.[2] Pollock either made do without paintbrushes or used them in an unconventional manner, and in doing so he paved the way for a number of painting styles that, as they made use of painting instruments other than brushes, stressed the very painting process itself. This of course does not allow for the reverse conclusion that would imply that any painting created with a brush cannot be processual. After Pollock, artists used their hands, sponges, spray guns, or even firearms to apply paint. Furthermore, Pollock changed the *position* of the canvas. A number of artists could be mentioned who made changes to the artistic process subsequent to this intervention, not (only) altering the position of the canvas, but even transforming the canvas's dynamic status. Alfons Schilling is one of them. Yet the example of Pollock also reveals something else: Once the artist becomes associated with a process—he or she need not even have invented it themselves—it is virtually impossible for another artist to use it in his or her work. Apart from the use of a particular material, nothing sets an artist apart more than the employment of his or her own process. Yet it is interesting to note that although Janet Sobel used the same drip painting process some years earlier, this hardly plays a role in how the technique that was favored by Pollock is seen today.[3] The close relationship between a painting process and individual biographies[4] may also be a reason why processes play almost no role whatsoever in broader surveys of painting, in contrast to monographs about individual artists.

Pollock's work may not, for the reasons mentioned above, have found many imitators, but this does not mean that it was without repercussions, for some aspects—such as the repositioning of the canvas—can also be found in subsequent works of art. For example, in describing Helen Frankenthaler's best-known painting *Mountains and Sea* (1952), Christopher Knight wrote, "The

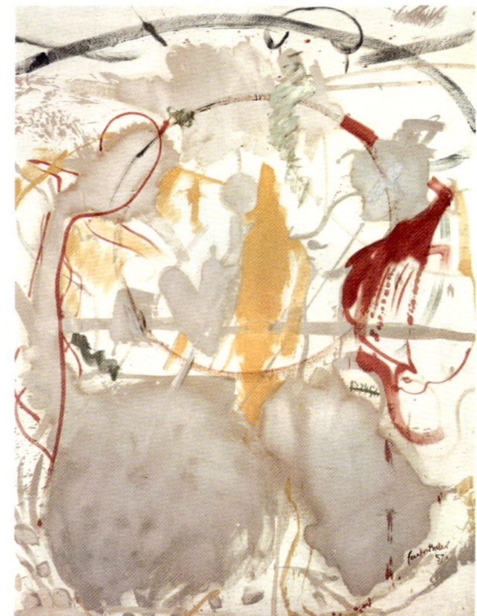 

Helen Frankenthaler
Seven Types of Ambiguity, 1957
Öl auf Leinwand / Oil on canvas
242,5 x 70,125 cm
© Geoffrey Clements / CORBIS

Robert Ryman
Ohne Titel (Untitled), 1961
Öl auf Leinwand / Oil on canvas
190 x 190 cm
Louisiana Museum of Modern Art

pictures pale wash of hues was composed by pouring thinned oil paints from a coffee can onto a large piece of canvas laid flat on the floor, then allowing them to soak directly into the raw cotton duck."[5] Regardlesss of the fact that Frankenthaler's example reveals the strange underexposure of the processual *as* a process—even if the term "stain painting," which describes the process as well as the result of paint being applied to an unprimed canvas, was used in the 1960s but *not* in the 1950s[6]—the difference between Pollock and Frankenthaler was that the processes used by Frankenthaler were not so closely linked to an overriding image, but clearly exhibit their processual character in the way that they co-exist: "[…] Frankenthaler seems to pull process itself away from image—farther […] than Pollock himself could allow […]."[7]

Frankenthaler passed on the processual aspect of Pollock's work to Kenneth Noland and Morris Louis,[8] who together with painters such as Jules Olitski or Larry Poons were grouped together under the rather vague label of post-painterly abstraction. Pollock, Frankenthaler, Louis, and, in the case of some of his works, Poons all share one common characteristic—these artists subjected the paint medium to the will of gravity. This submission to the forces of nature was by no means an attempt to seek a form of rapprochement with sculpture, for at that time sculpture was working *against* as opposed to *with* gravity. Instead, it represented an attempt to add paint *as* a material to the material world, which is entirely bound to the laws of gravity.

„Die blassen Farbtöne des Gemäldes entstanden, indem sie verdünnte Ölfarben aus einer Kaffeebüchse auf eine flach auf dem Boden liegende Leinwand goss, die Farben mit einem Schwamm verrieb und sie unmittelbar in den unversiegelten groben Baumwollstoff einsickern ließ."[5] Abgesehen davon, dass auch Frankenthalers Beispiel die seltsame Unterbelichtung des Prozesses *als* Prozess zeigt – wurde doch der Begriff „Stain-Painting", der Prozess und Resultat des Färbens ungrundierter Leinwand bezeichnet, im Unterschied zu den 1960er-Jahren in den 1950er-Jahren *nicht* verwendet –,[6] liegt der Unterschied zu Pollock darin, dass die verwendeten Prozesse nicht so sehr an eine übergeordnete Bildstruktur gebunden sind, sondern in ihrem Nebeneinander ihre Prozesshaftigkeit deutlich ausstellen: „[…] Frankenthaler scheint den Prozess an sich vom Bild wegzuführen – weiter […], als Pollock dies zulassen konnte […]."[7]

Frankenthaler vermittelte die prozessualen Anteile Pollocks an Kenneth Noland und Morris Louis,[8] die gemeinsam mit Malern wie Jules Olitski oder Larry Poons unter dem ebenso unscharfen wie schwer übersetzbaren Label „Post-Painterly Abstraction" subsumiert wurden. Gemeinsam ist Pollock, Frankenthaler, Louis und auch einigen Arbeiten von Poons die das Prozessuale ihrer Malerei betonende Unterwerfung des Malmaterials unter die Schwerkraft. Diese Unterwerfung war keine Annäherung an Prinzipien der Skulptur – die zu jener Zeit ja nicht *mit*, sondern *gegen* die Schwerkraft arbeitete –, sondern eine Eingliederung der Farbe *als* Material in die Welt des Materiellen an sich, die ja ohne Ausnahme der Schwerkraft unterliegt.

Entwicklungsgeschichtlich war dieser Schritt durch die Malerei der Moderne von langer Hand vorbereitet: „In [einer] Verselbstständigung und Verabsolutierung wurde die Farbe nicht mehr als Ersatz oder Darstellungsmittel, sondern als Produktions- und Konstruktionsmittel und somit als Material verwendet. Daher wurde auch die Art der Farbe, die Materialität der Farbe, ihr Pigment und so weiter, erstmals relevant, ebenso der Farbauftrag, zum Beispiel der Pinselstrich und seine Plastizität."[9]

Anmerkungen zu den „Anmerkungen zum Index"

Das Prozessuale ist nicht nur eine Funktion der Produktion, sondern dadurch, dass der Prozess am fertigen Bild abgelesen werden kann, auch eine Funktion der Rezeption, wobei nicht vergessen werden darf, dass, selbst wenn ein Bild seinen Entstehungsprozess nicht vollkommen offen legt, allein die *Frage* nach dem Prozess das Prozessuale in den Mittelpunkt der Rezeption rücken kann. Besonders gut eignen sich für eine solche Spurensuche die Bilder Robert Rymans, der den „Farbauftrag, [den] Pinselstrich und seine Plastizität" beziehungsweise die Materialität des Bildträgers und das Zusammenspiel dieser Elemente zum alleinigen Inhalt seiner Malerei machte. Rymans Version einer in den 1960er-Jahren seit Frank Stella sehr beliebten Sprachregelung lautete: „Was das Bild ist, ist genau das, was [man] sieht [...]."[10] Zur Beschreibung der Malerei Rymans kann der von Rosalind Krauss in ihrem zweiteiligen Aufsatz „Anmerkungen zum Index" im Anschluss an Roland Barthes' Fototheorie als Modus für die Kunst der 1970er-Jahre in die Diskussion eingebrachte Begriff des Index herangezogen werden: „Im Unterschied zu Symbolen stellen Indizes ihre Bedeutung aufgrund einer physischen Beziehung zu ihren Referenten her. Sie sind Markierungen oder Spuren einer besonderen Ursache, und diese Ursache ist das Ding, auf das sie sich beziehen, der Gegenstand, den sie bezeichnen. Unter der Kategorie des Index würden wir physische Spuren (wie Fußabdrücke) [...] fassen."[11] Als historischen Hintergrund für das Auftreten des Indexikalischen in der Kunst macht Krauss den abstrakten Expressionismus aus – schließlich sprach schon Clement

In terms of painting's historical development, this step had been prepared long in advance by modern painting: "In as much as it was made independent and absolute, paint was no longer used merely as a substitute or means of representation, but as a means of both production and construction, and thus as a material. Consequently, the type of paint, its materiality, its pigment, et cetera was made relevant for the first time. The same is true of the paint's application—the brush stroke and its plasticity, for example."[9]

Notes on "Notes on the Index"

The process, however, is not only a function of production. As the process can clearly be seen in the finished painting, it is also a function of its reception. Yet we must not forget that even if a painting does not completely divulge the manner in which it was created, we can make the processual aspect of central significance in terms of how the painting is received merely by *asking* about the nature of the process. Robert Ryman's paintings are particularly well-suited to this kind of examination, for the very substance of his painting can be boiled down to a combination of paint application, brush stroke, the plasticity of said brush stroke, the canvas's materiality, and the interplay of all of these elements. Ryman came up with his own version of a well-loved 1960s slogan first coined by Frank Stella, reworking "What you see is what you see" into: "What the painting is, is exactly what [you] see."[10] To describe Ryman's paintings, we can refer to Rosalind Krauss's two-part essay "Notes on the Index". Drawing on Roland Barthes' photographic theory as a mode to describe 1970s art, she introduced the notion of the index into the discourse: "As distinct from symbols, indexes establish their meaning along the axis of a physical relationship to their referents. They are the marks or traces of a particular cause, and that cause is the thing to which they refer, the object they signify. Into the category of the index, we would place physical traces (like footprints) [...]."[11] Krauss identifies abstract expressionism as historically paving the way for the appearance of the indexical in art—after all, Clement Greenberg did speak of "exhibited brush, knife, or finger marks" when referring to abstract expressionism[12]—and she also mentions Ryman, who adopted Pollock's "all-over" style of painting, as a direct successor to this approach. [13] Yet she does not fail to note that she is "not so much concerned here with the genesis of this condition within the arts, its historical process, as [she is] with its internal structure [...][14]. Krauss cites the photographic quality of Marcel Duchamp's work in her consideration of the indexical in art and, in the second part of "Notes on the Index", she also draws on the photographic condition in her analysis of abstract contemporary art. As a result, this serves to render the historical gap between Duchamp and 1970s art all the more visible. Yet although Krauss does *not* apply the structure that she describes to this period, her approach appears all the more historic in its rejection of the historical. While not openly addressing the issue, Krauss implies that the distinction between the painting of the 1960s and that of the 1970s rests in the tautological relationship between signifier and signified in 1970s abstract art that parallels the context-bound photography of the same era. Ryman's paintings with their subdued colors that direct the viewer's attention to the traces of the brush on the canvas, are also bound within a particular context. "The wall is the actual context—the actual background—without which the painting cannot be seen. [...] The white in the painting needs the white of the wall."[15] Yve-Alain Bois has a different reason for rejecting a purely indexical reading of Ryman's painting: "[T]he narrative of process establishes a primary meaning, an ultimate, originating referent that cuts off the interpretive chain."[16] Furthermore, in his reception of Ryman's work, Bois values the paradigm created by a *series* of paintings more than the indexical expressiveness of *individual* paintings.[17] In doing so, Bois raises an important point: Processes are not only "a priori systems"[18] that precede the work's completion and that are therefore latently conceptual, but they are also *repeatable*.

Greenberg in Bezug auf den abstrakten Expressionismus von „sichtbare[n] Pinsel-, Spachtel- oder Fingerspuren"[12] – und erwähnt auch Ryman, der von Pollock die All-over-Bildstruktur übernahm, als direkten Nachfolger dieses Ansatzes,[13] nicht ohne allerdings darauf hinzuweisen, dass es ihr nicht um die „Genese dieser Situation, [...] seine historische Entwicklung, sondern [um] seine innere Struktur"[14] gehe. Da Krauss' Referenz für das Indexikalische das Fotografische in der Arbeit von Marcel Duchamp ist und sie im zweiten Teil ihrer „Anmerkungen zum Index" die fotografische Kondition auch zur Beschreibung abstrakter Gegenwartskunst heranzieht, fällt die historische Lücke zwischen Duchamp und der Kunst der 1970er-Jahre besonders auf. Krauss wendet die von ihr beschriebene Struktur auf diesen Zeitraum *nicht* an, womit sich ihr Ansatz in seiner Ablehnung des Historischen erst recht als historisch zeigt. Den unausgesprochen mitgeführten Unterschied zur Malerei der 1960er-Jahre macht Krauss an der die tautologische Beziehung von Signifikat und Signifikant in der Fotografie parallelisierenden Kontextgebundenheit abstrakter Kunst der 1970er-Jahre fest, dabei ist ja auch die Malerei Rymans in ihrer zurückhaltenden Farbigkeit, die den Fokus umso mehr auf die Spuren auf dem Bildträger lenkt, an einen Kontext gebunden. „Die Wand ist der eigentliche Kontext, der eigentliche Bildgrund, ohne den das Bild nicht gesehen werden kann. [...] Das Weiß des Bildes bedarf des Weißes der Wand."[15] Yve-Alain Bois lehnt eine rein indexikalische Lesart von Rymans Malerei aus einem anderen Grund ab: „[D]as prozessuale Narrativ setzt eine Primärbedeutung fest, einen letztgültigen, grundlegenden Referenten, der die Interpretationskette kappt."[16] Darüber hinaus stellt Bois in seiner Ryman-Rezeption das Paradigma, das von einer *Serie* an Bildern erzeugt wird, über die indexikalische Aussagekraft *einzelner* Bilder[17] und spricht damit einen wichtigen Punkt an: Prozesse sind nicht nur „a priori Systeme"[18], die der Ausführung auch vorausgehen und dadurch latent konzeptuell sind, sondern sie sind auch *wiederholbar*.

Monochrome Malerei

Zwar hat auch Yves Klein eine ganze Reihe von
Prozessen in die Malerei eingeführt, das Prozessuale
an sich rückte allerdings erst nach dem Ende des
monochromen Bildes als Objekt, nachdem die
zunehmende, aber nicht vollständige Suspendierung
ästhetischer Differenz in einer paradoxen Bewegung
nicht die Flächigkeit des Bildes, sondern seinen
Objektcharakter betonte, in den Mittelpunkt. Die
noch bei Klein zu findende Behauptung einer Wirklichkeit außerhalb der materiellen Realität des Bildes
konnte in die Postmoderne nicht hinübergerettet
werden. Der Prozess des Malens, der in der monochromen Malerei durch den Verzicht auf jegliche
Komposition, die Beschränkung auf eine Farbe und
die Tatsache, dass meist nur „ein“ Prozess zur
Anwendung kommt, ohnehin sichtbarer ist als in
anderen Bildgattungen, füllte die entstandene Lücke.
Für Maler wie Joseph Marioni oder Günter Umberg
„ist der Anspruch der modernen Abstraktion, eine
wesentlichere Realität hinter der positiven Wirklichkeit der Dinge, eine kosmische, spirituelle oder
neuplatonische Welt überzeitlicher, ortloser und
immaterieller Empfindungen beziehungsweise Ideen
zeigen oder wenigstens symbolisieren zu können,
nicht mehr zu retten",[19] doch führte diese Erkennt-
nis weder zu einem reinen Positivismus noch zu
einem reinen Ästhetizismus. „[S]ie beharren auf
der sensuellen, phänomenalen oder subjektiven,
emotionalen Wirklichkeit des Gemäldes – der Realität der Wahrnehmung, der Empfindung oder
des Erlebnisses des Gemäldes jenseits von dessen
materieller Existenz."[20] – „Doch anerkennt auch
die ästhetische und essentialistische Haltung von
Marioni und Umberg die materielle Realität des
Gemäldes als den Ort und die Bedingung solchen
Erlebens [...]."[21] Über die Betonung des Prozesses
des Malens durch den Wegfall einer wie auch immer
gearteten außerbildlichen Wirklichkeit hinaus,
wurde in der monochromen Malerei der Postmoderne auch der Prozess des Malens selbst neu
besetzt, was sich am besten an Gerhard Merz'
Aussage: „Klein hat gemalt. Ich streiche an",[22]
ablesen lässt.

Monochrome Painting

Yves Klein may have introduced a number of
processes into painting, but the processual *itself*
was made the center of attention only after the
monochrome painting was no longer an object—
paradoxically only after the increasing yet still
incomplete suspension of aesthetic difference no
longer emphasized the surface of the image, but
the painting's character as an object. Klein's continued affirmation of a reality beyond the material
reality of a painting was unable to survive the
transition to postmodernity. As it is much more
visible in monochrome painting than in other
painting styles thanks to the renunciation of any
form of composition, the use of a single color, and
the fact that usually only "one" process is ever
applied, the painting process itself was able to fill
this gap. For painters such as Joseph Marioni or
Günter Umberg, "modern abstraction's ambition
of showing or at least symbolizing a more fundamental reality behind the actual material reality—
a cosmic, spiritual, or neo-Platonic world of trans-
temporal, nonspatial, and immaterial feelings or
ideas—can no longer be saved."[19] This insight,
however, led neither to a pure form of positivism,
nor did it create a form of pure aestheticism.
"They insist upon the painting's sensual, phenom-
enal, or subjective and emotional objectiveness—
the reality of the painting's perception, how it is
sensed or experienced goes beyond its material
existence."[20] "But Marioni and Umberg's aesthetic
and essentialist stance also acknowledges the
material reality of the painting as the place and
the prerequisite for such an experience [...]."[21]
In addition to the emphasis on the painting
process as a result of the loss of any form of
external reality beyond the confines of the image,
the monochrome painting of postmodernity also
serves to redefine the process of painting itself.
Gerhard Merz aptly summarized this notion as
follows: "Klein painted. I lay down coats of paint."[22]

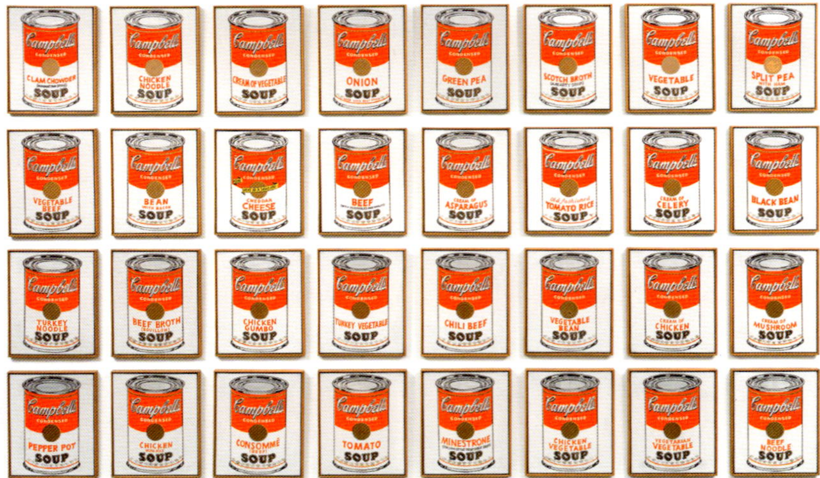

Andy Warhol
Campbell's Soup Cans, 1962
Synthetische Polymerfarbe
auf Leinwände
Synthetic polymer on canvases
32-teilig / In 32 parts:
Je / each 50,8 x 40,6 cm
Digital image © 2010,
The Museum of Modern Art,
New York/Scala, Florence

Industrial Production and Project Work

The processual aspect of painting can also gain importance when an artist integrates production processes into a work of art which, until that time, had not been employed in the creation of art. Andy Warhol adopted the structures inherent to industrial production as well as its accompanying features (the division of labor in the production process, assembly-line work, large-scale production, product uniformity, et cetera.) and integrated them into his own, mainly representational, output. It is important to note that the processual aspect of painting does not pertain only to a particular style of painting, nor does it apply only to abstract art. Warhol's use of the screen printing technique may have replaced the more established methods of applying paint to the canvas, but it is not the *real* processual element at work. Of much greater importance is Warhol's adaptation and subordination of the artistic process to the production processes taken from the world of industrial production. Whereas industrial products attempt to deny their own origins[23] and advertising does everything possible to hide or mystify the production process, many artists—beginning with Pollock—have displayed an increasing amount of transparency when it come to their chosen production process. Warhol's paintings do not necessarily display traces of their manufacture, but the process was extensively publicized in photographs and films. Whenever new painting processes are introduced—and this also applies to Yves Klein's Fire Paintings, Anthropometries, and Cosmogonies—a camera is usually somewhere nearby.

Industrielle Warenproduktion und Projektarbeit

Das Prozessuale kann auch durch die Übernahme eines bis zum Zeitpunkt der Übernahme außerhalb der Kunst liegenden Produktionsprozesses Bedeutung in einem malerischen Werkentwurf erlangen. Andy Warhol übernahm die Strukturen industrieller Warenproduktion und alle damit einhergehenden Implikationen (arbeitsteilige Produktion, Fließbandarbeit und die damit verbundenen hohen Stückzahlen, Warenförmigkeit der Endprodukte et cetera) für seine eigene, hauptsächlich gegenständliche malerische Produktion – das Prozessuale in der Malerei ist nicht nur nicht an einen bestimmten Stil, sondern auch nicht an die Ungegenständlichkeit gebunden. Der Siebdruck, die von Warhol verwendete Technik, ersetzt zwar etablierte Methoden, Farbe aufzutragen, ist aber dennoch nicht das *eigentliche* prozessuale Element, sondern dem verwendeten Produktionsprozess aus der Welt der Warenproduktion angepasst und untergeordnet. Während industrielle Produkte ihren Herstellungsprozess verleugnen[23] und auch in der Kommunikation industrieller Produkte alles daran gesetzt wird, den Herstellungsprozess zu verschleiern beziehungsweise zu mystifizieren, zeigt sich die schon bei Pollock zu beobachtende Transparenz im Umgang mit dem gewählten Produktionsprozess. Warhols Bilder zeigen nicht unbedingt die Spuren ihrer Herstellung, der Prozess wurde aber durch Fotos und Filme ausführlich kommuniziert. Wenn neue Prozesse in die Malerei eingeführt werden – und das trifft auch auf Yves Kleins Feuerbilder, Anthropometrien und Kosmogonien zu –, ist meist eine Kamera in der Nähe.

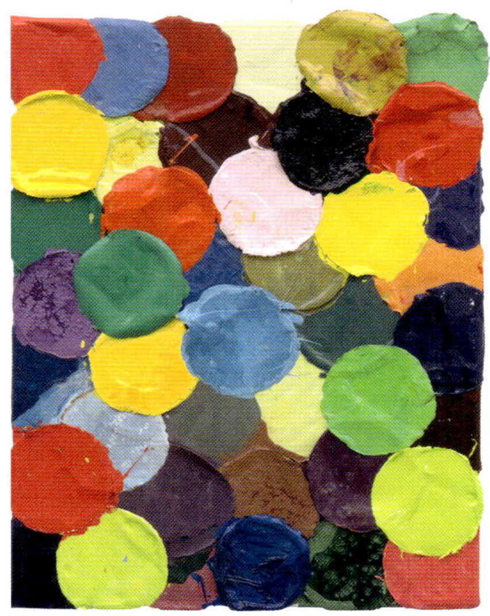

Bernard Frize
Suite Segond SF N5, 1980
Alkyd auf Leinwand / Alkyd on canvas
35 x 27 cm
Fotografie / Photography: Peter Cox
Collection of De Pont Museum of Contemporary Art

Warhols arbeitsteiliges Produzieren war für die bis heute nachfolgende Kunstproduktion derart folgenreich, dass der Aspekt der Arbeitsteilung, in seinem ubiquitären Charakter dem Prozessualen an sich nicht unähnlich, kaum zur diskursiven Unterscheidung künstlerischer Produktionen herangezogen wird beziehungsweise werden kann, geschweige denn in den fertigen Werken ablesbar ist. Eine Ausnahme hierzu bilden weite Teile des Werks des französischen Malers Bernard Frize. An den betreffenden Bildern ist nämlich klar ablesbar, dass sie nur von *mehr* als zwei Händen gemalt sein können, wie die meisten seiner Bilder deutliche Spuren ihres Produktionsprozesses zeigen und diese Prozesse über ihre Spuren dechiffrierbar werden. Frize legt seine arbeitsteilige Produktionsweise offen, macht sie selbst zum Bildinhalt und verweist damit, über die fordistische Fließbandarbeit Warhols hinausgehend, auf den das postfordistische Kreativsubjekt bestimmenden *Zwang* zur projektbezogenen Zusammenarbeit[24] – abstrakte Malerei muss also nicht außerhalb gesamtgesellschaftlicher Realitäten stehen.

Frize entwickelte seit Anfang der 1980er-Jahre eine Vielzahl originärer Prozesse: So klebte er die angetrockneten Häute offener Farbdosen auf Leinwände oder füllte Farben in rechteckige Behälter, um dann die sich nacheinander bildenden Farbhäute so lange auf Leinwände zu kleben, bis alle Farbe verbraucht war. Dort, wo Bois noch argumentieren konnte, dass Ryman nicht der Prozess *als solcher* interessiere,[25] überlässt sich Frize vollständig dem Prozessualen.

Sieht man einmal ab von Sigmar Polkes Experimenten mit hydro- und thermosensiblen Farben, die ihre Veränderbarkeit beibehalten[26] und so den

Warhol's introduction of the division of labor to the artistic process has had such a lasting impact on subsequent art production that the division of labor—its ubiquitous nature is not unlike that of the processual aspect of art—can hardly be used as a distinguishing criterion in artistic production, and it certainly cannot be detected in the finished works. An exception to this rule is provided by many of the French painter Bernard Frize's works. In these paintings, it is clear that they could only have been painted by *more* than two hands, just as most of his paintings display clear traces of the production process which allow us to decode the manner in which the artist worked. Frize reveals the division of labor in his production process and makes it a part of his painting's subject. In doing so, he refers beyond Warhol's assembly line production process to the *compulsion* of the post-Fordist creative subject to collaborate on artistic projects.[24] In short, abstract painting does not have to be confined to an existence beyond existing social realities.

Beginning in the early 1980s, Frize developed a number of original processes. He adhered the dried paint that formed on the tops of open paint cans to the canvas or poured paint into square-shaped containers and allowed the surface of the paint to dry into a skin. He then applied the skins that formed to the canvas until all of the paint was used up. Whereas Bois could still argue that Ryman was not interested in the process *as such*,[25] Frize had completely given himself over to the processual.

With the exception of Sigmar Polke's experiments with hydrosensitive and thermosensitive paints that maintain their malleable nature[26]—thus returning the notion of the process to its roots in chemistry as well as alchemy[27]—painting processes must at some point come to an end. The beginning of this end is the drying process, which Frize, admittedly, also understood how to use in his work. For example, he allowed a monochrome painted canvas to dry upside down attached to the ceiling in a horizontal position. Drops formed on the surface of the canvas and fell upon a crumpled canvas on the floor, thus creating an additional painting. Frize's "*materialistic* formalism"[28]—which not only consists of general attributes of his medium but also extends into the smallest details of the artistic means of production[29]—is mainly the result of the artist's political socialization in the late 1960s. Frize's style can be viewed as following in the tradition of the French group of painters "Supports/Surfaces,"[30] a group which also sprang up in the aftermath of May 1968.

Frize and Warhol's incorporation of social models of work and production is, however, not expended in the act of incorporation, but always entails some form of adaptation. "Successful artistic work should not be interpreted as the seismographic presentation of political, social, and aesthetic norms that show the elements of which they are constituted, but rather as the individual (performative) interpretation of these norms."[31]

Prozessbegriff an seine Ursprünge in Chemie und Alchemie[27] zurückführen, kommen Prozesse in der Malerei immer an ein Ende. Der Anfang dieses Endes ist der Trocknungsprozess, den Frize allerdings ebenso prozessual zu nutzen wusste. So ließ er eine monochrom bemalte Leinwand umgedreht in horizontaler Lage trocknen, wodurch sich kleine Noppen bildeten; die Farbe der an der Decke trocknenden Leinwand ließ Frize auf eine zerknitterte Leinwand am Boden tropfen, wodurch ein weiteres Bild entstand. Frizes „*materialistischer* Formalismus",[28] der nicht nur die generellen Konditionen seines Mediums beinhaltet, sondern bis ins kleinste Detail auch die Produktionsmittel,[29] verdankt viel der politischen Sozialisierung des Künstlers in den späten 1960er-Jahren und kann so in der Nachfolge der ebenfalls durch die Geschehnisse des Mai 1968 politisierten französischen Malergruppe „Supports/Surfaces"[30] gesehen werden.

Die Übernahme gesamtgesellschaftlicher Arbeits- und Produktionsmodelle durch Frize und Warhol erschöpft sich allerdings nicht in der Übernahme, sondern ist immer auch eine Umarbeitung: „Gelungenes künstlerisches Handeln sollte nicht nur als seismografische Präsentation politischer, sozialer und ästhetischer Normen aufgefasst werden, die das zeigt, was sie konstituiert, sondern auch als individuelle (performative) Interpretation dieser Normen."[31]

1   Vgl. Robert Morris, „Some Notes on the Phenomenology of Making", in: ders., *Continuous Project Altered Daily: The Writings of Robert Morris*, Cambridge, London 1993, S. 73.

2   Vgl. Anne M. Wagner, „Pollock's Nature, Frankenthaler's Culture", in: Kirk Varnedoe, Pepe Karmel (Hg.), *Jackson Pollock: New Approaches*, New York 1999, S. 191.

3   Vgl. William Rubin, „Jackson Pollock and the Modern Tradition, Part III", in: *Artforum* (April 1967), S. 29 f.

4   Vgl. Morris (wie Anm. 1), S. 73.

5   Christopher Knight, „Helen Frankenthalers übergroße Wasserfarben", in: *Texte zur Kunst* (September 1998), S. 170.

6   Vgl. Wagner (wie Anm. 2), S. 183.

7   Ebd., S. 194: "[...] Frankenthaler seems to pull process itself away from image – farther [...] than Pollock himself could allow [...]."

8   Vgl. ebd., S. 186.

9   Wolfgang Drechsler, Peter Weibel, „Malerei zwischen Präsenz und Absenz", in: dies. (Hg.), *Bildlicht. Malerei zwischen Material und Immaterialität*, Wien 1991, S. 101.

10   "What the painting is, is exactly what [you] see [...]." Zit. n.: Yve-Alain Bois, „Ryman's Tact", in: ders., *Painting as Model*, Cambridge, London 1990, S. 215.

11   Rosalind E. Krauss, „Anmerkungen zum Index: Teil 1", in: dies., *Die Originalität der Avantgarde und andere Mythen der Moderne*, Amsterdam, Dresden 2000, S. 251.

12   Clement Greenberg, „Nach dem Abstrakten Expressionismus", in: ders., *Die Essenz der Moderne. Ausgewählte Essays und Kritiken*, Amsterdam, Dresden 1997, S. 317.

13 Vgl. Rosalind E. Krauss, „Anmerkungen zum Index: Teil 2", in: *Die Originalität der Avantgarde* (wie Anm. 11), S. 267.
14 Ebd., S. 265.
15 Drechsler, Weibel (wie Anm. 9), S. 219.
16 "[T]he narrative of process establishes a primary meaning, an ultimate, originating referent that cuts off the interpretive chain." Bois (wie Anm. 10), S. 216.
17 Vgl. ebd., S. 220.
18 Morris (wie Anm. 1), S. 77.
19 Johannes Meinhardt, „Säkularisierte Moderne", in: Ingvild Goetz (Hg.), *Monochromie Geometrie*, München 1996, S. 7.
20 Ebd.
21 Ebd., S. 9.
22 Zit. n.: Beate Epperlein, *Monochrome Malerei*, Nürnberg 1997, S. 213.
23 Vgl. Dieter Hoffmann-Axthelm, *Theorie der künstlerischen Arbeit*, Frankfurt/M. 1974, S. 15.
24 Vgl. Ulrich Bröckling, *Das unternehmerische Selbst*, Frankfurt/M. 2007, S. 248–282.
25 Vgl. Bois (wie Anm. 10), S. 230.
26 Vgl. Ulli Seegers, „Unkontrollierbare Gäste", in: Kat. *Sigmar Polke. Werke & Tage*, Kunsthaus Zürich, 2005, S. 51.
27 Vgl. Peter Prechtl, Franz-Peter Burkard (Hg.), *Metzler Lexikon Philosophie*, Stuttgart, Weimar 2008, S. 490.
28 Yve-Alain Bois, „Introduction: Resisting Blackmail", in: *Painting as Model* (wie Anm. 10), S. xix.
29 Vgl. ebd.
30 Siehe Mick Finch, „Supports/Surfaces", in: *Contemporary Visual Arts*, 20 (1998), S. 48–53.
31 Judith Siegmund, *Die Evidenz der Kunst*, Bielefeld 2007, S. 85.

1 See Robert Morris, "Some Notes on the Phenomenology of Making," in: Morris, *Continuous Project Altered Daily: The Writings of Robert Morris*, London, 1993, p. 73.
2 See Anne M. Wagner, "Pollock's Nature, Frankenthaler's Culture," in: *Jackson Pollock: New Approaches*, (eds.) Kirk Varnedoe, Pepe Karmel, New York, 1999, p. 191.
3 See William Rubin, "Jackson Pollock and the Modern Tradition, Part III," in: *Artforum* (April 1967), p. 29–30.
4 See Morris, "Some Notes on the Phenomenology of Making," p. 73.
5 Christopher Knight, "Helen Frankenthalers übergroße Wasserfarben," in: *Texte zur Kunst* (September 1998), p. 170.
6 See Wagner, "Pollock's Nature, Frankenthaler's Culture," p. 183.
7 Ibid., p. 194
8 Ibid., p. 186.
9 Wolfgang Drechsler and Peter Weibel, "Malerei zwischen Präsenz und Absenz," in: *Bildlicht. Malerei zwischen Material und Immaterialität*, (eds.) Drechsler and Weibel, Vienna, 1991, p. 101.
10 Quoted in: Yve-Alain Bois, "Ryman's Tact," in Bois: *Painting as Model*, Cambridge MA, 1990, p. 215.
11 Rosalind E. Krauss, "Notes on the Index: Part 1", in: Krauss, *The Originality of the Avant-Garde and Other Modernist Myths*, Cambridge MA, 1986, p. 198.
12 Clement Greenberg, "After Abstract Expressionism," in: Greenberg, *The Collected Essays and Criticism: Modernism with a Vengeance, 1957–1969*, (ed.) John O'Brian, Chicago, 1997, p. 123.
13 See Rosalind E. Krauss, "Notes on the Index: Part 2", in: Krauss, *The Originality of the Avant-Garde and Other Modernist Myths*, Cambridge MA, 1986, p. 235.
14 Ibid., p. 210.
15 Drechsler and Weibel, "Malerei zwischen Präsenz und Absenz," p. 219.
16 Bois, "Ryman's Tact," p. 216.
17 See Ibid., p. 220.
18 Morris, "Some Notes on the Phenomenology of Making," p. 77.
19 Johannes Meinhardt, "Säkularisierte Moderne," in: *Monochromie Geometrie*, (ed.) Ingvild Goetz, Munich, 1996, p. 7.
20 Ibid.
21 Ibid., p. 9.
22 Quoted in: Beate Epperlein, *Monochrome Malerei*, Nuremberg, 1997, p. 213.
23 See Dieter Hoffmann-Axthelm, *Theorie der künstlerischen Arbeit*, Frankfurt, 1974, p. 15.
24 See Ulrich Bröckling, *Das unternehmerische Selbst*, Frankfurt, 2007, p. 248–282.
25 See Bois, "Ryman's Tact," p. 230.
26 See Ulli Seegers, "Unkontrollierbare Gäste," in: Cat. *Sigmar Polke. Werke & Tage*, Cologne, 2005, p. 51.
27 See Peter Prechtl and Franz-Peter Burkard (eds.), *Metzler Lexikon Philosophie*, Stuttgart, 2008, p. 490.
28 Yve-Alain Bois, "Introduction: Resisting Blackmail", in: *Painting as Model* (see note 10), p. xix.
29 See Ibid.
30 See Mick Finch, "Supports/Surfaces," in: *Contemporary Visual Arts*, no. 20, 1998, p. 48–53.
31 Judith Siegmund, *Die Evidenz der Kunst*, Bielefeld, 2007, p. 85.

Gabriel Hubmann

Aspekte von Prozess und Expansion in der westlichen Nachkriegskunst
Aspects of Process and Expansion in Postwar Western Art

Vom Werk zum Ereignis

Ab den 1950er-Jahren wurden in der Entwicklung der westlichen Nachkriegskunst verstärkt Vorgänge bemerkbar, die sich in unterschiedlichsten Ausformungen bis in die zeitgenössische Kunstproduktion hinein fortsetzten und wofür die zwei Begriffe des Ausstellungstitels – „Prozess" und „Expansion" – mögliche Beschreibungsformen darstellen. Einerseits wurde den fundamentalen Eigenschaften des Farbmaterials (etwa der Konsistenz der Farbe) und seinen Reaktionen auf äußere Einflüsse während des Schaffensprozesses (beispielsweise auf die Schwerkraft oder die Beschaffenheit des Bildträgers) immer mehr Beachtung geschenkt; andererseits wurden damit einhergehend das Medium Malerei und sein traditionelles Format – die rechteckige Leinwand – einer Untersuchung und Reflexion unterzogen, was in vielen Fällen zu objekthaften und räumlich-installativen Bezugnahmen führen sollte.[1]

Bereits in der Kunst der 1940er-Jahre kündigte sich eine Verschiebung von der traditionellen Kategorie des in der Zeit stabilen „Werks" hin zum transitorischen Ereignis an. Die Emphase des prozessualen Charakters künstlerischen Schaffens ging dabei mit einem forcierten Handlungs- und Performanzbegriff einher.[2] Um 1950 sollten der Tanz (eine zentrale Figur war dabei Merce Cunningham), Musik und Zufall (die essenziellen Elemente der künstlerischen Arbeit von John Cage) wichtige Bezugspunkte für die Kunst werden.[3] Doch nicht

From Work of Art to Event

From the 1950s onward, postwar western art increasingly began to show signs of developments that can still be found in various permutations in contemporary art today. The two concepts contained in the title of this exhibition, "process" and "expansion," represent two possible descriptions of these phenomena. For one thing, artists increasingly focused their attention on the fundamental properties of the paint (such as its consistency) and its response to external influences (such as gravity and the nature of the painting support) during the creative process. For another, the result of this focus was that the medium of painting itself, along with the rectangular canvas as its traditional format, became the subject of study and reflection. In many cases, this was to result in references to objects and spatial installations.[1]

It was possible as early as the 1940s to observe the first signs of a shift from the traditional category of the "work" of art, an object stable in time, to that of the transitory event. The emphasis on the processual character of artistic creativity went hand in hand with a greater focus on the concepts of action and performance.[2] Around the year 1950, important reference points for art were provided by dance (with Merce Cunningham as one of the key protagonists), music, and chance (the essential elements of the artistic output of John Cage).[3] But the processual character of art was not the only thing that the artists of the time wanted to emphasize. The observer also played a more active role in, for example, happenings, Fluxus actions, and participatory art.[4] At the same time, art became more open to spatial allusions in which the aim was to intensify the observer's physical experiences in relation to a work of art mounted on the wall.

"An Arena in Which to Act"

A comment by Harold Rosenberg underscores the fact that the school of gestural, informal postwar painting in the United States represented an important point of departure for this development. In 1952, Rosenberg remarked that more and more American painters had come to regard the canvas as an "arena" in which to act.[5] This remark was tantamount to the retrospective identification of a twofold transformation in American art of the 1940s. On the one hand, the space of representation was succeeded by a space for performance, action, and events,[6] and on the other hand, the term "arena" itself signified a tendency to shift the private into the public space. This development touches on a problem of postwar culture: In this context, the "arena" can be seen as a sphere of action that is surrounded and bounded by a large audience.[7]

But what is the origin of this explicit concept of performance and action? Research into this issue invariably turns up the photographs and films made by Hans Namuth in 1950 of Jackson Pollock moving like a dancer around a canvas spread out on the floor, repeatedly stepping onto it (thereby lending added definition to the image of the arena) and allowing paint to drip onto the canvas.[8] (fig. p. 28) The images recorded by Namuth—or the function they were intended to serve in the development of art theory—show that the process of producing a work of art was gaining significance compared with the finished product.[9] Viewers were intended to envisage in their mind's eye the production process that had given rise to the completed work, using the smears of color and trails of droplets to evoke the artist in motion. Thus the production process increas-

---

nur der prozessuale Charakter der Kunst sollte herausgestellt werden, auch der Betrachter wurde – etwa in Happenings, Fluxus-Aktionen oder in der Partizipationskunst – stärker eingebunden.[4] Dies wurde von einer Öffnung der Kunst hin zu räumlichen Bezügen begleitet, in denen die körperlichen Erfahrungen der Betrachter im Vergleich zu einem an der Wand fixierten Werk intensiviert werden sollten.

„An arena in which to act"

Dass die gestisch-informelle Nachkriegsmalerei in den USA einen wichtigen Ausgangspunkt für diese Öffnung bildete, lässt sich mit Blick auf eine Aussage Harold Rosenbergs genauer konturieren: 1952 hielt er fest, dass sich die Leinwand für immer mehr amerikanische Maler zu einer „Arena" gewandelt habe, in welcher man handelte,[5] womit er retrospektiv einen zweifachen Wandel in der amerikanischen Kunst der 1940er-Jahre markierte. Einerseits wurde der Raum der Darstellung abgelöst von einem Raum der Performanz, der Handlung und des Ereignisses („to act"),[6] andererseits zeigte der Begriff „arena" bereits eine tendenzielle Verschiebung des Privaten ins Öffentliche an, was an einen Problemkomplex der Nachkriegskultur rührt – die „Arena" kann in diesem Zusammenhang als Handlungsraum gesehen werden, der von einem großen Publikum umschlossen wird.[7]

Woher stammte nun aber dieser betonte Performanz- und Handlungsbegriff? Geht man der Frage nach, wird man unwillkürlich auf die von Hans Namuth im Jahr 1950 hergestellten Fotografien und Filme stoßen, die Jackson Pollock zeigen, wie er sich einem Tänzer gleich um die am Boden aufgelegte Leinwand bewegt, immer wieder auf sie hinaufsteigt (wodurch das Bild von einer „Arena" noch stärker Kontur gewinnt) und Farbe auf sie hinunterträufeln lässt.[8] (Abb. S. 28) Diese Aufnahmen – beziehungsweise die Funktion, die sie in der Theoriebildung erfüllen sollten – zeigen an, dass zunehmend die Herstellung eines Werks gegenüber dem fertigen Ergebnis an Wichtigkeit gewann.[9] Der Betrachter sollte das abgeschlossene Werk in seiner Imagination wieder in den Prozess der Fertigung zurückführen, indem er sich, ausgehend von den Farbschlieren und Tropfspuren auf der Leinwand, den Künstler in Bewegung vorstellte. In der amerikanischenNachkriegskunst wurde so der Produktionsprozess immer mehr zu einem inhaltlichen Aspekt der Werke[10] – und diese Entwicklung wurde über Medien wie Fotografie und Film auch öffentlich vermittelt.[11]

Neben der Betonung von Prozessualität und Handlung im Produktionsprozess eines Werks durch Rosenberg („to act") lässt sein Begriff „arena" nicht nur strukturelle Veränderungen in der Kunstwelt wie deren verstärkte Expansion in die Öffentlichkeit[12] anklingen, sondern kann in Verbindung mit dem von ihm forcierten Performanzcharakter durchaus als Expansion im Sinne einer Befragung, einer Reflexion des Mediums Malerei und seiner Grenzen an sich gelesen werden, was schließlich auch zur Überwindung des traditionellen Formats der viereckigen Leinwand führen sollte: So antizipierte Rosenberg mit seinem betonten Handlungsbegriff bereits Allan Kaprows Deutung von Pollocks Erbe als Überschreitung der Malerei,[13] worauf ich weiter unten zurückkommen werde.[14]

Krise des Staffeleibildes I (Dekor) und II (Horizontalität)

Jackson Pollocks Bild *Seven* von 1950 (Abb. S. 61) realisiert und radikalisiert zugleich in kleinem Format einen expansiven Zug seiner Malerei, der von Clement Greenberg bereits angesichts seiner größeren Leinwände konstatiert worden war. Greenberg hatte in seinem 1948 veröffentlichten Aufsatz „The Crisis of the Easel Picture" die unhierarchische Struktur der Maloberfläche, die dem dezentralisierten All-over-Bild (das zumeist mit Werken Pollocks assoziiert wird) zugrunde liege, mit dem eher negativ konnotierten Begriff des Dekors beschrieben und mit potenziell unendlicher Expansionsfähigkeit in Verbindung gebracht.[15] Durch das All-over werde das traditionelle Staffeleibild erschüttert, welches auf kompositorischen Zentren, auf Einheit und einer Isolierung von seinem Umfeld basiere (was es gänzlich unabhängig von Anforderungen der Dekoration mache). Greenberg spielte damit neben kompositorisch-formalen Aspekten auch auf die buchstäbliche Größe von Gemälden Pollocks an, die er immer

ingly became an aspect of the content of postwar American art.[10] And this development was communicated to the public through such media as photography and film.[11]

In addition to stressing process and action ("to act") in the production process of a work, Rosenberg's concept of the arena not only alludes to structural changes in the art world and its increasing expansion into the public sphere,[12] but can also—in conjunction with the performative character which he championed—be read as an expansion in the sense of a questioning of, and a reflection on, the medium of painting and its inherent limitations. Ultimately, this was to result in the demise of the traditional format of the square or rectangular canvas. Rosenberg's explicit concept of action anticipated Allan Kaprow's interpretation of Pollock's legacy as the transcendence of painting,[13] to which I will return later.[14]

The Crisis of the Easel Picture I (Decoration) and II (Horizontality)

Jackson Pollock's *Seven* (1950) (fig. p. 61) is both a realization and a small-format radicalization of the same expansive thrust in his art that Clement Greenberg had already identified in some of his larger-format canvases. In an essay published in 1948, "The Crisis of the Easel Picture," Greenberg had described the non-hierarchical structure of the painting support that underlies the decentralized all-over picture (which is typically associated with Pollock's works) in terms of the slightly disparaging concept of decoration and had suggested that its capacity for expansion was potentially unlimited.[15] In his view, the all-over picture shakes the foundations of traditional easel painting, which is based on compositional centers, unity, and a certain isolation from its surroundings (which makes it entirely independent of the requirements of decoration). With these comments, Greenberg was alluding both to formal compositional aspects of Pollock's work and to the literal size of his paintings, which he repeatedly described as "mural-like." Compared to these large paintings, in which the lines typically respect the

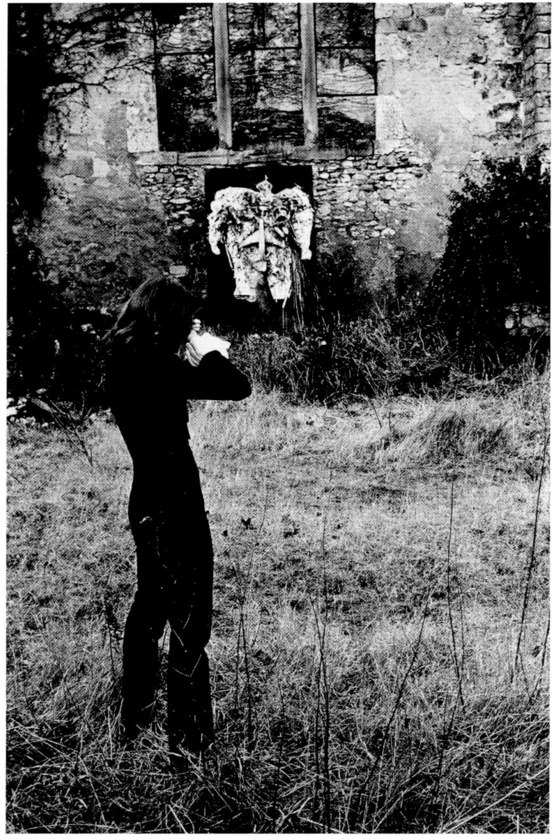

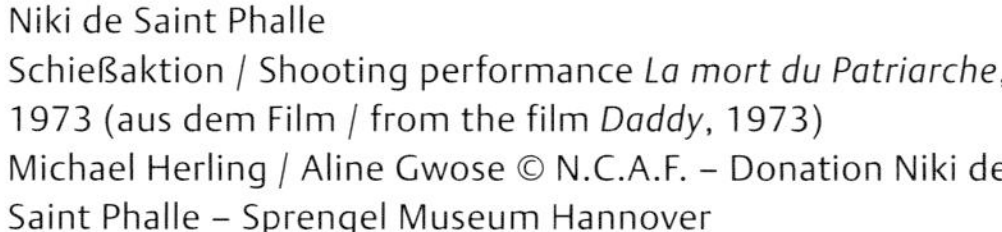

Niki de Saint Phalle
Schießaktion / Shooting performance *La mort du Patriarche*,
1973 (aus dem Film / from the film *Daddy*, 1973)
Michael Herling / Aline Gwose © N.C.A.F. – Donation Niki de
Saint Phalle – Sprengel Museum Hannover

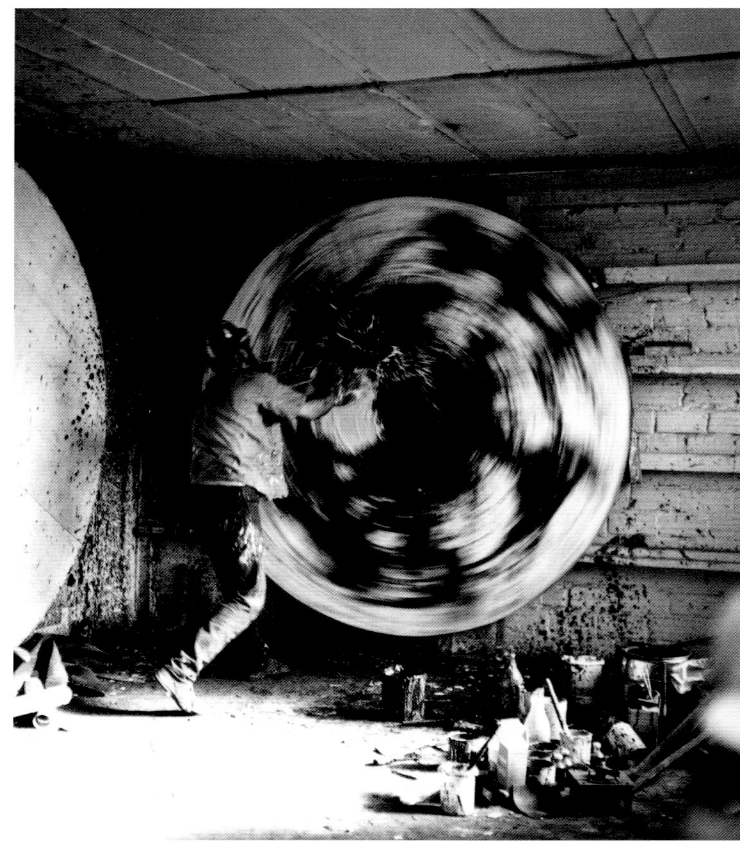

Alfons Schilling
Aktionsmalerei im Atelier / Action painting
in studio Rue de la Glacière, Paris 1962
© Alfons Schilling

borders of the image by becoming sparser towards
the edges, some of the black lacquer lines in the
small-format picture point beyond the edges and
thereby accentuate the expansive character of the
all-over structure of Pollock's larger canvases.[16]

Like the appearance of Pollock's works, his
style of working also exhibits an expansive character. In contrast to Greenberg, who ultimately
remained beholden to the traditional paradigm of
the vertically mounted picture despite—or perhaps because—of the crisis of easel painting,
Rosalind Krauss saw this as a radical departure
from the easel picture. In her 1999 essay for an
exhibition of Pollock's works in the MoMA,
Krauss stressed that the surfaces of Pollock's
works had had a horizontal orientation from the
very beginning, when he laid them out on the
ground for painting.[17] In contrast to the vertical
connotation of Greenberg's concept of the
"mural", Rosenberg had, according to Krauss,

wieder als „wandbildähnlich" („mural-like") bezeichnete. Gegenüber diesen großen Gemälden, in
denen sich die Linien meist zum Rand hin aus-
dünnen und ihn damit respektieren, weisen in dem
kleinformatigen Bild die schwarzen Lacklinien teilweise über den Rand hinaus und verdeutlichen so
den expansiven Charakterzug der All-over-Struktur
seiner größeren Leinwände.[16]

Neben der Gestalt seiner Werke weist auch die
Arbeitspraxis Pollocks einen expansiven Charakter
auf und wurde von Rosalind Krauss gegenüber
Greenberg, der letztlich trotz oder gerade wegen
der Krise des Staffeleibildes dem traditionellen -
Paradigma des vertikal angebrachten Bildes verhaftet
geblieben war, als radikaler Ausgang aus diesem
gewertet. Krauss betonte 1999 in ihrem Beitrag zu
einer Pollock-Ausstellung im MoMA, dass die Oberflächen von dessen Gemälden bereits von allem
Anfang an horizontal orientiert gewesen seien, als
er sie zum Bemalen auf den Boden legte.[17] Nach

Krauss hatte bereits Rosenberg gegenüber der (immer noch) vertikalen Konnotation von Greenbergs Wandbild mit seiner Betonung des Prozesses eine horizontale Dimension ausgemacht, die er später als „Arena" ausarbeiten sollte. Durch die waagrechte Lagerung der Leinwand entstanden nicht vertikale Rinnspuren, wie sie auf den Werken anderer abstrakter Expressionisten zu sehen sind, sondern eher Farbpfützen (wie im Bild *Seven*), die dauerhaft Zeugnis von der Orientierung der Leinwand während des Schaffensprozesses ablegen.[18] Für Krauss eröffnete Pollock damit vielen nachfolgenden Künstlern Arbeitstechniken, mit denen sie die Möglichkeiten von Horizontalität und den damit verbundenen Kräften der Gravitation für die Kunstproduktion ausloteten, deren Ergebnisse sich etwa in der Earth- oder Process-Art manifestierten.[19]

Das Erbe des abstrakten Expressionismus und des Action-Painting

Gegenüber Pollocks kleinformatigem Bild gibt es etliche Werke in der Ausstellung, die über den gesamten Bildkörper verteilte Rinnspuren aufweisen und somit dem von Krauss konturierten Paradigma des Vertikalen verpflichtet bleiben. *Dalet Rash* von Morris Louis aus dem Jahr 1958 (Abb. S. 86) steht exemplarisch für viele seiner Bilder, die wie Schleier wirken, da mehrere diaphane Farbschichten in ihnen übereinander gelegt sind. Louis ließ mit Terpentin verdünnte Farbe leicht angehobene und zu einem Trichter geformte Leinwände hinabrinnen – manchmal blieben Farbpfützen am unteren Bildrand sichtbar.[20] In Arbeiten Niki de Saint Phalles, des einzigen weiblichen Mitglieds der Nouveaux Réalistes, sollte sich gegenüber dem „dripping" Pollocks der Abstand zwischen Künstler und Werk noch weiter vergrößern. Die Einschusslöcher in ihrer Arbeit *Tir* (1961) (Abb. S. 91), die in der Ausstellung zu sehen ist, verweisen auf Saint Phalles künstlerisches Procedere: Sie hatte aus der Distanz mit einem Gewehr auf den Bildträger geschossen, in dem unter einer Gipsoberfläche Beutel fixiert waren, die beim Einschlagen der Kugeln Farbe verspritzten. Diese ergoss sich über das Objekt, welches von der Künstlerin anschließend umgedreht wurde, wodurch im gehängten Bild die

already identified a horizontal dimension in Pollock's work through his emphasis on process. He was later to develop this dimension in his concept of the "arena." The horizontal placement of the canvas naturally prevented the occurrence of the kind of vertical run marks that can be seen in the works of other abstract expressionists. Instead, Pollock's work exhibits puddles of color (these can be seen, for example, in *Seven*) that permanently testify to the orientation of the canvas during the creative process.[18] In Krauss' view, Pollock's work established new techniques with which many subsequent artists went on to explore the possibilities of using horizontality and the force of gravity in the production of art. The results of these explorations can be seen in such movements as earth art and process art.[19]

The Legacy of Abstract Expressionism and Action Painting

Several works in the exhibition differ from Pollock's small-format picture in that they exhibit run marks scattered over their entire area, thus remaining beholden to the paradigm of verticality as defined by Krauss. *Dalet Rash* by Morris Louis was painted in 1958 (fig. p. 86) and is typical of many of his pictures in that several diaphanous layers of color are superimposed on one another to create a veil-like appearance. Louis diluted paint with turpentine and allowed it to run down canvases that had been slightly elevated and rolled up into a funnel shape. Puddles of color sometimes remained visible at the bottom edge of the picture.[20] Compared to Pollock's "dripping" technique, the methods of Niki de Saint Phalle, the only woman among the nouveaux réalistes, opened up an even greater distance between the artist and the work. The bullet holes in her work *Tir* (1961) (fig. p. 91), which can be seen in the exhibition, are an indication of Saint Phalle's artistic *modus operandi*: She fired a gun from a distance at the painting support, which consisted of a plaster surface with bags attached underneath that squirted paint when punctured by the bullets. The paint poured over the object, which was

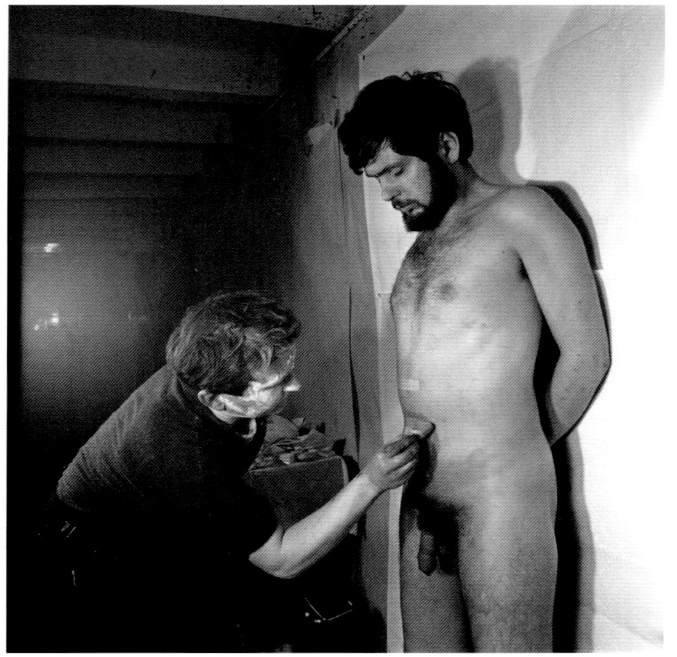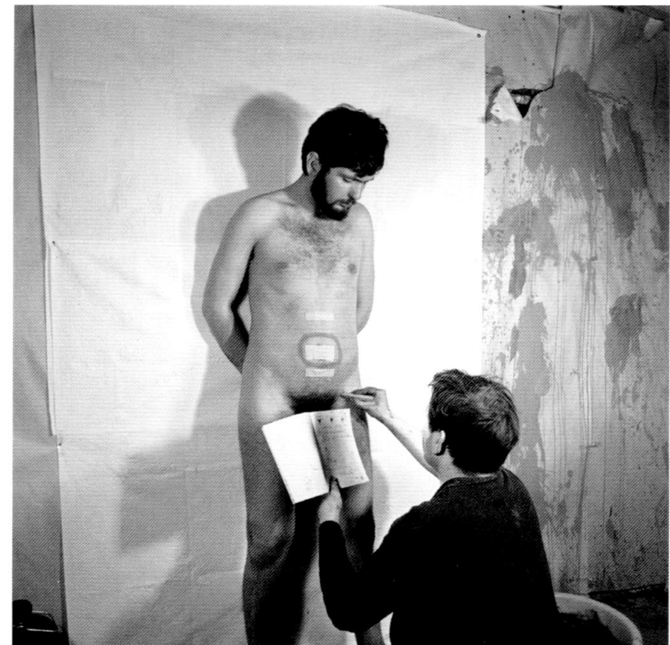

Hermann Nitsch, 10. Aktion (10th Action), 24.06.1965 / 24 June 1965
Fotografie / Photography: Ludwig Hoffenreich
Schenkung des Künstlers / Donated by the artist, 2007

subsequently turned upside-down by the artist, causing the flow marks to run upwards when the finished picture was mounted on the wall. Alfons Schilling, one of the precursors of Viennese actionism, poured or flung paint onto revolving discs, so that the run marks were created by centrifugal force (fig. p. 42, 62, 63).

The works by Louis, Saint Phalle, and Schilling are examples of a shift that took place in the 1950s and 1960s, when the expressive brush strokes of abstract expressionism, which were meant to be charged with the artist's entire being, were superseded by random material processes or rule-based procedures that partly suspended compositional intentions.[21] In the case of Louis, the artist's gesture was replaced by processes that were governed by chance, gravity, and the surface structure of the picture support. While Saint Phalle proceeded to radicalize the genre of action painting[22] by firing a gun at the picture support, she simultaneously forfeited the ability to exercise an immediate influence on the appearance of the work. Schilling integrated the picture support into the action painting process by setting it in motion, and, at the same time, broke with the rectangular shape of the picture support in favor of a tondo. While Louis allowed gravity to guide the flow of the paint, Saint Phalle added the kinetic energy of the

Fließspuren der Farbe nach oben weisen. Alfons Schilling, ein Wegbereiter des Wiener Aktionismus, schüttete beziehungsweise schleuderte Farbe auf sich drehende Scheiben, wobei sich durch die Zentrifugalkraft Verläufe bildeten (Abb. S. 42, 62, 63).

Die Werke von Louis, Saint Phalle und Schilling können exemplarisch für eine Verlagerung in den 1950er- und 1960er-Jahren stehen, als der ausdrucksstarke Pinselstrich des abstrakten Expressionismus, der vom ganzen Wesen des Künstlers aufgeladen sein sollte, von zufallsgeprägten materiellen Prozessen oder von regelbasierten Vorgangsweisen verdrängt wurde, die gleichermaßen kompositorische Überlegungen partiell suspendierten.[21] Bei Louis wurde die Geste des Künstlers ersetzt durch Vorgänge, die von Zufall, Gravitation und der Oberflächenbeschaffenheit des Bildträgers wesentlich bestimmt wurden. Saint Phalle sollte zwar das Action-Painting radikalisieren,[22] indem sie mit einem Gewehr auf den Bildträger schoss, brach damit aber gleichzeitig mit einem unmittelbaren Einfluss auf die Gestalt des Werks. Schilling wiederum integrierte den Bildträger selbst in das Action-Painting, indem er ihn in Bewegung versetzte und dabei gleichzeitig die Form des rechteckigen Bildträgers auf einen Tondo hin überschritt. Wurde bei Louis die Farbe von der Gravitation gelenkt, so bei Saint Phalle zusätzlich durch die kinetische Energie einschlagen-

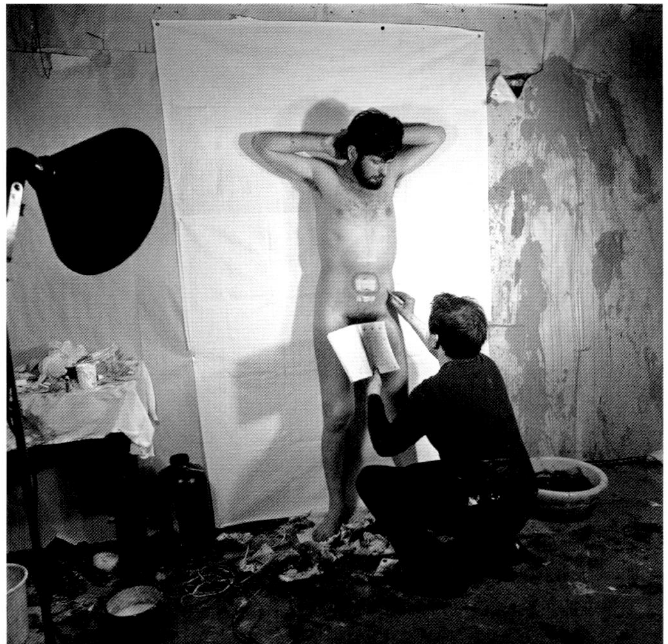 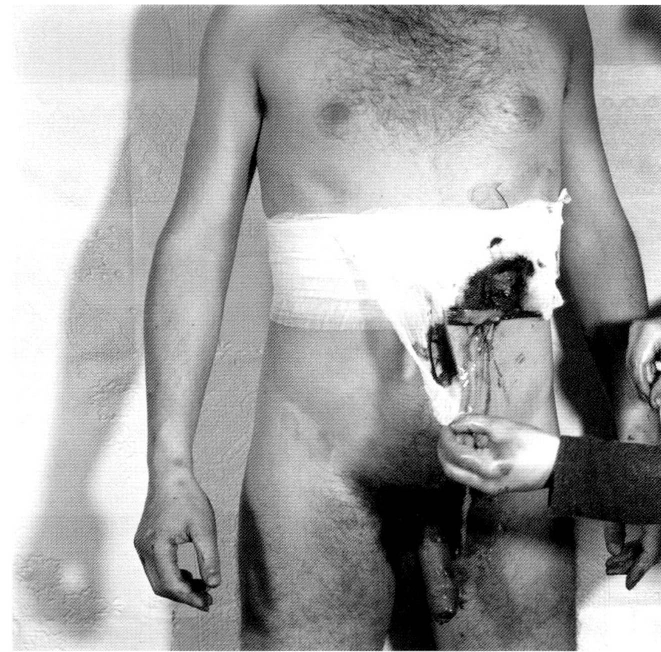

der Kugeln und bei Schilling wiederum durch die Zentrifugalkraft – in jedem Fall ist die Gestalt des Werks dem direkten Einfluss des Künstlers entzogen.[23]

Diese Positionen helfen zu verdeutlichen, dass im Gefolge des abstrakten Expressionismus eine vielfältige künstlerische Auseinandersetzung mit seinem Erbe wie einer expressiv-gestisch aufgeladenen Malerei und der damit einhergehenden Praxis des Action-Painting stattfand. Die Frage, die mit vielen Kunstwerken nach dem abstrakten Expressionismus in Verbindung gebracht werden kann, lautet deshalb, was mit dessen Erbe passierte und wie es aus- beziehungsweise umgedeutet wurde.[24] So wandten sich manche Künstler dezidiert von expressiven Gesten und einer Verdeutlichung des Malaktes ab, wie einige Vertreter der Post-Painterly Abstraction oder des Colourfield-Painting. Die Arbeit *Commissar Demikovsky* (1965) von Jules Olitski (Abb. S. 123) (einem der ersten Richtung zuzuordnenden Künstler) stellt mit ihrer glatten Oberfläche und der Tilgung sichtbarer Pinselspuren eine deutliche Abkehr vom stark gestisch verfassten abstrakten Expressionismus dar. Und Yves Klein sollte mit seinen monochrom blauen Bildern wie etwa *Monochrome Bleu* (1961) (Abb. S. 117) eher die Stofflichkeit des Bildträgers transzendieren als die Materialität eines Prozesses offen legen.[25] Andere wiederum, zum Beispiel die weiter oben genannten Künstler, bezogen sich zwar mitunter auf das Action-Painting und radikalisierten es, brachen dabei aber ebenfalls mit der expressiven Geste des

bullets and Schilling employed centrifugal force. In each case, the artist relinquished all direct influence on the appearance of the work.[23]

These examples help to illustrate the myriad of ways in which artists sought to grapple with the legacy of abstract expressionism, as well as with the school of expressive, gesturally charged painting and the accompanying practice of action painting. Thus we can ask what happened to the legacy of abstract expressionism and how it was interpreted, or reinterpreted, in many of the artworks created after this era.[24] Some artists, among them certain representatives of post-painterly abstraction and of colorfield painting, explicitly renounced expressive gestures and the disclosure of the act of painting as such. The painting *Commissar Demikovsky* (1965) by Jules Olitski (fig. p. 123), a representative of post-painterly abstraction, displays a smooth surface on which visible brush strokes were obliterated, representing a clear repudiation of the strongly gestural thrust of abstract expressionism. Yves Klein, with his monochrome blue pictures such as *Monochrome Bleu* (1961) (fig. p. 117), was more concerned with transcending the materiality of the painting support than with displaying the materiality of a process.[25] A number of other artists, such as those we mentioned earlier, did refer to and radicalize the genre of action painting, but, at the same time, broke with the expressive gesture of immediate artistic expression.

Cy Twombly's oeuvre also belongs in this context. Twombly radicalized action painting in

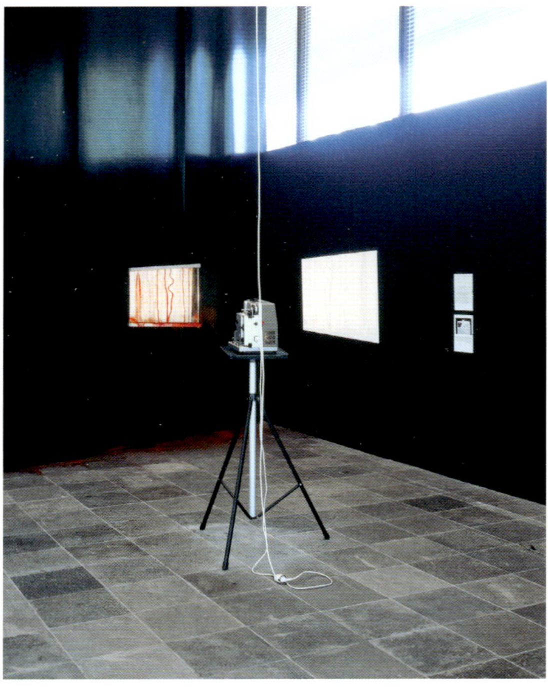

the sense that he furrowed and scored the painted stratum to impart a haptic quality to his lines.[26] In the painting *Untitled* (1968) (fig. p. 65), the lines reflect the movements of his body during the painting process. With these lines, which oscillate between written and pictorial logic, Twombly achieved a shift away from the expressive gesture of abstract expressionism.[27] A comparison of the scored lines in Twombly's paintings with graffiti evokes walls in public spaces that bear the scribble marks of unknown hands and thus resist any attempt to read them from a psychological perspective.[28] Instead of employing an individual, expressive gesture in his brush strokes, Twombly created allusions to an idiom that already existed before the commencement of the act of painting—the idiom of graffiti.[29]

Furthermore, the artists of the Viennese actionism movement became involved in the concept of action painting as a result of their fusion of informal painting and the idea of the body of the artist as a living picture support that becomes part of the action (for example, in the actions staged by Günter Brus)[30] (fig. p. 44, 149). Additionally, the processual element is likewise of fundamental significance here, as can be seen in Hermann Nitsch's large-format *Schüttbilder* (spill paintings). His cross-shaped *Kleiner Existenz-Altar* (1960) (fig. p. 87), which consists of separate individual pictures, features run marks in red paint on

unmittelbaren Künstlerausdrucks. In diesem Zusammenhang lässt sich auch das Werk Cy Twomblys nennen, der das Action-Painting insofern radikalisierte, als er die Malschicht durchfurchte und einritzte, womit er seinen Linien eine haptische Qualität verlieh[26] – auf seinem Bild *Untitled* von 1968 (Abb. S. 65) zeugen sie von den Bewegungen seines Körpers beim Malen. Mit diesen Linien, die zwischen skripturaler und bildlicher Logik oszillieren, vollzog Twombly aber eine Verschiebung gegenüber der expressiven Geste des abstrakten Expressionismus:[27] Der Vergleich von Twomblys eingeritzten Linien mit Graffiti lässt angesichts seiner Bilder an Wände im öffentlichen Raum denken, die von anonymer Hand bekritzelt wurden und sich somit einer psychologisierenden Lesart verschließen.[28] Statt eine expressiv-individuelle Gestik im Pinsel zu führen, sollte sich Twombly auf ein bereits vor dem Beginn des Malaktes bestehendes Idiom beziehen – nämlich Graffiti.[29]

Auch die Künstler des Wiener Aktionismus partizipierten mit der Fusion von informeller Malerei und dem Körper der Künstler als lebende Bildträger, die sodann in Aktion treten (man denke an die Aktionen von Günter Brus),[30] am Begriff des Action-Painting (Abb. S. 44, 149). Zudem hat das Prozessuale ebenfalls wesentliche Bedeutung, wie etwa in Hermann Nitschs großformatigen Schüttbildern ersichtlich wird. In seinem kreuzförmigen *Kleinen Existenz-Altar* von 1960 (Abb. S. 87), der aus einzelnen Bildern besteht, sind an jenen Flächen Rinnspuren roter Farbe zu finden, an denen die Arme des Gekreuzigten zu denken sind. Nitsch und Arnulf Rainer transponierten in manchen ihrer Werke die existenzialistisch aufgeladene Malerei des abstrakten Expressionismus in eine explizite (christliche) Ikonografie und machten sie dadurch mitunter etwas plakativ. Die Filminstallation *Expanded Cinema: abstract film Nr. 1* (1967/1968) von VALIE EXPORT scheint wiederum mit einem Problem zu spielen, an dem das Action-Painting laborierte, nämlich der unvermeidbaren Stilllegung der Malaktion in einem fertigen Bild, auf dem nur noch Spuren vom Malakt zeugen. EXPORT hält hingegen das Rinnen der Farbe buchstäblich am Laufen: Ein Filmprojektor wirft Licht auf einen in einem Becken stehenden Spiegel, über den immer wieder von neuem hochgepumpte Farbe rinnt – der angestrahlte Spiegel wirft ein Bild dieses Farbflusses auf die gegenüberliegende Seite der Wand.[31] Hier tritt wieder eine Brechung ein – das projizierte Bild an der Wand als „Endprodukt" ist eine seltsam flache und geisterhafte Erscheinung. In dieser Brechung und Vermittlung mag es sich mit dem ebenfalls 1967 entstandenen Werk *Untitled* von Willem de Kooning treffen, der darin die Farbe nicht mehr direkt auf das Zeitungspapier auftrug, sondern von einem anderen Träger darauf abdrückte.[32]

In der Nachfolge des abstrakten Expressionismus sollten noch viele Künstler in unterschiedlicher Art und Weise auf expressive Gesten und das Action-Painting Bezug nehmen. Manche künstlerische Positionen betonen dabei die Wichtigkeit der malerischen Geste und machen sie explizit sichtbar. Beispiele hierfür wären etwa Werke von Arnulf Rainer, in denen er mit heftigen Bewegungen Porträts übermalte – etwa in *Selbstporträt, übermalt* (1962) – und dadurch ein reizvolles Spiel mit dem Überdecken von Individualität durch Gesten eröffnet. Alfons Schillings Malerei *Ohne Titel* von 1960 steht ebenfalls in Zusammenhang mit einer informellen Bildsprache, die auf eine starke Körpermotorik setzte.[33] Vertreter der so genannten Neuen Malerei in Österreich wie Herbert Brandl, Erwin Bohatsch, Hubert Scheibl, Otto Zitko und Walter Vopava widmeten sich in den 1980er-Jahren ebenfalls einer gestisch

those surfaces where the viewer would expect to see the arms of the crucified figure. In some of their works, Nitsch and Arnulf Rainer transposed the existentially charged painting style of abstract expressionism into an explicit (Christian) iconography that sometimes became rather overblown. The film installation *Expanded Cinema: abstract film Nr. 1* (1967/1968) by VALIE EXPORT appears to be toying with a problem that dogged the genre of action painting: The unavoidable cessation of the painting process in a finished picture, on which only traces remain to testify to the process of its creation. In contrast, EXPORT literally keeps the paint running: A film projector casts light on a mirror standing in a basin, while a pump creates a continual stream of paint running down the mirror, and the image of this color flow is reflected onto the wall opposite.[31] Here another refraction takes place—the "end product" of the projected image on the wall has a strangely flat and ghostly appearance. A possible comparison might also be made, in terms of refraction and transmission, with *Untitled* produced by Willem de Kooning in the same year, in which the paint was not applied directly to the newspaper, but printed on to it from another painting support.[32]

In the aftermath of abstract expressionism, many other artists were to reference the relationship between expressive gesture and action painting in many different ways. Some of their artistic statements stressed the importance of the painterly gesture and made it explicitly visible. Examples of this phenomenon include works by Arnulf Rainer, who overpainted portraits— such as *Selbstporträt, übermalt* (1962)—with vigorous movements and in so doing played in an intriguing fashion with the idea of covering up individuality with gestures. The work of Alfons Schilling *Ohne Titel* (1960) is also associated with an informal visual language that is based on emphatic bodily movements.[33] In the 1980s, representatives of new painting in Austria such as Herbert Brandl, Erwin Bohatsch, Hubert Scheibl, Otto Zitko, and Walter Vopava likewise employed a markedly gestural style of painting. In Brandl's three-part work *Wasser* (1983), the gestural painting technique is not confined to an abstract and formal level, but simultaneously creates the motif of flowing water and correlates with it in its motion.[34] Some works that appear rigorously analytical or derivative at first glance—a characteristic that easily identifies them as postmodern works—often also exhibit an emphasis on the act of painting and on the use of the artist's entire body in the painting process. These works include the oeuvre of Bernard Frize *Mellegers & Van der Elsakor* (1989) (fig. p. 69).[35]

In the work of other artists, on the other hand, the painting process carries great weight but this is not instantly conspicuous. A good example of this kind of work is Brice Marden's *Tropézienne (Thinking Blue)* (1969/1979) (fig. p. 124). Here the artist mixed oil paint with hot wax, then applied several coats while leaving a narrow strip unpainted at the bottom edge in order to reveal the different layers and, with them, the working process. The different traces of this process showcase the materiality of the painting's surface and deliberately set Marden's work in contrast to the atmospheric, dematerialized color spaces that occur in the works of the post-painterly abstraction movement and in colorfield painting.[36]

Finally, there are works that reference a gestural or processual style of painting through postmodern, meditative refraction, the citation of expressive gestures, or the depiction of material processes. Works representing this style include David Reed's *# 348* (1995/1996) (fig. p. 70) and Miquel Mont's *S/T (Déversement no 7)*, which dates from the same year as Reed's picture. These artists initiate a discourse about the medium of painting and its specific qualities—a discourse that touches on the question of the significance and legitimacy of painting today. Finally, it should be noted that despite the distinctions we have drawn between the different artistic approaches, none of the artists mentioned here can be classified exclusively in terms of any single movement or position. Rather, an overlapping of many different styles can be observed in many of their works.

betonten Malweise. In Brandls dreiteiligem Werk *Wasser* (1983) bleibt die gestische Maltechnik nicht auf einer abstrakt-formalen Ebene, sondern schafft gleichzeitig das Motiv fließenden Wassers und korreliert mit diesem in einem Moment der Bewegung.[34] In manchen Werken, die auf den ersten Blick rigoros analytisch oder zitatartig erscheinen mögen – wodurch sie leicht der Postmoderne zuordenbar sind –, lässt sich mitunter ebenfalls eine Betonung des Malaktes, des ganzen Körpereinsatzes entdecken, etwa in den Werken Bernard Frizes, wie *Mellegers & Van der Elsakor* (1989, Abb. S. 69).[35]

Bei anderen Künstlern trägt der Malprozess wiederum zwar großes Gewicht, drängt sich aber dem Auge auf den ersten Blick nicht auf. Hierfür stellt *Tropézienne (Thinking Blue)* von Brice Marden aus dem Jahr 1969/1970 (Abb. S. 124) ein gutes Beispiel dar, in dem er Ölfarbe mit heißem Wachs vermischte, danach mehrere Schichten auftrug und am unteren Rand einen schmalen Streifen frei ließ, wodurch die verschiedenen Schichten und damit der Arbeitsprozess offen gelegt werden. Durch dessen verschiedene Spuren, welche die Oberfläche des Werks in ihrer Materialität erfahrbar machen, steht Marden in bewusstem Gegensatz zu atmosphärischen, entmaterialisierten Farbräumen, wie sie etwa in Werken der Post-Painterly Abstraction oder des Colourfield-Painting auftreten.[36]

Schließlich gibt es Werke, die in einer postmodernen reflexiven Brechung, einem Zitieren expressiver Gesten oder materieller Prozesse Bezug auf eine gestisch beziehungsweise prozessual verfasste Malweise nehmen. Als Vertreter wären hier etwa David Reed mit seinem Bild *# 348* von 1995/1996 (Abb. S. 70) oder Miquel Mont zu nennen, dessen Werk *S/T (Déversement no 7)* aus dem gleichen Jahr wie Reeds Bild stammt. Diese Künstler eröffnen einen Diskurs über das Medium Malerei und seine spezifischen Qualitäten, der an die Frage ihrer heutigen Bedeutung und Legitimität rührt. Abschließend ist zu dieser Differenzierung von Positionen anzumerken, dass die verschiedenen Künstler sich natürlich nicht ausschließlich *einer* Richtung oder Haltung zuordnen lassen, sondern in ihren Werken vielfältige Überschneidungen deutlich werden können.

Expansion der „Arena"

Wie bereits angedeutet wurde, lässt sich, ausgehend von einer verstärkten Betonung des prozessualen Charakters von Werken, eine Brücke zu einer Überschreitung des traditionellen Leinwandformats schlagen. Allan Kaprows Aufsatz „The Legacy of Jackson Pollock" von 1958 vermag eine solche Brücke zu bilden.[37] Darin konstatiert er, dass die Malerei Pollocks den nachfolgenden Künstlern neue Wege eröffnet habe, die Kaprow in einer Fortführung und Forcierung von Eigenschaften Pollock'scher Kunst sieht, die zuvor bereits von Rosenberg mit der Betonung des Prozessualen und von Greenberg mit der expansiven Wirkung beschrieben worden waren.[38] Pollock hatte Kaprow zufolge die Künstler schließlich an einem Ort gelassen, wo sie sich mit den Objekten des Alltags beschäftigen und diese in ihre Kunst integrieren mussten – in Happenings und Events sollte die bis dahin (in der amerikanischen Nachkriegskunst) ignorierte Welt wieder hineingenommen und thematisiert werden. Damit verlagerte Kaprow Rosenbergs „Arena", die doch noch auf die vier Seiten der Leinwand begrenzt gewesen war, in den Realraum[39] und wiederholte an dieser Stelle den klassisch-avantgardistischen Anspruch, die Kunst mit dem Leben zu verbinden.[40] Dies war ebenfalls bereits latent bei Rosenberg vorhanden, wenn auch „Leben" bei ihm wohl noch eher an das einzelne Künstlerindividuum gekoppelt gewesen war.[41]

Tatsächlich opponierten viele Künstler durch eine Verwendung banaler Alltagsobjekte in ihren Werken und die damit einhergehende Öffnung derselben Richtung Realraum gegen die vorherrschende modernistische Ideologie, die von Clement Greenberg und Michael Fried vertreten wurde und nach der sich ein authentisches Kunstwerk vor dem mondänen Treiben der Welt möglichst abzuschotten habe.[42] Claes Oldenburg sollte in seine plastischen Werke wie etwa *Street Head – I and the Big Man* (1959) Straßenmüll integrieren und in Aktionen wie *Store* (1961) den (Konsum-)Alltag in den Raum der Kunst überführen. Robert Rauschenberg kombinierte in seinen Assemblagen und *Combine Paintings* – etwa in *Diplomat* (1960) (Abb. S. 197) – Zitate des expressiven Pinselstrichs mit Alltagsobjekten und

The Expansion of the "Arena"

As we have seen, the heightened emphasis on the processual character of artworks can serve as a bridge for transcending the confines of the traditional canvas format. Allan Kaprow's 1958 essay, "The Legacy of Jackson Pollock," is capable of creating such a bridge.[37] In the essay, Kaprow observes that Pollock's paintings opened up new paths for the artists who succeeded him. Kaprow sees these paths as involving the continuation of and emphasis on certain properties of Pollock's art that were previously described by Rosenberg in terms of an emphasis on the processual and by Greenberg in terms of expansive impact.[38] According to Kaprow, Pollock had transported artists to a place where they were compelled to study objects from everyday life and integrate them into their art. The everyday world, which had hitherto been ignored in postwar American art, was to be incorporated and showcased by means of happenings and events. In this way, Kaprow transferred Rosenberg's "arena," which was still limited to the four edges of the painter's canvas, into real space[39] and reiterated the classical/avant-garde demand that art should be related to life.[40] This demand was covertly present even in Rosenberg's thought, although in his mind, "life" was probably still pegged to the personality of the individual artist.[41]

In fact, many artists employed banal, everyday objects in their works and simultaneously opened up their art towards real space as a gesture of opposition against the dominant modernist ideology, which was championed by Clement Greenberg and Michael Fried and which held that authentic works of art should isolate themselves as much as possible from the mundane activities of the world.[42] Claes Oldenburg was to integrate roadside refuse in his sculptural works, such as *Street Head—I and the Big Man* (1959) and translate everyday (consumer) reality into art in the context of actions such as *Store* (1961). Robert Rauschenberg's assemblages and *combine paintings*—such as *Diplomat* (1960) (fig. p. 197) — combined quotations of expressive brush stroke techniques with everyday objects. In Leo Steinberg's view, this combination served to illustrate a change of orientation from an explicitly vertical image surface that should create the optical illusion of providing a view of a three-dimensional space (Alberti's window) to an opaque, implicitly horizontal receptor surface onto which the information and data of the world is written.[43]

The expansion of panel painting into the third dimension usually went hand in hand with an increasing emphasis on multi-materiality. This can be observed in works such as Rauschenberg's *combine paintings* and his assemblages as well as the works of Lucio Fontana, Antoni Tàpies, and Jean Dubuffet.[44] Fontana's *Concetto Spaziale* (1957) features sand on the canvas as well as perforations that pierce the surface of the picture.[45] The artist had employed similar methods in other works, all of which he described as *Concetti Spaziali*, and in all of which he had cut slits into the canvas.[46] Both methods—the perforations and the slits—draw attention to the reverse side of the canvas and its physical character, turning empty space into a positive element of the work.[47] When discussing the methods by which artists transcended traditional painting formats after World War II and broke through into real space, one should not neglect to mention such important precursors as Pablo Picasso, Vladimir Tatlin, Marcel Duchamp, and Kurt Schwitters.[48]

In retrospect, it may seem as though the logic of medium specificity had led modernism itself to the point where artists acknowledged the specificity of their works in an affirmation of the material painting support and then subsequently began to transform them into picture objects.[49] Jasper Johns presented a model of painting in which figure and background blended into a single picture object[50]—*Target* (1967) (fig. p. 205) is a good example of this phenomenon. The rings of the target take up almost the complete picture, making the representation of the object begin to resemble the object itself. Frank Stella began to stress this fusion of figure and background from 1961 onwards in his *shaped canvases*. To create this effect in these works, he was still employing

machte damit für Leo Steinberg einen Orientierungswechsel deutlich, nämlich von einer explizit vertikalen Bildfläche, die sich optisch-illusionistisch auf einen Ausblick öffnen sollte (das Alberti'sche Fenster), hin zu einer opaken, implizit horizontal ausgerichteten Rezeptoroberfläche, in die sich die Informationen und Daten der Welt einschreiben.[43]

Die Erweiterung des Tafelbildes in die dritte Dimension war meist mit einer verstärkten Multimaterialität verbunden – Beispiele hierfür sind neben Rauschenbergs *Combine Paintings* und Assemblagen etwa die Arbeiten von Lucio Fontana, Antoni Tàpies und Jean Dubuffet.[44] In Fontanas Werk *Concetto Spaziale* von 1957 sind neben Sand auf der Leinwand Perforationen zu finden, die die Bildoberfläche durchlöchern.[45] Ähnliches hatte er in anderen Werken gemacht, die er allesamt als *Concetti Spaziali* bezeichnete und in denen er die Leinwand aufschlitzte.[46] Beides, das Durchlöchern und das Aufschlitzen, macht auf die Rückseite der Leinwand, ihre Körperlichkeit aufmerksam: Der leere Raum wird damit zu einem positiven Element der Arbeit.[47] Bei all der Rede von der Überschreitung des traditionellen Formats der Malerei hin zum Realraum in der Kunst nach dem Zweiten Weltkrieg dürfen aber natürlich wichtige Vorläufer nicht außer Acht gelassen werden: etwa Pablo Picasso, Wladimir Tatlin, Marcel Duchamp oder Kurt Schwitters.[48]

Im Rückblick mag es so erscheinen, als hätte die Logik der Medienspezifität den Modernismus selbst an einen Punkt geführt, wo die Künstler das Spezifische ihrer Werke in einer Affirmation des materiellen Trägers erkannten und diese daraufhin in Bildobjekte transformierten.[49] Jasper Johns präsentierte ein Malereimodell, das Figur und Grund zu einem einzelnen Bildobjekt verschmolz[50] – *Target* von 1967 (Abb. S. 205) ist hierfür ein gutes Beispiel. Die Ringe der Zielscheibe füllen darin beinahe das ganze Bildformat aus und nähern die Repräsentation eines solchen Objekts dem Gegenstand selbst an. Frank Stella forcierte seit 1961 diese Figur-Grund-Fusion in seinen *Shaped Canvases* noch durch die Bildstreifen gleicher Breite, deren Verlauf sich von der Form des Leinwandumfanges ableitet.[51] Stellas „geformte Leinwände" sollten schließlich zu einer Einsatzstelle des Minimalismus werden und von

Donald Judd in seinem Aufsatz „Specific Objects"
(1965) als Ausgangspunkt für eine Überschreitung
des Mediums Malerei hin zu dreidimensionalen
Objekten gelesen werden.[52] Judds „specific objects"
sind Hybridwerke aus Malerei und Skulptur respektive weder das eine noch das andere,[53] beziehen sich
aber mit „specific" paradoxerweise noch auf die
modernistische Logik der Medienspezifität. Ein spä-
teres Werk von Judd, *Untitled* (1989, Abb. S. 239),
hängt zwar wie ein Bild an der Wand, tritt aber in
seiner Dreidimensionalität wie eine Skulptur hervor.
In der Minimal Art beziehungsweise in Happenings
und Fluxus-Aktionen sowie in Installationen[54] sollten sich die Betrachter in realräumlichen Bezügen
bewegen und auf eine ganz andere Art und Weise
körperlich aktiviert werden als vor einem Werk,
das flach an der Wand hängt.

Mit der Minimal Art wird auch ein gewisser
Bruch mit kulturellen Voraussetzungen sichtbar.
Wurde nach dem Zweiten Weltkrieg im amerikanischen Kunstschaffen noch an europäische Vorkriegs-
phänomene wie Abstraktion und Surrealismus
angeknüpft, so richtete sich die Minimal Art ausdrücklich gegen die expressive Geste des abstrakten
Expressionismus (und seine Wurzeln) sowie gegen
einen relationalen Kompositionsbegriff, der als
europäischer Ballast angesehen wurde.[55] An die
Stelle der Bezugnahme auf Europa trat im Minimalismus eine Anknüpfung an den Konstruktivismus
der russischen Avantgarde.[56] Doch die rigorosen
geometrischen Strukturen des Minimalismus waren
nicht von langer Dauer: Sie sollten von postminima-
listischen Strömungen wie der Process-Art wieder
aufgeweicht werden.[57]

stripes of equal width whose orientation was
derived from the shape of the edges of the canvas.[51] Stella's *shaped canvases* would ultimately
become a focus of minimalism and would be read
by Donald Judd, in a 1965 essay titled "Specific
Objects," as a point of departure for moving
beyond the medium of painting toward the three-
dimensional object.[52] Judd's "specific objects" are
hybrid works that combine painting and sculpture, or perhaps they are neither one nor the
other.[53] Their "specific" aspect, however, paradoxically references the modernist logic of medium
specificity. A later work by Judd, *Untitled* (1989)
(fig. p. 239) is mounted on the wall like a painting, but juts out three-dimensionally from the
wall like a sculpture. In minimal art, happenings
and Fluxus actions, as well as in installations,[54] the
aim is to make observers move between reference
points in real space and become physically active
in an entirely different way than if they were
contemplating a flat, wall-mounted work of art.

Minimal art also reveals a certain departure
from cultural presuppositions. While American art
after World War II still built on prewar European
phenomena such as abstraction and surrealism,
minimal art explicitly opposed the expressive gesture of abstract expressionism (and of its roots)
along with a relational concept of composition,
which was regarded as European ballast.[55] In minimalism, references to European art were replaced
by a focus on the constructivism of the Russian
avant-garde.[56] However, the rigorous geometric
structures of minimalism were not destined to last
long, and were soon softened by post-minimalist
movements such as process art.[57]

1   Die Gründe für diese Intensivierung prozessual beziehungsweise expansiv verfasster Phänomene in der westlichen Nachkriegskunst sind komplex und gleichermaßen von sozialen Kontexten und kunstimmanenten Entwicklungen determiniert. In der geistigen Krisensituation nach dem Zweiten Weltkrieg, die eine Krise künstlerischer Darstellung mit einschloss, avancierten gegenüber den strengen naturalistischen Kunstvorgaben totalitärer Regime jene künstlerischen Formen zu einem Zeichen von Befreiung, in denen sich ein von abbildenden Aufgaben entbundener Umgang mit dem Malmaterial manifestierte – was etwa in prozessual verfassten Werken der Fall war (vgl. zur Loslösung von einer Begrenzung auf naturalistische Darstellung etwa die Lit. in Anm. 5). Zudem etablierten sich in der Nachkriegszeit Kulturen, die sich mit der Geschwindigkeit und Flüchtigkeit des modernen Lebens auseinandersetzten, wie etwa die Beat-Generation in den USA. Mit Blick auf eine kunstimmanente Entwicklung lassen sich immer wieder Abstoßbewegungen von vorangegangenen Kunstformen beobachten, wie es etwa die Betonung des Prozessualen und der Veränderung der Werkgestalt in der Zeit durch die Process-Art verdeutlicht, was als Antithese zu den strengen geometrischen Formen der Minimal Art gesehen werden kann. Aspekte der Expansion waren im amerikanischen Kunstschaffen (etwa in der Minimal Art) zuweilen mit einer Kritik an einem traditionellen, Europa zugeordneten Bildbegriff und einer angestrebten Loslösung von diesem verknüpft (vgl. dazu die Lit. in Anm. 53).

2   Zu diesem „shift" vgl. etwa Erika Fischer-Lichte, *Ästhetik des Performativen*, Frankfurt/M. 2004. Diese Verschiebung spiegelt sich auf theoretischer Ebene auch in der Verdrängung einer objektivistisch orientierten Werkästhetik durch eine Theorie der ästhetischen Erfahrung wider. Vgl. Juliane Rebentisch, *Ästhetik der Installation*, Frankfurt/M. 2003, S. 9 f. In diesem Zusammenhang ist auch auf John Deweys Buch, *Art as Experience* zu verweisen, das bereits 1934 veröffentlicht wurde.

3   Eine Schlüsselrolle spielte hierbei das Black Mountain College in North Carolina, an dem unter anderen Cunningham und Cage zusammenarbeiteten. Vgl. Achim Hochdörfer, „To Let the World Come in Again. Das Black Mountain College/Pop Art/Fotorealismus. Schwerpunkte der Österreichischen Ludwig Stiftung", in: Kat. *Die Sammlung*, Museum Moderner Kunst Stiftung Ludwig Wien, 2001, S. 203–229, hier: S. 206 f. Cunningham sollte etwa wichtige Impulse für die Performance-Art liefern. Vgl. Patrick Werkner, *Kunst seit 1940. Von Jackson Pollock bis Joseph Beuys*, Wien, Köln, Weimar 2007, S. 54.

4   Zur Beteiligung des Betrachters vgl. etwa Lars Blunck, *Between Object & Event. Partizipationskunst zwischen Mythos und Teilhabe*, Weimar 2003.

5   "At a certain moment, the canvas began to appear to one American painter after another as an arena in which to act—rather than as a space in which to reproduce, re-design, analyze, or 'express' an object, actual or imagined." Harold Rosenberg, „The American Action Painters", in: *Art News*, 51/8 (1952), S. 22 f. u. S. 48–50. Hier zit. n.: ders., *The Tradition of the New* (1960), New York 1994, S. 23–39, hier: S. 25.

6   "(…) the nature of painting had shifted from a space for picturing things to an 'arena in which to act' (…)." David Joselit, *American Art Since 1945*, London 2003, S. 9. Nach seiner Deklaration des Bildraums als „Arena" fügt Rosenberg hinzu: "What was to go on the canvas was not a picture but an event." (Wie Anm. 5, S. 25.)

7   Zum komplexen Verhältnis der beiden Sphären des Privaten und Öffentlichen, die sich durch neue Medien in der amerikanischen Nachkriegskultur überschneiden, vgl. Joselit, *American Art* (wie Anm. 6), S. 12. Die Verlinkung von (privater) Bild-„Arena" und Öffentlichkeit sowie die damit einhergehenden Expansionsbewegungen der Kunstwelt sind von Joselits Ausführungen informiert.

8   Zu diesen Aufnahmen vgl. etwa Thomas Dreher, *Performance Art nach 1945. Aktionstheater und Intermedia*, München 2001, S. 59–63.

9   Robert Morris drückte es in den späten 1960er-Jahren folgendermaßen aus: "Of the Abstract Expressionists, only Pollock was able to *recover process and hold on to it as part of the end form of the work*. Pollock's recovery of process involved a profound rethinking of the role of both material and tools in making." (Hervorhebung v. G. H.) Zit. n. dem Eintrag von Rosalind Krauss zum Jahr 1949 in: Hal Foster u. a. (Hg.), *Art since 1900. Modernism Antimodernism Postmodernism*, London 2004, S. 355–359, hier: S. 358.

10   "These painters allowed the process of making their art to stand as a fundamental aspect of its 'content.'" Joselit, *American Art* (wie Anm. 6), S. 9. Vgl. auch ebd., S. 33.

11   Vgl. Dreher, *Performance Art* (wie Anm. 8), S. 63, sowie Werkner, *Kunst seit 1940* (wie Anm. 3), S. 25 u. S. 55.

12   Im Bereich der Kunst haben in den letzten Jahrzehnten vielfältigste Expansionsbewegungen stattgefunden – seien es aufgeblähte Blasen des Marktes, das Verschieben von Kunstwerken aus dem White Cube in die Öffentlichkeit zwecks Werbung, die stetig ansteigende Größe von Museumsbauten oder die immersiven Wirkungen von Werken selbst, die mitunter ans Spektakel grenzen – wie etwa James Turrells Lichträume. Vgl. zu derartigen strukturellen Veränderungen auch Rosalind Krauss, „The Cultural Logic of the Late Capitalist Museum", in: *October*, 54 (1990), S. 3–17, sowie ihren Eintrag zum Jahr 1976 in: Foster u. a. (Hg.), *Art since 1900* (wie. Anm. 9), S. 576–579.

13   Vgl. Blunck, *Between Object & Event* (wie Anm. 4), S. 11, sowie Werkner, *Kunst seit 1940* (wie Anm. 3), S. 43.

14   Das Beispiel Pollocks kann dazu dienen, die Aufmerksamkeit für künstlerische Phänomene zu schärfen, in denen sich Überschneidungen beziehungsweise Übergänge von Prozess und Expansion zeigen, die in einer vielfältigen Weise zu einer Auslotung des Mediums Malerei und damit auch zu dessen Überschreitung führen können.

15   "Although it still remains easel painting somehow, at least when successful, and will still hang dramatically on a wall, *this sort of painting comes closest of all to decoration—to wallpaper patterns capable of being extended indefinitely—and in so far as it still remains easel painting it infects the whole notion of this form with ambiguity." (Hervorhebung v. G. H.) Clement Greenberg, „The Crisis of the Easel Picture" (1948), in: ders., *The Collected Essays and Criticism*, Bd. 2: *Arrogant Purpose: 1945–1949*, Chicago 1986, S. 221–225, hier: S. 223. An dieser zitierten Stelle scheint sich eine gewisse Skepsis bemerkbar zu machen, die in der Sorge um die festen Grenzen der (autonomen) Kunst begründet liegen mag, um die Grenzen zwischen hehrer Kunst und mondäner Umwelt, zwischen Hochkunst und angewandter Kunst und so weiter. Vgl. dazu Stefan Neuner, *Maskierung der Malerei. Jasper Johns nach Willem de Kooning*, München 2008, S. 96–98 u. S. 116 f., Anm. 37 u. Anm. 38.

16   Zu diesem Bild und seinem expansiven Charakter vgl. den Eintrag von Friedrich Tietjen in Kat. *Die Sammlung* (wie Anm. 3), S. 110.

17 Rosalind Krauss, „The Crisis of the Easel Picture", in: Kat. *Jackson Pollock. New Approaches*, Museum of Modern Art New York, 1999, S. 155–179.

18 Auch wenn Pollock seine Leinwände beim Bemalen vertikal gedacht haben mag.

19 Als Hauptbeispiel in ihrem Text wählt Krauss *Casting*, ein Frühwerk von Richard Serra aus dem Jahr 1969. Darin führte dieser Pollocks Geste des Träufelns von Farbe auf die am Boden liegende Leinwand fort, indem er geschmolzenes Blei gegen die Kante zwischen Boden und Wand warf, das in seiner erstarrten Form zu einem Index für das Ereignis des wiederholten Werfens wurde – durch diesen Index der Wiederholung, der auf die Offenheit der Serie verweist, widersetzt sich das Werk auch einer institutionellen Rahmung und Stillstellung, was ihm eine zusätzliche expansive Dimension verleiht.

20 Vgl. Joselit, *American Art* (wie Anm. 6), S. 37 u. S. 39.

21 Vgl. ebd., S. 34–40, S. 42 u. S. 45, sowie den Eintrag von Rosalind Krauss zum Jahr 1953 in: Foster u. a. (Hg.), *Art since 1900* (wie Anm. 9), S. 368–372. Vgl. ebenfalls Ulf Küster, „Action Painting – Myth and Reality", in: Fondation Beyeler (Hg.), *Action Painting. Jackson Pollock*, Ostfildern 2008, S. 12–19, bes. S. 18.

22 Pollock stellte mit seiner Maltechnik neben Saint Phalle auch für Georges Mathieu, César oder die Gutai-Gruppe einen wichtigen Vorläufer dar. Vgl. Werkner, *Kunst seit 1940* (wie Anm. 3), S. 24 u. S. 92. Vgl. zu dieser Einflussgeschichte auch Dreher, *Performance Art* (wie Anm. 8), S. 68–70 u. S. 77 f.

23 Dies ist natürlich bereits bei Pollocks „Dripping"-Technik gegenüber dem traditionellen Schema Auge/Hand/Pinsel/Leinwand der Fall; verglichen mit den zuletzt vorgestellten Positionen, besteht aber im Fall Pollocks noch ein weit größerer Grad an Steuerung und somit auch an kompositorischen Entscheidungen.

24 Hierbei ist jedoch darauf zu achten, dass etwa die Strömung des abstrakten Expressionismus in den USA und verwandte europäische Kunstentwicklungen der gleichen Zeit wie Informel und Tachismus voneinander unabhängig entstanden sind (auch wenn der Tachismus mitunter als „Version" des abstrakten Expressionismus bezeichnet wird, beispielsweise im Glossar von *Art since 1900* [wie Anm. 9]). Aber selbst wenn von keiner unmittelbaren Beeinflussung durch oder einer direkten Bezugnahme auf das Erbe des abstrakten Expressionismus gesprochen werden kann, lohnt es sich, die verschiedenen künstlerischen Positionen miteinander zu vergleichen und in Beziehung zu setzen.

25 Vgl. den Eintrag von Tietjen in Kat. *Die Sammlung* (wie Anm. 3), S. 126. Kleins *Anthropometrien* hingegen eröffnen sehr wohl eine haptisch-taktile Dimension.

26 Schon im Zusammenhang mit der Malpraxis Willem de Koonings, einer Vorzeigefigur des Action-Painting und des abstrakten Expressionismus, war von Gewalt gegenüber dem Bildträger gesprochen worden.

27 Vgl. dazu Joselit, *American Art* (wie Anm. 6), S. 36 f. u. S. 39, sowie den Eintrag von Krauss zum Jahr 1953 (wie Anm. 21), S. 371 f.

28 Vgl. den Eintrag von Stefan Neuner in Kat. *Die Sammlung* (wie Anm. 3), S. 234.

29 Vgl. Joselit, *American Art* (wie Anm. 6), S. 40. Unbestritten ist dabei, dass sich in Graffiti höchst individuelle Ausdrücke erzielen lassen – hier geht es wohl eher um anonymes Gekritzel, das sich einer Zuordnung an ein Individuum verweigert. Dennoch hat Twombly natürlich ein eigenes, unverwechselbares künstlerisches Idiom geschaffen.

30 Vgl. dazu Hanno Millesi, „Bemerkungen zum Wiener Aktionismus, seinen Vorgängern und Nachfolgern sowie seinem Umfeld", in: Kat. *Die Sammlung* (wie Anm. 3), S. 159–185, hier: S. 173.

31 Vgl. zu diesem Werk den Eintrag von Hanno Millesi in Kat. *Die Sammlung* (wie Anm. 3), S. 196.

32 Vgl. zu diesem monotypischen Herstellungsverfahren des Werks Susanne Neuburger, „An der Schwelle zum letzten Jahrhundertdrittel. Das neue Museum des 20. Jahrhunderts, seine Sammlungspolitik und die Sammlungsbestände des Museums moderner Kunst von der Nachkriegszeit bis in die sechziger Jahre", in: Kat. *Die Sammlung* (wie Anm. 3), S. 95–109, hier: S. 104.

33 Vgl. Millesi, „Bemerkungen zum Wiener Aktionismus" (wie Anm. 30), S. 169.

34 Den Hinweis auf diese Korrelation verdanke ich Rainer Fuchs.

35 Vgl. Robert Fleck, „Action Painting – Today", in: Fondation Beyeler (Hg.), *Action Painting* (wie Anm. 21), S. 178–184, bes. S. 181.

36 Vgl. zu diesem Werk Hochdörfer, „To Let the World Come in Again" (wie Anm. 3), S. 213.

37 Allan Kaprow, „The Legacy of Jackson Pollock" (1958), in: ders., *Essays on the Blurring of Art and Life*, Berkeley 1993, S. 1–9.

38 Die Spannung zwischen einer Identifikation mit dem Künstler in Bewegung und den gegenständlichen Malspuren (von denen diese ausgeht) entfernt laut Kaprow Pollocks Kunst weit von einer abgeschlossenen Malerei. Den buchstäblich expansiven Charakter Pollock'scher Kunst sollte Kaprow insofern forcieren, als er einen gänzlich von der Malerei Pollocks bedeckten Ausstellungsraum imaginierte, die so zu einem Environment würde.

39 Vgl. Joselit, *American Art* (wie Anm. 6), S. 34 u. S. 50 f.

40 Damit arbeitete er auch gegen Greenberg, der sich ja mit einem Beharren auf Kunstautonomie gegen eine Vermischung verschiedener ästhetischer Sphären wie Kunst und Leben gestellt hatte (s. auch Anm. 15).

41 "The act-painting is of the same metaphysical substance as the artist's existence. The new painting has broken down every distinction between art and life." Rosenberg, „The American Action Painters" (wie Anm. 5), S. 28.

42 Vgl. dazu Hochdörfer, „To Let the World Come in Again" (wie Anm. 3). Natürlich war aber die vorangegangene Kunst nicht so rein und puristisch wie angenommen. Jackson Pollock etwa hatte in *Full Fathom Five* (1947) ein Impasto gelegt, angereichert mit Gegenständen wie Nägeln, Knöpfen, Schlüsseln, Zigaretten et cetera. Und Morris Louis hatte mit seinen Rinnbildern mehr die Materialität von Leinwand und Farbe betont als das „rein Optische", das Greenberg darin sehen wollte. Vgl. den Eintrag von Jörg Wolfert in Kat. *Die Sammlung* (wie Anm. 3), S. 112. Greenbergs Begriff des „Optischen" kann als eine Gegenreaktion auf literalistische Strömungen um 1960 verstanden werden, die die Körperlichkeit beziehungsweise Objekthaftigkeit von Kunstwerken betonten, wie es etwa Jasper Johns' Bildobjekte vorführten. Vgl. dazu Krauss, „The Crisis of the Easel Picture", (wie Anm. 17), S. 164 f.

43 Vgl. den Eintrag von Heike Eipeldauer in Kat. *Die Sammlung* (wie Anm. 3), S. 230. Zu Leo Steinbergs Begriff der „flatbed picture plane",
    der in diesem Zusammenhang zentral ist, vgl. ders., *Other Criteria. Confrontations with Twentieth-Century Art* (1972), Chicago 2007,
    S. 55–91, bes. S. 82 ff. Rosalind Krauss hatte in ihrem Beitrag zur Pollock-Ausstellung (Anm. 17) Fragen der (impliziten) Orientierung
    von Kunstwerken und deren Verhältnis zum Betrachter wieder aufgegriffen; Steinberg und Krauss arbeiteten damit beide gegen
    Greenbergs Begriff des „Optischen" und seine modernistische Kunsttheorie. Vgl. dazu auch Hochdörfer, „To Let the World Come in
    Again" (wie Anm. 3), S. 229.
44 Vgl. Neuburger, „An der Schwelle zum letzten Jahrhundertdrittel" (wie Anm. 32), S. 98.
45 Vgl. den Eintrag von Thomas Trummer in Kat. *Die Sammlung* (wie Anm. 3), S. 116.
46 Dies sind Formen der Problematisierung des Mediums Malerei, die auch dessen Status als Endziel künstlerischer Tätigkeit infrage stellen.
    Vgl. Dreher, *Performance Art* (wie Anm. 8), S. 72.
47 Diese Tendenz, die Körperlichkeit des Bildträgers zu betonen, sollte allerdings im Fotorealismus Ende der 1960er-Jahre konterkariert
    werden, der die materielle Oberfläche des Werks eben nicht affirmieren, sondern in einem täuschenden Illusionismus auflösen wollte.
    Vgl. dazu Hochdörfer, „To Let the World Come in Again" (wie Anm. 3), S. 225. Den Hinweis auf diese Gegenströmung verdanke ich
    Martin de la Iglesia.
48 Picasso öffnete um 1911 mit seinen Collagen die Bildfläche hin zum Realraum und stellte mit seiner *Gitarre* (1912–1913) ein Objekt her.
    Beeinflusst von Picassos kubistischen Konstruktionen, entwickelte Tatlin 1914/1915 seine *Eckreliefs*. Duchamp schuf einerseits Werke,
    die in den Raum ausgreifen, aber immer noch am Begriff der Malerei partizipieren (wie etwa sein *Großes Glas*), und lieferte andererseits
    wichtige Vorbilder für Installationen. Schwitters hatte mit seinem *Merzbau* in den 1920er- und 1930er-Jahren an einer Innenrauminstal-
    lation gearbeitet. Zu Schwitters als Vorläufer der Objektkunst um 1960 vgl. Werkner, *Kunst seit 1940* (wie Anm. 3), S. 46 u. S. 49.
49 Vgl. zu dieser Klimax und der gleichzeitigen Öffnung des medienspezifischen Paradigmas den Eintrag von Rosalind Krauss zum Jahr 1960
    in: Foster u. a. (Hg.), *Art since 1900* (wie Anm. 9), S. 439–444, hier: S. 444, sowie dies., „The Crisis of the Easel Picture" (wie Anm. 17),
    S. 164 f. Auch die in diesem Text behandelten Aspekte von Prozess und Expansion können mitunter als Endpunkte und Überschreitun-
    gen der medienspezifischen Logik betrachtet werden, die von ihr zwar verdeckt, aber gleichzeitig befördert wurden. Spezifität meinte
    so im Falle Pollocks eine Dramatisierung der materiellen Natur der Farbe im Malakt, was ja eine wichtige Basis für die Überschreitung
    des Mediums Malerei bildete. Vgl. Joselit, *American Art* (wie Anm. 6), S. 11. Greenberg selbst ging angesichts der literalistischen Strö-
    mungen der 1960er-Jahre, die doch ihrerseits nur die Konsequenzen aus seiner materialistisch gedachten „flatness" gezogen hatten,
    zum Begriff des „Optischen" über, der die Materialität des Bildträgers wiederum transzendieren sollte (s. auch Anm. 42). Vgl. zu diesem
    Wandel der Terminologie Greenbergs den Eintrag von Krauss zum Jahr 1960 in: Foster u. a. (Hg.), *Art since 1900* (wie Anm. 9),
    S. 439–444.
50 Vgl. den Eintrag von Hal Foster zum Jahr 1958 in: ders. u. a. (Hg.), *Art since 1900* (wie Anm. 9), S. 404–410.
51 Vgl. ebd., S. 409.
52 Vgl. den Eintrag von Rosalind Krauss zum Jahr 1965 in: Foster u. a. (Hg.), *Art since 1900* (wie Anm. 9), S. 492–495, hier: S. 493.
53 Vgl. Eva Badura-Triska, „Minimal und die Folgen. Aspekte der Kunst der sechziger Jahre", in: Kat. *Die Sammlung* (wie Anm. 3),
    S. 255–277, hier: S. 263.
54 Vgl. dazu Rebentisch, *Ästhetik der Installation* (wie Anm. 2).
55 Vgl. Badura-Triska, „Minimal und die Folgen" (wie Anm. 53), S. 264. Andere Künstler hatten sich ja bereits einige Zeit vorher das
    Vermeiden kompositorischer Erwägungen zur Aufgabe gemacht. Wandte sich die Minimal Art zwar gegen den Subjektivismus des
    abstrakten Expressionismus, so machte sie sich doch gleichzeitig eine Steigerung körperlicher Erfahrung zum Ziel, die in anderer Form
    von Künstlern wie Kaprow, ausgehend vom abstrakten Expressionismus, entwickelt worden war.
56 Vgl. dazu den Eintrag von Hal Foster zum Jahr 1962 in: ders. u. a. (Hg.), *Art since 1900* (wie Anm. 9), S. 470–474. Ich danke Rainer Fuchs
    für den Hinweis auf diese kulturellen Brüche und Neuanknüpfungen.
57 Vgl. dazu Badura-Triska, „Minimal und die Folgen" (wie Anm. 53), S. 266.

1   The reasons for this intensification of processual and expansive phenomena in postwar western art are complex and have their roots in social contexts on the one hand and in immanent developments in the art world itself on the other. The state of intellectual crisis after World War II was also a crisis of artistic representation. The art forms that developed into gestures of liberation from the rigidly naturalist artistic standards stipulated by totalitarian regimes were the ones that relieved themselves of any obligation to representationalism in painting. This phenomenon can be observed, for example, in the case of processual works (on the abandonment of the limits of naturalistic representation, see the literature cited in note 5). Additionally, the postwar period saw the rise of cultures that studied the speed and evanescence of modern life, such as the beat generation in the United States. As regards developments immanent in the art world itself, one can observe repeated efforts by new movements to shrug off those that had gone before. One example of this phenomenon is the emphasis that process art placed on the processual and on the changes in the appearance of a work of art over time, which can be viewed as an antithesis to the rigidly geometric forms of minimal art. In the case of American art movements (such as minimal art), aspects of expansion were sometimes linked with criticism of a traditional outlook—which was perceived as European— on the concept of the picture and with attempts to break free from it (see the literature cited in note 53).

2   On this shift, see, for example, Erika Fischer-Lichte, *Ästhetik des Performativen*, Frankfurt, 2004. The shift is reflected on the theoretical level in the displacement of an objectivist aesthetic of the work by a theory of aesthetic experience. See Juliane Rebentisch, *Ästhetik der Installation*, Frankfurt, 2003, p. 9f. In this context, see also John Dewey's book *Art as Experience*, which was published in 1934.

3   The Black Mountain College in North Carolina, where Cunningham and Cage and others worked together, played a key role here. See Achim Hochdörfer, "To Let the World Come in Again. Das Black Mountain College/Pop Art/Fotorealismus. Schwerpunkte der Österreichischen Ludwig Stiftung", in: Cat. *Die Sammlung*, Museum Moderner Kunst Stiftung Ludwig Wien, Vienna, 2001, p. 203–229, here: p. 206f. Cunningham was to provide important impulses for the development of performance art. See Patrick Werkner, *Kunst seit 1940. Von Jackson Pollock bis Joseph Beuys*, Vienna, Cologne, Weimar, 2007, p. 54.

4   On the participation of the observer see, for example, Lars Blunck, *Between Object & Event: Partizipationskunst zwischen Mythos und Teilhabe*, Weimar, 2003.

5   "At a certain moment, the canvas began to appear to one American painter after another as an arena in which to act—rather than as a space in which to reproduce, re-design, analyze, or 'express' an object, actual or imagined." Harold Rosenberg, "The American Action Painters," in: *Art News*, 51/8 (1952), p. 22f. & p. 48–50. Quoted here from Harald Rosenberg, *The Tradition of the New* (1960), New York, 1994, p. 23–39, here: p. 25.

6   "(...) the nature of painting had shifted from a space for picturing things to an 'arena in which to act' (...)." David Joselit, *American Art Since 1945*, London, 2003, p. 9. After declaring the picture area to be an "arena," Rosenberg adds: "What was to go on the canvas was not a picture but an event." (loc. cit. in note 5, p. 25.)

7   On the complex relationship between the private and public spheres that overlap in postwar American culture due to the impact of the new media, see Joselit, *American Art* (see note 6), p. 12. The links between the (private) picture "arena" and the public sphere and the concomitant expansionist movements in the art world are informed by Joselit's remarks.

8   On these films and photographs, see for example Thomas Dreher, *Performance Art nach 1945. Aktionstheater und Intermedia*, Munich, 2001, p. 59–63.

9   In the late 1960s, Robert Morris put it as follows: "Of the Abstract Expressionists, only Pollock was able to *recover process and hold on to it as part of the end form of the work*. Pollock's recovery of process involved a profound rethinking of the role of both material and tools in making." (emphasis by G. H.) Quoted from Rosalind Krauss' entry for the year 1949 in: Hal Foster et al. (eds.), *Art since 1900. Modernism Antimodernism Postmodernism*, London, 2004, p. 355–359, here: p. 358.

10 "These painters allowed the process of making their art to stand as a fundamental aspect of its 'content.'" Joselit, *American Art* (see note 6), p. 9. See also Ibid., p. 33.

11 See Dreher, *Performance Art* (see note 8), p. 63, and Werkner, *Kunst seit 1940* (see note 3), p. 25 & p. 55.

12 In the field of art, the last few decades have seen a wide variety of expansionist movements—the inflated bubbles on the art market, the shifting of works of art from the white cube into the public sphere for advertising purposes, the continual increase in the size of museum buildings, and the immersive effects of the works themselves that sometimes, as in the case of James Turrell's light spaces, border on public spectacles. On these kinds of structural changes, see also Rosalind Krauss, "The Cultural Logic of the Late Capitalist Museum, " in: *October*, 54 (1990), p. 3–17, and her entry for the year 1976 in: Foster et al. (eds.), *Art since 1900* (see note 9), p. 576–579.

13 See also Blunck, *Between Object & Event* (see note 4), p. 11, and Werkner, *Kunst seit 1940* (see note 3), p. 43.

14 The example of Pollock can serve to heighten awareness of those artistic phenomena that display areas of overlap and transition between process and expansion. These overlaps and transitions can trigger an exploration of the medium of painting and even its transcendence in many different ways.

15 "Although it still remains easel painting somehow, at least when successful, and will still hang dramatically on a wall, *this sort of painting comes closest of all to decoration—to wallpaper patterns capable of being extended indefinitely*—and in so far as it still remains easel painting it infects the whole notion of this form with ambiguity." (Emphasis by G. H.) Clement Greenberg, "The Crisis of the Easel Picture" (1948), in: Clement Greenberg, *The Collected Essays and Criticism*, Vol. 2: *Arrogant Purpose: 1945–1949*, (ed.) John O'Brian, Chicago, 1986, p. 221–225, here: p. 223. The passage quoted here seems to exude a certain skepticism, which may be rooted in a concern for the fixed borders of (autonomous) art, the boundaries between sublime art and the mundane environment, between high art and applied art, and so forth. See also Stefan Neuner, *Maskierung der Malerei. Jasper Johns nach Willem de Kooning*, Munich, 2008, p. 96–98 & p. 116f., note 37 and note 38.

16 On this picture and its expansive character, see the entry by Friedrich Tietjen in: Cat. *Die Sammlung* (see note 3), p. 110.

17   Rosalind Krauss, "The Crisis of the Easel Picture," in: Cat. *Jackson Pollock. New Approaches*, Museum of Modern Art, New York, 1999, p. 155–179.

18   Even though Pollock may have had a vertical conception of his canvases while he was painting.

19   Krauss chose *Casting*, an early work by Richard Serra from the year 1969, as the main example in her text. In this work, Serra took up and modified Pollock's gesture of dribbling paint onto a canvas spread out on the floor by throwing molten lead at the seam between the floor and the wall. As it solidified, the lead became an index for the repeated act of throwing—and through this index of repetition, which points towards the openness of the series, the work resists any attempt at institutional framing and immobilization and thus acquires an added expansive dimension.

20   See Joselit, *American Art* (see note 6), p. 37 & p. 39.

21   See Ibid., p. 34–40, p. 42, & p. 45, as well as the entry by Rosalind Krauss for the year 1953 in: Foster et al. (eds.), *Art since 1900* (see note 9), p. 368–372. See also Ulf Küster, "Action Painting – Myth and Reality," in: Fondation Beyeler (ed.), *Action Painting. Jackson Pollock*, Ostfildern, 2008, p. 12–19, esp. p. 18.

22   Pollock's painting technique was an important precursor, along with Saint Phalle, to George Mathieu, César, and the Gutai Group. See Werkner, *Kunst seit 1940* (see note 3), p. 24 & p. 92. On the history of this influence see also Dreher, *Performance Art* (see note 8), p. 68–70 & p. 77f.

23   This is of course also the case in Pollock's "dripping" technique compared to the traditional schema of eye/hand/brush/canvas. Compared to the positions just described, however, Pollock still retains a far higher degree of control and thus also a greater power over compositional decision.

24   It must be noted, however, that the movement of abstract expressionism in the United States and related developments in European art at the same time, such as informel and tachisme, developed independently of one another (even if tachisme is described as a "version" of abstract expressionism in some literature, such as the glossary of *Art since 1900* [see note 9]). But even if it is impossible to speak of an immediate influence by, or direct references to the heritage of, abstract expressionism, it is rewarding to compare the various different artistic positions and to relate them to one another.

25   See the entry by Tietjen in: Cat. *Die Sammlung* (see note 3), p. 126. In contrast, Klein's *Anthropometries* do open up a haptic, tactile dimension.

26   Even the painting practice of Willem de Kooning, one of the leading figures of action painting and abstract expressionism, had prompted observations that violence was being done to the painting support.

27   See Joselit, *American Art* (see note 6), p. 36f. & p. 39, as well as the entry by Krauss for the year 1953 (see note 21), p. 371f.

28   See the entry by Stefan Neuner in: Cat. *Die Sammlung* (see note 3), p. 234.

29   See Joselit, *American Art* (see note 6), p. 40. It is indisputable that graffiti permits a very high degree of individual expression, although we are here most likely dealing with anonymous scribbles that resist any identification with an individual. Nevertheless, Twombly did of course create an original, unmistakably artistic idiom.

30   See Hanno Millesi, "Bemerkungen zum Wiener Aktionismus, seinen Vorgängern und Nachfolgern sowie seinem Umfeld," in: Cat. *Die Sammlung* (see note 3), p. 159–185, here: p. 173.

31   On this work, see the entry by Hanno Millesi in: Cat. *Die Sammlung* (see note 3), p. 196.

32   On the monotype procedure used to create the work, see Susanne Neuburger, "An der Schwelle zum letzten Jahrhundertdrittel. Das neue Museum des 20. Jahrhunderts, seine Sammlungspolitik und die Sammlungsbestände des Museums moderner Kunst von der Nachkriegszeit bis in die sechziger Jahre," in: Cat. *Die Sammlung* (see note 3), p. 95–109, here: p. 104.

33   See Millesi, "Bemerkungen zum Wiener Aktionismus" (see note 30), p. 169.

34   Thanks to Rainer Fuchs for pointing out this correlation.

35   See Robert Fleck, "Action Painting – Today," in: Fondation Beyeler (ed.), *Action Painting* (see note 21), p. 178–184, esp. p. 181.

36   On this work, see Hochdörfer, "To Let the World Come in Again" (see note 3), p. 213.

37   Allan Kaprow, "The Legacy of Jackson Pollock" (1958), in: Kaprow, *Essays on the Blurring of Art and Life*, Berkeley, 1993, p. 1–9.

38   According to Kaprow, the tension between an identification with the artist in motion and the concrete traces of the painting process (which the former takes as its point of departure) means that Pollock's art is far removed from being complete. Kaprow promoted the literally expansive character of Pollock's art in the sense that he imagined an exhibition space that was completely covered with Pollock's painting and was thus transformed into an environment.

39   See Joselit, *American Art* (see note 6), p. 34 & p. 50f.

40   With this he was working against Greenberg, who had insisted on the autonomy of art and opposed the mingling of different aesthetic spheres such as art and life (see also note 15).

41   "The act-painting is of the same metaphysical substance as the artist's existence. The new painting has broken down every distinction between art and life." Rosenberg, "The American Action Painters" (see note 5), p. 28.

42   On this, see Hochdörfer, "To Let the World Come in Again" (see note 3). But the art that had gone before was not, of course, as purist and unadulterated as he assumed. For example, in *Full Fathom Five* (1947) Jackson Pollock had used an impasto enriched with objects such as nails, buttons, keys, cigarettes, and other objects, while the flow pictures of Morris Louis emphasized the materiality of the paint and canvas more than the "purely optical" aspect that Greenberg wanted to see in them. See the entry by Jörg Wolfert in: Cat. *Die Sammlung* (see note 3), p. 112. Greenberg's concept of the "optical" may be seen as a reaction against literalist movements around the year 1960 that stressed the materiality and physical nature of works of art, as can be seen in Jasper John's picture objects. See also Krauss, "The Crisis of the Easel Picture," (see note 17), p. 164 f.

43   See the entry by Heike Eipeldauer in: Cat. *Die Sammlung* (see note 3), p. 230. On Leo Steinberg's concept of the "flatbed picture plane," which is of crucial significance in this context, see Steinberg's, *Other Criteria. Confrontations with Twentieth-Century Art* (1972), Chicago,

2007, p. 55–91, esp. p. 82ff. In her essay for the Pollock exhibition (see note 17), Rosalind Krauss had returned to the questions of the (implicit) orientation of artworks and their relationship to the observer. Thus both Steinberg and Krauss opposed Greenberg's concept of the "optical" and his modernist art theory. See also Hochdörfer, "To Let the World Come in Again" (see note 3), p. 229.

44 See Neuburger, "An der Schwelle zum letzten Jahrhundertdrittel" (see note 32), p. 98.

45 See the entry by Thomas Trummer in: Cat. *Die Sammlung* (see note 3), p. 116.

46 These approaches to the medium of painting also question its status as the ultimate goal of artistic activity. See Dreher, *Performance Art* (see note 8), p. 72.

47 This tendency to stress the corporeality of the picture support was to be countered by the photorealism of the late 1960s. Far from affirming the material surface of the work, this movement strove to dissolve it by means of deceptive illusionism. See Hochdörfer, "To Let the World Come in Again" (see note 3), p. 225. I am grateful to Martin de la Iglesia for pointing out this counter-current.

48 Around the year 1911, Picasso opened up the surface of the image towards real space in his collages and produced an object with his work titled *Guitar* (1912–1913). Under the influence of Picasso's cubist constructions, Tatlin developed his *Eckreliefs* in 1914/1915. Duchamp created works that extend into space but still fall under the definition of painting (for example, his *The Large Glass*, but also provided important prototypes for installations. Schwitters worked on an interior installation titled *Merzbau* in the 1920s and 1930s. For a discussion on Schwitters as a precursor of object art around 1960 see Werkner, *Kunst seit 1940* (see note 3), p. 46 & p. 49.

49 On this climax and the simultaneous opening of the medium-specific paradigm, see the entry by Rosalind Krauss for the year 1960 in: Foster et al. (eds.), *Art since 1900* (see note 9), p. 439–444, here: p. 444, as well as Krauss, "The Crisis of the Easel Picture" (see note 17), p. 164f. The aspects of process and expansion examined in this text can sometimes be regarded as endpoints and transcendences of the logic of medium specificity, a logic which they simultaneously obscured and promoted. Thus specificity, in Pollock's case, signified a dramatization of the material nature of color in the act of painting, which served as an important basis for transcending the medium of painting. See Joselit, *American Art* (see note 6), p. 11. In the face of the literalist movements of the 1960s, which themselves had done nothing more than to draw the inevitable conclusions from Greenberg's materialistically conceived "flatness," Greenberg himself adopted the concept of the "optical," which again aimed to transcend the materiality of the painting support (see also note 42). On this shift in Greenberg's terminology, see the entry by Krauss for the year 1960 in: Foster et al. (eds.), *Art since 1900* (see note 9), p. 439–444.

50 See the entry by Hal Foster for the year 1958 in: Foster et al. (eds.), *Art since 1900* (see note 9), p. 404–410.

51 See Ibid., p. 409.

52 See the entry by Rosalind Krauss for the year 1965 in: Foster et al. (eds.), *Art since 1900* (see note 9), p. 492–495, here: p. 493.

53 See Eva Badura-Triska, "Minimal und die Folgen. Aspekte der Kunst der sechziger Jahre," in: Cat. *Die Sammlung* (see note 3), p. 255–277, here: p. 263.

54 See Rebentisch, *Ästhetik der Installation* (see note 2).

55 See Badura-Triska, "Minimal und die Folgen" (see note 53), p. 264. Other artists had tackled the task of avoiding compositional considerations some time earlier. While minimal art did oppose the subjectivism of abstract expressionism, it also aimed at a heightening of corporeal experience that had been developed in a different form by artists such as Kaprow on the basis of abstract expressionism.

56 See the entry by Hal Foster for the year 1962 in: Foster et al. (eds.), *Art since 1900* (see note 9), p. 470–474. I am indebted to Rainer Fuchs for the reference to these cultural breaks and new beginnings.

57 See Badura-Triska, "Minimal und die Folgen" (see note 53), p. 266.

Aktion, Gestus, Spur / Action, Gesture, Trail

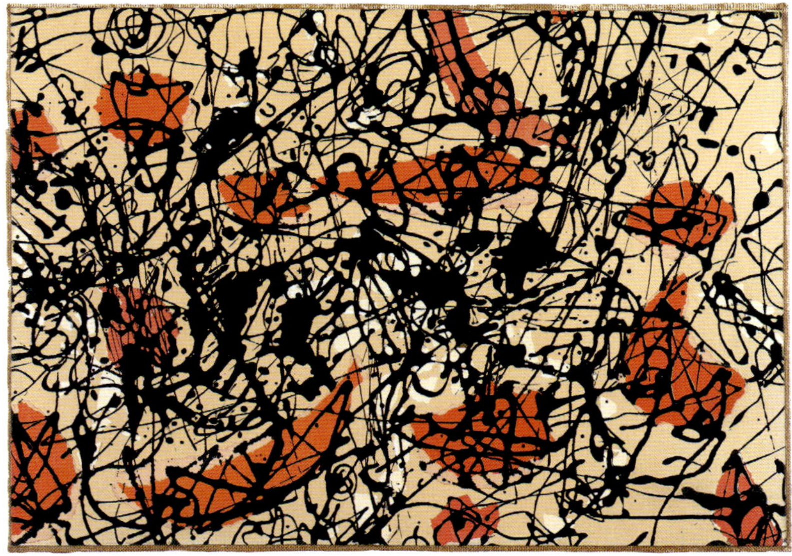

Jackson Pollock
Seven (Sieben), 1950
Email auf brauner Malpappe, Papier auf Leinwand
Enamel on brown board, paper on canvas
33 x 50 cm
Erworben / Acquired in 1993

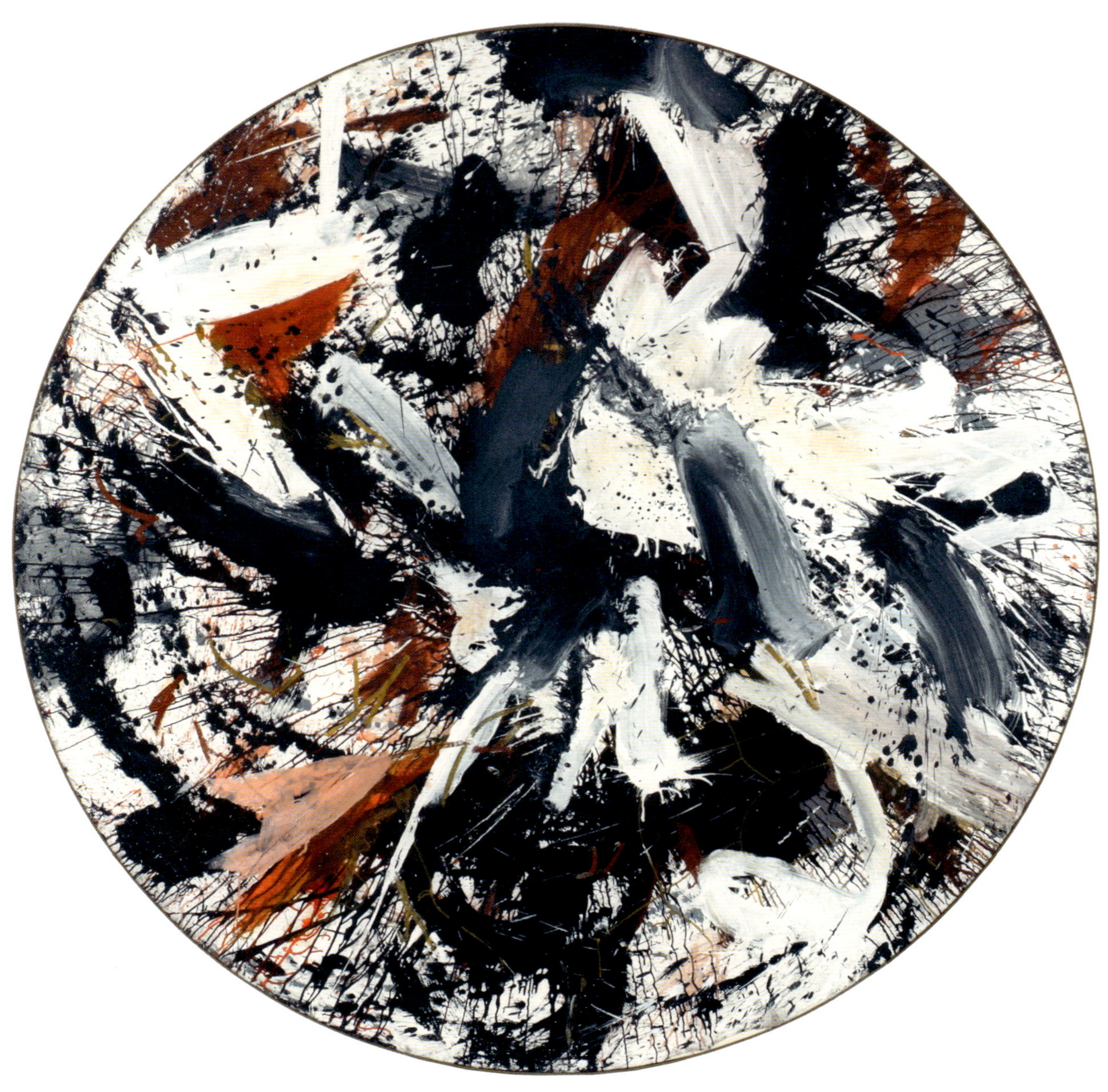

Alfons Schilling
Ohne Titel (Untitled), 1962
Acryl, Pulverfarbe auf Molino / Acrylic, powder paint on molino
Ø 221,5 cm
Erworben / Acquired in 1994

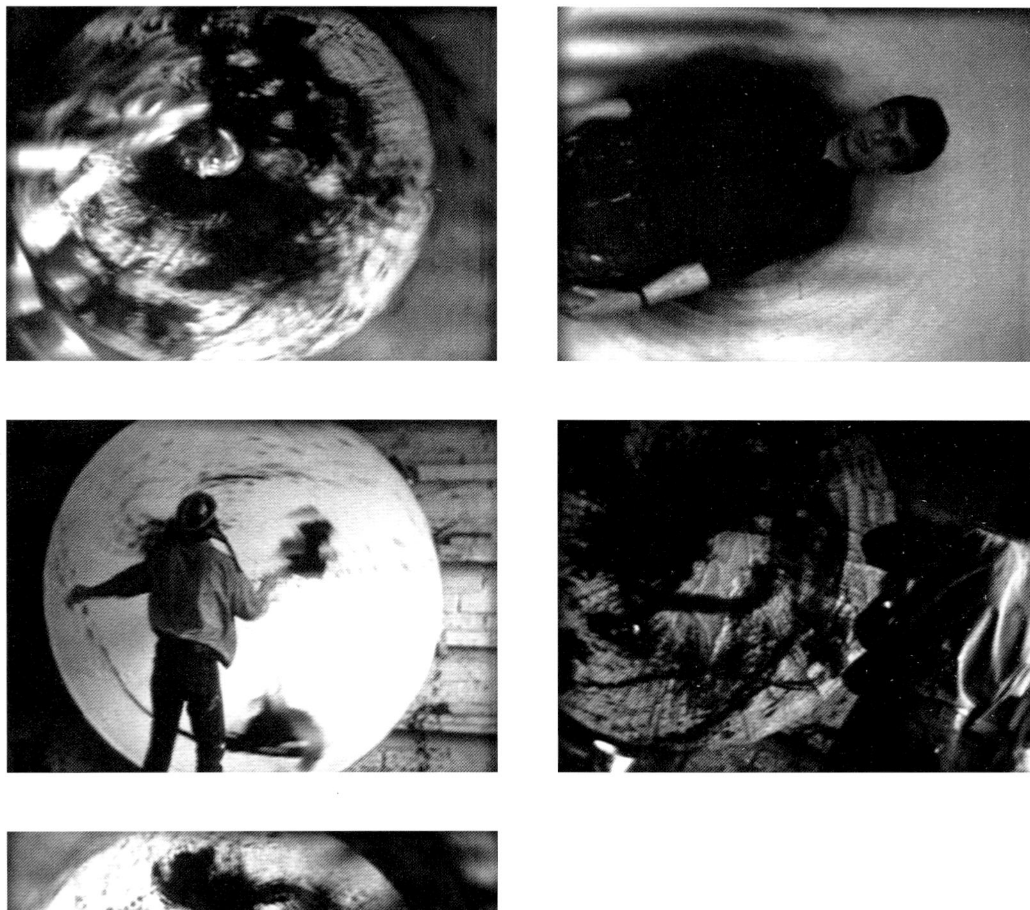

Alfons Schilling
Cosmos Action Painting / Desperate Motion, 1962
8-mm-Film, S/W, Ton / 8mm film, b&w, sound, 12 min
Filmstills / Film stills
Regie / Directed by Niklaus Schilling
Erworben / Acquired in 2009

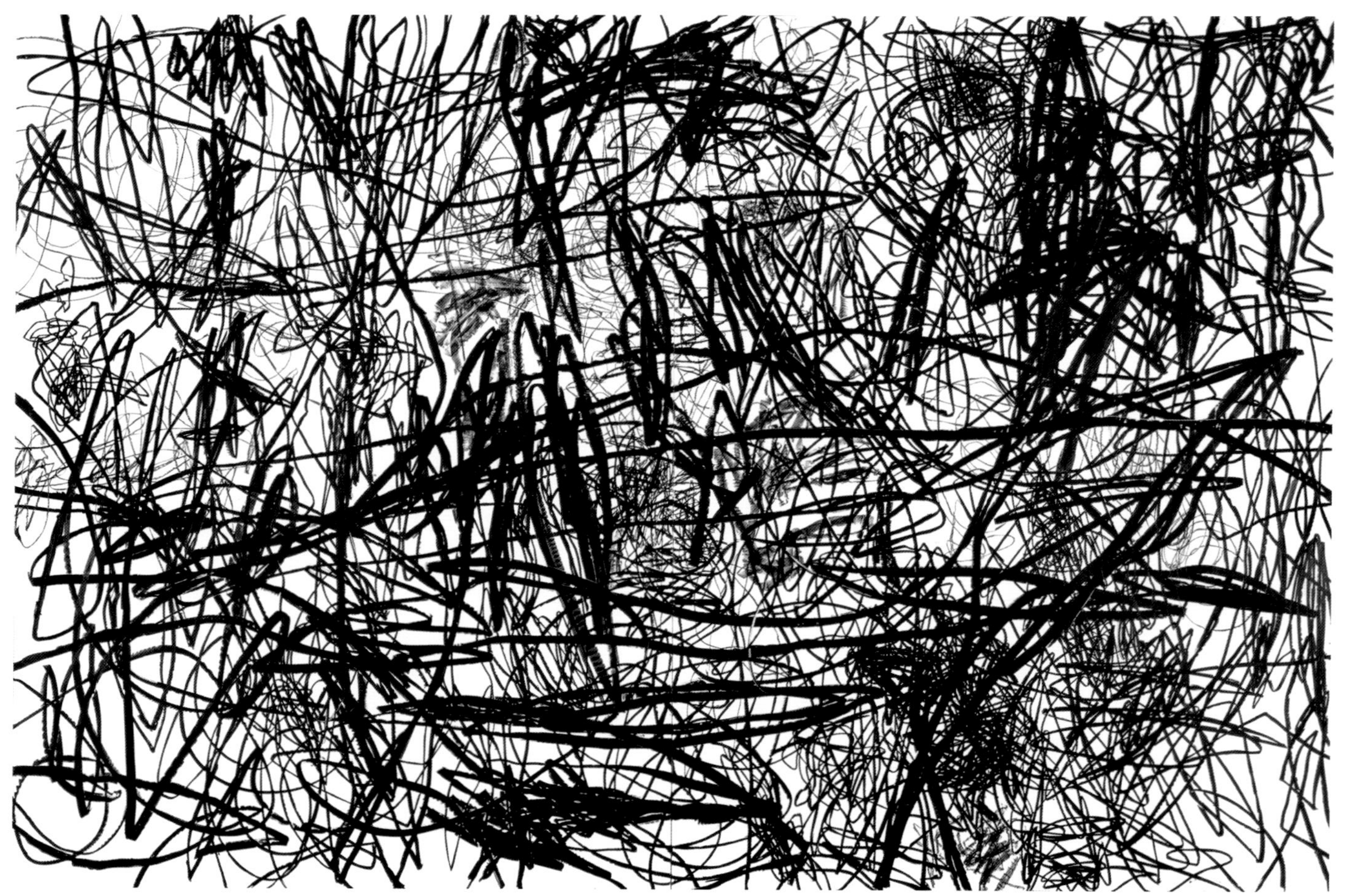

Otto Zitko
Ohne Titel (Untitled), 1996
Öl auf Aluminium / Oil on aluminum
300 x 440 cm
Erworben / Acquired in 1997

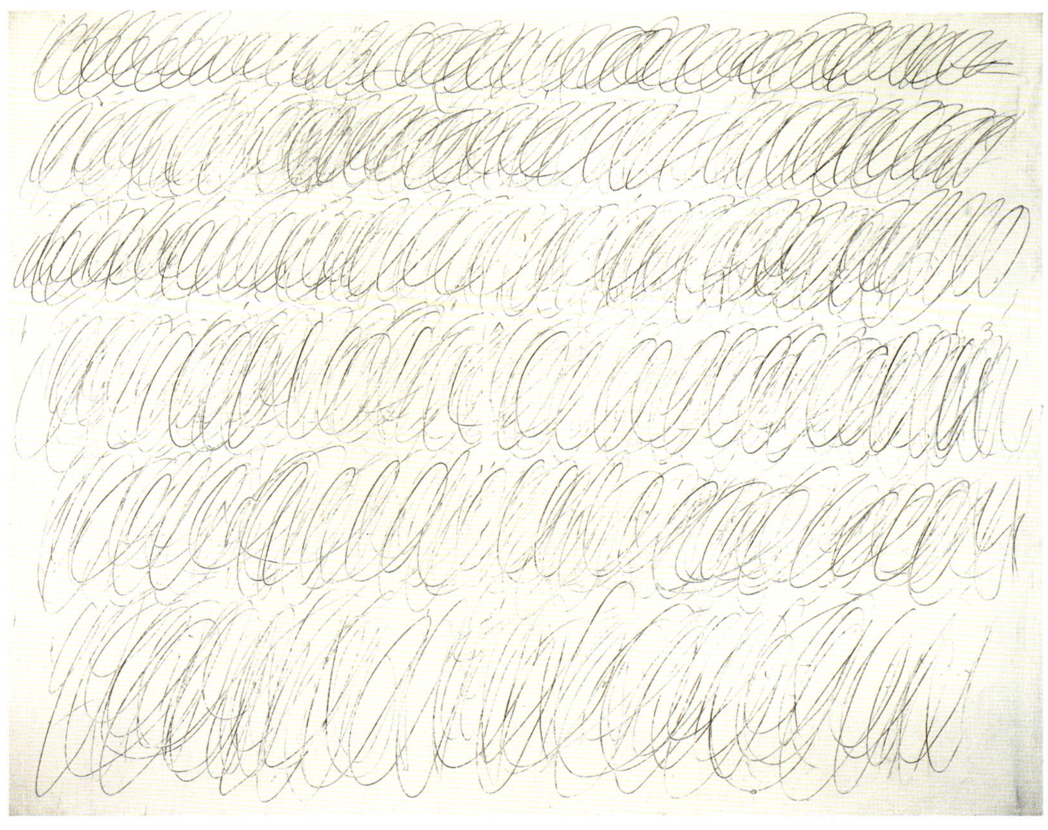

Cy Twombly
Ohne Titel (Untitled), 1968
Wandfarbe auf Ölbasis, Wachskreide auf Leinwand
Oil-based wall paint, wax crayon on canvas
175 x 218 cm
Leihgabe der Österreichischen Ludwig-Stiftung
On loan from the Austrian Ludwig Foundation, seit / since 1991

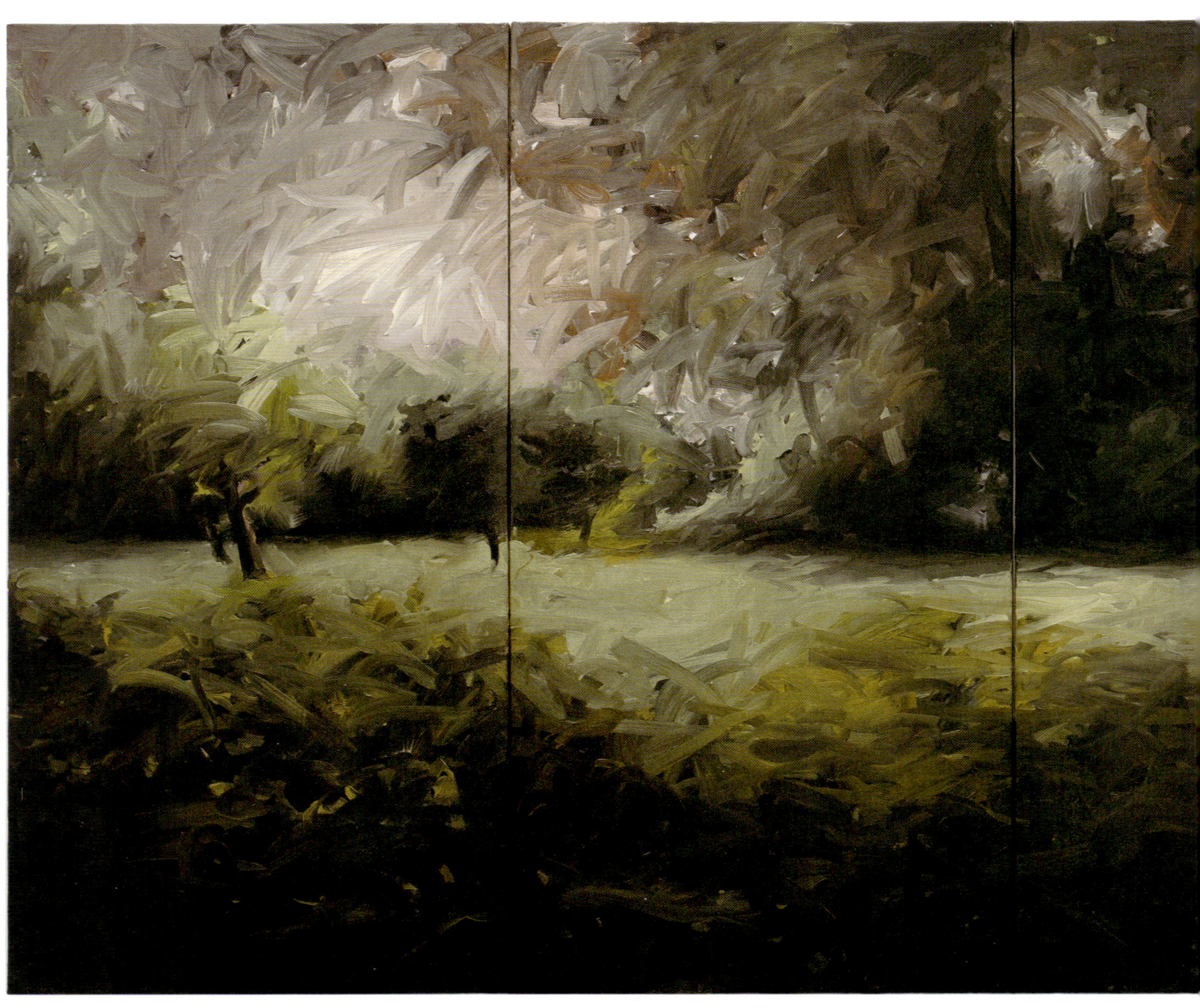

Gerhard Richter
Das Parkstück, 1971
Öl auf Leinwand / Oil on canvas
5-teilig / In five parts: 250 x 625 cm
Leihgabe der Sammlung Ludwig, Aachen
On loan from the Ludwig Collection, Aachen
seit / since 1978

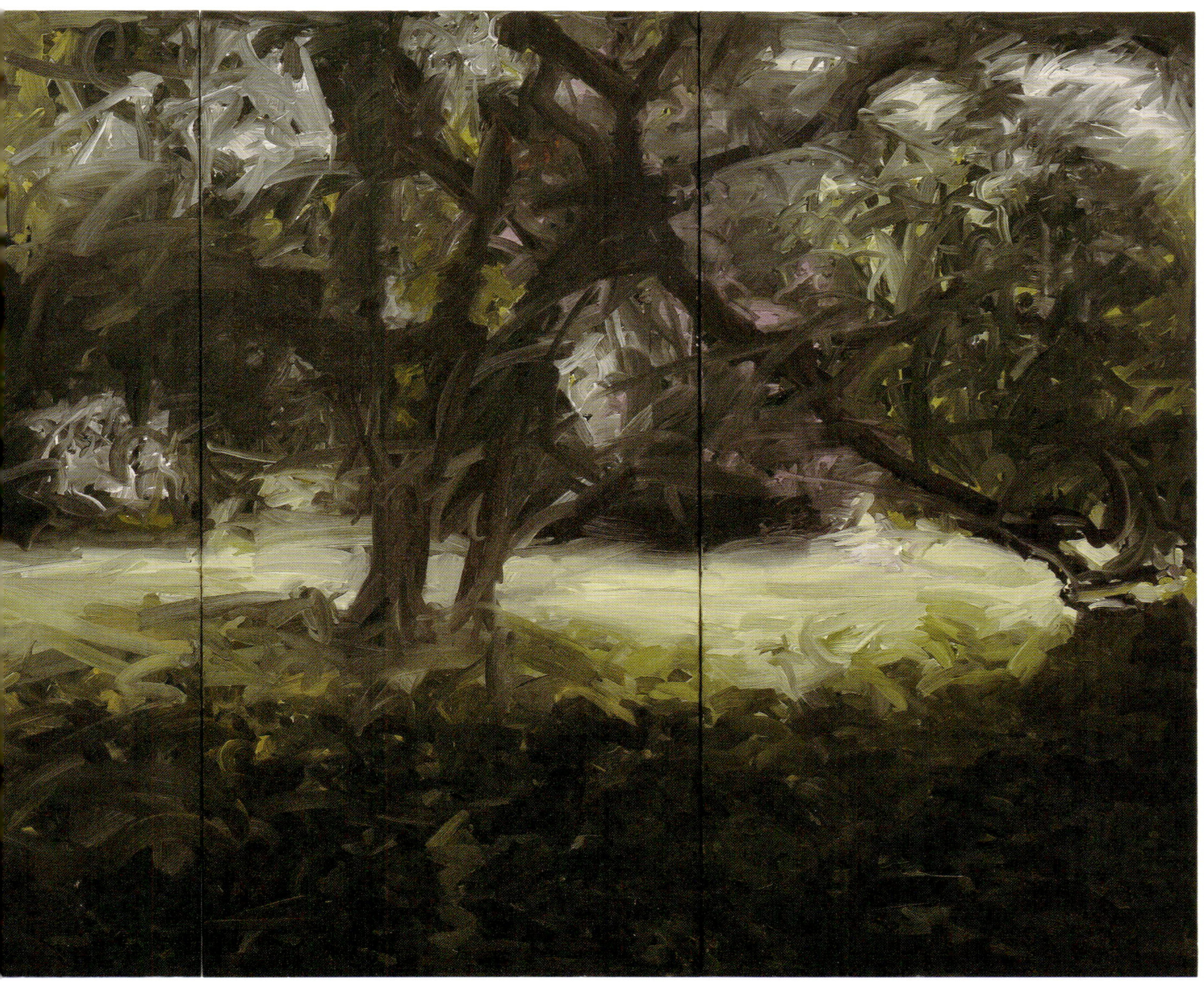

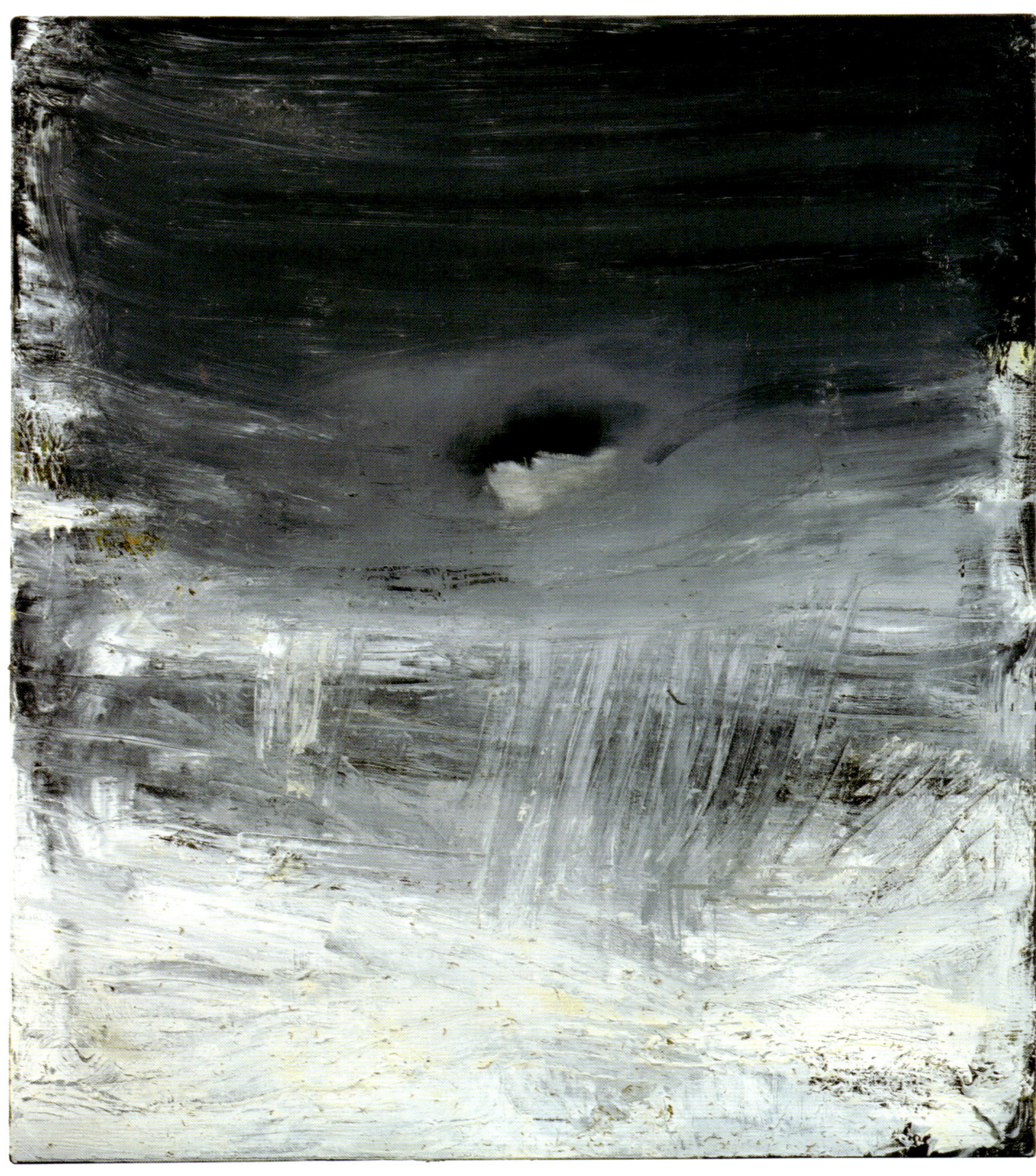

Herbert Brandl
Ohne Titel (Untitled), 1991
Öl auf Leinwand / Oil on canvas
221 x 191 cm
Schenkung der Gesellschaft der Freunde der bildenden Künste
Donated by the Society of the Friends of Fine Arts Vienna, 1993

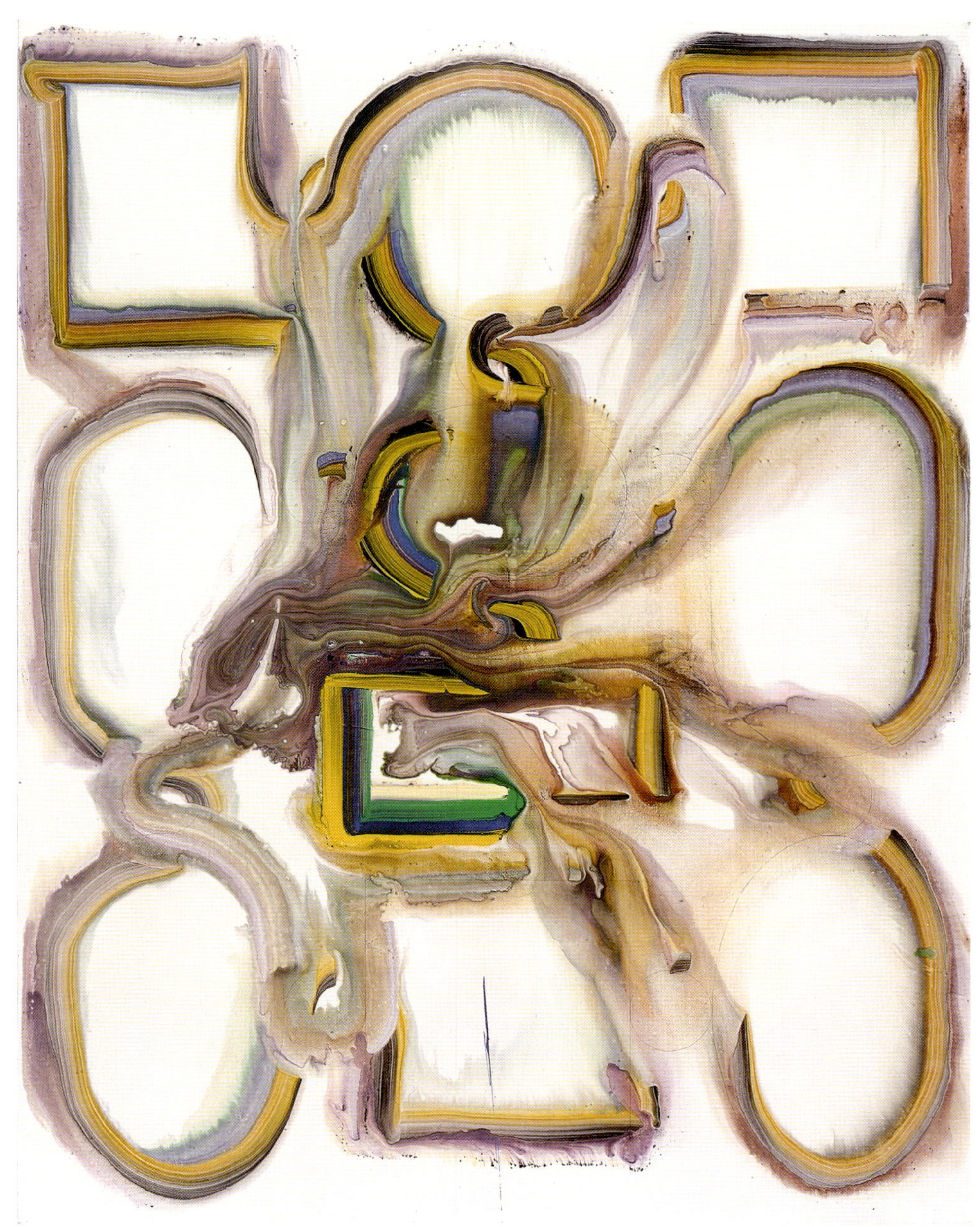

Bernard Frize
Mellegers & Van der Elsakor, 1989
Acryl, Harz auf Leinwand / Acrylic, resin on canvas
240 x 185 cm
Erworben / Acquired in 1998

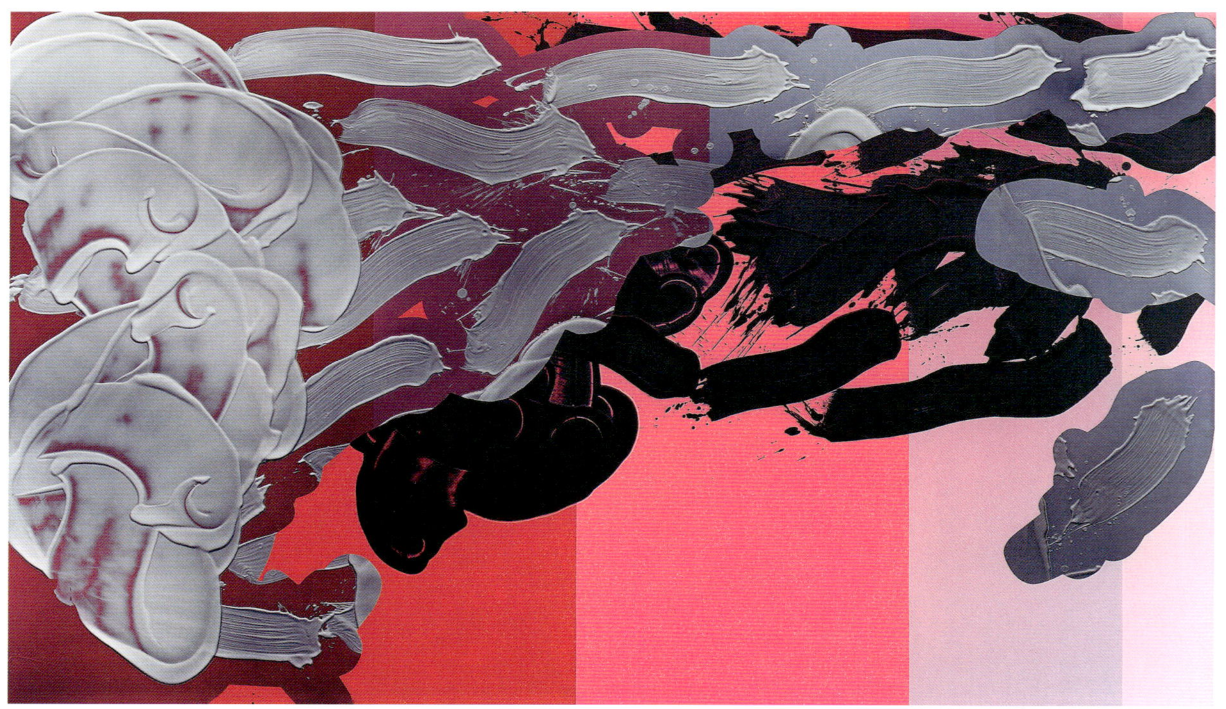

David Reed
348, 1995/1996
Öl, Alkyd auf Leinen / Oil, alkyd on linen
154 x 259 cm
Erworben / Acquired in 1998

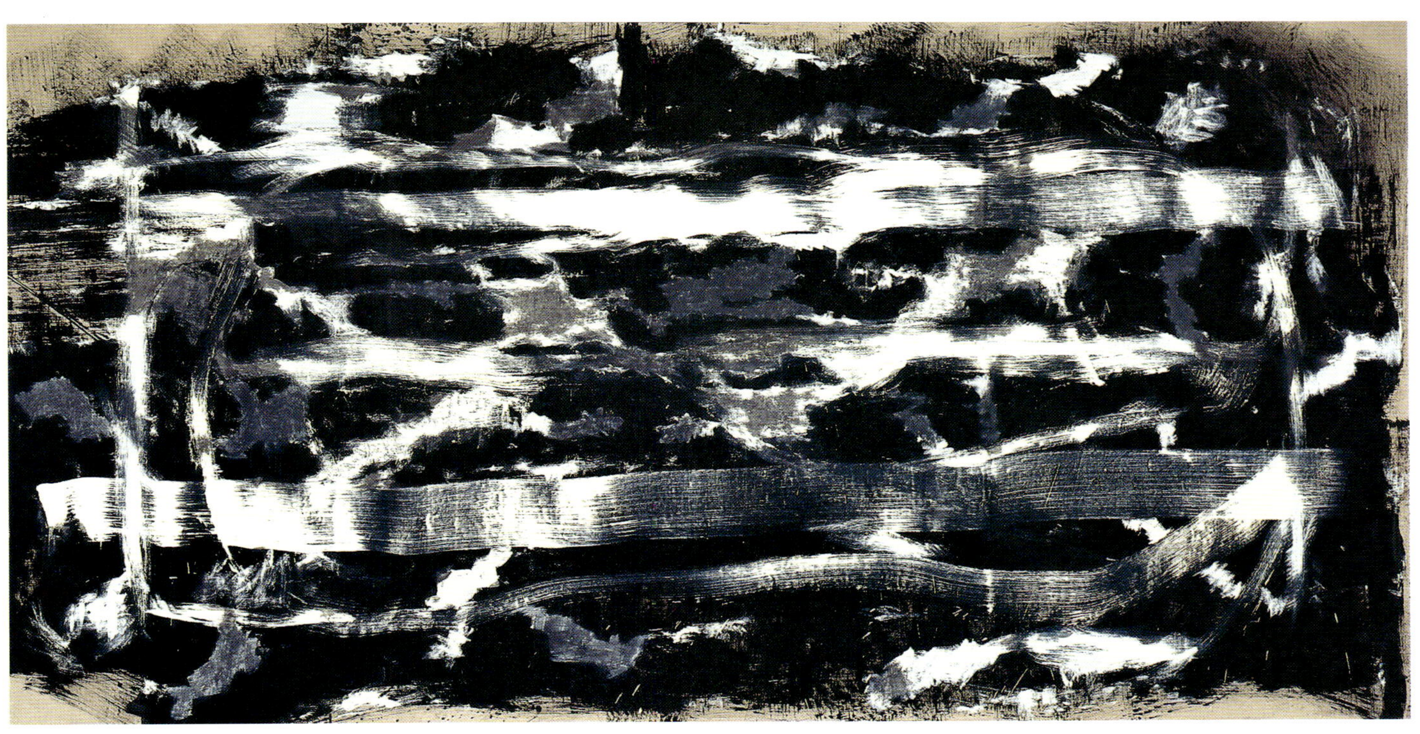

Walter Vopava
Ohne Titel (Untitled), 1991
Dispersion auf Leinwand / Emulsion paint on canvas
300 x 530 cm
Erworben / Acquired in 1992

Andreas Eriksson
Ohne Titel (Untitled), 2007
Mischtechnik auf Leinwand / Mixed media on canvas
75,1 x 42,3 cm
Schenkung Bâloise-Gruppe und Basler Versicherungen Österreich
Donated by the Bâloise Group and Basler Versicherungen Austria, 2008

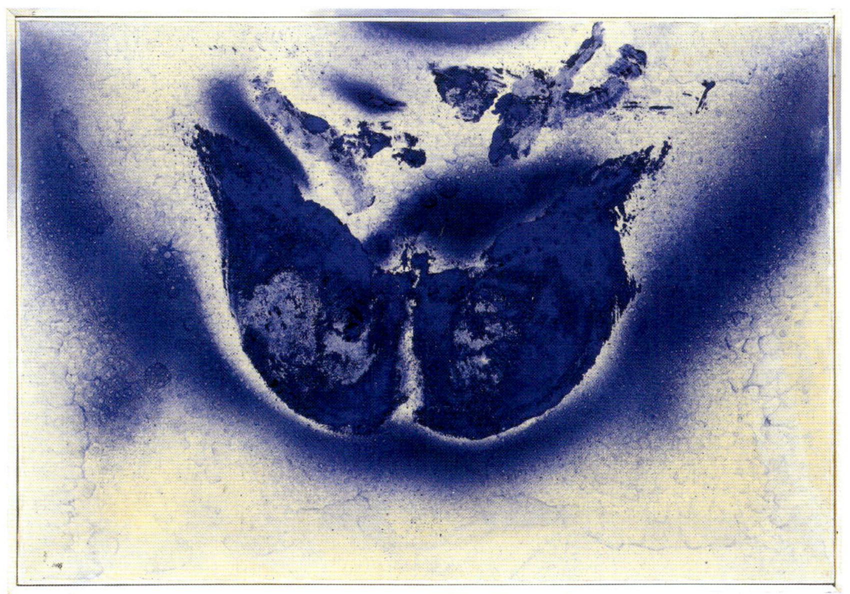

Yves Klein
ANT 120, 1960
Pigment, Kunstharz auf Papier auf Leinwand
Pigment, synthetic resin on paper on canvas
55 x 75 cm
Erworben / Acquired in 1998

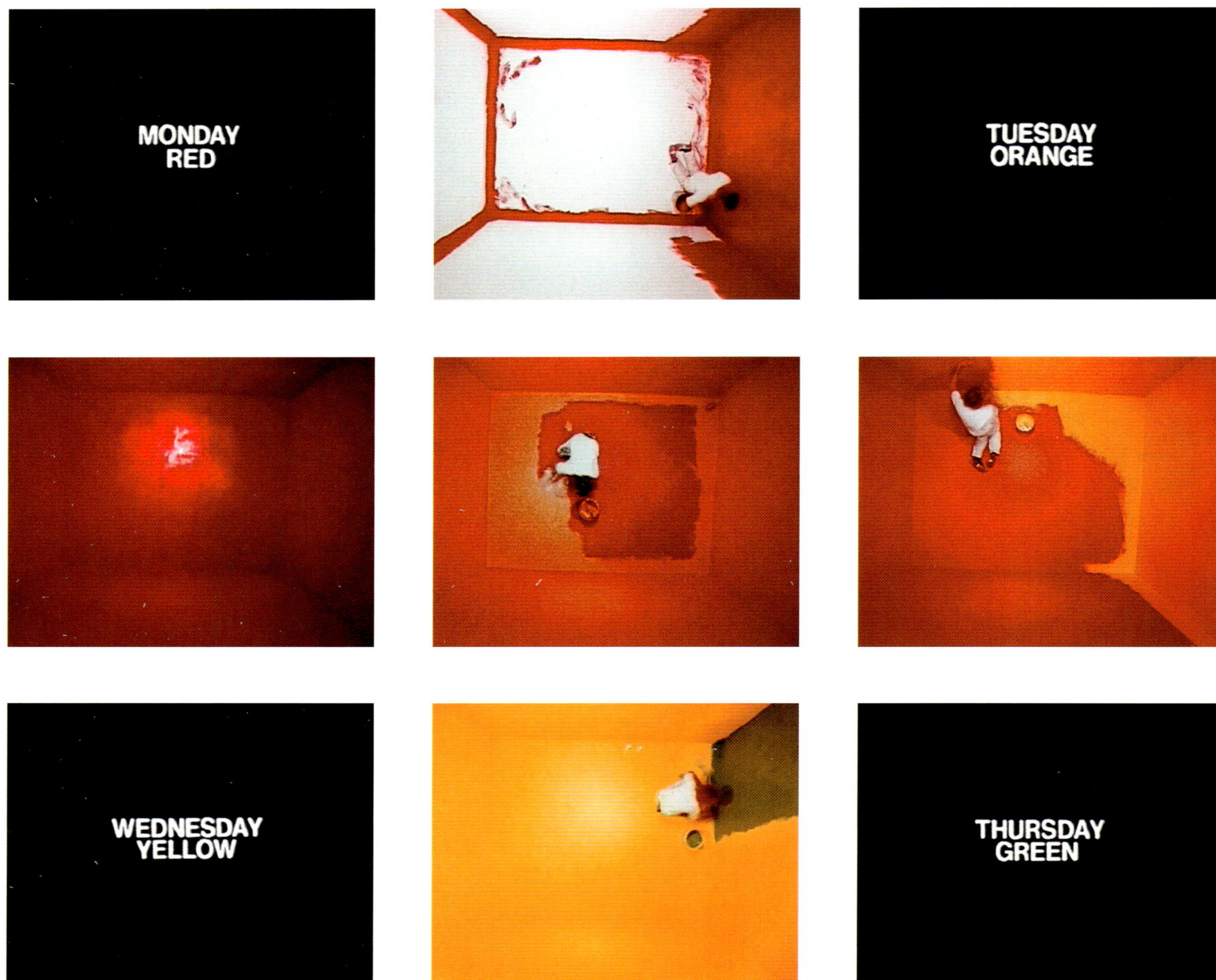

John Baldessari
Six Colorful Inside Jobs, 1977
16-mm-Film, Farbe / 16mm film, color, 32:53 min
Fimstills / Film stills
Erworben / Acquired in 2005

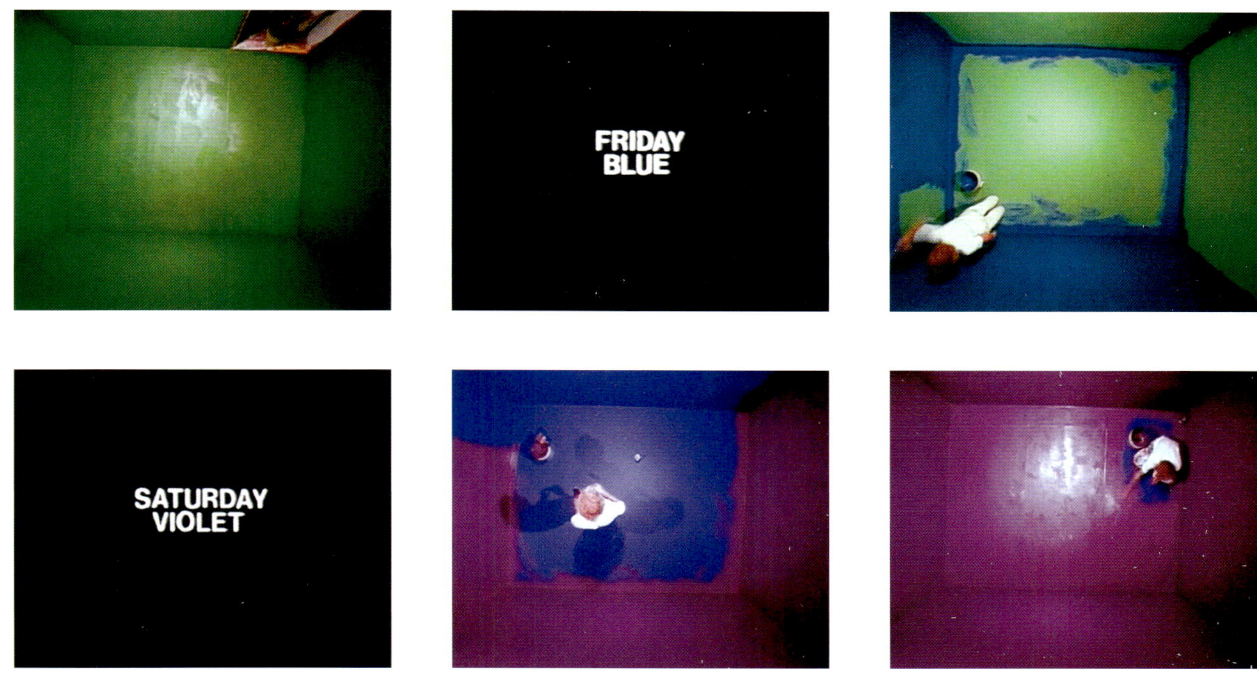
FRIDAY
BLUE

SATURDAY
VIOLET

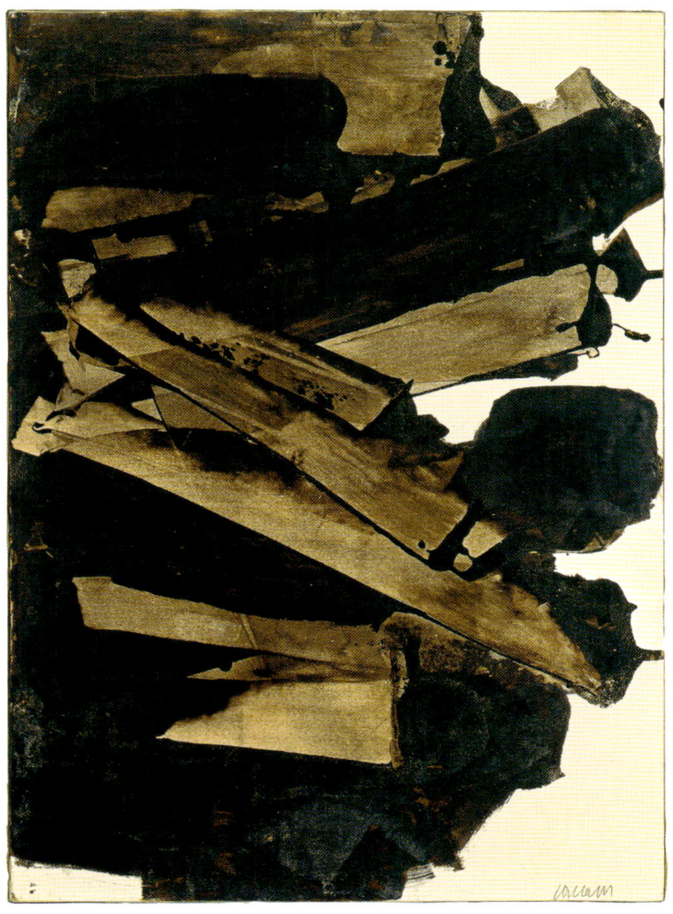

Pierre Soulages
Peinture (Bild / Painting), 1959
Nussbeize auf Papier auf Leinwand / Nut stain on paper on canvas
76 x 56 cm
Erworben / Acquired in 1963

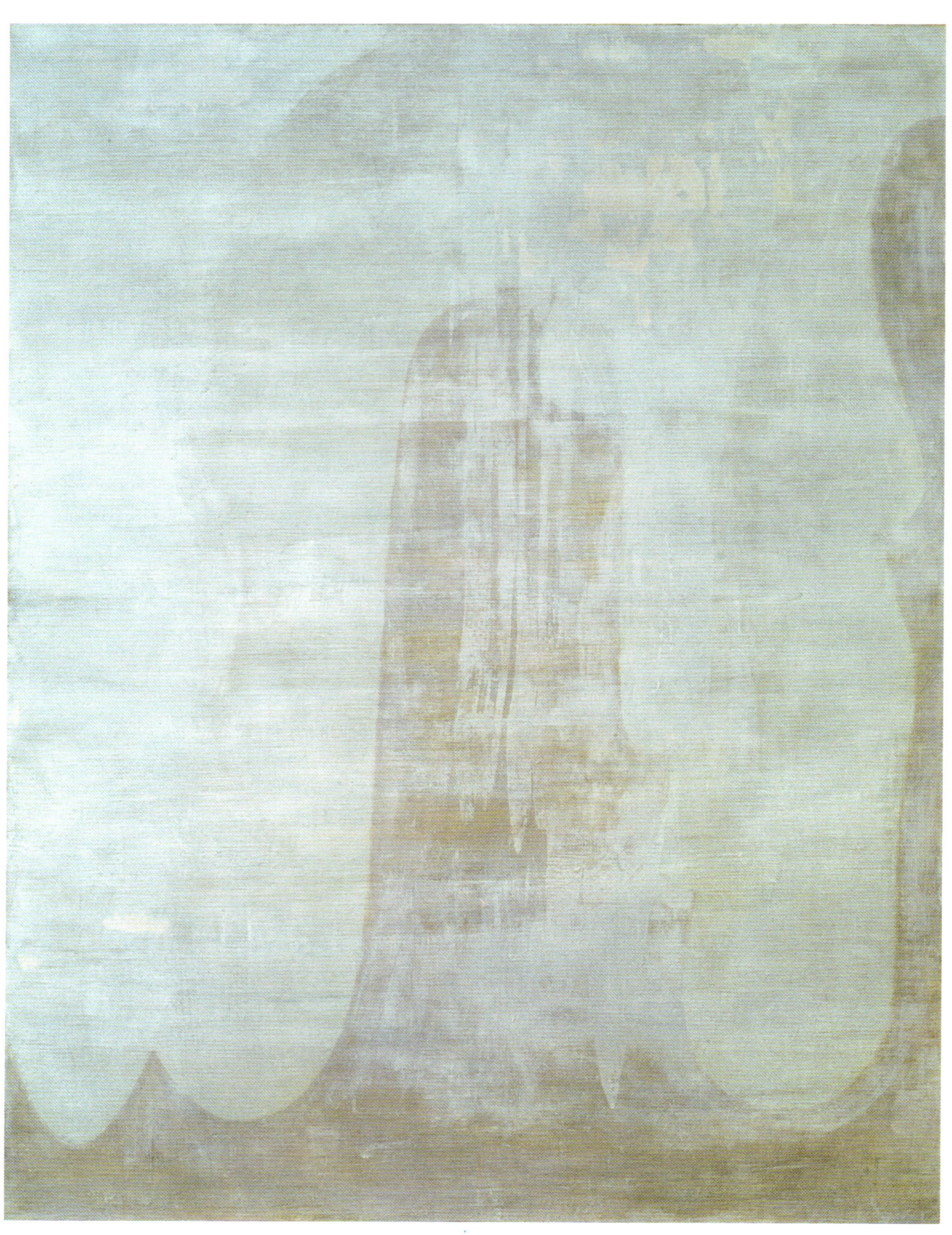

Erwin Bohatsch
Ohne Titel (Untitled), 1994
Acryl, Öl auf Leinwand / Acrylic, oil on canvas
250 x 190 cm
Erworben / Acquired in 1997

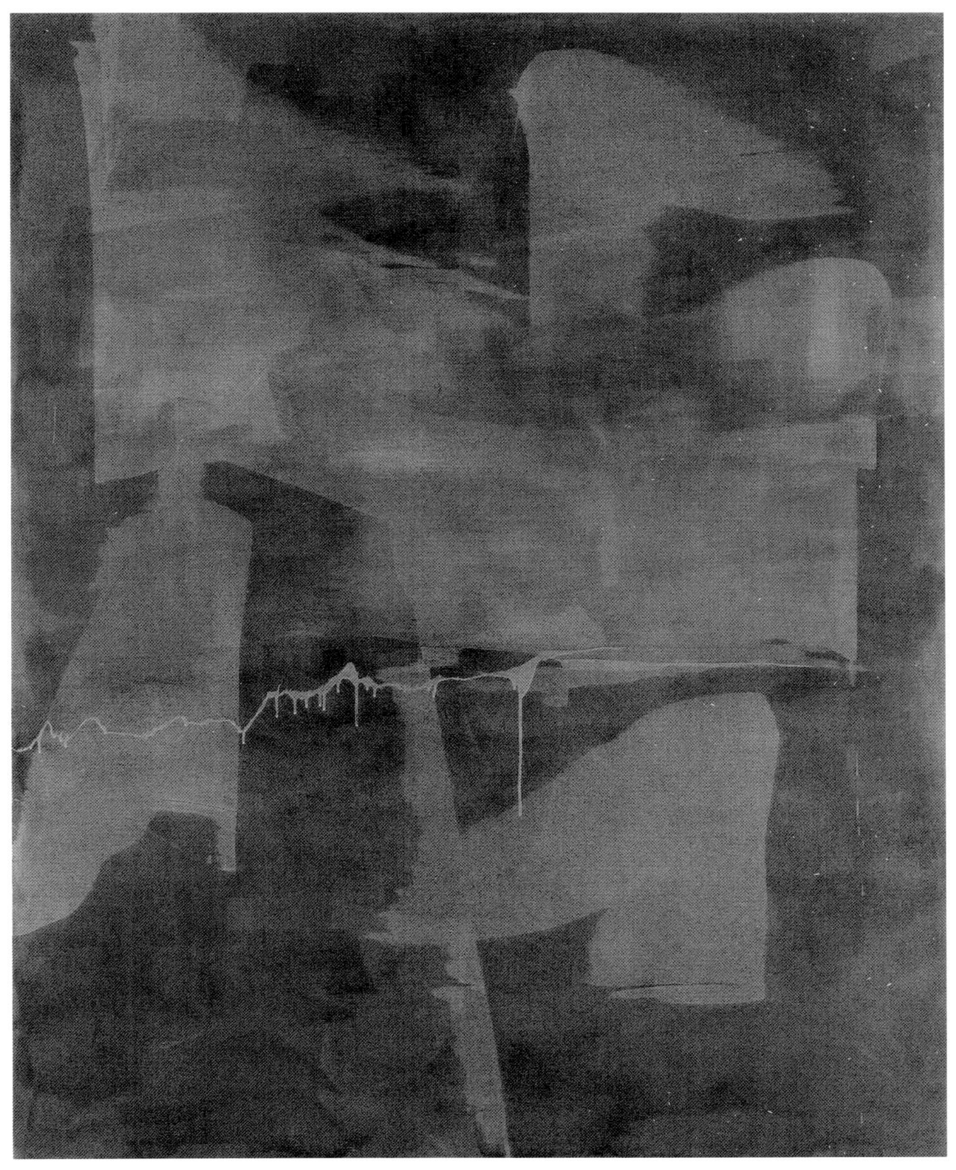

Erwin Bohatsch
Ohne Titel (Untitled), 1999
Acryl, Öl auf Leinwand / Acrylic, oil on canvas
240 x 190 cm
Erworben / Acquired in 1999

Erwin Bohatsch
Ohne Titel (Untitled), 1999
Acryl, Öl auf Leinwand / Acrylic, oil on canvas
190 x 150 cm
Erworben / Acquired in 1999

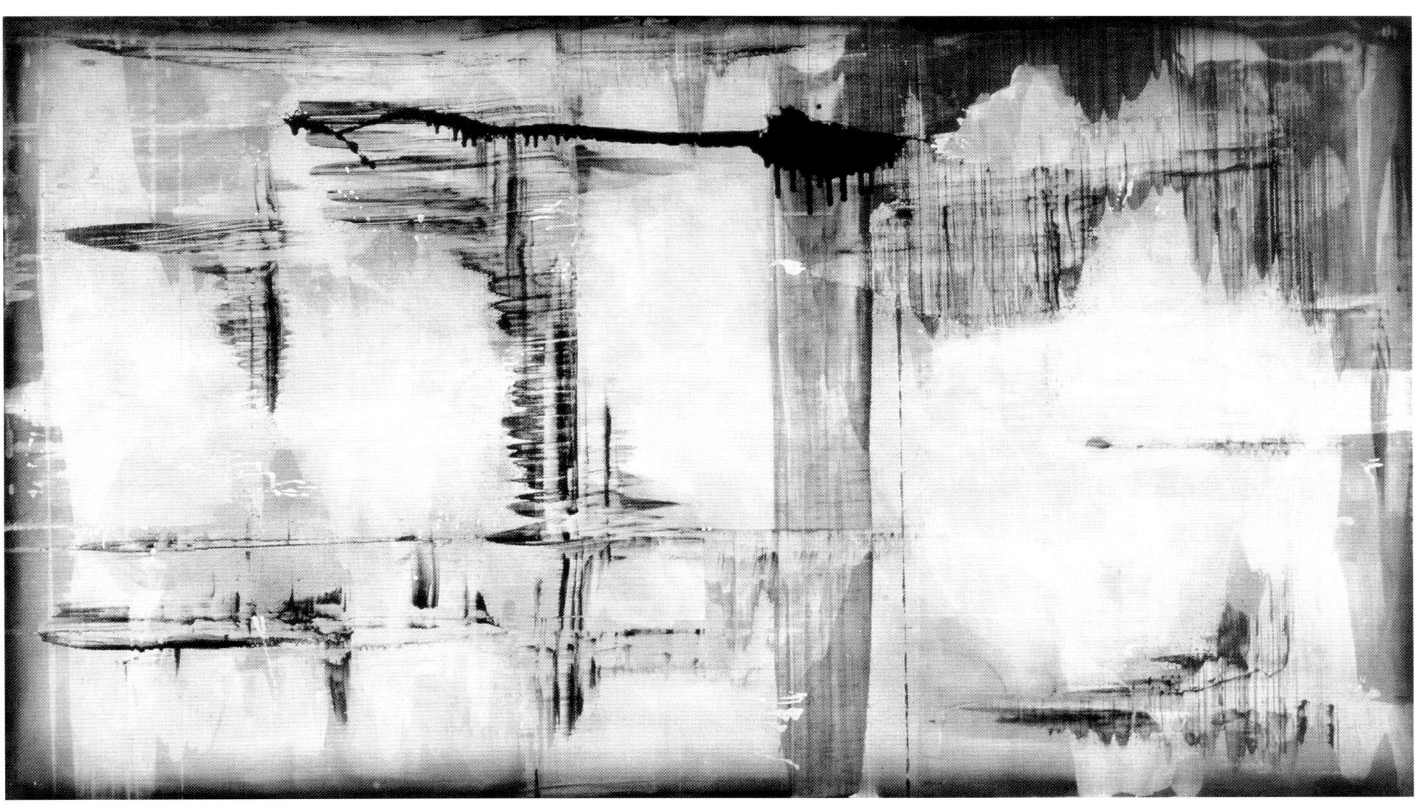

Erwin Bohatsch
Sequenz III (Sequence III), 2006
Acryl, Öl auf Leinwand / Acrylic, oil on canvas
190,4 x 330,2 cm
Schenkung des Künstlers / Donated by the artist, 2006

Der Lauf der Farbe / The Flow of Paint

Joseph Marioni
Red Painting (Rotes Gemälde), 1993
Acryl auf Leinen / Acrylic on linen
180 x 170 cm
Erworben / Acquired in 1993

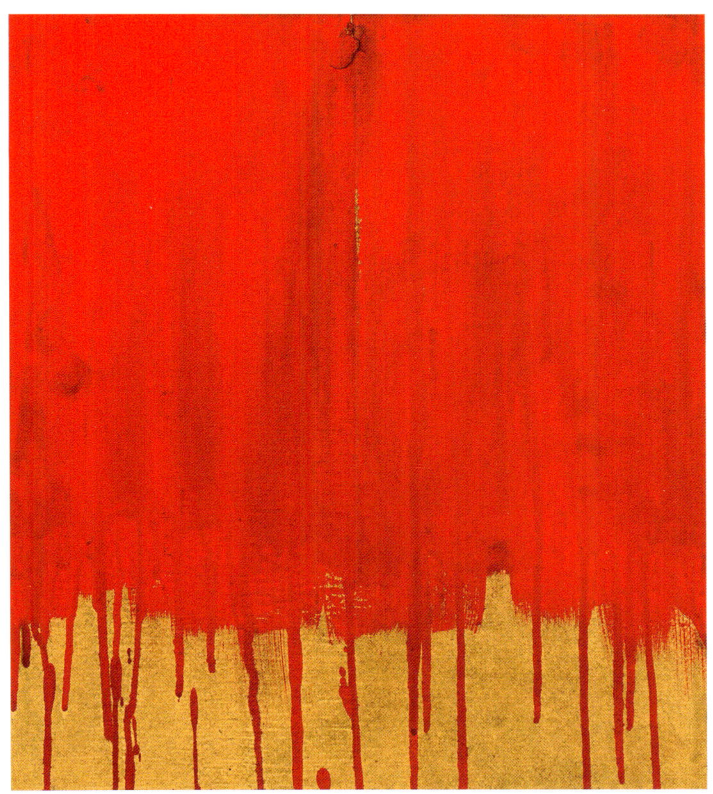

Yves Klein
D 54, 1957
Pigment auf Karton und Kunstharz
Pigment on cardboard and synthetic resin
40 x 35 cm
Erworben / Acquired in 1999

Morris Louis
Dalet Rash, 1958
Acryl auf Leinwand / Acrylic on canvas
233 x 337 cm
Leihgabe der Österreichischen Ludwig-Stiftung
On loan from the Austrian Ludwig Foundation, seit / since 1997

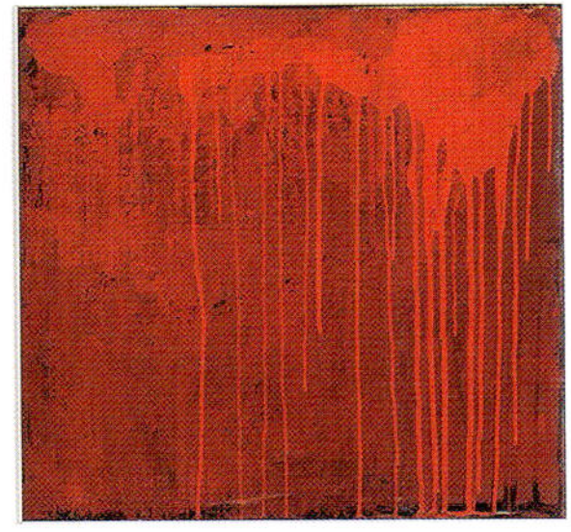

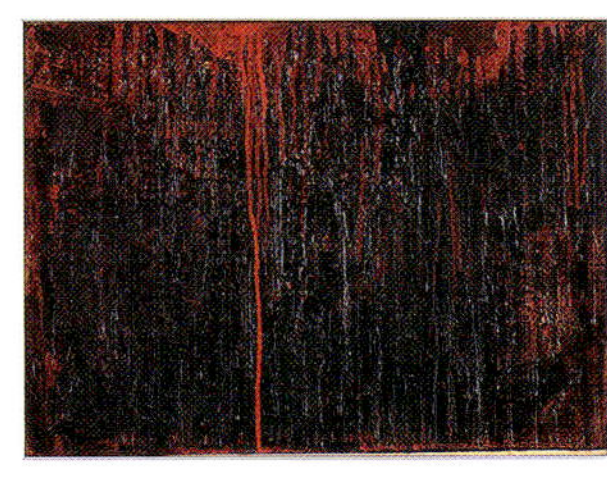

Hermann Nitsch
Kleiner Existenz-Altar (Small Existence Altar), 1960
Acryl auf Holz / Acrylic on wood
7-teilig / In seven parts: 310 x 248 cm
Erworben / Acquired in 1983

Hermann Nitsch
Kleines Schüttbild (Small Spill Painting), 1986
Grundierung, Öl auf Jute / Primer, oil on jute
106 x 80 cm
Schenkung des Künstlers / Donated by the artist, 1987

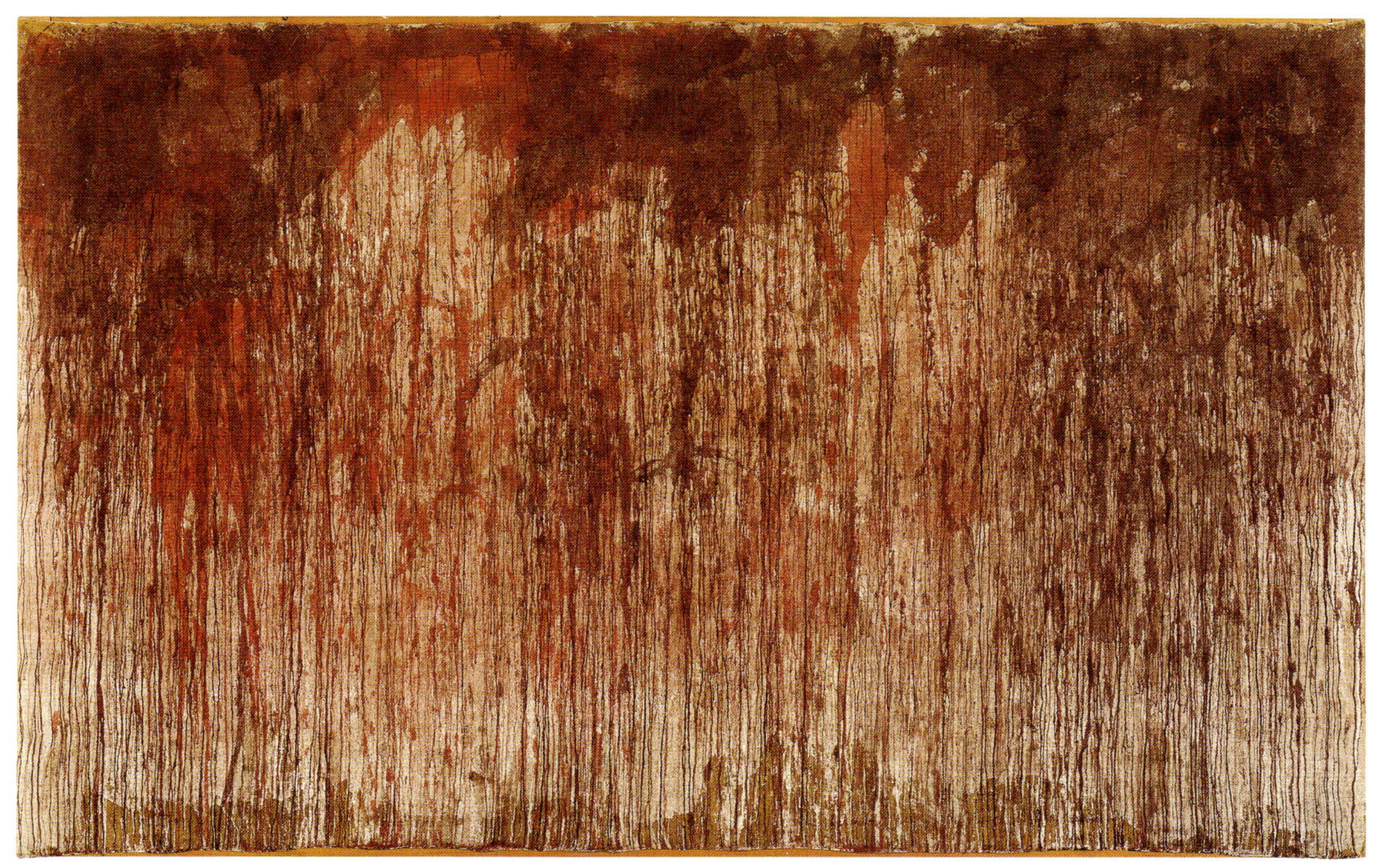

Hermann Nitsch
Kreuzwegstation (Station of the Cross), 1960
Dispersion, Schlämmkreide auf Leinwand
Dispersion paint and whitening chalk on canvas
190 x 297 cm
Leihgabe der Artothek des Bundes
On loan from the Artothek des Bundes, seit / since 1976

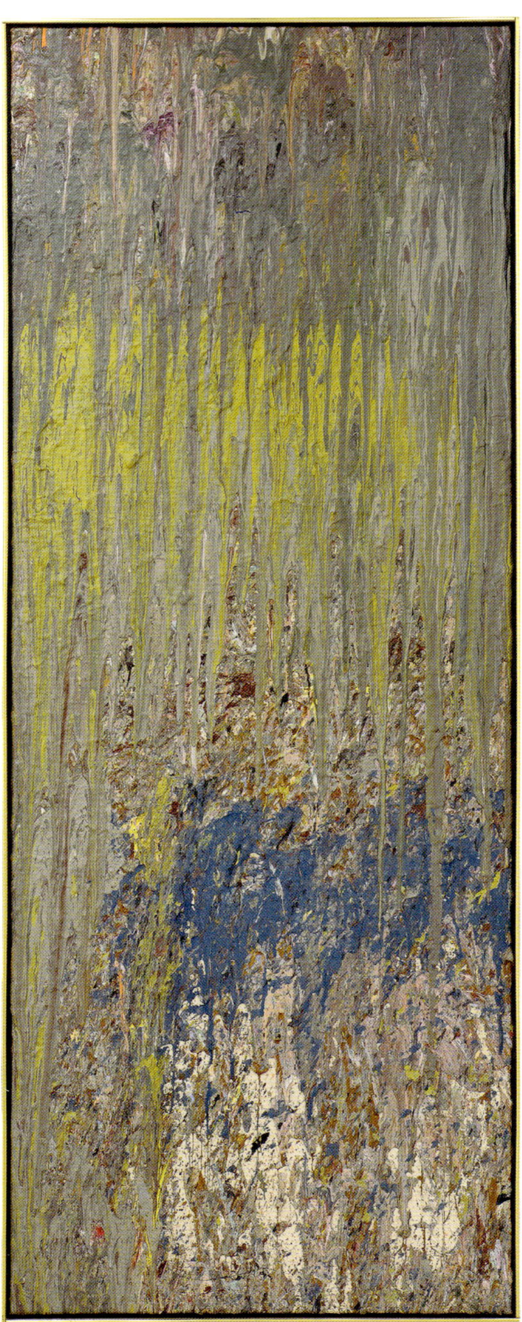

Larry Poons
Absent Dinner (Fehlendes Abendessen), 1979
Acryl auf Leinwand / Acrylic on canvas
233 x 88 cm
Erworben / Acquired in 1980

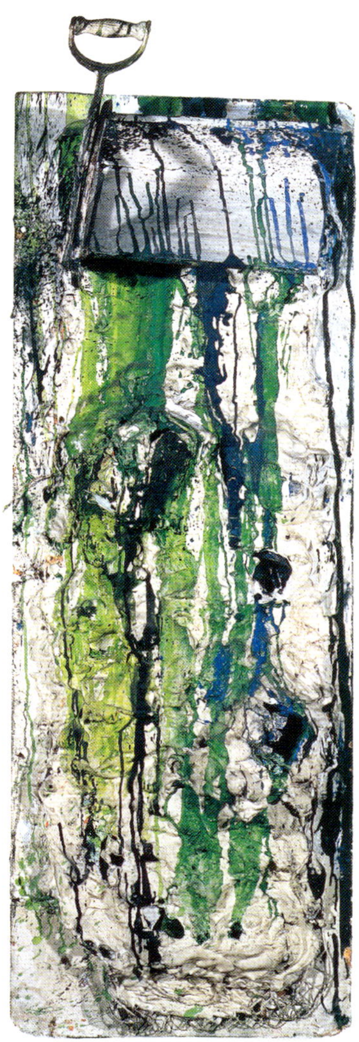

Niki de Saint Phalle
Tir (Schuss / Shot), 1961
Farbe, Brotschneidemaschine, Gips, Glas und verschiedene Materialien, auf Holzplatte fixiert
Paint, bread cutter, plaster, glas and various materials mounted on wooden board
145 x 44 x 33 cm
Ehemals Sammlung Hahn / Former Hahn Collection, Köln / Cologne
Erworben / Acquired in 1978

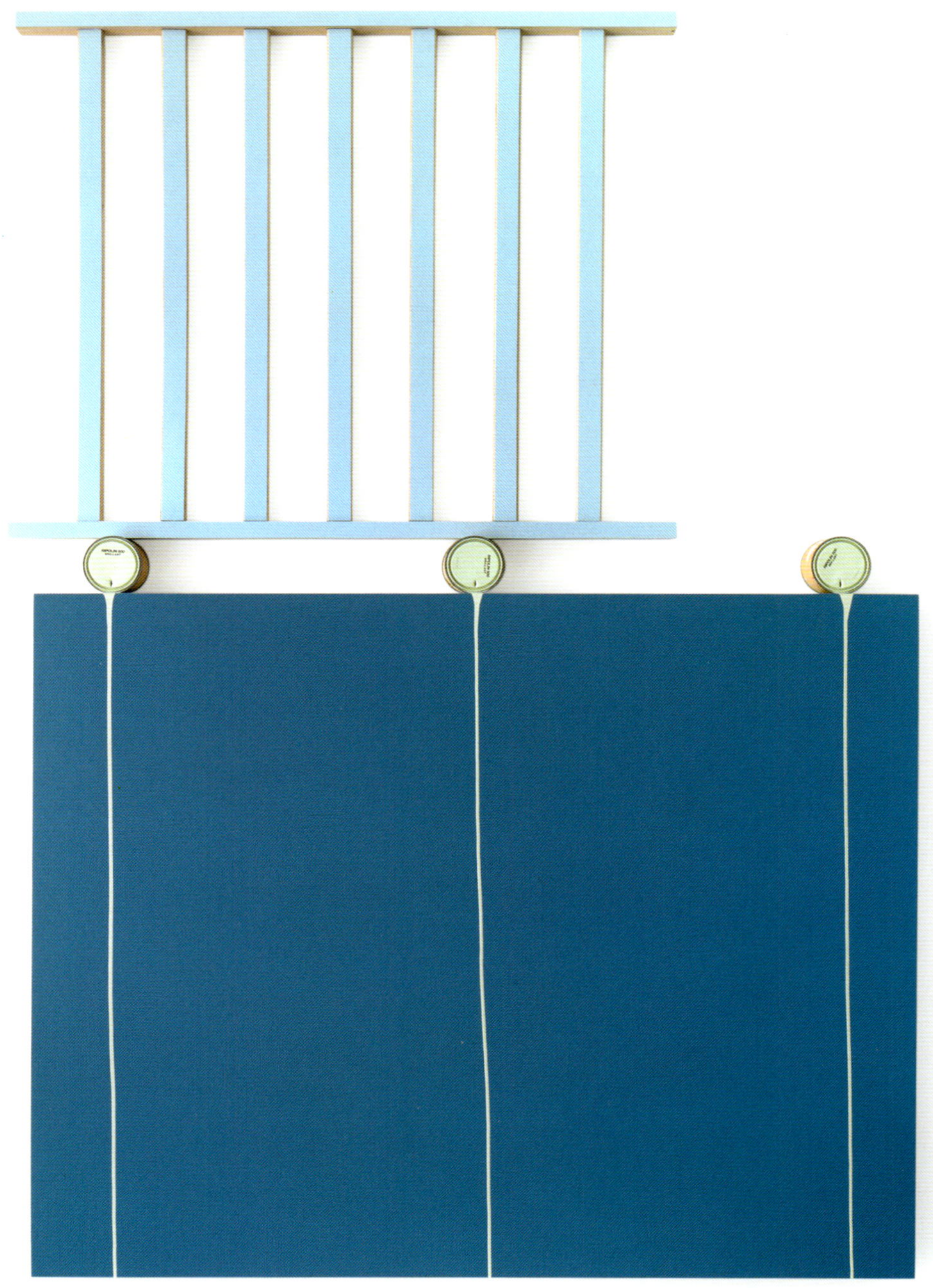

Noël Dolla
Ripolin No-No, 1993
Mischtechnik, Acryl, Lack auf Holz, Blechdosen
Mixed media, acrylic, lacquer on wood, tin cans
221 x 150 x 12 cm
Erworben / Acquired in 1994

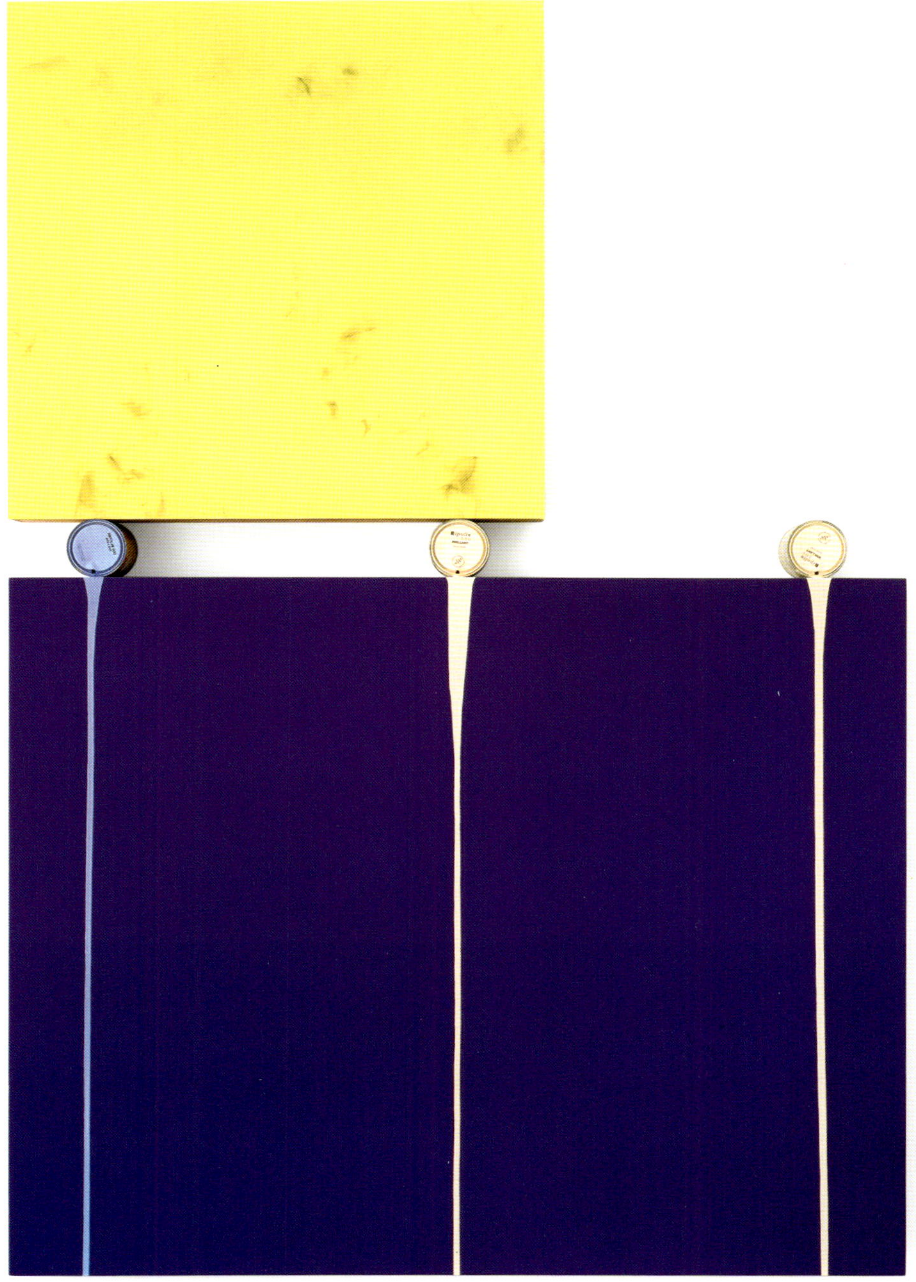

Noël Dolla
Ripolin Non-Non, 1993
Mischtechnik, Acryl, Lack auf Holz, Blechdosen
Mixed media, acrylic, lacquer on wood, tin cans
221 x 150 x 12 cm
Erworben / Acquired in 1994

Material und Struktur der Farbe
The Materiality and Structure of Paint

Dezsö Korniss
Zöld ezüst (Grün Silber / Green Silver), 1962
Öl, Email auf Leinwand / Oil, enamel on canvas
141 x 271 cm
Erworben / Acquired in 1991

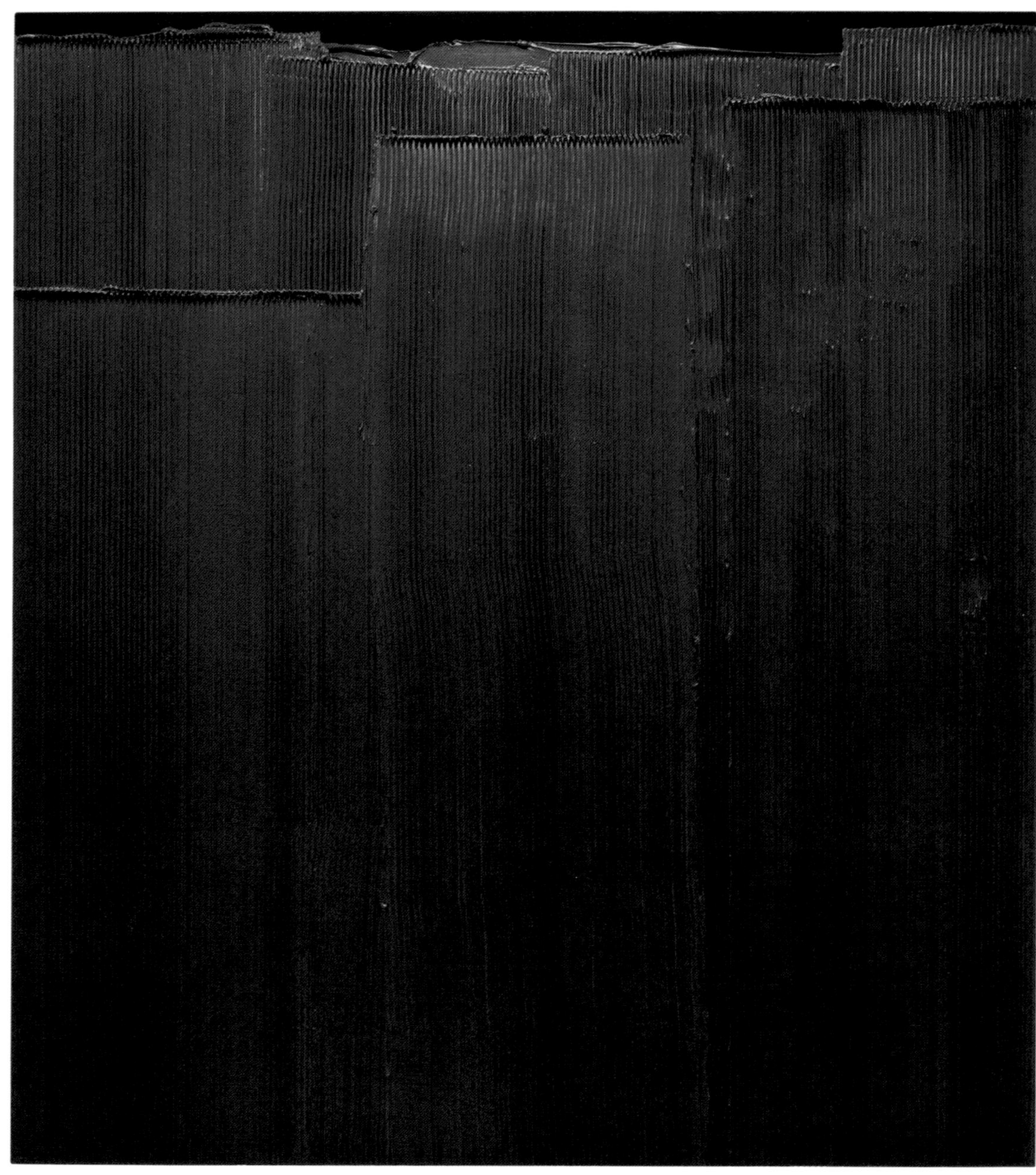

Jakob Gasteiger
Ohne Titel (Untitled), 2000
Lack auf Acryl auf Leinwand / Lacquer on acrylic on canvas
281 x 240,5 cm
Erworben / Acquired in 2001

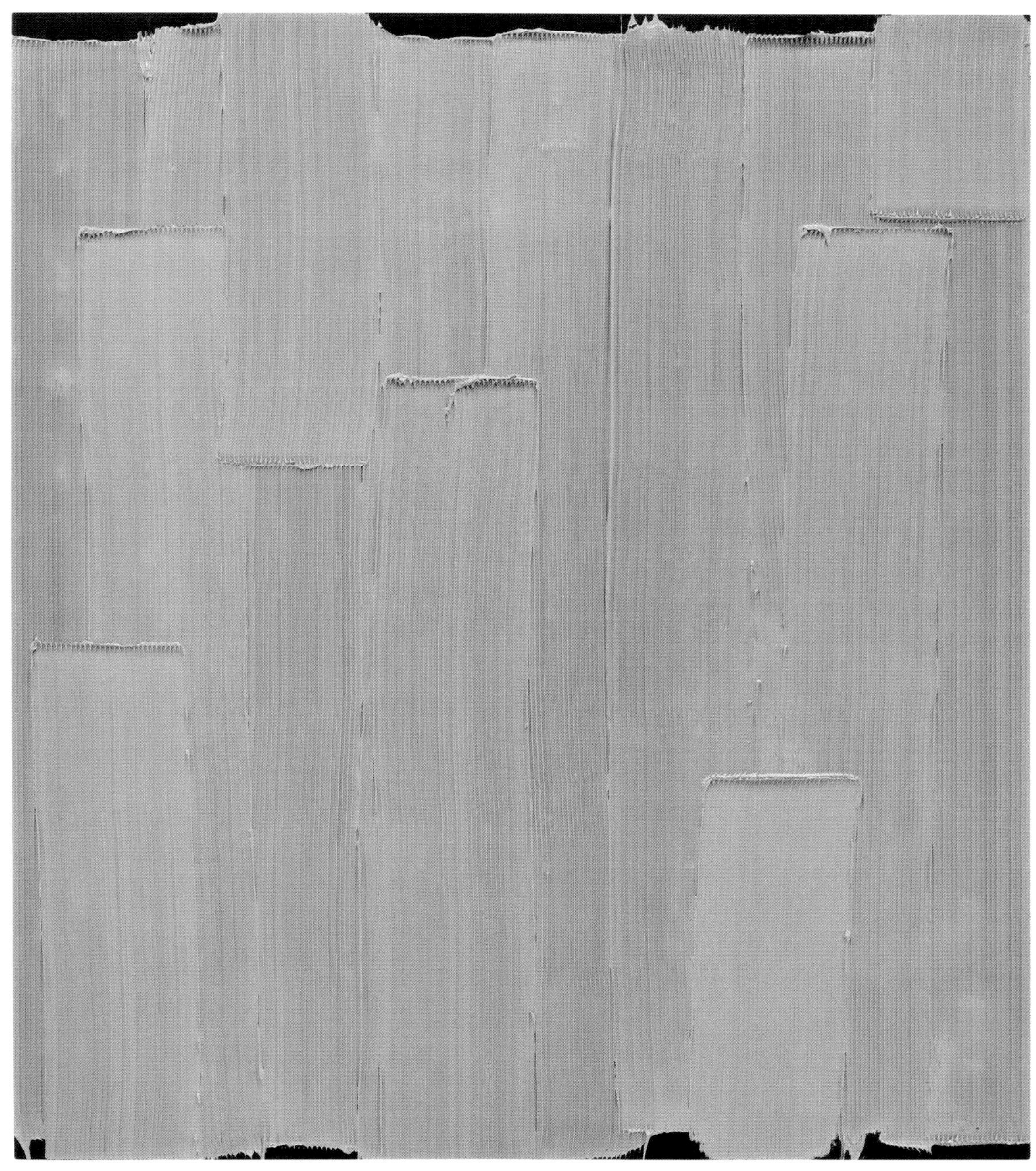

Jakob Gasteiger
Ohne Titel (Untitled), 2000
Lack auf Acryl auf Leinwand / Lacquer on acrylic on canvas
280 x 240 cm
Erworben / Acquired in 2001

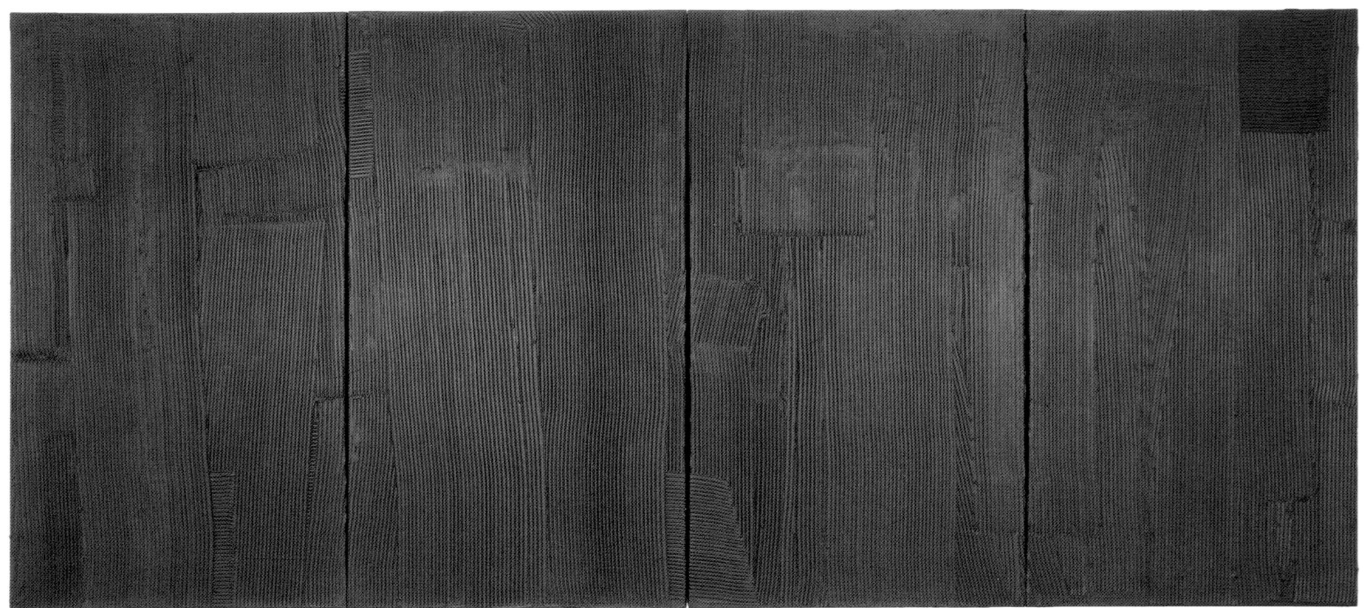

Jakob Gasteiger
Ohne Titel (Untitled), 1991
Öl auf Acryl auf Leinwand / Oil on acrylic on canvas
4-teilig / In four parts: je / each 220 x 120 cm
Erworben / Acquired in 1993

Jakob Gasteiger
Ohne Titel (Untitled), 1991
Öl auf Acryl auf Leinwand / Oil on acrylic on canvas
2-teilig / In two parts: je / each 200 x 120 cm
Leihgabe der Artcthek des Bundes
On loan from the Artothek des Bundes, seit / since 1992

Josef Danner
Ohne Titel (Untitled), 1992
Mischtechnik auf Leinwand / Mixed media on canvas
180 x 150 cm
Erworben / Acquired in 1992

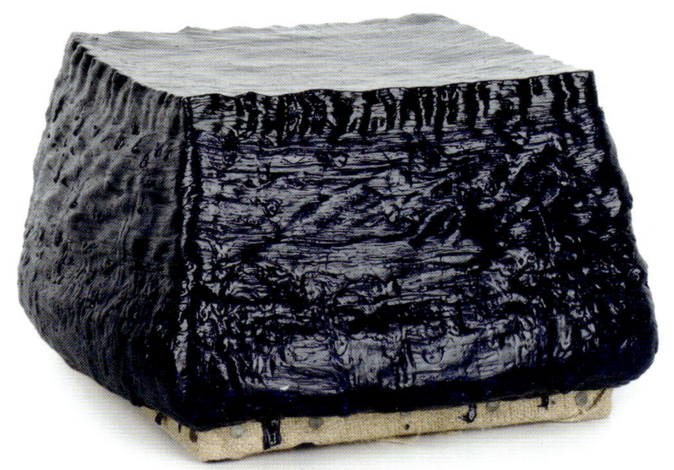

Christian Stock
Blaues Würfelbild (Blue Cube Painting),
Juli 1989–Mai 1990 / July 1989–May 1990
Acryl auf Leinwand / Acrylic on canvas
15 x 15 x 15 cm
Erworben / Acquired in 1990

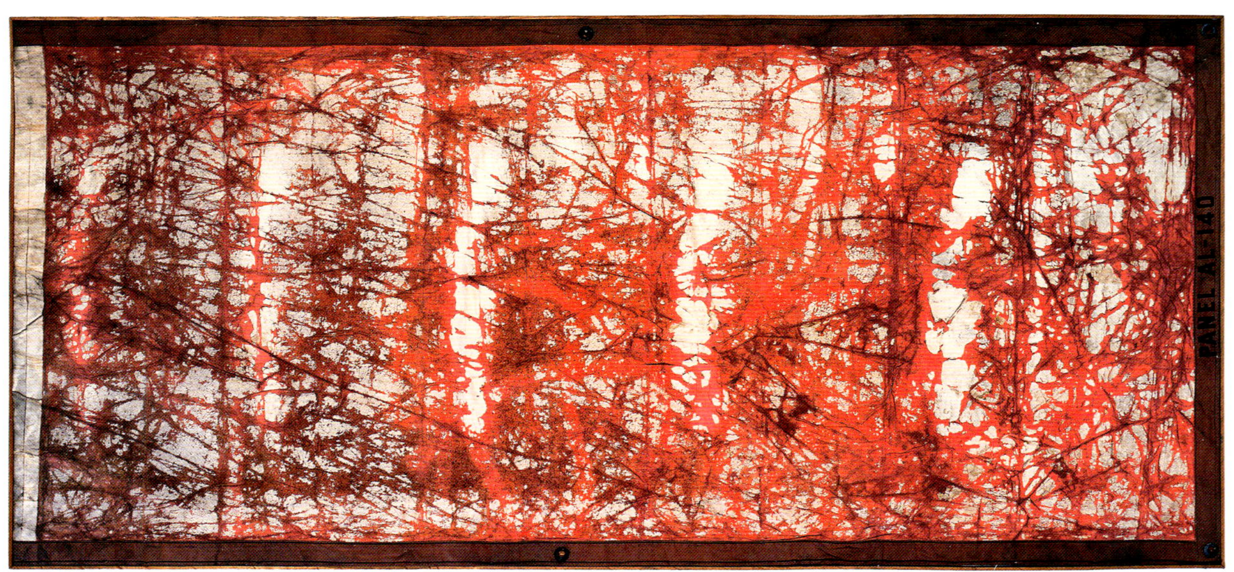

Gérard Deschamps
Bâche de Signalisation (Plane / Tarpaulin), 1961
Plane mit abgeblätterter Farbe, Randverstärkungen und Metallösen, auf Sperrholzplatte
Tarpaulin with peeling paint, reinforced edges and metal eyelets, on plywood panel
79 x 168 cm
Ehemals Sammlung Hahn / Former Hahn Collection, Köln / Cologne
Erworben / Acquired in 1979

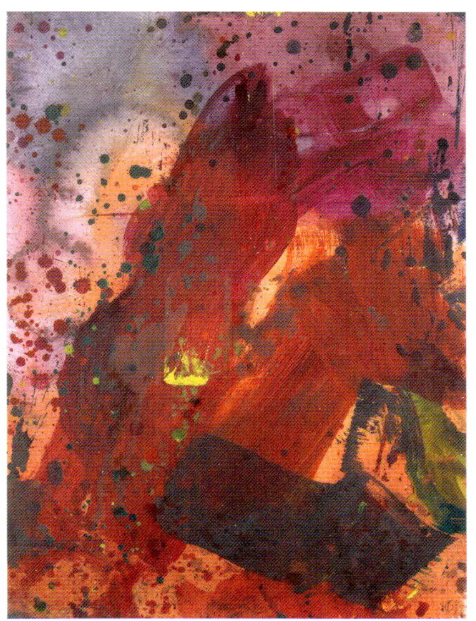

Herbert Brandl
Schmierage, 2010
Öl, Acryl auf Papier / Oil, acrylic on paper
76 x 56 cm
Schenkung des Künstlers / Donated by the artist, 2010

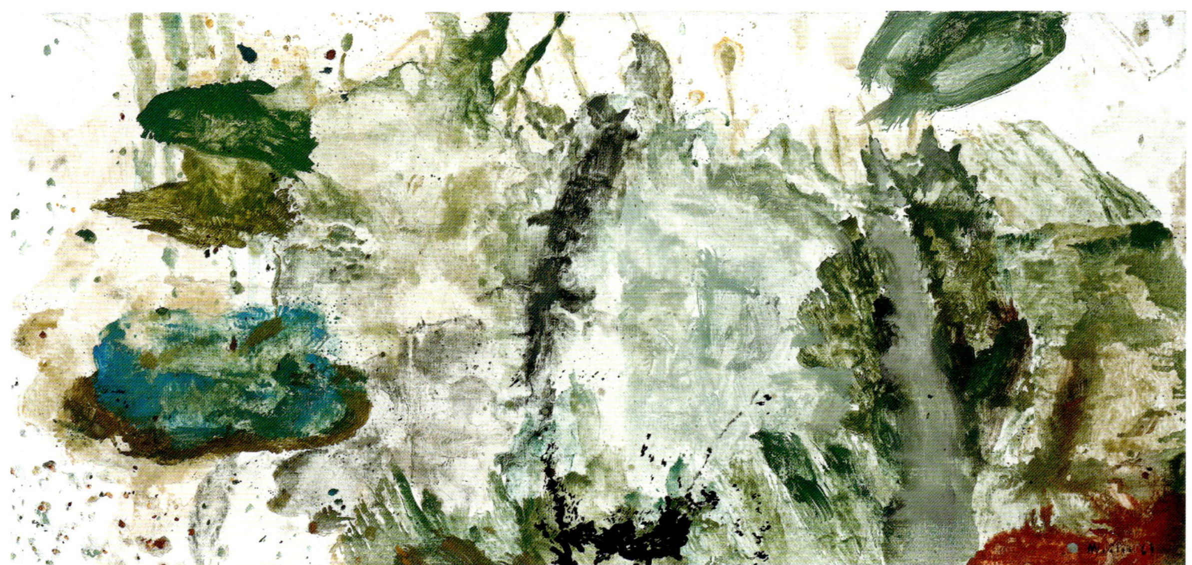

Max Weiler
Wie eine Landschaft, Hochmoor, neblig, sumpfig, dunstig, nass, Gras, Kräuter, Moos.
Aus dem Werkblock „Wie eine Landschaft", großformatigen Übersetzungen von Ausschnitten aus
Probierpapieren (Like a landscape, upland moor, foggy, boggy, hazy, damp, grass, herbs, moss.
From the group of works "Like a Landscape", large format transpositions of cut-out segments
from various wipe-off sheets), 1964
Eitempera auf Leinwand / Egg tempera on canvas
96 x 196 cm
Leihgabe der Artothek des Bundes / On loan from the Artothek des Bundes, seit / since 1979

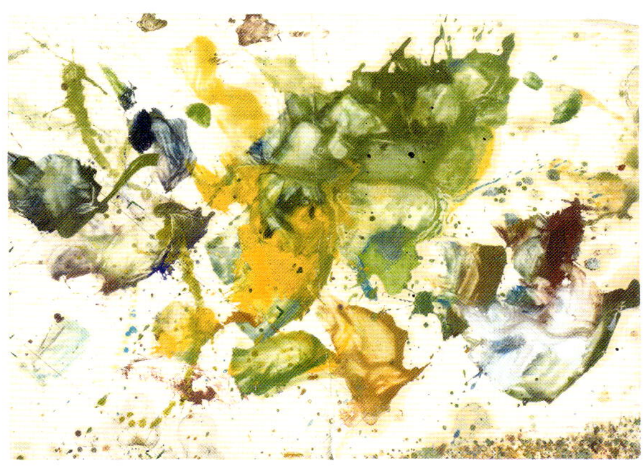

Max Weiler
Probierpapier mit Motiveingrenzung für die Übersetzung in Gemälde
(Wipe-off sheet with motif fields for integrating into paintings), 1960er-Jahre / 1960s
Eitempera, Bleistift auf Papier / Egg tempera, pencil on paper
29,8 x 38,9 cm
Schenkung / Donated by Yvonne Weiler, 2010

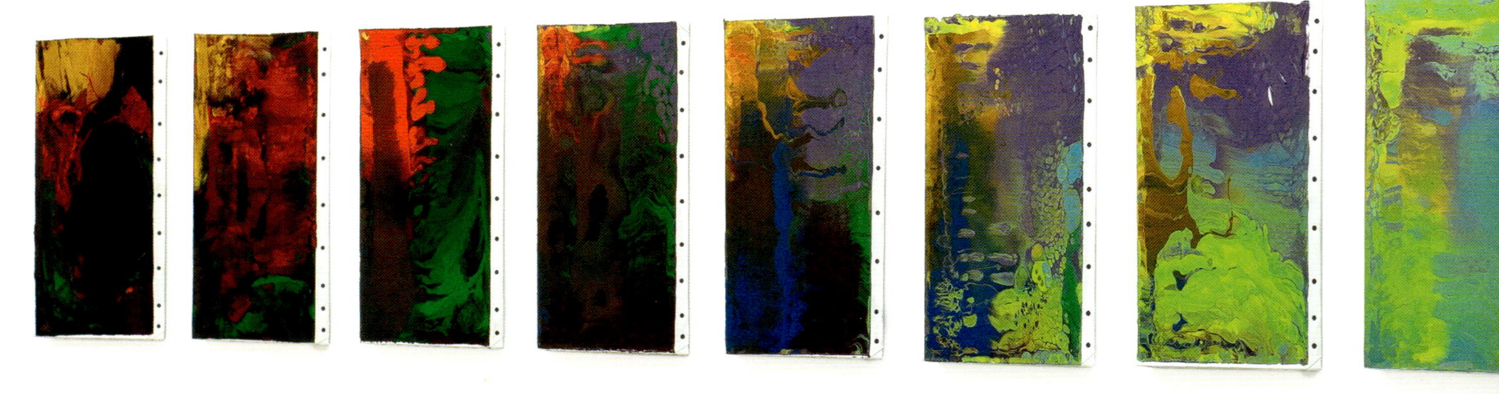

Bernard Frize
Suite G, 1991/1992
Alkydharz auf Leinwand / Alkyd resin on canvas
13-teilig / In 13 parts: je / each 41 x 33 cm
Erworben / Acquired in 1996

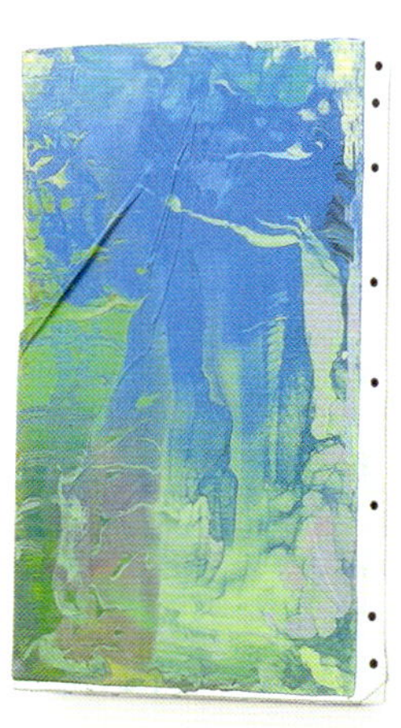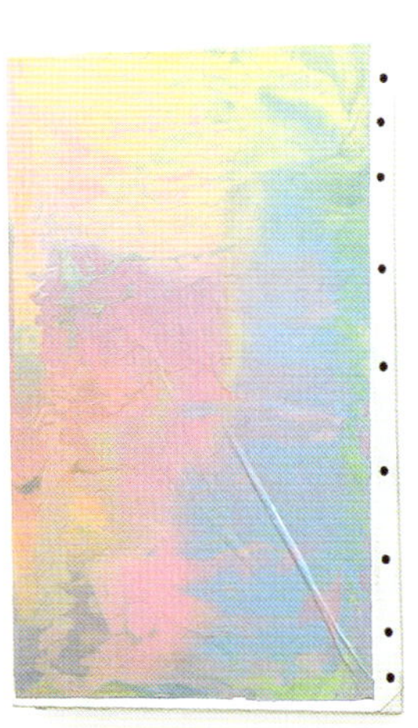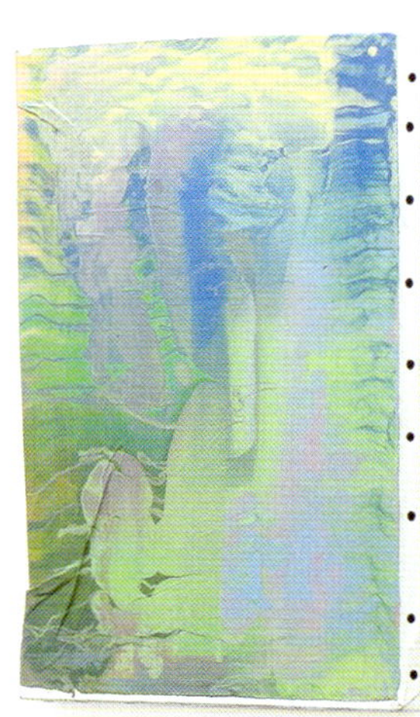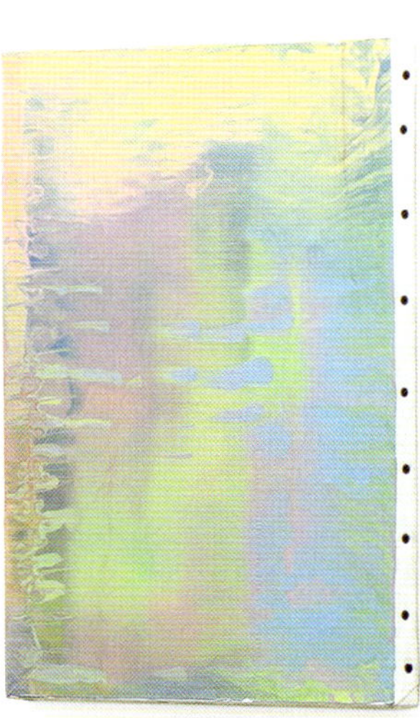

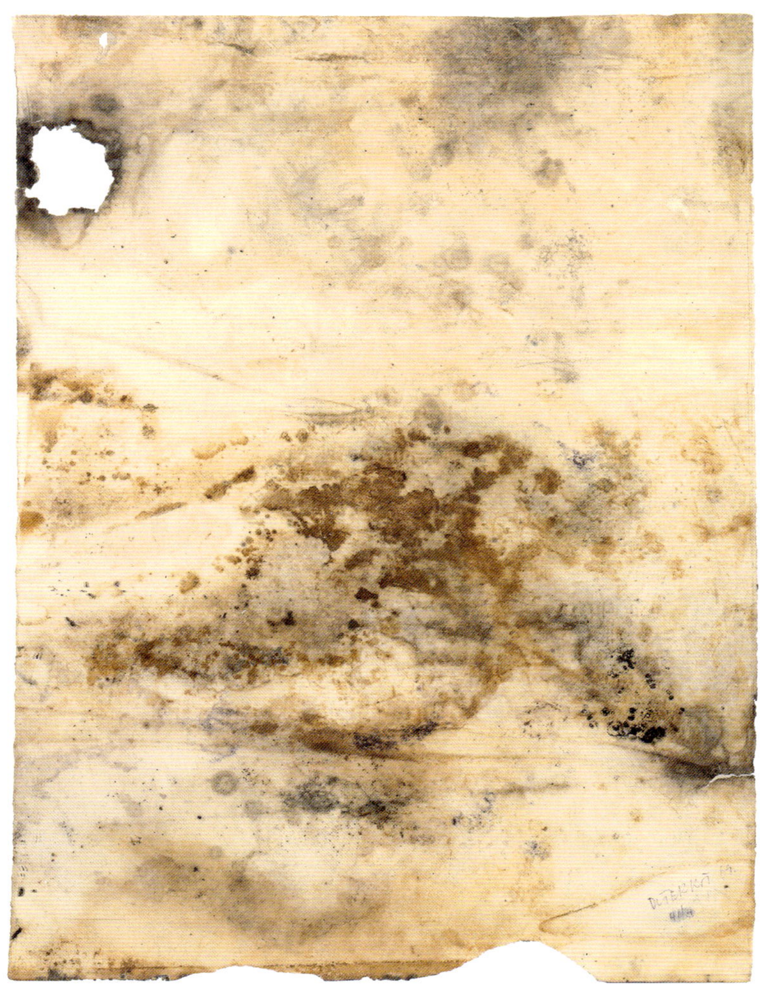

Dieter Roth
Schimmelgraphik (Mold Image), 1969
Schimmelemulsionen auf Büttenpapier / Mold emulsions on handmade paper
108 x 80 cm
Ehemals Sammlung Hahn / Former Hahn Collection, Köln / Cologne
Erworben / Acquired in 1978

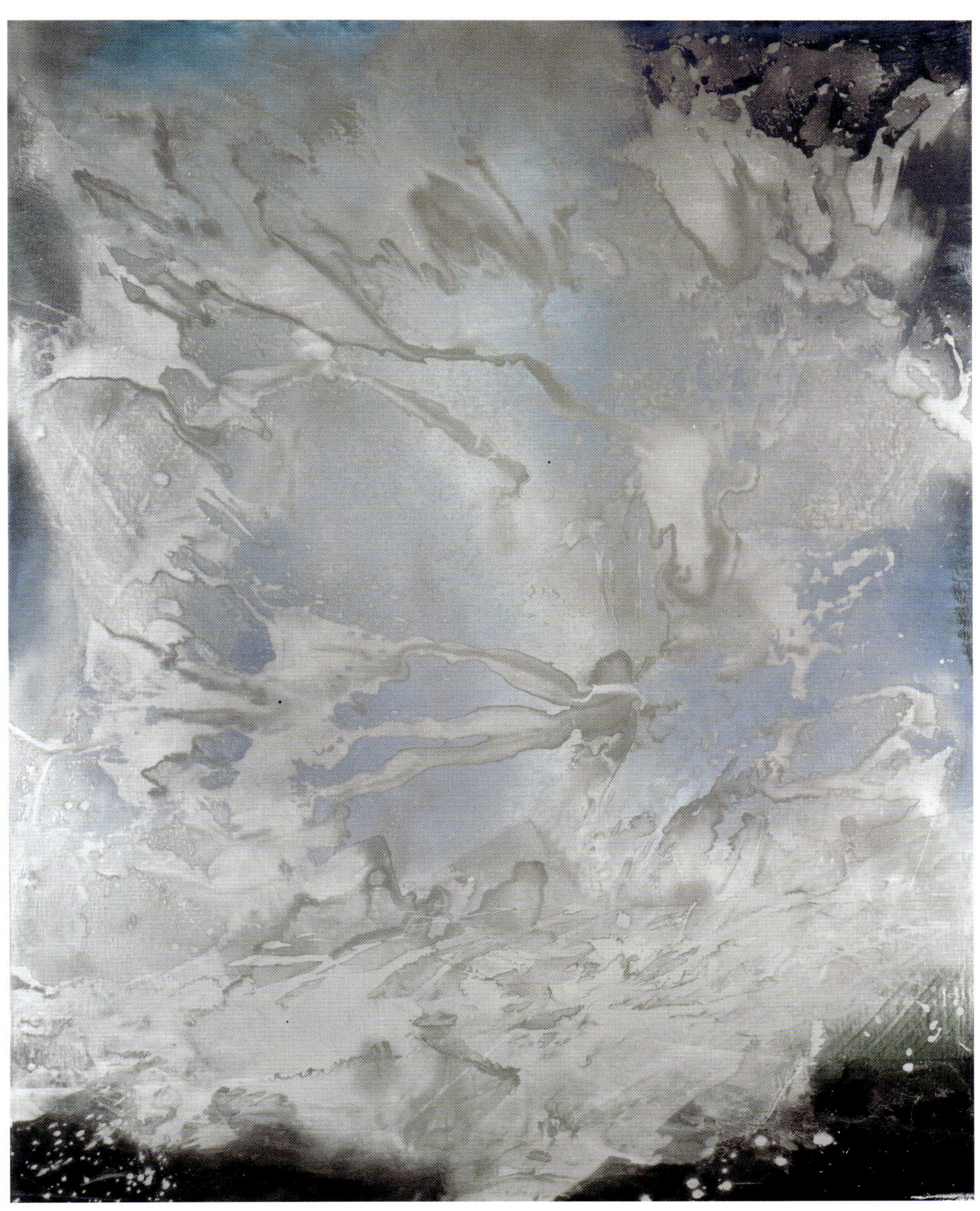

Hubert Scheibl
Nicotin on Silverscreen, 2009/2010
Öl auf Leinwand / Oil on canvas
240 x 190 cm
Schenkung des Künstlers / Donated by the artist

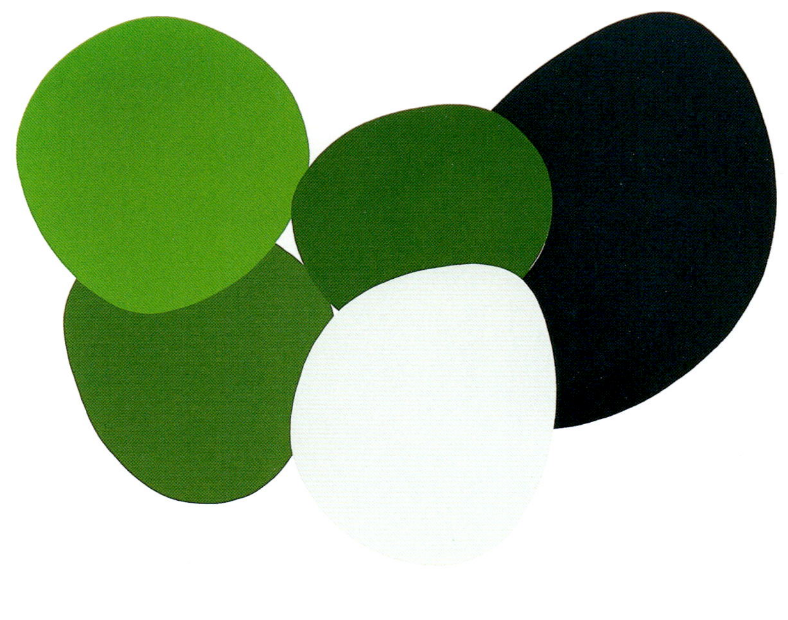

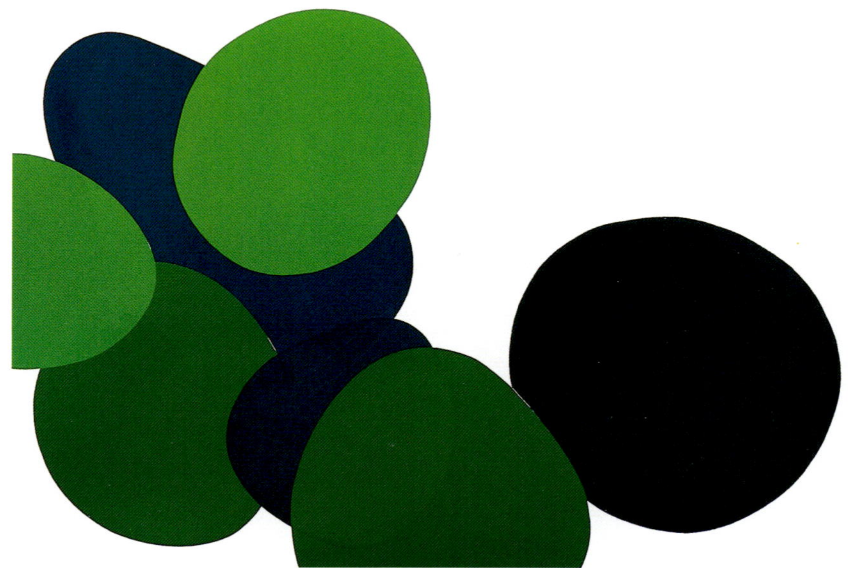

Andreas Reiter Raabe
Pools, 2001
Acryl auf Leinwand / Acrylic on canvas
240 x 160 cm
Schenkung der Gesellschaft der Freunde der bildenden Künste
Donated by the Society of the Friends of Fine Arts Vienna, 2001

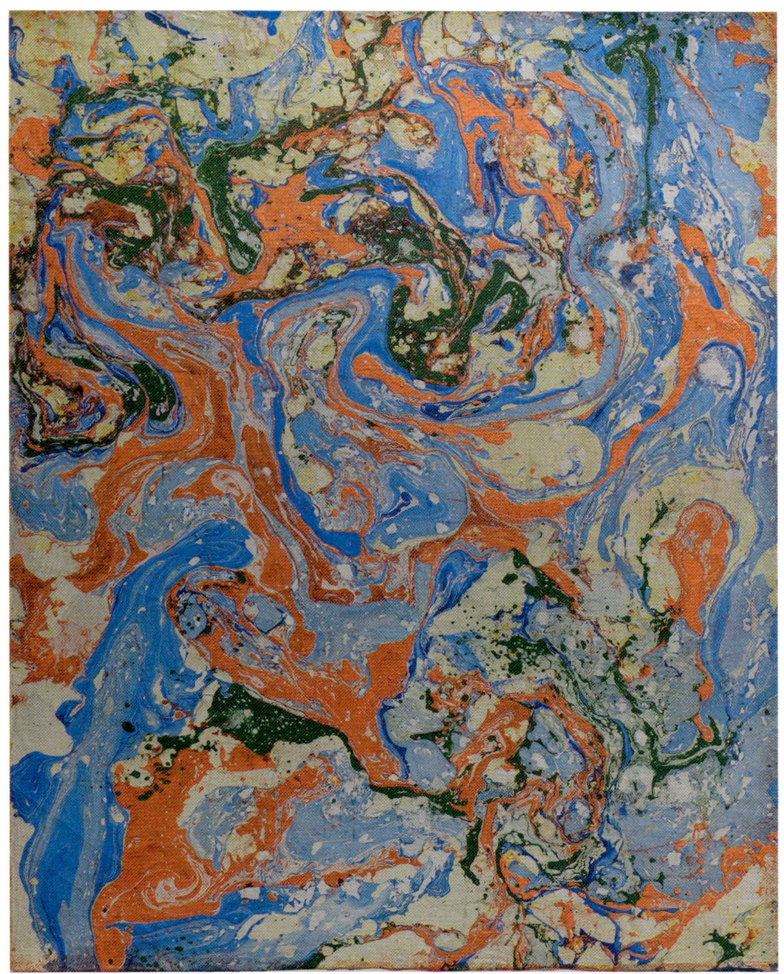

Lois Weinberger
Ohne Titel (Untitled), 1989
Kunstharzlack, Öl auf Leinwand / Acrylic lacquer, oil on canvas
129 x 100 cm
Erworben / Acquired in 1992

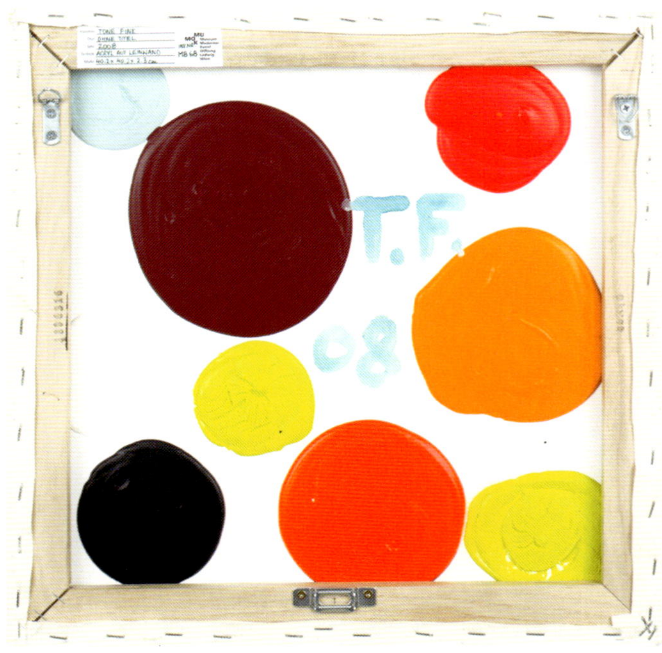

Tone Fink
Ohne Titel (Untitled), 2008
Acryl auf Leinwand / Acrylic on canvas
Vorderseite / Front; 40,2 x 40,2 cm
Schenkung des Künstlers / Donated by the artist, 2008

Ohne Titel (Untitled), 2008
Acryl auf Leinwand / Acrylic on canvas
Rückseite / Reverse; 40,2 x 40,2 cm
Schenkung des Künstlers / Donated by the artist, 2008

Tone Fink
Kreiszentriert (Circle Centered), 1994
Acryl, Quarzsand auf Leinwand / Acrylic, quartz sand on canvas
50 x 40 cm
Schenkung des Künstlers / Donated by the artist, 2008

Ohne Titel (Untitled), 1989
Acryl auf Leinwand / Acrylic on canvas
40,2 x 30,2 cm
Schenkung des Künstlers / Donated by the artist, 2008

Arnulf Rainer
Übermalung violett (Paintover Violet), 1961
Öl, Kreide auf Leinwand / Oil, chalk on canvas
201 x 81 cm
Erworben / Acquired in 1983

Yves Klein
Monochrome Bleu (Monochrom Blau / Monochrome Blue), 1961
Pigment auf Molino auf Spanplatte / Pigment on molino on particle board
72 x 54 cm
Erworben / Acquired in 1982

Rudolf Schwarzkogler
Ohne Titel (Untitled), 1962
Acryl, Schnur auf Sackleinen / Acrylic, string on burlap
120,5 x 100 cm
Leihgabe der Österreichischen Ludwig-Stiftung
On loan from the Austrian Ludwig Foundation, seit / since 1984

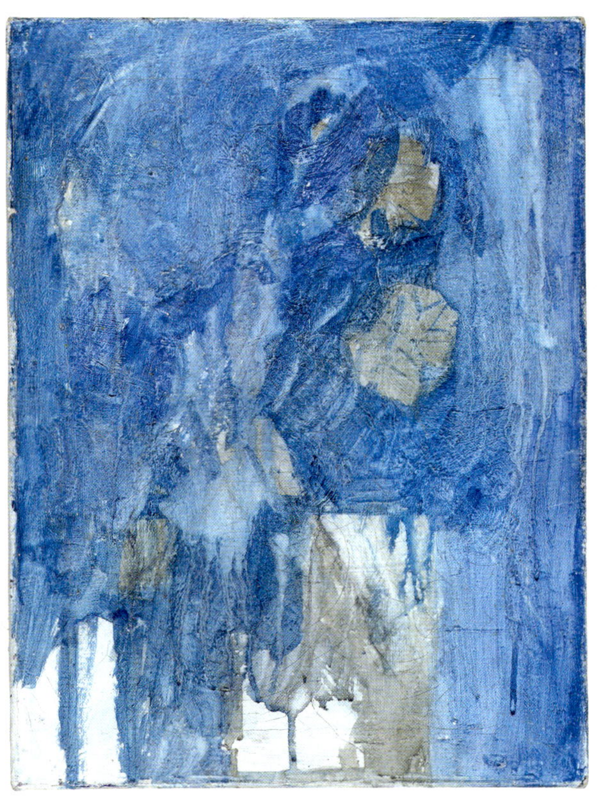

Rudolf Schwarzkogler
Ohne Titel (Untitled), 1962
Acryl auf Leinwand / Acrylic on canvas
55,5 x 40 cm
Leihgabe der Österreichischen Ludwig-Stiftung
On loan from the Austrian Ludwig Foundation, seit / since 1984

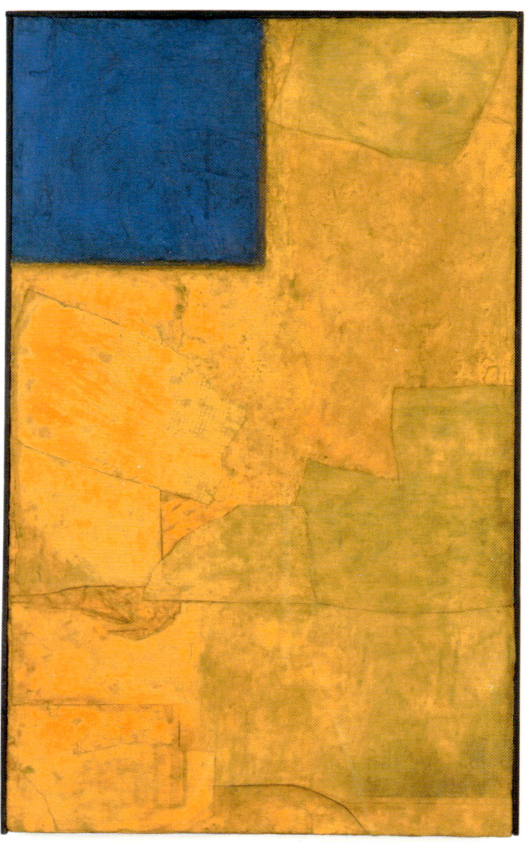

Rudolf Schwarzkogler
Ohne Titel (Untitled), 1962/63
Acryl, Gips und Papierstücke auf Holz
Acrylic, plaster and scraps of paper on wood
77 x 46 cm
Leihgabe der Österreichischen Ludwig-Stiftung
On loan from the Austrian Ludwig Foundation, seit / since 1984

Rudolf Schwarzkogler
Ohne Titel (Untitled), 1962/63
Öl, Acryl, Spachtelmasse und Schnur auf Holz
Oil, acrylic, filler and string on wood
77 x 43,3 cm
Leihgabe der Österreichischen Ludwig-Stiftung
On loan from the Austrian Ludwig Foundation, seit / since 1984

Thomas Kaminsky
Ohne Titel (Untitled), 1978
154 x 165 cm
Eitempera auf Leinwand / Egg tempera on canvas
Sammlung / Collection Dieter und Gertraud Bogner
im / at MUMOK, seit / since 2007

Jules Olitski
Commissar Demikovsky (Kommissar Demikovsky), 1965
Acryl auf Leinwand / Acrylic on canvas
244 x 213 cm
Leihgabe der Österreichischen Ludwig-Stiftung
On loan from the Austrian Ludwig Foundation, seit / since 1999

Brice Marden
Tropézienne (Thinking Blue), 1969/1970
Öl, Wachs auf Leinwand / Oil, wax on canvas
175,5 x 92 cm
Leihgabe der Österreichischen Ludwig-Stiftung
On loan from the Austrian Ludwig Foundation, seit / since 1981

Gerhard Richter
Grau Nr. 349/3 (Gray No. 349/3), 1973
Öl auf Leinwand / Oil on canvas
250 x 200 cm
Leihgabe der Österreichischen Ludwig-Stiftung
On loan from the Austrian Ludwig Foundation, seit / since 1987

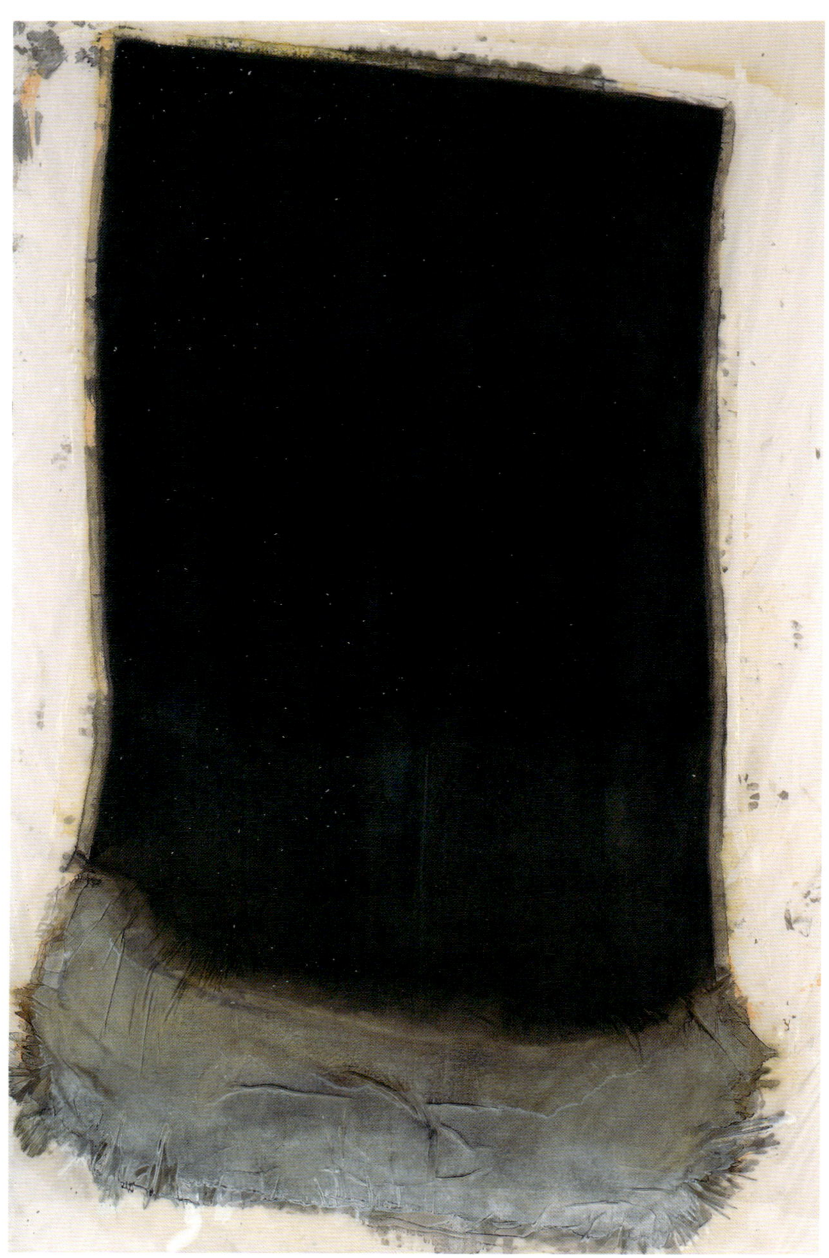

Gotthard Graubner
Schwarze Haut (Black Skin), 1969
210 x 135 cm
Öl auf Perlon / Oil on Perlon
Leihgabe der Österreichischen Ludwig-Stiftung
On loan from the Austrian Ludwig Foundation, seit / since 1991

Norbert Fleischmann
Ohne Titel (Untitled), 1994
Pigment, Acrylbinder auf Holz / Pigment, acrylic binder on wood
180 x 120 cm
Erworben / Acquired in 1999

Expansion

Rainer Fuchs

Malerei jenseits des Bildes
Zur Expansion und Überschreitung der Malerei um 1960

Transcending the Edge of the Picture
Expansion and Transgression in Painting around 1960

Vorbemerkung

Um 1960 tauchen neue Formen von Bildobjekten mit Realitäts- und Raumbezügen auf, die von einer Krise traditioneller Malerei- und Bildvorstellungen zeugen. Diese Krise der Malerei und die Versuche ihrer Überwindung fallen mit dem Aufkommen neuer handlungs-, sprach- und mediengestützter Kunstformen zusammen, die überkommene Auffassungen von Werk und Autorschaft sowie die gängigen musealen und kunstbetrieblichen Präsentations- und Distributionsformen infrage stellen und neu verhandeln. Einen konsistenten und kontinuierlich entwickelten Diskurs der Malerei, der in dieser Umbruchsituation einer Selbstbestätigung hätte dienen können, wird man dabei vergeblich suchen. Malerei hatte sich längst als ein Bündel aus unterschiedlichen Techniken und Bildbezügen erwiesen, sie war in ihren voneinander abweichenden europäischen und amerikanischen Spielformen der Abstraktion ohnehin nur als in sich heterogener Kollektivsingular fassbar. Außerdem waren es nicht nur die Protagonisten der Malerei, sondern vor allem deren theorieaffine Gegner, die in ihren Abgrenzungsstrategien ex negativo die Definitionen und Kommentare zur Malerei mitbestimmten.

Die zeitgenössische Kritik an den Abstraktionen der Malerei berief sich auf einen neuen Wirklichkeitsbegriff, um Kunst und Leben miteinander zu verschränken. Dies erfolgte auf unterschiedliche

Preliminary Remarks

New kinds of picture objects began to appear from about 1960 that referred to reality and space in ways that testified to a crisis in traditional ideas about painting and pictures. This crisis in painting, together with the attempts that were made to surmount it, coincided with the appearance of new forms of art. Based on action, language, and the media, these new forms challenged and renegotiated traditional ideas about art works and authorship, as well as conventional ways of presenting and distributing art in museums and the art industry. However, they did not give rise to the kind of consistent, continually developing discourse that might have helped to affirm and validate the identity of painting as a discipline during the upheavals of the time. Painting had long been recognized as encompassing a raft of different techniques and pictorial relationships, and the medium could no longer be comprehended as anything but an intrinsically heterogeneous, collective singular given the divergent forms of abstract painting that had developed in Europe and America. And it was not only painters themselves, but also, and indeed primarily, their theory-loving opponents who helped to shape definitions of and commentaries on painting ex negativo with their strategies of disassociation.

Contemporary critics of abstractions in painting invoked a new concept of reality in order to relate art to life. This was done in a variety of ways as abstract expressionism gave way to minimal art and pop art in the United States and art informel and lyrical abstraction were superseded by the realistic European movements of *nouveau réalisme*, Fluxus, Viennese actionism, and arte povera. The geometrical abstractions of the neo-avant-garde in what was then the Soviet Bloc display a critical relationship to reality, representing a form of resistance to the empty propaganda art of socialist realism. Notwithstanding their diversity, all these movements and approaches were accompanied by a desire to bring art back down to earth—they dealt with spatial and representational relationships that made the idea of the painted picture as a bounded, two-dimensional terrain of symbolic color seem outdated and challenged artists to transform it. These strategies of transgression and amplification in painting, collectively termed "expansion," will be examined in the remarks that follow, with special reference to the works in the MUMOK collection. Another possibility for critical reflection on and renewal of the discipline of painting lay in the study of the material and processual preconditions as the true themes and motifs of works of art. Both aspects, the expansive and the processual, could also overlap and be dependent on each other.

From Abstract Expressionism to Specific Objects

Abstract expressionism proved that the specifically processual element in painting contained an expansive dynamism that transcended the limits of the square or rectangular canvas. The critic and art theorist Clement Greenberg cited painters like Mark Tobey and Jackson Pollock, whose streaked and dripped paint tended to run beyond the edges of their pictures and undermined the tradition of the easel picture, which cut "the illusion of a box-like cavity into the wall behind it."[1] Greenberg saw this as a consequence of the liberation of color that had begun in the impressionist period and

Weise im Übergang vom abstrakten Expressionismus zur Minimal und Pop-Art in den Vereinigten Staaten sowie in der Ablöse des Informel und der lyrischen Abstraktion durch die realitätsorientierten, europäischen Strömungen des Nouveau Réalisme, des Fluxus, des Wiener Aktionismus und der Arte povera. In den geometrischen Abstraktionen der Neoavantgarde im ehemaligen Ostblock zeigte sich ein kritischer Wirklichkeitsbezug als Widerstand gegen die hohle Propagandakunst des sozialistischen Realismus. Die trotz ihrer Differenziertheit in all diesen Richtungen und Ansätzen erkennbaren Intentionen, in der Kunst wieder auf den Boden der Realität und der Tatsachen zurückzukehren, gehen mit Raum- und Objektbezügen einher, die das gemalte Bild als flächenhaft begrenztes Terrain von symbolischer Farbkraft überholt erscheinen ließen und dessen Transformationen herausforderten. Diese als „Expansion" titulierten Strategien der Überschreitung und Erweiterung von Malerei und Bild stehen im Folgenden, fokussiert auf die Sammlung des MUMOK, zur Debatte. Die Thematisierung der materiellen und prozessualen Rahmenbedingungen als eigentlicher Werkinhalte und -motive war eine weitere Möglichkeit der kritischen Selbstreflexion und Erneuerung der Malerei. Beide Aspekte, das Expansive und das Prozessuale, konnten einander auch überlagern und bedingen.

Vom abstrakten Expressionismus zu spezifischen Objekten

Dass gerade das Prozessuale in der Malerei eine expansive, die Grenzen des Bildgevierts sprengende Dynamik beinhaltet, stellte der abstrakte Expressionismus unter Beweis. So berief sich der Kritiker und Theoretiker Clement Greenberg auf Maler wie Mark Tobey und Jackson Pollock, die mit ihren schlierenartig aufgetropften Farbverläufen, die tendenziell über die Bildränder hinausreichten, die Tradition des Staffeleibildes und dessen „guckkastenartigen Hohlraum, der sich in die dahinter liegende Wand eingräbt", unterliefen.[1] Greenberg sah darin eine Folge der im Impressionismus einsetzenden Befreiung der Farbe zu ihrer immer flächenhafteren und abstrakteren Anwendung, die allerdings auch die

Integrität und die Grenzen der Malerei und des Bildes aushöhlte: „Monet und Pissarro hatten bereits sehr früh eine Art der Malerei vorweggenommen, die heute von einigen unserer ‚avantgardistischsten‘ Künstler praktiziert wird und die die Identität des Staffeleibildes in gerade dieser Hinsicht bedroht: das ‚dezentralisierte‘, ‚polyfone‘, ‚all-over‘ Bild, dessen Oberfläche sich aus einer Vielzahl identischer oder ähnlicher Elemente zusammensetzt und das sich in dieser Weise ohne größere Variation über die gesamte Leinwand wiederholt und auf Anfang, Mitte und Ende zu verzichten scheint."[2]

Aber auch jene abstrakten Expressionisten, die der Farbe geometrische oder sonstige reduktive, durchwegs aber großflächige Spielräume boten, begünstigten bildüberschreitende Gestaltungs- und Wahrnehmungsweisen. Die geronnenen und sich überlagernden Farbschleier bei Morris Louis vermittelten Greenberg „das Gefühl, dass die Farbe nicht nur quasi körperlos und daher etwas noch ausschließlicher Optisches ist, sondern zugleich die Bildfläche öffnet und erweitert" und „den Bildraum über den Bildrand hinaus in den Raum außerhalb des Bildes ausströmen [lässt]".[3]

Doch war Greenberg nicht bereit, die Konsequenz seiner Erkenntnisse, nämlich die Berechtigung neuer, raum- und objektbezogener Formen von Malerei, auch tatsächlich zu akzeptieren, sondern blieb dabei, dass „das Erschaffen eines Bildes [...] das bewusste Herstellen oder Auswählen einer planen Fläche und deren bewusste Abgrenzung und Begrenzung" sei.[4] Deutlich wird seine Ablehnung innovativer Bildkonzepte auch, wenn er bei Kenneth Noland in den Kreisscheiben, Rhomben und Kreuzformen zwar „eine kreisende Bewegung" erkennt, „die über die unbemalten Flächen und über die vier Ränder des Bildes hinauswirbelt", zugleich aber festhält, dass „das [...] Bild nur gelingen [kann], wenn es letzten Endes [...] die Begrenztheit des Bildraumes mit all seiner Rechteckigkeit und Flächigkeit und Opazität wieder bestätigt".[5] Die Beschränkung auf das Bildgeviert und die Ausgrenzung außerbildlicher Wirklichkeit als Interpretationsansatz gingen bei Greenberg Hand in Hand. Er wollte die Malerei auf das beschränkt wissen, „was in der visuellen Erfahrung gegeben ist", und sie sollte sich „auf

had led to the increasingly abstract and flat application of color that simultaneously undermined the integrity and the limits of painting and the picture, writing: "Monet and Pissarro anticipated (...) a mode of painting now practiced by some of our most advanced artists, that threatens the identity of the easel picture at precisely these points: the decentralized, polyphonic, all-over picture, which, with a surface knit together of a multiplicity of identical or similar elements, repeats itself without strong variation from one end of the canvas to the other and dispenses, apparently, with beginning, middle, and ending."[2]

But even those abstract expressionists who confined their colors to geometrical or otherwise reductive, but invariably large, surfaces were aiding the development of methods of composition and perception that transcended the limits of the picture. The coagulated, overlapping veils of color in the works of Morris Louis gave Greenberg "a sense not only of color as somehow disembodied, and therefore purely optical, but also of color as a thing that opens and expands the picture frame" and "[...] causes pictorial space to leak through— or rather, to seem about to leak through—the framing edges of the picture into the space beyond them."[3]

Greenberg was unwilling, however, to accept the consequence of his analysis and acknowledge the validity of new, space-related and object-related forms of painting. Rather, he continued to hold that "the making of a picture means [...] the deliberate creating or choosing of a flat surface, and the deliberate circumscribing or limiting of it."[4] His rejection of innovative concepts of the picture is similarly evident in his remarks on the work of Kenneth Noland, where he concedes that "the discs, diamonds and crossed arms create a revolving movement that spins out over unpainted surfaces and beyond the four sides of the picture," but also remarks that "[...]the picture succeeds, when it does succeed, by reaffirming in the end (like any other picture that succeeds) the limitedness of pictorial space as such, with all its rectangularity and flatness and opacity."[5] For Greenberg, his definition of the picture as bounded by its four sides was inseparable from his interpretive approach that excluded the reality outside the picture. He held that painting should be confined to "what is given in visual experience, and make no reference to anything given in any other order of experience."[6] This hermeticism of the visual, which Greenberg believed should be apprehended as a scientific axiom in the tradition of Kantian critical philosophy, revealed the weakness of the foundations on which he sought to defend his conception of painting and art against the up-and-coming iconoclasts of pop art and minimal art.

Greenberg aimed to preserve the picture, and the discipline of painting, as autonomous and essentially unique entities even though he had himself recognized and described their inherent expansive qualities. By contrast, the theorists of minimal art propagated—in their expression of reservations against painting—the notion of the expansive as the elimination of the picture or its transformation into objects that might or might not have any relationship with the wall. Greenberg's championing of the flat and bounded character of the painting is the diametrical opposite of Donald Judd's apologia for the three-dimensional and the non-painterly, which he saw as being realized in the form of "specific objects" in his own oeuvre: "Three dimensions are real space. That gets rid of the problem of illusionism and literal space, space in and around marks and colors—which is riddance [sic] of one of the salient and most objectionable relics of European art. The several limits of painting are no longer present."[7] Under the influence of contemporary gestalt psychology, and obsessed by the idea of a holistic gestalt in artistic form, Judd became convinced that painting was an unsuitable medium for realizing these intentions. In Judd's view, even innovative propositions such as those of Jackson Pollock, Barnett Newman, Mark Rothko, Kenneth Noland, Clyfford Still, and Ad Reinhardt—who together created a new type of painting whose large-scale forms and simple elements he acknowledged as representing "nearly an entity, one thing"[8]—embodied "only a beginning." He

nichts beziehen, was in einer anderen Art von Erfahrung gründet".[6] Diese Hermetik des Visuellen, die Greenberg noch dazu als wissenschaftliches Axiom in der Tradition des Kant'schen Kritizismus verstanden wissen wollte, verriet, auf welch schwachen Fundamenten er seinen Malerei- und Kunstbegriff gegenüber den aufkommenden Bilderstürmern der Pop-Art und der Minimal Art zu verteidigen trachtete.

Suchte Greenberg das Bild und die Malerei als autonome Entitäten von essenzieller Eigenheit zu bewahren, obwohl er die ihnen eigenen expansiven Momente selbst erkannt und beschrieben hatte, so propagierten die Programmatiker der Minimal Art in ihren Vorbehalten gegenüber der Malerei die Vorstellung des Expansiven als Auslöschung oder Transformation des Bildes in Gestalt von Objekten mit oder ohne Wandbezug. Greenbergs Einsatz für die Flächigkeit und Begrenztheit des Gemäldes steht Donald Judds Apologie des Dreidimensionalen und des Nichtmalerischen diametral gegenüber, die er in seinen Arbeiten als „specific objects" realisiert sah: „Drei Dimensionen machen realen Raum aus. Das befreit uns vom Problem des Illusionismus und des nur bezeichneten Raums, der sich in Markierungspunkten und Farbbezügen manifestiert. So verschwindet eines der ausgeprägtesten Relikte europäischer Kunst, und eines der unerwünschtesten zugleich. Die verschiedenen Grenzen, die das Gemälde bestimm(t)en, sind gefallen."[7] Beeinflusst von der zeitgenössischen Gestaltpsychologie und besessen von der Idee einer ganzheitlichen Gestalt der künstlerischen Form, gelangte Judd zur Überzeugung, dass die Malerei zur Einlösung dieser Intentionen ungeeignet sei. Auch innovative Positionen wie bei Jackson Pollock, Barnett Newman, Mark Rothko, Kenneth Noland, Clyfford Still und Ad Reinhardt, die einen neuen Gemäldetypus schufen, der mit seinen großflächigen Formen und einfachen Elementen, wie Judd selbst bemerkte, „nahezu ein Ding-an-sich, eine Identität"[8] darstelle, verkörperten für ihn doch nur „Züge eines Aufbruchs", dessen „bessere Zukunftsaussichten"[9] er außerhalb der Malerei im Objekthaften und in der Verwendung neuer, industriell produzierter Materialien sah.

Der Unterschied zwischen Bild und Objekt manifestierte sich für Judd im Verhältnis der Proportionen innerhalb des Werks. Um den Eindruck von Malerei zu vermeiden, entschied er sich, seinen Wandobjekten mehr Tiefe als Höhe zu geben, sodass der Eindruck des Auskragens von der Wand dominierte und das gewöhnlich für Malerei typische Anliegen der Bilder an der Wand abgeschwächt beziehungsweise vermieden wurde: „[…] mir wurde klar, dass ich meine Vorstellungen umsetzen könnte, indem ich die Objekte in den Raum erweiterte, und dass sich der Malereibezug komplett vermeiden ließ, wenn sie weiter hineinragen würden, als sie hoch wären."[10] Damit lieferte er eine Definition von Expansion als Überschreitung der Malerei, die sich geradezu mathematisch verifizieren ließ.

Dass Malerei und Bild wandlungsfähige Kategorien sind, die nicht an das flache Bildgeviert gebunden sind, beziehungsweise dass etwas Malerei sein konnte und doch zugleich Objekt, lag aber ebenfalls in den Programmatiken der Minimal Art begründet. Es war die viel beschworene „literalness", eine Nüchternheit, die sowohl auf der Verweigerung narrativer und anthropomorpher Referenzen als auch auf der Tilgung von hierarchischen Kompositionsregeln und Spuren manueller Fertigung gründete, die ein neues Verständnis und eine veränderte Produktion von Malerei zulassen konnte, wie Frank Stellas Haltung eindrücklich vermittelte: „Meine Malerei basiert darauf, dass nur das da ist, was da zu sehen ist. Tatsächlich handelt es sich um ein Objekt. […] Meine Bilder sollen dem Betrachter nichts anderes vermitteln als den auch für mich wesentlichen Umstand, dass die ganze Idee völlig klar zu sehen ist … Was man sieht, ist, was man sieht."[11] Stella begriff also Malerei jenseits narrativer Bezüge als Erstellung nüchtern-objekthafter Gebilde, die aufgrund ihrer Selbstbezogenheit genau jene Wahrnehmungswahrnehmung auslösen konnten, die auch Zielbestimmung der Objekte der Minimal Art war. Dass dieser Wahrnehmungsbegriff jedoch die wirklichkeitsfremde Vorstellung eines geschichtsneutralen Betrachters einschloss, sollte bald zu einem der Kritikpunkte an der Minimal Art werden.

Für Stellas Ansatz fand auch Robert Morris rechtfertigende Worte. Dazu bezog er einen Automatismus,

deemed "a better future" to lie "outside painting"[9] in the world of objects and in the use of new, industrially manufactured materials.

Judd held that the difference between pictures and objects manifested itself in the relationship of the proportions within the work. To avoid creating the impression of painting, he chose to make his wall-mounted objects deeper than they were high, so that the overriding impression was of a cantilever projecting from the wall instead of—or at least to a lesser degree—a work lying flush against the wall, as was typical in paintings. In an interview with John Coplans, he commented: "[…] [I]t occurred to me that the idea would work if the pieces were projected, and that the painting situation would be completely avoided if they projected more than they were wide, top to bottom."[10] In this way, he formulated a definition of expansion as a transgression of painting that is practically mathematically verifiable.

However, the character of painting and painted pictures as mutable categories that are not limited to the flat four-sided surface of the picture was rooted in the programmatic claims of minimal art, as was the fact that a work could be simultaneously a painting and an object. It was the frequently invoked principle of literalness—an austerity arising both from the rejection of narrative and anthropomorphic references and from the abolition of hierarchical rules of composition and traces of manual production—that provided scope for a new understanding and a change in the production of painting. This is clearly reflected in the position of Frank Stella: "My painting is based on the fact that only what can be seen there is there. It really is an object. […] All I want anyone to get out of my paintings, and all I ever get out of them, is the fact that you can see the whole idea without any confusion […] What you see is what you see."[11] Thus Stella regarded painting, stripped of its narrative references, as involving the production of austere, object-like constructs whose self-referentialism could trigger the perception of perception itself, which was precisely the goal of the objects of minimal art. However, minimal art was soon to come under criticism because this concept of perception included the unrealistic idea of a historically neutral observer.

Robert Morris defended Stella's approach, relating the automated process that was to place the discipline of painting on a more objective footing not only to its processual manifestation in the works of Jackson Pollock. He ascribed it also to the object-like paintings of Jasper Johns and Frank Stella on the grounds that these artists also sought to express an internal logic between the production of the work and its form that abrogated the detested affectation of artistic genius. Morris wrote: "The automated process has taken a variety of forms in various artists' works. Jasper Johns focused very clearly on two possible ways for painting. One was to identify a prior flat image of a target or flag with the total physical limit of the painting. [...] These, and Stella's subsequent notched striped paintings, present total systems, internally coherent. Both imply a set of necessary sequential steps which, when taken, complete the work. [...] At those points where automation is substituted for a previous, 'all made by hand' homologous set of steps, the artist has stepped aside for more of the world to enter into the art."[12] However the idea that the retreat of artistic subjectivity automatically favored the triumphal march of realism into art threatened to degrade the artistic element to something passive and was more closely connected with materialistic theories of reflection than Morris would have liked.

For Morris, the character of the object and illusionism—the latter linked to the discipline of painting—ultimately represented an insurmountable dichotomy. Stella was able to put this dichotomy to productive use in his *shaped canvases;* Morris, however, decided against painting and in favor of the object. Before committing himself to this decision, however, he created picture-like and relief-like wall-hung works, such as *Untitled* (1964) (fig. p. 207), whose apparative character alludes to Duchamp's ready-mades with their sexual connotations while also recalling the representational expansions of painting of Jasper Johns and Jim Dine.

der die Malerei auf objektivere Grundlagen stellen sollte, nicht nur auf ihre prozessuale Ausformung bei Jackson Pollock; er schrieb ihn ebenso den objekthaften Malereien von Jasper Johns und Frank Stella zu, weil auch sie einer inneren Logik zwischen Werkproduktion und Werkform zum Ausdruck verhalfen, die das verhasste geniale künstlerische Getue außer Kraft setzte: „Automatisierte Prozesse haben unterschiedliche Formen in den Arbeiten diverser Künstler angenommen. Jasper Johns konzentrierte sich ganz offensichtlich auf zwei mögliche Arten des Malens. Eine war, das von vornherein flache Bild einer Zielscheibe oder Flagge mit der totalen physischen Begrenztheit des gemalten Bildes zu identifizieren. [...] Diese wie auch Stellas folgende gekerbte und gestreifte Bilder führen totale Systeme vor, die in sich kohärent sind. Beide implizieren eine Reihe bestimmter notwendiger Schritte, die, so sie ausgeführt werden, die Arbeit vervollständigen. [...] Dort, wo Automation vorher ‚gänzlich handgemachte' Prozesse ersetzt, ist der Künstler beiseite getreten, um der Welt größeren Raum in der Kunst zu schaffen."[12] Die Vorstellung, dass der Rückzug künstlerischer Subjektivität automatisch den Einzug der Wirklichkeit in die Kunst begünstige, drohte jedoch das Künstlerische zu einer passiven Angelegenheit zu degradieren und stand materialistischen Widerspiegelungstheorien näher, als dies Morris lieb sein konnte.

Der Objektcharakter einerseits und der an die Malerei gebundene Illusionismus andererseits bildeten für Morris letztlich einen unüberwindlichen Gegensatz. Stella vermochte diesen in seinen *Shaped Canvases* für sich produktiv zu nutzen, Morris hingegen entschied sich gegen die Malerei und für das Objekt. Zuvor schuf er aber noch bild- und reliefartige Wandarbeiten wie *Untitled* (1964) (Abb. S. 207), die sich in ihren apparativen Anspielungen auf Duchamps Readymades und deren sexuelle Konnotationen beziehen, zugleich aber auch an die gegenständlichen Erweiterungen der Malerei bei Jasper Johns und Jim Dine anschließen.

Das Spiel mit der Doppelbödigkeit der Malerei als Medium der Darstellung von anderem, in der aber immer auch sie selbst zum Thema wird, hat Jasper Johns sowohl in seinen reliefhaften wie auch seinen „flachen" Malereien vor Augen geführt. Seine

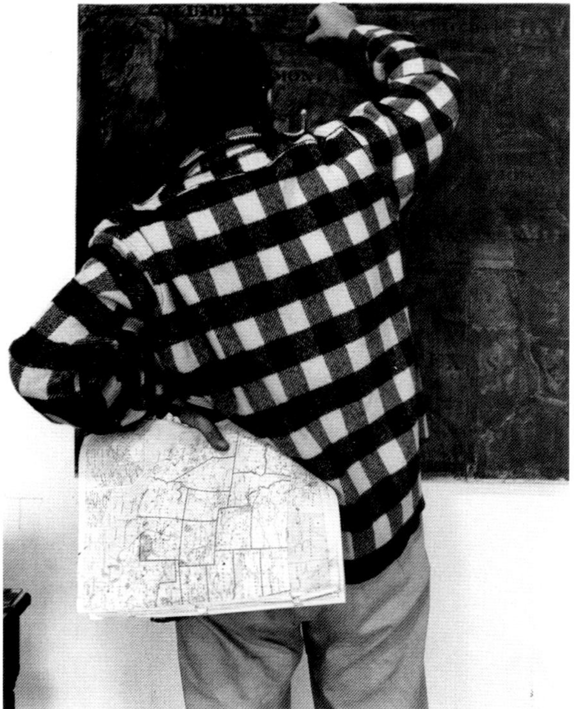

Jasper Johns, New York 1964
Fotografie / Photography: Ugo Mulas

Flaggenbilder sind zu Ikonen dieser Form von Malerei als Überlagerung von Selbst- und Fremddarstellung geworden: „Die schon in der herkömmlichen gegenstandslosen Malerei thematische Identität von zweidimensionaler Darstellung und dargestellter Zweidimensionalität findet im ‚shaped canvas', [...] gegenständlich wie bei Johns oder gegenstandslos wie bei Stella, ihre extreme Radikalisierung."[13]

Neben Jasper Johns hat Robert Rauschenberg mit seinen *Combine Paintings* wie *Diplomat* (1960) (Abb. S. 197) als einer der Begründer der Pop-Art und der Pioniere eines realitätsbezogenen Bildbegriffes die Malerei in ein erweitertes Feld gestellt. Bereits in seinen *White Paintings* fand die Einbeziehung des Realen auch ohne Objektzitate statt, weil sich die weiße Farbe als ein subtiler Spiegel für die Außenwelt erwies, deren Reflexe sich in zarten Nuancen in die Bildoberflächen einschreiben konnten. John Cages stille Kompositionen, in denen sich die Alltaggeräusche verfingen, waren dafür ein prägendes Vorbild.

Unverhohlen expandiert auch Jim Dines *Yellow Oil Can* (1962) (Abb. S. 202) ins Realräumliche. Das klassische Bildgeviert der Malerei und der Trichter erscheinen nicht nur mit einer Schnur vernabelt, sondern auch durch die Monochromie zu einer Einheit verklammert. In den objektbeladenen Bildern von Rauschenberg und Dine zeigte sich, dass das Eindringen der Wirklichkeit in die Kunst und deren

Both in his relief-like works and in his "flat" paintings, Jasper Johns flirted with the ambiguity of painting—a medium that both serves to represent something else and also always has itself as its own subject. His flag paintings became icons of this form of painting as the superimposition of self-representation and the representation of the other. "The thematic identity of the two-dimensional representation and the representation of two-dimensionality, which is an issue even in conventional non-representational art, is radicalized to the extreme in the *shaped canvas* both in representational works such as those of Johns and in non-representational ones like those of Stella."[13]

Like Jasper Johns, Robert Rauschenberg, one of the founders of pop art and a pioneer of a reality-based concept of the picture, also expanded the scope of painting with his *combine paintings*, such as *Diplomat* (1960) (fig. p. 197). Even works as early as the *White Paintings* incorporate the element of the real even without depicting specific objects, in that the white paint functions as a subtle mirror for the outside world whose reflections could play across the surface of the pictures in delicate nuances. One of the crucial inspirations for these works were the silent compositions of John Cage, in which everyday noises became part of the performance.

· Jim Dine's *Yellow Oil Can* (1962) (fig. p. 202), too, unashamedly expands out into real space. The funnel and the classical quadrangle of the painting are not only connected with a string as though with an umbilical cord, but are also subsumed into a unit by the monochrome colors. The object-laden pictures of Rauschenberg and Dine showed that the penetration of reality into art and the literal jutting out of art into the real world were complementary phenomena that revealed art to be as real as reality was riddled with artistic constructs.

Dan Flavin used light to demonstrate that it was possible to transcend the debate about the primacy of the picture or the object and achieve a form of art that expanded painting. Initially, he abolished the boundaries of the picture by screwing light bulbs on to his work *Icons* that quite literally generated a luminous aura. Later he placed standardized neon tubes at particularly sensitive spatial points, creating colorful atmospheres of light that showed the genre of painting to be a volatile, expansive medium. In this way, Flavin contradicted not only the orthogonal parameters of space and architecture, but also those of picture-bound painting. His fluorescent tubes created: "a buoyant and relentless gaseous image which, through brilliance, somewhat betrayed its physical presence into approximate invisibility."[14] It would be difficult to find a more precise way of dematerializing the painting and simultaneously placing the observer within the chromatic picture." (fig. p. 240)

From Lyrical Abstractions to Socio-Poetic Realities

In Europe, too, artists turned away from abstract painting and increasingly began to favor approaches that expanded the discipline of painting and its product, the picture, with the aim of expressing a new relationship to reality in a process supported by texts and theory. Just as American artists defined themselves in relation to European modernism and its successors, so the European art movements and individual

buchstäbliches Auskragen in die Welt komplementäre Erscheinungen waren, in denen sich die Kunst als ebenso real erwies, wie die Wirklichkeit als künstlich gespicktes Konstrukt erkennbar wurde.

Wie man auch jenseits der Debatte über die Vorherrschaft zwischen Bild und Objekt zu einer malereierweiternden Kunst kommen konnte, führte Dan Flavin mittels Licht vor Augen. Entgrenzte er zunächst in seinen *Icons* das Bild durch angeschraubte Glühbirnen, die buchstäblich eine leuchtende Aura erzeugten, so entwarf er schließlich mit standardisierten Neonröhren an neuralgischen Stellen des Raumes farbig luminöse Atmosphären, in denen sich Malerei als flüchtig expansives Medium erwies. Flavin konterkarierte damit nicht nur die orthogonalen Parameter von Raum und Architektur, sondern auch jene der bildgebundenen Malerei, entwarf er doch mit seinen Leuchtröhren „ein schwebendes und anhaltend gasförmiges Bild, das durch seine Leuchtkraft die physische Gegenwart fast bis zur Unkenntlichkeit verleugnete".[14] Präziser konnte man die Malerei nicht entmaterialisieren und zugleich den Betrachter ins farbige „Bild" stellen. (Abb. S. 240)

Von lyrischen Abstraktionen zu soziopoetischen Realitäten

Die Abkehr von abstrakter Malerei und die Forcierung malerei- beziehungsweise bilderweiternder Ansätze vollzog sich auch in Europa unter der Prämisse eines neuen Wirklichkeitsbezuges als text- und theoriegestützter Prozess. Und ebenso wie sich die Amerikaner in ihren Selbstdefinitionen auf die europäische Moderne und deren Nachfolger bezogen, spiegelt sich in den hier relevanten europäischen Kunstrichtungen und Einzelpositionen Amerika als Vorbild wie auch als Gegenwelt wider. Wir haben es dabei mit einem geteilten Europa zu tun, in dem die diametralen gesellschaftspolitischen Systeme auch divergierende Realismus- und Abstraktionskonzepte mit sich brachten. Während im westlichen Teil Europas die abstrakte Malerei verlassen wurde, um die Realität ins Werk zu setzen, waren es um 1960 im osteuropäischen Bereich abstrakte Tendenzen, die als Zeichen einer leichten politischen Liberalisierung nach dem Sturz des stalinistischen Regimes in den so genannten „sanften Diktaturen" gegen den realitätsverklärenden sozialistischen Realismus aufgeboten wurden.

Doch wenden wir uns zunächst dem Westen Europas zu. Wie jenseits des Atlantiks ging auch hier die neue Interdisziplinarität in der Kunst mit Manifesten und Selbstbeschreibungen einher. Doch anders als die Programmatiker der Minimal und Concept-Art kennzeichnet die europäischen Szenen eine „Theorie der Nichttheorie",[15] so als ob sich darin die Einsicht spiegeln würde, dass man den alten und akademischen Ordnungsschemata am besten entgeht, wenn man nicht gleich wieder zu kategorischen Festschreibungen übergeht. Auch deshalb lassen sich die im Nouveau Réalisme, in der Arte povera, im Fluxus und Wiener Aktionismus vertretenen europäischen Realismuskonzeptionen nicht unter einer griffigen Formel subsumieren. Wenn hier dennoch von „soziopoetischen Realitäten" als Klammerbegriff die Rede ist, dann um auf das breite Spektrum und die vielfältigen Verknüpfungen von soziokulturellen, gesellschaftskritischen und poetischen Aspekten in diesen Kunstrichtungen als kleinsten gemeinsamen Nenner Bezug zu nehmen. Doch weder sind diese Richtungen in sich homogen, noch erschöpft sich in den Arbeiten ihrer Protagonisten die Geschichte malereiexpansiver Ansätze.

Die bemerkenswerteste Einzelposition jenseits dieser Gruppierungen, die hier auch deshalb vorweg genannt sei, weil sie zeitliche Priorität besaß, nimmt Friedrich Kiesler ein. Er hatte bereits ab den 1920er-Jahren engen Kontakt zur amerikanischen Architektur- und Kunstszene. Als Grenzgänger zwischen den Kontinenten gehörte er auch zu den Pionieren eines offenen Kunstbegriffs, in dem die Malerei eine erweiterte und zugleich lebensintegrative Funktion erhielt. Bereits ab 1947 schuf er mit den so genannten *Galaxies* mehrteilige Bildobjekte, die als Transmitter zwischen Malerei, Skulptur und Architektur gedacht waren und seine Sensibilität für Präsentationsweisen und Raumbezüge als Interpretations- und Rezeptionsrahmen der Kunst verrieten. Ausgangs- und Bezugsthema der *Galaxies* war Kieslers Theorie des Correalismus als Ausdruck seiner Überzeugung von den Wechselbeziehungen zwischen urbanen Strukturen, Gebäuden und ihren technischen und

artists looked to America both for their models and their antitheses. But we must remember that Europe itself was a divided continent, and the diametrical contrasts between its two socio-political systems also gave rise to divergent concepts of realism and abstraction. While western Europe abandoned abstract painting in order to reinstate reality in art, eastern European art brought abstract tendencies into play that opposed the idealization of reality that was a compulsory element of socialist realism. This development was symptomatic of the cautious political liberalization that came with the break with Stalinism.

Let us turn first to western European art. Here, as on the other side of the Atlantic, the new interdisciplinary art went hand in hand with the publication of manifestos and with self-analysis. In contrast to the theories of minimal and concept art, however, the art scene in Europe was characterized by a "theory of non-theory"[15]—almost as though European art had realized that the best way to evade the old, academic order of things was by refraining from replacing it with yet another categorical, normative scheme. This is one reason why the concepts of realism that are reflected by nouveau réalisme, arte povera, Fluxus, and Viennese actionism cannot be summed up in a single, concise definition. My use, nevertheless, of the concept of "socio-poetic realities" as a blanket expression here aims to encompass the broad spectrum and the manifold interrelationships of socio-cultural, socio-critical, and poetic aspects as a common denominator of these forms of art. It should not, however, be taken to mean that these movements were homogeneous or that the oeuvres of their protagonists document every known strategy for expanding the discipline of painting.

The most remarkable single figure outside the boundaries of these groups, whom we will mention first because he predated them chronologically, was Friedrich Kiesler, who was in close contact with the American art and architecture scenes as early as the 1920s. As a traveler between the continents, he was also one of the pioneers of an open concept of art in which painting acquired an extended function that simultaneously integrated it into real life. From 1947 onwards he was already creating multi-part picture objects—his *Galaxies*—whose purpose was to serve as "transmitters" between painting, sculpture, and architecture. Furthermore, these works revealed his sensitivity to the function of presentation methods and spatial relationships as frameworks for the interpretation and reception of art. The point of departure and the frame of reference of Kiesler's *Galaxies* was the artist's theory of "correalism" as an expression of his belief in the interrelationships between urban structures, buildings, and their technical and artistic features. His *Endless House*, which was never realized but which is documented in numerous models, sketches, and descriptions, is a vision of a detached family home as the seed of new lifestyles and represents not only a focus of his "correalism", but also the conceptual essence of the *Galaxies*, the interplay of whose pictorial elements Kiesler compared to the structures of a family: "Every element is a special unit in its own right, just as every member of a family has a separate individuality. But their strong cohesion (to form a whole) is inborn, no matter how diverse the personalities of the family members might be."[16] Both the relationship of the parts to the overall scenario and the functionality of the interstitial and empty spaces as integrative components of the work as a whole reveal Kiesler's intention of achieving a flowing amalgamation of structures—as a sign that even "the traditional division of the fine arts into painting, sculpture, and architecture must be broken down and transcended."[17] The fragmentation of the quadrangle of the picture into separate, correlating pictures with an interdisciplinary focus illustrates an attempt to expand the picture and the discipline of painting. It is significant that the blending of centrifugal and centripetal forces in this attempt alludes to cosmic spheres. Kiesler's rigorously universalist thought did not content itself with interpreting *Galaxies* as a construct of internal interrelationships, but also included the role of the observer who has "the freedom either to take in all the elements at once or to concentrate his attention on only a part of them."[18] Kiesler thus thematized both practically and theo-

künstlerischen Ausstattungen. In der Vision seines *Endless House*, eines zwar niemals realisierten, aber in zahlreichen Modellen, Zeichnungen und Beschreibungen dokumentierten Einfamilienhauses als Keimzelle neuer Lebensweisen, zentriert sich nicht nur sein Correalismus, sondern liegt auch die konzeptuelle Essenz der *Galaxies*, deren Bildbestandteile in ihrem Zusammenspiel von Kiesler mit familiären Strukturen verglichen wurden: „Jedes Element ist eine spezielle Einheit in sich selbst, so wie jedes Mitglied einer Familie eine eigene Individualität besitzt. Doch ihr starker Zusammenhalt (zu einem Ganzen) ist angeboren, egal wie unterschiedlich die Charaktere der Mitglieder sein mögen."[16] In der Verbindung der Einzelteile zum Gesamtszenario sowie in der Bestimmung der Zwischen- und Leerräume als integrativer Bestandteile des Werkganzen zeigt sich Kieslers Absicht einer fließenden Verschmelzung der Werkstrukturen – als Zeichen dafür, dass auch „die traditionelle Trennung der bildenden Kunst in Malerei, Skulptur und Architektur aufgelöst und überwunden"[17] werden sollte. Das Aufbrechen des Bildgevierts in korrelierende Einzelbilder mit gattungsübergreifender Ausrichtung umschreibt einen Versuch der Expansion von Bild und Malerei, der in seiner Verschmelzung zentrifugaler und zentripetaler Kräfte bezeichnenderweise auf kosmische Sphären anspielt. Kieslers universalistisches Denken machte konsequenterweise nicht bei den *Galaxies* als internem Beziehungsgefüge Halt, sondern bezieht auch die Rolle des Betrachters, der „die Freiheit [hat], alle Elemente gleichzeitig wahrzunehmen oder sein Interesse auf nur einen Teil zu konzentrieren",[18] in seine Überlegungen ein. Lange bevor die Minimalisten ihre gestaltpsychologisch begründeten Wahrnehmungstheorien zur Grundlage ihre Produktionsrichtlinien machten, hatte also Kiesler den Zusammenhang zwischen Werkform und Rezeptionsästhetik praktisch und theoretisch thematisiert.

Anders als bei Kiesler, der Künstler und Theoretiker in einem war, bestimmte im Nouveau Réalisme und der Arte povera die Arbeitsteilung zwischen singulären Theoretikern und ihren Künstlern das Programm. Im Falle des Nouveau Réalisme war es Pierre Restany, dessen Manifeste sich wie kämpferisch pathetische Pamphlete lesen, in denen

Duchamps Erfindung des Readymade als traditions-verachtende Geste in ein wirklichkeitsbejahendes, gesellschaftsanalytisches und die Gegenstandswelt ästhetisierendes Grundmotiv umgedeutet wird. Diese Ästhetisierung der Wirklichkeit hatte Duchamp entgegen seinen eigenen Aussagen durch die äußerst berechnende Auswahl seiner Gegenstände grundge-legt. Was Restany und die neuen Realisten zudem mit Duchamp und ihren amerikanischen Kollegen verband, war die Abkehr von introspektiven und subjektiven Allüren zugunsten einer intellektuali-sierten und automatisierten Werkgestaltung: „Weg vom Pinsel, weg von der persönlichen Handschrift, weg vom Hochstilisieren des kreativen Aktes […]. Ob Yves Klein anstelle von Pinseln Rollen für die Herstellung seiner sensibilisierten Bildtafeln be-nutzte […], ob Jean Tinguely Zeichenmaschinen, die mechanisch, ohne Unterlass ‚abstrakte Bilder‘ produzierten, oder ob César seine Kompressionen einfach vom Autofriedhof […] transferierte, dies alles wurde vom Kritiker [Pierre Restany] als Spitzen, die gegen die Abstraktion gerichtet waren, herausgestrichen.“[19]

Bemerkenswerterweise war Yves Klein, der nicht zu den Reaktivisten des Readymade zählte, sondern die Malerei und die Farbe unter der Prämisse der Monochromie als räumlich-energetisches Phänomen neu definierte, entscheidend für Restanys Bruch mit der Abstraktion. Restany zeigte sich äußerst beein-druckt von Kleins Ausstellung *Le Vide* (1958), in der die Immaterialisierung von Farbe zur Imprägnie-rung eines Raumes und damit zur Neubestimmung der Malerei als ein kosmisches All-over vollzogen wurde. „Die kosmische Energie, wenn sie einmal in der reinen Farbe festgehalten worden ist, kann in die Unendlichkeit ihres Ursprungs, das heißt in den freien Raum, zurückkehren. Wichtig ist lediglich, dass der Künstler, der sich ihrer für eine bestimmte Zeit bemächtigt hat, ihre Spur bewahrt und kennt-lich macht.“[20] Als Befreier und Dompteur der Farbe hat Klein durch persönliche Selbstinszenierung die räumlich denkbar expansivste Form von Malerei ge-schaffen und damit Restany darin bestärkt, im Rah-men seines Readymade-Begriffes auch gleich „die Welt als Gemälde“[21] zu betrachten. Restanys Welt-Gemälde-Konzeption und Kleins kosmisch orientierter

retically the relationship between form and the aesthetics of reception long before the minimalists made their theories of perception, rooted in gestalt psychology, the basis of their production guidelines.

Unlike Kiesler, who was both an artist and a theorist, the programs of nouveau réalisme and arte povera were characterized by a division of labor between individual theorists and the artists who followed them. The theorist of nouveau réal-isme was Pierre Restany, whose manifestos read like militantly melodramatic pamphlets in which Duchamp's invention of the ready-made as an expression of contempt for tradition was reinter-preted as a reality-affirming, socially analytical motif that aestheticized the world of objects. Although Duchamp denied it, he himself had made this aestheticization of reality a fundamental principle of his art by the extremely calculating selection of his objects. What Restany and the artists of nouveau réalisme had in common with Duchamp and their American counterparts was the rejection of introspective and subjective affec-tations in favor of an intellectualized, automated method of production. "Away from the brush, away from personal signatures, away from the idealization of the creative act [...]. No matter whether it was Yves Klein's use of rollers instead of brushes for his sensitized panel pictures [...], Jean Tinguely's creation of drawing machines that automatically and incessantly produced 'abstract pictures' or César's simple transference of his compressions from the car junk yard, the critic [Pierre Restany] focused on all these things as jabs aimed against abstraction."[19]

It should be noted that Yves Klein, who was not one of those artists who sought to reactivate the ready-made, but who redefined painting and color as a spatial and energetic phenomenon on the basis of the monochrome, was instrumental in bringing about Restany's break with abstraction. The latter was extremely impressed by Klein's exhibition *Le Vide* (1958), in which the immateri-alization of color was used to impregnate a space and thus redefine the discipline of painting as a cosmic all-over. "Once cosmic energy has been

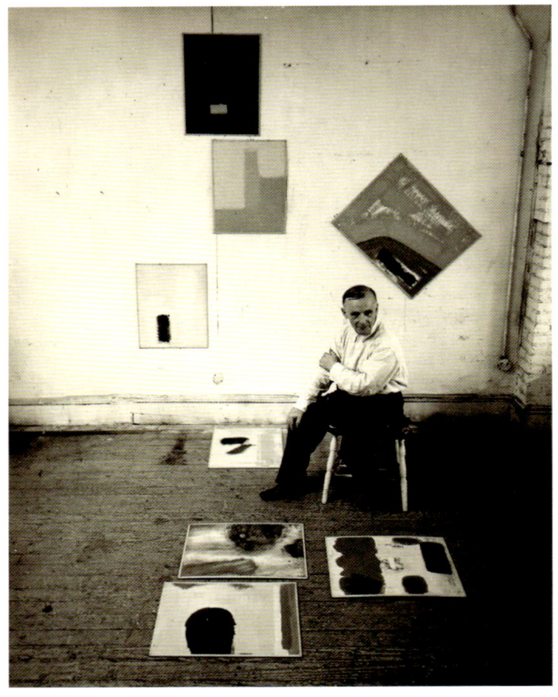

Friedrich Kiesler in 8-teiliger *Galaxy* (Floor and Wall Piece)
in seinem Atelier / Friedrich Kiesler in 8-part *Galaxy*
(Floor and Wall Piece) in his studio, 1952
Österreichische Friedrich und Lillian Kiesler-Privatstiftung
Austrian Frederick and Lillian Kiesler Private Foundation, 2010

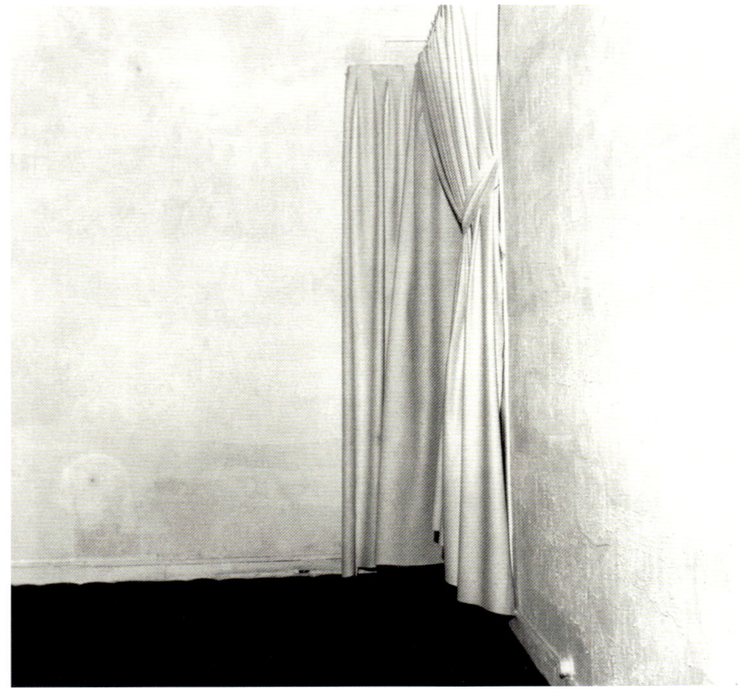

Yves Kleins Ausstellung / Yves Klein's exhibition
*La Spécialisation de la sensibilité à l'état matière première en
sensibilité picturale stabilisée*, genannt / known as *Le Vide*,
Paris, Galerie Iris Clert, 28.04.–12.05.1958
Yves Klein Archives

captured in pure color, it is able to return to the
infinity of its origin, that is, into free space. The
only thing that matters is that the artist who takes
possession of it for a certain time preserves its
traces and makes them recognizable." [20] As the
liberator and tamer of color, Klein used strategies
of self-dramatization to create the most spatially
expansive form of painting imaginable, and in
so doing confirmed Restany in the belief that his
concept of the ready-made encompassed the idea
of "the world as a painting."[21] Restany's world-as-
painting and Klein's cosmic concept of painting
represent the extremes of an expansive concept
of painting. Compared to Klein's intentions, the
approach of his fellow artist César—who gave
public performances in which he used the
expanding properties of polyurethane foam in
his *Expansions dirigées* to create a new method
of painting that incorporated objects and made
references to space and time—appears positively
sober and modest. With respect to Restany's global
conception of painting, however, Cèsar's works
seem to encompass the wider whole in a small-
scale format.

    Restany not only supported his new realists
in their role as representatives of the new avant-

Malereibegriff sind Extremkonzepte expansiver
Malereiauffassung. Nüchtern und bescheiden nimmt
sich gegen Kleins Absichten der Ansatz seines Künst-
lerkollegen César aus, bei öffentlichen Auftritten in
seinen *Expansions dirigées* Polyurethanschaumstoff
und dessen sich ausdehnende Eigenschaften für
eine neue Form objekt-, raum- und zeitbezogener
Malerei zu nutzen. In Hinsicht auf Restanys globales
Malereiverständnis scheinen sie jedoch das große
Ganze im Kleinen zu enthalten.

    Restany bestärkte seine neuen Realisten nicht
nur in ihrer Rolle als Neoavantgardisten gegenüber
den in traumatischer Erinnerungsarbeit verstrickten
Malern der lyrischen Abstraktion, sondern er über-
höhte diesen Avantgardismus noch durch den Vergleich mit den amerikanischen „Neodadaisten"
(Restany) Robert Rauschenberg und Jasper Johns als
freundschaftlich verbundenen Zeitgenossen. Selbst-
redend sah er sich und die seinen als die radikaleren
und kompromisslosen Traditionsbrecher, weil sie
nicht wie die Amerikaner Duchamps Readymade-
Erbe in einen abstrakt expressionistischen Kontext
überführt und damit entschärft hätten, sondern sich
mit „der direkten Aneignung der Wirklichkeit"[22]
jeden Kompromiss versagt hätten. Wie überzogen
und selbstgerecht diese Aussagen waren, zeigen die

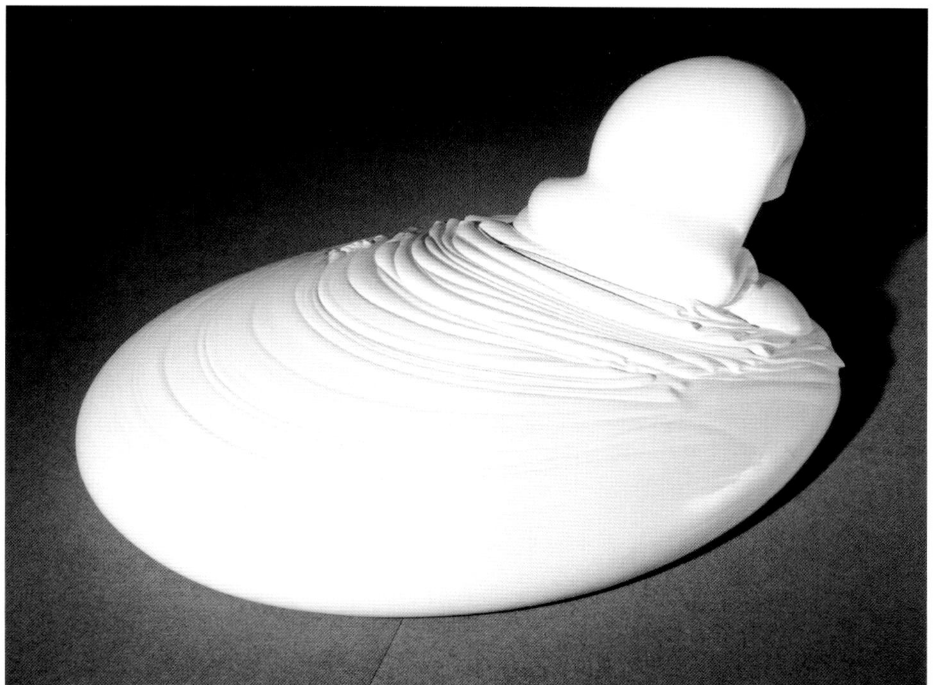

César
Expansion n°14,1970
Polyurethan / Polyurethane, 100 x 270 x 220 cm
© Collection Centre Pompidou, Dist. RMN / Philippe Migeat

Arbeiten des Nouveau Réalisme mit ihrem äußerst breiten Spektrum an Verbindungen von Realitätszitaten mit traditionellen Bild- und Malereikonzepten. Martial Raysses *Ciné* (1964) (Abb. S. 194) in dem Neonschrift, Fundgegenstände und ein Plakatsujet in eine bildhaft malerische Aura zurückgebunden sind, ist nur ein bezeichnendes Beispiel dafür.

Vergleichbar mit dem Nouveau Réalisme formierten sich auch bei der Arte povera die Künstler um einen charismatischen Theoretiker und Kurator. Hier war es Germano Celant, der aber anders als Restany die Kunst nicht auf die Bejahung zivilisatorischer Errungenschaften einschwor, sondern im Gegenteil von einer „Zeit der Unkultur"[23] sprach, in der es galt, sich auf die vormoderne Zivilisation und ihre Mythen zu besinnen. Damit sollte eine Synthese von Natur und Kultur herbeigeführt werden, mit der man der gesellschaftlichen Entfremdung Paroli bieten konnte. Einer unkritischen Wissenschafts- und Fortschrittsgläubigkeit begegnete die Arte povera aber nicht mit naiver Weltflucht, sondern indem natürliche Materialien und zivilisatorische Errungenschaften gleichermaßen als Zeichen- und Sprachsysteme begriffen und verwendet wurden. Auch die Auseinandersetzung mit Malerei fand – wenn überhaupt – unter sprachlichen Vorzeichen statt und

garde vis-a-vis the painters of lyrical abstraction, who were caught up in processing the trauma of the recent past, but also exalted this avant-gardism by comparing it with the American "Neodadaists" (Restany) Robert Rauschenberg and Jasper Johns, whom he saw as friendly, like-minded contemporaries. It goes without saying that he was convinced that he and his circle were the more radical and uncompromising iconoclasts, since they had not defused Duchamp's legacy of the ready-made by transferring it into the context of abstract expressionism, as the Americans had done, but had instead foregone every possibility of compromise by the "direct appropriation of reality."[22] The exaggerated and self-righteous nature of these claims is shown by the works of nouveau réalisme, with their extremely broad spectrum of links between allusions to reality and traditional concepts of painting and the picture. One such exemplary work is Martial Raysse's *Ciné* (1964) (fig. p. 194), which integrates neon lettering, objets trouvés, and a poster motif into a picturesque aura.

As was the case in nouveau réalisme, the artists of arte povera gathered around a charismatic theorist and curator. Unlike his counterpart Restany, however, Germano Celant did not expect art to commit itself to the affirmation of the achievements of civilization, but instead spoke of an uncultured age[23] in which it was necessary to recall pre-modern civilization and its myths. The aim was to achieve a synthesis between nature and culture that would be able to resist social estrangement. However, arte povera responded to an uncritical faith in science and progress not by resorting to escapism, but by interpreting and using natural materials and the products of civilization as semiotic and linguistic systems. Furthermore, its critical engagement with painting took place—when it took place at all—from a linguistic perspective and resulted in picture objects that took the form of linguistically inspired images full of poetical allusions, such as Pino Pascali's *Il muro del sonno* (1966) (fig. p. 187). The pillows covered in white paint form a wall-like construction of repeating elements that differ from one another, however, in minor details. Pascali had a special interest in differences within structural similarities and used them to make reference to the dangers lurking in a superficial way of seeing that is inured to nuance. Thus the "wall of sleep" refers not only to a poetic visualization of objects in the tradition of concrete poetry, but also to the generalized mistrust of arte povera toward all forms of leveling and the decline of critical discernment in a time of superficial consumerism. Significantly, Pascali—who was initially intrigued by American pop art but then adopted a critical attitude to the genre—regarded his art as opposing to America's euphoric enthusiasm for progress: "The Americans can afford the luxury of nailing something to a picture and calling it complete. [...] We are in a different situation. There is still an intellectual element. We want to choose, we don't want to be drawn into something."[24] This type of expansion of painting, therefore, is fueled not by the joyous affirmation of industrial and mercantile products, but by misgivings about them. Pascali's comments also read like a paraphrase of Yoko Ono's *Painting to Hammer a Nail* (fig. p. 203) (MUMOK exhibit, executed in 2005), in which an instruction becomes a trigger for art that expands pictorial limits. He himself, however,

führte, wie bei Pino Pascalis *Il muro del sonno* (1966) (Abb. S. 187), zu Bildobjekten als Sprachbildern voll poetischer Anspielungen. Die mit weißer Farbe übermalten Polster formieren sich zu einem mauerartigen Gebilde einander wiederholender und doch in Details voneinander abweichender Elemente. Pascali war gerade an den Unterschieden innerhalb struktureller Ähnlichkeiten interessiert und lieferte damit einen Verweis auf die Tücken eines oberflächlichen und gegen Nuancen abgestumpften Blicks. So verweist seine „Mauer des Schlafes" nicht nur auf eine poetische Visualisierung von Dingen in der Tradition konkreter Poesie, sondern auch auf ein von der Arte povera generell eingemahntes Misstrauen gegen die Nivellierung und das Einschlafen kritischen Unterscheidungsvermögens in Zeiten oberflächlichen Konsumierens. Bezeichnenderweise verstand Pascali, der anfangs von der amerikanischen Pop-Art fasziniert war und dann auf kritische Distanz zu ihr ging, seine Kunst als Opposition zur Fortschrittseuphorie amerikanischer Prägung: „Die Amerikaner können es sich leisten, irgendetwas auf ein Bild zu nageln, und das Bild ist fertig. [...] Wir befinden uns in einer anderen Situation. Es existiert noch ein geistiges Element, man möchte wählen, sich nicht hineinziehen lassen."[24] Diese Art der Erweiterung von Malerei und Bild nährt sich also nicht aus der freudigen Bejahung des Industriellen und Merkantilen, sondern aus dem Misstrauen dagegen. Pascalis Kommentar liest sich außerdem wie eine Paraphrase auf Yoko Onos Arbeit *Painting to Hammer a Nail* (Abb. S. 203) (MUMOK-Exponat, ausgeführt 2005), in der eine Handlungsanweisung der Auslöser bilderweiternder Kunst ist. Pascali selbst jedoch überzieht oder ersetzt die Malerei und das Bild nicht durch Objekte, sondern verfährt umgekehrt: Die Objekte sind mit weißer Farbe überzogen, sie unterliegen buchstäblich der Malerei, so als ob die Erinnerung an Vergangenes sich als Korrektiv über die Gegenwart und ihre Dingwelt legen würde.

Die theoretisch vermittelte Theorielosigkeit als Erkennungszeichen von Gruppenidentität verband Nouveau Réalisme und Arte povera mit dem Fluxus. Als Amalgam aus unterschiedlichen innovativen Ansätzen von Theater, Musik, Film, Malerei und Skulptur war die Grenzüberschreitung von Kunstformen so sehr Programm der Fluxus-Bewegung, dass deren Protagonisten gerade die Sinnlosigkeit einer konkreten Richtungsdefinition für sinnvoll erachteten. „Das Wichtigste an Fluxus ist, dass niemand weiß, was es ist […]. Es soll wenigstens etwas geben, das die Experten nicht verstehen. Ich sehe Fluxus, wo ich auch hingehe."[25] Diese Ablehnung von Kategorisierungen gründete in einer Kritik an „den bis dahin dominierenden Schulen der Abstraktion", die jeglichen Inhalt aus der Kunst verbannt und „sie somit für unser normales Leben und unsere alltäglichen Sorgen moralischer, sozialer, spiritueller und praktischer Art" nutzlos gemacht hätten.[26] Auch für die Fluxus-Künstler war also primär die abstrakte Malerei jenes Feindbild, das sie in ihrem Drang bestärkte, Kunst und Leben ineinander überzuführen. Wie für Pop-Art und Nouveau Réalisme war auch für sie neben Duchamp und dem Dadaismus der Grenzgänger John Cage die zentrale Orientierungsfigur inmitten selbst proklamierter Richtungslosigkeit. Doch war die Fluxus-Bewegung nicht nur zwischen den Kunstgattungen, sondern – bedenkt man die Nationalitäten ihrer Protagonisten – auch zwischen den Kontinenten angesiedelt. George Maciunas definierte die Fluxus-Ziele als soziale und nicht als ästhetische. Kollektivismus, Anonymität, Antiindividualismus, Kritik am Warencharakter des Kunstwerks und Antieuropäismus als Synonym für die Ablehnung der Tradition des L'art pour l'art waren seine Grundprinzipien für künstlerisches Verhalten, denen aber sein eigenes Geltungsbedürfnis widersprach, das zu zahlreichen gruppeninternen Konflikten führte. Seine Prinzipien standen jedenfalls im Gegensatz sowohl zu Restanys optimistischer Daseinsbejahung und ästhetisierender Sicht der Wirklichkeit wie auch zum marktkonformen Geniekult der Pop-Art.

Wolf Vostell, dessen Werk repräsentativ in der MUMOK-Sammlung vertreten ist, war als eines der Gründungsmitglieder auch einer der engagiertesten Gesellschaftskritiker und wollte nicht nur die Grenzen zwischen Kunst und Leben verwischen, sondern mit seinen Arbeiten das Publikum auch dazu bringen, „einen gesellschaftlichen Gedankengang zu denken, keinen Kunstgedanken".[27] Vostell, der neben seiner künstlerischen Arbeit als Herausgeber von Zeitschriften und Büchern, als Theoretiker und

does not overlay or replace painting and pictures with objects, but rather does the opposite: The objects are covered in white paint, so that they are literally subordinated to painting as though the memory of things past had been laid over the present and its representational world as a corrective cover.

The theoretically transmitted freedom from theory as a badge of group identity was what nouveau réalisme and arte povera had in common with Fluxus. As an amalgam of divergent innovative approaches to theater, music, film, painting, and sculpture, Fluxus was so dominated by its programmatic transcendence of individual art forms that its protagonists considered even the pointlessness of a specific definition of their movement to have a point. Robert Watts once commented that the most important thing about Fluxus was that nobody knew what it was, stressing that there should be at least one thing that the experts don't understand. He, himself, said that he saw Fluxus wherever he went.[25] This rejection of all categorization was rooted in a criticism of the hitherto dominant schools of abstraction, which were accused of having banished all content from art, thus robbing it of relevance for people's normal lives and everyday worries about moral, social, spiritual, and practical issues.[26] The Fluxus artists also, therefore, saw abstract painting as their main enemy, an enemy that confirmed them in their quest to merge art and life. Like pop art and nouveau réalisme, Fluxus, too, looked not only to Duchamp and Dadaism, but also to the cross-disciplinary pioneer John Cage as a guiding light in an environment of self-proclaimed lack of direction. However, Fluxus was situated not only between art genres but, given the nationalities of its protagonists, between the continents as well.

George Maciunas defined the goals of Fluxus as being social rather than aesthetic. His fundamental principles for artistic behavior were collectivism, anonymity, anti-individualism, criticism of the commodified character of the artwork, and anti-Europeanism as a synonym of the tradition of art for art's sake. Maciunas' own craving for recognition contradicted, however, his own principles, resulting in many internal conflicts within Fluxus. At any rate, his principles contrasted both with Restany's optimistic affirmation of existence and aestheticizing view of reality, as well as with the market-oriented cult of genius that was prevalent in pop art.

Wolf Vostell, representative examples of whose works are in the MUMOK collection, was both one of the founder members of Fluxus and one of its most dedicated social critics who strove not only to blur the borders between art and life in his works, but also to persuade the audience to "think social thoughts, not artistic ones."[27] Vostell was not only an artist, but also a publisher of magazines and books, and his theoretical work and media criticism made him one of the key figures in artistic discourse. He judged social life to be a process of dissolution and attrition full of self-destructive energies, and therefore related the concept of décollage to the reality of life as a whole, viewing his own artistically charged poster décollages as acts of indictment, protest, and rebellion of consciousness against the contradictions and absurdities of bourgeois capitalist society. His actionist approach to art can be seen in the fact that he did not confine himself to expanding the décollages into material collages and paintings, but also incorporated them into performances and actions. Thus the script for his project *Das Theater ist auf der Straße* (Paris, 1958) calls for the participants to take undamaged portions of texts from the posters and read them out loud until crowds gathered, who would then help to continue destroying the posters.[28] Painting could hardly be anything but a marginal phenomenon in such an agitative and participatory environment, even if it was perceived as being located within a wider context.

The ideological bandwidth of Fluxus is reflected, in exemplary fashion, in the difference between Vostell and Geoffrey Hendricks, who began in the mid-1960s to paint blue-white skies over objects such as animal skulls, clothing, shoes, washboards, cars, and chairs (fig. p. 188, 189). Inspired by the trompe l'oeil painting technique of Roman baroque ceilings about which he had

Medienkritiker zu einer zentralen Diskursfigur avancierte, bewertete das gesellschaftliche Leben als Auflösungs- und Verschleißprozess voll selbstzerstörerischer Energien. Er bezog daher den Begriff der Decollage auf die gesamte Lebensrealität und verstand seine eigenen malerisch aufgeladenen Plakatabrisse als Anklage, Protest und Rebellion des Bewusstseins gegen die Widersprüche und Widersinnigkeiten der kapitalistisch-bürgerlichen Zivilisation. Sein aktionistischer Anspruch an die Kunst zeigte sich unter anderem darin, die Decollagen nicht nur zu Materialcollagen und -malereien zu erweitern, sondern sie auch in Aktionen überzuführen. So forderte er in seinen Aktionsanweisungen zu seinem Projekt *Das Theater ist auf der Straße* (Paris, 1958) die Teilnehmer auf, unversehrte Textteile von Plakaten lautstark zu lesen, bis sich Menschenansammlungen gebildet hatten, die dann weiter an der Zerstörung dieser Plakate mitwirken sollten.[28] Malerei konnte in einem solch agitativ und partizipatorisch ausgerichteten Denken – auch wenn sie in einem erweiterten Feld angesiedelt wurde – bestenfalls als Randnotiz fungieren.

Die ideologische Bandbreite von Fluxus spiegelt sich beispielhaft im Vergleich Vostells mit Geoffrey Hendricks, der ab Mitte der 1960er-Jahre Gegenstände wie Tierschädel, Kleidung, Schuhe, Waschbretter, Autos, Stühle et cetera mit blau-weißen Himmeln übermalte (Abb. S. 188, 189). Angeregt von römischen Barockdecken mit ihrer scheinräumlichen Malerei, über die er eine Diplomarbeit verfasst hatte, erweiterte er nicht nur die Malerei ins Objekthafte, sondern löste zugleich die verwendeten Gegenstände in atmosphärisch-malerische Gebilde auf. Die Durchdringung von Gegensätzen, die Verbindung des Sphärisch-Unendlichen mit dem Endlich-Realen, des Räumlichen mit dem Körperlichen verraten ein von fernöstlichem Denken inspiriertes Schaffen, das der gesellschaftlichen Entfremdung mit philosophisch gelassener Haltung begegnet. Wenn er in einigen Performances selbst seinen nackten Körper als Himmel übermalte und sich in die Erde grub, dann ging es dabei um ein Zurückfinden zu sich selbst in eine universelle Geborgenheit und Einheit mit den Elementen und der Natur – ein Anspruch, der auch im Zusammenhang mit Hendricks' Selbstfindung als homoerotischer Persönlichkeit zu sehen ist.

Hendricks war in einigen Aktionen von Hermann Nitsch als Akteur eingebunden und hat ihn bei der Realisierung einer Aktion in New Jersey gegen örtlichen Widerstand unterstützt.[29] Den Wiener Aktionismus hat Nitsch selbst im Vergleich zum „kühlen, konzeptuell bestimmten" Fluxus als „extrem sinnlich, expressiv, exzessiv, dramatisch"[30] beschrieben und sein *Orgien Mysterien Theater* als „religiösphilosophisches Unternehmen" den „politischideologischen Zielsetzungen"[31] der Fluxus-Künstler gegenübergestellt.

Die Erweiterung der Malerei zu realzeitlichen und körperbezogenen Handlungen ist eine grundsätzliche Errungenschaft des Wiener Aktionismus, die von seinen einzelnen Protagonisten unterschiedlich formuliert wurde. Entgrenzung der Malerei bedeutet bei Nitsch, sie als ekstatischen Prozess zu inszenieren und die Bildfläche zu verlassen, um reale Geschehnisse in Form von Abreaktionsspielen entstehen zu lassen, die therapeutische Wirkung entfalten sollen. Nitsch stellt sich selbst in die Tradition archaischer Rituale, er bezieht sich auf die antike und christliche Mythologie und verknüpft die kathartischen Mythen ihrer Opfer- und Märtyrerlegenden mit tiefenpsychologischem Diagnose- und Therapiewillen. Therapieziele waren aber nicht nur die einzelnen Teilnehmer an seinen Aktionen, sondern im Grunde die österreichische Nachkriegsgesellschaft, die in der geistigen Enge eines verlogenen und geschichtsverdrängenden Katholizismus erstarrt war und die schon damit Probleme hatte, den verspäteten Nachholbedarf an gestisch-abstrakter Malerei mit Körperbezügen durch Künstler wie Maria Lassnig und Arnulf Rainer zu verkraften. Aber nicht nur in der Verwandlung in theatralische Aktionen lag Nitschs Beitrag zur Expansion der Malerei, sondern auch in der Transformation des Bildes in altarartige skulpturale Hybriden oder Materialcollagen wie in der *Reliktmontage mit blutigen Tüchern* (1964) (Abb. S. 185), die Resultate seiner Aktionen waren.

Das Leiden an dieser Gesellschaft und die Wut an ihrer Ignoranz zeigte sich bei Otto Muehl unter anderem in der Zerstörung eines Tafelbildes, durch Zerschneiden der Leinwand, Zertrümmern des Rahmens und das Verschnüren der so entstandenen

written a degree thesis, he not only expanded painting into the realm of objects, but also dissolved the objects he used into atmospheric, picturesque formations. The interpenetration of opposites and the connection of the celestial infinite with finite reality and of the spatial with the corporeal reveals a creative drive inspired by eastern thought that responds to social estrangement with philosophical serenity. When he painted a sky on his own nude body in some of his performances and burrowed into the earth in others, he was concerned with the quest for the self and with a return to universal security and unity with the elements and nature—an aim that must also be analyzed in connection with Hendricks' discovery of himself as a homoerotic personality.

Furthermore, Hendricks participated in some of the actions of Hermann Nitsch, whom he defended against resistance from the local community during a performance in New Jersey. [29] Nitsch himself described Viennese actionism in comparison with the "cool, conceptually dominated" Fluxus as "extremely sensually expressive, excessive, dramatic"[30] and contrasted his *Orgien Mysterien Theater*, which he described as a "religious and philosophical project" with the "politically ideological aims"[31] of the Fluxus artists.

The expansion of painting to encompass realtime, physical acts is one of the fundamental achievements of Viennese actionism and was formulated in different ways by different protagonists of the movement. Nitsch aimed to dissolve the boundaries of painting by presenting the act of painting as an ecstatic process and by abandoning the plane of the picture in order to allow real events to unfold in the form of abreactive, cathartic games that served a therapeutic purpose. Nitsch felt himself to be following the tradition of archaic rituals. He alluded to classical mythology and Christian themes, linking the cathartic myths of their stories of sacrifice and martyrdom with the diagnoses and therapies of depth psychology. His therapeutic intentions were not, however, directed exclusively at the individuals who participated in his actions, but rather at postwar Austrian society as a whole, which he saw as

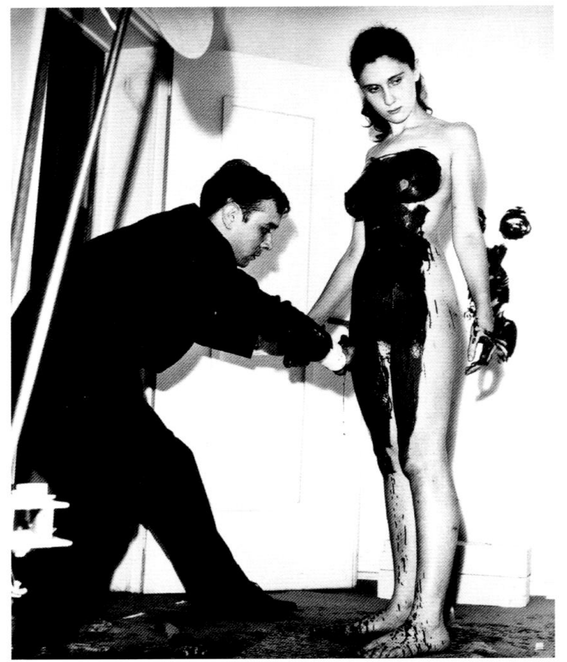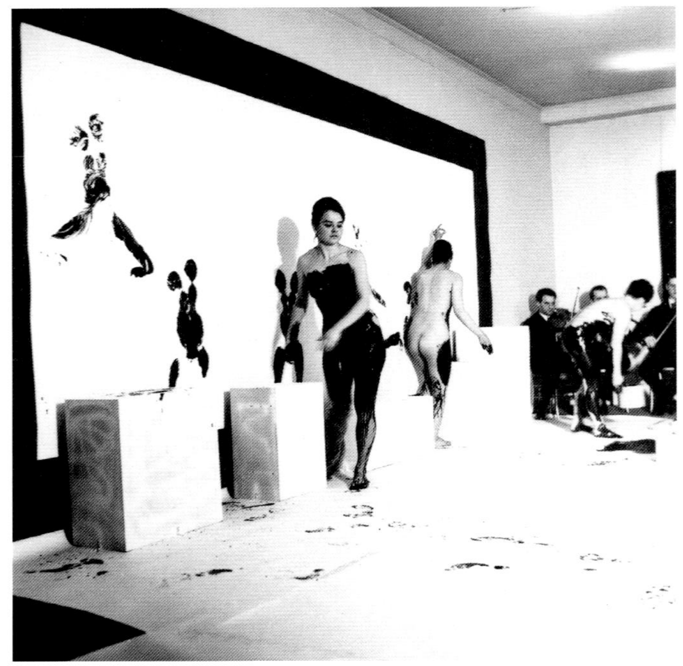

being trapped in the intellectual straitjacket of a mendacious Catholicism that denied history and even had difficulty dealing with the belated adoption of gesturally abstract, body-oriented painting by artists like Maria Lassnig and Arnulf Rainer. But Nitsch's contribution to the expansion of painting was not limited to its transformation into theatrical performance actions. He also transformed painting into altar-like, sculptural hybrids or material collages such as *Reliktmontage mit blutigen Tüchern* (1964) (fig. p. 185), which resulted from his performances.

The destruction of a panel painting by slashing the canvas, smashing the frame, and parceling up the resultant pieces was, for example, one of the ways in which Otto Muehl's oeuvre revealed the suffering caused by society and expressed fury at its ignorance. This was done with the aim of depicting painting, ultimately, as a material action and documenting the process on film. "The material action is painting that has expanded beyond the borders of the picture. The human body [...] or a space becomes the 'canvas.'"[32] Thus painting was defined as a real-time process involving actors—as a "picture" that continually changes in time and space, in which bodies and colors constantly coalesce into one another, just as the borders between art and the documentation of art became indistinct as both real actionism and its interpretation on film equally attained the status of art. This approach shares its concept of the model

Teile mit dem Ziel, Malerei letztlich als Materialaktion zu inszenieren und filmisch zu dokumentieren. „Die Materialaktion ist über die Bildfläche hinausgewachsene Malerei. Der menschliche Körper [...] oder ein Raum wird zur ‚Bildfläche'."[32] So wurde Malerei als ein realzeitlicher Prozess mit Akteuren definiert, als ein sich permanent in Zeit und Raum veränderndes „Bild", in dem Körper und Farben unablässig ineinander gleiten, ebenso wie die Grenze zwischen Kunst und ihrer Dokumentation verschwamm, da der reale Aktionismus und dessen filmische Interpretation gleichermaßen Kunststatus erlangten. Die Modelle als lebende Pinsel hat dieser Ansatz mit den Anthropometrien Yves Kleins gemein, der orgiastisch-rauschhafte Umgang mit Geschlechtlichkeit und Körperlichkeit unterscheidet Muehl allerdings von der analytisch-distanzierten Choreografie des Franzosen.

Das priesterliche Gehabe Nitschs und das autoritär inszenierte Laisser-faire Muehls waren sowohl Rudolf Schwarzkogler wie auch Günter Brus fremd. Aber die im Vergleich zu den anderen Aktionisten statisch und arrangiert wirkenden Arbeiten Schwarzkoglers begründeten sich ebenso als eine Erweiterung des Malaktes in eine Totalaktion als „räumlich-zeitliches Gebilde".[33] Für Brus war die gestische Malerei selbst Ausgangspunkt und Gegenstand einer Transformation ins Zeiträumliche unter aktionistisch-existenzialistischen Prämissen. Seine Verräumlichung der Malerei kulminierte in Formen der Selbstbemalung und deren Zurschaustellung im

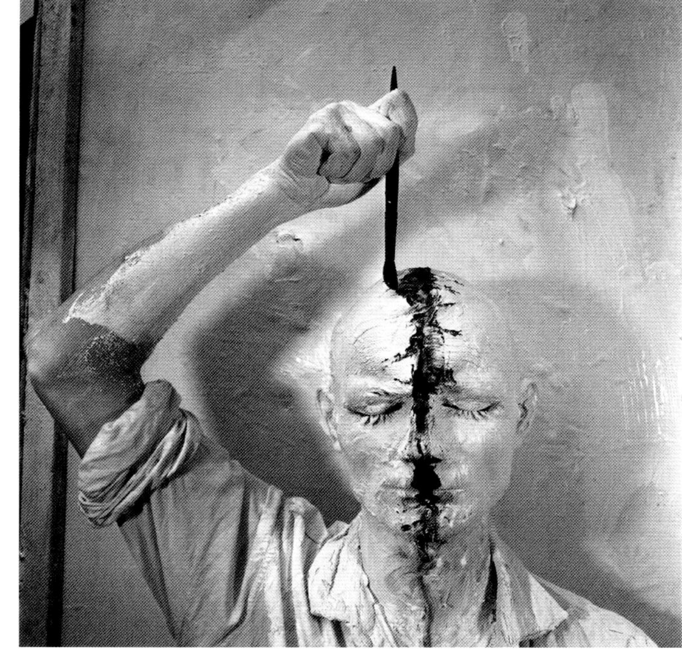

Yves Klein bei der Herstellung einer *Anthropometrie* in seiner
Wohnung / during the making of an *Anthropometry* in his
apartment, 14, rue Campagne-Première, Paris, 1960
Yves Klein Archives

Erste öffentliche Anthropometrie-Aktion bei Robert Godet /
First public *Anthropometry* performance in the home of
Robert Godet, Paris, Île Saint-Louis, 05.06.1958
Performance Anthropométrie de l'epoque bleue (Anthropometrie
der blauen Epoche / Anthropometrie of the Blue Period), Galerie
international d'Art contemporain, Paris, 09.03.1960
Yves Klein Archives

Günter Brus, Aktion / Action Selbstbemalung (Self-Painting), 1964
Fotografie / Photography: Ludwig Hoffenreich
Schenkung des Künstlers / Donated by the artist, 2006

öffentlichen Raum – wie im *Wiener Spaziergang*
(1965) (Abb. S. 183). Als wandelndes Gemälde formulierte Brus eine Expansion der Malerei, die das
abstrakte Schwarz-Weiß so auf den Körper übertrug,
dass es die konkrete Bedeutung eines schmerzhaften
Schnittes annehmen und selbst mit Lucio Fontanas
aufgeschlitzten Leinwänden in Verbindung gebracht
werden konnte.[34] Mit seiner Anmerkung, dass
„Selbstbemalung [...] bewältigte Selbstverstümmelung [...], unendlich ausgekostete Selbstentleibung"
sei,[35] betonte Brus mit dem selbstzerstörerischen
zugleich den kathartischen Effekt seiner – auf den
Körper und den damit durchschrittenen Raum –
erweiterten Malerei.

Auch im Umfeld und jenseits des Wiener Aktionismus fand hierzulande die Demontage der Tafelbildmalerei in Materialbildern und Bildobjekten
ihren Ausdruck. Adolf Frohner, der anfangs ein
Nahverhältnis zum Aktionismus hatte, schuf mit aufgerissenem und bildhaft dekonstruiertem Mobiliar
wie dem *Schwarzen Sessel* (1962) (Abb. S. 179) Sinnbilder für körperliche Verwundbarkeit und Vergänglichkeit. In solchen Bildkörpern wird das Innere
nach außen gekehrt und die Außenhaut der Dinge
für den Blick in das Innere existenzieller Befindlichkeit durchlässig gemacht. Alfons Schilling führte mit
seinen Rotationsbildern (Abb. S. 62, 63) einen Automatismus ein, der seiner Malerei die existenzielle
Schwere aktionistischer Daseinsanalyse ersparte, und
Oswald Oberhuber ließ im *Rahmenbild* (1953) (Abb.
S. 177) mit der Verwendung eines leinwandbefreiten

as a living paintbrush with the *Anthropometries* of
Yves Klein, although Muehl's orgiastic, Dionysian
approach to sexuality and the body bears no
resemblance to the analytical detachment of
Klein's choreography.

Both the priestly demeanor affected by Nitsch
and Muehl's authoritarian imposition of the
principle of anything goes were foreign both to
Rudolf Schwarzkogler and Günter Brus. But even
Schwarzkogler's works, which seem static and
deliberately arranged in comparison to those of
other actionists, also justified themselves as
expanding the act of painting in a total action to
create a "spatial and temporal construct."[33] For
Brus, gestural painting itself was the point of
departure and the object of a transformation into
the temporal and spatial under actionist and existentialist premises. His spatialization of painting
culminated in forms of self-painting and their
exhibition in the public space, for example in
Wiener Spaziergang (1965) (fig. p. 183). As a walking painting, Brus formulated an expansion of
painting that transferred the abstract colors of
black and white onto his body in such a way that
it could take on the specific significance of a
painful incision and could even be associated with
Lucio Fontana's slashed canvases.[34] In asserting
that "self-painting [...] is controlled self-mutilation [...] and eternally enjoyable suicide,"[35] Brus
stressed both the self-destructive and the cathartic
effect of his style of expanded painting, which

extends to the body and to the space the body moves through.

In the vicinity of the Viennese actionists and beyond, the dismantling of panel painting was also expressed in Austrian art in the form of material paintings and picture objects. Adolf Frohner, who initially had a close relationship to actionism, created furniture objects such as *Schwarzer Sessel* (1962) (fig. p. 179) that were torn open and deconstructed to become symbols of physical vulnerability and transience. Such picture objects turn the object partially inside out, making its external skin permeable to allow a view of the interior of existential affective states. Alfons Schilling's Rotationsbilder (fig. p. 62, 63) introduced an automatism that allowed his paintings to escape the existential weight of an actionist analysis of being. Similarly, Oswald Oberhuber's *Rahmenbild* (1953) (fig. p. 177), which consisted of a picture frame devoid of a canvas, gave a glimpse of the dialectical interlinking of the interior and the exterior, of work and space, without resorting to the pathos of depth psychology.

Max Weiler's *Flügelbild: Große Blume* (1968) (fig. p. 174) shows that even abstraction could serve to expand the picture without undermining the traditional definition of painting, if it incorporated references to nature and landscapes. He put three-dimensional folds into the surface of works like this one, as though to give the fissured, airily transparent structures of his nature scenes a more authentic appearance and to allegorize the process of growth and blossoming. Subsequently, however, he abandoned this practice, while Bernard Schultze displayed a more consistent rigor in expanding his paintings from the traditions of art informel into the spatial dimension of sculpture. In the late 1950s he developed his increasingly pastose pictures into color reliefs that resembled overhead views of fissured, organ-like topographies, and subsequently began to produce polychrome, fibrous constructs which he called *Migofs* (fig. p. 175). This artificial word, which he invented to describe artistic structures that fluctuated between painting, relief, and sculpture, deliberately evaded any semblance of unambiguous

Bilderrahmens Einsichten in die dialektische Verzahnung von Innen und Außen, von Werk und Raum ohne tiefenpsychologisches Pathos aufblitzen.

Dass auch die Abstraktion mit Natur- und Landschaftsbezügen einer Erweiterung des Bildes Raum geben konnte, ohne das traditionelle Malereiverständnis infrage zu stellen, zeigt Max Weilers *Flügelbild: Große Blume* (1968) (Abb. S. 174). Wie um den zerklüfteten und luftig-transparenten Strukturen seiner Naturschilderungen ein authentischeres Erscheinungsbild zu geben und den Prozess des Wachsens und Blühens zu versinnbildlichen, faltete er in Arbeiten wie dieser die Bildfläche räumlich auf, ließ jedoch in der Folge wieder davon ab.

Mit nachhaltigerer Konsequenz hingegen erweiterte Bernard Schultze die Malerei aus der Tradition des Informel heraus ins Räumlich-Skulpturale. Er übersteigerte in den späten 1950er-Jahren seine immer pastoser werdenden Bilder zu Farbreliefs, die wie zerfurchte und organoide Topografien aus der Vogelperspektive erscheinen, bevor er zu farbigfaserigen Gebilden überging, die er als *Migofs* (Abb. S. 175) bezeichnete. Damit ordnete er diesen zwischen Malerei, Relief und Skulptur changierenden Kunstgebilden ein Kunstwort zu, das seinerseits mit Absicht jede Eindeutigkeit vermied. Schultze verfolgte jedoch keinen Ausstieg aus dem Bild durch Einbindung realer Gegenstände wie im Nouveau Réalisme oder in der Pop-Art, sondern zielte auf eine Fortsetzung der Malerei mit anderen Mitteln, er „malt ja nicht mit Gegenständen, sondern macht seine in der autonomen Ausdruckskraft der Farbe wurzelnde Malerei handgreiflich wirklich, ohne von ihren ästhetischen Möglichkeiten irgendetwas aufgeben zu müssen".[36] Die Vergegenständlichung des Bildes hing dabei offensichtlich mit der Verdinglichung der Farbe zusammen, das heißt mit der Vorstellung, „dass die Farbe Pigment sein müsste, über die Form gespannt, untrennbar mit ihr verbunden, wie es in der Erscheinungswelt rundum zu sehen ist".[37] Farbe dient hier nicht nur der Illustration, sondern ist selbst „ein Ding in Gestalt eines organisch verlaufenden Fließprozesses, der für den Moment der Bildwerdung exemplarisch zum Erstarren gebracht ist".[38] Die *Migofs* verkörpern als farbig erstarrte, zwischen Bild und Raum vermittelnde Hybriden die „Gleichzeitigkeit von Wachsen und Verderben, Aufblühen und Verrotten, Schönheit und Grimasse, Bewunderung und Ekel".[39] Ihr Wirklichkeitsbegriff orientiert sich am Werden und Vergehen der Natur als objektivem Faktum und an den Erfahrungen des Krieges beziehungsweise der Nachkriegszeit als geschichtlichem Hintergrund.

Abstraktion als Befreiung vom sozialistischen Realismus

Die Fortsetzung avantgardistischer Kunst bemaß sich im ehemaligen Ostblock an ihrer Distanz zum Realismus, der als Synonym für Propagandakunst jegliche innovative Dimension eingebüßt hatte. Doch selbst nach der „harten Diktatur" waren radikale Positionen der Abstraktion, die auch im Zusammenhang eines erweiterten Bild- und Malereibegriffes von Interesse sind, bis in die späten 1970er-Jahre weitgehend verpönt. Die Diskreditierung der jungen zeitgenössischen Abstraktion durch die staatliche Kulturpolitik erfolgte unter anderem dadurch, dass man die klassische Abstraktion und den Konstruktivismus der Moderne als gesellschaftspolitisch linke und engagierte Kunst gegen die vorgeblich bloß formale, inhaltsleere und nihilistische Haltung der jungen Künstler ausspielte. Eine andere Form der Neutralisierung abstrakter Kunst bestand in ihrer Abmilderung zur angewandten Abstraktion in Form mehr oder weniger dekorativen Fassadenschmucks.[40] Zu dieser ablehnenden und neutralisierenden Haltung gegenüber der zeitgenössischen Abstraktion trug wesentlich die Niederschlagung des Prager Frühlings 1968 bei, in deren Folge mit der Abschaffung der Wirtschaftsreformen und der Rückkehr zu zentralistisch-repressiven Strukturen in der Administration auch eine Beschränkung kultureller und künstlerischer Freiheit spürbar wurde. Davon waren insbesondere die Tschechoslowakei und Ungarn betroffen, während beispielsweise in Polen die Tradition der Abstraktion sichtbar blieb. Dort bildete das Muzeum Sztuki in Lodz, das die geometrische Abstraktion als historisches und gegenwärtiges Phänomen in seiner Sammlungs- und Ausstellungspolitik hochhielt, ein Zentrum des intellektuellen Austausches.

definition. However, Schultze's aim was not to depart from the concept of the picture by incorporating real-life objects in the manner of nouveau réalisme and pop art; rather, he wanted to achieve a continuation of painting by different means. He did not "paint with objects, but made his painting, rooted as it was in the autonomous expressiveness of the paint, palpably real without forfeiting any part of its aesthetic possibilities."[36] The objectification of the picture was obviously connected with the reification of the paint—with the idea that "the paint ought to be pigment, stretched across the form and inextricably linked to it, just as we see everywhere in the visible world [...]."[37] Here the paint is not only a tool for illustration, but represents "an object in the shape of an organic flow process that solidifies in the moment of the picture's creation [...]."[38] The *Migofs*, polychrome, solidified hybrids of picture and space, embody the "simultaneity of growth and decline, blossoming and decay, beauty and grimace, admiration and revulsion."[39] Their concept of reality is based upon the waxing and waning of nature as an objective fact and the historical experiences of the war and postwar years.

Abstraction as Liberation from Socialist Realism

The yardstick of continuing avant-garde art in the former Soviet Bloc countries was its distance from realism, which had become a synonym for propaganda art and had thus forfeited any kind of innovative dimension. But even after hardline, Stalinist cultural policy had come to an end, radical forms of abstraction, which are of interest in connection with an extended definition of painting and the picture, were largely frowned upon until the late 1970s. One of the ways in which state policies on art discredited the young movement of contemporary abstraction was by playing off classical abstraction and the constructivism of the modern age as socio-politically leftwing and committed art, on the one hand, against the allegedly purely formal, meaningless, nihilist attitude of the young abstract artists, on the other. Another way in which abstract art was neutralized was by water-

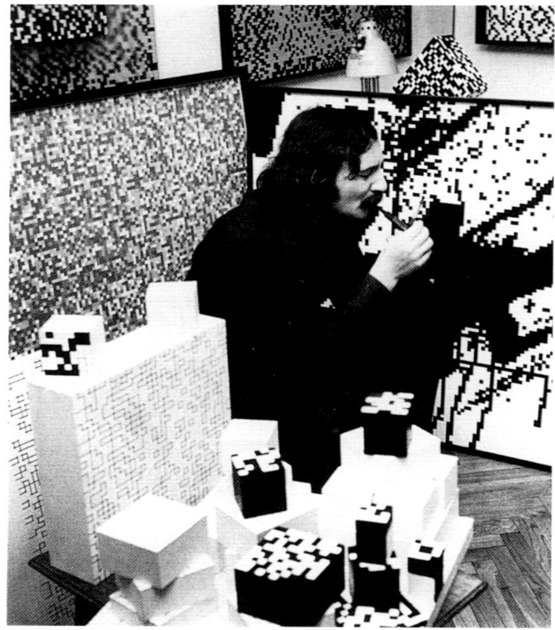

Ryszard Winiarski im Atelier / in the studio, 1969

Zbigniew Gostomski
Environment, 1968
Installationsansicht / Installation view at Foksal Gallery
Courtesy of the artist and the Foksal Gallery, Warsaw

ing it down by using it in an applied fashion to adorn façades, indeed with varying success in terms of its decorative effect.[40] This deprecatory and neutralizing attitude to contemporary abstraction was significantly reinforced by the suppression of the Prague Spring in 1968, in the aftermath of which the reversal of economic reform and the return to centralized, repressive administrative structures went hand in hand with increased constraints on cultural and artistic freedom. Czechoslovakia and Hungary were particularly affected, while Poland, for example, was one of the countries in which the abstract tradition remained visible. The Muzeum Sztuki in Lodz in Poland, which supported geometric abstraction as a historical and contemporary phenomenon in its acquisition and exhibition policies, became a center of intellectual exchange.

When this museum was founded in 1931, Henryk Stażewski was one of its driving forces together with Michel Seuphor and the members of the a.r. group (real avant-garde—revolutionary artists). As a member of international artists' groups such as cercle et carrée and abstraction—création and as a friend of Piet Mondrian and Jean Arp, Stażewski became a crucial link between Poland's avant-garde and the international art scene even before World War Two. As an interior designer and stage designer, he incorporated considerations of space and motion, as crucial elements, into his own artworks from the very beginning. When the liberalization of the post-

Als dieses Museum 1931 gegründet wurde, war Henryk Stażewski neben Michel Seuphor und den Mitgliedern der Gruppe „a.r." („wirkliche Avantgarde – revolutionäre Künstler") die treibende Kraft. Als Mitglied internationaler Künstlergruppen wie „Cercle et Carré" und „Abstraction-Création" sowie durch seine Freundschaft mit Piet Mondrian und Jean Arp fungierte Stażewski schon vor dem Zweiten Weltkrieg als zentrales internationales Bindeglied für die polnische Avantgarde. Als Innenarchitekt und Bühnenbildner war für ihn der Umgang mit Raum und Bewegung von Beginn an auch wesentlich in seinem bildnerischen Schaffen. Als er im Zuge der Lockerungen in der poststalinistischen Ära Ende der 1950er-Jahre seine Arbeit an der geometrischen Abstraktion wieder aufnahm, erweiterte er seine Bilder zu Reliefs mit dynamisch schwingenden Formen. Serielle Strukturen und industrielle Materialien verweisen zudem auf einen bild- und malereierweiternden Werkbegriff, der sich auch in seinen monochromen Kompositionen Ende der 1960er-Jahre zeigte. Diese Arbeiten thematisieren zudem rezeptionsästhetische Fragestellungen, da ihre Erscheinung vom Lichteinfall und vom Betrachterstandpunkt abhängt. Das *Relief* (1965) (Abb. S. 252) in der Sammlung des MUMOK nimmt mit seiner dynamisch verräumlichten Oberfläche Auflösungen orthogonaler Bildstrukturen vorweg, wie sie später beispielsweise bei François Morellet auftauchen (Abb. S. 253).

Neben Stażewski haben in Polen unter anderen auch Zbigniew Gostomski und Richard Winiarski im Rahmen der geometrischen Abstraktion seit den

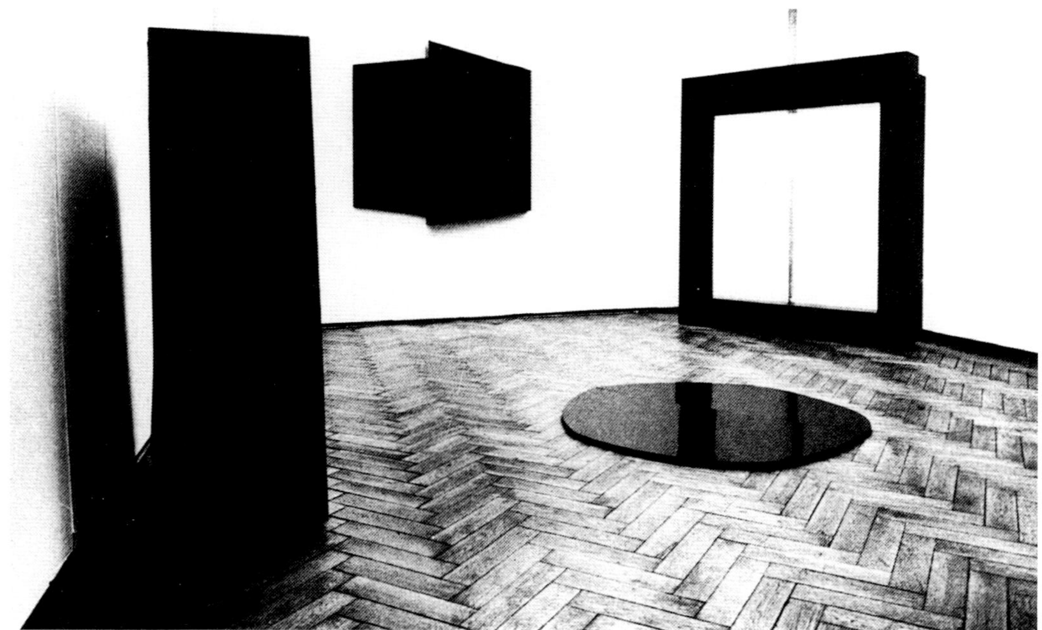

1960er-Jahren bilderweiternde und raumbezogene Arbeiten geschaffen. Winiarski hat dabei Prinzipien der Mathematik und Aleatorik als Spielsysteme eingesetzt, die zu raster- und schachbrettartigen Bildstrukturen führten. Chaos und Ordnung, Zufall und Logik, manuelle Malerei und technoide Erscheinung interferieren in seinen Arbeiten aus schwarzen und weißen Quadraten. Diese Bilder sind aber nicht nur in sich gerastert, sondern mitunter auch durchbrochen, weisen abgestufte Ränder auf oder bestehen aus getrennten Teilen. Das Spiel mit mathematisch berechneten Zufällen mündet also in Bildelemente, die ihrerseits wie Spielsteine korrespondieren und, falls sie von der Decke inmitten des Raums gehängt werden, auch skulpturale und installative Eigenschaften annehmen können. Kunst ist dabei für Winiarski ein System der „Unübersichtlichkeit", mit dessen Hilfe die Regeln der Mathematik und Kybernetik gebrochen und gleichsam von außen betrachtet werden können.[41]

In so genannten *optischen Objekten* und einem *Umgebungsbild* hat Gostomski in den 1960er-Jahren die geometrische Abstraktion auf Bildobjekte mit Raumbezug angewandt. Das *Umgebungsbild*, 1968 in der Warschauer Foksal-Galerie ausgeführt, verrät schon im Titel die raumaffine Auflösung des Bildes in mehrere mit dem Umraum verknüpfte Komponenten geometrischer und monochromer Art. Der Betrachter findet sich selbst in ein verräumlichtes Bilderszenario eingeschrieben, in dem das Wahrnehmen als raumzeitliches Erlebnis die Werkdeutung mitbestimmt. Der sich aufdrängende Vergleich mit

Stalinist era allowed him to return to geometric abstraction at the end of the 1950s, he expanded his pictures into reliefs with dynamically oscillating forms. Additionally, he incorporated serial structures and industrial materials, which indicate a definition of the artwork that expanded the concepts of painting and the picture. This is also illustrated by his monochrome compositions from the late 1960s. These works also deal with the aesthetics of reception, as their appearance depends on the angle of the light and the observer's viewpoint. With its dynamic three-dimensional surface, *Relief* (1965) (fig. p. 252), which is part of the MUMOK collection, anticipates the dissolution of orthogonal pictorial structures that was to appear later in the works of artists like Francois Morellet (fig. p. 253).

Zbigniew Gostomski and Richard Winiarski were among the other Polish artists, apart from Stażewski, who expanded the realm of the picture and took space into account in their works within the post-1960s geometric abstraction movement. Winiarski employed mathematical and aleatoric principles as gaming systems, which gave rise to grids and chessboard-like structures in his pictures. Chaos and order, chance and logic, manual painting and technoid appearance interfere with one another in the black and white squares that make up his works. But these pictures not only contain internal grids; they are also frequently punctuated, with graduated edges or with separate parts making up a whole. This game with mathematically calculated, chance elements results in picture elements that correspond to one another like gaming pieces and, in the case of works suspended from the ceiling, may also take on the properties of sculptures and installations. For Winiarski, art was a complex, confusing system that could help to break the rules of mathematics and cybernetics and allow them to be viewed from the outside. [41]

In the 1960s, Gostomski created *optical objects* and *Environment*, in which he applied the principles of geometric abstraction to spatially oriented picture objects. *Environment* (1968) was executed in Foksal Gallery in Warsaw. Its title reveals the spatial dissolution of the picture into several geometrical and monochrome components that are linked with the surrounding space. The observer finds him or herself included in a spatialized picture scenario in which perception, as a space-time experience, also determines the interpretation of the work. Although Gostomski's works bear an obvious relationship with minimal art, this is not the only American art movement to which obvious allusions can be found in his oeuvre. As an interdisciplinary artist who referenced both music and literature in the structure of his picture objects, he alluded, for example, to John Cage's "Lecture on Nothing" (1976) in his works. His picture objects and installations tested the boundaries of painting without explicitly invoking their programmatic dissolution. "My work also encompasses reflection about the putative end of painting, although I personally do not believe in such an end as long as we still have pigment."[42]

The works of Stażewski, Winiarski, and Gostomski exhibit the recognizable intention to realize developmental models in the "universe of abstract art" that will enable the synthesis of opposites and attempt to create organic relationships. According to Goshka Gawlik, these intentions are "generally the result of concern for the loss of coherence between mind and nature as a result of advancing processes of social abstraction."[43] Thus abstraction as a social phenomenon was met with an abstraction in art that extends into real space in order to metaphorically

der Minimal Art ist aber nicht der einzige evidente Bezug zur amerikanischen Kunst im Werk Gostomskis. Als interdisziplinär arbeitender Künstler, der sich zur Strukturierung seiner Bildobjekte auf musikalische und literarische Werke als Grundlagen bezog, hat er unter anderem auch John Cages „Lecture on Nothing" (1976) verarbeitet. Mit seinen Bildobjekten und -installationen ging er an die Grenzen der Malerei, ohne gleich deren programmatisches Ende zu beschwören: „Meine Arbeit umfasst auch die Reflexion über ein mutmaßliches Ende der Malerei, woran ich persönlich jedoch nicht glaube, solange es Pigment gibt."[42]

Die in den Arbeiten von Stażewski, Winiarski und Gostomski erkennbaren Absichten, im „Universum der abstrakten Kunst" Entwicklungsmodelle zu verwirklichen, die Synthesen des Gegensätzlichen ermöglichen und organische Zusammenhänge herzustellen versuchen, resultieren, so Goschka Gawlik, „zumeist aus der Sorge um den Verlust der Kohärenz von Geist und Natur aufgrund der voranschreitenden gesellschaftlichen Abstraktionsprozesse".[43] Gegen die Abstraktion als gesellschaftliches Phänomen wurde also eine Abstraktion der Kunst aufgeboten, die real in den Raum ausgreift, um ihn metaphorisch zurückzugewinnen. So betrachtet, verweisen die bewegt dynamischen Formen der Arbeiten dieser Künstler auf die Dynamik der Gesellschaft als Zusammenspiel vielteiliger, heterogener und in ständigem Wechsel begriffener Komponenten.

Konnte sich in Polen die Skulpturalisierung und Verräumlichung der Malerei auf eine Kontinuität der Abstraktion seit der Moderne berufen, so war in der Tschechoslowakei die Tradition surrealistisch-symbolistischer Ansätze so prägend, dass die Erweiterung narrativ-figurativer Malerei durch abstrakte Strukturen als „antiromantische Tendenz"[44] erschwert war. Bei Künstlern wie Karel Malich und Stanislav Kolíbal, die solche Stilbrüche und Gattungsüberschreitungen vollzogen, tauchen Werkentwürfe auf, die Prozessualität und Subjektivität in Form kosmisch-energetischer Kräfte (Malich) oder existenzieller Spannungen (Kolíbal) zu visualisieren versuchen, zugleich aber auch eine Objektivierung von Empfindsamkeit und Introspektion durch geometrisierende Abstraktionen vornehmen.

Malichs „hypersensitive Raum-, Energie- und Lichtwahrnehmung"[45] findet ihren Ausdruck in technisch exakt ausgeführten Reliefbildern, die monochrom lackiert sind und jegliche individuell subjektive Handschrift verweigern. Diese als *Korridore* (Abb. S. 245) betitelten Arbeiten verkörpern in ihren subtilen Übergängen, Wölbungen und Einkerbungen die Idee der Durchdringung von Materie und Raum, von Form und Energie. Auf ihnen soll das Licht in unterschiedlichen Schattierungen und Farbschwingungen als physikalisch-kosmische Energie sichtbar werden. Der Raum als „autonomes, immaterielles Feld von Licht- und Energiespuren"[46] findet also seine sinnfällig Übersetzung in malerei- und bilderweiternden Arbeiten, die in der Tradition des Konstruktivismus und Suprematismus stehen. In Malichs Darstellung energetischer Spannungen scheint Kasimir Malewitschs Vorstellung der Form und des Materials als eines energetischen Potenzials ebenso durch wie dessen elementaristische Auffassung vom ökonomischen Prinzip, dem alle Beziehungen im terrestrischen und kosmischen Bereich unterliegen.

Balance und prekäre Stabilität öffnen in Kolíbals Arbeiten ein Spannungsfeld, in dem auch auf das permanent gefährdete Gleichgewicht menschlicher Existenz verwiesen wird. Zur Thematisierung dieser Dialektik von Stabilität und Instabilität als Labilität wählte der Künstler in den 1960er-Jahren vorwiegend Gips, da dieser ein form- und veränderbares, zwischen unterschiedlichen materiellen Zuständen existierendes Material ist: „Ich habe Gips gern, weil er nichts ist. Er gibt uns keinen Gedanken ein, sondern gehorcht unseren Gedanken."[47] Zur Materialisierung von Gedanken und Zwischenzuständen, in denen Materielles und Geistiges zugleich repräsentiert sind, verwendete Kolíbal wie in *A Travers* (1974) (Abb. S. 250) auch Fäden in Zusammenhang mit aufgespannten Leinwänden. Er setzte die Fäden als materialisierte Linien ein und überführte damit Malerei in ein fragiles skulpturales Gewebe, das auf die Bedrohtheit des Menschen anspielt. „Auf einer Leinwand habe ich die Linie durch einen gespannten Faden ersetzt: Man kann ihn abreißen, er ist sehr gefährdet und trotzdem materieller als eine mit Bleistift gezogene Linie."[48] Diese subtile Expansion des

reconquer it. Viewed from this perspective, the dynamic forms in the works of these artists point to the dynamism of society as an interplay of manifold, heterogeneous, and constantly changing components.

While the expansion of painting in spatial and sculptural directions in Poland could draw on a continuous tradition of abstraction since classical modernism, Czechoslovakia had such a strong tradition of surrealist and symbolist approaches that the extension of narrative and figurative painting by abstract structures was impeded by being perceived as an "anti-romantic tendency."[44] Artists who undertook these changes of style and shifts in genre, among them Karel Malich and Stanislav Kolíbal, developed layouts that sought to visualize the processual and subjective nature of the work in the form of cosmic and energetic forces (Malich) or existential tension (Kolíbal) while simultaneously objectivizing sensitivity and introspection by means of geometric abstractions.

Malich's "hypersensitive perception of space, energy, and light"[45] is expressed in technically precise relief pictures, which are painted in monochrome and bear no trace of an individual, subjective artistic hallmark. These works, titled *Corridors* (fig. p. 245), display subtle transitions, curvatures, and indentations that embody the idea of the interpenetration of matter and space, form and energy. Their surfaces are intended to make light visible as a physical, cosmic energy in the form of varying shades and color waves. Space as an "autonomous, immaterial field of traces of light and energy"[46] is thus translated into the form of artworks that expand painting and the picture and that reflect the tradition of constructivism and suprematism. Malich's depiction of energetic tensions reflects both Kazimir Malevich's concept of form and material as energy potentials and his elementaristic idea of the economic principle to which all relationships in the terrestrial and cosmic spheres are subject.

In Kolíbal's works, balance and precarious stability delineate a charged environment that also encompasses references to the perpetually threatened equilibrium of human existence. To express this dialectic of stability and instability as lability, the artist worked primarily in plaster during the 1960s, since this material is malleable and mutable and fluctuates between different states of matter. In 1967 he praised the material's qualities: "I like plaster because it is nothing. It does not suggest ideas to us, but obeys our thoughts."[47] To materialize thoughts and interstitial states in which mind and matter are represented simultaneously, Kolíbal also used threads and stretched canvases, for example in *A Travers* (1974) (fig. p. 250). He used the threads as materialized lines, thus transferring painting into a fragile sculptural web that alludes to the threatened condition of humankind. "On one of the canvases I replaced the line with a stretched thread. You can break it, it is highly vulnerable, but it is still more material than a line drawn in pencil."[48] This subtle expansion of the picture hangs by the proverbial thread here—the thread of an abstraction of the anthropomorphic and existential against the background of a socio-politically repressive system.

These are only a few positions among many that arose in the countries of eastern Europe. Taken together with developments in the west, they confirm the virulence of expansive tendencies in painting and definitions of the picture around the year 1960 that transcended the barriers between political systems. Painting thus became a multi-layered, expansive concept long before the decline of the neue Wilde style of flat painting in the 1980s. Its expansive tendencies predate this period, and to this day they continue to form the basis for new and contemporary outlooks on painting beyond the confines of the picture.

Bildes hängt hier sprichwörtlich am Faden einer Abstraktion des Anthropomorphen und Existenziellen vor dem Hintergrund einer gesellschaftspolitisch repressiven Situation.

Damit sind nur einige Positionen aus dem osteuropäischen Bereich genannt, die – sieht man sie mit den Entwicklungen im Westen zusammen – eine in mehrfachem Sinn systemübergreifende Virulenz expansiver Malerei- und Bildbestimmungen um 1960 belegen. Von Malerei zu sprechen bedeutet also nicht erst ab den 1980er-Jahren – nach dem Ende der Konjunktur der neuen wilden Malerei als Flachware –, einen vielschichtigen Begriff bildüberschreitender Art im Mund zu führen. Diese Geschichte hat schon davor begonnen und bildet die Grundlage für neuere und gegenwärtige Positionen der Malerei jenseits des Bildes.

1   Clement Greenberg, „Die Krise des Staffeleibildes" (1948), in: ders., *Die Essenz der Moderne. Ausgewählte Essays und Kritiken*, Dresden 1997, S. 149–155, hier: S. 149 f.

2   Ebd., S. 151.

3   Clement Greenberg, „Louis und Noland" (1960), in: *Die Essenz der Moderne* (wie Anm. 1), S. 279–288, hier: S. 284.

4   Clement Greenberg, „Modernistische Malerei" (1960), in: *Die Essenz der Moderne* (wie Anm. 1), S. 265–278, hier: S. 276.

5   Greenberg, „Louis und Noland" (wie Anm. 3), S. 285 f.

6   Greenberg, „Modernistische Malerei" (wie Anm. 4), S. 274.

7   Donald Judd, zit. n.: Kat. *Don Judd*, Kunstverein Hannover, 1970, S. 40.

8   Ebd., S. 38.

9   Ebd., S. 40.

10 "[...] it occurred to me that the idea would work if the pieces were projected, and that the painting situation would be completely avoided if they projected more than they were wide, top to bottom." Donald Judd, zit. n.: „Don Judd: An Interview with John Coplans", in: Kat. *Don Judd*, Pasadena Art Museum, 1971, S. 19–44, hier: S. 25.

11 "My painting is based on the fact that only what can be seen there is there. It really is an object. [...] All I want anyone to get out of my paintings, and all I ever get out of them, is the fact that you can see the whole idea without any confusion... What you see is what you see." Frank Stella, zit. n.: „Questions to Stella and Judd. Interview by Bruce Glaser. Edited by Lucy R. Lippard", in: *Art News* (September 1966); wieder abgedruckt in: Gregory Battcock (Hg.), *Minimal Art. A Critical Anthology*, New York 1968, S. 148–164, hier: S. 158.

12 "The automated process has taken a variety of forms in various artists' works. Jasper Johns focused very clearly on two possible ways for painting. One was to identify a prior flat image of a target or flag with the total physical limit of the painting. [...] These, and Stella's subsequent notched striped paintings, present total systems, internally coherent. Both imply a set of necessary sequential steps which, when taken, complete the work. [...] At those points where automation is substituted for a previous, 'all made by hand' homologous set of steps, the artist has stepped aside for more of the world to enter into the art." Robert Morris, „Some Notes on the Phenomenology of Making: The Search for the Motivated", in: ders., *Continuous Project Altered Daily. The Writings of Robert Morris*, Cambridge/MA, London 1993, S. 71–93, hier: S. 87 u. S. 89.

13 Walter Kambartel, „Einführung", in: ders., *Robert Morris. Felt Piece*, Stuttgart 1971, S. 13.

14 Dan Flavin, „,... in Tageslicht oder kühlem Weiß.' Eine autobiographische Skizze", in: Gregor Stemmrich (Hg.), *Minimal Art. Eine kritische Retrospektive*, Basel 1995, S. 162–170, hier: S. 167.

15 Bettina Ruhrberg, „Arte Povera: zur Genese eines Begriffs und zur Rezeption einer ,Bewegung'", in: Ingvild Goetz, Christiane Meyer-Stoll (Hg.), *Arte Povera. Arbeiten und Dokumente aus der Sammlung Goetz 1958 bis heute*, Ditzingen-Heimerdingen 1997, S. 17–27, hier: S. 17.

16 Friedrich Kiesler, zit. n.: Dieter Bogner, *Friedrich Kiesler. Inside the Endless House*, Wien 1997, S. 16.

17 Ebd.

18 Ebd.

19 Peter Vetsch, „Der Kunstkritiker und ,seine' Künstler. Pierre Restany und der Nouveau Réalisme", in: Kat. *1960, les Nouveaux Réalistes*, MAM/Musée de la Ville de Paris; Kunsthalle Mannheim; Kunstmuseum Winterthur, 1986, S. 38–41, hier: S. 40.

20 „La prise en compte réaliste d'une situation nouvelle. Ein Interview mit Pierre Restany von Sylvain Lecombre", in: *1960, les Nouveaux Réalistes* (wie Anm. 19), S. 18–23, hier: S. 19.

21 Vetsch, „Der Kunstkritiker und ,seine' Künstler" (wie Anm. 19), S. 40.

22 „La prise en compte réaliste d'une situation nouvelle" (wie Anm. 20), S. 21.

23 Germano Celant, zit. n.: Carolyn Christov-Bakargiev, „Arte Povera oder der Raum der Elemente", in: Goetz, Meyer-Stoll (Hg.), *Arte Povera* (wie Anm. 15), S. 9–16, hier: S. 11.

24 „,Ich tue so, als würde ich Skulpturen machen' – Interview mit Pino Pascali und Carla Lonzi" (1967), in: Goetz, Meyer-Stoll (Hg.), *Arte Povera* (wie Anm. 15), S. 145–157, hier: S. 151.

25 Robert Watts, zit. n.: Kat. *Fluxus – Aspekte eines Phänomens*, Kunst- und Museumsverein Wuppertal, 1982, S. 9.

26 Henry Martin, „Fiat Flux", in: Kat. *Fluxers*, Museum für moderne Kunst Bozen, 1992, S. 11–23, hier: S. 17.

27 Wolf Vostell, zit. n.: Jürgen Schilling, *Aktionskunst. Identität von Kunst und Leben? Eine Dokumentation*, Luzern, Frankfurt/M. 1978, S. 127.

28 Vgl. ebd., S. 119.

29 Vgl. Hermann Nitsch, „Berührungen zwischen Fluxus, Wiener Aktionismus und O. M. Theater", in: Kat. *Fluxus Subjektiv*, Galerie Krinzinger, Wien, 1990, S. III/3–III/9, hier: S. III/4.

30 Ebd., S. III/5.

31 Ebd.

32 Otto Muehl, zit. n.: Schilling, *Aktionskunst* (wie Anm. 27), S. 157.

33 Ebd., S. 161.

34 Vgl. ebd., S. 162. Der Vergleich stammt von Peter Weibel.

35 Günter Brus, zit. n.: Peter Weibel, VALIE EXPORT (Hg.), *Wien. Bildkompendium Wiener Aktionismus und Film*, Frankfurt/M. 1970, S. 246.

36 Jörn Merkert, „Der innere Monolog als Faden im Labyrinth", in: Kat. *Bernard Schultze. Im Labyrinth*, Städtische Kunsthalle Düsseldorf u. a., 1980, S. 50.

37 Bernard Schultze, zit. n.: Wolfgang Rothe (Hg.), *Wegzeichen im Unbekannten. Neunzehn deutsche Maler zu Fragen der zeitgenössischen Kunst*, Heidelberg 1962, S. 38 f.

38 Eberhard Roters, zit. n.: Kat. *Die Welt der Migofs. Bernard Schultze*, Staatliche Kunsthalle Baden-Baden, 1974, S. 9, 42.

39 Lothar Romain, „Migofs und Migof-Labyrinthe", in: Lothar Romain, Rolf Wedewer, *Bernard Schultze*, München 1991, S. 42.

40 Vgl. Lóránd Hegyi, „Ostkunst – Staatskunst. Offizielle Kunst und der Status der abstrakten Kunst in den ehemaligen Ostblockländern", in: Kat. *Reduktivismus. Abstraktion in Polen, Tschechoslowakei, Ungarn 1950–1980*, Museum Moderner Kunst Stiftung Ludwig Wien, 20er Haus, 1992, S. 23–42, hier: S. 38.

41 Vgl. Goschka Gawlik, „Moderate Abstraktion", in: *Reduktivismus* (wie Anm. 40), S. 85–95, hier: S. 91.

42 Zbigniew Gostomski (1977), zit. n.: Jaromir Jedlinski, „Die einfachsten Formen in der Kunst", in: *Reduktivismus* (wie Anm. 40), S. 65–72, hier: S. 68.

43 Gawlik, „Moderate Abstraktion" (wie Anm. 41), S. 95.

44 Jiri Sevcik, „Reduktion als positives Prinzip in der ‚apokalyptischen Narrativität'", in: *Reduktivismus* (wie Anm. 40), S. 125–135, hier: S. 126.

45 Ebd., S. 132.

46 Ebd., S. 131.

47 Stanislav Kolíbal (1967), zit. n. ebd., S. 135.

48 „Interview Stanislav Kolíbal und Stella Rollig", in: *Reduktivismus* (wie Anm. 40), S. 150.

1   Clement Greenberg, "The Crisis of the Easel Picture" (1948), in: Greenberg, *The Collected Essays and Criticism*, Vol. 2: *Arrogant Purpose: 1945–1949*, (ed.) John O'Brian, Chicago, 1986, p. 221–225, here: p. 221.

2   Ibid., p. 222.

3   Clement Greenberg, "Louis und Noland" (1960) in: Greenberg,*The Collected Essays and Criticism* (see note 1), p. 94–100, here: p. 97.

4   Clement Greenberg, "Modernist Painting" (1960), in: Greenberg, ibid. (see note 1), p. 85–93, p. 92.

5   Clement Greenberg, "Louis und Noland", ibid. (see note 3), p. 98.

6   Clement Greenberg, "Modernist Painting", ibid. (see note 4), p. 91.

7   Donald Judd, "Specific Objects" in: *Theories and Documents of Contemporary Art: A Sourcebook of Artists' Writings*, (ed.) Kristine Stilles and Peter Selz, Berkeley, Los Angeles and London, 1996, p. 114–117, here: p. 116 ("Specific Objects" was originally published in: *Arts Yearbook*, vol. 8, 1965, p. 74–82).

8   Ibid., p. 115.

9   Ibid., p. 40.

10 "Don Judd: An interview with John Coplans", in. Cat: *Don Judd*, Pasadena Art Museum, 1971, p. 19–44, here: p. 25.

11 "Questions to Stella and Judd: Interview by Bruce Glaser. Edited by Lucy R. Lippard", in: *Art News* (September 1966); reprinted in: *Minimal Art. A Critical Anthology*, (ed.) Gregory Battcock, New York, 1968, p. 148–164, here: p. 158.

12 Robert Morris, "Some Notes on the Phenomenology of Making: The Search for the Motivated", in: Morris, *Continuous Project Altered Daily – The Writings of Robert Morris*, Cambridge/MA, London, 1993, p. 71–93, here: p. 87–89.

13 Walter Kambartel, "Introduction", in Kambartel, *Robert Morris – Felt Piece*, Stuttgart, 1971, p. 13.

14 Cited by Alex Potts, "Dan Flavin: '… in cool white' and 'infected with a blank magic'" in: *Dan Flavin: A New Light*, (ed.) Jeffrey Weis, Washington 2006, p. 1–25, here: p. 11–12. Dan Flavin, "'… in daylight or cool white': an autobiographical sketch" was originally published in *Artforum*, vol. 4, no. 4, December 1965, p. 21–24.

15 Bettina Ruhrberg, "Arte Povera: zur Genese eines Begriffs und zur Rezeption einer Bewegung", in: *Arte Povera: Arbeiten und Dokumente aus der Sammlung Goetz 1958 bis heute*, (eds.) Ingvild Goetz, Christiane Meyer-Stoll, Ditzingen-Heimerdingen, 1997, p. 17–27, here: p. 17.

16 Friedrich Kiesler, quoted by Dieter Bogner, *Friedrich Kiesler 1890–1965: Inside the Endless House*, Vienna, 1997, p. 16.

17 Ibid.

18 Ibid.

19 Peter Vetsch, "Der Kunstkritiker und 'seine' Künstler: Pierre Restany und der Nouveau Réalisme", in Cat: *1960: les Nouveaux Réalistes*, MAM/Musée de la Ville de Paris; Kunsthalle Mannheim; Kunstmuseum Winterthur, 1986, p. 38–41, here p. 40.

20 "La prise en compte réaliste d'une situation nouvelle: Ein Interview mit Pierre Restany von Sylvain Lecombre" (translated by Rolf Appel), in: *1960: les Nouveaux Réalistes* (see note 19), p. 18–23, here: p. 19.

21 Vetsch, "Der Kunstkritiker und 'seine' Künstler" (see note 19), p. 40.

22 "La prise en compte réaliste d'une situation nouvelle (see note 20), p. 21.

23 Germano Celant quoted by Carolyn Christov-Bakargiev, "Arte Povera oder der Raum der Elemente", in: *Arte Povera*, (eds.) Goetz, Meyer-Stoll (see note 15), p. 9–16, here: p. 11.

24 "'Ich tue so, als würde ich Skulpturen machen': Interview mit Pino Pascali and Carla Lonzi" (1967), in: *Arte Povera* (see note 23), p. 145–157, here: p. 151.

25 Robert Watts in: *Fluxus – Aspekte eines Phänomens*, Kunst- und Museumsverein Wuppertal, 1982, p. 9.

26 Henry Martin, "Fiat Flux", in: *Fluxers*, Museum für moderne Kunst Bozen, Bolzano, 1992, p. 11–23, here: p. 17

27 Wolf Vostell quoted by Jürgen Schilling, *Aktionskunst: Identität von Kunst und Leben? Eine Dokumentation*, Lucerne and Frankfurt, 1978, p. 127.

28 Cf. ibid., p 119.

29 Cf. Hermann Nitsch, "Berührungen zwischen Fluxus, Wiener Aktionismus und O.M. Theater", in: Cat. *Fluxus Subjektiv*, Galerie Krinzinger, Vienna, p. III/3–III/9, here: p. III/ 4.

30 Ibid., p. III/5.

31 Ibid.

32 Otto Muehl quoted in: Schilling, *Aktionskunst* (see note 27), p. 157

33 Ibid., p.161.

34 Cf. ibid., p. 162. The comparison was made by Peter Weibel.

35 Günter Brus quoted in: *Wien. Bildkompendium Wiener Aktionismus und Film,* (eds.) Peter Weibel, VALIE EXPORT, Frankfurt, 1970, p. 246.

36 Jörn Merkert, "Der innere Monolog als Faden im Labyrinth", in: Cat. *Bernard Schultze "Im Labyrinth"*, Städtische Kunsthalle Düsseldorf et al., 1980, p. 50.

37 Bernard Schultze quoted in: *Wegzeichen im Unbekannten: Neunzehn deutsche Maler zu Fragen der zeitgenössischen Kunst,* (ed.) Wolfgang Rothe, Heidelberg, 1962, p. 38f..

38 Eberhard Roters quoted in: Cat. *Die Welt der Migofs: Bernard Schultze*, Staatliche Kunsthalle Baden-Baden, 1974, p. 9, p. 42.

39 Lothar Romain, "Migofs und Migof-Labyrinthe", in: Lothar Romain, Rolf Wedewer, *Bernard Schultze*, Munich, 1991, p. 42.

40 Cf. Lóránd Hegyi, "Ostkunst – Staatskunst: Offizielle Kunst und der Status der abstrakten Kunst in den ehemaligen Ostblockländern", in: Cat. *Reduktivismus: Abstraktion in Polen, Tschechoslowakei, Ungarn 1950–1980*, Museum Moderner Kunst Foundation Ludwig Vienna, 20er Haus, 1992, p. 23–42, p. 38.

41 Goschka Gawlik, "Moderate Abstraktion", in: *Reduktivismus*, (see note 41), p. 85–95, p. 91.

42 Zbigniew Gostomski (1977), quoted in: Jaromir Jedlinski, "Die einfachsten Formen in der Kunst", in: *Reduktivismus*, (see note 40), p. 65–72, here: p. 68.

43 Gawlik, "Moderate Abstraktion", (see note 40), p. 95

44 Jiri Sevcik, "Reduktion als positives Prinzip in der 'apokalyptischen Narrativität'", in: *Reduktivismus*, (see note 40), p. 125–135, here: p. 126.

45 Ibid., p 132.

46 Ibid., p. 131.

47 Ibid., p. 135.

48 Stanislav Kolíbal (1967), in ibid., p. 150

Ines Gebetsroither

Das ist (k)eine Malerei. Beispiele zwischen Überschreitung und Wiederholung

This Is (Not) Painting. Examples at the Intersection between Transgression and Repetition

„[…] denn wie wäre es der Mühe wert, sich *des* Vergangenen zu erinnern, das nicht ein Gegenwärtiges werden kann.“
Søren Kierkegaard, *Furcht und Zittern*, 1843

"[. . .] for what is worthwhile in remembering the past that cannot become a present?"
Søren Kierkegaard, *Fear and Trembling*, 1843

Endspiele

„Tatsächliche Transgression ist unmöglich geworden, und gleichzeitig wächst das Verlangen nach ihr. Eifrig absorbiert die ‚Kultur der Faszination‘ spätestens seit den 1960er-Jahren alles, was auch nur ansatzweise transgressiv sein könnte. Kriminelle und politisch Radikale schreiben Bestseller. ‚Avantgarde‘-Künstler treten in Fernsehnachrichtensendungen auf, während der Moderator Transsexuelle interviewt.“[1] Diese Feststellung stammt vom New Yorker Neo-Geo-Künstler Peter Halley; er formulierte sie 1985 in seinem Essay „After Art".

Sowohl dem Prozess als auch der Expansion, also dem Fokussieren der Malerei auf ihre Entstehung und ihren infiniten Status sowie ihrer Ausdehnung ins Objekthafte, Räumliche, liegt, so scheint es mir, vor allem ein Versprechen zugrunde: jenes der Überschreitung der Grenzen zwischen Kunst und Leben. Die Transgression ist jene Verheißung, die der westlichen Kunst nach der Moderne eine Relevanz außerhalb ihrer selbst (zurück-)geben sollte. Die Kunst praktizierte sie auf unterschiedliche Weise – die Minimal Art etwa mit einem neuen Interesse am

Endgames

"As the reality of transgression becomes an impossibility, the demand for transgression increases. Since the '60s at least, the culture of fascination has been all too eager to absorb any remaining acts of transgression or near transgression that might be attempted. Criminals and radicals write bestsellers. 'Avant-garde' artists appear on the television news program *20/20*, while transsexuals are interviewed by the talk show host." These remarks were written by the neo-geo artist Peter Halley from New York and were first published in 1985 in an essay titled "After Art."[1]

Both process and expansion—in other words, both the focus of a painting on its creation and infinite status and its expansion into the realm of objects and space—appear to me to be based primarily on one promise, namely that of surmounting the borders between art and life. Transgression is that promise by which it was hoped that postwar western art would acquire or regain relevance outside its own borders. Transgression was practiced in art in a variety of ways. Minimal art, for example, developed a new interest in the body, time, and perception as well as in the production process and the questioning of categories such as painting and sculpture. Process art, concept art, happenings and performances, site-specific art, and institutional criticism took up this interest. All these movements arose in an artistic environment that was characterized by belief in the possibility and necessity of transgressing "toward the world" and thereby being able to change the world. "What art holds in its hands today is mutable stuff," wrote Robert Morris.[2] The limits of art—which had previously been defended ardently by art critics like Clement Greenberg—had become permeable.

This was followed by disillusionment in the mid-1980s. Taking pop art, for example, as their point of departure for analyzing the disappearance of the real, theorists like Jean Baudrillard and Fredric Jameson began to find an echo in the art world itself. Jameson held that, in the case of Warhol's works, the issue was no longer one of content, but of a "fundamental transformation both in the specific world of the objects, which has become a series of texts or simulacra, and in the placement and the uniqueness of the subject." He added that the disavowal of affect led in Warhol's *Diamond Dust Shoes* to a kind of "return of what was repressed, an oddly compensatory, decorative cheerfulness."[3] Baudrillard, whose theories were to play a very influential role in the neo-geo movement, held that the principle of reality had been totally displaced by the principle of simulation. In his view, art had lost its peculiar claim on the principle of aesthetics, which could now be found everywhere at every level of (predominantly capitalist) society.[4]

To return to the passage by Peter Halley that I quoted at the outset, transgression now seems impossible in the sense that reality itself has become artificial and has been turned into an aesthetic principle. According to Baudrillard, art and industry can exchange their symbols as they see fit. But what does this caesura, this endgame, this break with reality, mean for the art of painting?

Körper, an der Zeitlichkeit und der Wahrnehmung oder am Produktionsprozess sowie mit der Infragestellung von Kategorien wie Malerei und Skulptur; Prozesskunst, Konzeptkunst, Happening und Performance, ortsspezifische Kunst, Institutionskritik bauten darauf auf. Alle diese Strömungen entstanden in einem künstlerischen Umfeld, das geprägt war von der Vorstellung einer möglichen und notwendigen Transgression „zur Welt" hin, die dadurch auch verändert werden könnte: „Was die Kunst jetzt in Händen hält, ist verwandelbarer Stoff", schrieb Robert Morris.[2] Die – von Kunstkritikern wie Clement Greenberg vordem noch vehement verteidigten – Grenzen der Kunst waren durchlässig geworden.

Mitte der 1980er-Jahre kam dann die Ernüchterung: Theoretiker wie Jean Baudrillard oder Fredric Jameson fanden, nicht zuletzt die Pop-Art als einen Ausgangspunkt ihrer Analysen über das Verschwinden des Realen nehmend, Widerhall auch in der Kunstwelt. Jameson konstatierte anhand von Arbeiten Warhols, dass es nicht mehr um Fragen des Inhalts gehe, sondern um eine „fundamentale Wandlung sowohl in der eigentlichen Welt der Objekte, die zu einer Serie von Texten oder Simulakren geworden ist, als auch in Bezug auf den Standort und die Eigenart des Subjekts"; in Warhols *Diamond Dust Shoes* gebe es als Folge einer Verleugnung des Affekts eine Art „Wiederkehr des Verdrängten, eine eigenartig kompensierende, dekorative Heiterkeit".[3] Baudrillard, der nolens volens zur theoretischen Leitfigur der Neo-Geo-Bewegung werden sollte, sah das Realitätsprinzip vom Prinzip der Simulation vollends überrollt. Die Kunst habe ihr Vorrecht auf das Prinzip der Ästhetik verloren, dieses finde sich nun überall, auf allen Ebenen der (vom Kapitalismus geprägten) Gesellschaft.[4]

Überschreitung, um auf das eingangs wiedergegebene Zitat Peter Halleys zurückzukommen, scheint nunmehr insofern unmöglich, als Realität selbst künstlich, zum ästhetischen Prinzip geworden ist. Kunst und Industrie, so Baudrillard, könnten ihre Zeichen beliebig austauschen. Doch was bedeuten diese Zäsur, dieses Endspiel, dieser Bruch mit dem Realen für die Malerei?

Peter Halley absorbiert die austauschbar gewordenen Zeichen in einem malerischen Werk, das selbst nur noch simulakralen Charakter besitzt (Abb. S. 268, 269). Seine schematischen Darstellungen von Schaltkreisen, Flussdiagrammen oder Gitterstäben nehmen formal den modernistischen „grid" (beziehungsweise die modernistische Formensprache) auf, unterlegen ihn aber mit Bedeutungen des (post-)industriellen, spätkapitalistischen Zeitalters. Doch eine potenzielle Kritik an diesem wird überstrahlt vom Glanz fluoreszierender Day-Glo-Farben – eine oxymoronische Rhetorik, die unentwegt zwischen kritischer Distanz und Affirmation flirrt und darüber hinaus die Malerei als künstlerische Kategorie ad absurdum führt. Die Malerei als Medium, jeglicher künstlerischen Notwendigkeit beraubt, ist per se austauschbar geworden oder, wie Hal Foster schreibt, „zum appropriierten Objekt, zum Readymade".[5] Und dennoch stellt sich die Frage, ob nicht gerade in diesem Punkt die Überschreitung zum Realen hin sogar in einer äußersten Konsequenz vollzogen wird; ob nicht das Liebäugeln beziehungsweise die Komplizenschaft mit den realen Bedingungen einer (kapitalistischen) Gesellschaft die eigentliche Grenzüberschreitung darstellt; Neo-Geo war – und das ist in diesem Kontext wohl nicht unerheblich – auf dem Kunstmarkt sehr erfolgreich. Transgression betrifft hier nicht mehr das Medium, sondern eine Haltung oder – besser – eine Art para-kritisches Sichverhalten gegenüber Bedingungen des Marktes, deren sich auch und gerade die Kunst nicht entziehen, ja, die sie für sich nutzbar machen kann.

Erinnerungen an die Malerei

Unter dem Eindruck der New Yorker Neo-Geo-Bewegung begann der österreichische Künstler Gerwald Rockenschaub Anfang der 1980er-Jahre mit Malereien in Öl auf Leinwand oder Holz, die, jeweils auf wenige, meist ungebrochene Farben reduziert, piktogrammartige Formen aufweisen: etwa die schematische Darstellung eines sich lösenden Tropfens, eines zerfließenden Spiegeleis oder einfacher geometrischer Formen. In den Arbeiten auf Holz wird – ähnlich wie bei den *Shaped Canvases* von Frank Stella, Kenneth Noland oder auch Peter Lowe – das Trägermaterial zur bestimmenden Form. Aber anders als bei den genannten Künstlern wird

Peter Halley absorbs the now-interchangeable symbols into a kind of painting that itself has been reduced to a simulacrum (fig. p. 268, 269). His schematic representations of circuits, flow diagrams and lattices take up the formal language of the modernist "grid" (or modernist formal language in general), but infuse it with the meanings of the (post-) industrial, late capitalist age. Any potential criticism of this age, however, is drowned out by the radiance of fluorescent Day-Glo colors—an oxymoronic rhetoric that constantly flits back and forth between critical detachment and affirmation and makes nonsense of the genre of painting as an artistic category. The medium of painting, now stripped of any vestige of artistic necessity, has become interchangeable per se. In the words of Hal Foster, it has become "an appropriated object, a ready-made."[5] And yet the question remains whether this is not precisely the point where the transgression towards the real is accomplished with the greatest stringency; whether flirting or collaborating with the real conditions of (capitalist) society does not represent the true act of transgression. In this context, it is not insignificant that neo-geo was highly successful on the art market. Here, transgression applies less to the medium than to an attitude—or, more accurately, to a kind of para-critical behavior towards the conditions of the market which even art, and perhaps especially art, cannot escape, but can put to use for its own ends.

Reminiscences of Painting

Influenced by the neo-geo movement in New York, the Austrian artist Gerwald Rockenschaub began in the early 1980s to produce paintings in oil on canvas or wood that used a very restricted range of, usually unmixed, colors and depicted forms reminiscent of pictograms, such as schematic representations of a falling drop of water, an egg spreading out in the frying pan, or simple geometric shapes. In his works on wood, the painting support became the dominating shape, in a manner similar to the *shaped canvases* of Frank Stella, Kenneth Noland, and Peter Lowe.

Unlike these artists, however, Rockenschaub transferred this shape into the realm of representationalism by creating, for example, the form of a ladder, a window frame, or a drop. In contrast, the paint was used in such a manner that it only played a very reduced representational role, for example to fill out the form of lips in red or to paint a window frame brown. It is noteworthy that some of these works display "flowing" (albeit clearly outlined) shapes with a downward-streaming appearance, as though the finished work were alluding to liquid paint running down the vertically suspended canvas. One can almost see droplets forming, and the paint looks as though it has not yet had time to dry. Does this evoke the "memory" of a kind of painting that no longer seems to be possible in this form? A kind of painting that emphatically exposed its own materiality and the act of painting—or, to quote Leo Steinberg and his allusion to the abstract expressionist Morris Louis, "a kind of painting that submits to the same force of gravity to which our own natural existence is subject"?[6]

Gerwald Rockenschaub gave up painting in 1987, at the precise moment when the American art market bubble burst and there was a dramatic slump in art sales.[7] It was as if an economic phenomenon from beyond the realm of artistic activity proper had had an impact on decisions—not limited to pragmatic ones—immanent in the process of art production itself.[8] Rockenschaub turned to materials such as Plexiglas, acrylic lacquer, and color foils, continuing to use his previous, emblematic formal language in this new medium, as he still does today. In between, his painting reached a temporary endpoint, or even a zero point. In 1989 he began to produce colorless, transparent, or tinted Plexiglas panels. Mounted on the wall with metal screws (fig. p. 260, 261), these panels seemed to do away with the last traces of the painting process (brush strokes, pigments, etc.) along with the debates about categories that had accompanied the art of painting for so long, such as transparency vs. opacity, background vs. figure, "expression," and the act of painting. And yet their shape and vertical mount-

diese Form in die Gegenständlichkeit überführt, indem sie zum Beispiel eine Leiter, einen Fensterrahmen oder einen Tropfen bildet; der Farbauftrag hingegen besitzt nur einen reduzierten formgebenden beziehungsweise darstellerischen Charakter, wenn etwa die Form einer Lippe durchgängig rot bemalt ist oder die des Fensters braun. Auffällig ist, dass einige dieser Werke „fließende" (wenn auch fest umrissene) Formen aufweisen, ein Nach-unten-Rinnen darstellen, als würde auf noch flüssige Farbe angespielt, welche die vertikal hängende Leinwand hinabläuft: Da scheinen sich Tropfen gerade zu formieren und Farben wohl noch nicht trocken zu sein. Wird damit die „Erinnerung" an eine Malerei evoziert, die so nicht mehr möglich zu sein scheint? Eine Malerei nämlich, die ihre eigene Materialität und den zugrunde liegenden Malakt emphatisch offen legte, oder, wie es Leo Steinberg mit dem Verweis auf den abstrakten Expressionisten Morris Louis formulierte, „eine Malerei, die sich derselben Schwerkraft fügte, der auch unser natürliches Dasein unterworfen ist"?[6]

Gerwald Rockenschaub gab 1987 das Malen auf, just zu jenem Zeitpunkt, als nach einer überhitzten Atmosphäre am US-amerikanischen Kunstmarkt der große Börsencrash folgte, mit dem auch ein dramatischer Einbruch von Kunstverkäufen einherging[7] – als ob dieses „außerhalb" der künstlerischen Arbeit per se liegende Faktum Einfluss auf werkimmanente (und durchaus nicht nur pragmatische) Entscheidungen genommen hätte.[8] Rockenschaub wechselte zu Materialien wie Plexiglas, Kunstharzlack oder Farbfolien, welche die erwähnte emblematische Formensprache bis heute in einem anderen Medium weiterführen. Dazwischen liegt ein vorübergehender End- oder Nullpunkt: 1989 stellte er erstmals farblose, transparente beziehungsweise gefärbte Plexiglasscheiben aus, die mit Metallschrauben an der Wand befestigt wurden (Abb. S. 260, 261) – die letzten „malerischen" Spuren (wie Pinselstrich, Pigment et cetera) scheinen getilgt, ebenso wie die Diskussionen um Kategorien wie Transparenz/Opazität, Bildgrund/malerisches Motiv, „Ausdruck" oder Malakt, die die Malerei so lange begleitet haben. Dennoch bleibt eine Reminiszenz an das Gemälde: die vertikale Hängung eines Bildgevierts. Das absolute

Gerwald Rockenschaub
1983
Öl auf Leinwand / Oil on canvas
40 x 35 cm
© Archiv Gerwald Rockenschaub, Berlin

Gemälde, schrieb Arthur C. Danto, sei wohl „überhaupt kein Gemälde mehr, ebenso wie die höchste Schauspielkunst, wie sich Proust-Leser erinnern können, die Abwesenheit von Schauspielerei ist".[9] Tatsächlich liegt Rockenschaubs malerischer „Nullpunkt" weit entfernt von modernistischen Vorstellungen des Absoluten im Sinne eines „reinen Mediums"; sehr nahe aber an Kategorien, die jenseits der Frage nach dem Medium liegen, wie Effizienz oder Konsumierbarkeit.

Allegorien des Malens

Was in den Arbeiten Rockenschaubs getilgt ist, taucht bei anderen Künstlern umso vehementer und beharrlicher auf – wenn auch nicht ungebrochen –: der Pinselstrich. Als Ausdruck der Einzigartigkeit, Spontaneität, Originalität, des inneren Gefühls des Künstlers stand er nach dem Zweiten Weltkrieg symbolhaft für eine Art letztes Refugium von Freiheit und Individualität in einer industrialisierten Gesellschaft. Er repräsentierte wie auch Kleckse oder „drips" die Substanz der Farbe selbst, so wie die Leinwand ein Aktionsfeld darstellte – alles Zeichen für die „aktive Präsenz des Künstlers", wie Meyer Schapiro schrieb.[10] Eine erste Brechung mit diesem Bild vollzog 1965 Roy Lichtenstein, der in *Little Big Painting* (Abb. S. 167) den expressiven Pinselstrich ins Popformat übersetzte: Der „künstlerische Ausdruck" gerann so zum emblematischen Zeichen. Am „Pinselstrich" scheinen also gewisse Trans-

ing harks back to the painting. An absolute painting, in the opinion of Arthur C. Danto, would be "no longer a painting at all, just as the highest level of acting skill, as readers of Proust will recall, is the absence of acting."[9] In fact, Rockenschaub's "zero point" of painting is far removed from the modernist notions of the absolute as a "pure medium," but it does come very close to categories that do not deal with the issue of the medium, such as efficiency or consumability.

Allegories of Painting

While Rockenschaub expunged the brush stroke from his work, this manifested itself all the more vehemently and tenaciously in other artists' work, albeit not without exception. In postwar art, the brush stroke became a symbol for a kind of last refuge of freedom and individuality in an industrialized society, expressing the artist's uniqueness, spontaneity, originality, and inner feeling. Like splashes or drips, it represented the substance of the paint itself, just as the canvas represented a field of action—each was a sign, in Meyer Schapiro's words, of the "active presence of the artist."[10] Roy Lichtenstein, in 1965, was one of the first to break with this image when he transferred the expressive brush stroke into the pop art format in his *Little Big Painting* (fig. p. 167), causing "artistic expression" to coalesce into an emblematic sign. Thus it seems that certain translation processes were set in motion with respect to the brush stroke, which evidently not only points to the specific act of painting—it *is* painting.

In the works of the American artist David Reed, too, the brush stroke becomes a motif of sorts. In the 1970s, Reed began to draw a paintbrush across a surface of still-wet white paint in even, horizontal strokes. His *brushstroke paintings*, which display single or multiple rows of brush strokes, illustrate the production process as such: The canvas captures the underlying physical motion with all its concentration—and with all its irregularities. Thus Reed's paintings are not abstract in the strict sense. Rather, they illustrate the brush stroke just as Lichtenstein's paintings do. Unlike Lichtenstein's works, however, which imitate the completely different medium of screen printing and thus represent a clear line of demarcation between the actual brush stroke and the represented one, this ontological difference is blurred in the works of Reed. In his later paintings, such as *# 348* (1995/1996) (fig. p. 70), the painting process (the stroking of the brush across the canvas) is sometimes still identical with the subject of the painting. At other times, however, the brush stroke has become reduced to representation: It is represented, but it no longer constitutes a material reality. Thus Reed's works show how the brush stroke gradually changes from a quasi-automatic self-manifestation into a simulation, a formula full of pathos. The medium of painting turns into a revenant, as it were: It asserts its presence, and that presence simultaneously exposes it as a phantasm.

Bernard Frize's works also draw attention, albeit in a different way, to this sense of shifting between presence and absence, between self-affirmation and abnegation (fig. p. 35, 108). "The strokes you see hold the memory of the order and manner in which an exchange has taken place, just as the sticky trail of snails or the match struck against the box leave their traces. They represent nothing. They duplicate and materialise what time renders invisible in a space which is not its own," Frize wrote about his work.[11] In his paintings the brush strokes manifest themselves as traces on the picture ground in a manner akin to Reed's early

lationsprozesse in Gang gesetzt zu werden. Offenkundig verweist er nicht nur auf den jeweiligen Akt des Malens, er ist die Malerei.

Auch in den Arbeiten des amerikanischen Künstlers David Reed wird er zum „Motiv": In den 1970er-Jahren begann dieser, mit dem Pinsel in einer gleichmäßigen horizontalen Bewegung über eine noch nasse weiße Farbfläche zu streichen. In seinen *Brushstroke Paintings*, die eine oder mehrere Reihen von Pinselstrichen enthalten, ist der Herstellungsprozess dieser Malereien per se abgebildet, auf der Leinwand ist die zugrunde liegende körperliche Bewegung festgehalten, mit all ihrer Konzentration, aber auch allen Unregelmäßigkeiten. So sind Reeds Malereien im Grunde nicht abstrakt, vielmehr bilden sie wie Lichtensteins Malerei den Pinselstrich ab. Aber im Gegensatz zu dieser, die ein anderes Medium, den Siebdruck, imitiert und so eine klare Abgrenzung zwischen tatsächlichem und dargestelltem Pinselstrich markiert, ist bei Reed diese ontologische Differenz verwischt. In seinen späteren Arbeiten, etwa in *# 348* (1995/1996) (Abb. S. 70), fällt der malerische Prozess, der Malakt (das Streichen des Pinsels über die Leinwand), noch teils in eins mit dem Dargestellten – teils aber ist der Pinselstrich hier nur mehr Repräsentation: Er ist dargestellt, aber keine materielle Realität mehr. So kippt der Pinselstrich bei Reed langsam von einer quasiautomatisierten Selbstmanifestation über in eine Simulation, eine pathetische Floskel. Die Malerei gerät zur Wiedergängerin: Sie behauptet eine Präsenz, die sie im selben Augenblick als Trugbild entblößt.

Dieses „shifting" zwischen Anwesenheit und Abwesenheit, zwischen Selbstaffirmation und -negation bedienen, wenn auch auf andere Weise, die Arbeiten von Bernard Frize (Abb. S. 35, 108). „Die Spuren, die man betrachtet, halten die Ordnung und die Art, in der ein Austausch stattgefunden hat, im Bewusstsein, etwa so, wie der Schleim von Schnecken oder das am Stiefel angezündete Streichholz Spuren hinterlässt. Sie stellen nichts dar. In einem Raum, der ihnen nicht mehr gehört, vervielfältigen und materialisieren sie, was die Zeit unsichtbar macht", schrieb Frize zu seiner Malerei.[11] In seinen Arbeiten manifestiert sich der Pinselstrich –

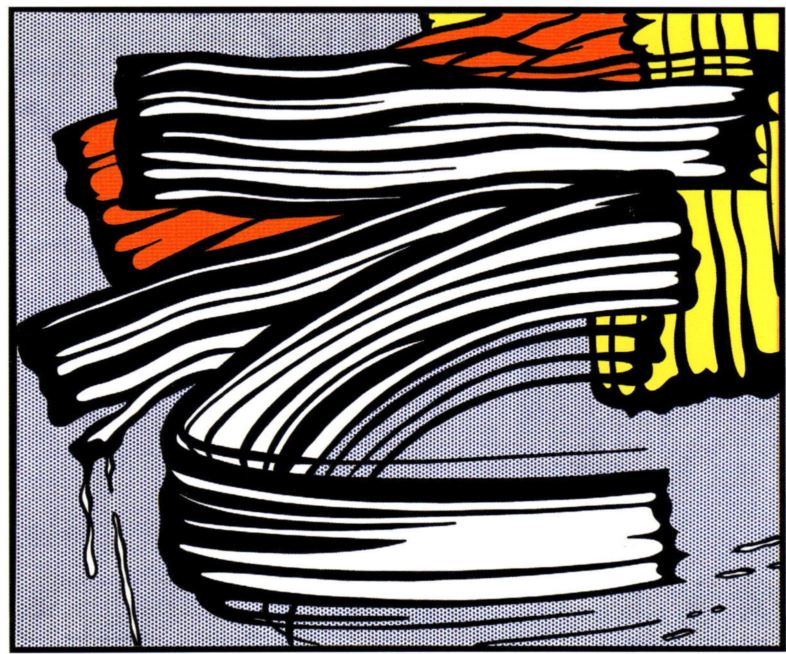

Roy Lichtenstein
Little Big Painting, 1965
Öl und Magna auf Leinwand
Oil and Magna on canvas
172,7 x 203,2 cm
© Estate of Roy Lichtenstein

ähnlich wie in den frühen Werken Reeds – als Spur auf dem Bildgrund. Frize überlässt dabei Originalität und Autonomie, die beiden modernistischen Imperative, dem Material, der Farbe: Er bewahre etwa 50 Glasbehälter mit Farben auf, und jede Farbe werde selbst ihre „Chance auf Originalität und Autonomie" ergreifen.[12]

Der Prozess des Malens, in einer Art Écriture automatique auf der Leinwand materialisiert, leugnet – und das unterscheidet die Arbeiten Frizes von jenen Reeds – die Präsenz eines malenden Subjekts. Der Betrachter wird im Unklaren darüber gelassen, wie die Spuren zustande gekommen sind – wie viele und wessen Hände etwa im Spiel waren (in den Malakt werden bei Frize zum Teil mehrere Personen mit einbezogen). Der Automatismus bietet also keinen direkten Draht zu einem individuellen Künstlersubjekt, er dient weder dem Hervorrufen noch der Tilgung eines – wie immer gearteten – Ausdrucks. Frizes Malereien evozieren vielmehr *Vorstellungen vom Malakt*; der Prozess ist das, was der Betrachter imaginiert. Die Malerei findet statt, aber in einem Raum, der ihr nicht mehr gehört, ermöglicht durch einen Künstler, der dem Prozess, dem Entstehen der Malerei, alle künstlerische Integrität überträgt. Der Künstler, schrieb Heidegger, bleibe „gegenüber dem Werk etwas Gleichgültiges, fast wie ein im Schaffen sich selbst vernichtender Durchgang für den Hervorgang des Werkes".[13]

Wir haben es hier mit Scharnieren zu tun, die die Malerei in einen unbestimmten Status zwischen

works. Frize cedes originality and autonomy— the two modernist imperatives—to the material, which in this case is the paint, saying that he keeps approximately fifty glass containers of paint and that each color seizes its own "opportunity for originality and autonomy."[12]

The difference between the works of Frize and Reed is that in Frize's case, the process of painting, materialized on the canvas in a process analogous to automatic writing, denies the presence of a protagonist who paints. The viewer remains uncertain of how the traces of painting came into being, of how many hands were involved and to whom the hands belonged—in some of Frize's works, several people participated in the painting process. Thus the automatism does not provide a direct line to an individual artist, nor does it serve to bring forth or to eliminate an expression of any kind. Rather, Frize's paintings evoke conceptions of the painting process. The process is that which is imagined by the observer. The act of painting takes place, but it takes place in a space that is no longer its own and is enabled by an artist who transfers all artistic integrity to the process, to the act of creating the painting. Heidegger wrote that the artist remained "inconsequential as compared with the work, almost like a passageway that destroys itself in the creative process for the work to emerge."[13]

We are dealing here with hinges that maneuver the medium of painting into an indeterminate status between presence and absence. The result is a state of infinitely prolonged teetering on the edge; any solution, any decision of whatever kind, is postponed and eternally arrested at the level of a promise. We are moving within a rhetorical space.

Another example can be found in works by Bertrand Lavier in which everyday objects are covered with a very thick layer of paint. In an act of extreme stringency, a wall clock, a piano, and a refrigerator are painted in the colors that each object has in real life: The clock is black, white, red, and transparent; the piano is black and white; the refrigerator is red (fig. p. 212). And so we are confronted with an Italian SMEG "frigo," as large as life and as red as the original—but the red we see is the paint applied by the artist. The materiality of the paint echoes the color of the original object. Is this a tautology? What happens here to the relationship between object and representation when the representation is literally overlaid onto the object? The object presents (or performs) itself like a ready-made, but it is also the medium, or vehicle, for a portrayal. The portrayal or representation, however, is here reduced to the materiality of the paint, to the brush stroke. Enmeshed in an indissoluble liaison, the medium of painting needs the real object both as a reference and as a painting support. The tautological moment—the semantic repetition—is confined here, in fact, to the paint itself. The object as such forms part of an irresolvable game of either-or between painting and reality. The fridge is real and/or painted. But this also means that the presence of both, the painted fridge and the real one, is indirect and refracted. The presence of both is sentimental—experiencing either presence is dependent on memory. It is no coincidence that Lavier once remarked in an interview about his work: "There is a kind of nostalgia for the present in them."[14]

Rediscovering Painting

How can we reconquer the lost realm of painting? Even more than the examples already mentioned, the works of Jessica Stockholder seem to require a distinction to be drawn between painting and the

Präsenz und Absenz manövrieren. Die Folge ist ein ins Unendliche ausgedehnter Zustand des Kippens; eine „Lösung", also eine wie immer geartete Entscheidung, ist aufgeschoben und befindet sich im anhaltenden Zustand der Versprechung. Wir bewegen uns in einem rhetorischen Raum.

Ein weiteres Beispiel sind Arbeiten Bertrand Laviers, in denen Alltagsobjekte pastos mit Farbe überzogen werden. In äußerster Konsequenz sind eine Wanduhr, ein Klavier oder ein Kühlschrank in den Farben bemalt, die ihnen jeweils ohnehin eigen sind: die Uhr schwarz, weiß, rot, transparent, das Klavier schwarz und weiß, der Kühlschrank rot (Abb. S. 212). So steht ein italienischer „frigo" der Marke SMEG in seiner vollen Größe da, knallrot wie das Original, aber eben mit roter Farbe bedeckt. Das Material Farbe wiederholt die Farbigkeit des ursprünglichen Objekts. Eine Tautologie? Was passiert hier mit dem Verhältnis zwischen Objekt und Darstellung, wenn die Darstellung das Objekt buchstäblich überlagert? Das Objekt präsentiert (oder performiert) sich selbst (wie ein Readymade), aber es ist auch Träger einer Darstellung. Doch die Darstellung, die Repräsentation, ist hier in Wirklichkeit auf die Materialität der Farbe, den Pinselstrich reduziert. Die Malerei braucht, in eine unlösbare Liaison verstrickt, das reale Objekt als Referenz und als Träger gleichermaßen. Das tautologische Moment, also die semantische Wiederholung, bezieht sich hier tatsächlich nur auf die Farbe; das Objekt selbst ist Teil eines nicht entscheidbaren Und-oder-Spiels zwischen Malerei und Realität. Der Kühlschrank ist real und/oder gemalt. Dies bedeutet allerdings auch, dass die Präsenz von beidem, von Gemaltem wie von Realem, mittelbar und gebrochen ist. Beider Präsenz ist eine sentimentale; sie zu erfahren setzt Erinnerung voraus. Nicht zufällig sagte Lavier einmal in einem Interview zu seinen Arbeiten: „Es gibt da eine Art Nostalgie für die Gegenwart."[14]

Malerei wieder finden

Wie den verlorenen Raum der Malerei zurückerobern? Mehr noch als bei den vorangegangenen Beispielen scheint es angesichts der Arbeiten Jessica Stockholders notwendig, zwischen der Malerei und dem Malerischen zu unterscheiden, zwischen dem buchstäblich Gemalten und Momenten, die der Malerei entlehnt, aber auch außerhalb des Mediums anzutreffen sind. Stockholders Arbeiten transferieren das, was man als das „Malerische" bezeichnen könnte, in das Medium Installation. In *Nit Picking Trumpets of Iced Blue Vagaries* (1997) (Abb. S. 216) bilden verschiedene dreidimensionale Elemente beziehungsweise Gegenstände ein komplexes Zusammenspiel von Farben, Formen und Relationen. Die Installation dominieren elf Seitenwände von Kühlkammern, die, auf langen Holzstäben befestigt, übereinander geschichtet liegen respektive gegen die Wand gelehnt sind. In verschiedenen Farben flächig, aber nicht vollständig bemalt, sind sie maßgebliche Bestandteile einer Komposition, die auf nichts Inhaltliches verweist, auch wenn sie reale Gebrauchsgegenstände integriert. Weitere Komponenten der Arbeit sind 34 Stapel von blauen Kunststoffeimern unterschiedlicher Höhe, die sich, in mehreren Reihen angeordnet, am Rand der Installation befinden, ein gemusterter Teppich, eine bemalte Fläche aus Karton, ein Teil einer Schaukel und anderes Material.

Stockholders Arbeit basiert auf einer Verschiebung, die zugleich materiell wie rhetorisch ist: Sie lässt buchstäblich Objekte antreten, die aufeinandertreffen und sich zueinander in Beziehung begeben, wie es Formen und Farben in der Malerei bildlich tun, etwa in der konstruktivistischen Malerei. Die Verschiebung besteht aber nicht allein in der Überführung einer zweidimensionalen Komposition in eine dreidimensionale, sondern ist eine Form von Übertragung, die Bestandteile der Malerei in einem anderen Medium erinnert und reaktiviert.[15] Dass Stockholder dabei das Medium Malerei verlässt, ist eine notwendige Voraussetzung für diese Reaktivierung. „Ich setze das Malerische einem Kontext der ständigen Bedrängnis aus", meinte Stockholder in einem Interview.[16]

Stockholders Installationen integrieren häufig Gegenstände, die im Haushalt oder in den Gemischtwarenabteilungen von Supermärkten zu finden sind, verschiedenfarbige Wollknäuel, Plastikkörbe, Haartrockner, Kunststofftischdecken, Stoffe, Kabel oder Spielzeuge, die, teilweise bemalt und sorgfältig in

painterly, between the literal, painted image and elements that are borrowed from the medium of painting, but that can also be found outside it. Stockholder's works transfer the element that one might describe as "painterly" into the medium of installation. In her *Nit Picking Trumpets of Iced Blue Vagaries* (1997) (fig. p. 216), various different three-dimensional elements or objects combine to form a complex interplay of colors, forms, and relationships. The installation is dominated by eleven side panels from cold storage rooms. Mounted on long wooden rods, these panels lie stacked on top of one another or propped up against the wall. Painted in part with large expanses of various colors, they represent significant portions of a composition that references no specific content despite integrating real-life objects. Other components of the installation include blue plastic buckets stacked in 34 piles of different heights that are arranged in several rows at the edge of the installation; an ornamental rug; a piece of painted cardboard; part of a swing; and other materials.

Stockholder's work is based on a shift that is simultaneously material and rhetorical. She brings objects into play that literally collide and enter into relationships with one another in the same way that shapes and colors do pictorially in constructivist painting, for example. But the shift consists not only of the transfer of a two-dimensional composition into the realm of three dimensions. Rather, it is a form of transference that recalls and reactivates components of the art of painting in a different medium.[15] The fact that Stockholder abandons the medium of painting in the process is a necessary prerequisite for this reactivation. "I place the pictorial in a context where it's always being poked at," Stockholder said in an interview.[16]

Stockholder's installations frequently include objects that can be found in the home or in the household department of the supermarket, such as balls of yarn in different colors, plastic baskets, hairdryers, plastic tablecloths, fabric, cables, and toys. Partly painted and carefully placed in a compositional context, these objects play a formal role within the installation that is similar to that of other items, such as painted walls and structural elements that do *not* belong to the world of consumer goods. Although it is tempting to describe these goods as ready-mades, it would not be entirely accurate to do so. A ready-made conveys the significance and the function of the real object even if the object is placed into a new context. In Stockholder's case, however, the objects lose this reference. Instead, they are transferred into a new formal system of reference; in a sense, they are drained of their former meaning. However, Stockholder's works do achieve a different act of transgression. Although the composition denies the referentialism of the object (just as the "transparency" of classical painting denied the materiality of paint and canvas), it does constitute a systemic whole that visualizes the world beyond, the world of reality. "There is an attempt to bring the city inside the gallery, not to erase fiction, but to inform and expand it," the artist said of her own work.[17] In Stockholder's works, expansion means evoking (everyday) reality with the methods of painting—but on a level *outside* this reality and outside of painting.

Perhaps this outside space is the only remaining place for a genre of painting that does not shut itself away from the present. In this context one should not forget the *Flache Arbeiten* (1996/1997) by the Swiss artist Adrian Schiess (fig. p. 266), in which the medium of painting is virtually placed at the mercy of its own materiality and non-fictionality. Panels spray-painted with automotive paint lie just above the level of the floor. Their monochrome, reflective surfaces mirror the surrounding space in a relationship of continual exchange while simultaneously "coloring" their surroundings. They no longer claim to generate a "painterly" space that exists beyond the realm of reality; rather, they are a fragment and a projection surface for a reality—of whatever kind—that draws no distinction between outside and inside or between now and then.

einen kompositorischen Zusammenhang gebracht, innerhalb der Arbeit eine ähnliche formale Rolle spielen wie auch andere Elemente, etwa bemalte Wände oder Konstruktionsteile, die ihren Ursprung *nicht* in der Warenwelt haben. Obwohl es nahe liegt, Erstere als Readymades zu bezeichnen, trifft dies nicht ganz die Sache. Ein Readymade führt die Bedeutung und Funktion des realen Objekts mit sich, auch wenn dieses in einen neuen Kontext gebracht ist. Bei Stockholder aber verlieren die Gegenstände diese Referenz, sie werden vielmehr in ein neues, formales Bezugssystem überführt, werden sozusagen entleert. Einen anderen Transgressionsakt vollziehen Stockholders Arbeiten dennoch: Die Komposition verleugnet zwar die Referenzialität des Gegenstands (sowie die „Transparenz" der klassischen Malerei die Materialität der Farbe beziehungsweise der Leinwand negierte), aber sie vergegenwärtigt als systemisches Ganzes die Welt außerhalb, die Realität. „Wenn ich versuche, die Stadt in die Galerie zu bringen, tue ich das nicht, um das Fiktionale zurückzudrängen, sondern um es zu beeinflussen und zu erweitern", wie die Künstlerin selbst sagt.[17] Expansion bedeutet in Stockholders Arbeiten, (Alltags-)Realität mit den Mitteln der Malerei aufzurufen – allerdings *außerhalb* dieser Realität und auch außerhalb der Malerei.

Vielleicht ist dieses Außerhalb nunmehr der einzig mögliche Ort für eine Malerei, die sich einer Gegenwart nicht versperrt, die ihre eigene Vergegenwärtigung zustande bringt. Erinnert sei hier auch an die *Flachen Arbeiten* (1996/1997) des Schweizer Künstlers Adrian Schiess (Abb. S. 266), welche die Malerei ihrer eigenen Dinglichkeit und Fiktionslosigkeit geradezu ausliefern: Mit Autolack farbig gespritzte Platten liegen knapp über dem Boden. Ihre monochromen, spiegelnden Oberflächen nehmen in einer permanenten Austauschbeziehung den sie umgebenden Raum auf, „färben" jedoch auch gleichzeitig die Umgebung. Sie geben nicht mehr vor, einen „malerischen" Raum zu erzeugen, der sich jenseits des Realen befände, sondern sie sind Bruchstück und Projektionsfläche einer – wie immer gearteten – Wirklichkeit, in der Außen und Innen, Jetzt und Früher ohnehin nicht unterschieden sind.

1   "As the reality of transgression becomes an impossibility, the demand for transgression increases. Since the '60s at least, the culture of fascination has been all too eager to absorb any remaining acts of transgression or near transgression that might be attempted. Criminals and radicals write bestsellers. 'Avant-garde' artists appear on the television news program *20/20*, while transsexuals are interviewed by the talk show host." Peter Halley, *Collected Essays 1981–1987*, Zürich, New York 1989, S. 114.

2   Robert Morris, „Anmerkungen über Skulptur IV: Jenseits der Objekte", in: Charles Harrison, Paul Wood (Hg.), *Kunsttheorie im 20. Jahrhundert. Band II: 1940–1991*, Ostfildern-Ruit 2003, S. 1.065.

3   Fredric Jameson, „Postmoderne: Zur Logik der Kultur im Spätkapitalismus", in: Andreas Huyssen, Klaus Scherpe (Hg.), *Postmoderne: Zeichen eines kulturellen Wandels*, Reinbek 1986, S. 45.

4   Vgl. Jean Baudrillard, „Towards the Vanishing Point of Art", in: ders., *The Conspiracy of Art*, Cambridge/MA 2005, S. 98–110. Auf Deutsch unter demselben Titel in: Florian Rötzer, Sara Rogenhofer (Hg.), *Kunst machen? Gespräche und Essays*, München 1990, S. 201–210.

5   Hal Foster, „The Art of Cynical Reason", in: ders., *The Return of the Real*, Cambridge/MA 1996, S. 99.

6   Leo Steinberg, *Other Criteria*, New York 1972, S. 84.

7   Vgl. Jörg Heiser, „Öffentlicher Dienst/Privatvergnügen", in: Kat. *Gerwald Rockenschaub: 1980–2004*, Museum Moderner Kunst Stiftung Ludwig Wien, 2004, S. 299.

8   Vgl. ebd., S. 299 f. Ab diesem Zeitpunkt begann Rockenschaub auch verstärkt in anderen Bereichen zu arbeiten, etwa in der Werbung, als Designer oder als DJ.

9   Arthur C. Danto, „Morris Louis", in: ders., *Reiz und Reflexion*, München 1994, S. 59.

10 Meyer Schapiro, „The Liberating Quality of Avant-Garde Art", zit. n.: Hal Foster u. a. (Hg.), *Art since 1900. Modernism Antimodernism Postmodernism*, London 2004, S. 351.

11 Bernard Frize, in: Kat. *Bernard Frize. Size Matters*, Musée d'art contemporain, Nîmes; Museum Moderner Kunst Stiftung Ludwig Wien u. a., 1999, S. 159.

12 Ebd., S. 135.

13 Martin Heidegger, *Der Ursprung des Kunstwerkes*, Stuttgart 2008, S. 35.

14 Bertrand Lavier im Interview mit Daniel Birnbaum, in: Kat. *Bertrand Lavier*, Musée d'art moderne de la Ville de Paris, 2002, S. 116.

15 In diesem Punkt besteht auch ein wesentlicher Unterschied etwa zu den Arbeiten eines Robert Rauschenberg oder Werken des Nouveau Réalisme.

16 "I place the pictorial in a context where it's always being poked at." Zit. n.: Barry Schwabsky, Lynne Tillman, Lynne Cooke, *Jessica Stockholder*, London 1995, S. 117.

17 Ebd., S. 76: "There is an attempt to bring the city inside the gallery, not to erase fiction, but to inform an expand it."

1   Peter Halley, *Collected Essays 1981–1987*, Zurich, New York, 1989, p. 114.

2   Robert Morris, "Notes on Sculpture 4: Beyond Objects," in: *Art in Theory: 1900–1990* (eds.) Charles Harrison and Paul Wood, Malden, MA, 1999, p. 872.

3   Fredric Jameson, *Postmodernism, or, the Cultural Logic of Late Modernism*, Durham NC., 1991, p. 10.

4   Cf. Jean Baudrillard, "Towards the Vanishing Point of Art," in: Ibid., *The Conspiracy of Art*, Cambridge, MA, 2005, p. 98–110.

5   Hal Foster, "The Art of Cynical Reason," in: Ibid., *The Return of the Real*, Cambridge, MA, 1996, p. 99.

6   Leo Steinberg, *Other Criteria*, New York, 1972, p. 84.

7   Cf. Jörg Heiser, "Öffentlicher Dienst/Privatvergnügen," in: Cat. *Gerwald Rockenschaub: 1980–2004*, Museum Moderner Kunst Stiftung Ludwig Wien, 2004, p. 299.

8   Cf. ibid., p. 299f. From this point onwards, Rockenschaub also began to step up his involvement in other fields too, such as advertising, design, and disc jockey work.

9   Arthur C. Danto, "Morris Louis," in: Danto, *Encounters and Reflections: Art in the Historical Present*, Berkeley and Los Angeles, 1997, p. 48.

10 Meyer Schapiro, "The Liberating Quality of Avant-Garde Art," quoted in: Hal Foster et al. (eds.), *Art since 1900. Modernism Antimodernism Postmodernism*, London, 2004, p. 351.

11 Bernard Frize, in: Cat. *Bernard Frize. Size Matters*, Musée d'art contemporain, Nîmes; Museum Moderner Kunst Stiftung Ludwig Wien et al., 1999, p. 159.

12 Ibid., p. 135.

13 Martin Heidegger, "The Origin of the Work of Art" in: Heidegger, *Poetry, Language and Thought*, trans. Albert Hofstadter, New York, 1971, p. 40.

14 Bertrand Lavier in an interview with Daniel Birnbaum, in: Cat. *Bertrand Lavier*, Musée d'art moderne de la Ville de Paris, 2002, p. 116.

15 On this point, Stockholder's works also differ significantly from those of artists like Robert Rauschenberg and the works of nouveau réalisme.

16 Quoted in: Barry Schwabsky, Lynne Tillman, Lynne Cooke, *Jessica Stockholder*, London, 1995, p. 117.

17 Ibid., p. 76.

Bildentgrenzung und Realitätsbezüge

Transgressing the Boundaries of the Picture
and References to Reality

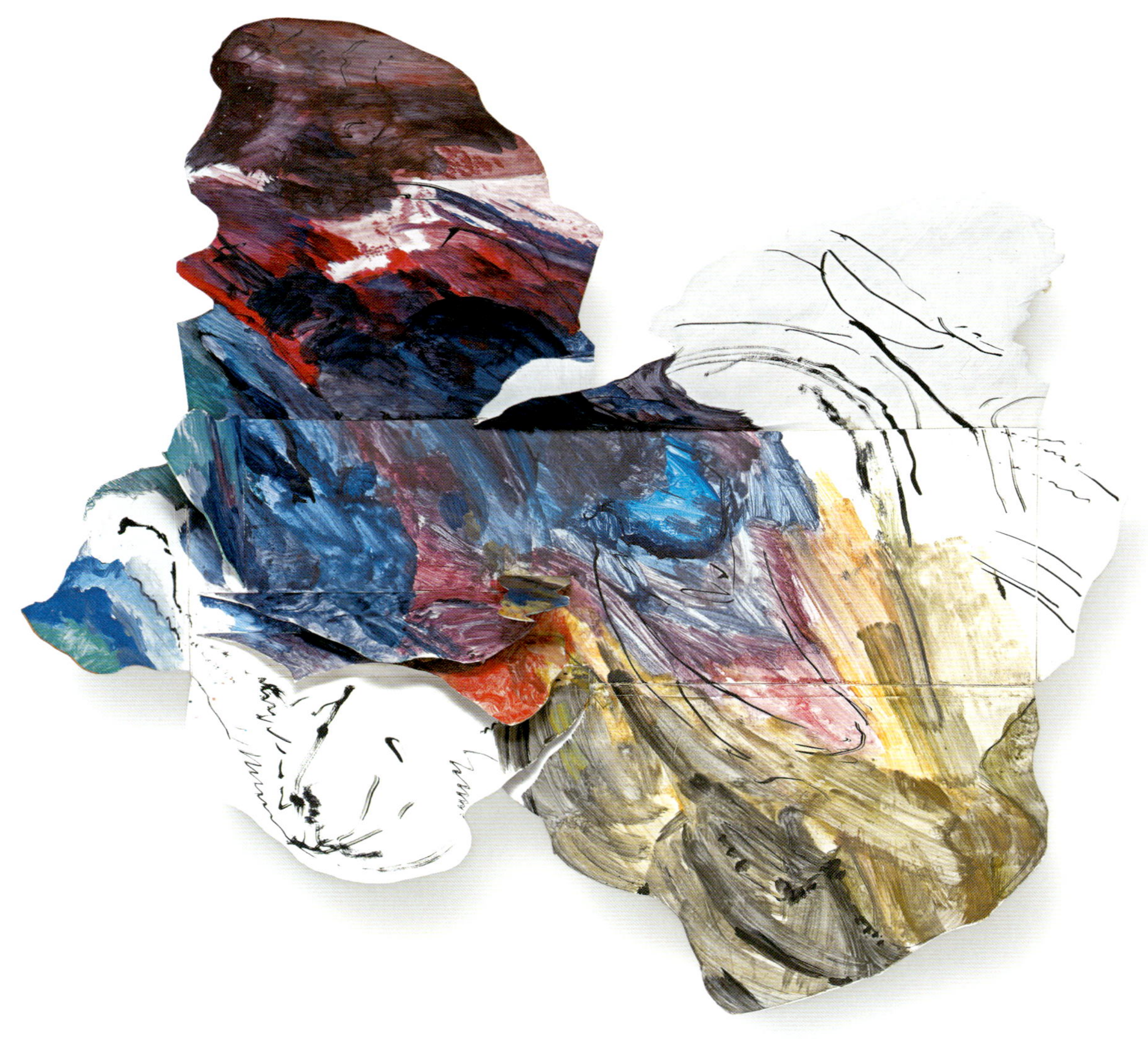

Max Weiler
Flügelbild: Große Blume (Polyptych: Large Flower), 1968
Eitempera auf Spanplatte und Karton / Egg tempera on chipboard and cardboard
Grundfläche / Area / 50 x 150 cm, mit geöffneten Flügeln / with opened panels: 210 x 176 cm
Leihgabe der Artothek des Bundes / On loan from the Artothek des Bundes, seit / since 1970

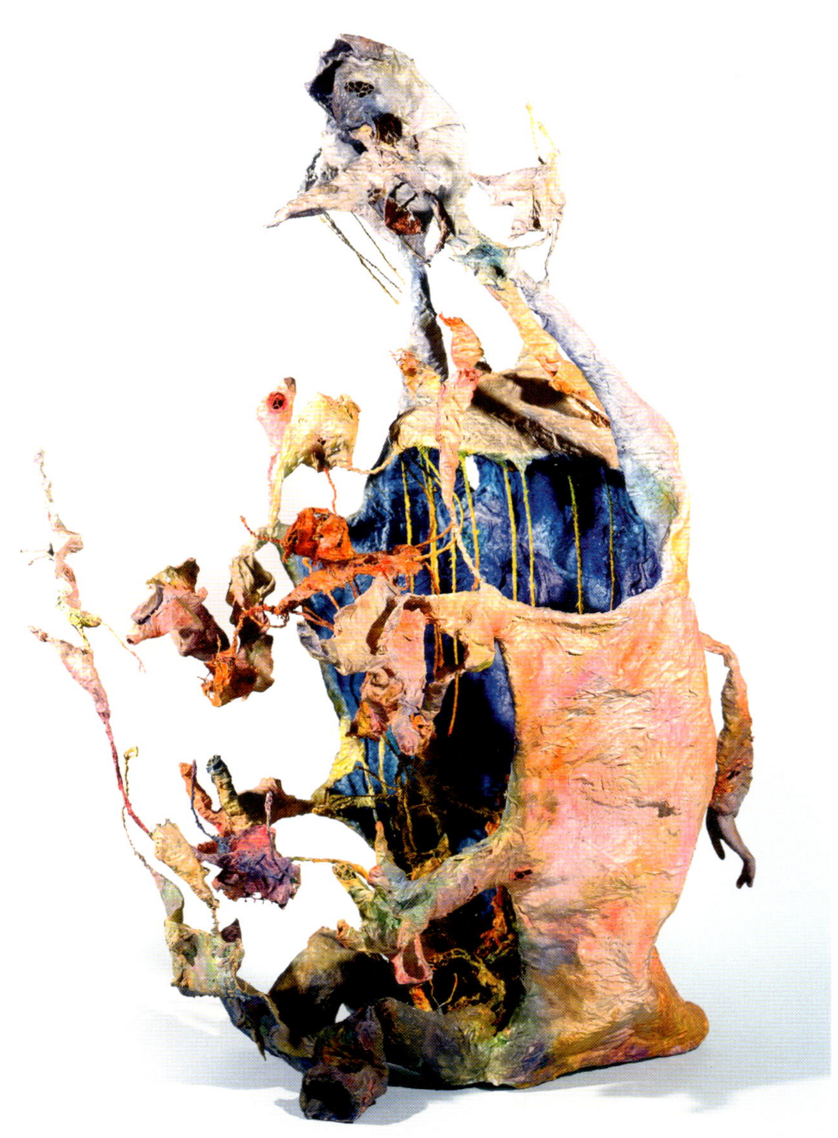

Bernhard Schultze
Migof-Mantel-Stilleben, 1964–1971
Öl auf Draht, Eisen, Holz, Kunststoff, Hand einer Schaufensterpuppe und diverse Materialien
Oil on wire, iron, plastic, hand of a shop window mannequin and various materials
180 x 140 x 120 cm
Ehemals Sammlung Hahn / Former Hahn Collection, Köln / Cologne
Erworben / Acquired in 1978

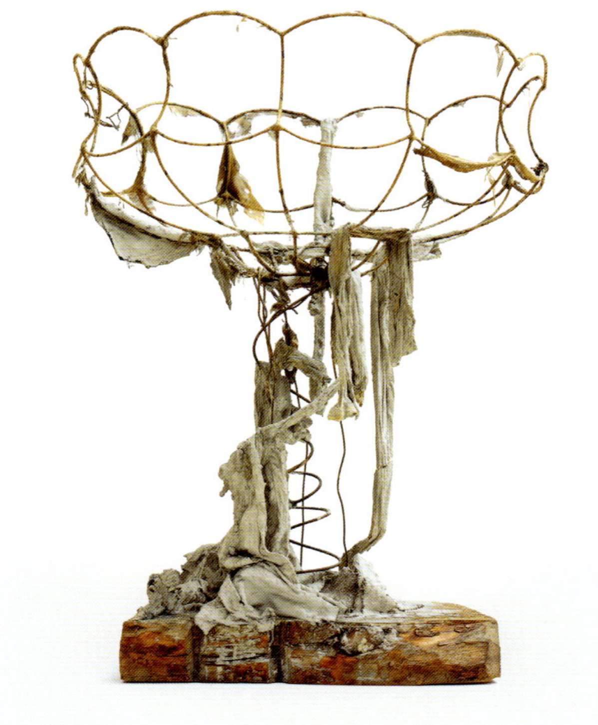

Oswald Oberhuber
Ende (End), 1951
Holz, Draht, Stoff, Gips / Wood, wire, fabric, plaster
Ø 60 cm, 90 cm
Erworben / Acquired in 1968

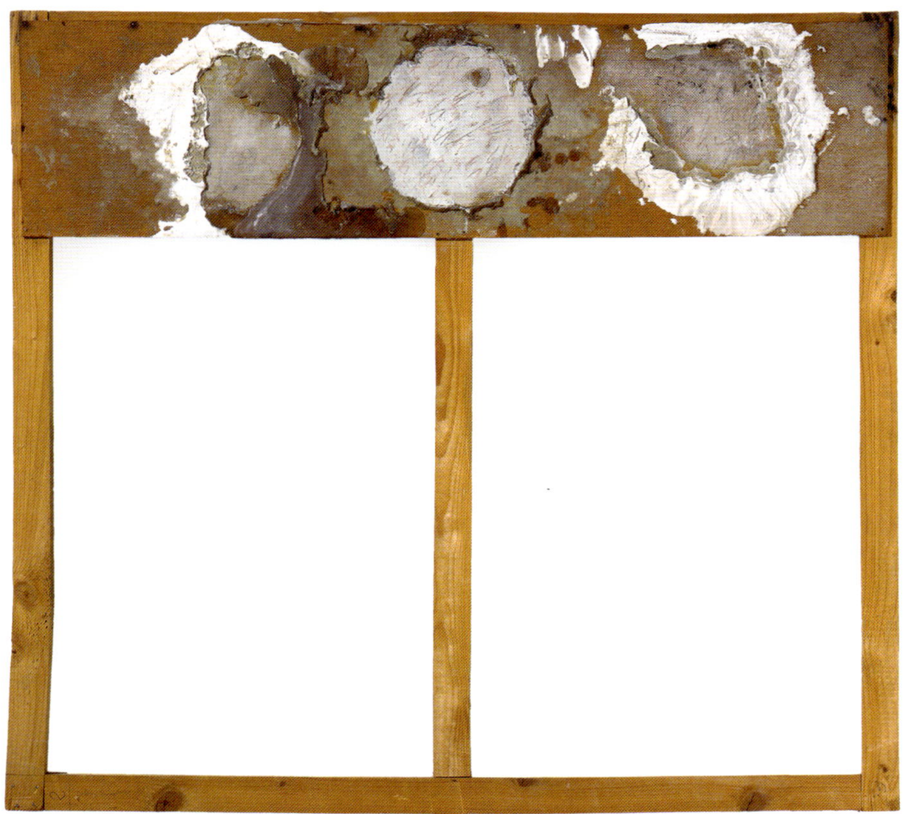

Oswald Oberhuber
Rahmenbild (Frame Picture), 1953
Gips, Ton und Wachs auf Hartfaserplatte auf Holz
Plaster, clay and wax on high-density fiberboard on wood
93 x 100 x 2,5 cm
Erworben / Acquired in 1978

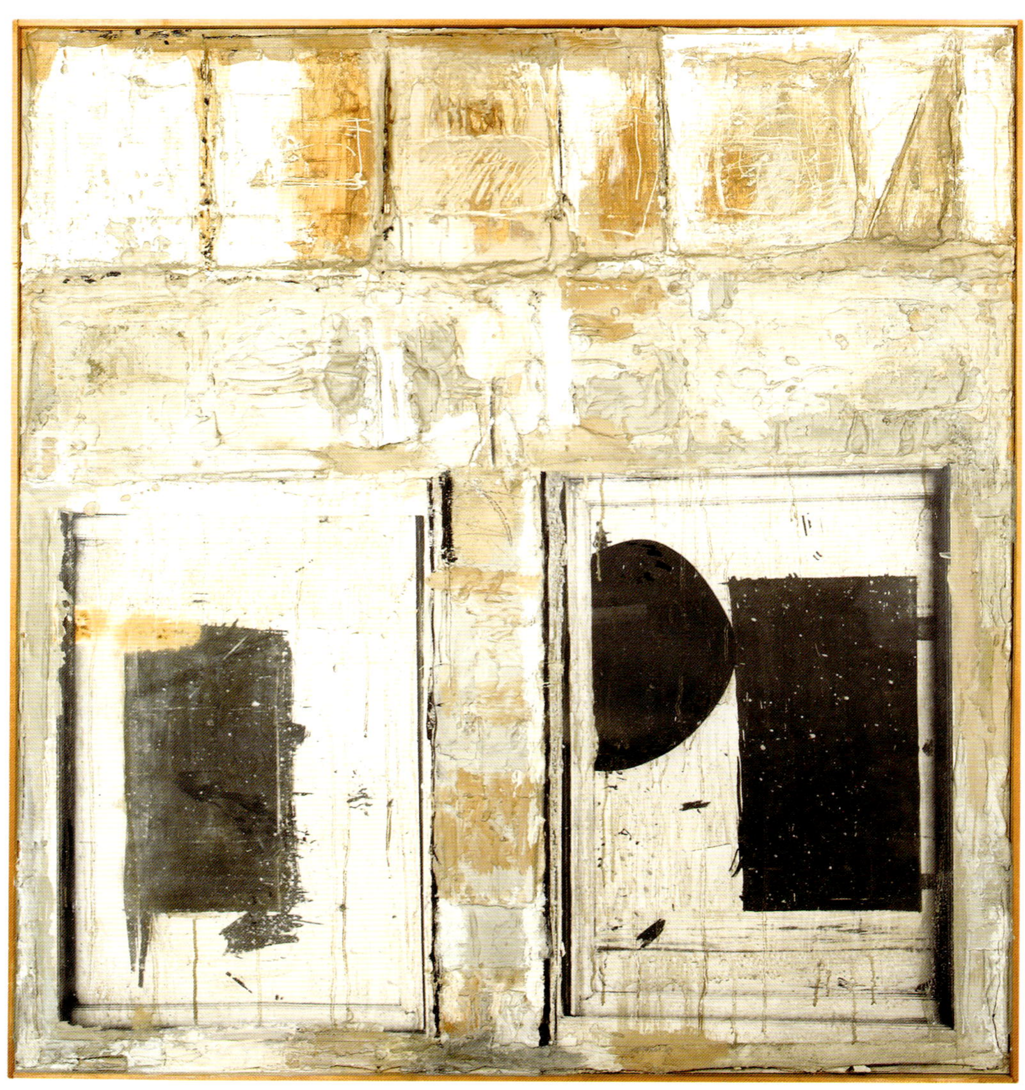

Adolf Frohner
Wandbild Arena (Wall Painting Arena), 1965
Fotografie, Zement und PVC auf Leinwand / Photography, cement and PVC on canvas
152,8 x 140,5 x 4,5 cm
Leihgabe der Artothek des Bundes / On loan from the Artothek des Bundes, seit / since 1967

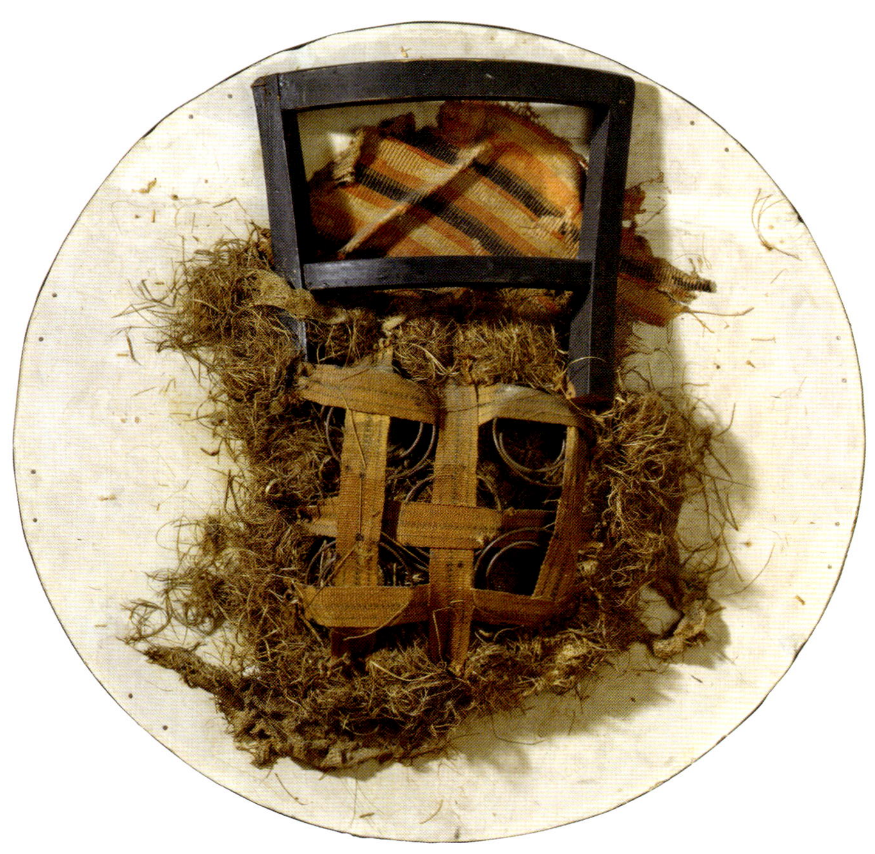

Adolf Frohner
Schwarzer Sessel (Black Armchair), 1962
Draht, Holz, Jute und Seegras auf Holz auf Leinen
Wire, wood, jute and seagrass on wood on linen
Ø 94 cm, 17,5 cm
Leihgabe der Österreichischen Ludwig-Stiftung
On loan from the Austrian Ludwig Foundation, seit / since 1981

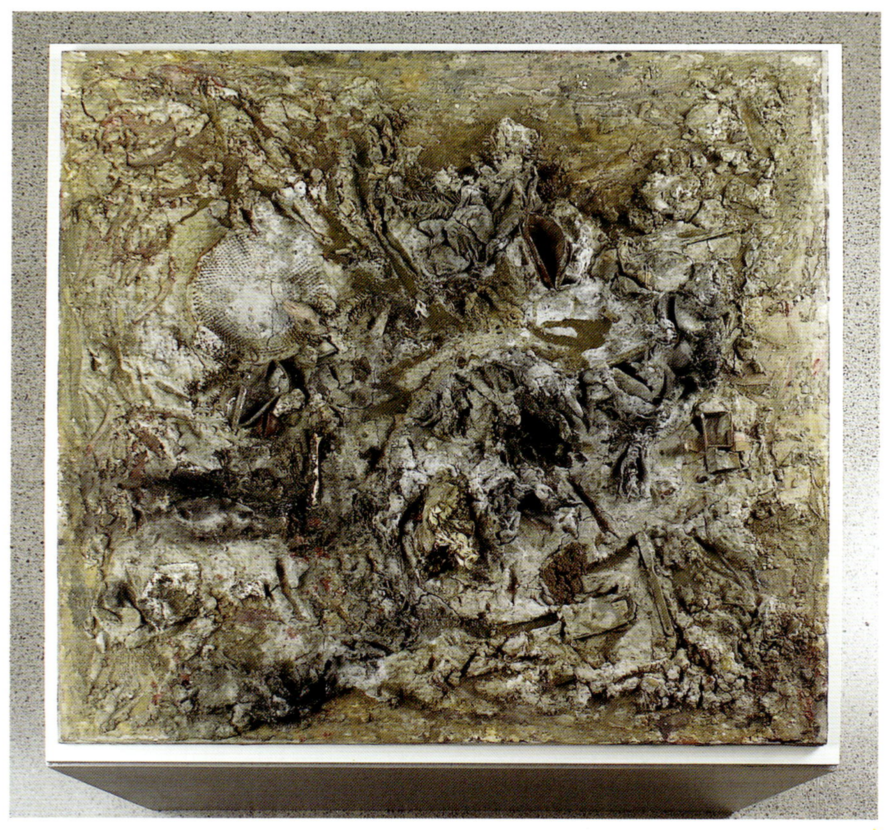

Otto Muehl
Materialbild Ölsardine (Material Picture Sardine), 1961/1962
Gips, Sand, Pigment, Papier, Sardinendose, Stoff, verschiedene Materialien
Plaster, sand, pigment, paper, sardine can, fabric, various materials
114 x 105 x 8 cm
Erworben / Acquired in 2003

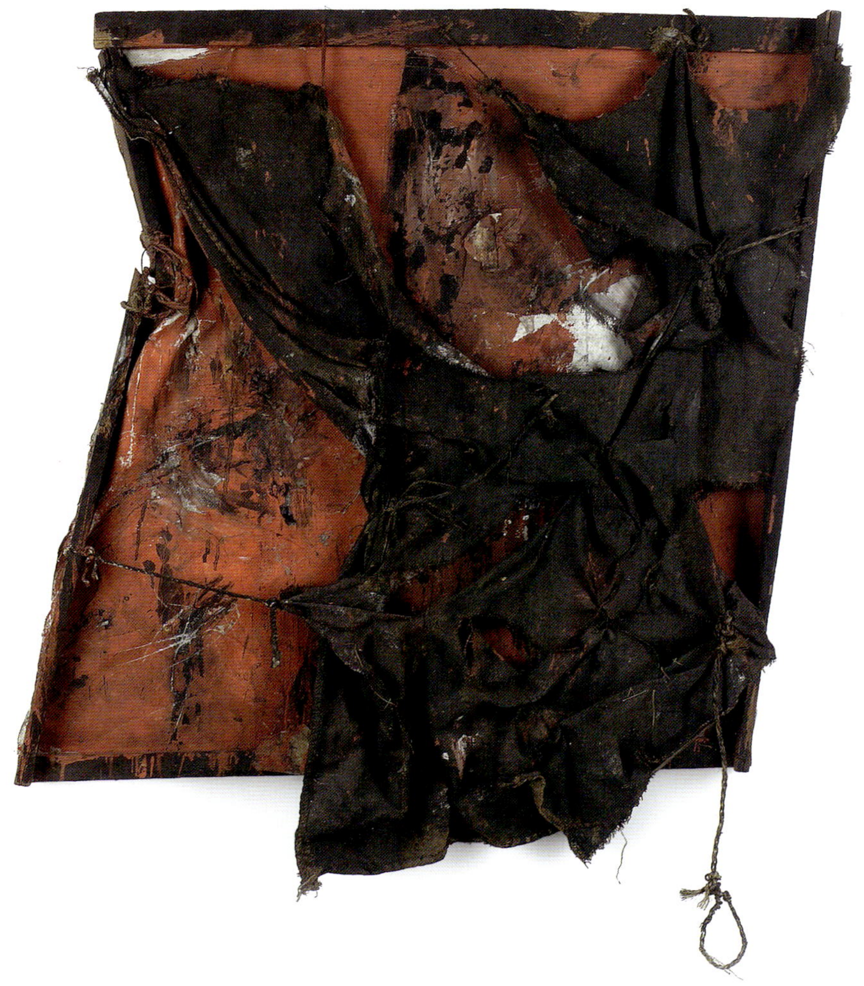

Otto Muehl
Brand in der Kohlenhandlung (Fire at the Coal Merchants), 1961
Dispersion, Jute, Holz, Papier, Schnur / Emulsion paint, jute, wood, paper, string
120 x 110 x 18 cm
Erworben / Acquired in 2003

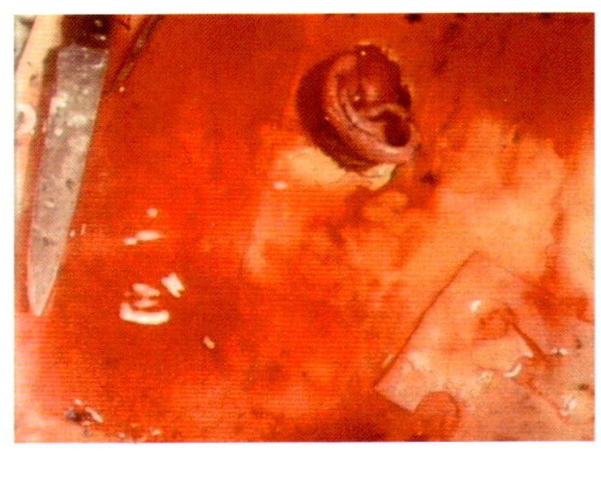 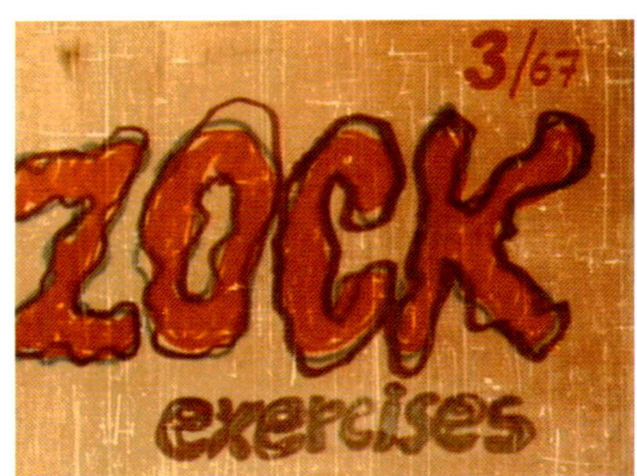

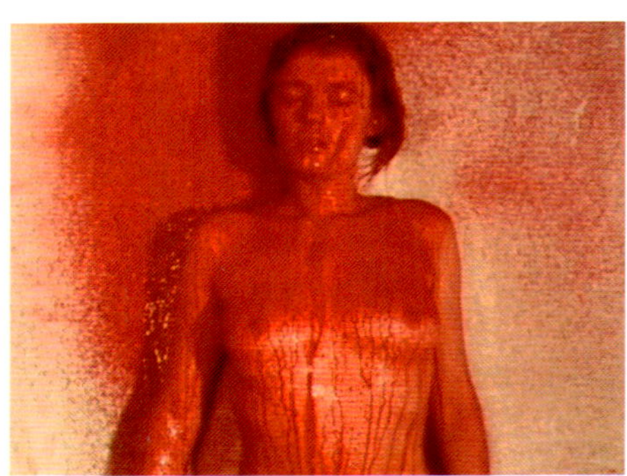 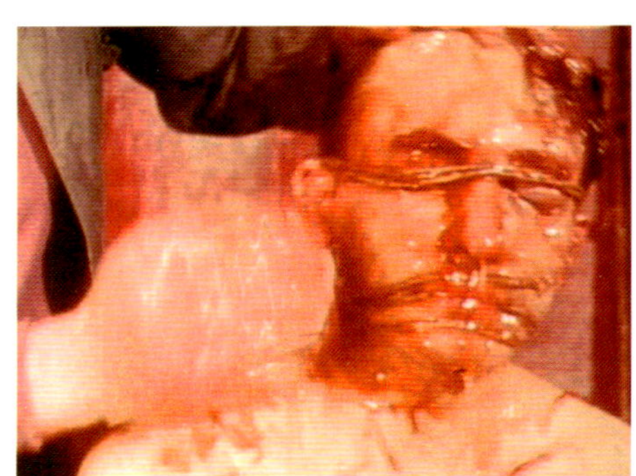

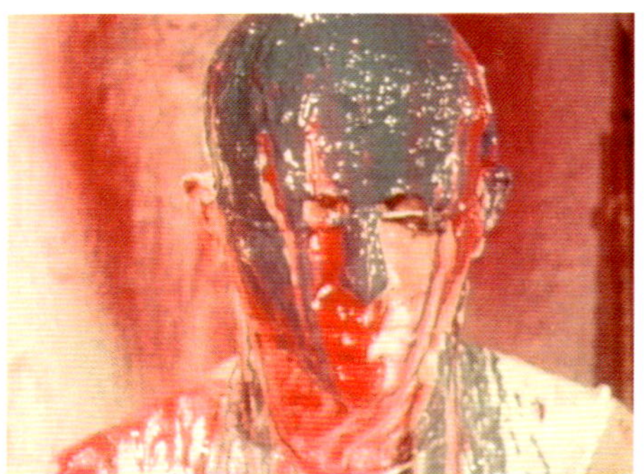 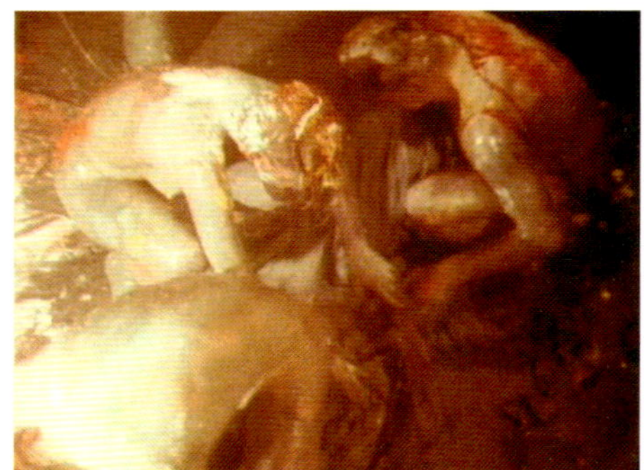

Otto Muehl
Zock-Exercises (Das Ohr / La Dolorosa / Kardinal / Michelangelo), 1967
16-mm-Film, Farbe, Ton / 16mm film, color, sound, 12 min
Erworben mit Unterstützung der Gesellschaft der Freunde der bildenden Künste
Acquired with funding from the Society of the Friends of Fine Arts Vienna, 2009

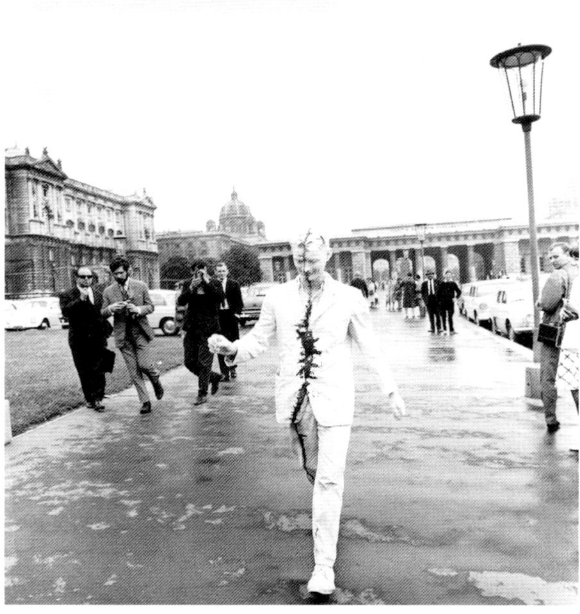 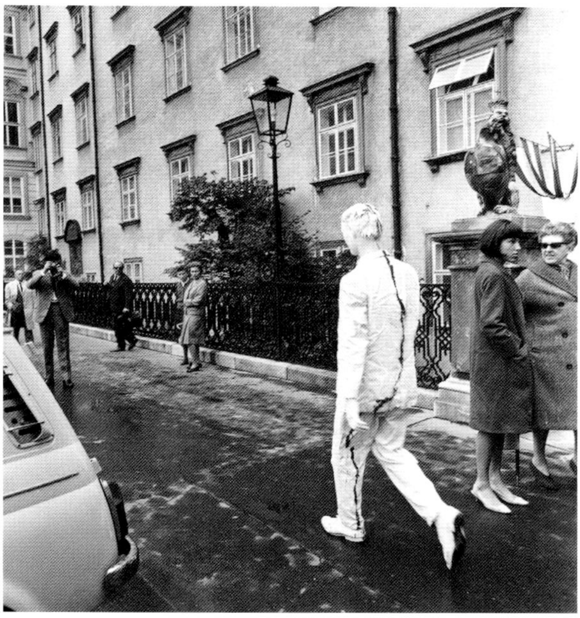

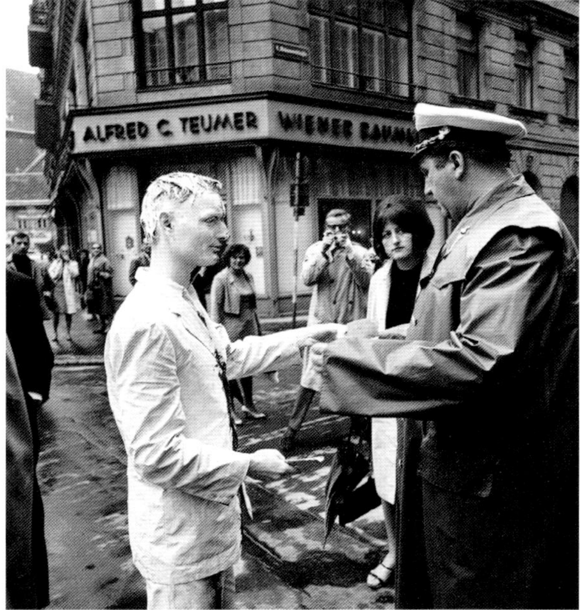 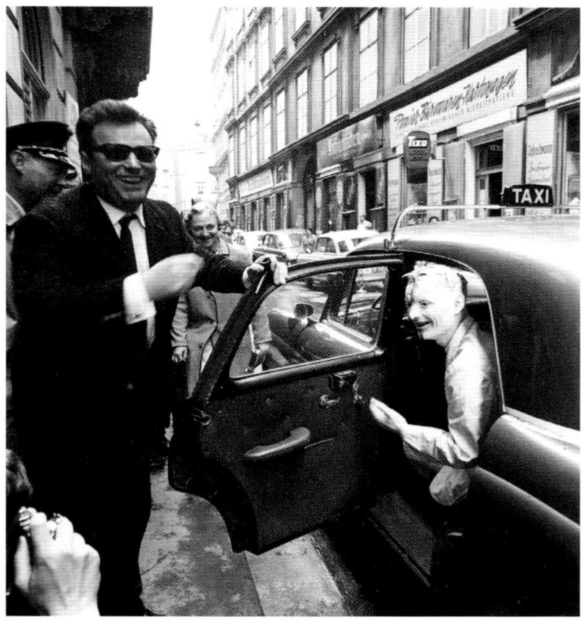

Günter Brus
Aktion Wiener Spaziergang (Action Vienna Walk), 1965
Serie von S/W-Fotografien, je 30,5 x 24 cm (Detail)
Series of b&w photographs, each 30,5 x 24 cm (detail)
Schenkung des Künstlers / Donated by the artist, 2006

Rudolf Schwarzkogler
Ohne Titel (Sigmund-Freud-Bild) (Untitled [Sigmund Freud Picture]), 1965
Lack, Schnur, Korkstöpsel, Rasierklinge auf Pressspanplatte
Lacquer, string, cork stopper, razor blade on particle board
108 x 53 x 5,5 cm
Leihgabe der Österreichischen Ludwig-Stiftung
On loan from the Austrian Ludwig Foundation, seit / since 1984

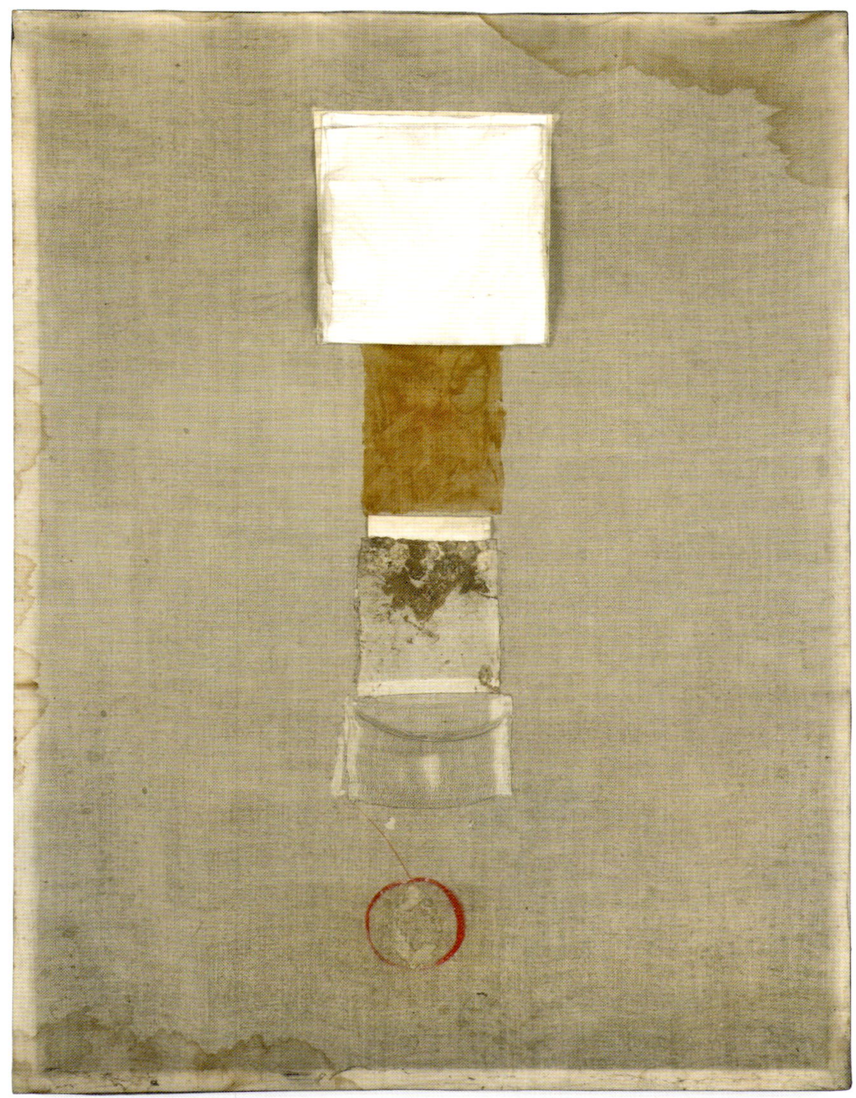

Hermann Nitsch
Reliktmontage mit blutigen Tüchern (Relic Montage with Bloody Cloths), 1964
Blut, Kreide, Mullbinde, Papier und Stoff auf Molino
Blood, chalk, muslin bandage, paper and fabric on molino
109 x 81 cm
Schenkung / Donated by Ernst Ploil, Wien / Vienna, 2006

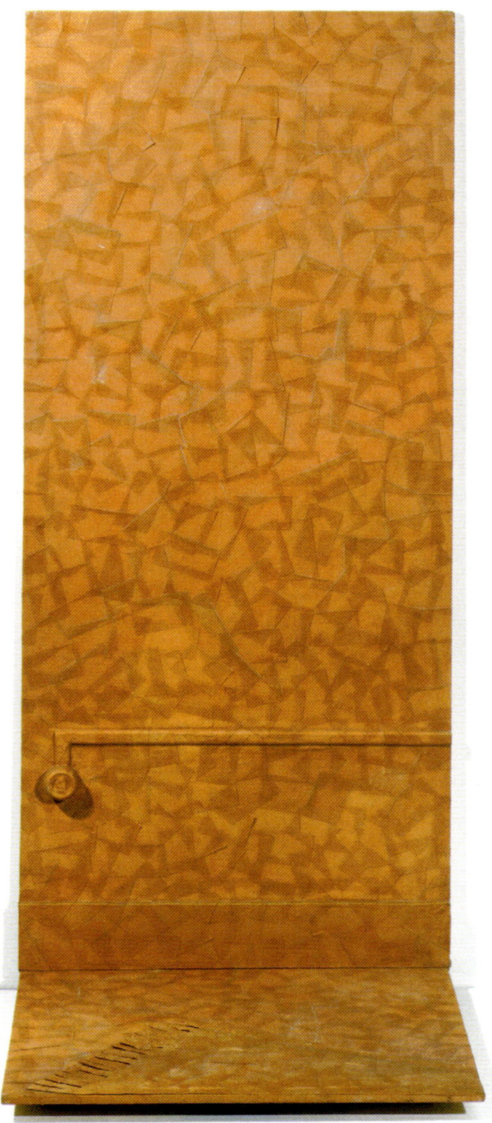

Erik Dietman
Wand-Boden-Stück (Wall-Floor-Piece), 1964
Leukoplast auf Holz, Teppich und Steckdose
Sticking tape on wood, carpet and power outlet
Wandplatte / Wall panel: 140 x 60 x 6 cm, Bodenplatte / Floor panel: 53 x 60 x 3,5 cm
Ehemals Sammlung Hahn / Former Hahn Collection, Köln / Cologne
Erworben / Acquired in 1978

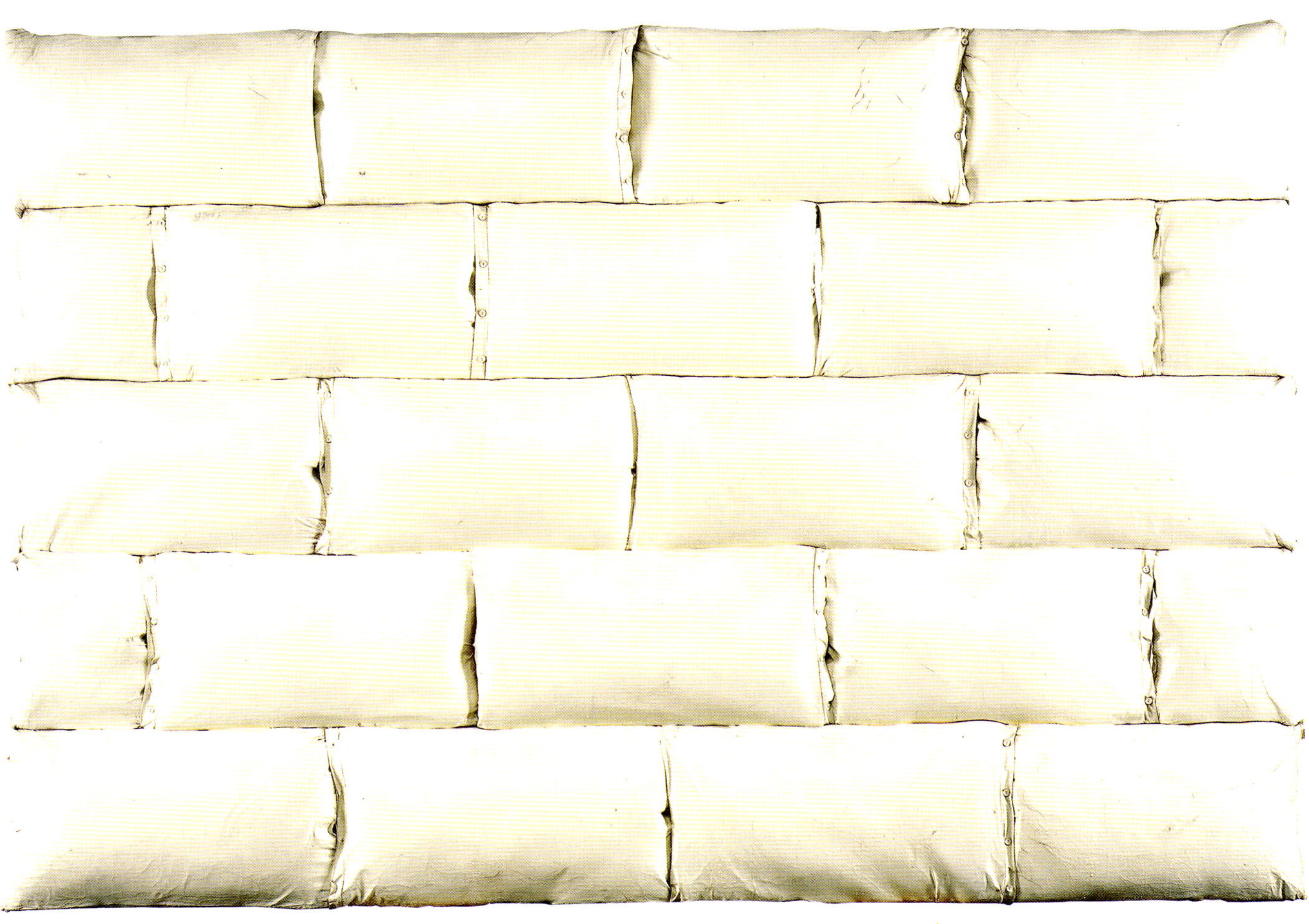

Pino Pascali
Il muro del sonno (Die Mauer des Schlafes / The Wall of Sleep), 1966
Kissen, Schaumstoff, Farbe und Holz / Cushions, foam rubber, paint and wood
250 x 230 x 19 cm
Leihgabe der Österreichischen Ludwig-Stiftung
On loan from the Austrian Ludwig Foundation, seit / since 1981

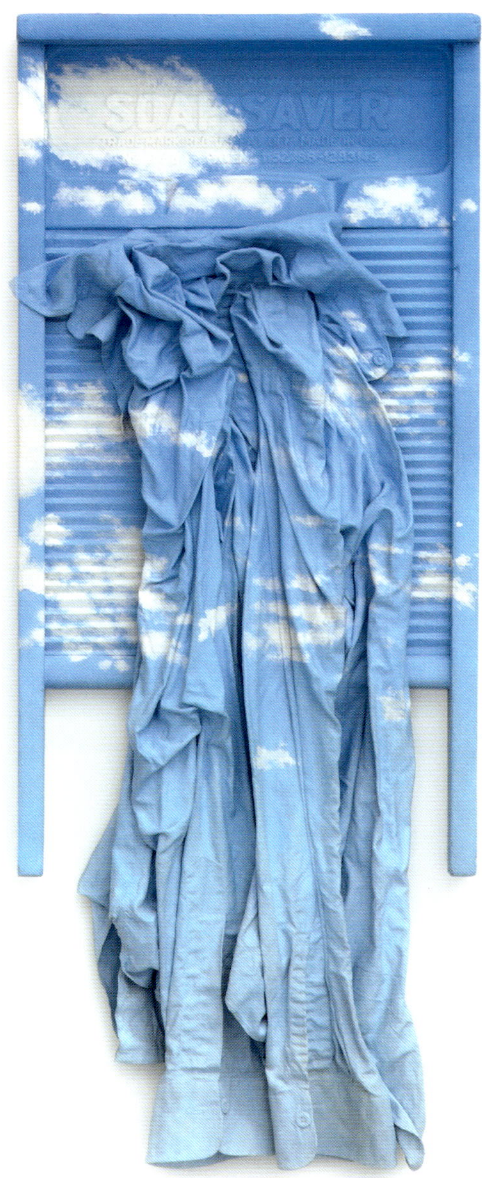

Geoffrey Hendricks
Soap Saver (Seifensparer), 1965
Acryl auf Waschbrett und Stoff / Acrylic on washboard and fabric
89 x 34 x 8 cm
Ehemals Sammlung Hahn / Former Hahn Collection, Köln / Cologne
Erworben / Acquired in 1978

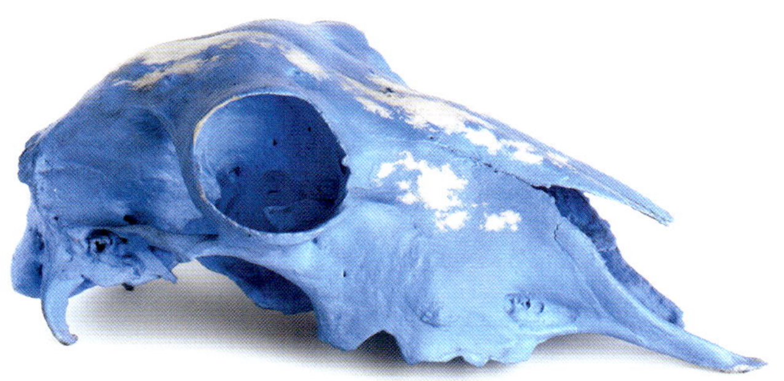

Geoffrey Hendricks
Skull (Schädel), 1967
Acryl auf Tierschädel / Acrylic on animal skull
12 x 22 x 9 cm
Ehemals Sammlung Hahn / Former Hahn Collection, Köln / Cologne
Erworben / Acquired in 1978

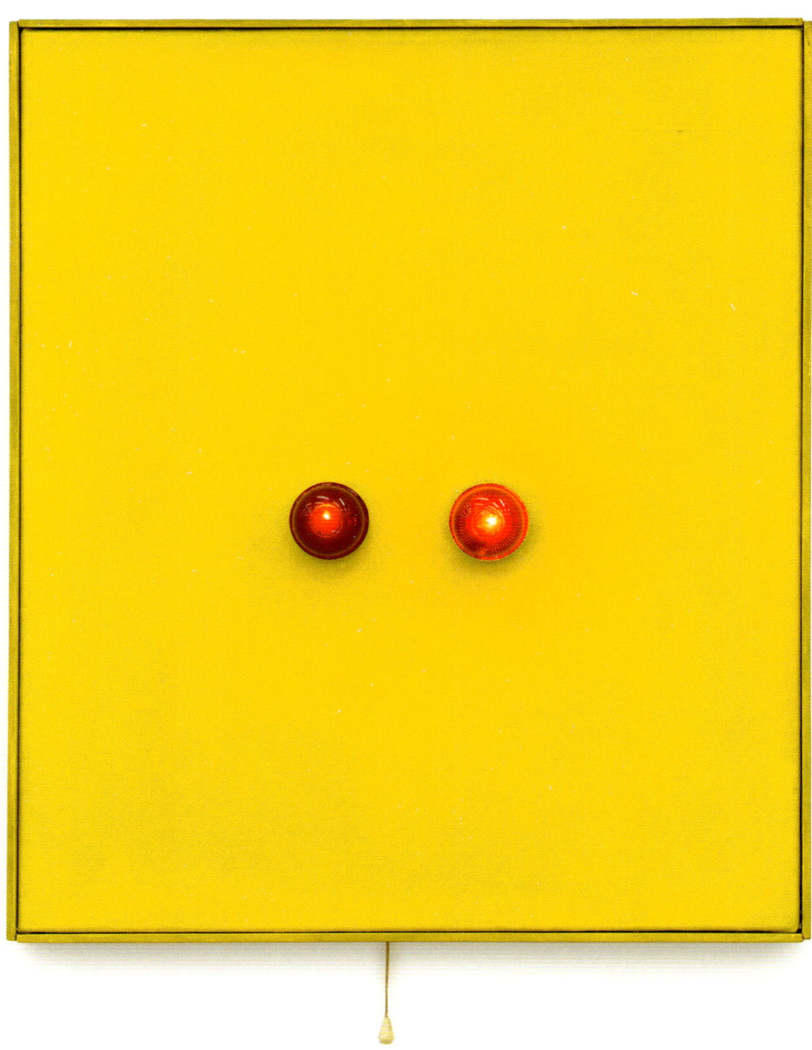

Hans Joachim Dietrich
Zwei Blinker (Two Flashing Lights), 1964
Öl auf Leinwand und Keilrahmen, Blinkglühlampen, Kordel, Batterie
Oil on canvas and canvas stretcher, blinking lights, cord, battery
68,2 x 51,5 x 7 cm
Ehemals Sammlung Hahn / Former Hahn Collection, Köln / Cologne
Erworben / Acquired in 1978

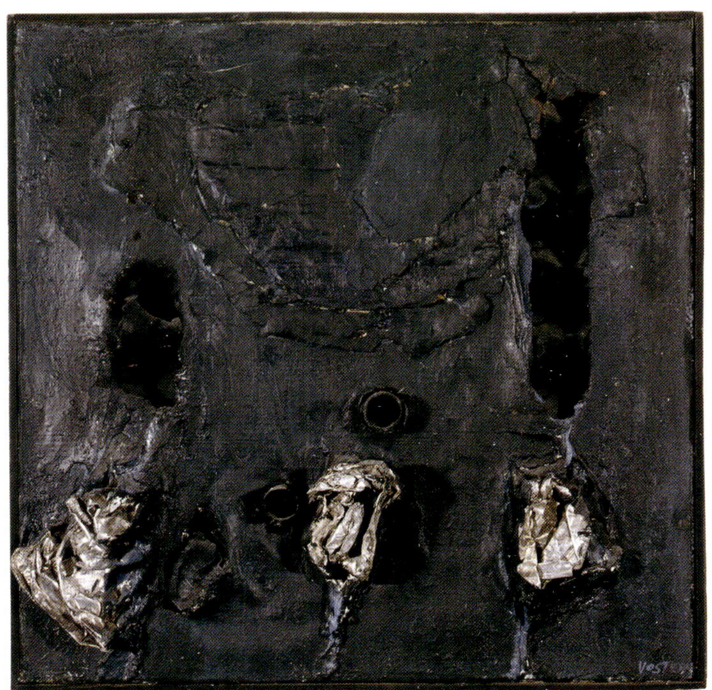

Wolf Vostell
Transmigracion N. 8, 1960
Öl, decollagierte Plakatreste, Metall, Eierkarton auf Leinwand, montiert auf Keilrahmen
Oil, decollaged poster remnants, metal, egg boxes on canvas mounted on a stretcher
41 x 41 x 10 cm
Ehemals Sammlung Hahn / Former Hahn Collection, Köln / Cologne
Erworben / Acquired in 1978

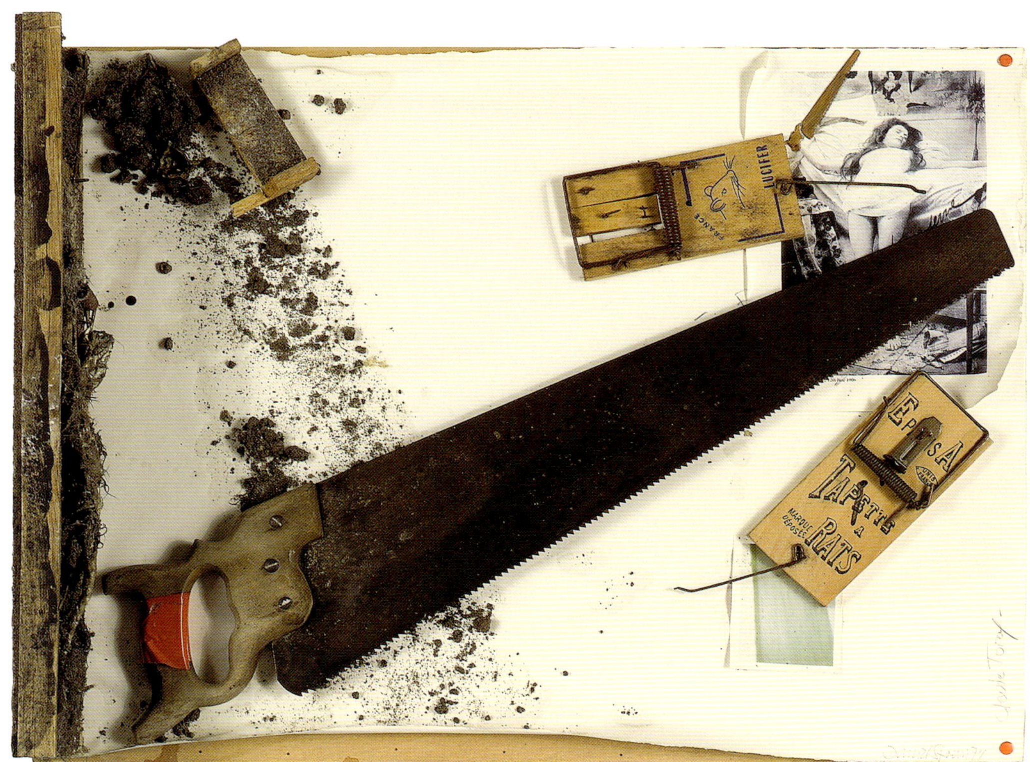

Daniel Spoerri
Le rat du Canard – Pour un canard sauvage (Die Ratte der Ente – für eine Wildente / The Duck's Rat—for a Wild Duck), 1974
S/W-Fotografie, Fuchsschwanzsäge, Rattenfalle, verschiedene Materialien auf Papier auf Holz montiert
b&w photograph, saw, rat trap, various materials on paper mounted on wood
57 x 76 x 15 cm
Ehemals Sammlung Hahn / Former Hahn Collection, Köln / Cologne
Erworben / Acquired in 1978

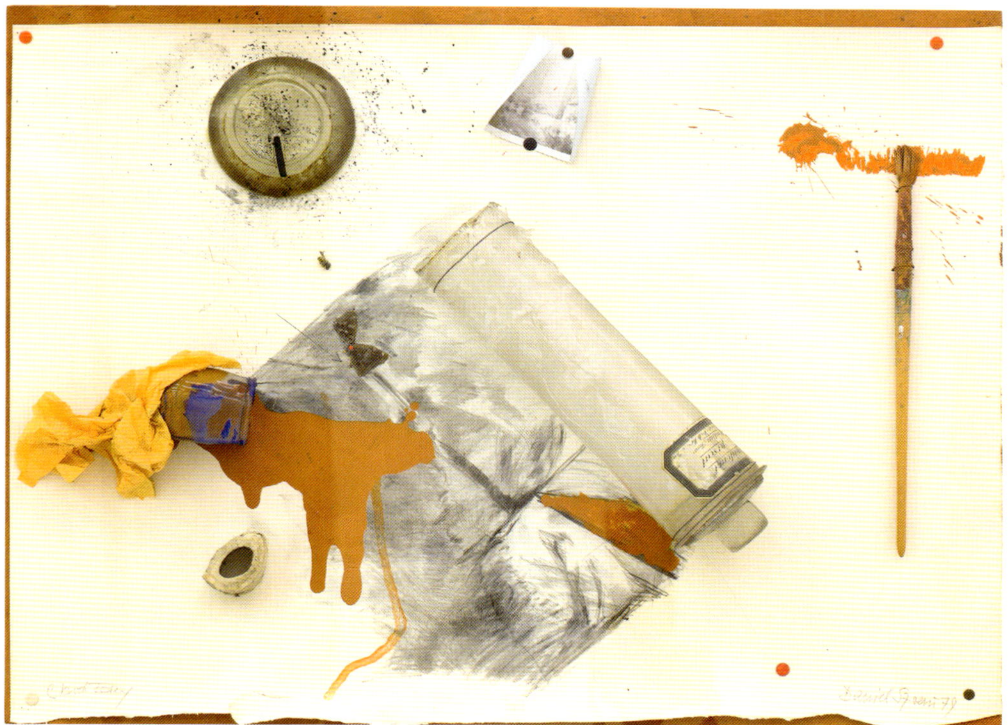

Daniel Spoerri
Où est la vipère – Une page d'histoire (Wo ist die Viper – eine Seite der Geschichte / Where Is the Viper—A Page of History), 1974
Glas, Knochen, Schmetterling, Pinsel, Farbe, verschiedene Materialien auf Papier auf Holz montiert
Glass, bone, butterfly, paintbrush, paint, various materials on paper mounted on wood
57 x 76 x 14 cm
Ehemals Sammlung Hahn / Former Hahn Collection, Köln / Cologne
Erworben / Acquired in 1978

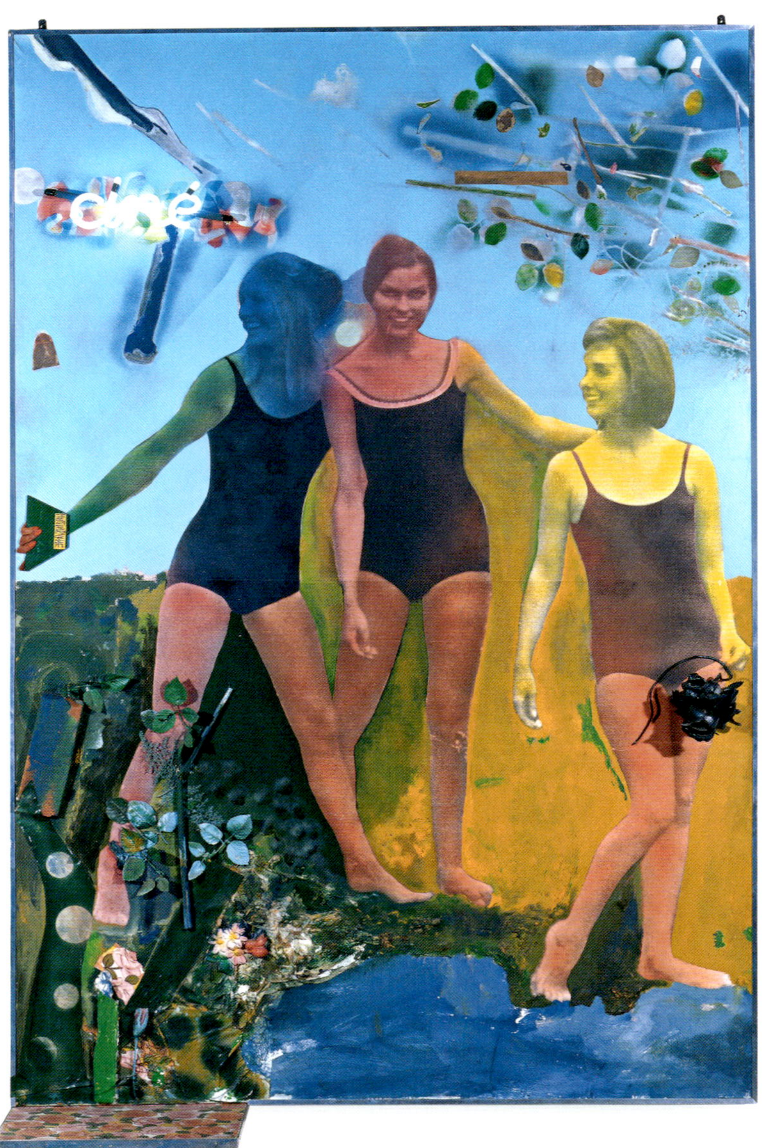

Martial Raysse
Ciné (Kino / Cinema), 1964
Kunststoffblume, Neonröhre und verschiedene Materialien, montiert auf kolorierte Fotografie auf Leinwand
Artificial flowers, neon lamp and various materials, mounted on colored photo on canvas
197 x 131 x 30,5 cm
Ehemals Sammlung Hahn / Former Hahn Collection, Köln / Cologne
Erworben / Acquired in 1978

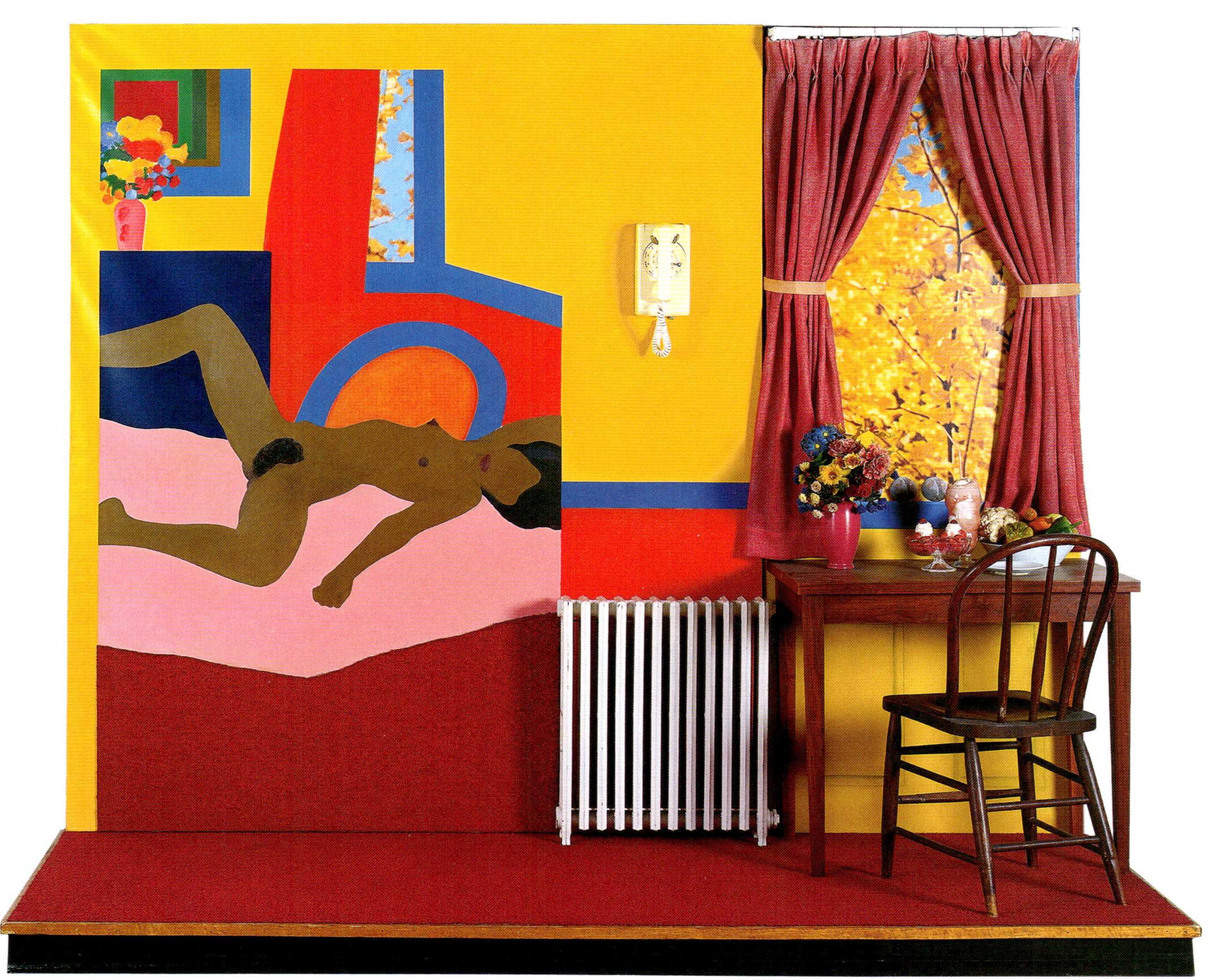

Tom Wesselmann
Great American Nude No. 54 (Großer amerikanischer Akt Nr. 54), 1964
Verschiedene Materialien, Tonbandaufnahme leiser Straßengeräusche
Various materials, tape recording of quiet street sounds
214 x 260 x 133 cm
Leihgabe der Österreichischen Ludwig-Stiftung
On loan from the Austrian Ludwig Foundation, seit / since 1981

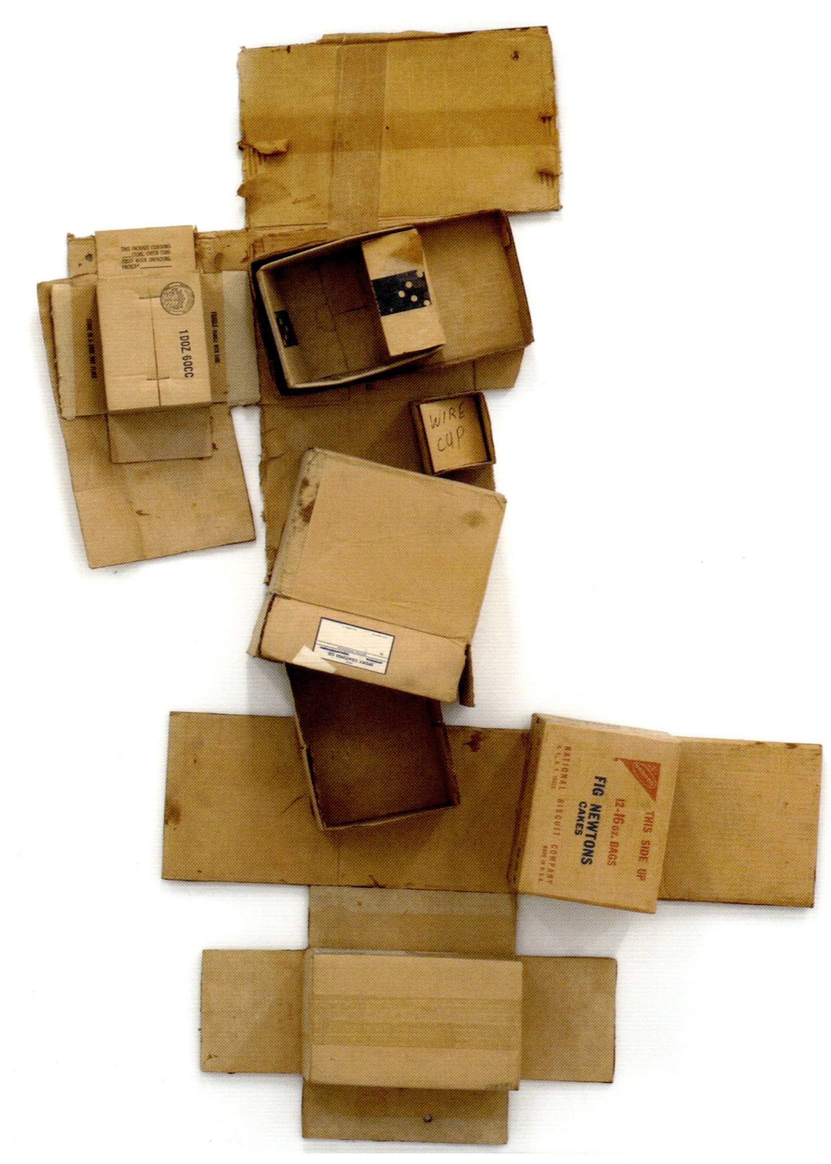

Robert Rauschenberg
Spanish Stuffed Mode Plus, 1971
Pappkartons auf Holz montiert / Cardboard boxes mounted on wood
174 x 128 x 20 cm
Leihgabe der Österreichischen Ludwig-Stiftung
On loan from the Austrian Ludwig Foundation, seit / since 1981

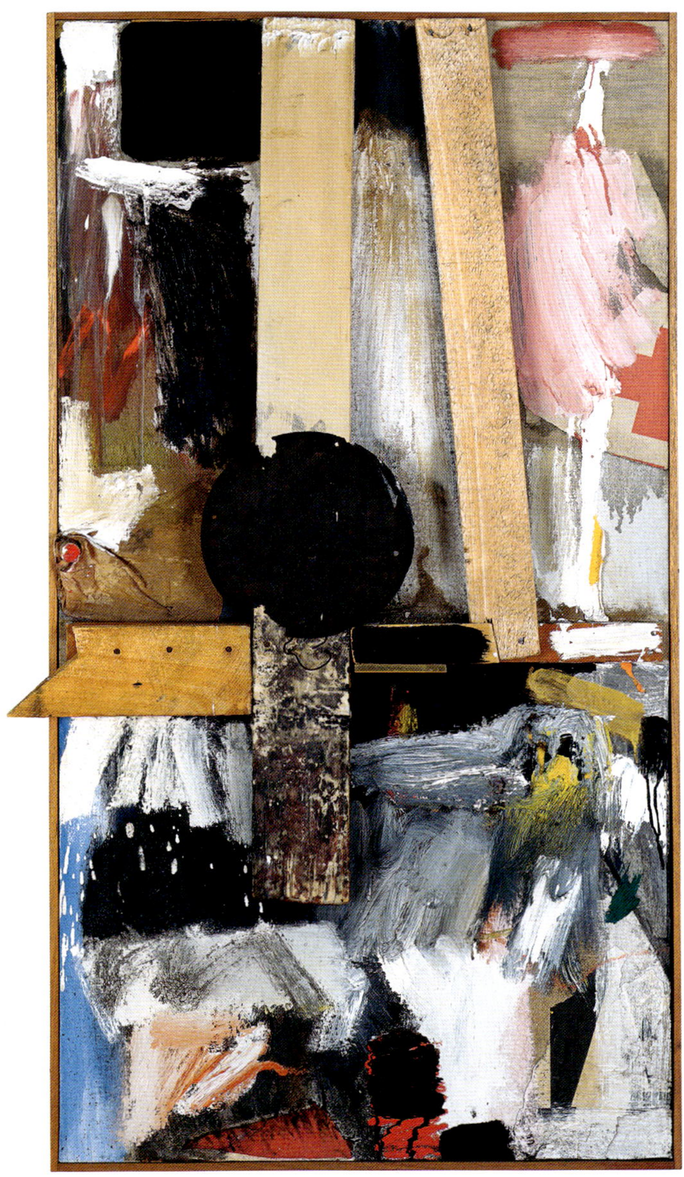

Robert Rauschenberg
Diplomat, 1960
Öl auf Leinwand, verschiedene Materialien / Oil on canvas, various materials
125 x 67 x 11 cm
Leihgabe der Österreichischen Ludwig-Stiftung
On loan from the Austrian Ludwig Foundation, seit / since 1991

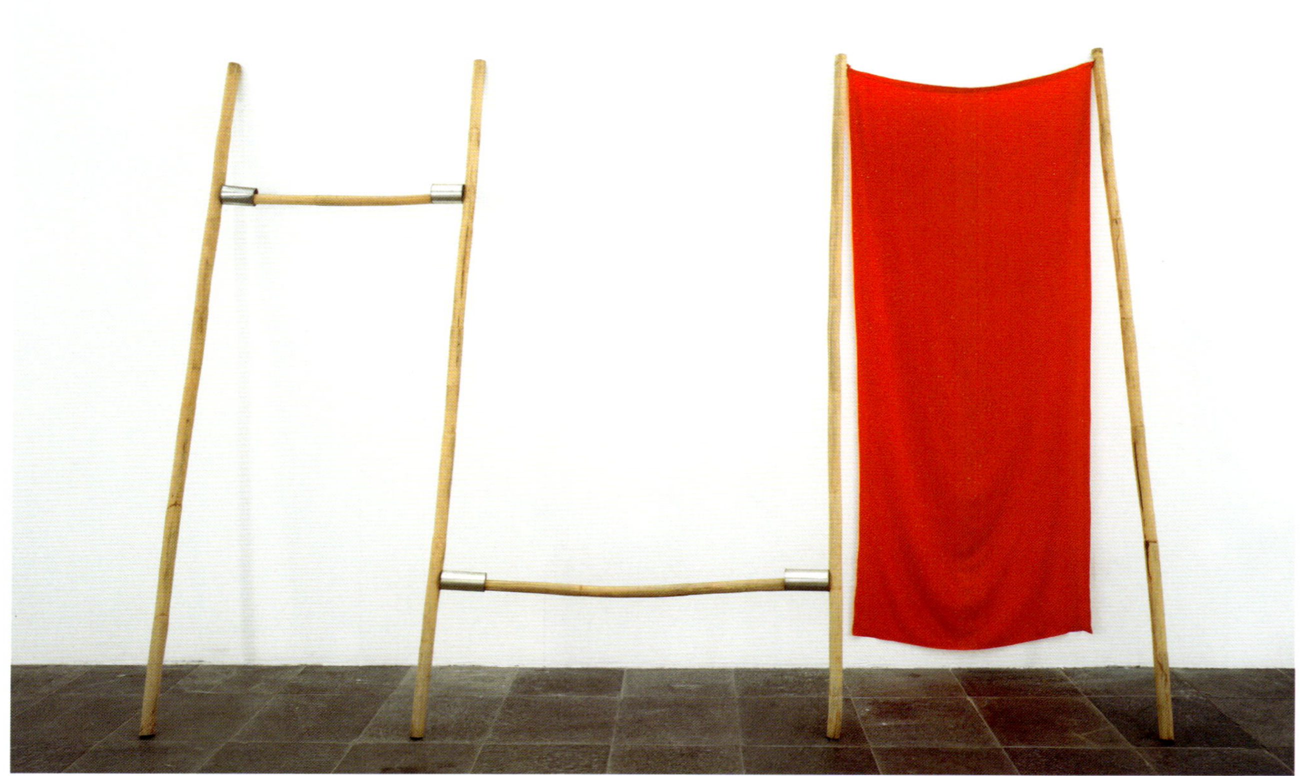

Robert Rauschenberg
Brim (Krempe), 1976
Holz, Seide, Konservendosen / Wood, silk, tin cans
93 x 130 x 26 cm
Leihgabe der Österreichischen Ludwig-Stiftung
On loan from the Austrian Ludwig Foundation, seit / since 1981

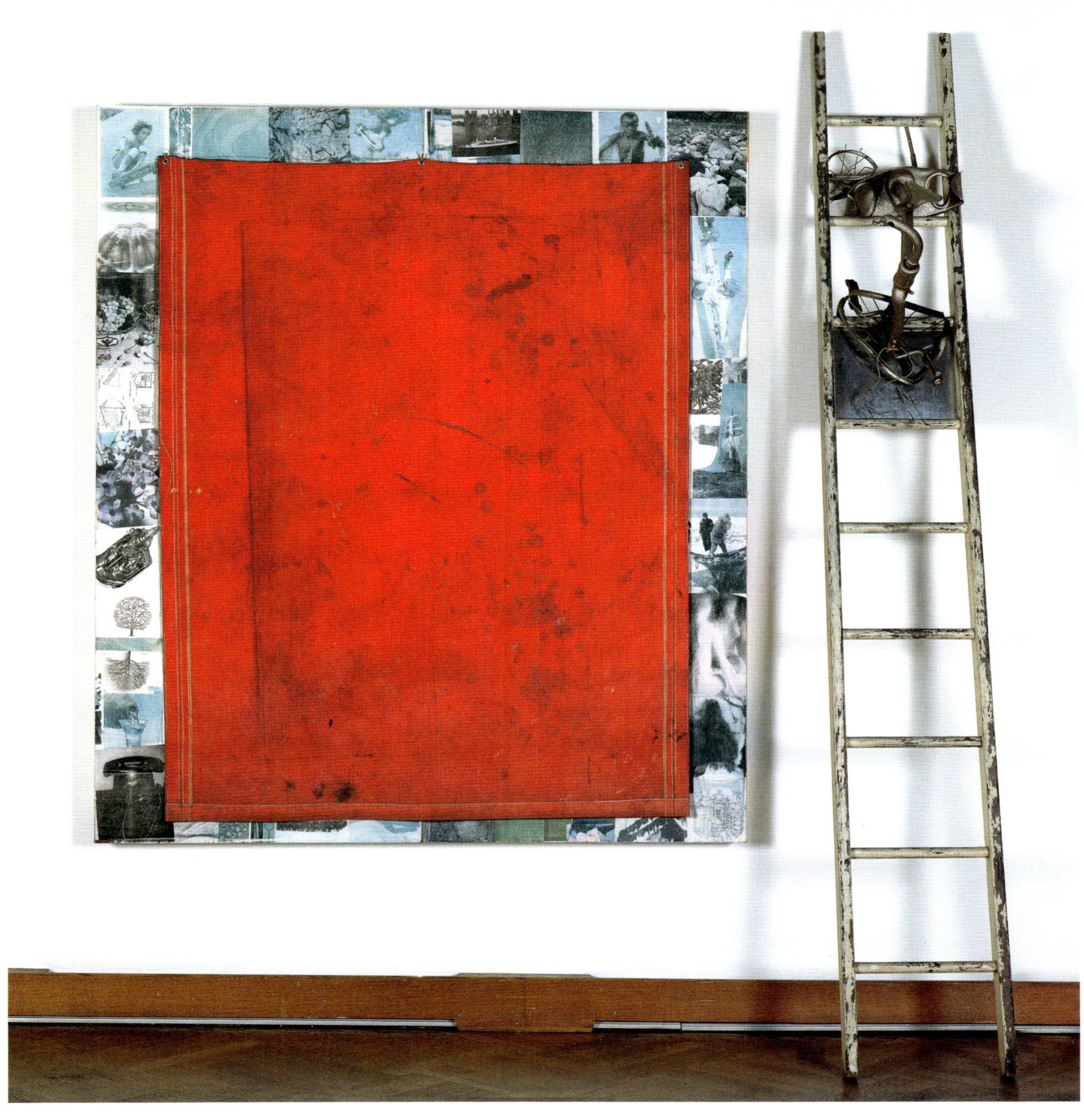

Robert Rauschenberg
Mango Ice Cave (Scale) (Mango Eishöhle [Skala]), 1977
Verschiedene Materialien / Various materials
299 x 235 x 110 cm
Leihgabe der Österreichischen Ludwig Stiftung
On loan from the Austrian Ludwig Foundation, seit / since 1991

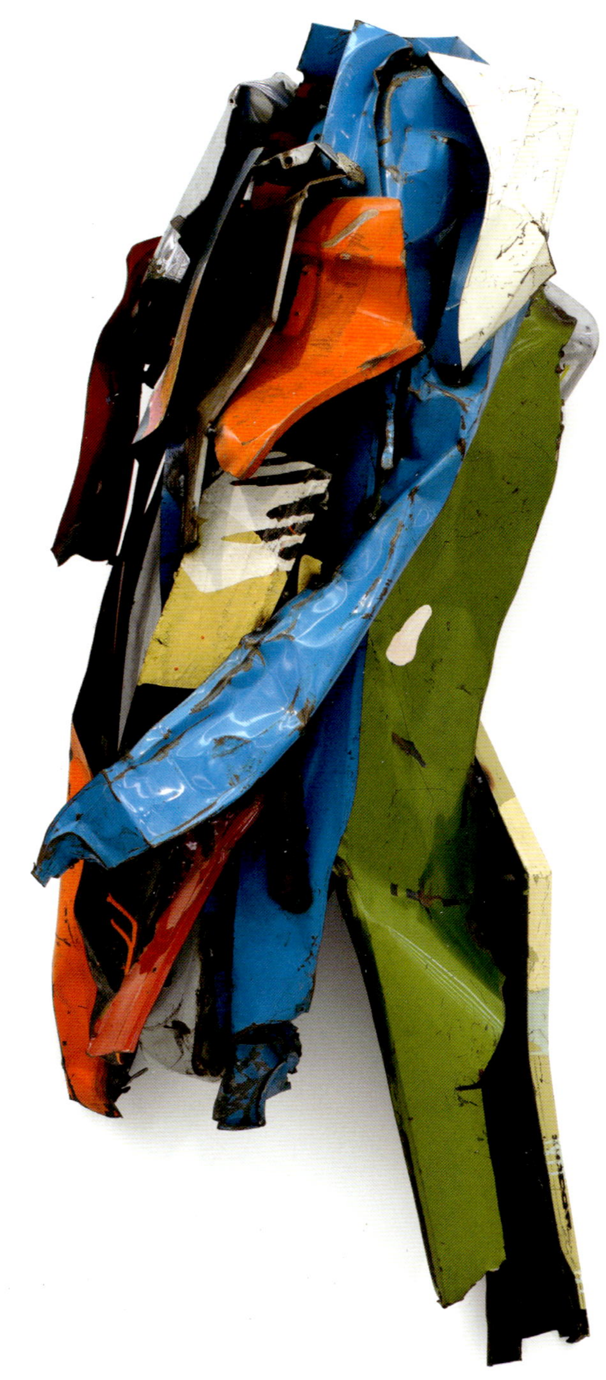

John Chamberlain
American Star, 1978
Stahlblech, lackiert und verchromt
Painted and chromed steel
203 x 89 x 74 cm
Leihgabe der Österreichischen Ludwig-Stiftung
On loan from the Austrian Ludwig Foundation, seit / since 1981

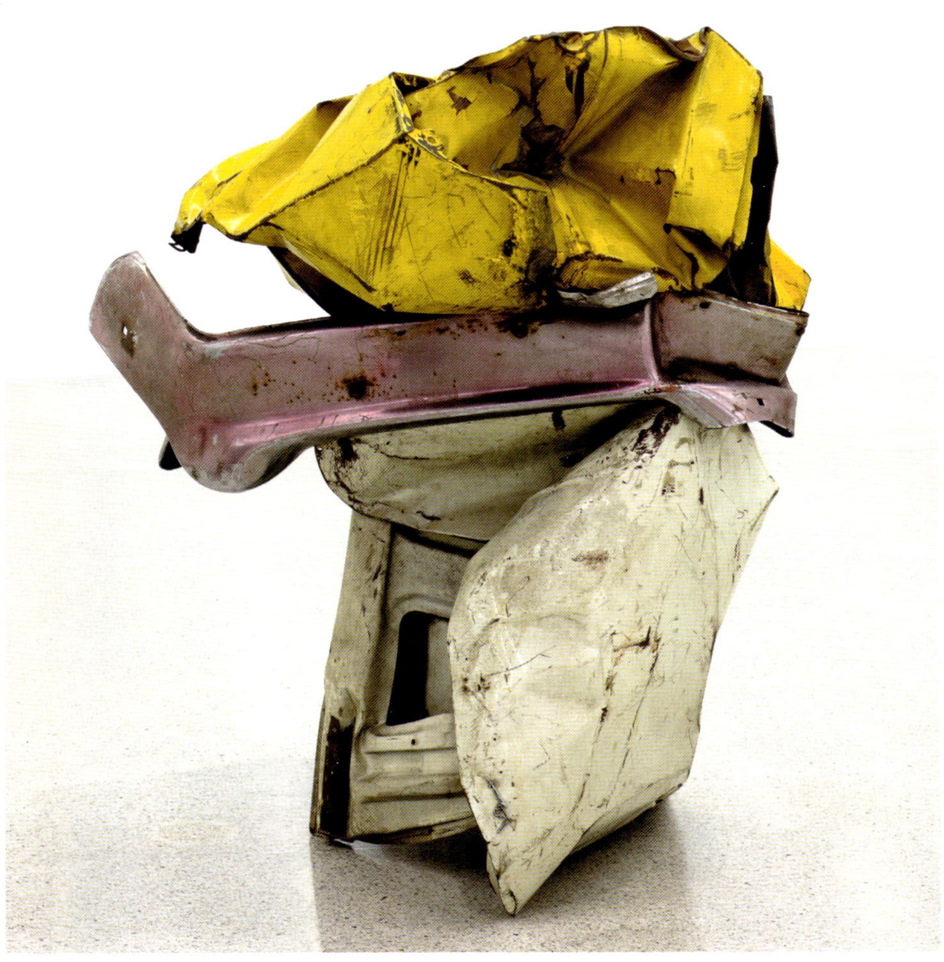

John Chamberlain
Trixie Dee, 1963
Stahlblech, lackiert und verchromt / Painted and chromed steel
138 x 135 x 125 cm
Ehemals Sammlung Hahn / Former Hahn Collection, Köln / Cologne
Erworben / Acquired in 1978

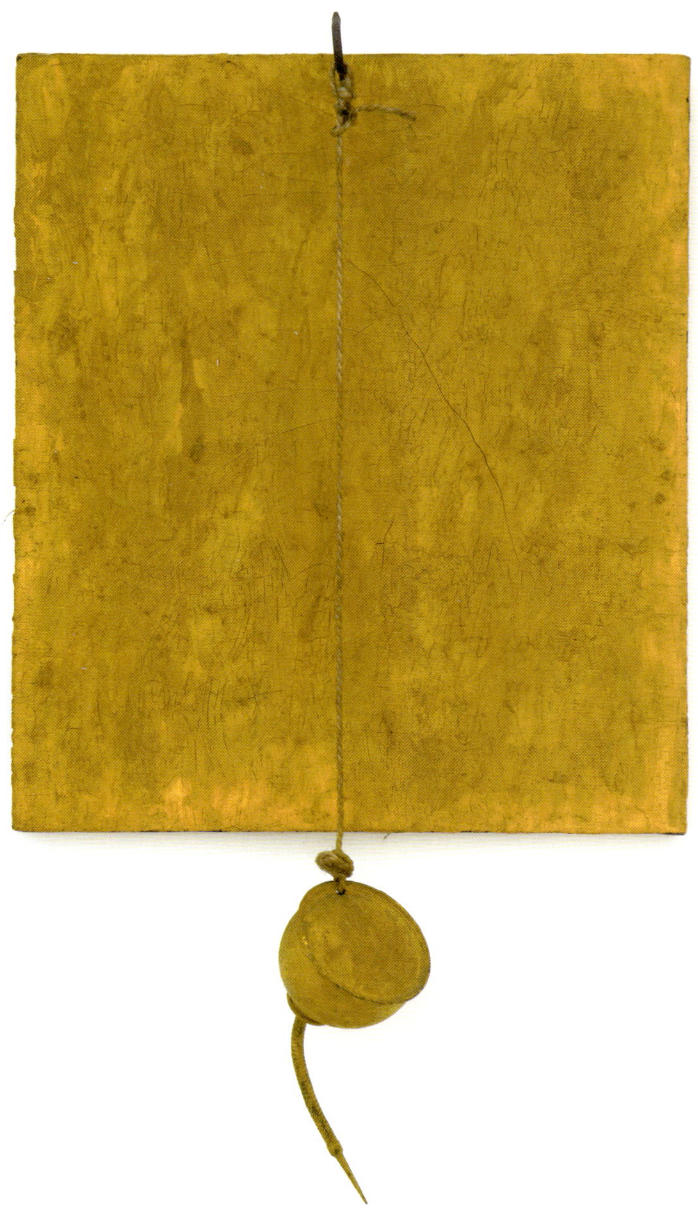

Jim Dine
Yellow Oil Can (Gelbe Ölkanne), 1962
Öl auf Leinwand, Ölkanne, Haken, Kordel / Oil on canvas, oil can, hook, cord
94 x 51 x 31 cm
Ehemals Sammlung Hahn / Former Hahn Collection, Köln / Cologne
Erworben / Acquired in 1978

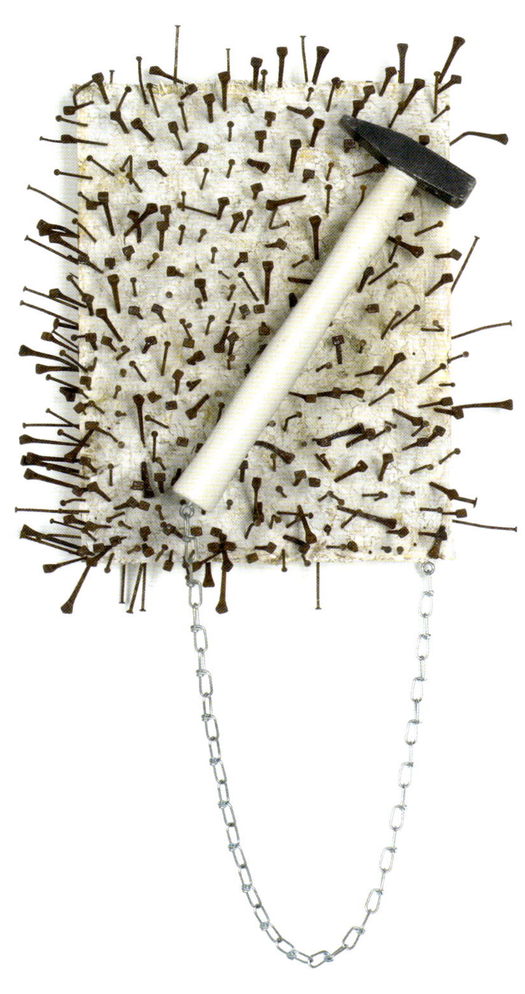

PAINTING TO HAMMER A NAIL

Hammer a nail into a mirror, a piece of
glass, a canvas, wood or metal every
morning. Also, pick up a hair that came
off when you combed in the morning and
tie it around the hammered nail. The
painting ends when the surface is covered
with nails.

1961 winter

Yoko Ono
Painting to Hammer a Nail (Bild, um einen Nagel einzuschlagen), 2005
Eisennägel, Gewebe, Hammer, Haare, Kette, Farbe und Kunstharz auf Holz
Iron nails, cloth, hammer, hair, chain, paint and acrylic lacquer on wood
35 x 27 x 11 cm
Schenkung der Künstlerin / Donated by the artist, 2008

Painting to Hammer a Nail (Bild, um einen Nagel einzuschlagen), 1961/1990
Siebdruck auf Acrylgrundierung auf Leinwand
Screen print on acrylic primer on canvas
72 x 100 cm
Leihgabe der Österreichischen Ludwig-Stiftung
On loan from the Austrian Ludwig Foundation, seit / since 1993

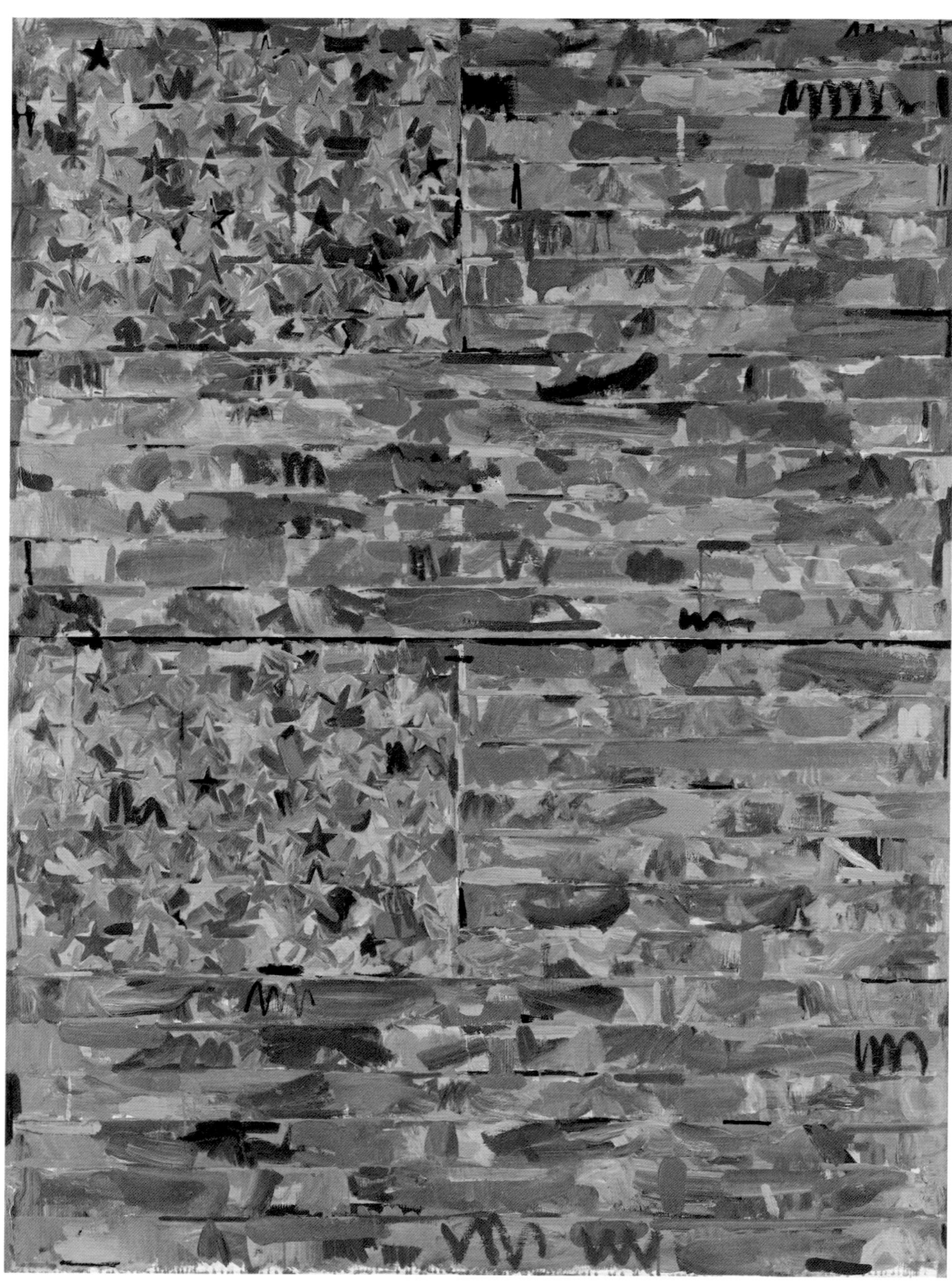

Jasper Johns
Two Flags (Zwei Flaggen), 1959
Acryl auf Leinwand / Acrylic on canvas
200 x 145 cm
Leihgabe der Sammlung Ludwig
On loan from the Ludwig Collection, Aachen
seit / since seit 1978

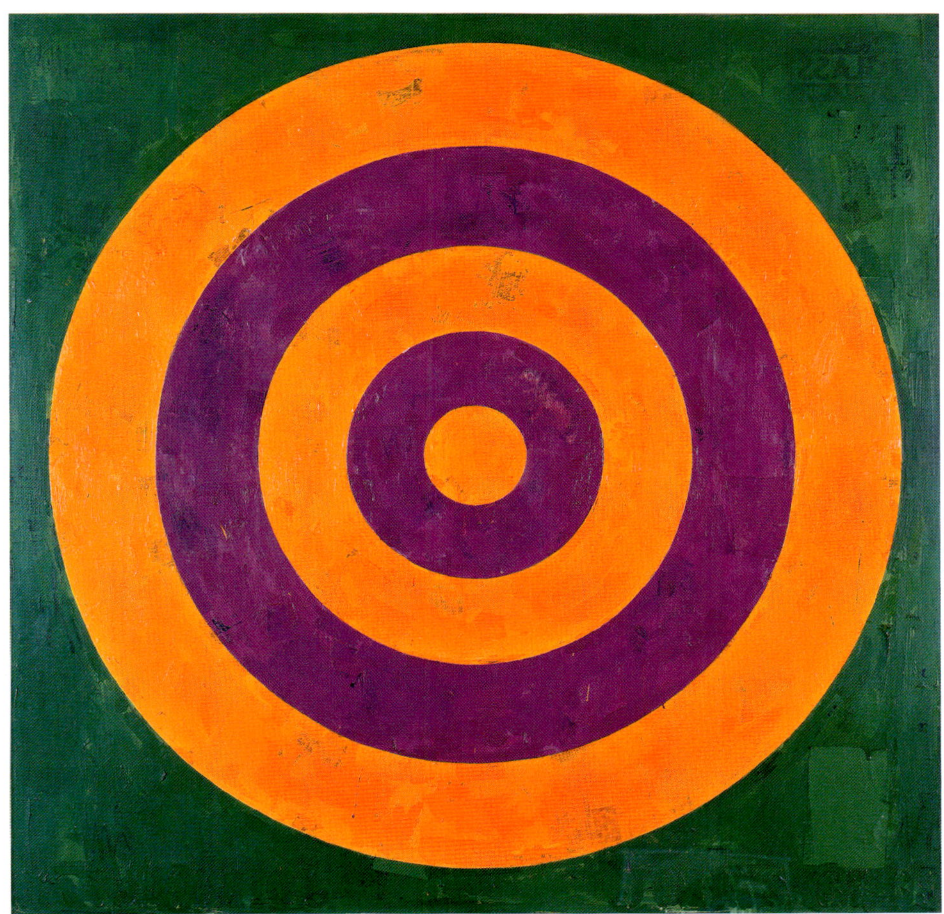

Jasper Johns
Target (Zielscheibe), 1967–1969
Öl, Collage, Transfertechnik auf Leinwand
Oil, collage, transfer technique on canvas
152 x 152 cm
Leihgabe der Österreichischen Ludwig-Stiftung
On loan from the Austrian Ludwig Foundation, seit / since 1981

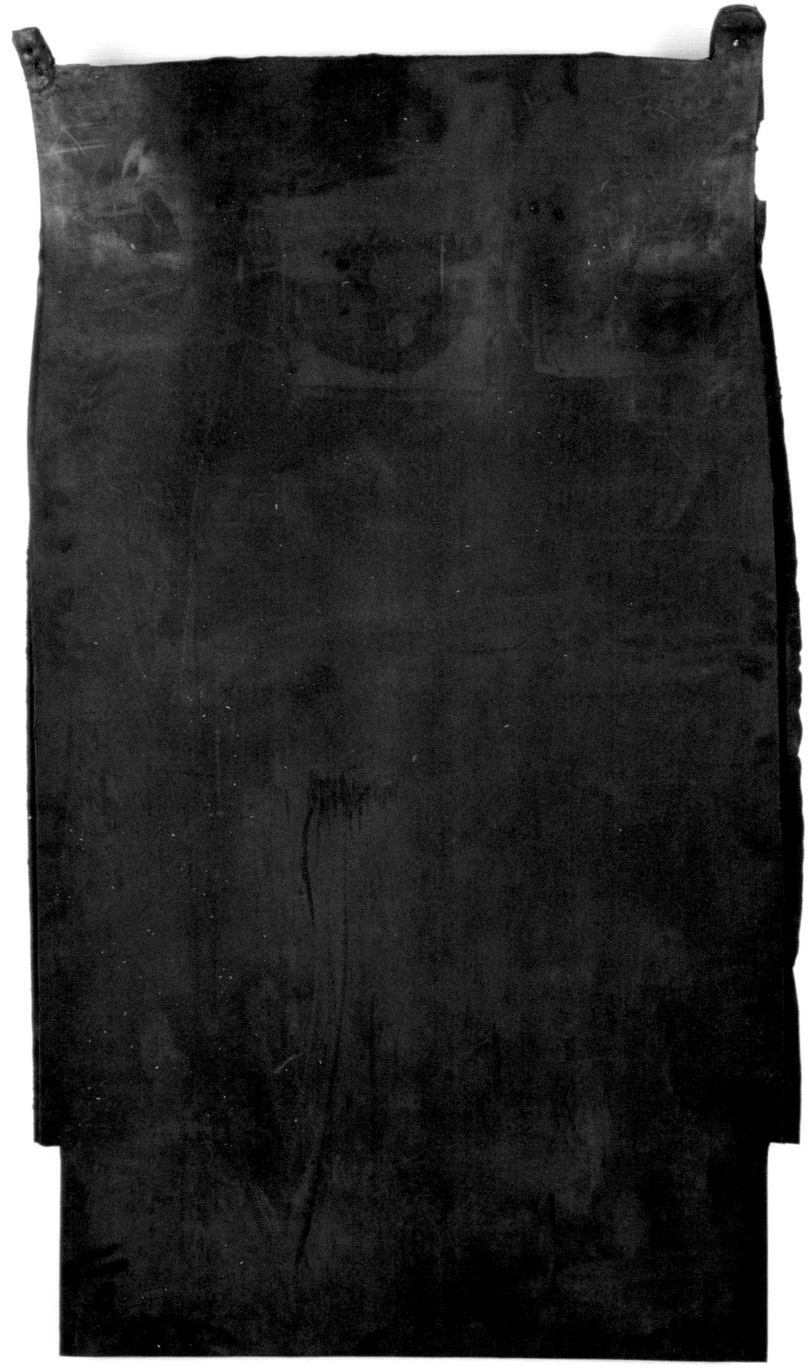

Richard Serra
Remnant (Mat) (Rest [Matte]), 1968
Vulkanisierter Gummi / Vulcanized rubber
200 x 95 x 3 cm
Leihgabe der Österreichischen Ludwig Stiftung
On loan from the Austrian Ludwig Foundation, seit / since 1981

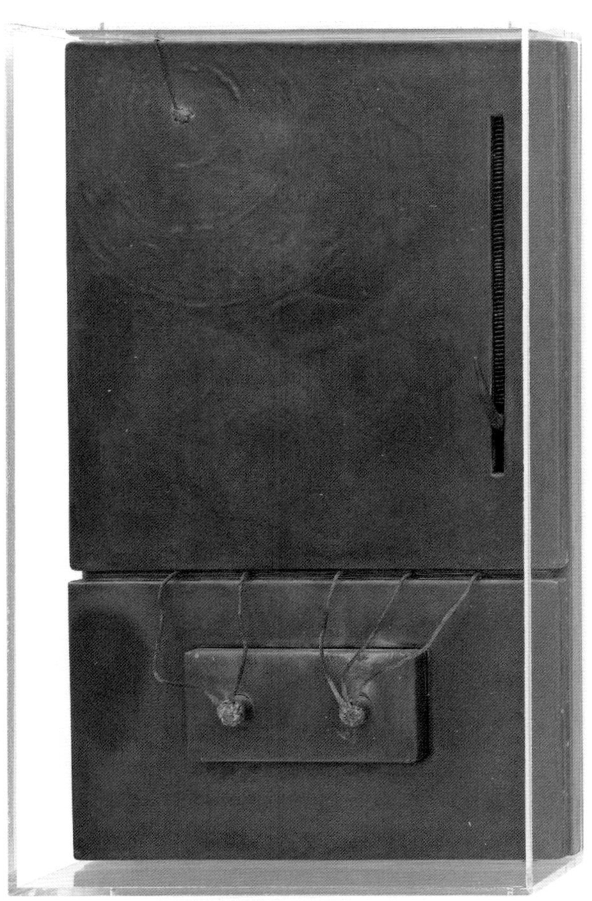

Robert Morris
Ohne Titel (Untitled), 1964
Blei, Draht, Feder / Lead, wire, metal spring
67 x 40 x 6 cm
Leihgabe der Österreichischen Ludwig-Stiftung
On loan from the Austrian Ludwig Foundation, seit / since 1981

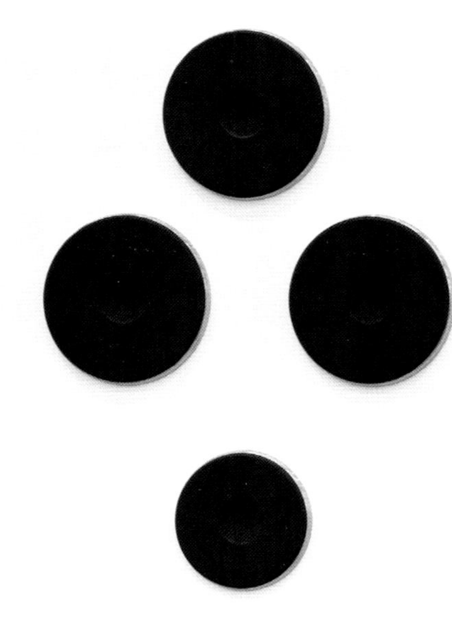

Rosemarie Trockel
Ohne Titel (Untitled), 1991
Email auf Stahl, Herdplatten
Enamel on steel, hot plates
90 x 70 x 10 cm
Erworben / Acquired in 1998

John M. Armleder
Ohne Titel (Untitled), 1987
Aluminiumjalousien, Dispersion auf Leinwand
Aluminum blinds, emulsion paint on canvas
200 x 700 x 3 cm
Erworben / Acquired in 2001

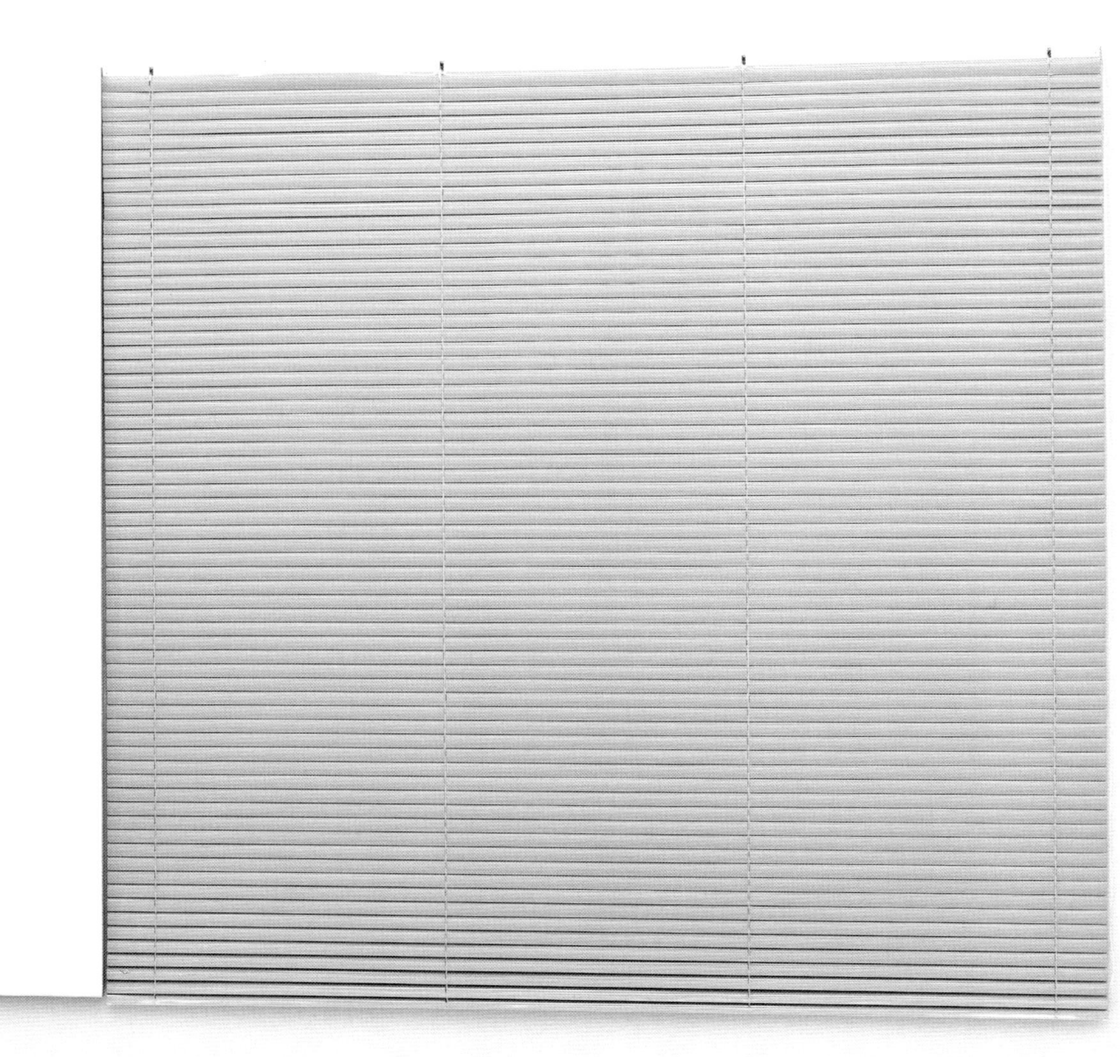

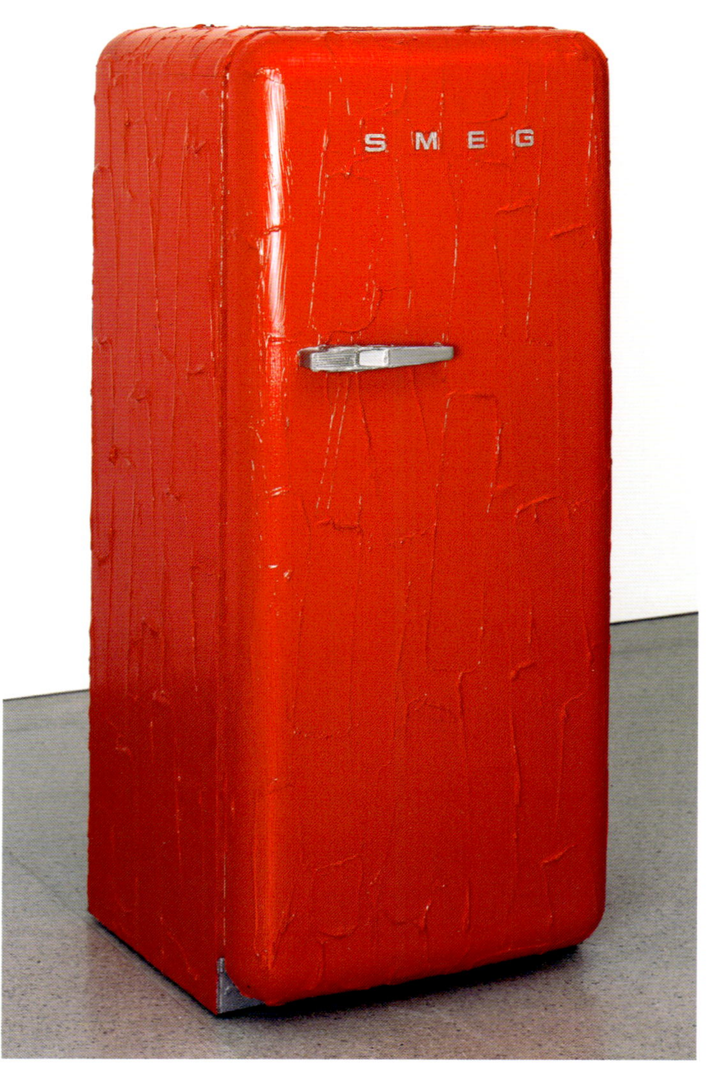

Bertrand Lavier
SMEG, 1997
Acryl auf Kühlschrank / Acrylic on refrigerator
145 x 61 x 72 cm
Erworben / Acquired in 1998

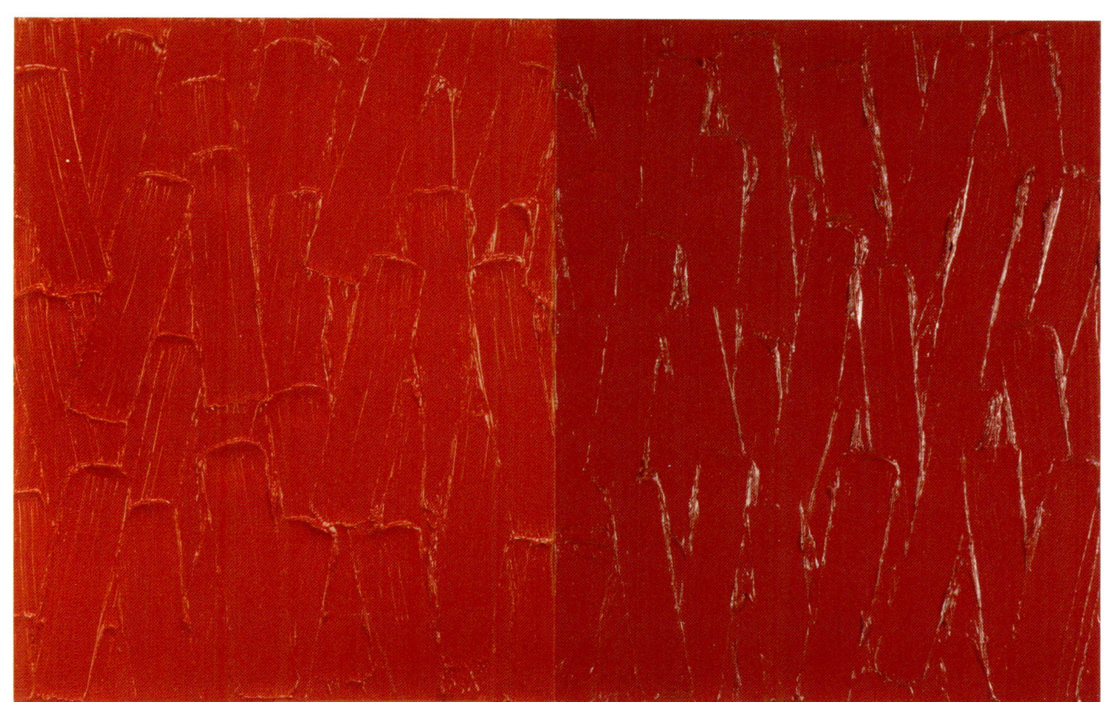

Bertrand Lavier
Cadmium (Kadmium), 1991
Acryl, Cibachrome auf Aluminium
Acrylic, cibachrome on aluminum
98 x 150 cm
Erworben / Acquired in 1994

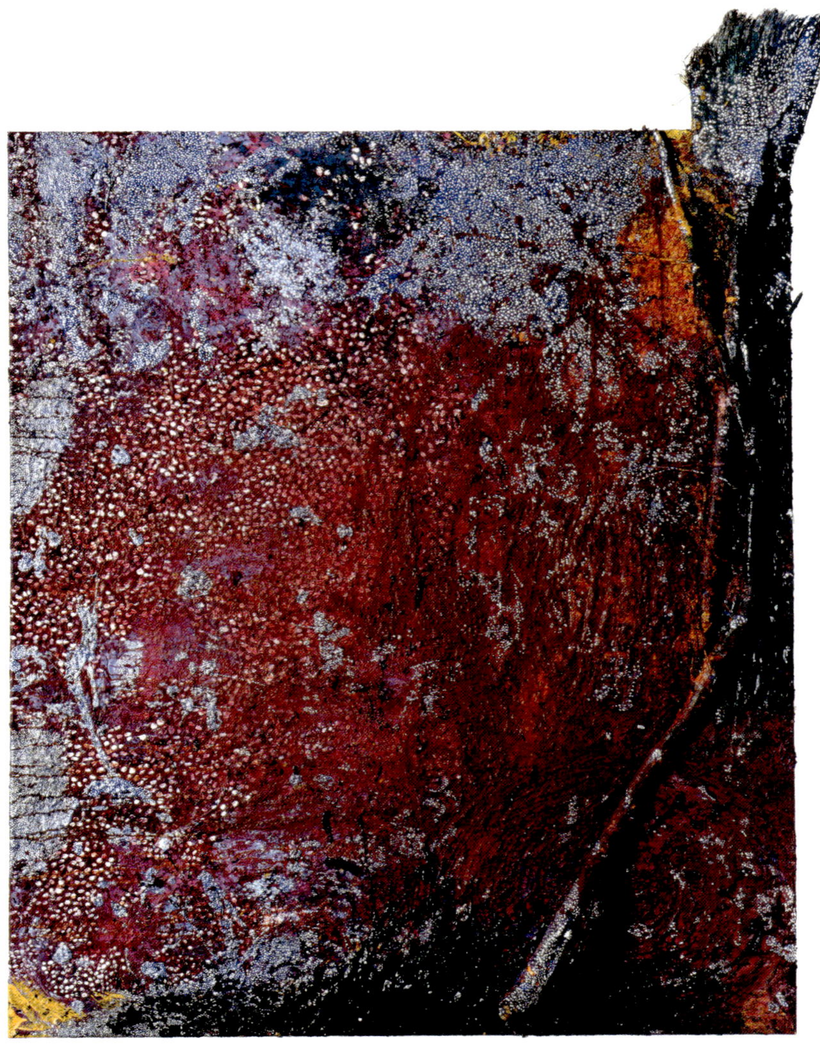

Michael Buthe
Westfälische Landschaft (Westphalian Landscape), 1990/1991
Mischtechnik auf Leinwand / Mixed media on canvas
180 x 150 x 25 cm
Erworben / Acquired in 1992

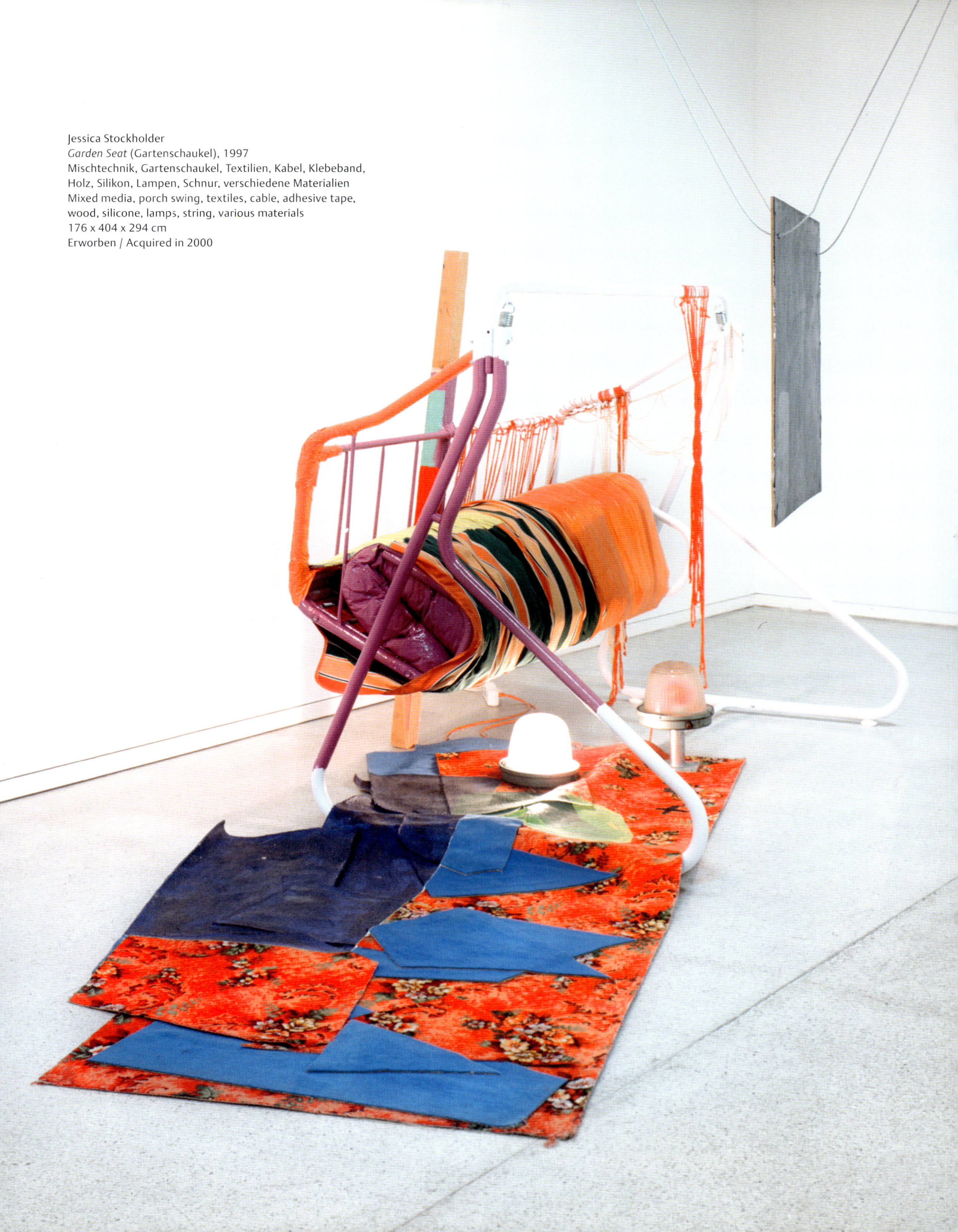

Jessica Stockholder
Garden Seat (Gartenschaukel), 1997
Mischtechnik, Gartenschaukel, Textilien, Kabel, Klebeband,
Holz, Silikon, Lampen, Schnur, verschiedene Materialien
Mixed media, porch swing, textiles, cable, adhesive tape,
wood, silicone, lamps, string, various materials
176 x 404 x 294 cm
Erworben / Acquired in 2000

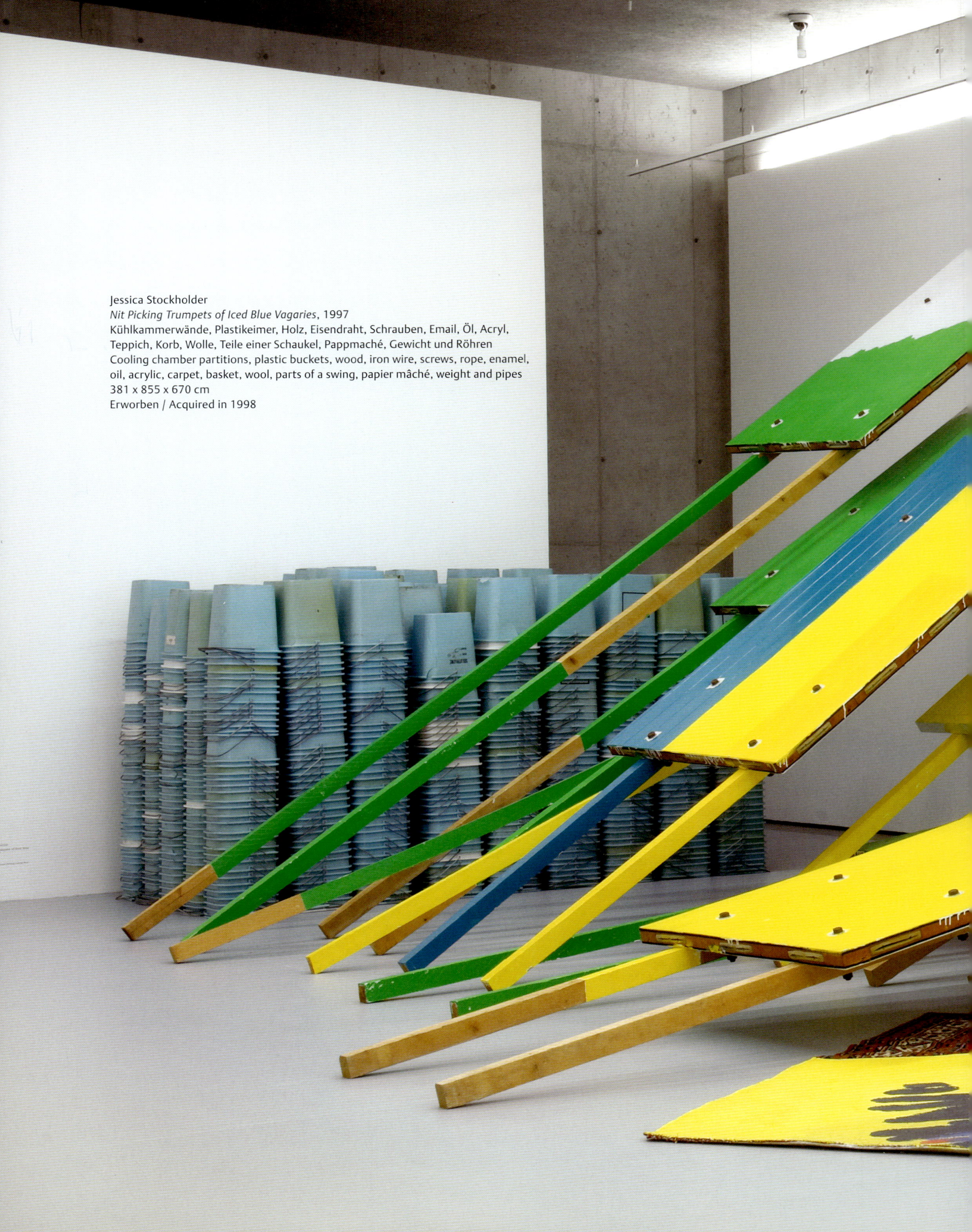

Jessica Stockholder
Nit Picking Trumpets of Iced Blue Vagaries, 1997
Kühlkammerwände, Plastikeimer, Holz, Eisendraht, Schrauben, Email, Öl, Acryl,
Teppich, Korb, Wolle, Teile einer Schaukel, Pappmaché, Gewicht und Röhren
Cooling chamber partitions, plastic buckets, wood, iron wire, screws, rope, enamel,
oil, acrylic, carpet, basket, wool, parts of a swing, papier mâché, weight and pipes
381 x 855 x 670 cm
Erworben / Acquired in 1998

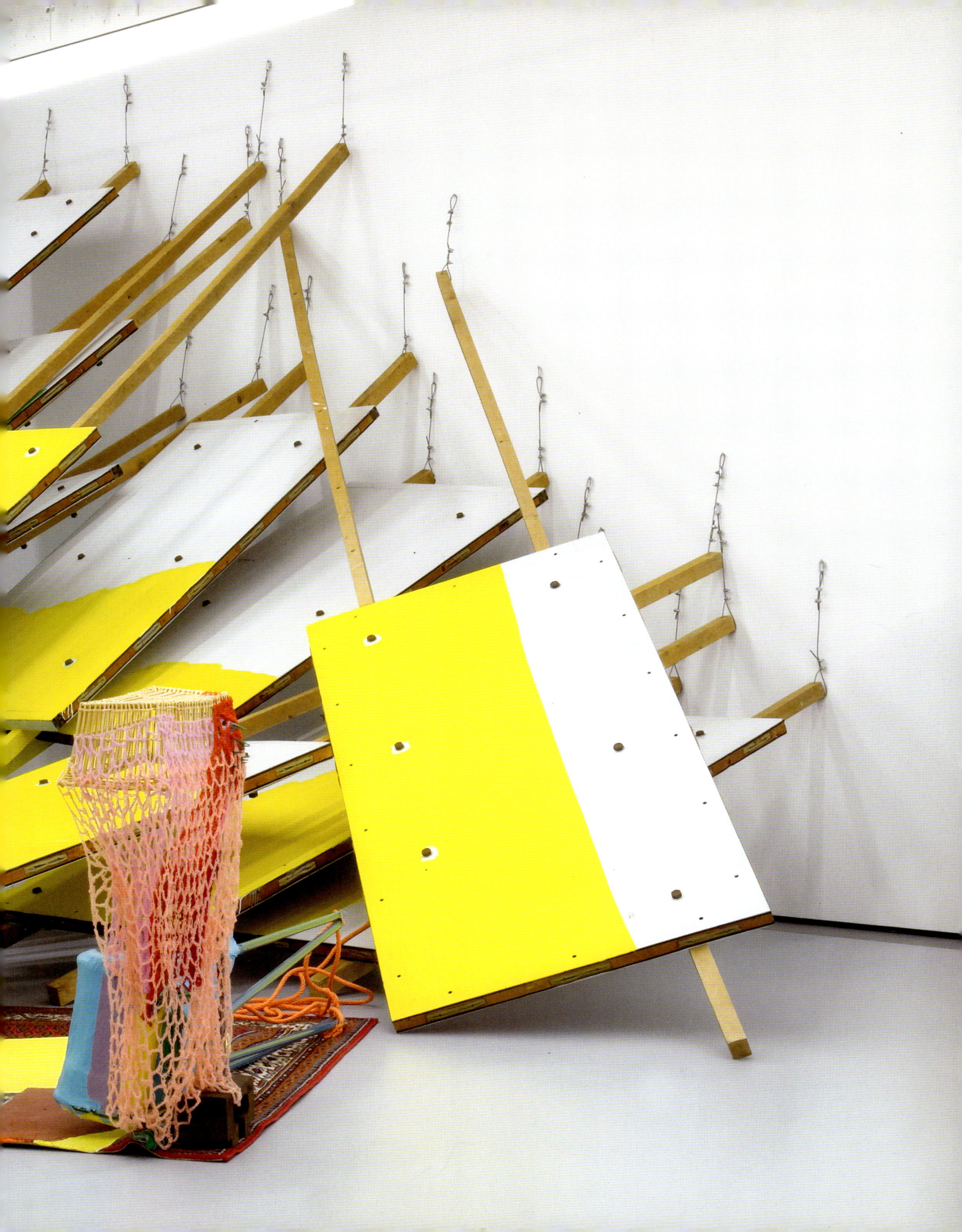

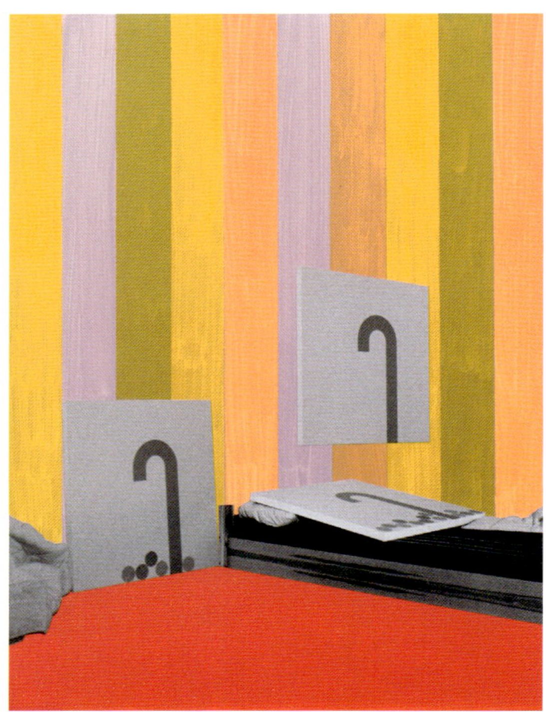

Christian Hutzinger
Ohne Titel (Untitled), 2004
Acryl auf Leinwand / Acrylic on canvas
40 x 30 cm
Erworben / Acquired in 2001

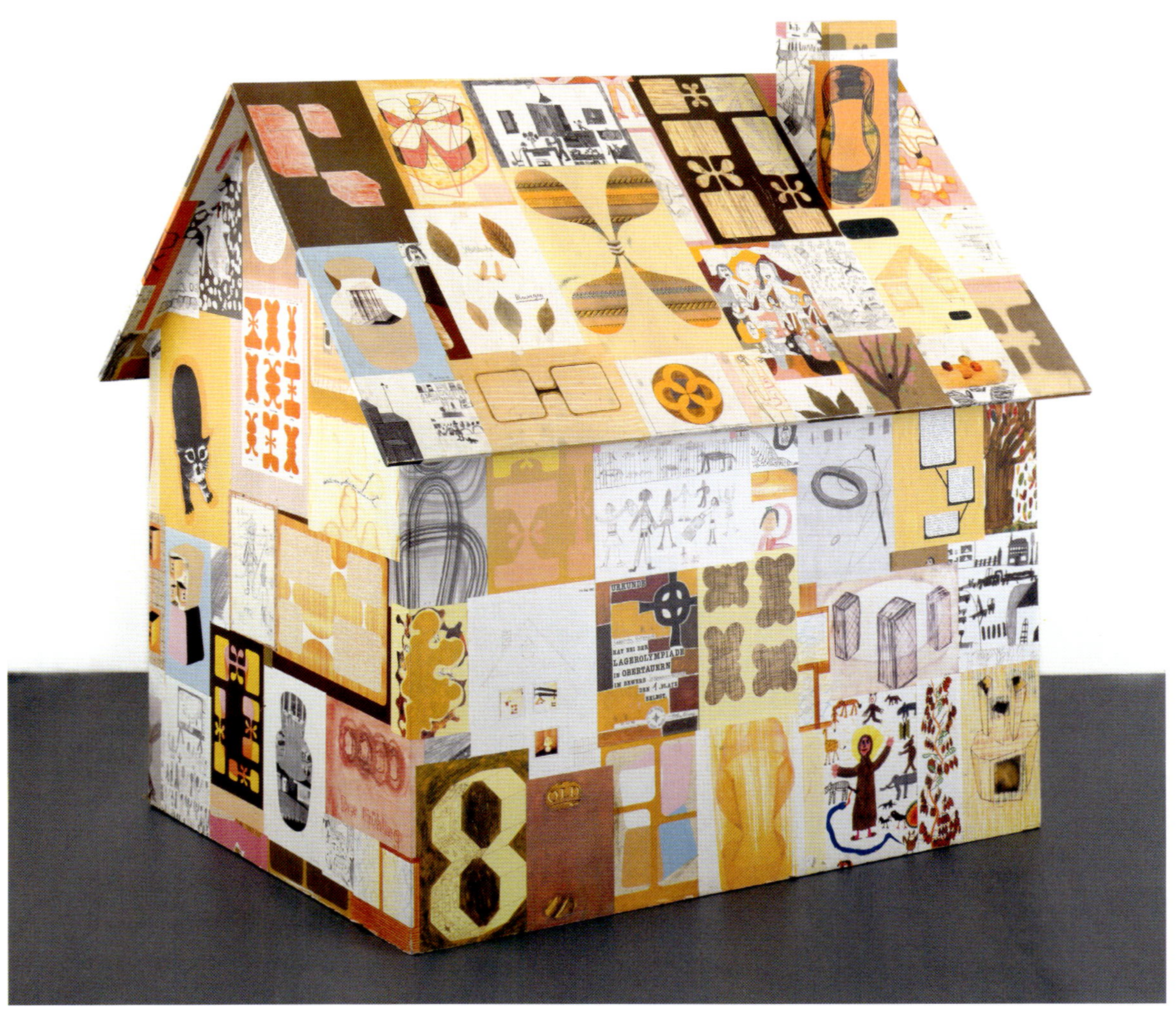

Christian Hutzinger
Mein Haus (My House), 1995
141 x 103 x 136 cm
Laserkopien auf Holz / Laser copies on wood
Erworben / Acquired in 2001

Reduktive Geometrien und Raumbezüge
Reductive Geometries and Spatial References

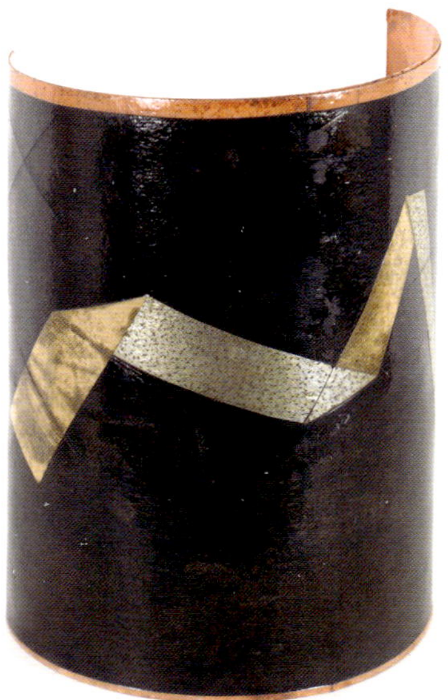

Hermann Glöckner
Dreimal gebrochener Keil auf Schwarz (Thrice Broken Wedge on Black), 1933–1935
Holz, Lack, Metall / Wood, lacquer, metal
17,5 x 12 x 9 cm
Erworben / Acquired in 1992

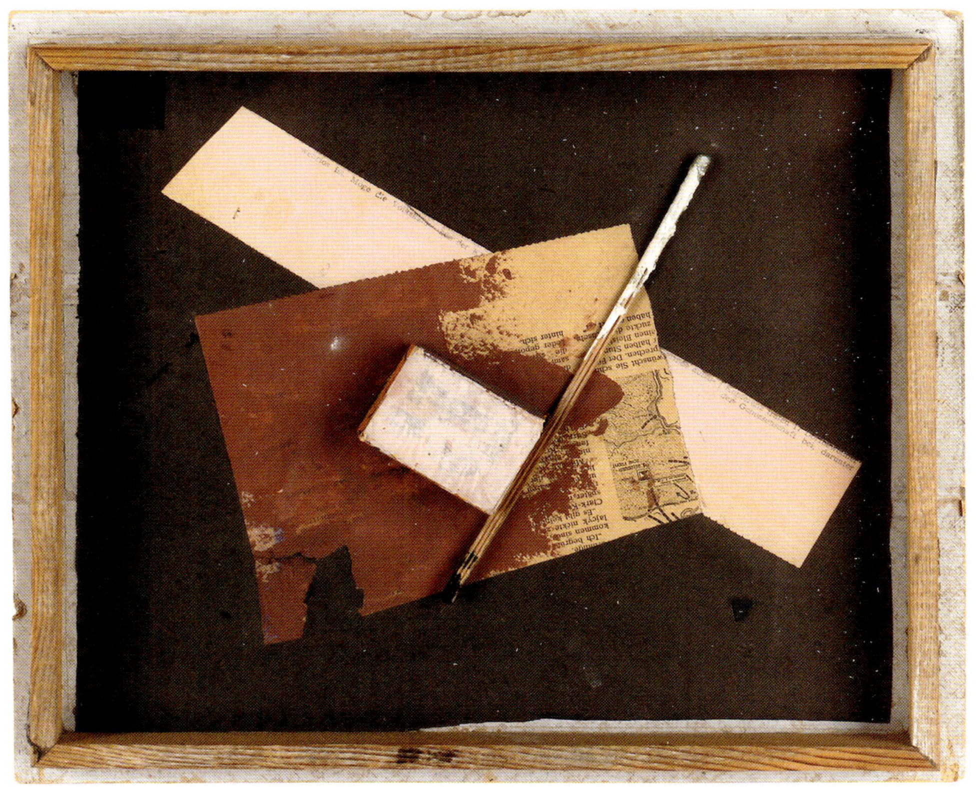

Hermann Glöckner
Materialbild (Material Picture), 1956
Farbe, Zeitungspapier, Streichholzschachtel, Holz
Paint, newsprint, match box, wood
26,7 x 32 x 4 cm
Erworben / Acquired in 1991

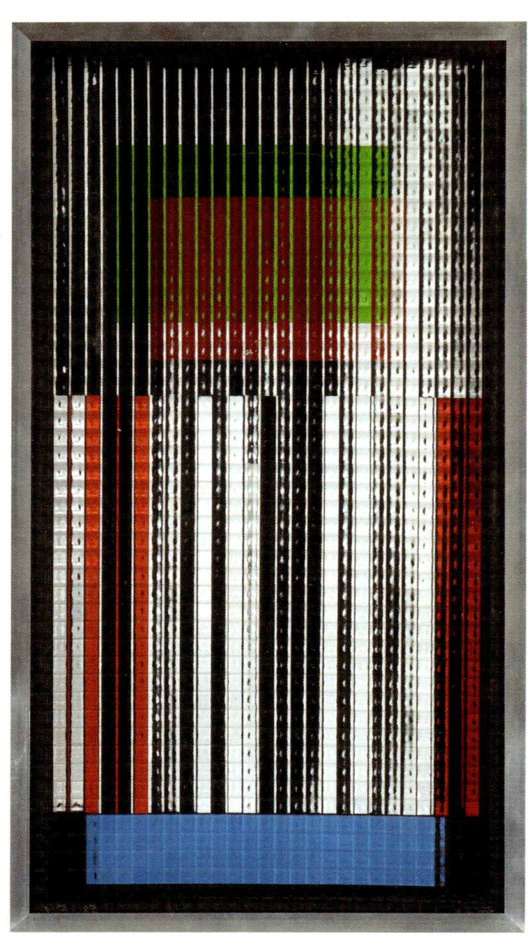

Marc Adrian
WV 15, 1958–1960
Hinterglasmontage / Montage behind glass
Holz, Glas, Ölfarbe / Wood, glass, oil paint
76 x 43,3 x 5,4 cm
Sammlung / Collection Dieter und Gertraud Bogner
im / at the MUMOK, seit / since 2007

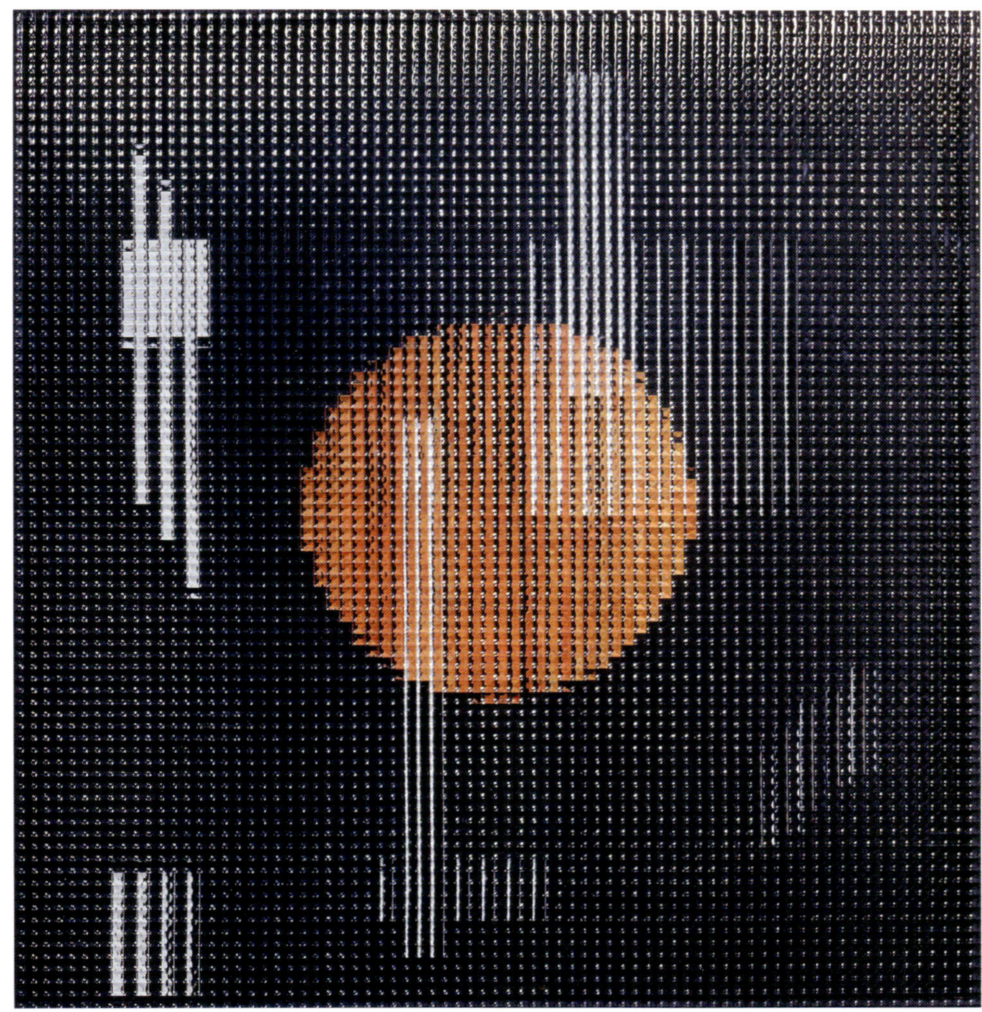

Marc Adrian
i 3, 1959–1961
Hinterglasmontage / Montage behind glass
Holz, Glas, Metallfolien / Wood, glass, metal foils
108 x 101,2 x 5 cm
Leihgabe der Artothek des Bundes /
On loan from the Artothek des Bundes, seit / since 1962

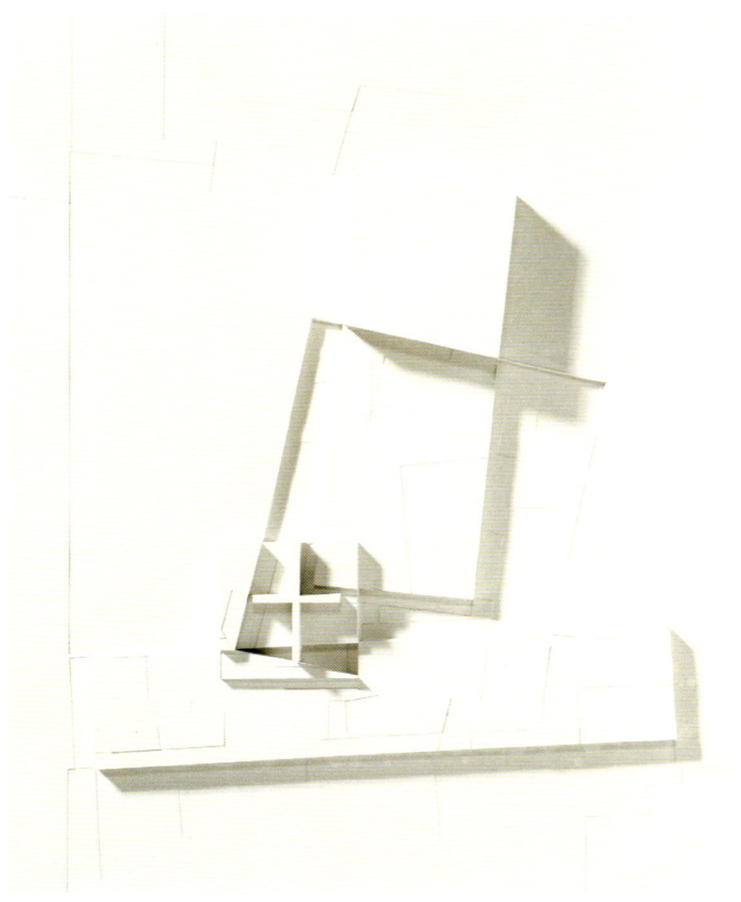

György Jovánovics
Hommage à Moholy Nagy Q-VIII, 1996
Gips / Plaster
95,5 x 76,3 x 10 cm
Erworben / Acquired in 1996

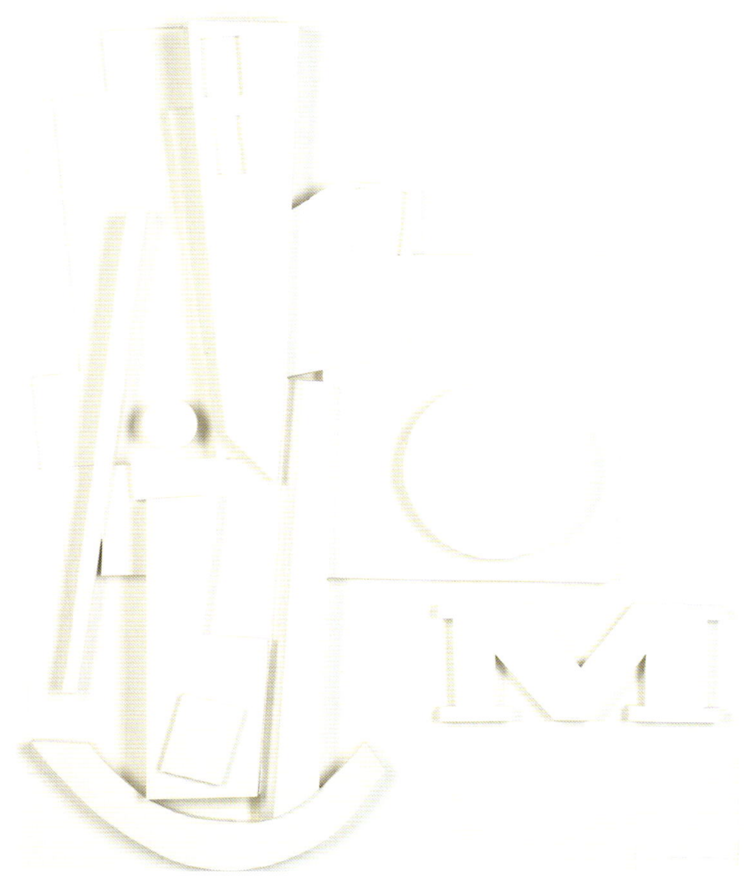

György Jovánovics
Kassák I., 1996
Gips / Plaster
96,5 x 78,5 x 11 cm
Schenkung der Gesellschaft der Freunde der bildenden Künste
Donated by the Society of the Friends of Fine Arts, Wien / Vienna, 2001

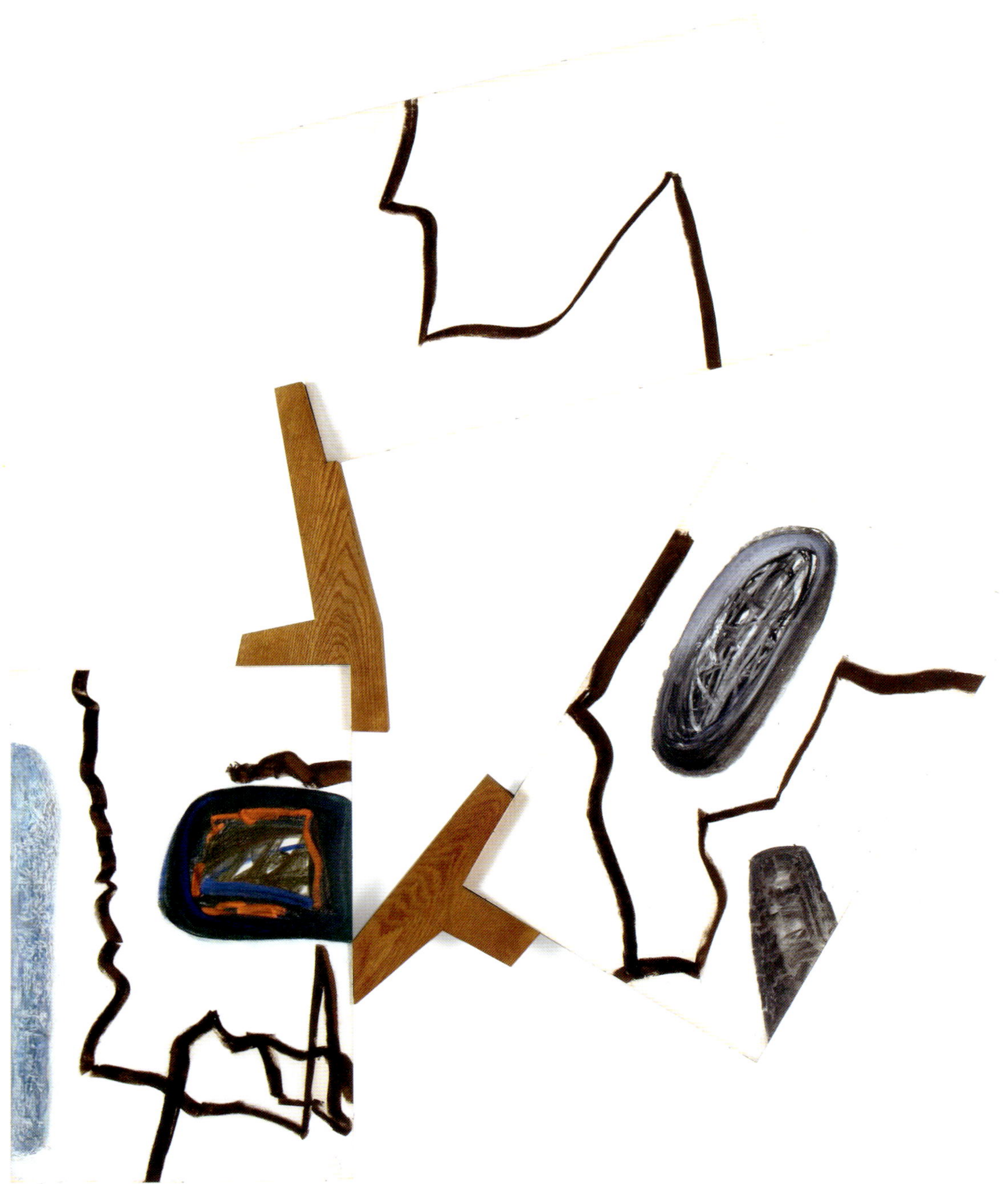

Friedrich Kiesler
Galaxy F (Galaxie F), 1960
Gouache, Kohle und Pastell auf Papier, auf Karton und Holz montiert
Gouache, charcoal, and pastel on paper, mounted on cardboard and wood
198 x 163 x 17,5 cm
Erworben / Acquired in 1988

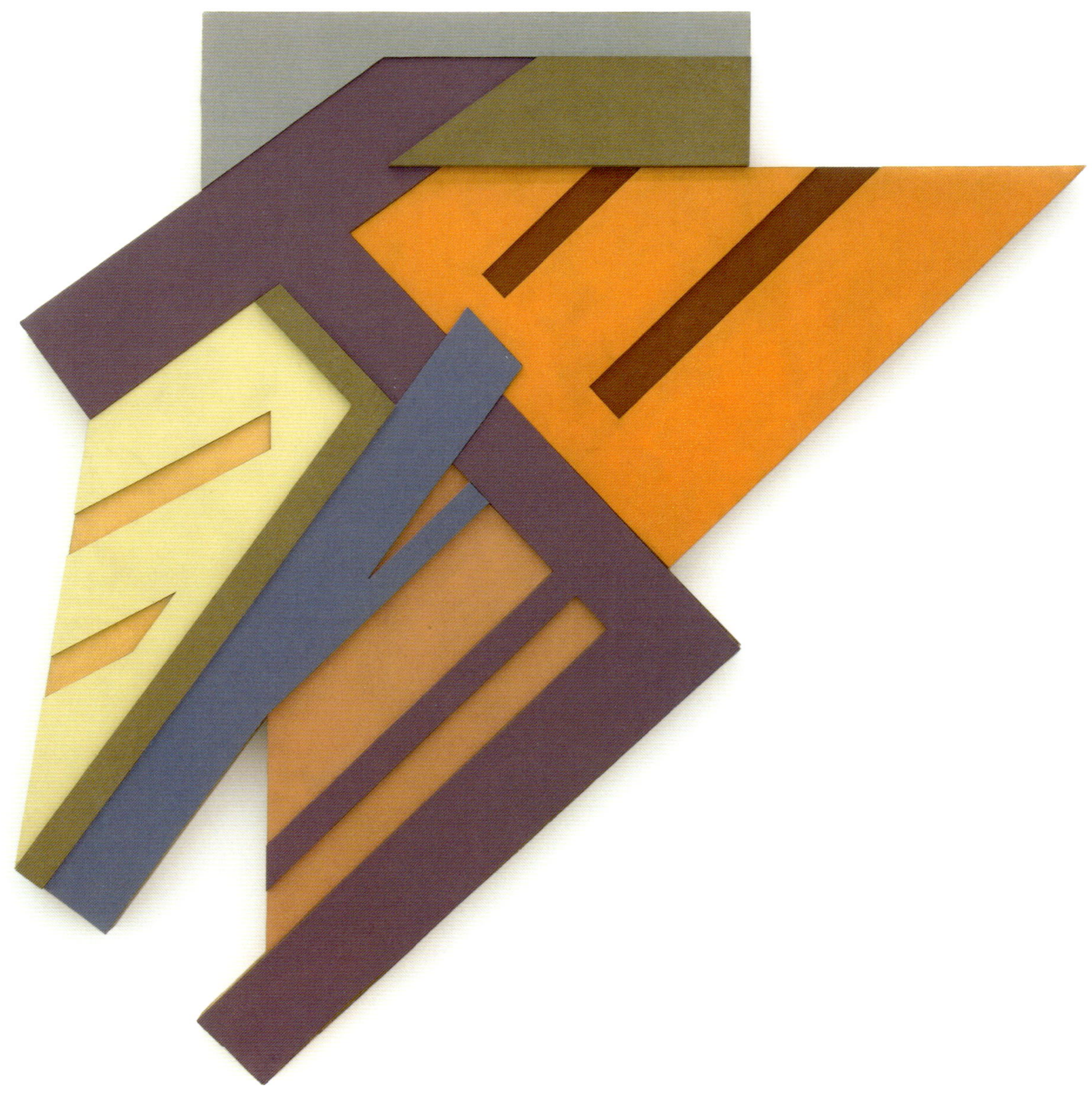

Frank Stella
Lipsko II, 1972
Mischtechnik / Mixed media
249 x 238,5 cm
Leihgabe der Österreichischen Ludwig-Stiftung
On loan from the Austrian Ludwig Foundation, seit / since 1998

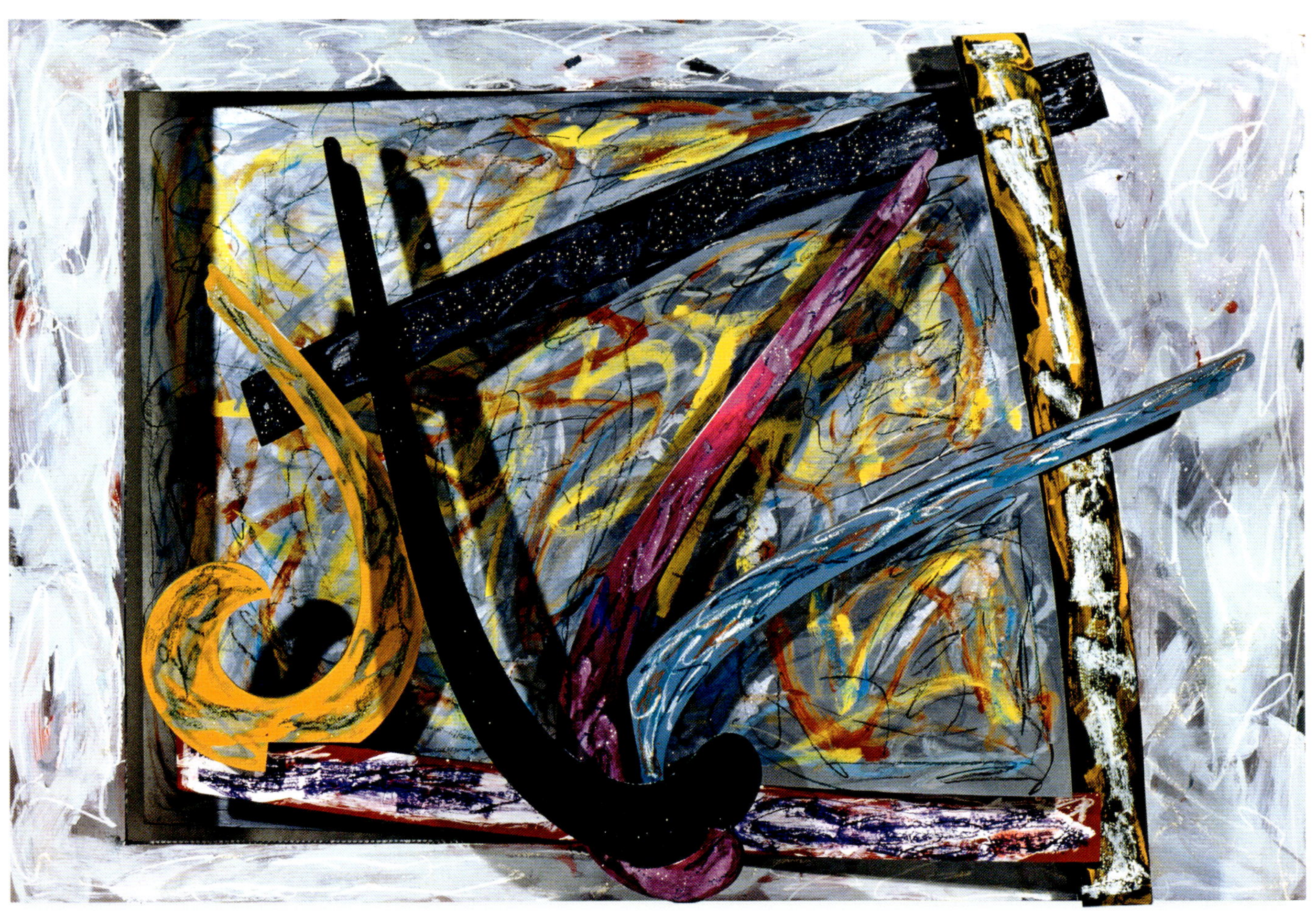

Frank Stella
Newells Hawaiian Clearwater, 1976
Kunstharzlack auf Aluminium / Acrylic lacquer on aluminum
152 x 214 x 27 cm
Leihgabe der Österreichischen Ludwig Stiftung
On loan from the Austrian Ludwig Foundation, seit / since 1991

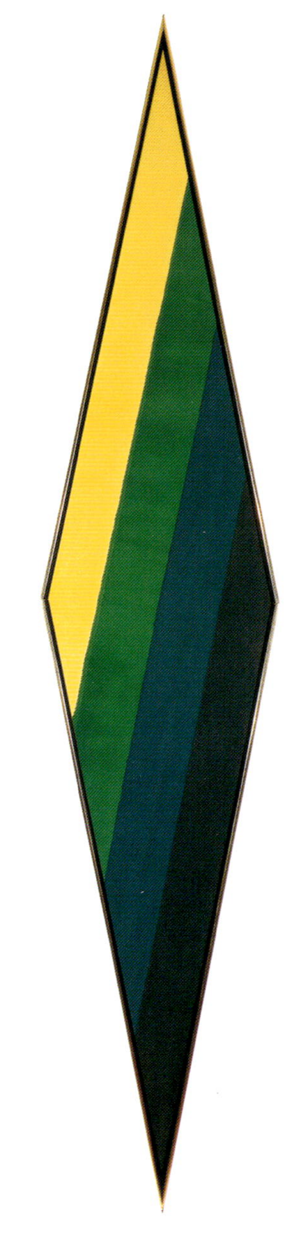

Kenneth Noland
Thaw (Das Auftauen), 1966
Acryl auf Leinwand / Acrylic on canvas
255 x 49 cm
Erworben / Acquired in 1993

Kenneth Noland
Eternal Scholar (Ewiger Student), 1969
Acryl auf Leinwand / Acrylic on canvas
163 x 397 x 4 cm
Erworben / Acquired in 1996

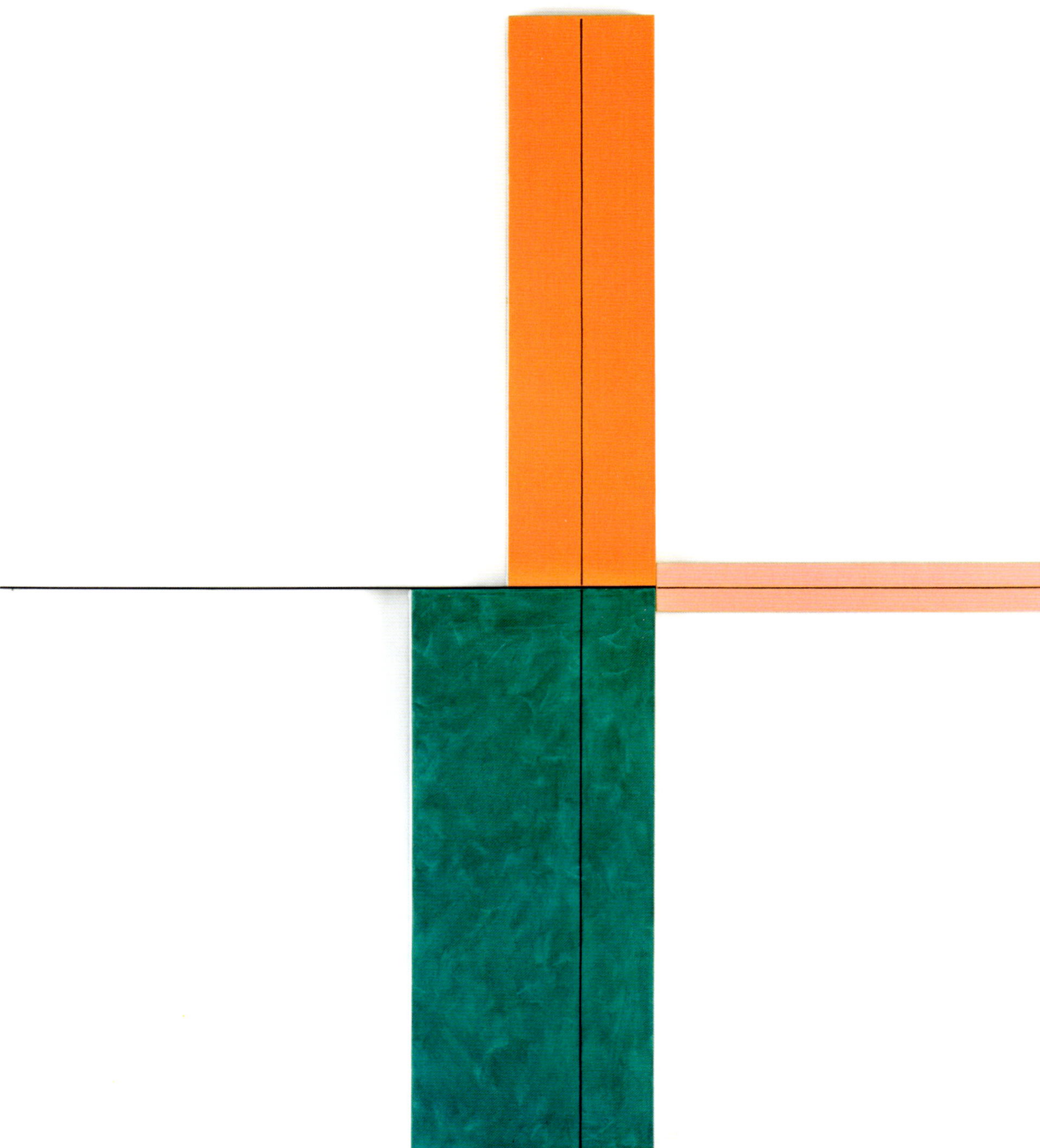

234

Robert Mangold
Plus Minus Painting (Plus Minus Bild), 1982
Acryl auf Leinwand, Aluminium / Acrylic on canvas, aluminum
304 x 323 x 3,5 cm
Erworben / Acquired in 1985

Hartmut Böhm
Paraliel, Innen – Außen I (Parallel, Inside – Outside), 1981/1982
Lasur auf Holzfaserplatte / Glaze on wood fiberboard
100 x 250 x 1,8 cm
Sammlung / Collection Dieter und Gertraud Bogner
im / at the MUMOK, seit / since 2007

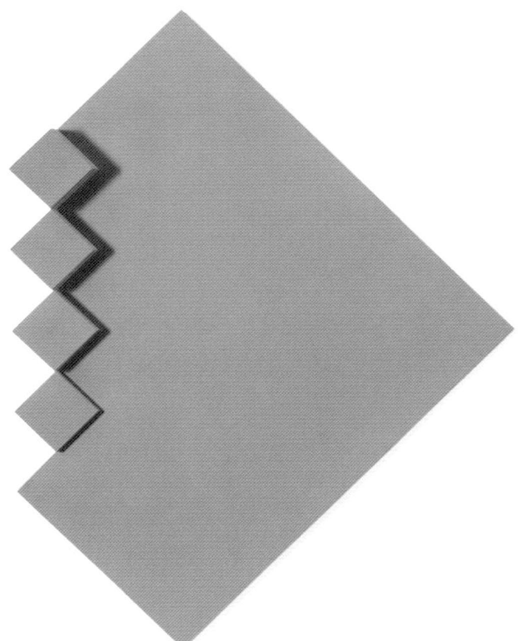

Peter Lowe
Ohne Titel (Untitled), 1976
Acryl auf Holzfaserplatte / Acrylic on wood fiberboard
50,8 x 50,8 x 7,9 cm
Sammlung / Collection Dieter und Gertraud Bogner
im / at the MUMOK, seit / since 2007

Peter Lowe
Ohne Titel (Untitled), 1978
Acryl auf Holzfaserplatte / Acrylic on wood fiberboard
50,2 x 50,2 x 7,9 cm
Sammlung / Collection Dieter und Gertraud Bogner
im / at the MUMOK, seit / since 2007

Ohne Titel (Untitled), 1979
Acryl auf Holzfaserplatte / Acrylic on wood fiberboard
50,8 x 50,8 x 7,9 cm
Sammlung / Collection Dieter und Gertraud Bogner
im / at the MUMOK, seit / since 2007

Jo Baer
Tenebrosa, 1971
Acryl auf Leinwand / Acrylic on canvas
55 x 245 cm
Leihgabe der Österreichischen Ludwig-Stiftung
On loan from the Austrian Ludwig Foundation, seit / since 1981

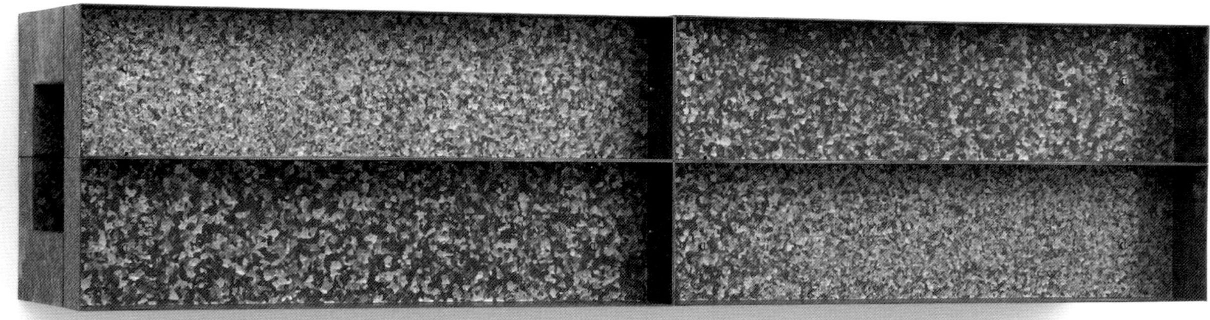

Donald Judd
Ohne Titel (Untitled), 1989
Verzinktes Blech / Galvanized tin
30 x 121 x 30 cm
Erworben / Acquired in 1995

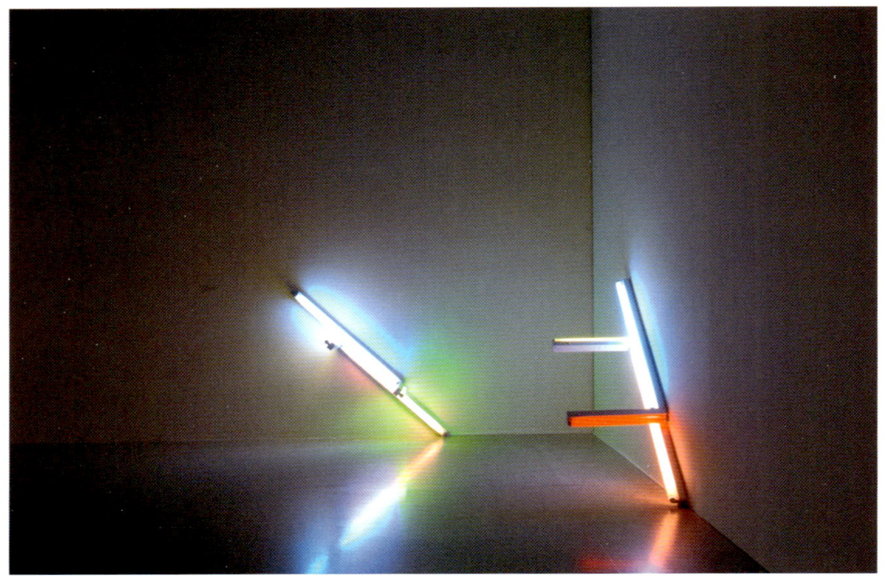

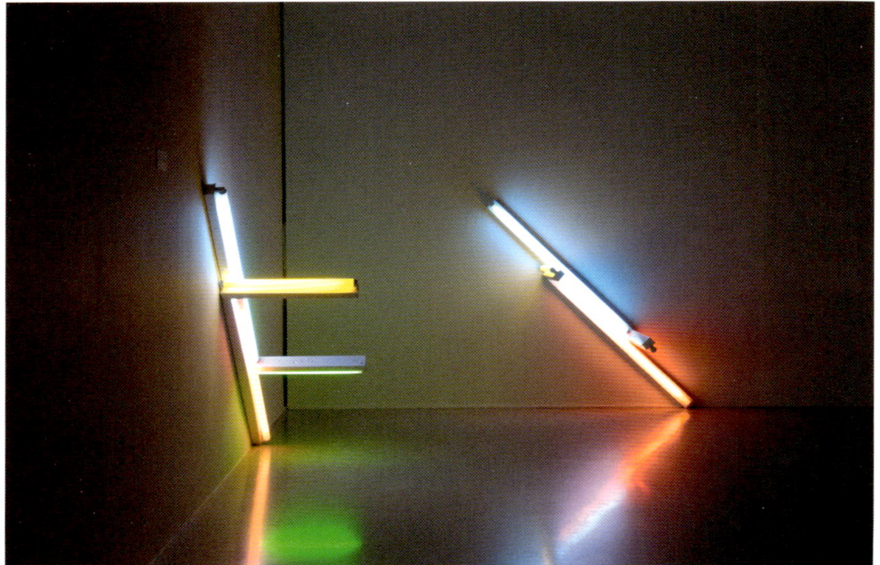

Dan Flavin
Untitled (To my friend De Wain Valentine)
Ohne Titel (Für meinen Freund De Wain Valentine), 1990
Neonröhren, Metall / Neon lights, metal
140 x 140 x 62 cm
Erworben / Acquired in 1993

Untitled (To my friend De Wain Valentine)
Ohne Titel (Für meinen Freund De Wain Valentine), 1990
Neonröhren, Metall / Neon lights, metal
140 x 140 x 62 cm
Erworben / Acquired in 1993

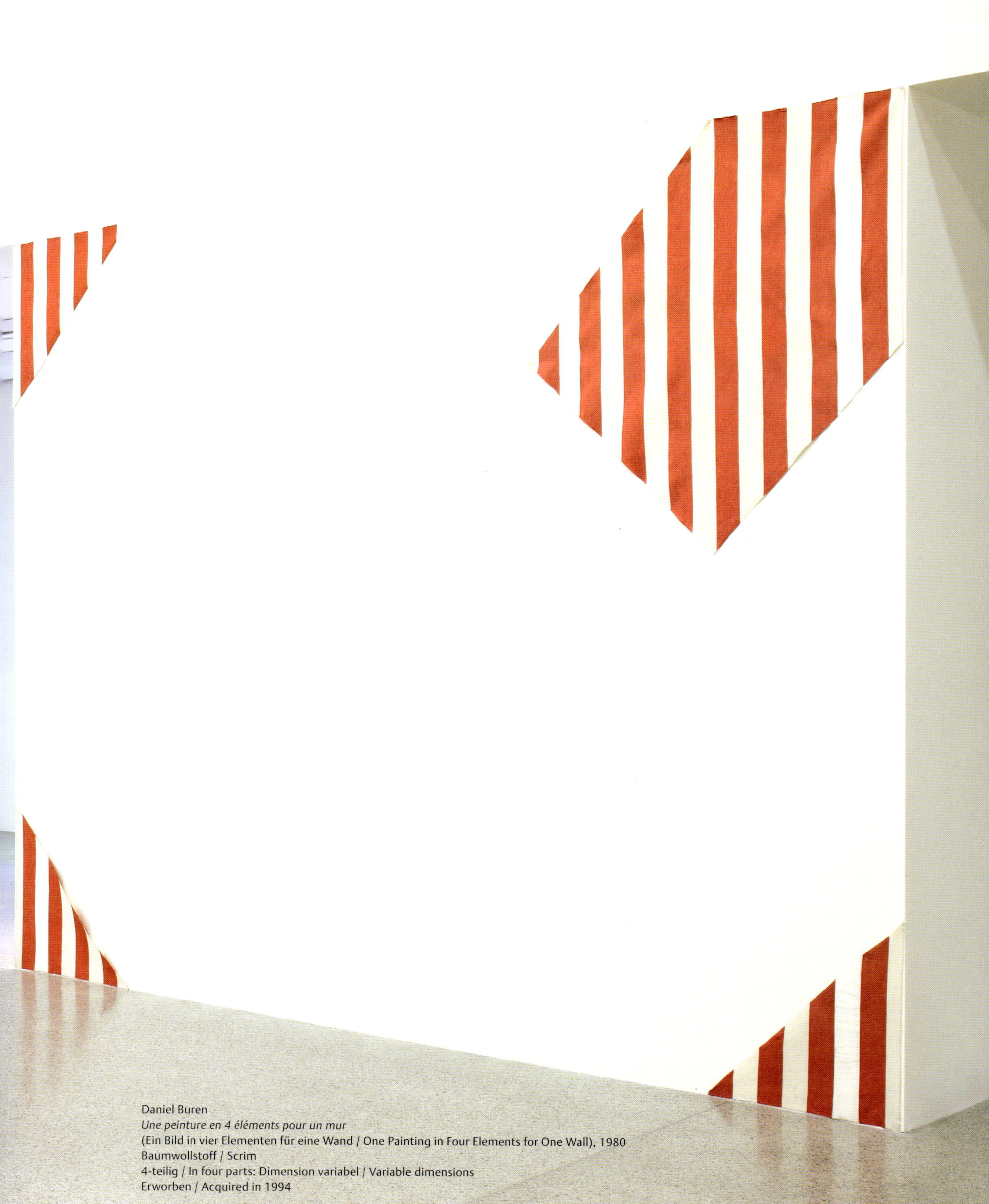

Daniel Buren
Une peinture en 4 éléments pour un mur
(Ein Bild in vier Elementen für eine Wand / One Painting in Four Elements for One Wall), 1980
Baumwollstoff / Scrim
4-teilig / In four parts: Dimension variabel / Variable dimensions
Erworben / Acquired in 1994

Alan Charlton
Painting in 20 Parts (Bild in 20 Teilen), 1990
Acryl auf Leinwand / Acrylic on canvas
153 x 625 cm
Erworben / Acquired in 1992

Karel Malich
Schwarzes Relief (Black Relief), 1968/1969
Lack, Kunststoff auf Holz / Lacquer, plastic on wood
90 x 64 x 8 cm
Erworben / Acquired in 1994

Karel Malich
Modrý koridor (Blauer Korridor / Blue Corridor), 1966
Lack auf Holz / Lacquer on wood
95 x 158 x 8 cm
Erworben / Acquired in 2002

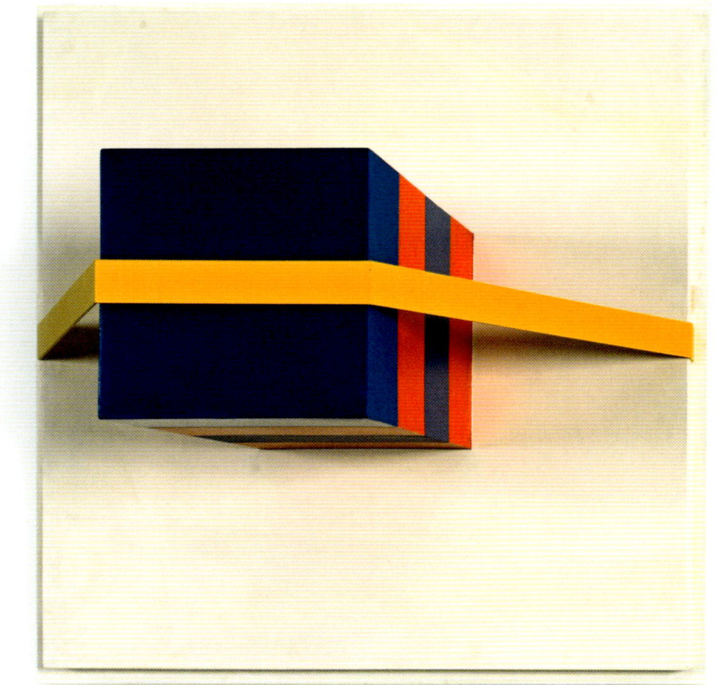

Roland Goeschl
Farbformumklammerung (Colored Object in a Clinch), 1975
Kunststein, Metall, Kunstharzlack / Artificial stone, metal, acrylic lacquer
100 x 100 x 70 cm
Leihgabe der Artothek des Bundes
On loan from the Artothek des Bundes, seit / since 1979

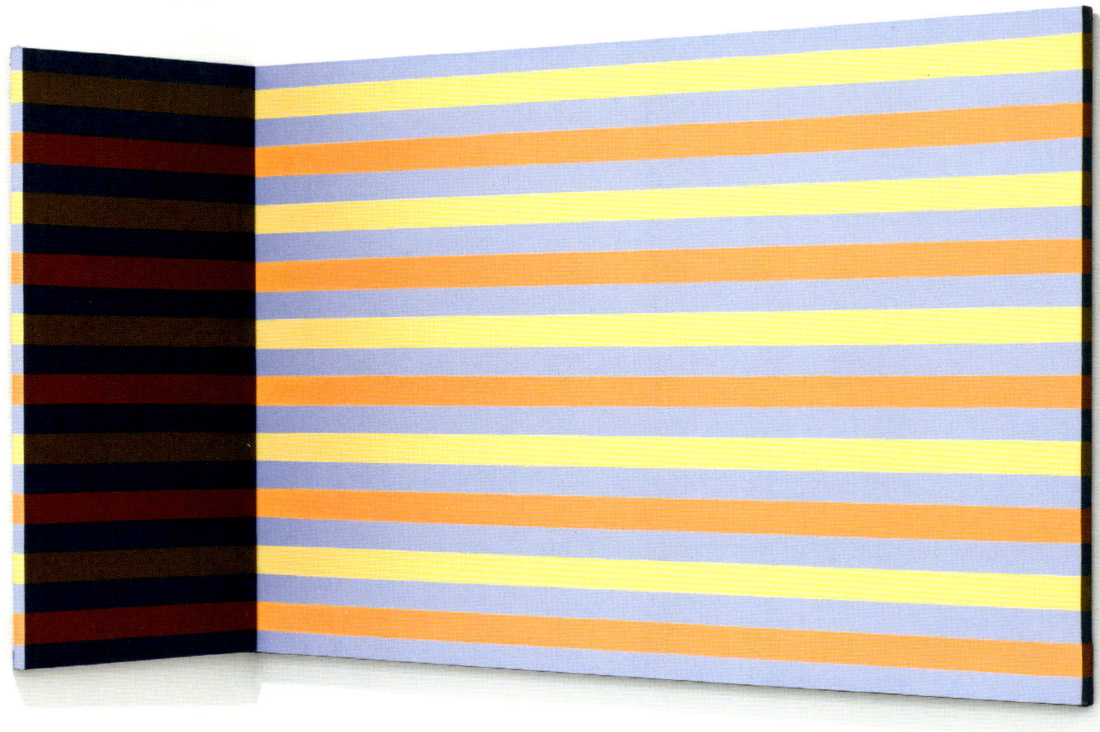

Jorrit Tornquist
Licht und Schatten (Light and Shadow), 1979
Acryl auf Leinwand / Acrylic on canvas
80 x 132,1 x 40 cm
Sammlung / Collection Dieter und Gertraud Bogner
im / at the MUMOK, seit / since 2007

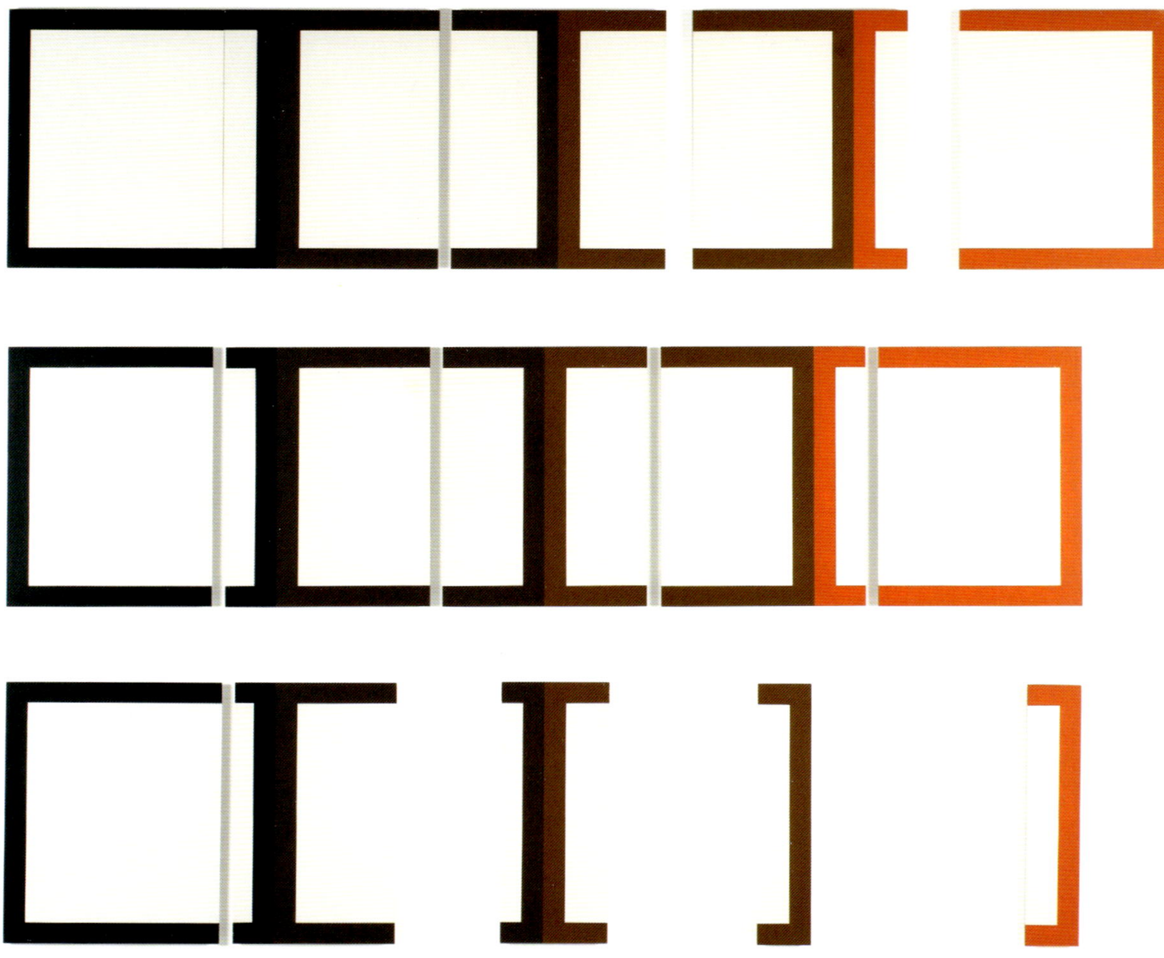

Dóra Maurer
4-ből 5 (5 aus 4 / 5 out of 4), 1978
Acryl auf Spanplatte / Acrylic on particle board
180 x 208,5 x 2,8 cm
Sammlung / Collection Dieter und Gertraud Bogner
im / at the MUMOK, seit / since 2007

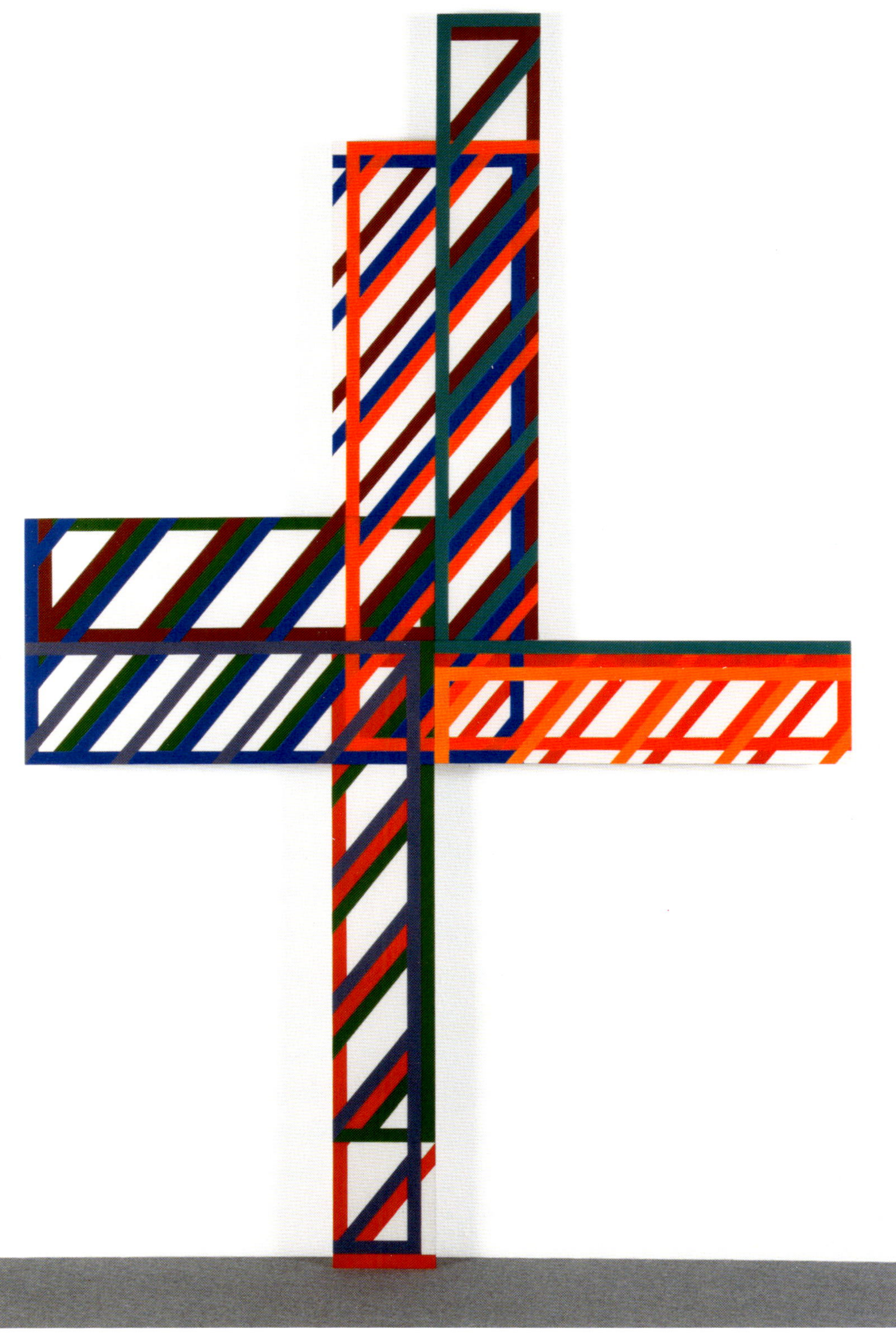

Dóra Maurer
Kvázi-kép No. 86 (Quasi-Bild Nr. 86 / Quasi-Image No. 86), 1983
Acryl auf Spanplatte / Acrylic on particle board
200 x 128 x 4 cm
Sammlung / Collection Dieter und Gertraud Bogner
im / at the MUMOK, seit / since 2007

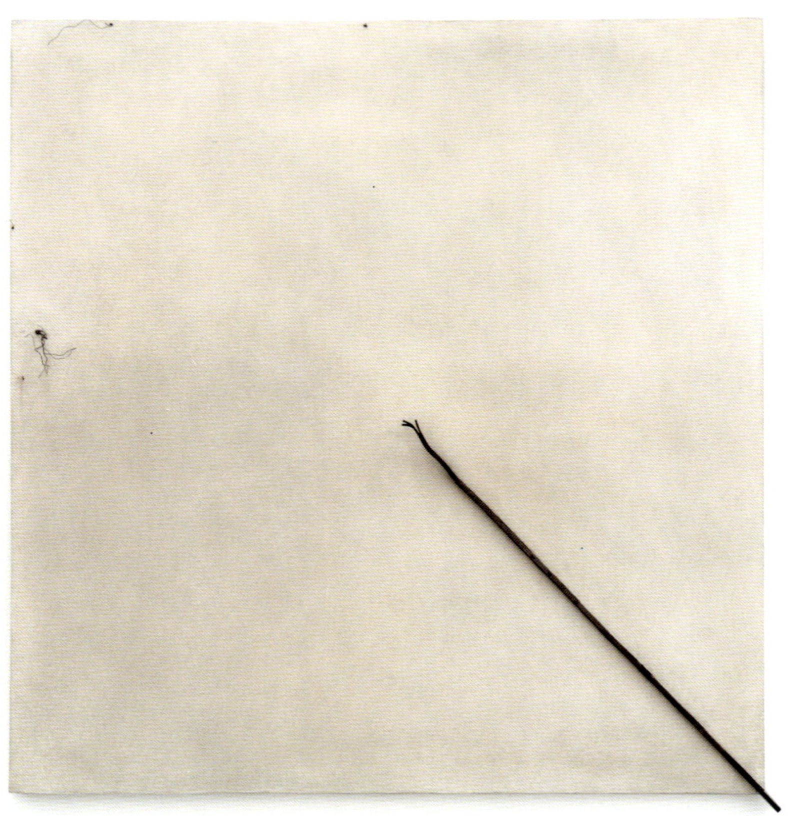

Stanislav Kolíbal
A Travers, 1974
Gips, Draht, Eisen und Faden auf Holz
Plaster, wire, iron and thread on wood
83 x 77,3 x 8 cm
Sammlung / Collection Dieter und Gertraud Bogner
im / at the MUMOK, seit / since 2007

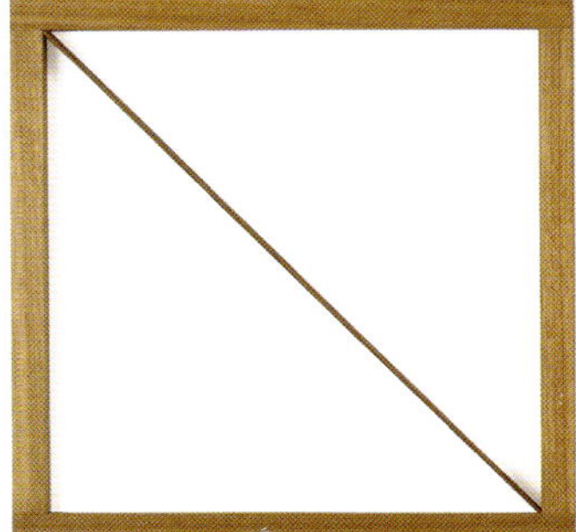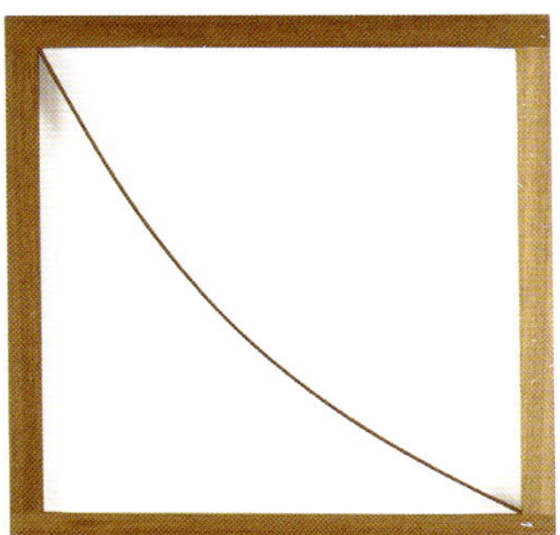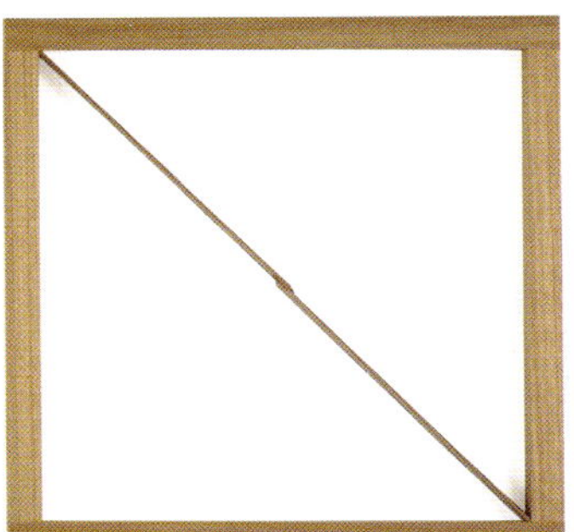

José Bréval
50:49:49, 1980
Holz / Wood
3-teilig / In three parts: 50 x 50 cm, 49 x 49 cm, 49 x 49 cm
Sammlung / Collection Dieter und Gertraud Bogner
im / at the MUMOK, seit / since 2007

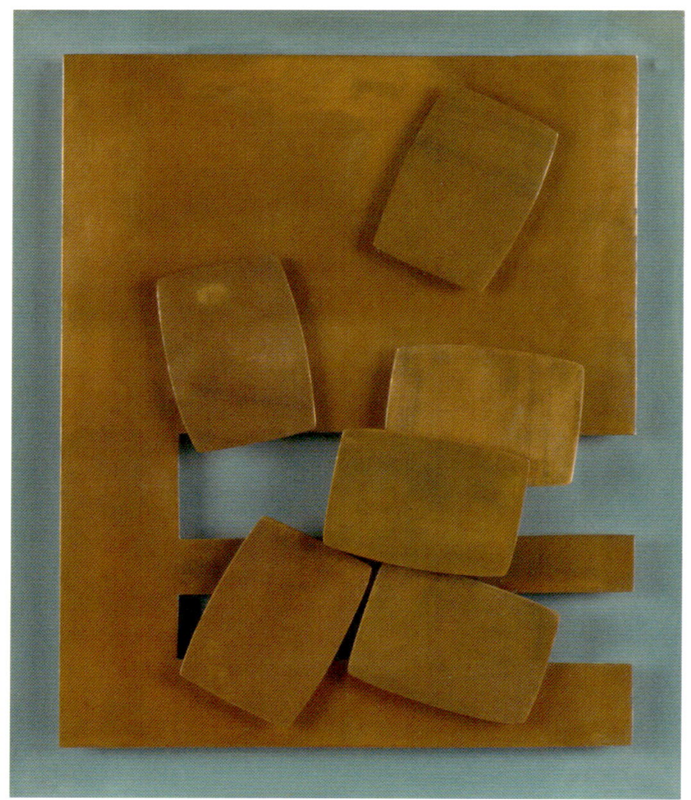

Henryk Stażewski
Relief, 1965
Kupfer, Holzplatte, Acryl / Copper, wooden board, acrylic
45 x 37 x 2 cm
Erworben / Acquired in 1992

François Morellet
Défiguration (nach Tizians Kirschenmadonna), 1989
Grundierung auf Leinwand auf Holz / Primer on canvas on wood
250 x 210 x 4,5 cm
Sammlung / Collection Dieter und Gertraud Bogner
im / at the MUMOK, seit / since 2007

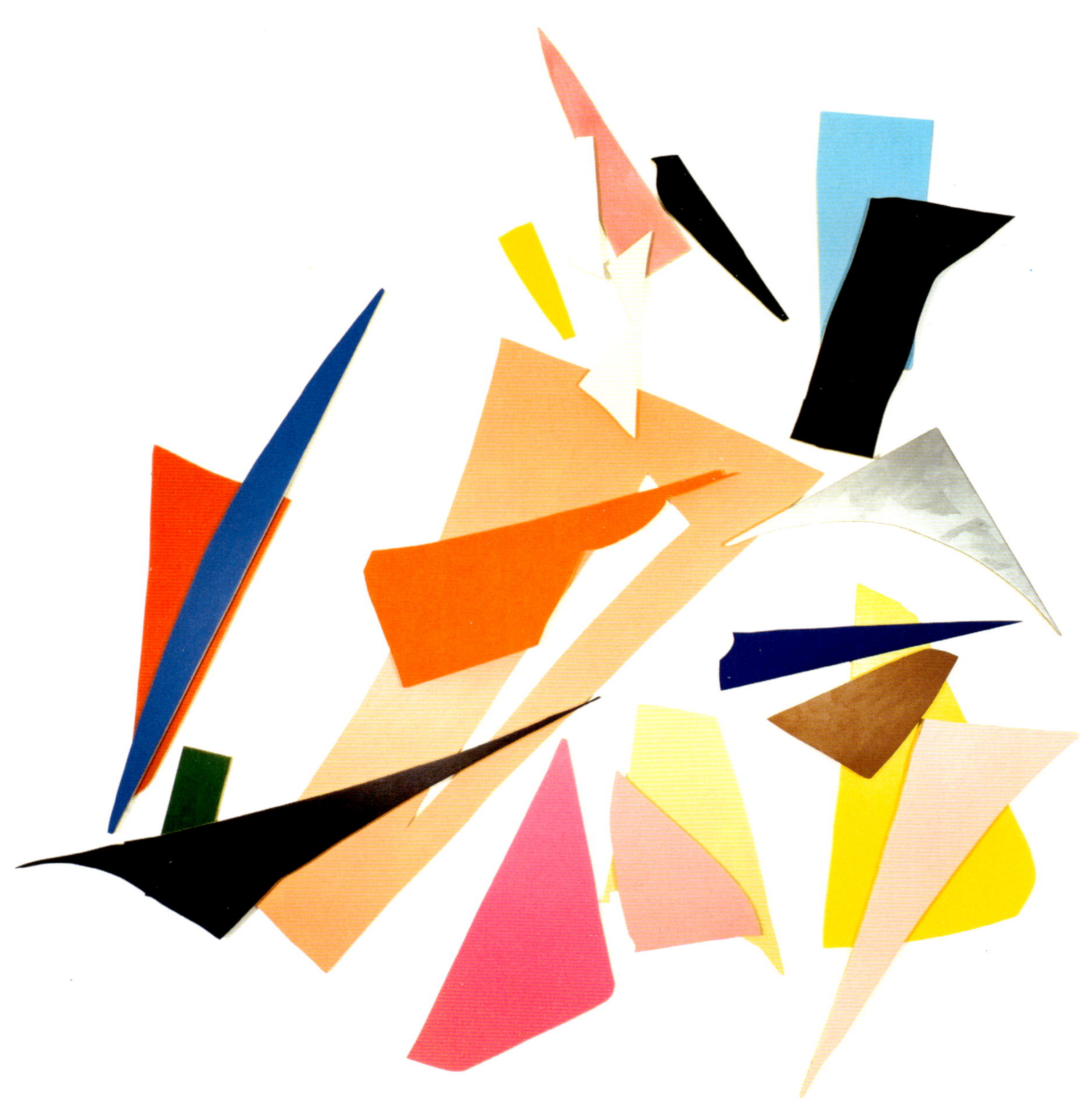

Imi Knoebel
Ohne Titel (Untitled), 1978
Acryl auf Holz / Acrylic on wood
360 x 340 x 6 cm
Leihgabe der Österreichischen Ludwig-Stiftung
On loan from the Austrian Ludwig Foundation
seit / since 1981

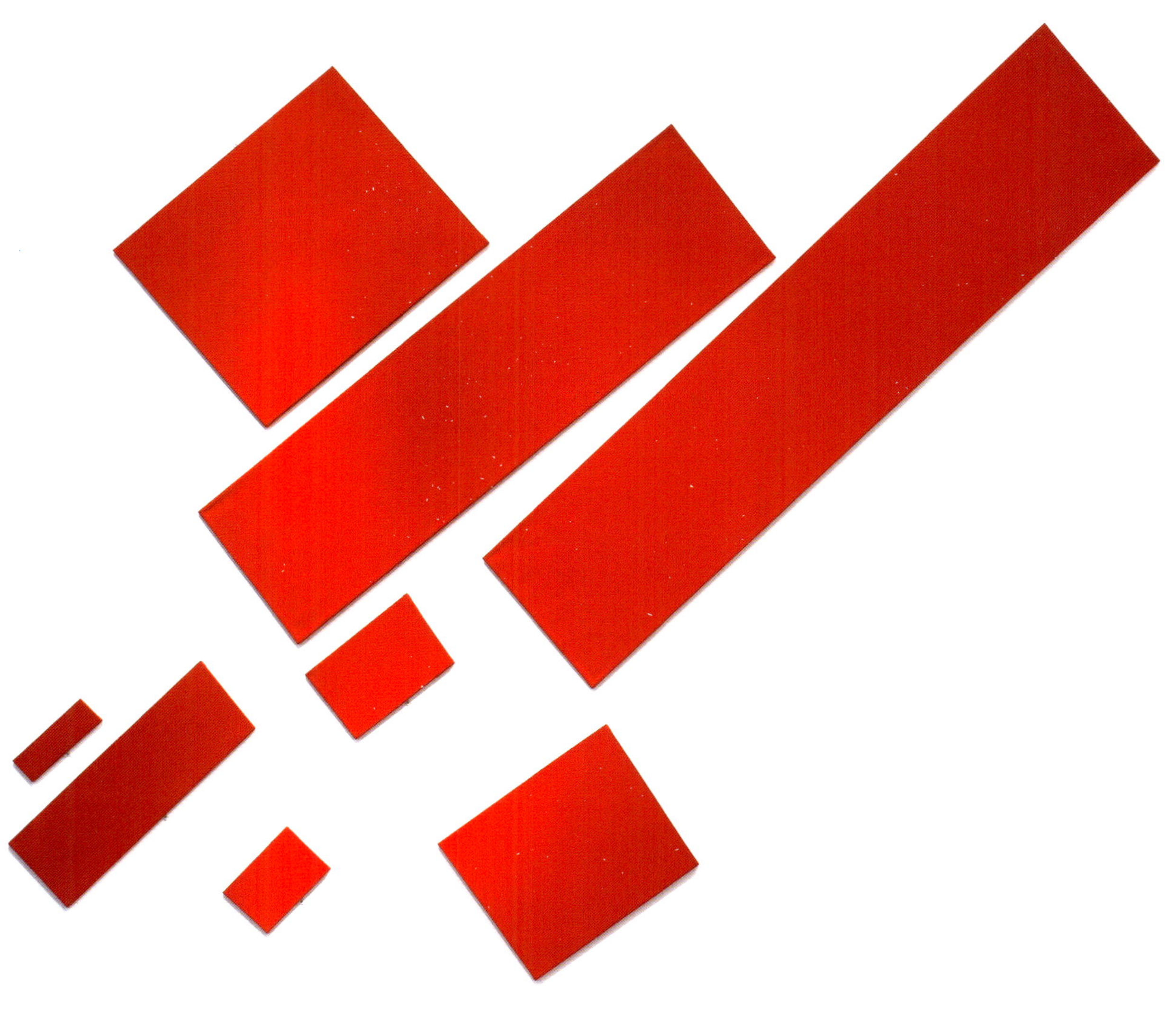

Claudio Parmiggiani
Otto idee rosse (Vienna rossa)
(Acht rote Ideen [Rotes Wien] / Eight Red Ideas [Red Vienna]), 1976
Öl auf Leinwand / Oil on canvas
350 x 350 cm
Erworben / Acquired in 1988

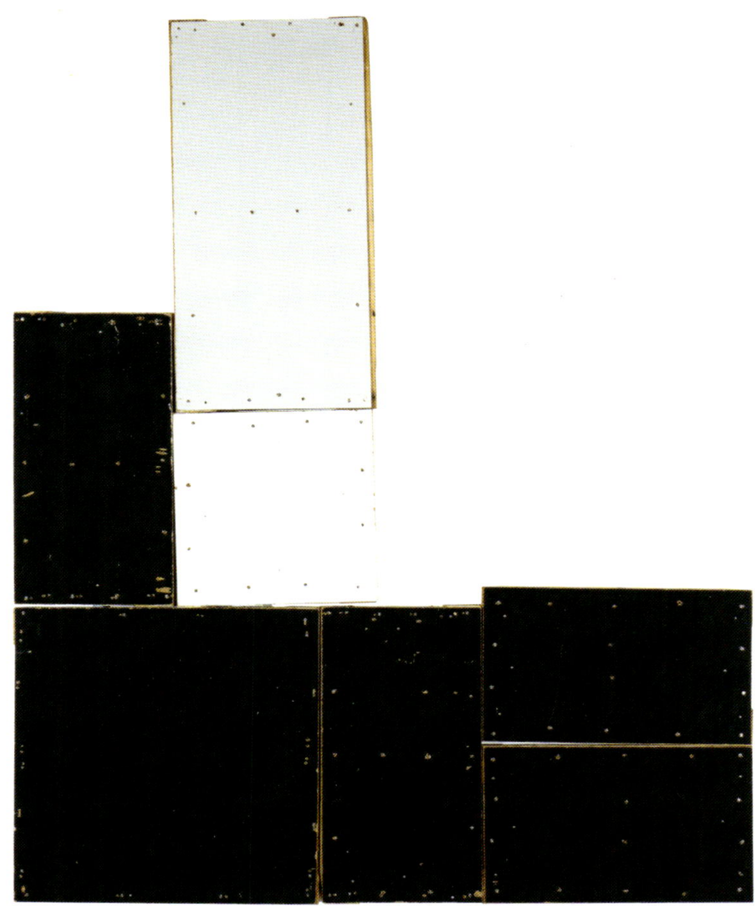

Jirí Kovanda
Ohne Titel (Untitled), 1991
Kunststoff auf Holz / Plastic on wood
130 x 110 x 3 cm
Erworben / Acquired in 1999

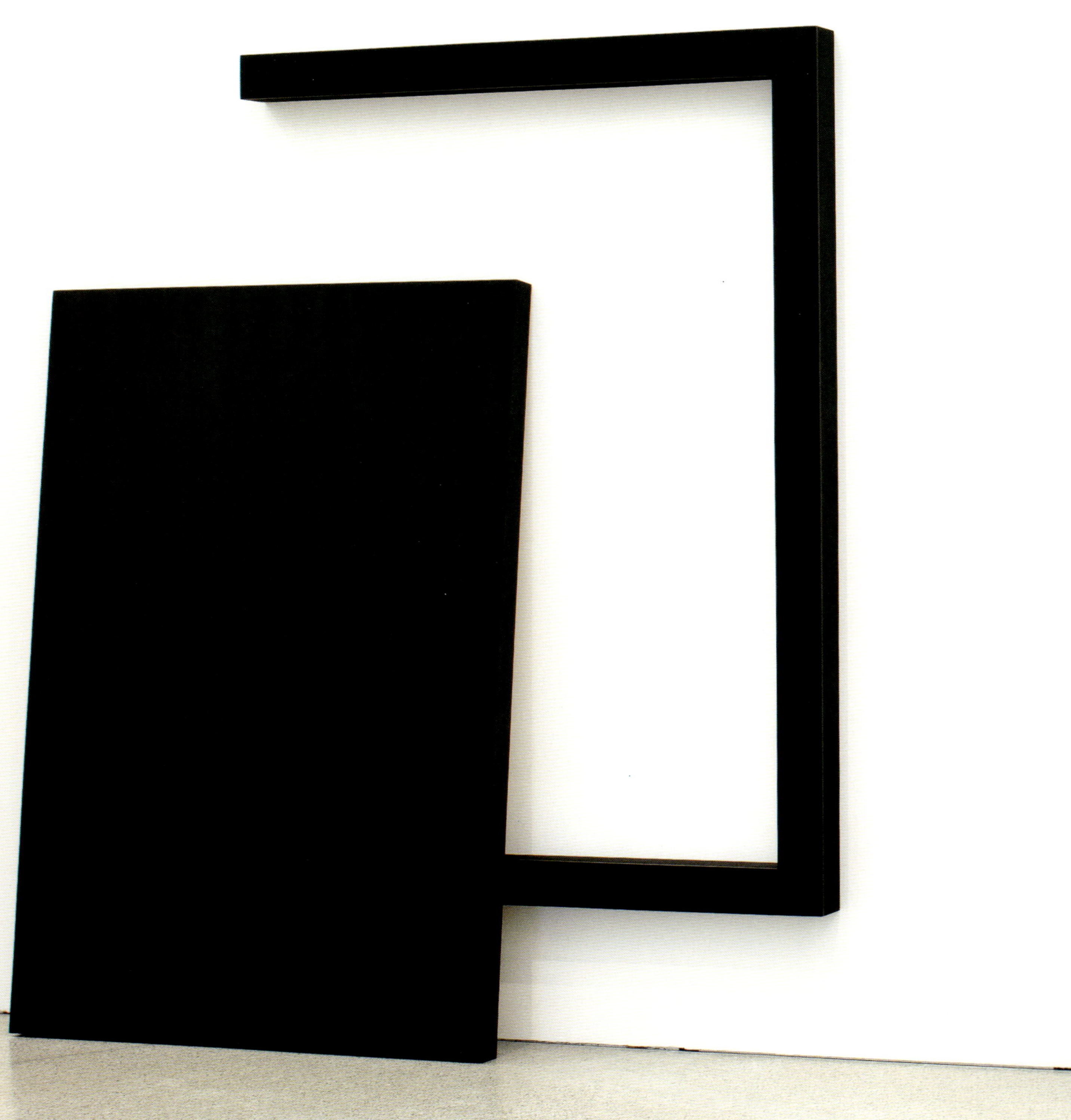

Heinrich Dunst
Ohne Titel (Untitled), 1996
Acryl auf Leinwand auf Sperrholz / Acrylic on canvas on plywood
4-teilig / In four parts: 225 x 160 x 12 cm, 201 x 136 x 8 cm, 215 x 45 x 45 cm, 75 x 60 x 10 cm
Erworben / Acquired in 1998

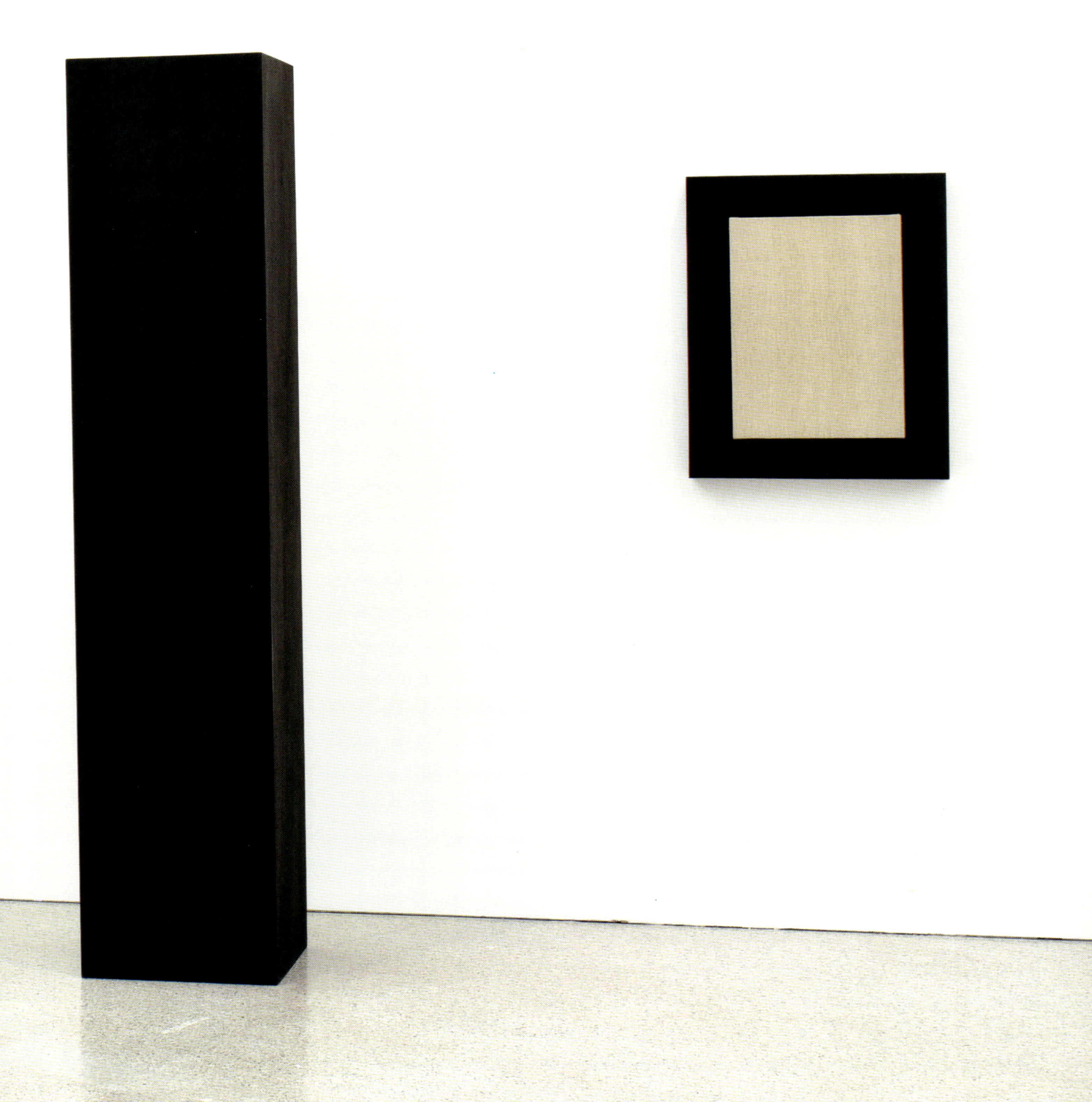

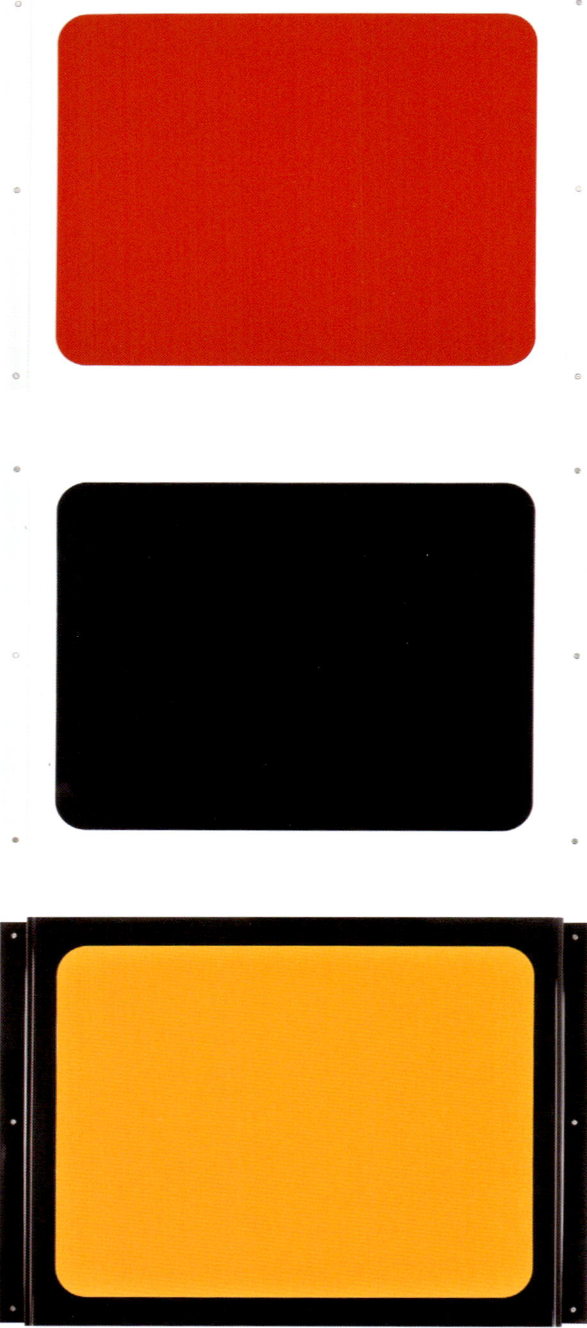

Gerwald Rockenschaub
2002
Acrylglasobjekte in verschiedenen Farben, Metallschrauben, Beilagscheiben
Acrylic glass objects in various colors, metal screws, washers
Je / each 110 x 150 x 8 cm
Erworben mit Unterstützung der Kommunalkredit AG
Acquired with funding from the Kommunalkredit AG, 2004

Gerwald Rockenschaub
1992
Farblose, transparente Acrylglasplatte, Metallschrauben, Beilagscheiben
Colorless, transparent acrylic glass sheet, metal screws, washers
205 x 304 x 6 cm
Erworben / Acquired in 1992

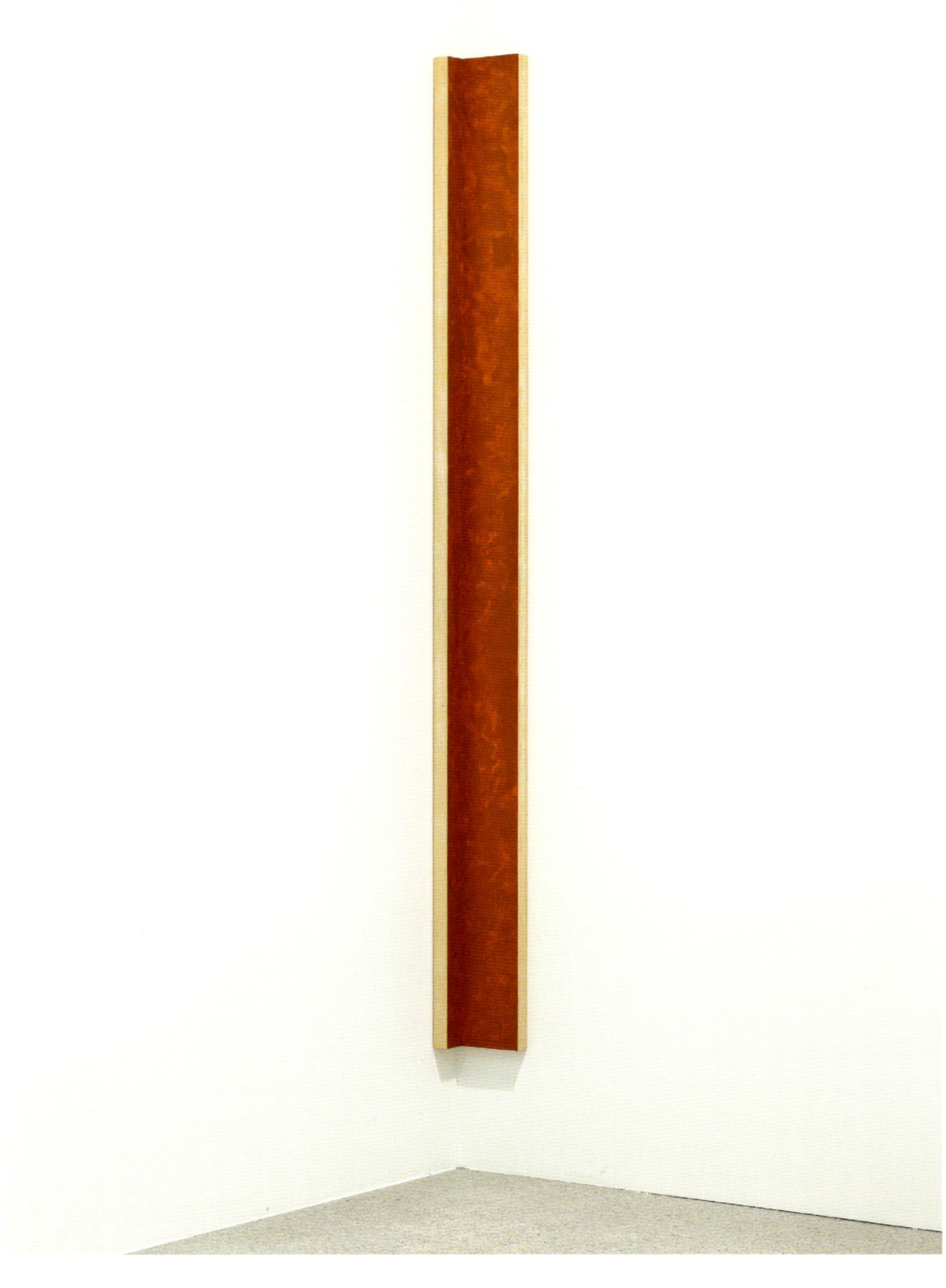

Leo Zogmayer
Rot (Red), 1998
Acryl auf Sperrholz / Acrylic on plywood
241 x 20 x 4 cm
Erworben / Acquired in 2000

Christian Eckart
Curved Monochrome Painting # 2003
(Geschwungenes monochromes Bild # 2003), 1995
Autolack auf Aluminium / Car paint on aluminum
176 x 107 x 33 cm
Erworben / Acquired in 1997

Curved Monochrome Painting # 2005
(Geschwungenes monochromes Bild # 2005), 1995
Autolack auf Aluminium / Car paint on aluminum
176 x 107 x 33 cm
Erworben / Acquired in 1997

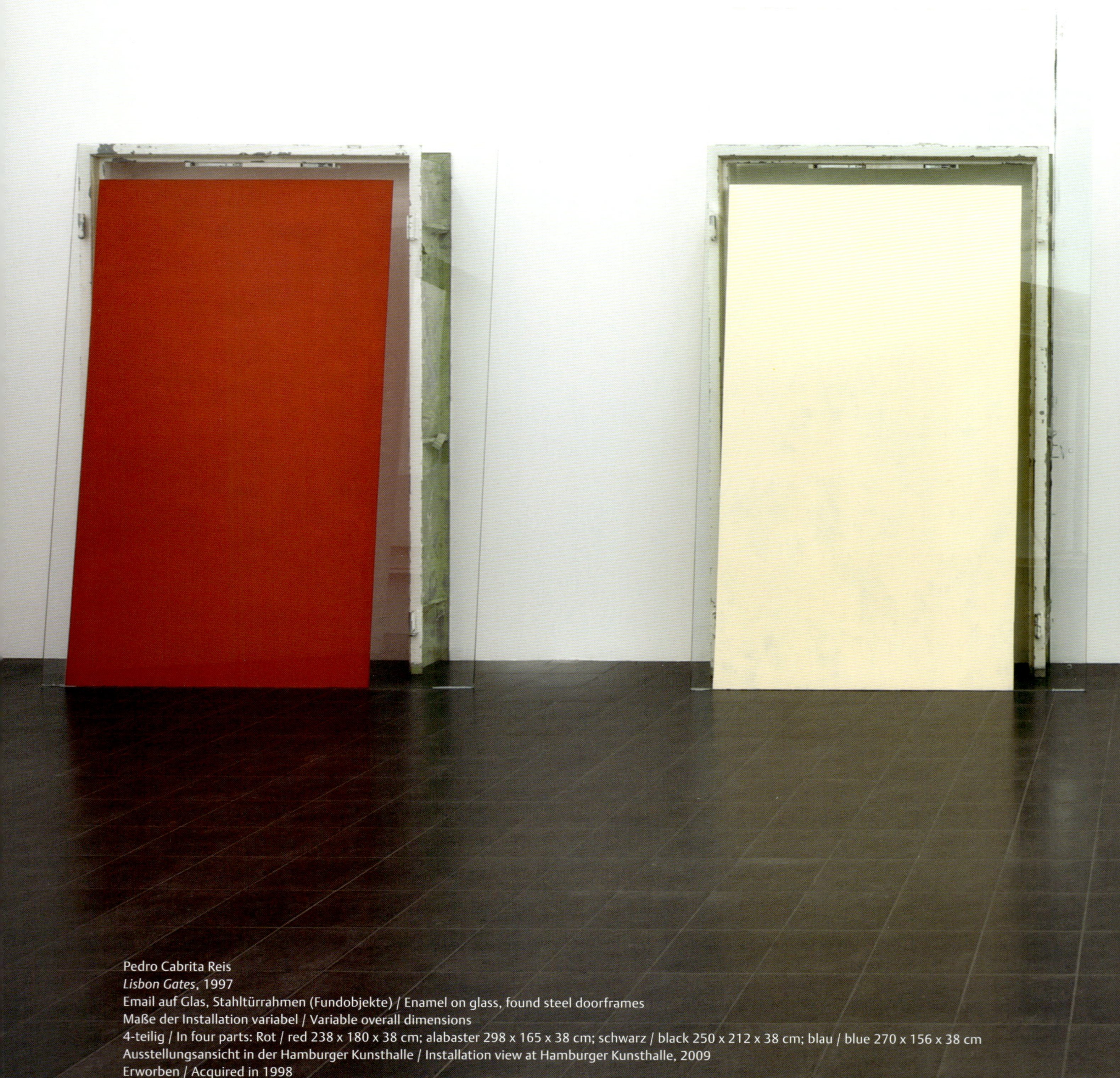

Pedro Cabrita Reis
Lisbon Gates, 1997
Email auf Glas, Stahltürrahmen (Fundobjekte) / Enamel on glass, found steel doorframes
Maße der Installation variabel / Variable overall dimensions
4-teilig / In four parts: Rot / red 238 x 180 x 38 cm; alabaster 298 x 165 x 38 cm; schwarz / black 250 x 212 x 38 cm; blau / blue 270 x 156 x 38 cm
Ausstellungsansicht in der Hamburger Kunsthalle / Installation view at Hamburger Kunsthalle, 2009
Erworben / Acquired in 1998

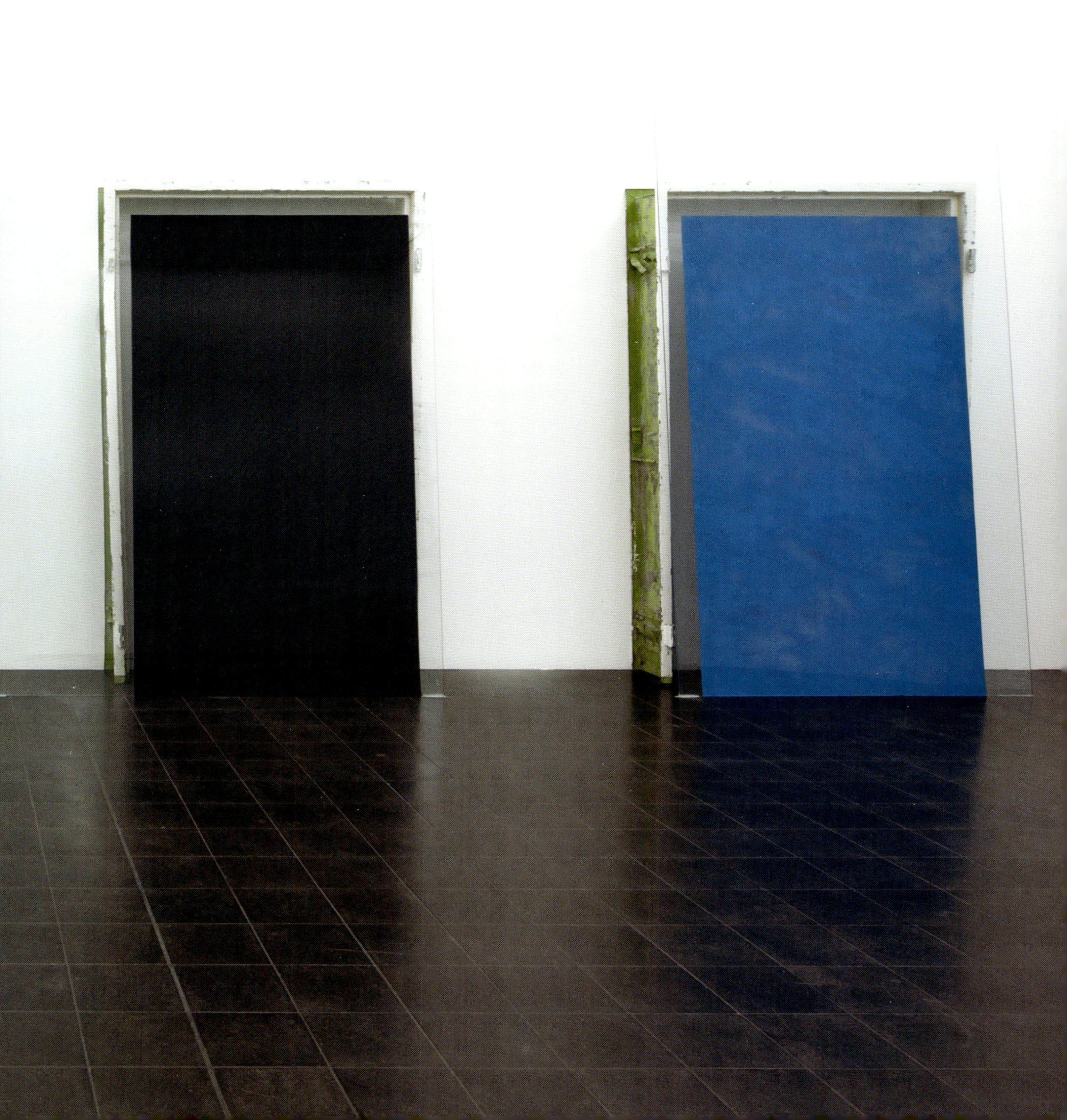

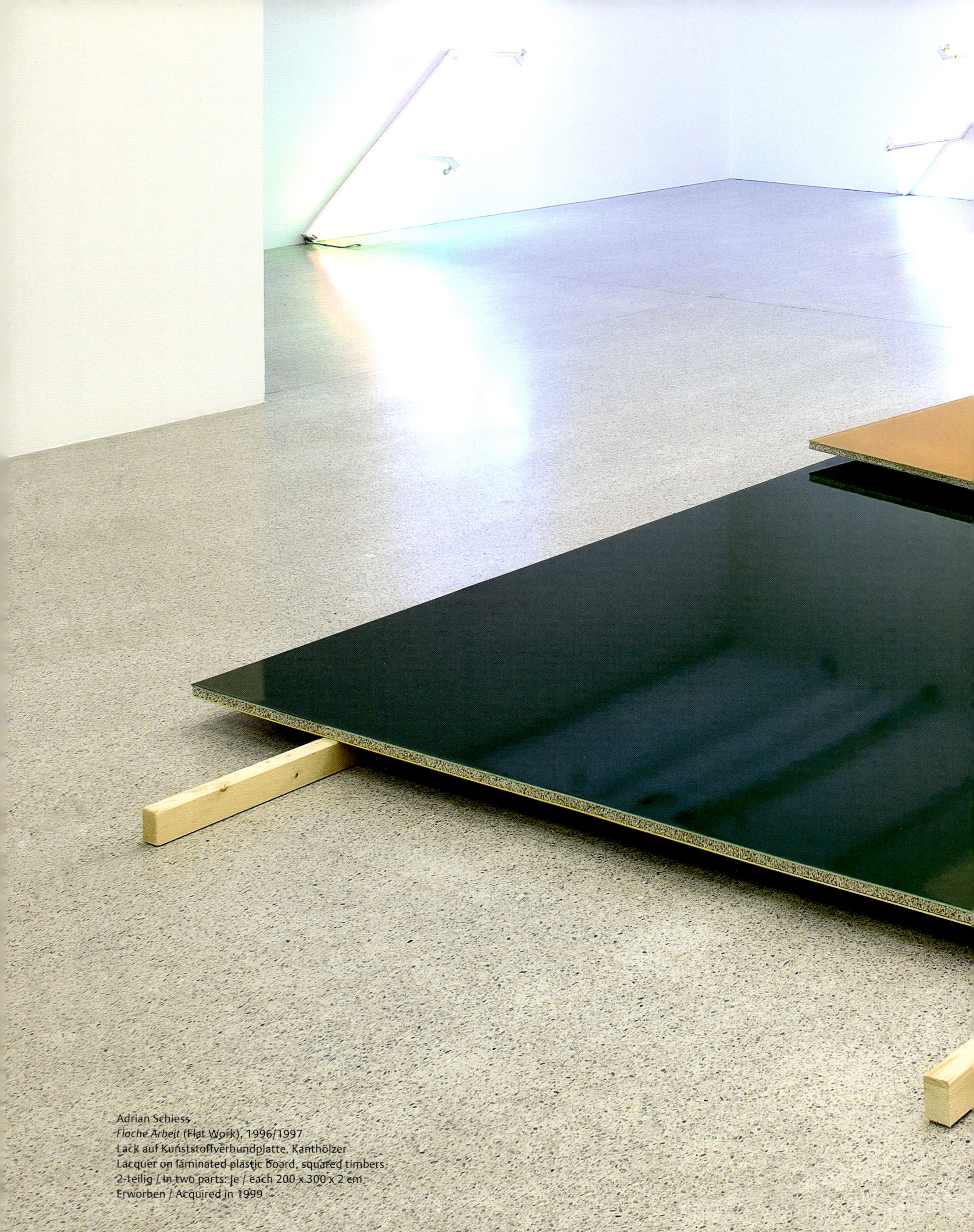

Adrian Schiess
Flache Arbeit (Flat Work), 1996/1997
Lack auf Kunststoffverbundplatte, Kanthölzer
Lacquer on laminated plastic board, squared timbers
2-teilig / In two parts: Je / each 200 x 300 x 2 cm
Erworben / Acquired in 1999

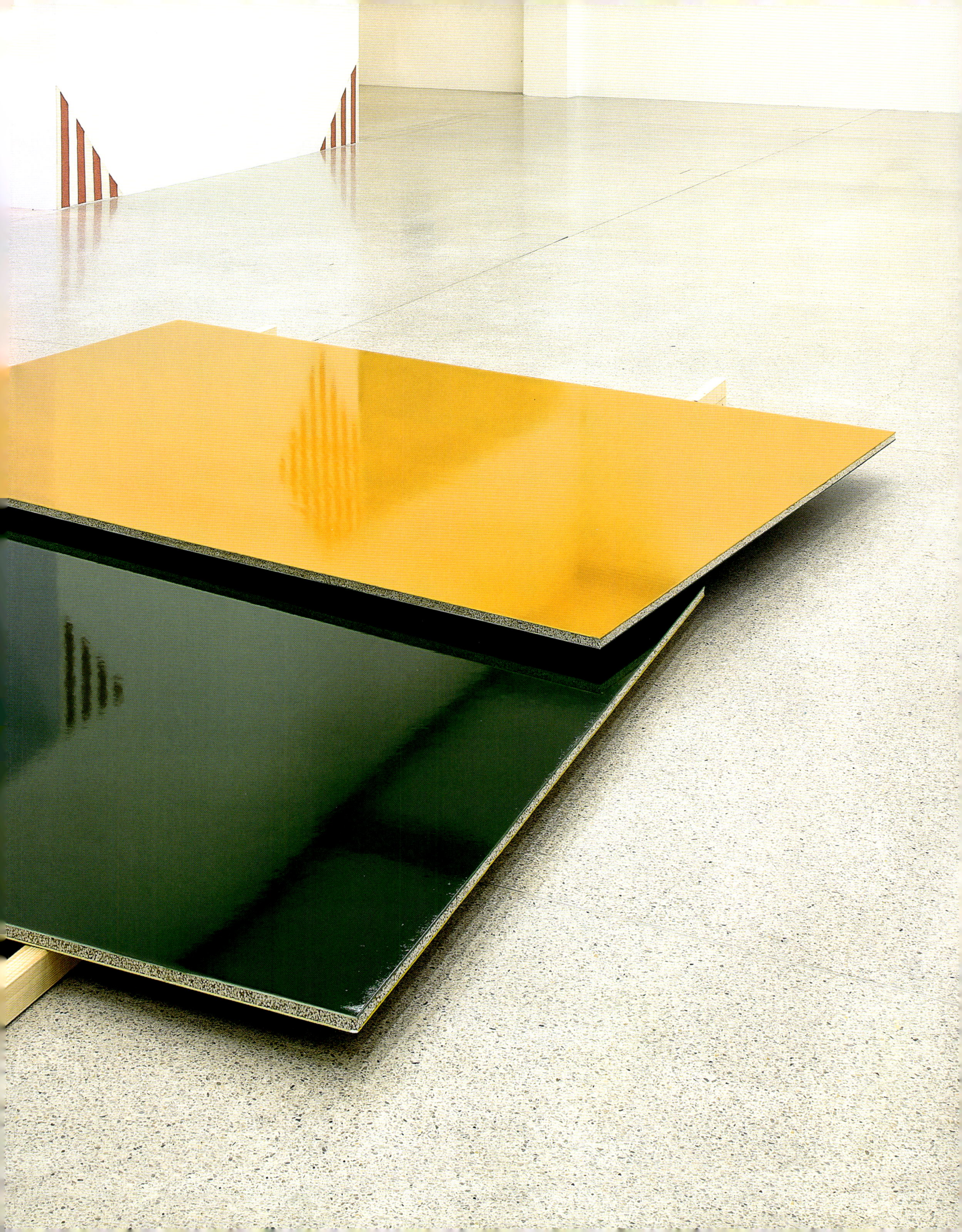

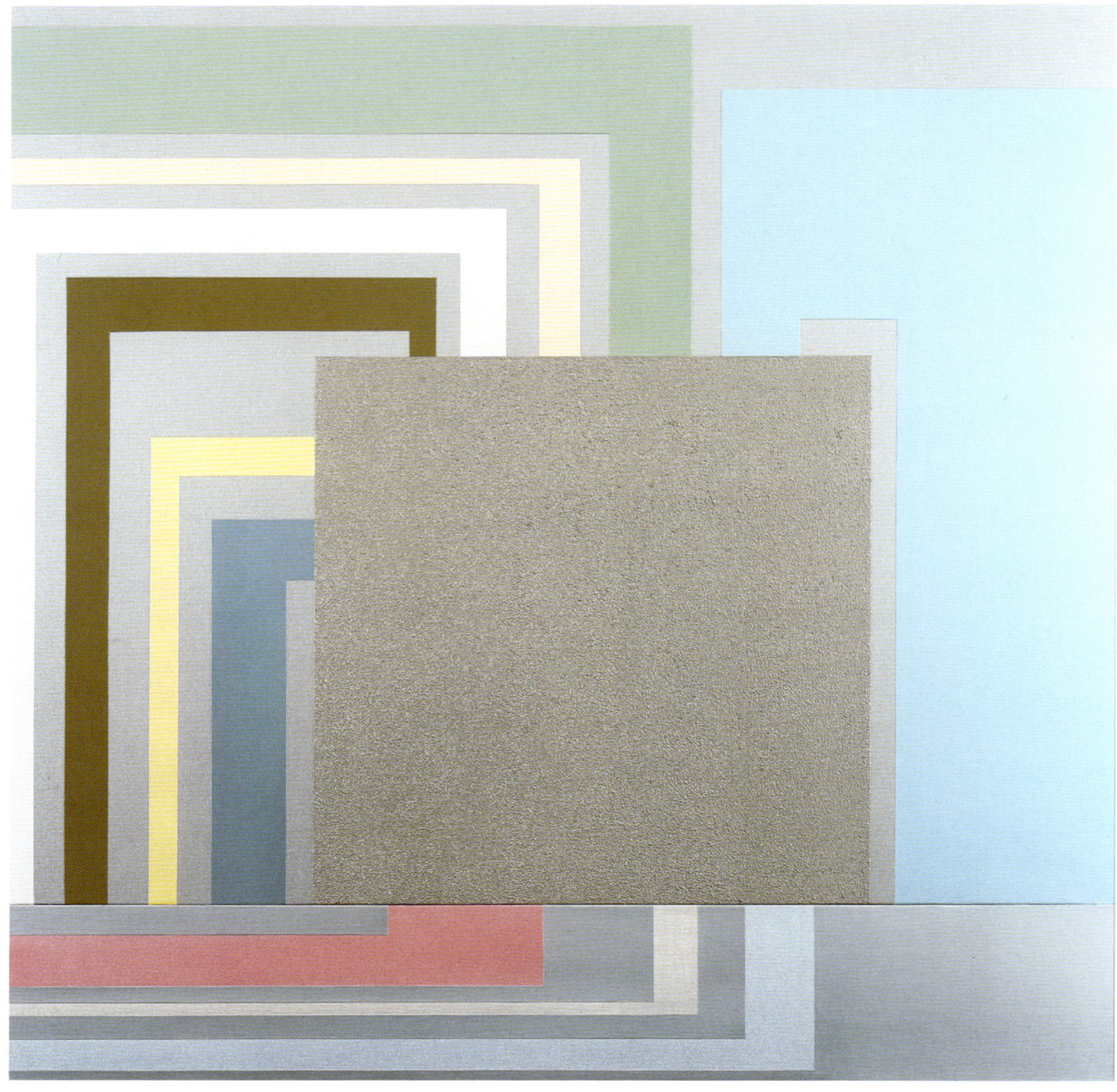

Peter Halley
Low Heat, 2000
Acryl auf Leinwand / Acrylic on canvas
218 x 218 cm
Schenkung der Gesellschaft der Freunde der bildenden Künste
Donated by the Society of the Friends of Fine Arts, Wien / Vienna, 2001

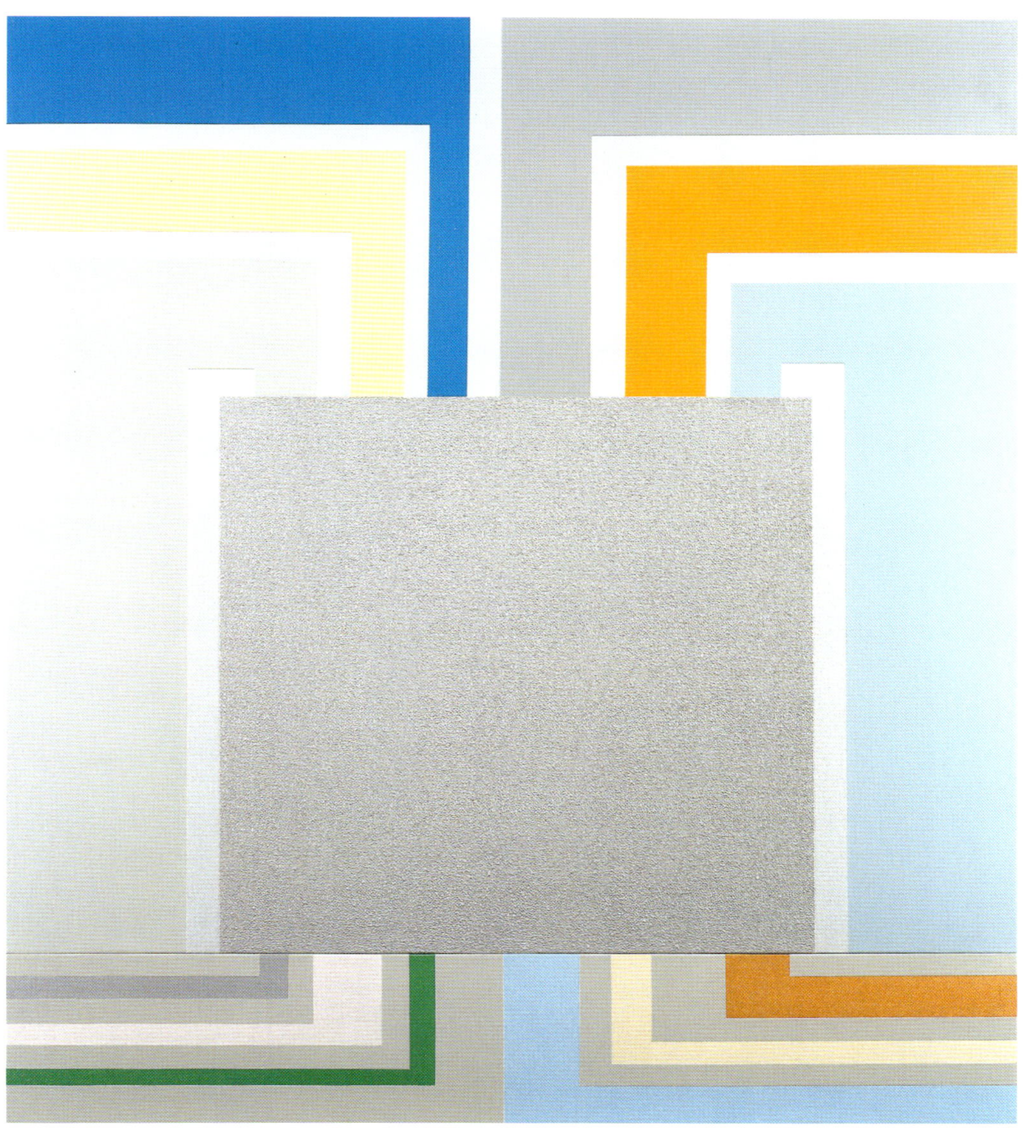

Peter Halley
Light History, 2000
Acryl auf Leinwand / Acrylic on canvas
244 x 216 cm
Leihgabe der Österreichischen Ludwig Stiftung
On loan from the Austrian Ludwig Foundation, seit / since 2001

Thomas Jocher
Bildbild (Picturepicture), 1995
Öl auf Leinwand / Oil on canvas
95 x 135 cm
Erworben / Acquired in 1997

Thomas Jocher
Bildbild (Picturepicture), 1995
Öl auf Leinwand / Oil on canvas
140 x 100 cm
Erworben / Acquired in 1997

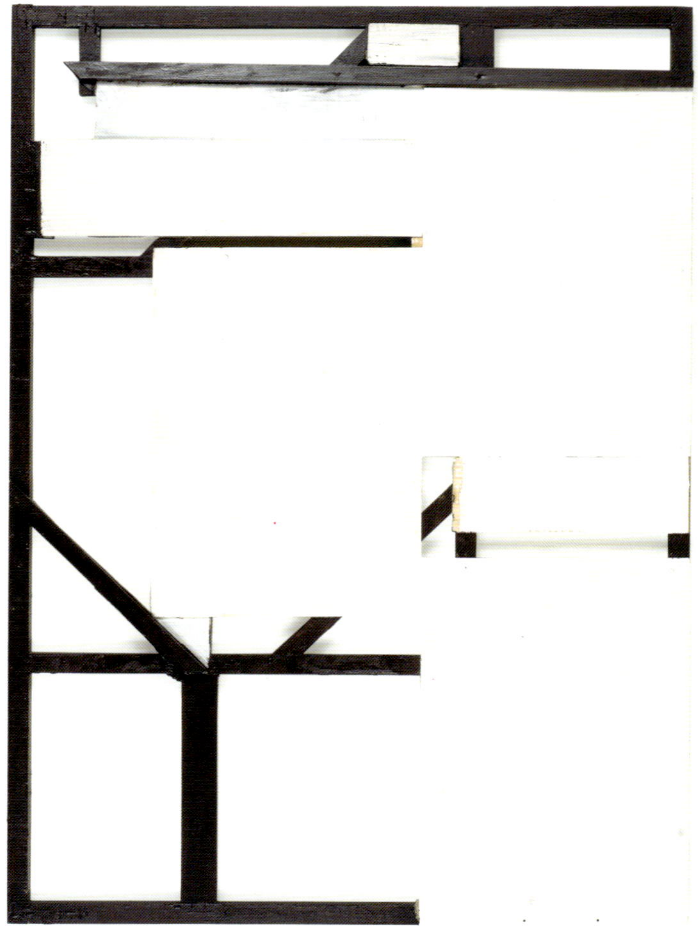

Florian Schmidt
Untitled 1 (Governance), 2008
Holz, Metall, Kunststoff, Karton, Metallfolie, Heißsiegelkleber, Nägel, Acrylmasse, Dispersion
Wood, metal, plastic, cardboard, metal foil, hot glue, nails, acrylic filler, emulsion paint
105 x 75,2 x 5 cm
Erworben mit Unterstützung des BKA, Sektion Kunst
Acquired with support of BKA, Sektion Kunst, 2009

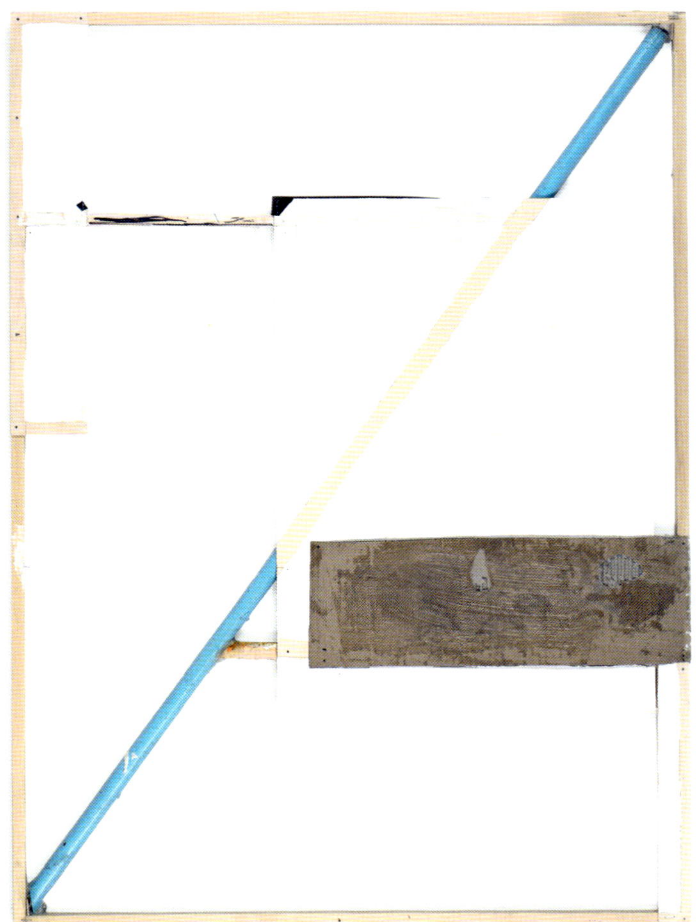

Florian Schmidt
Untitled 3 (Governance), 2008
Lack, Dispersion auf Holz / Lacquer, emulsion paint on wood
105 x 75,2 x 5 cm
Erworben mit Unterstützung des BKA, Sektion Kunst
Acquired with support of BKA, Sektion Kunst, 2009

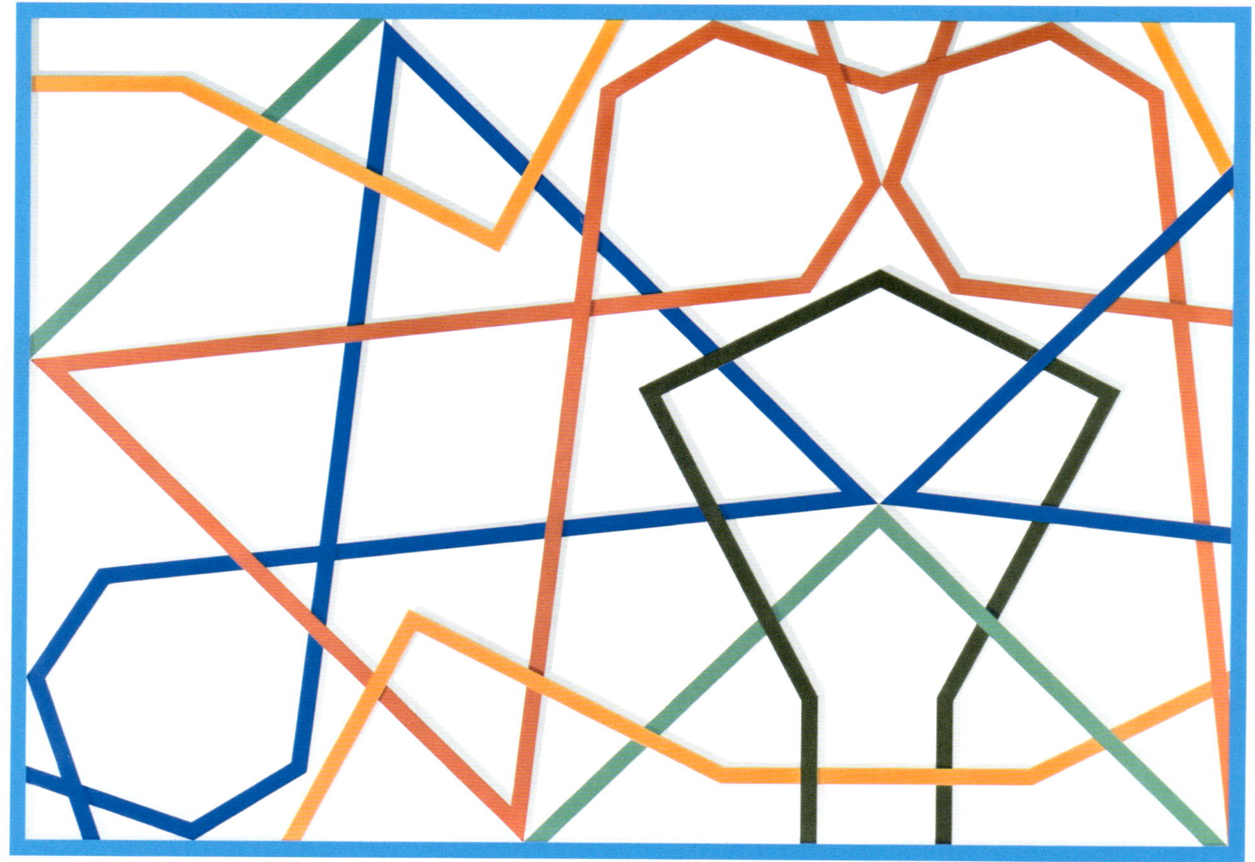

Walter Obholzer
Otaku 6, 1998
Tempera auf Aluminium / Tempera on aluminum
160 x 218 cm
Erworben / Acquired in 2001

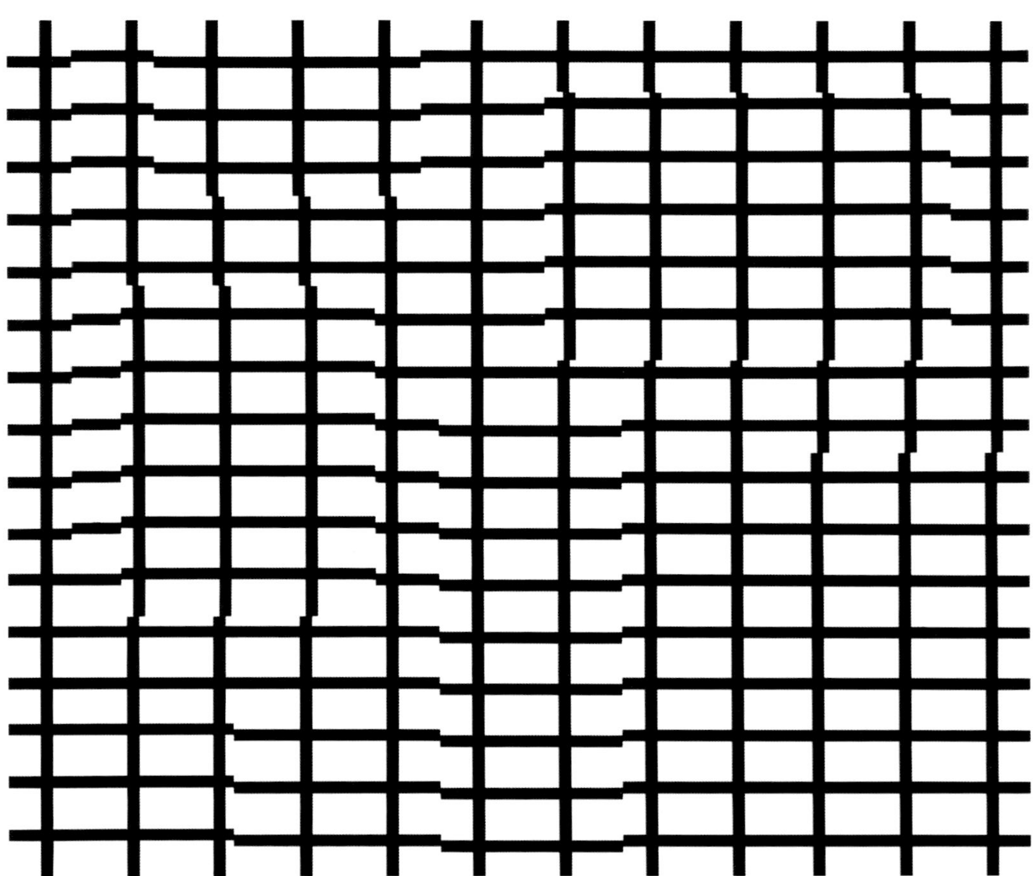

Esther Stocker
Ohne Titel (EST 27_03) (Untitled [EST 27_03]), 2003
Acryl auf Baumwolle / Acrylic on cotton
140 x 160 cm
Erworben mit Unterstützung des BKA, Sektion Kunst
Acquired with support of BKA, Sektion Kunst, 2007

Ausstellung / Exhibition

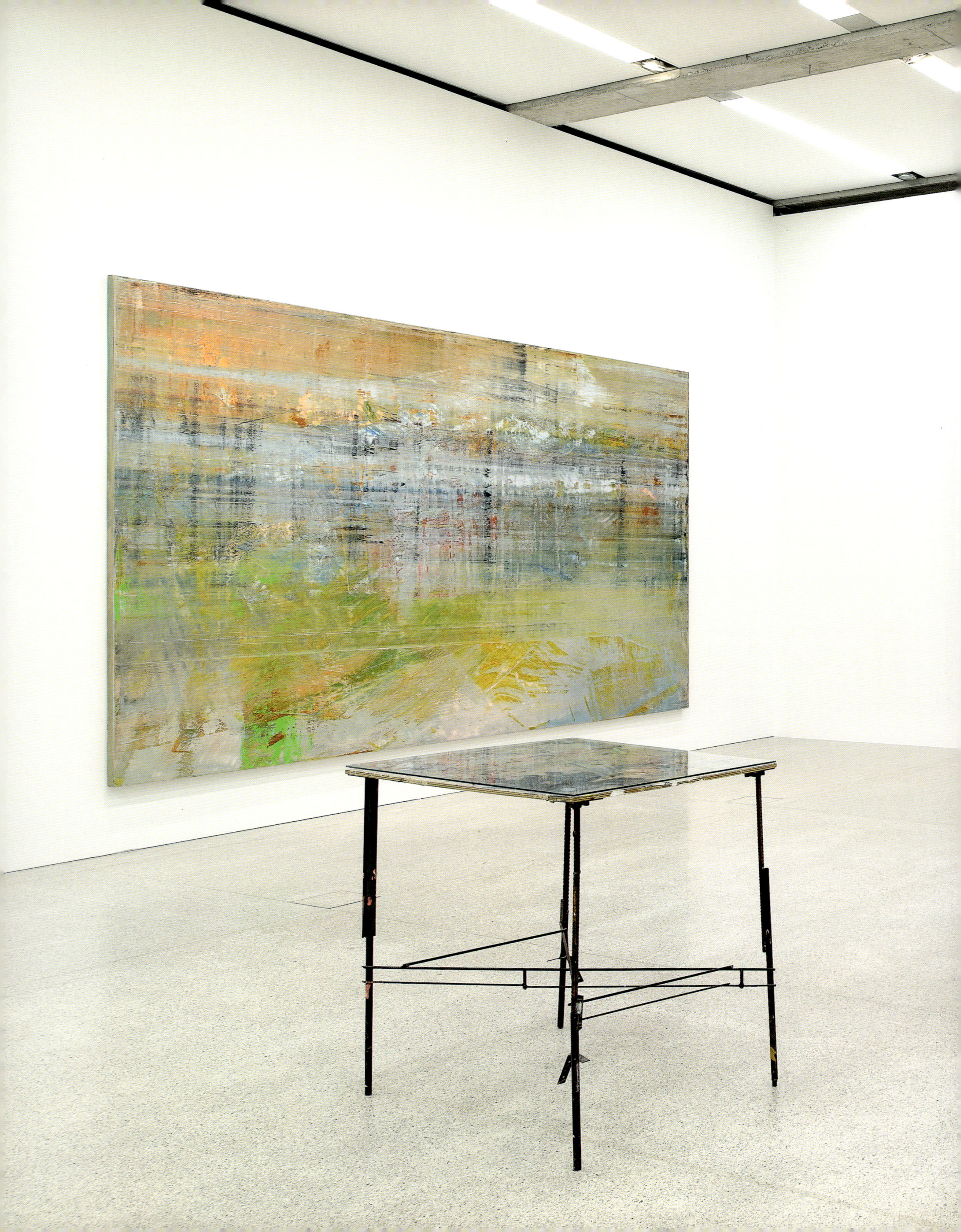

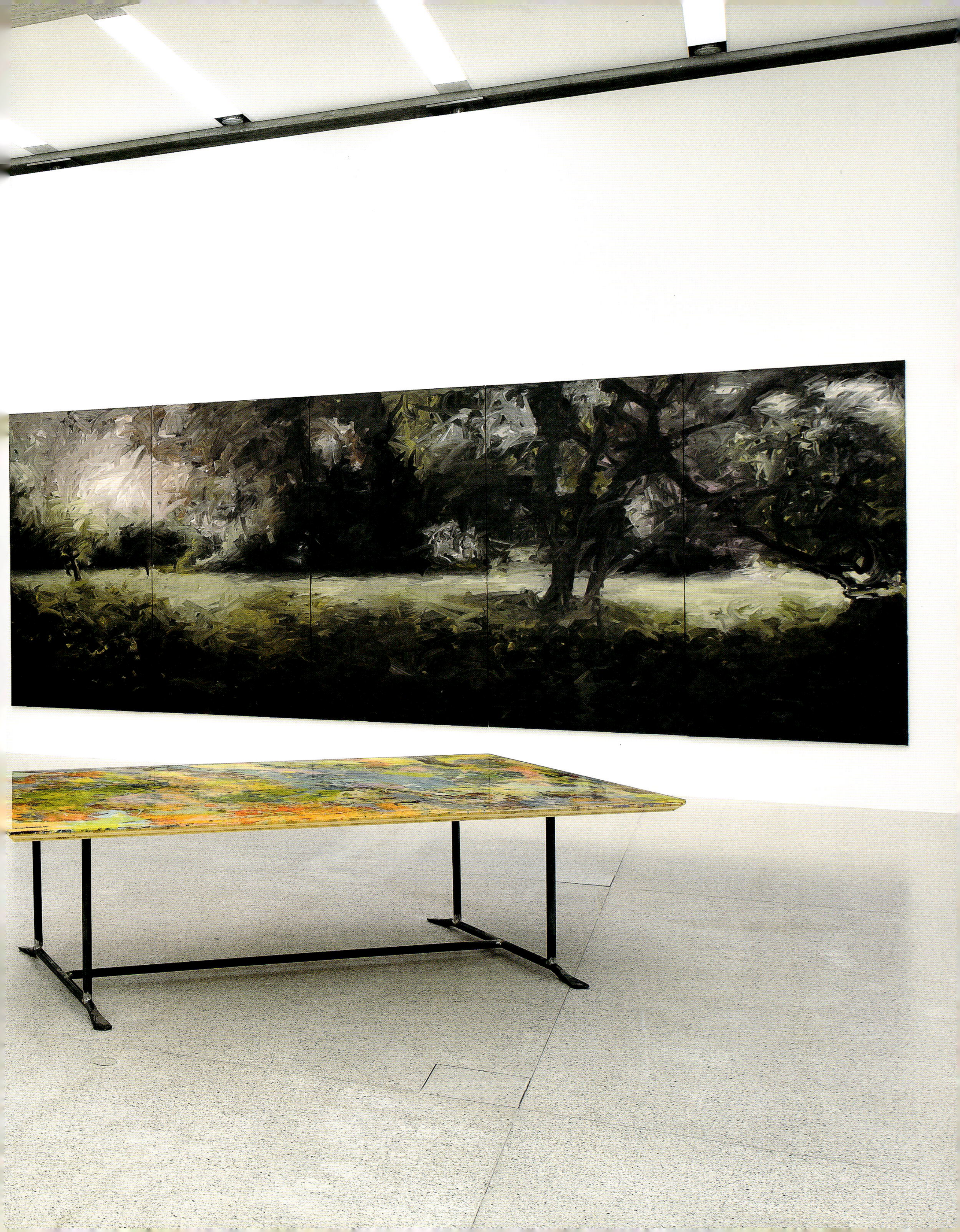

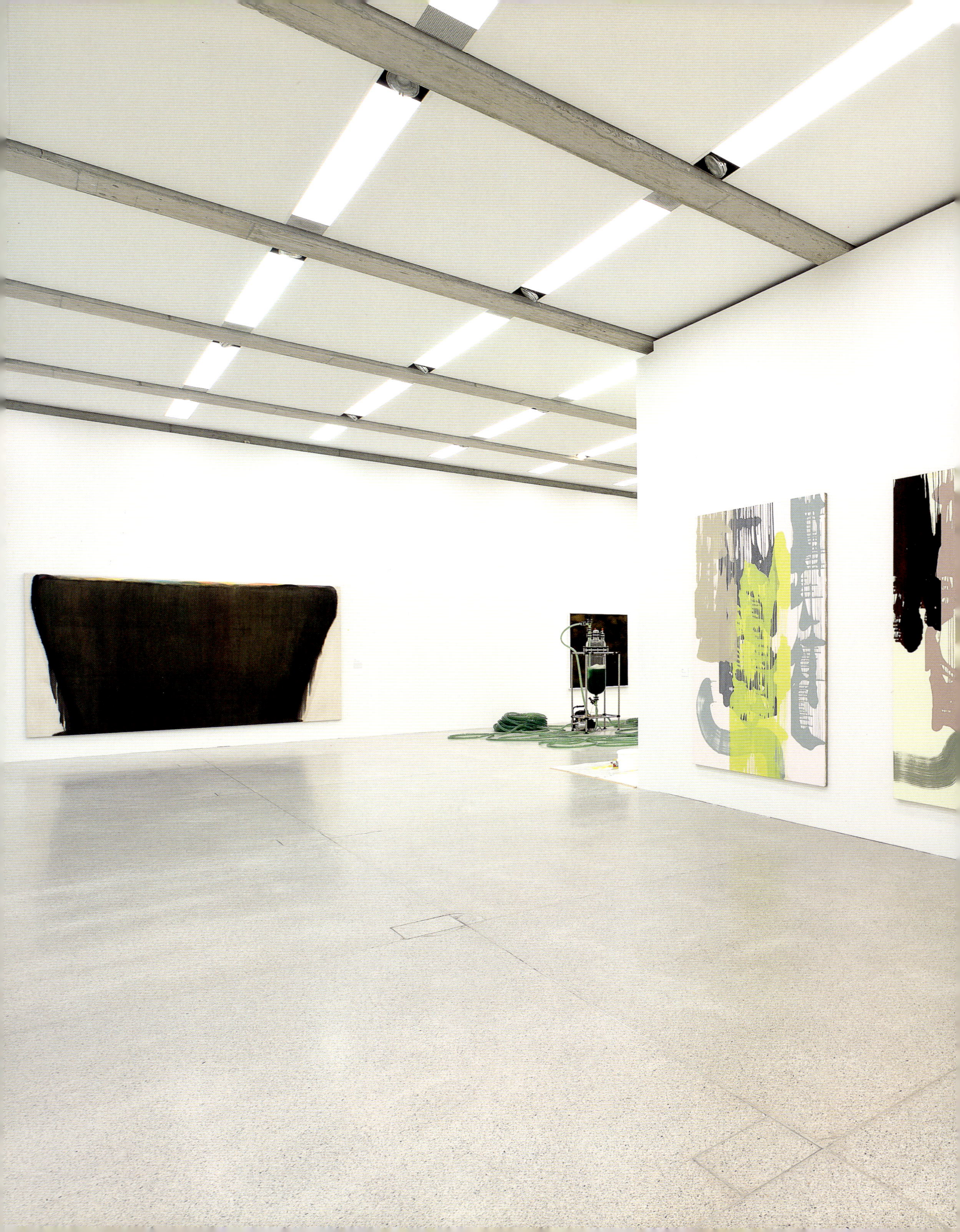

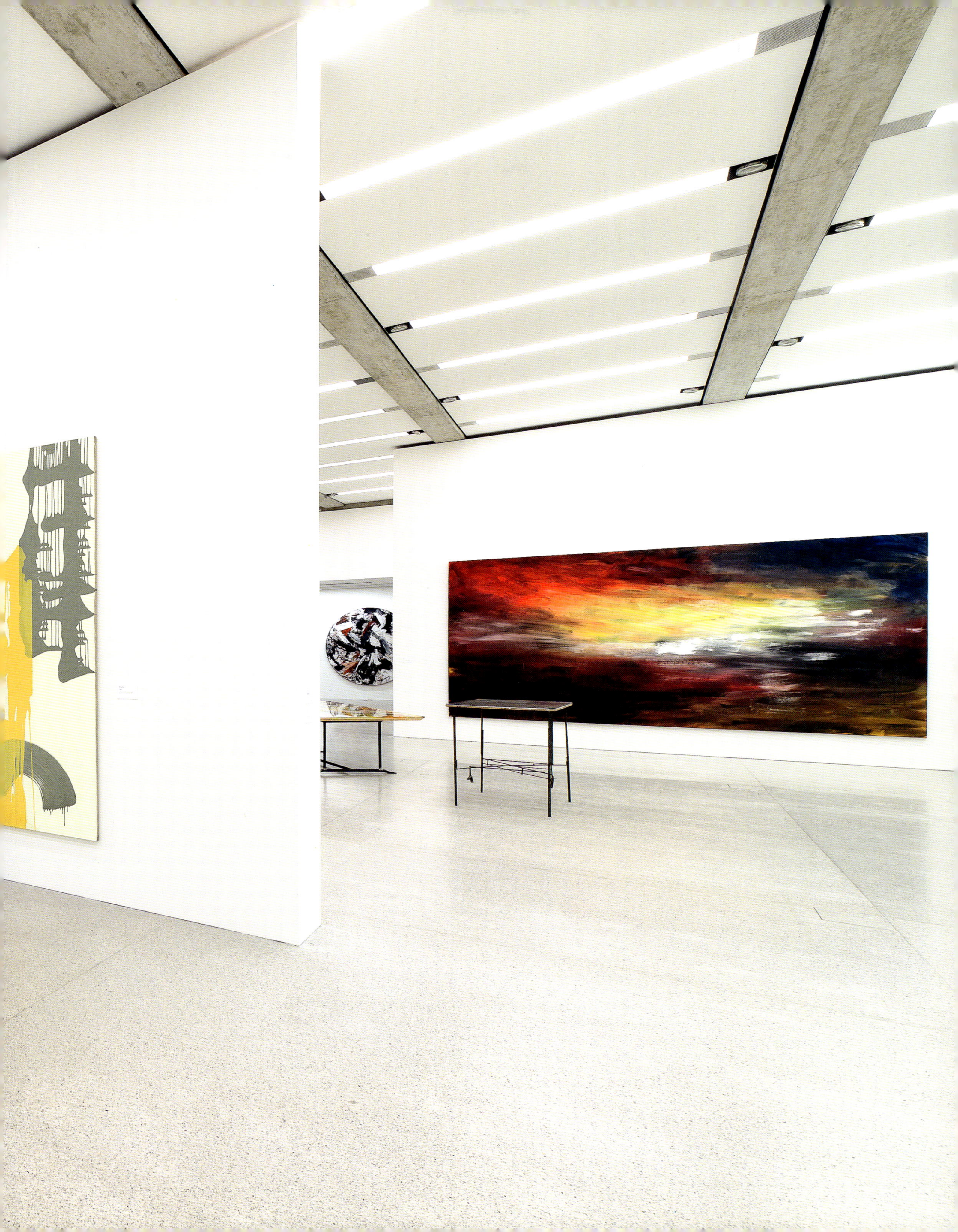

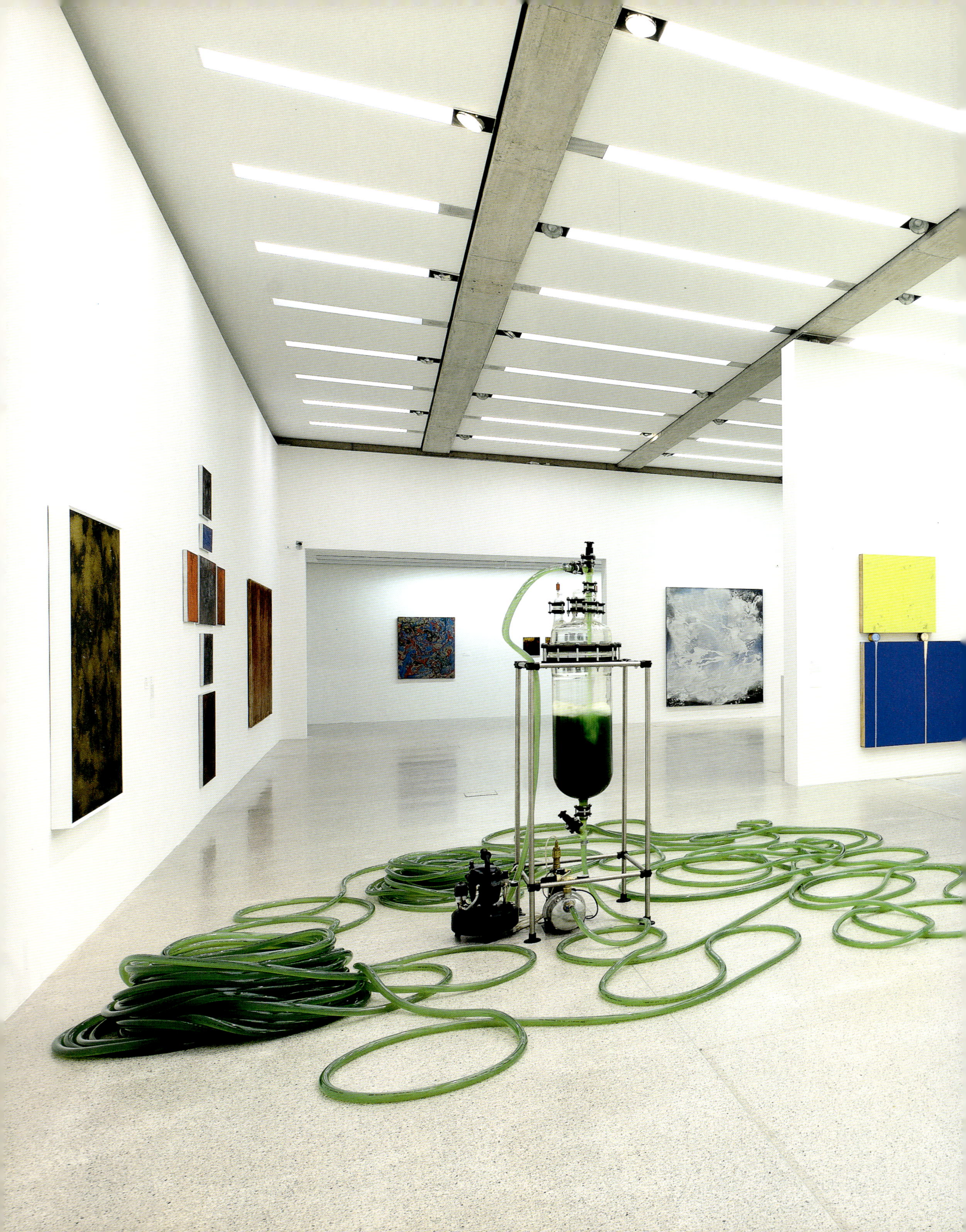

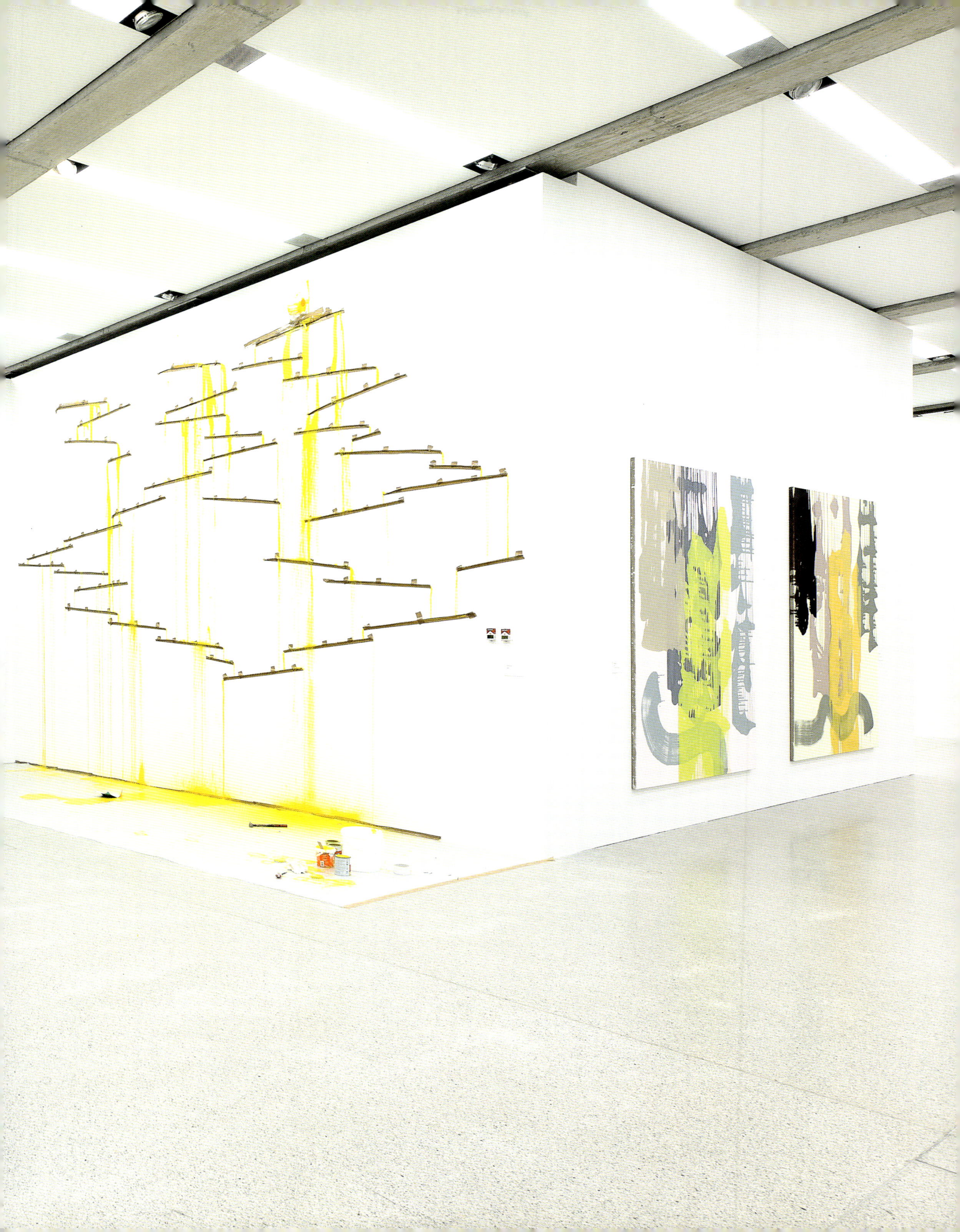

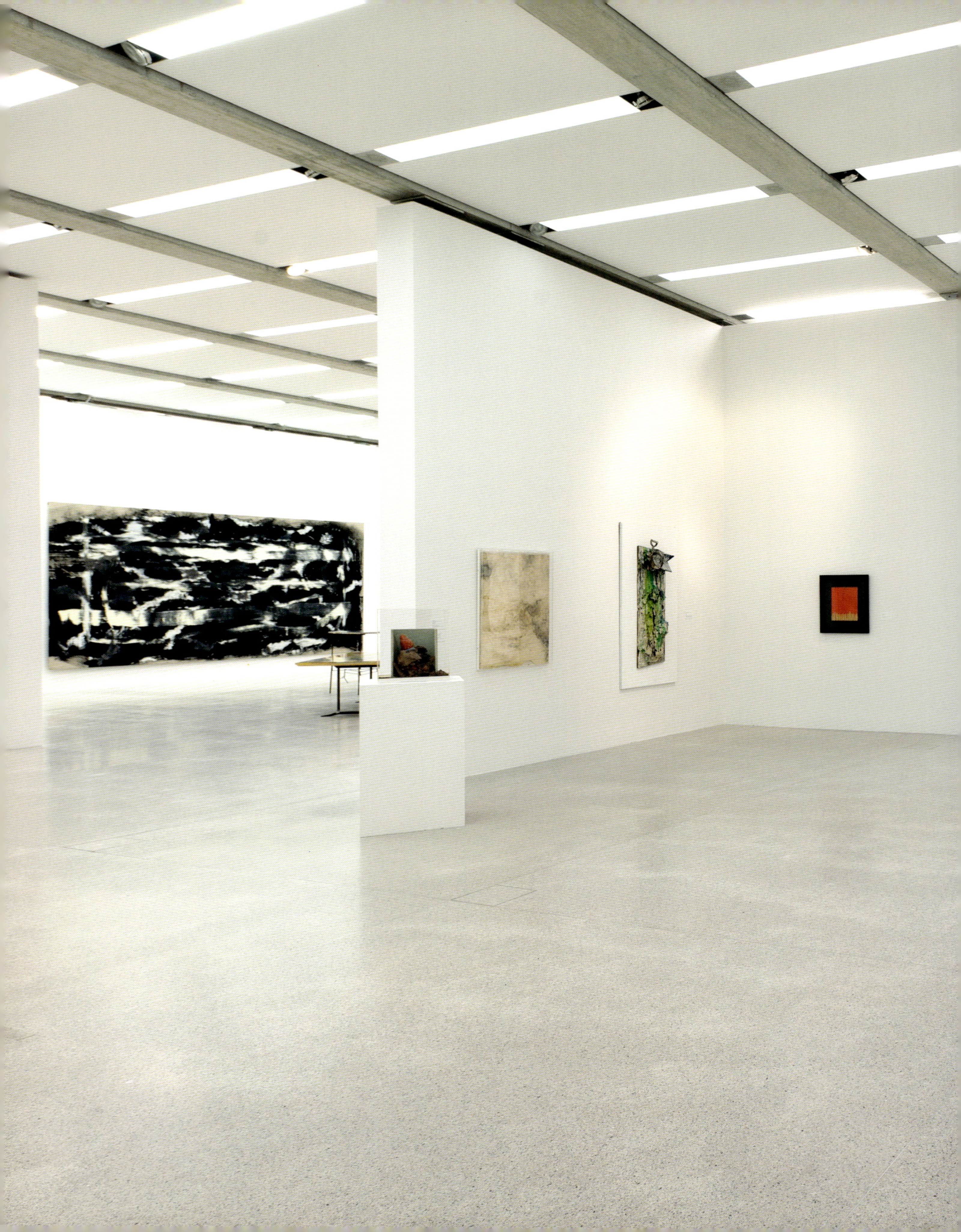

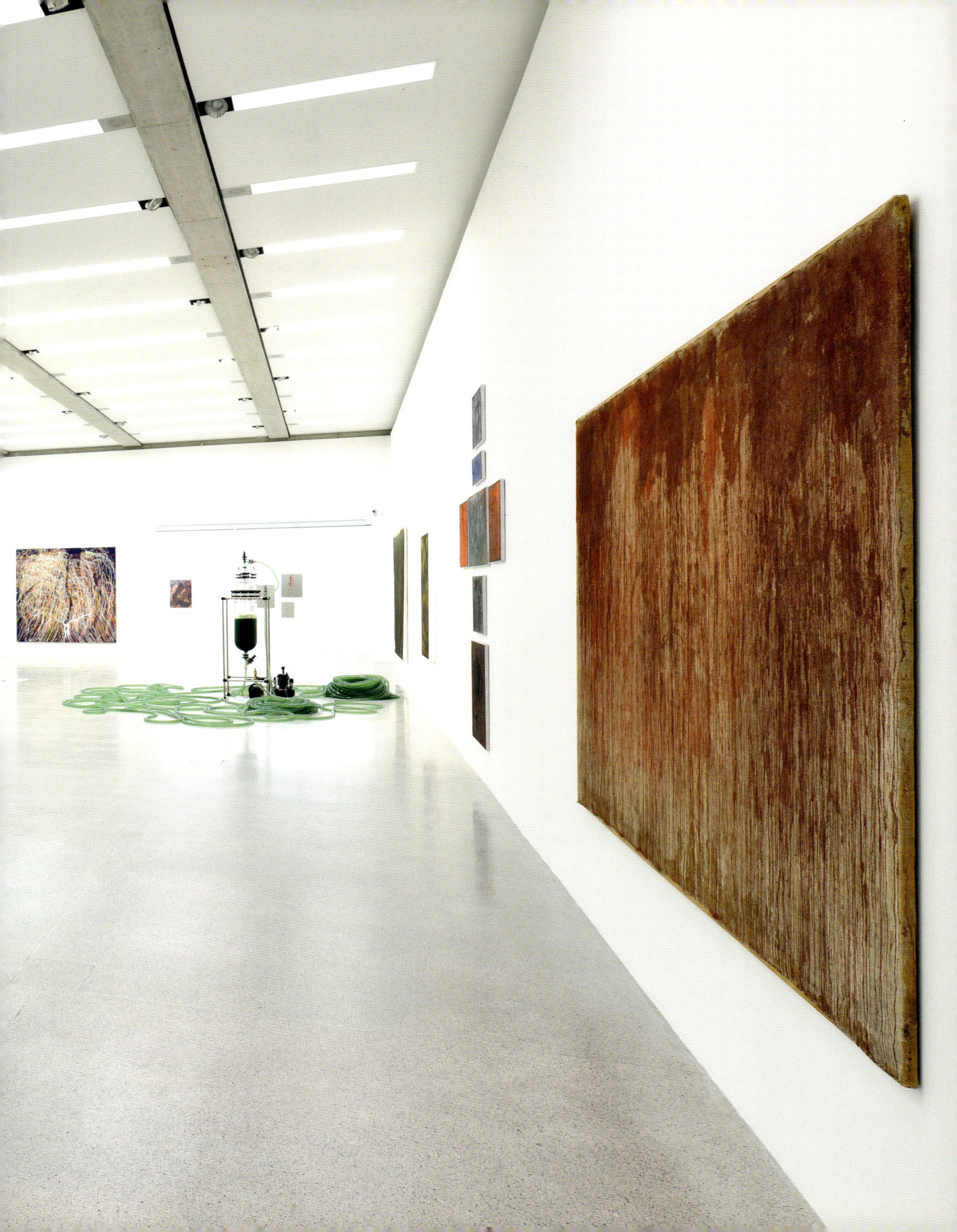

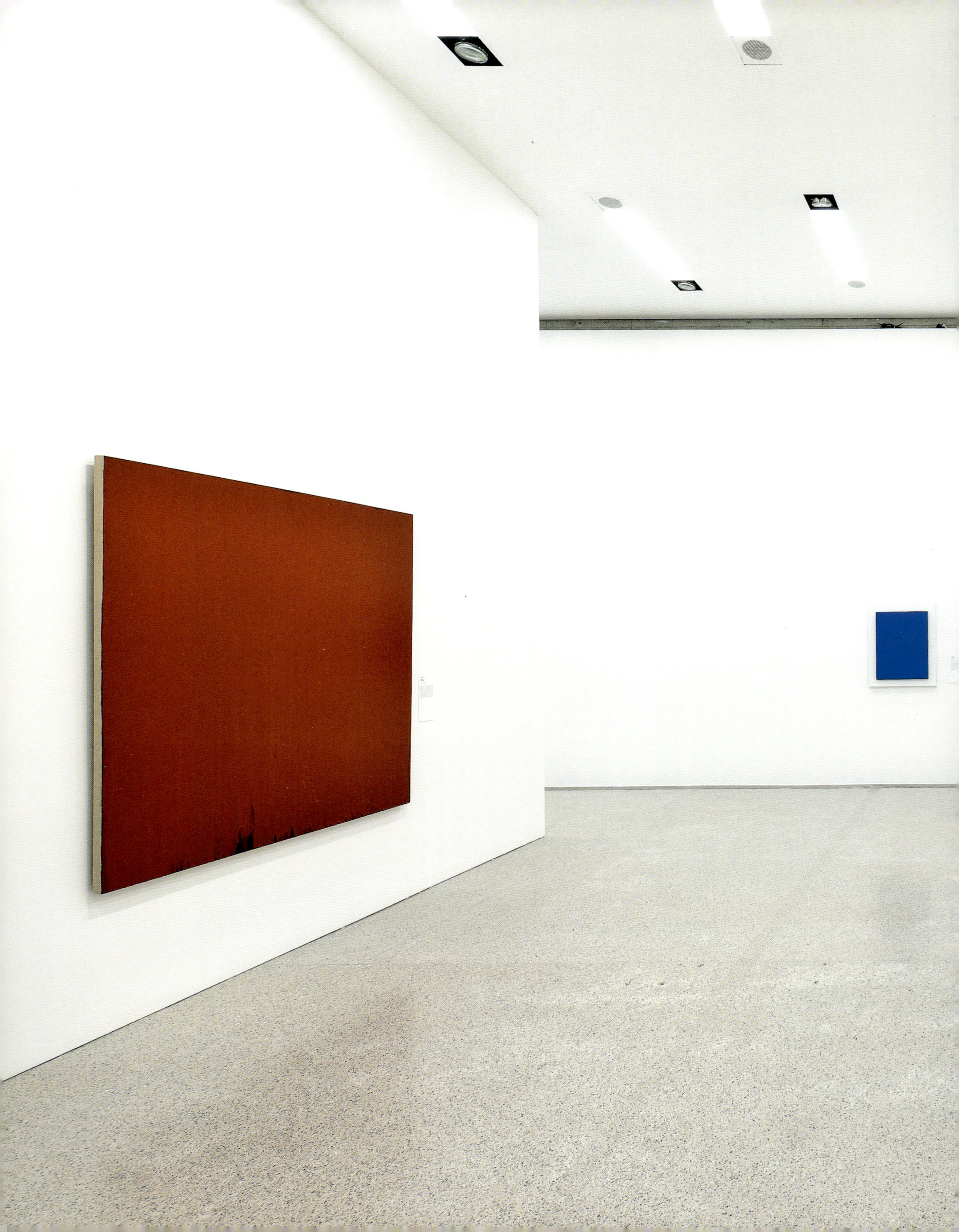

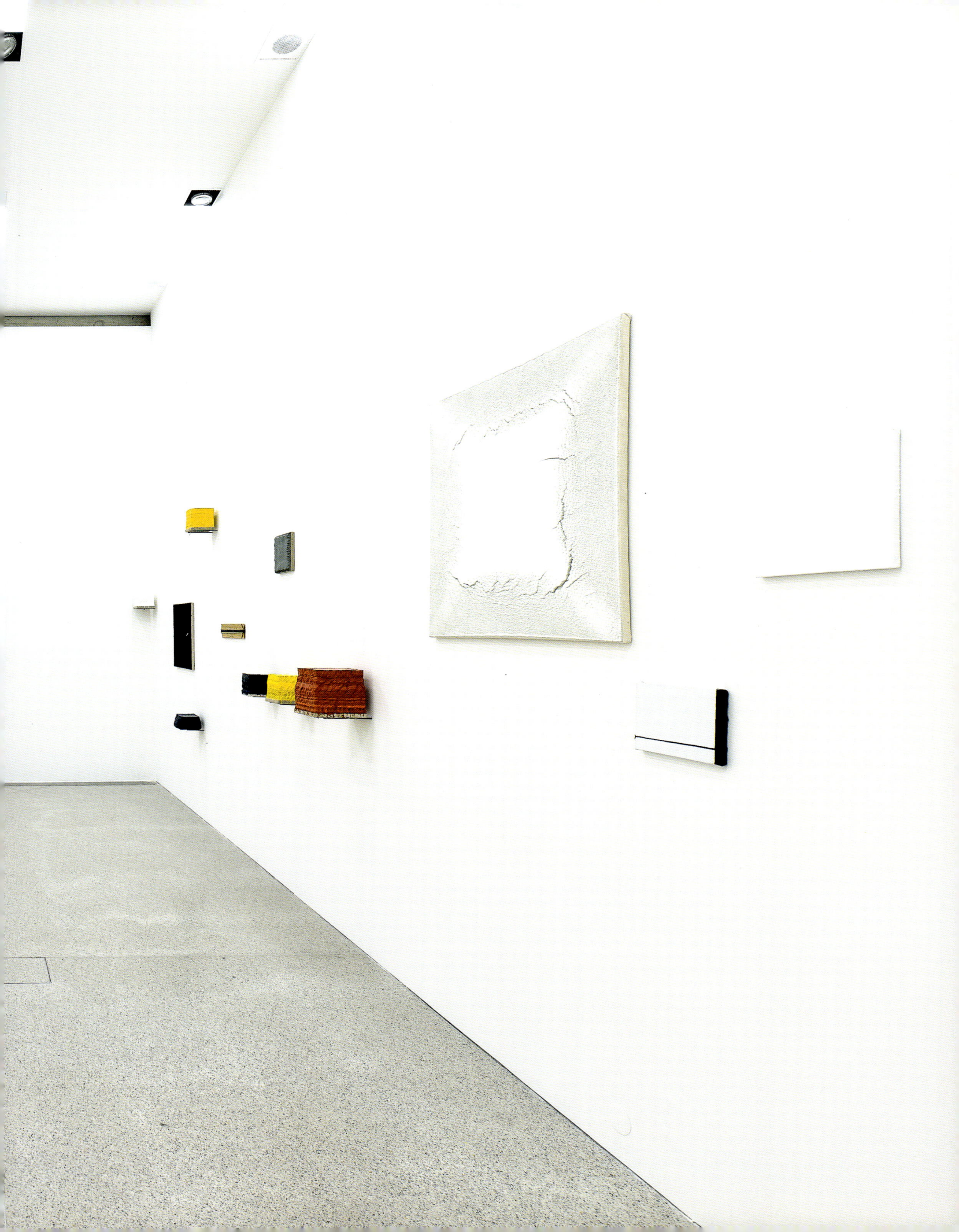

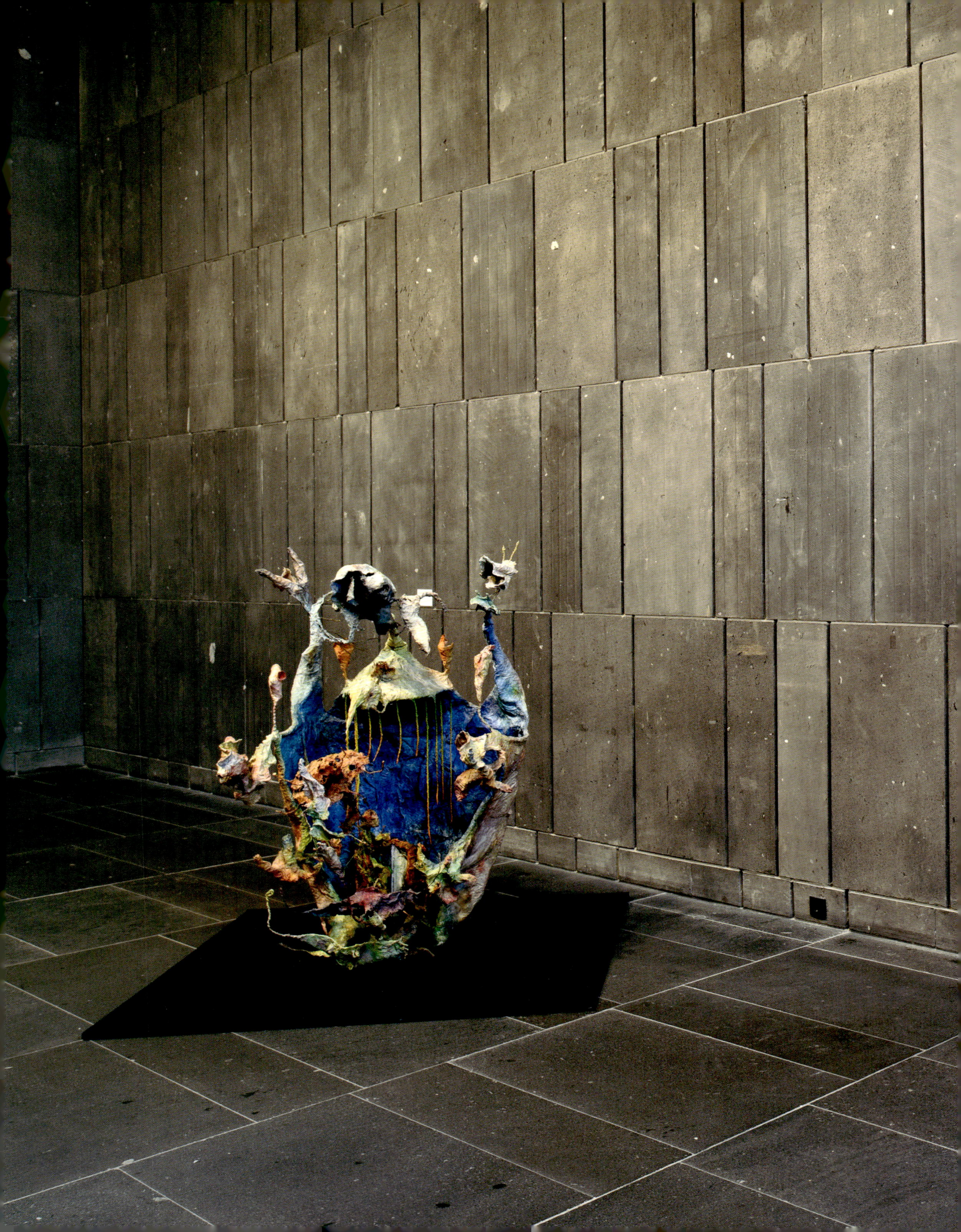

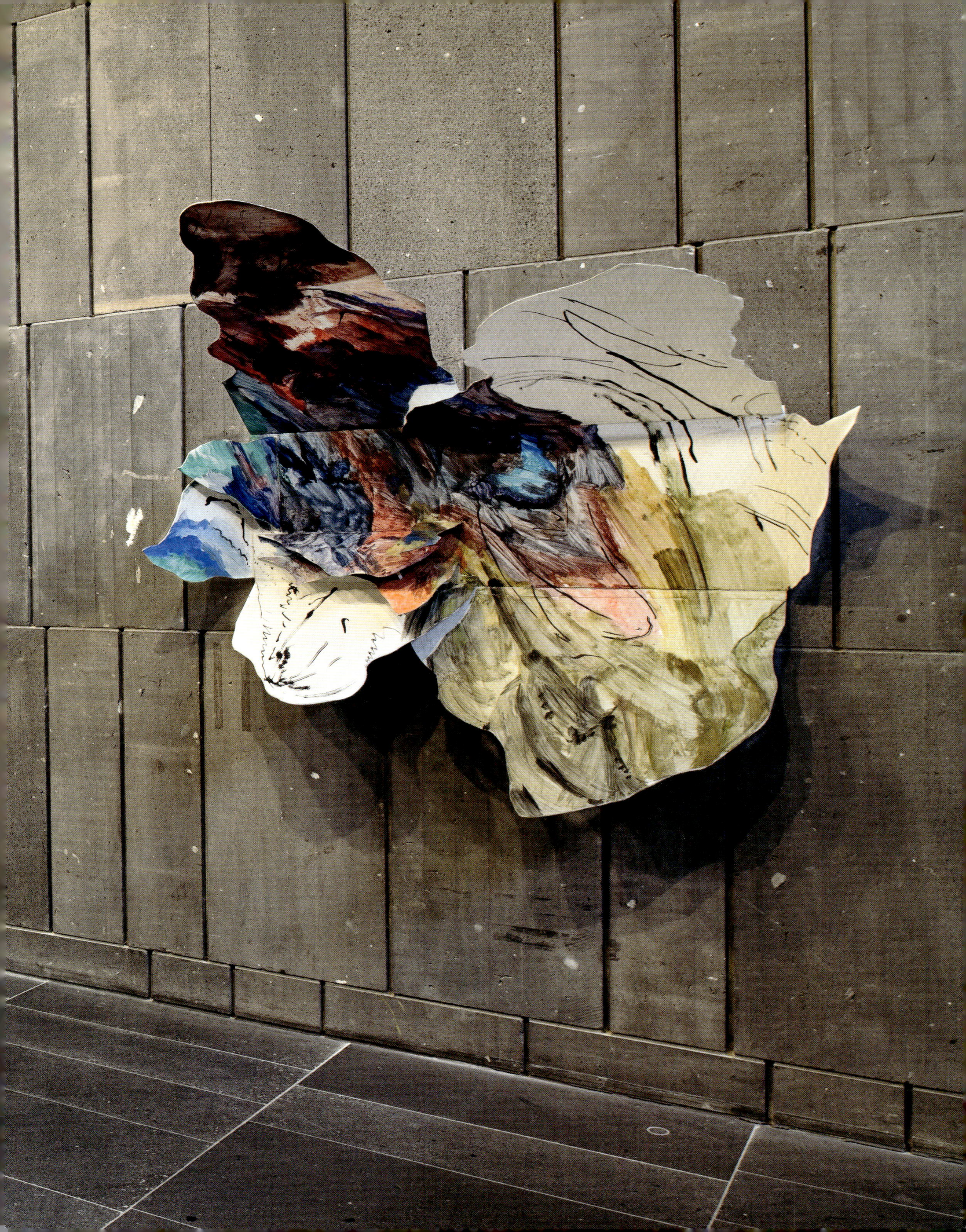

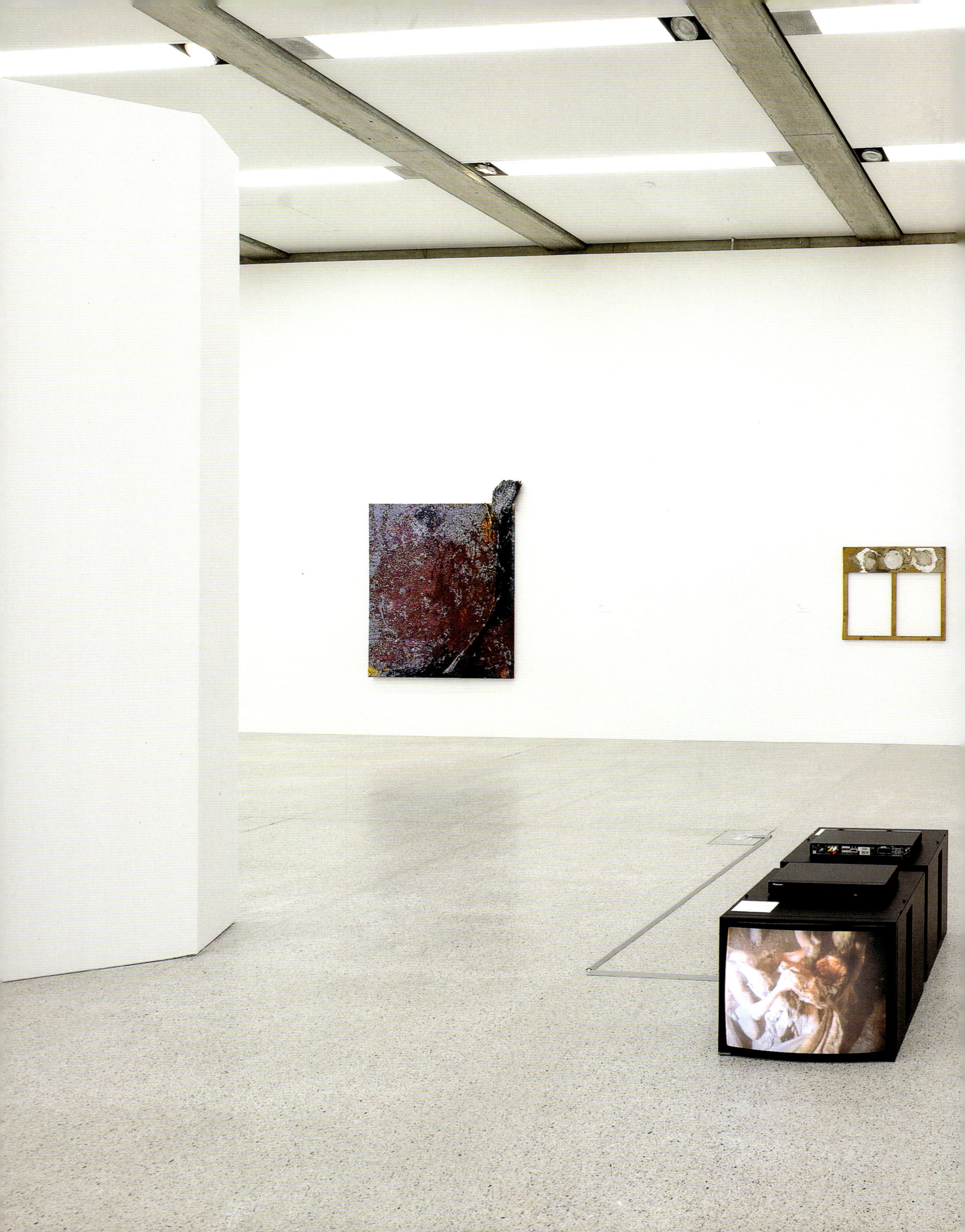

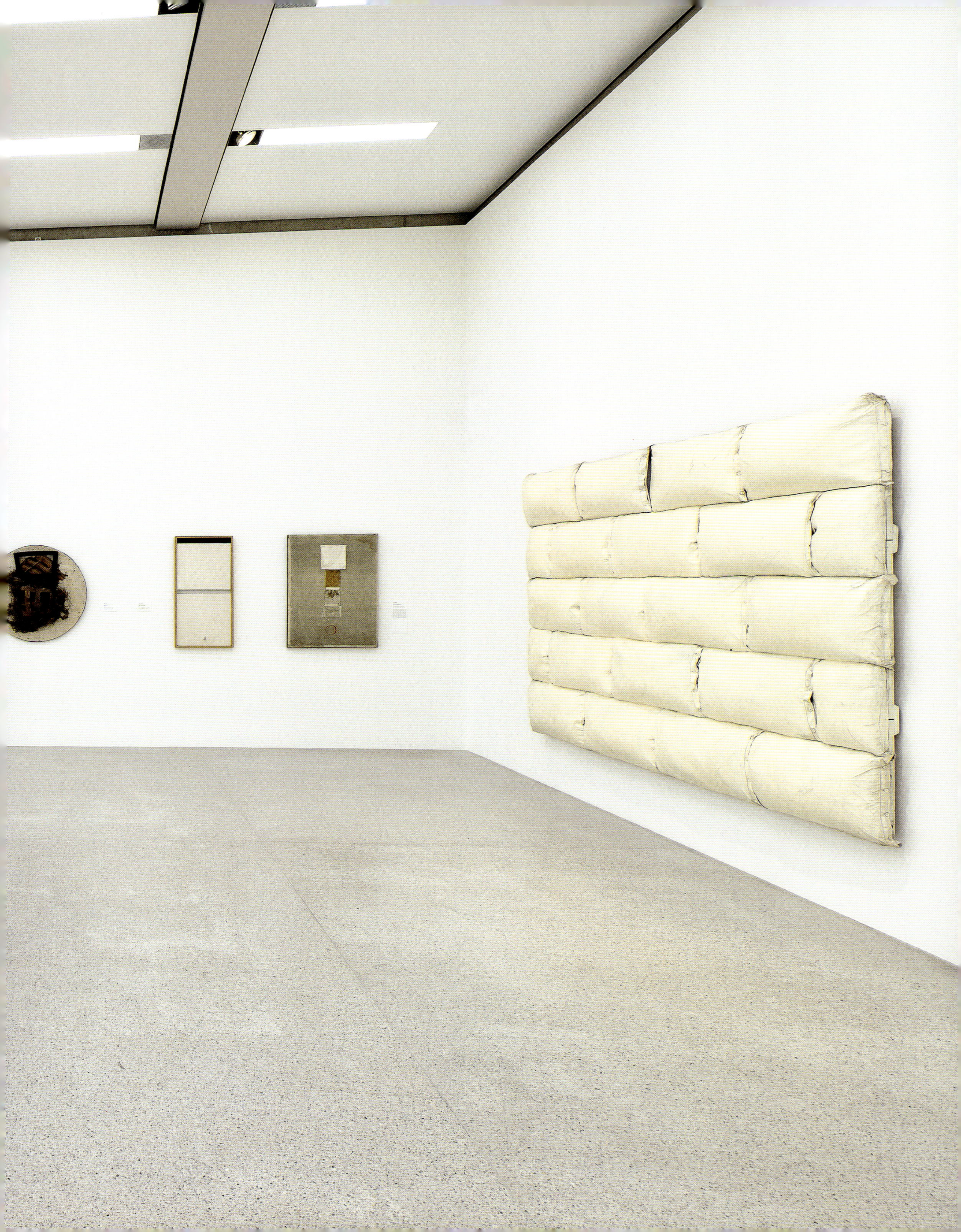

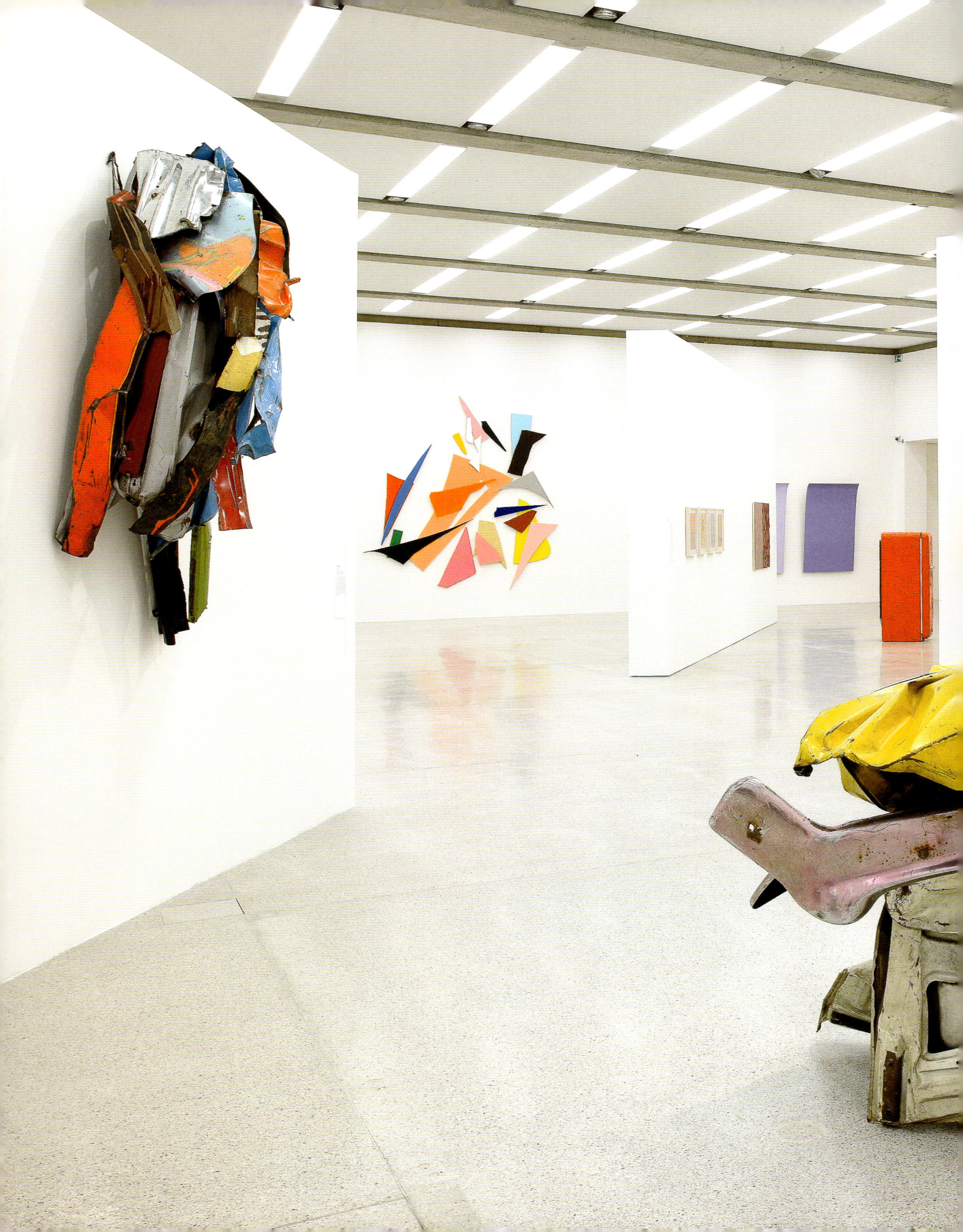

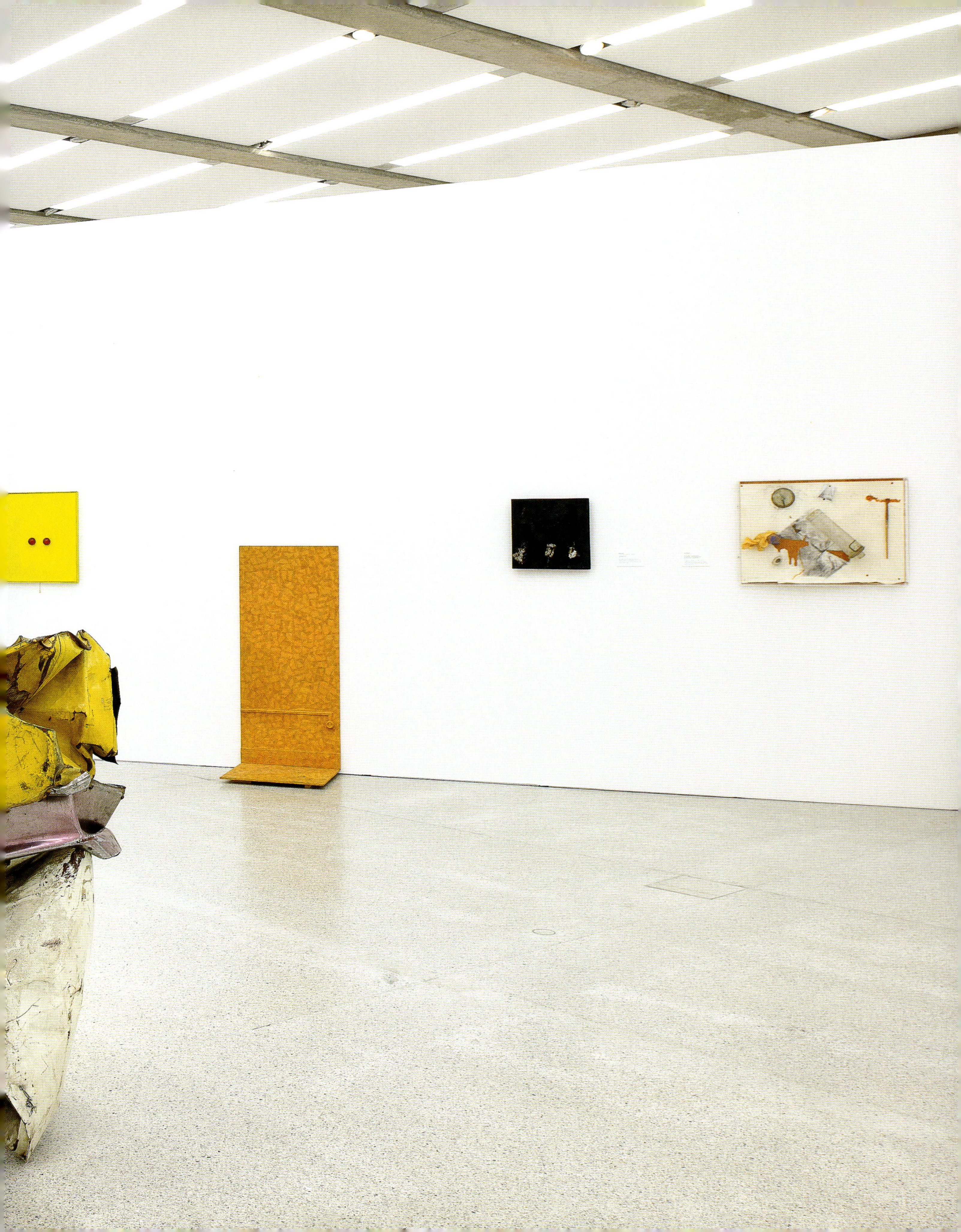

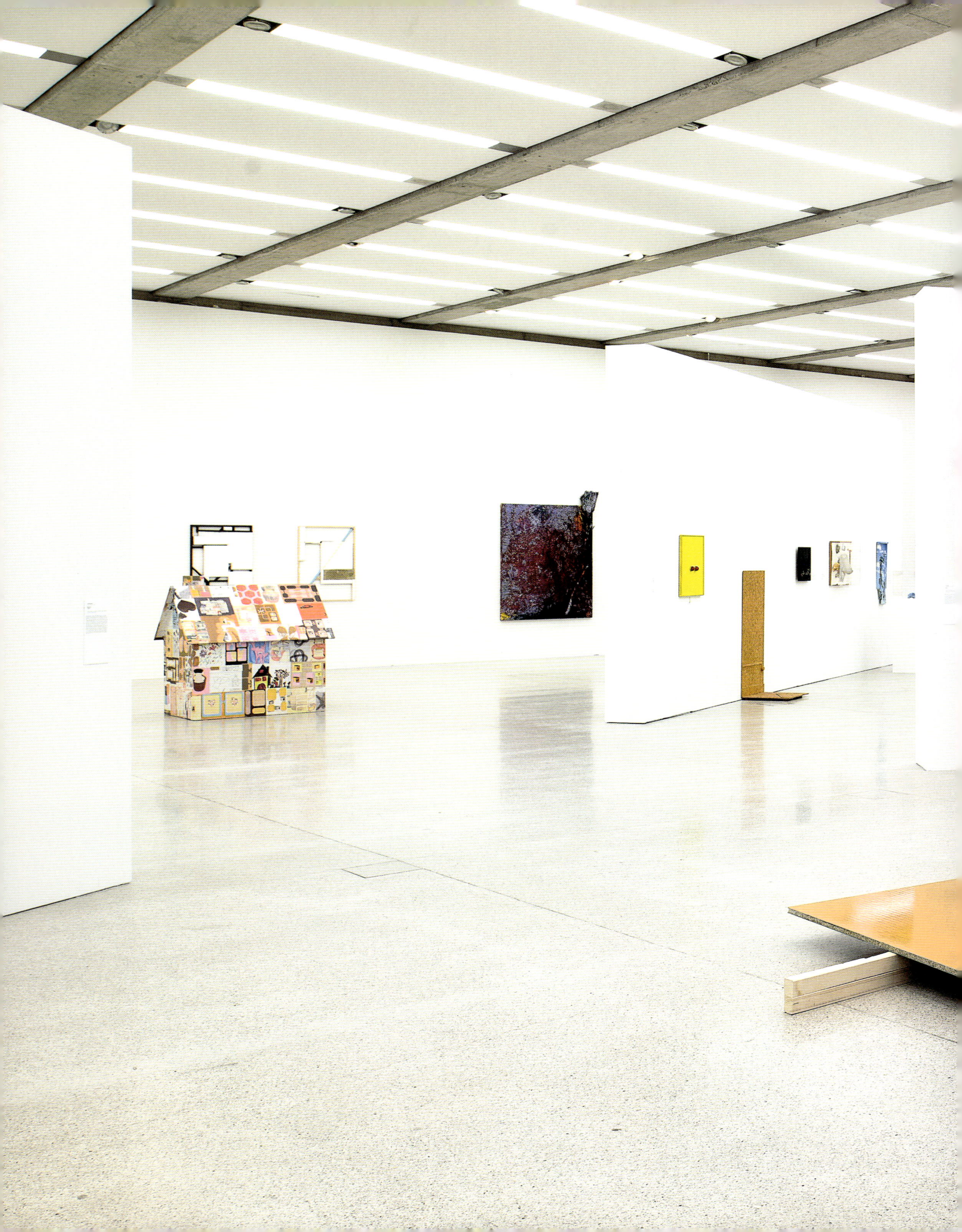

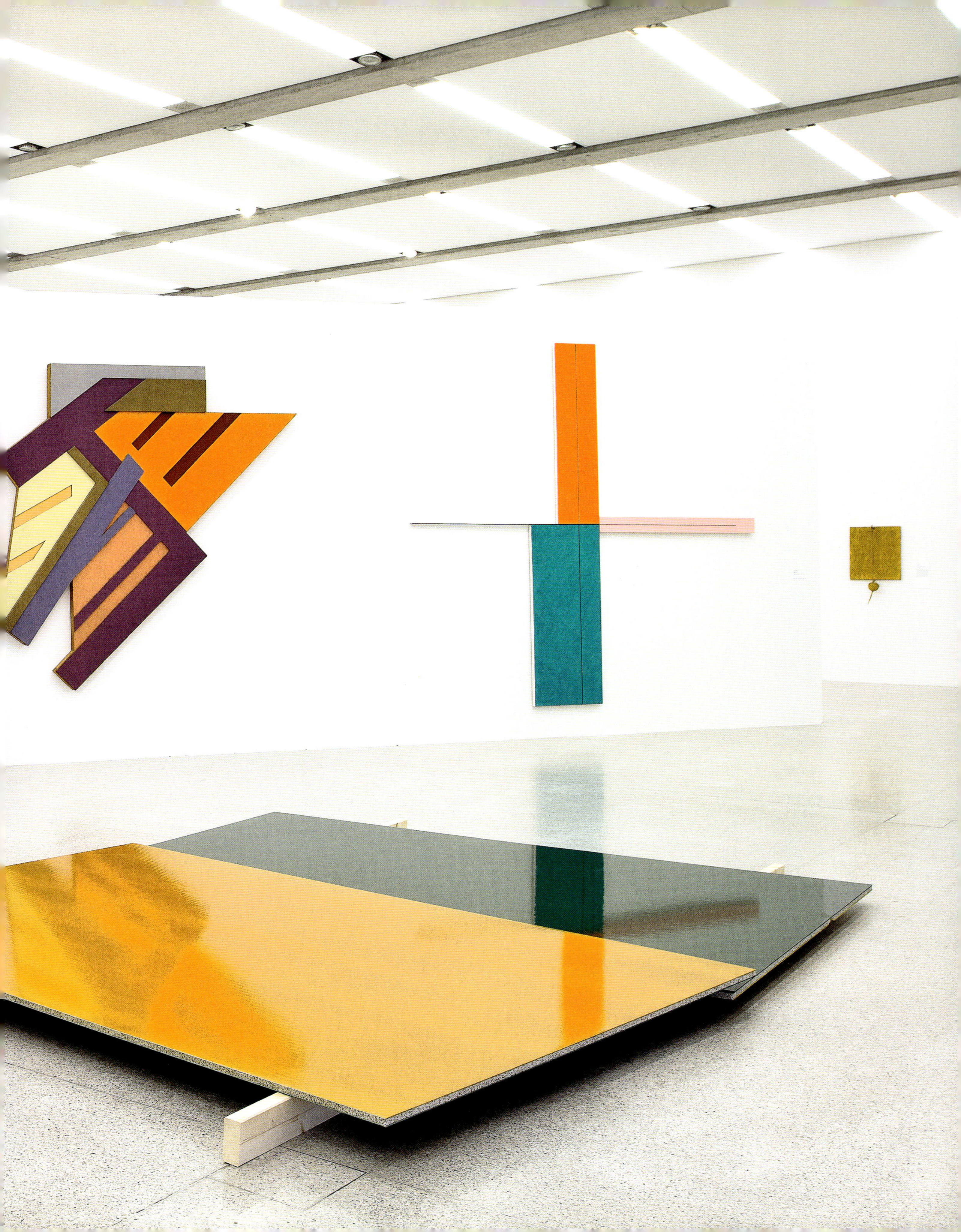

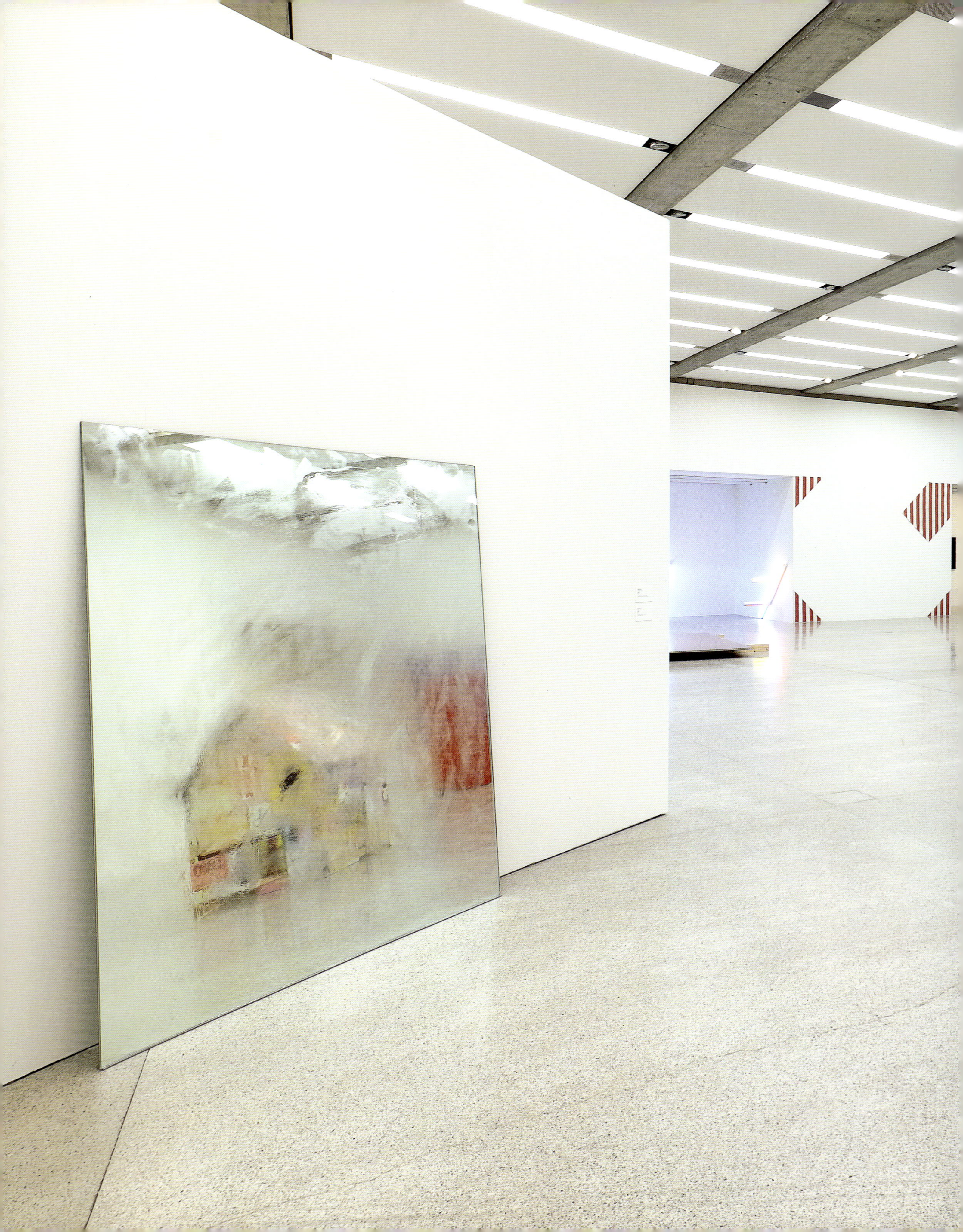

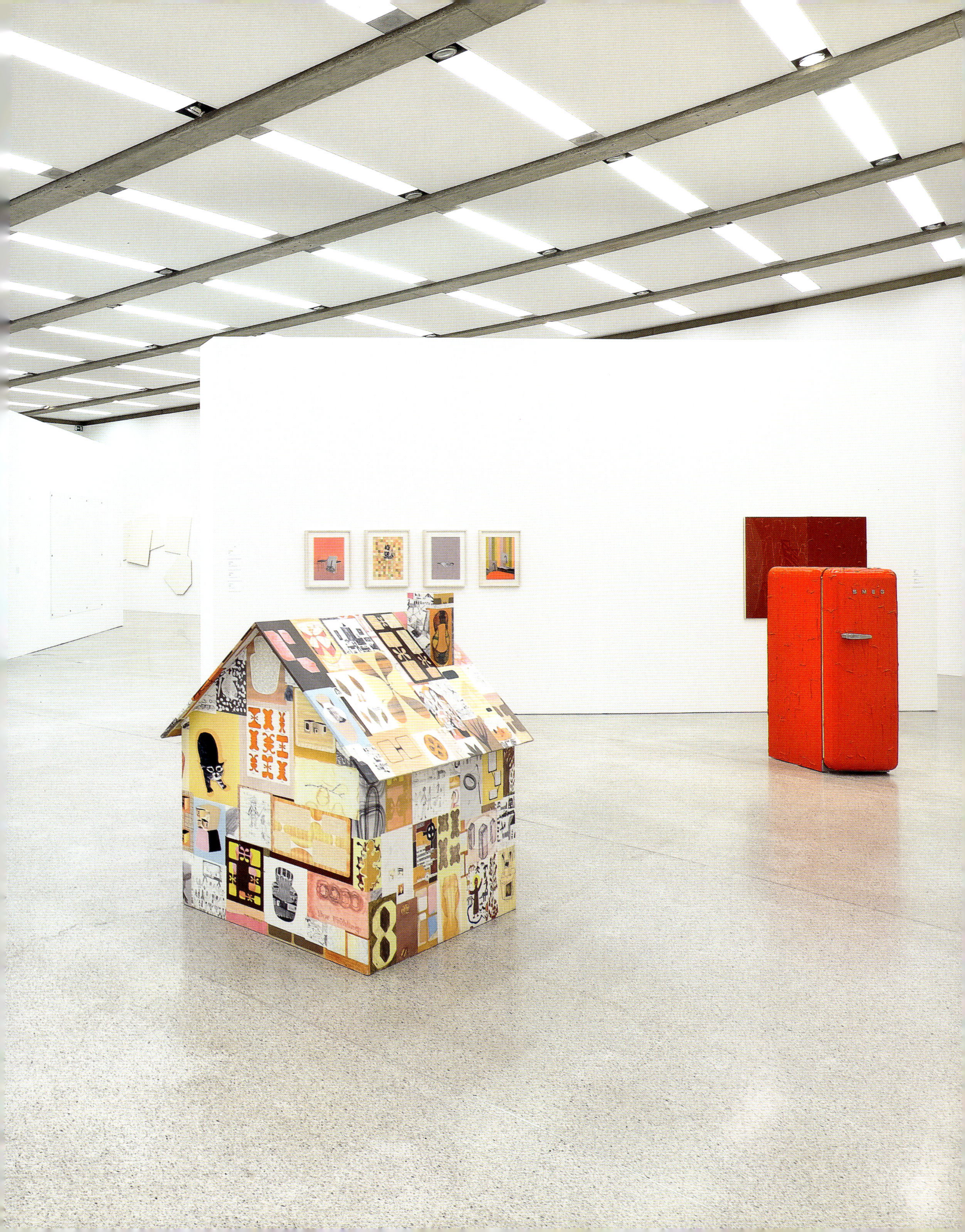

Appendix

Werke in der Ausstellung / Works in the Exhibition

Werke der Sammlung / Works of the MUMOK Collection

John M. Armleder
Ohne Titel (Untitled), 1987
Aluminiumjalousien, Dispersion auf Leinwand
Aluminum blinds, emulsion paint on canvas
200 x 700 x 3 cm
Erworben / Acquired in 2001

John Baldessari
Six Colorful Inside Jobs, 1977
16-mm-Film transferiert auf DVD, Farbe
16mm film transferred to DVD, color,
32:53 min
Erworben / Acquired in 2005

Erwin Bohatsch
Ohne Titel (Untitled), 1994
Acryl, Öl auf Leinwand / Acrylic, oil on canvas
250 x 190 cm
Erworben / Acquired in 1997

Erwin Bohatsch
Sequenz III (Sequence III), 2006
Acryl, Öl auf Leinwand / Acrylic, oil on canvas
190,4 x 330,2 cm
Schenkung des Künstlers
Donated by the artist, 2006

Daniel Buren
Une peinture en 4 éléments pour un mur
(Ein Bild in vier Elementen für eine Wand /
One Painting in Four Elements for One Wall), 1980
Baumwollstoff / Scrim
4-teilig / In four parts: Dimension variabel
Variable dimensions
Erworben / Acquired in 1994

Günter Brus
Wiener Spaziergang (Vienna Walk), 1965
16-mm-Film transferiert auf DVD, S/W, stumm
16mm film transferred to DVD, b&w, silent,
01:45 min
Mit freundlicher Genehmigung von
With permission by Günter Brus

Michael Buthe
Westfälische Landschaft
(Westphalian Landscape), 1990/1991
Mischtechnik auf Leinwand
Mixed media on canvas
180 x 150 x 25 cm
Erworben / Acquired in 1992

John Chamberlain
American Star, 1978
Stahlblech, lackiert und verchromt
Painted and chromed steel
203 x 89 x 74 cm
Leihgabe der Österreichischen Ludwig-Stiftung
On loan from the Austrian Ludwig Foundation,
seit / since 1981

John Chamberlain
Trixie Dee, 1963
Stahlblech, lackiert und verchromt
Painted and chromed steel
138 x 135 x 125 cm
Ehemals Sammlung Hahn
Former Hahn Collection, Köln / Cologne
Erworben / Acquired in 1978

Alan Charlton
Painting in 20 Parts (Bild in 20 Teilen), 1990
Acryl auf Leinwand / Acrylic on canvas
153 x 625 cm
Erworben / Acquired in 1992

Josef Danner
Ohne Titel (Untitled), 1992
Mischtechnik auf Leinwand
Mixed media on canvas
180 x 150 cm
Erworben / Acquired in 1992

Gérard Deschamps
Bâche de Signalisation (Plane / Tarpaulin), 1961
Plane mit abgeblätterter Farbe, Randverstär-
kungen und Metallösen, auf Sperrholzplatte
Tarpaulin with peeling paint, reinforced edges
and metal eyelets, on plywood panel
79 x 168 cm
Ehemals Sammlung Hahn
Former Hahn Collection, Köln / Cologne
Erworben / Acquired in 1979

Erik Dietman
Wand-Boden-Stück (Wall-Floor-Piece), 1964
Leukoplast auf Holz, Teppich und Steckdose
Sticking tape on wood, carpet and power outlet
Wandplatte / Wall panel: 140 x 60 x 6 cm,
Bodenplatte / Floor panel: 53 x 60 x 3,5 cm
Ehemals Sammlung Hahn
Former Hahn Collection, Köln / Cologne
Erworben / Acquired in 1978

Hans Joachim Dietrich
Zwei Blinker (Two Flashing Lights), 1964
Öl auf Leinwand und Keilrahmen, Blinkglüh-
lampen, Kordel, Batterie / Oil on canvas and
canvas stretcher, blinking lights, cord, battery
68,2 x 51,5 x 7 cm
Ehemals Sammlung Hahn
Former Hahn Collection, Köln / Cologne
Erworben / Acquired in 1978

Jim Dine
Yellow Oil Can (Gelbe Ölkanne), 1962
Öl auf Leinwand, Ölkanne, Haken, Kordel
Oil on canvas, oil can, hook, cord
94 x 51 x 31 cm
Ehemals Sammlung Hahn
Former Hahn Collection, Köln / Cologne
Erworben / Acquired in 1978

Noël Dolla
Ripolin Non-Non, 1993
Mischtechnik, Acryl, Lack auf Holz, Blechdosen
Mixed media, acrylic, lacquer on wood, tin cans
221 x 150 x 12 cm
Erworben / Acquired in 1994

Heinrich Dunst
Ohne Titel (Untitled), 1996
Acryl auf Leinwand auf Sperrholz
Acrylic on canvas on plywood
4-teilig / In four parts: 225 x 160 x 12 cm,
201 x 136 x 8 cm, 215 x 45 x 45 cm,
75 x 60 x 10 cm
Erworben / Acquired in 1998

Christian Eckart
Curved Monochrome Painting # 2003
(Geschwungenes monochromes Bild # 2003),
1995
Autolack auf Aluminium / Car paint on aluminum
176 x 107 x 33 cm
Erworben / Acquired in 1997

Christian Eckart
Curved Monochrome Painting # 2005
(Geschwungenes monochromes Bild # 2005),
1995
Autolack auf Aluminium / Car paint on aluminum
176 x 107 x 33 cm
Erworben / Acquired in 1997

Andreas Eriksson
Ohne Titel (Untitled), 2007
Mischtechnik auf Leinwand
Mixed media on canvas
75,1 x 42,3 cm
Schenkung Bâloise-Gruppe und Basler
Versicherungen Österreich, 2008
Donated by the Bâloise Group and Basler
Versicherungen Austria, 2008

Tone Fink
Kreiszentriert (Circle Centered), 1994
Acryl, Quarzsand auf Leinwand
Acrylic, quartz sand on canvas
50 x 40 cm
Schenkung des Künstlers
Donated by the artist, 2008

Tone Fink
Ohne Titel (Untitled), 1989
Acryl auf Leinwand / Acrylic on canvas
40,2 x 30,2 cm
Schenkung des Künstlers
Donated by the artist, 2008

Tone Fink
Ohne Titel (Untitled), 2008
Acryl auf Leinwand / Acrylic on canvas
40,2 x 40,2 cm
Schenkung des Künstlers
Donated by the artist, 2008

Dan Flavin
Untitled (To my friend De Wain Valentine)
Ohne Titel (Für meinen Freund De Wain
Valentine), 1990
Neonröhren, Metall / Neon lights, metal
140 x 140 x 62 cm
Erworben / Acquired in 1993

Dan Flavin
Untitled (To my friend De Wain Valentine)
Ohne Titel (Für meinen Freund De Wain
Valentine), 1990
Neonröhren, Metall / Neon lights, metal
140 x 140 x 62 cm
Erworben / Acquired in 1993

Bernard Frize
Mellegers & Van der Elsakor, 1989
Acryl, Harz auf Leinwand
Acrylic, resin on canvas
240 x 185 cm
Erworben / Acquired in 1998

Bernard Frize
Suite G, 1991/1992
Alkydharz auf Leinwand / Alkyd resin on canvas
13-teilig / In 13 parts: je / each 41 x 33 cm
Erworben / Acquired in 1996

Adolf Frohner
Schwarzer Sessel (Black Armchair), 1962
Draht, Holz, Jute und Seegras auf Holz auf Leinen
Wire, wood, jute and seagrass on wood on linen
Ø 94 cm, 17,5 cm
Leihgabe der Österreichischen Ludwig-Stiftung
On loan from the Austrian Ludwig Foundation,
seit / since 1981

Jakob Gasteiger
Ohne Titel (Untitled), 2000
Lack auf Acryl auf Leinwand
Lacquer on acrylic on canvas
281 x 240,5 cm
Erworben / Acquired in 2001

Jakob Gasteiger
Ohne Titel (Untitled), 2000
Lack auf Acryl auf Leinwand
Lacquer on acrylic on canvas
280 x 240 cm
Erworben / Acquired in 2001

Hermann Glöckner
Dreimal gebrochener Keil auf Schwarz
(Thrice Broken Wedge on Black), 1933–1935
Holz, Lack, Metall / Wood, lacquer, metal
17,5 x 12 x 9 cm
Erworben / Acquired in 1992

Geoffrey Hendricks
Skull (Schädel), 1967
Acryl auf Tierschädel / Acrylic on animal skull
12 x 22 x 9 cm
Ehemals Sammlung Hahn
Former Hahn Collection, Köln / Cologne
Erworben / Acquired in 1978

Geoffrey Hendricks
Soap Saver (Seifensparer), 1965
Acryl auf Waschbrett und Stoff
Acrylic on washboard and fabric
89 x 34 x 8 cm
Ehemals Sammlung Hahn
Former Hahn Collection, Köln / Cologne
Erworben / Acquired in 1978

Christian Hutzinger
Mein Haus (My House), 1995
141 x 103 x 136 cm
Laserkopien auf Holz / Laser copies on wood
Erworben / Acquired in 2001

Christian Hutzinger
Ohne Titel (Untitled), 2004
Acryl auf Leinwand / Acrylic on canvas
40 x 30 cm
Erworben / Acquired in 2001

György Jovánovics
Hommage à Moholy Nagy Q-VIII, 1996
Gips / Plaster
95,5 x 76,3 x 10 cm
Erworben / Acquired in 1996

György Jovánovics
Kassák I., 1996
Gips / Plaster
96,5 x 78,5 x 11 cm
Schenkung der Gesellschaft der Freunde der
bildenden Künste / Donated by the Society of
the Friends of Fine Arts, Wien / Vienna, 2001

Donald Judd
Ohne Titel (Untitled), 1989
Verzinktes Blech / Galvanized tin
30 x 121 x 30 cm
Erworben / Acquired in 1995

Friedrich Kiesler
Galaxy F (Galaxie F), 1960
Gouache, Kohle und Pastell auf Papier,
auf Karton und Holz montiert
Gouache, charcoal, and pastel on paper,
mounted on cardboard and wood
198 x 163 x 17,5 cm
Erworben / Acquired in 1988

Yves Klein
D 54, 1957
Pigment auf Karton und Kunstharz
Pigment on cardboard on synthetic resin
40 x 35 cm
Erworben / Acquired in 1999

Yves Klein
ANT 120, 1960
Pigment, Kunstharz auf Papier auf Leinwand
Pigment, synthetic resin on paper on canvas
55 x 75 cm
Erworben / Acquired in 1998

Yves Klein
Monochrome Bleu (Monochrom Blau /
Monochrome Blue), 1961
Pigment auf Molino auf Spanplatte
Pigment on molino on particle board
72 x 54 cm
Erworben / Acquired in 1982

Imi Knoebel
Ohne Titel (Untitled), 1978
Acryl auf Holz / Acrylic on wood
360 x 340 x 6 cm
Leihgabe der Österreichischen Ludwig-Stiftung
On loan from the Austrian Ludwig Foundation,
seit / since 1981

Stanislav Kolíbal
A Travers, 1974
Gips, Draht, Eisen und Faden auf Holz
Plaster, wire, iron and thread on wood
83 x 77,3 x 8 cm
Sammlung / Collection Dieter und Gertraud
Bogner im / at the MUMOK, seit / since 2007

Jiří Kovanda
Ohne Titel (Untitled), 1991
Kunststoff auf Holz / Plastic on wood
130 x 110 x 3 cm
Erworben / Acquired in 1999

Bertrand Lavier
Cadmium (Kadmium), 1991
Acryl, Cibachrome auf Aluminium
Acrylic, cibachrome on aluminum
98 x 150 cm
Erworben / Acquired in 1994

Bertrand Lavier
SMEG, 1997
Acryl auf Kühlschrank / Acrylic on refrigerator
145 x 61 x 72 cm
Erworben / Acquired in 1998

Morris Louis
Dalet Rash, 1958
Acryl auf Leinwand / Acrylic on canvas
233 x 337 cm
Leihgabe der Österreichischen Ludwig-Stiftung
On loan from the Austrian Ludwig Foundation,
seit / since 1997

Peter Lowe
Ohne Titel (Untitled), 1978
Acryl auf Holzfaserplatte
Acrylic on wood fiberboard
50,2 x 50,2 x 7,9 cm
Sammlung / Collection Dieter und Gertraud
Bogner im / at the MUMOK, seit / since 2007

Peter Lowe
Ohne Titel (Untitled), 1979
Acryl auf Holzfaserplatte
Acrylic on wood fiberboard
50,8 x 50,8 x 7,9 cm
Sammlung / Collection Dieter und Gertraud
Bogner im / at the MUMOK, seit / since 2007

Karel Malich
Schwarzes Relief (Black Relief), 1968/1969
Lack, Kunststoff auf Holz
Lacquer, plastic on wood
90 x 64 x 8 cm
Erworben / Acquired in 1994

Robert Mangold
Plus Minus Painting (Plus Minus Bild), 1982
Acryl auf Leinwand, Aluminium
Acrylic on canvas, aluminum
304 x 323 x 3,5 cm
Erworben / Acquired in 1985

Brice Marden
Tropézienne (Thinking Blue), 1969/1970
Öl, Wachs auf Leinwand / Oil, wax on canvas
175,5 x 92 cm
Leihgabe der Österreichischen Ludwig-Stiftung
On loan from the Austrian Ludwig Foundation,
seit / since 1981

Joseph Marioni
Red Painting (Rotes Gemälde), 1993
Acryl auf Leinen / Acrylic on linen
180 x 170 cm
Erworben / Acquired in 1993

Dóra Maurer
Kvázi-kép No. 86 (Quasi-Bild Nr. 86 /
Quasi-Image No. 86), 1983
Acryl auf Spanplatte / Acrylic on particle board
200 x 128 x 4 cm
Sammlung / Collection Dieter und Gertraud
Bogner im / at the MUMOK, seit / since 2007

François Morellet
Défiguration (nach Tizians Kirschenmadonna),
1989
Grundierung auf Leinwand auf Holz
Primer on canvas on wood
250 x 210 x 4,5 cm
Sammlung / Collection Dieter und Gertraud
Bogner im / at the MUMOK, seit / since 2007

Robert Morris
Ohne Titel (Untitled), 1964
Blei, Draht, Feder / Lead, wire, metal spring
67 x 40 x 6 cm
Leihgabe der Österreichischen Ludwig-Stiftung
On loan from the Austrian Ludwig Foundation,
seit / since 1981

Otto Muehl
Zock-Exercises (Das Ohr / La Dolorosa /
Kardinal / Michaelangelo), 1967
16-mm-Film transferiert auf DVD, Farbe, Ton
16mm film transferred to DVD, color, sound,
12:00 min
Erworben mit Unterstützung der Gesellschaft
der Freunde der bildenden Künste / Acquired
with funding from the Society of the Friends
of Fine Arts Vienna, 2009

Hermann Nitsch
Kleiner Existenz-Altar (Small Existence Altar),
1960
Acryl auf Holz / Acrylic on wood
7-teilig / In seven parts: 310 x 248 cm
Erworben / Acquired in 1983

Hermann Nitsch
Kreuzwegstation (Station of the Cross), 1960
Dispersion, Schlämmkreide auf Leinwand
Dispersion paint and whitening chalk on canvas
190 x 297 cm
Leihgabe der Artothek des Bundes / On loan
from the Artothek des Bundes, seit / since 1976

Hermann Nitsch
Reliktmontage mit blutigen Tüchern
(Relic Montage with Bloody Cloths), 1964
Blut, Kreide, Mullbinde, Papier und Stoff auf
Molino / Blood, chalk, muslin bandage, paper
and fabric on molino
109 x 81 cm
Schenkung / Donated by Ernst Ploil,
Wien / Vienna, 2006

Oswald Oberhuber
Rahmenbild (Frame Picture), 1953
Gips, Ton und Wachs auf Hartfaserplatte auf Holz
Plaster, clay and wax on high-density fiberboard
on wood
93 x 100 x 2,5 cm
Erworben / Acquired in 1978

Jules Olitski
Commissar Demikovsky
(Kommissar Demikovsky), 1965
Acryl auf Leinwand / Acrylic on canvas
244 x 213 cm
Leihgabe der Österreichischen Ludwig-Stiftung
On loan from the Austrian Ludwig Foundation,
seit / since 1999

Pino Pascali
Il muro del sonno (Die Mauer des Schlafes /
The Wall of Sleep), 1966
Kissen, Schaumstoff, Farbe und Holz
Cushions, foam rubber, paint and wood
250 x 230 x 19 cm
Leihgabe der Österreichischen Ludwig-Stiftung
On loan from the Austrian Ludwig Foundation,
seit / since 1981

Jackson Pollock
Seven (Sieben), 1950
Email auf brauner Malpappe, Papier auf Leinwand
Enamel on brown board, paper on canvas
33 x 50 cm
Erworben / Acquired in 1993

Larry Poons
Absent Dinner (Fehlendes Abendessen), 1979
Acryl auf Leinwand / Acrylic on canvas
233 x 88 cm
Erworben / Acquired in 1980

Arnulf Rainer
Übermalung violett (Paintover Violet), 1961
Öl, Kreide auf Leinwand / Oil, chalk on canvas
201 x 81 cm
Erworben / Acquired in 1983

Robert Rauschenberg
Diplomat, 1960
Öl auf Leinwand, verschiedene Materialien
Oil on canvas, various materials
125 x 67 x 11 cm
Leihgabe der Österreichischen Ludwig-Stiftung
On loan from the Austrian Ludwig Foundation,
seit / since 1991

Robert Rauschenberg
Spanish Stuffed Mode Plus, 1971
Pappkartons auf Holz montiert
Cardboard boxes mounted on wood
174 x 128 x 20 cm
Leihgabe der Österreichischen Ludwig-Stiftung
On loan from the Austrian Ludwig Foundation,
seit / since 1981

David Reed
 # 348, 1995/1996
Öl, Alkyd auf Leinen / Oil, alkyd on linen
154 x 259 cm
Erworben / Acquired in 1998

Gerhard Richter
Das Parkstück, 1971
Öl auf Leinwand / Oil on canvas
5-teilig / In five parts: 250 x 625 cm
Leihgabe der Sammlung Ludwig, Aachen
On loan from the Ludwig Collection, Aachen,
seit / since 1978

Gerhard Richter
Grau Nr. 349/3 (Gray No. 349/3), 1973
Öl auf Leinwand / Oil on canvas
250 x 200 cm
Leihgabe der Österreichischen Ludwig-Stiftung
On loan from the Austrian Ludwig Foundation,
seit / since 1987

Gerwald Rockenschaub
1992
Farblose, transparente Acrylglasplatte,
Metallschrauben, Beilagscheiben
Colorless, transparent acrylic glass sheet,
metal screws, washers
205 x 304 x 6 cm
Erworben / Acquired in 1992

Dieter Roth
Schimmelgraphik (Mold Image), 1969
Schimmelemulsionen auf Büttenpapier
Mold emulsions on handmade paper
108 x 80 cm
Ehemals Sammlung Hahn
Former Hahn Collection, Köln / Cologne
Erworben / Acquired in 1978

Dieter Roth
Gartenzwerg als Eichhörnchenfutterplastik
(Garden Gnome as Squirrel Feed Sculpture), 1969
Gartenzwerg, zylindrisch in Schokolade einge-
gossen, Lederkasten, verschiedene Materialien
Garden gnome, cylindrically molded in
chocolate, leather box, various materials
34 x 27 x 22 cm
Ehemals Sammlung Hahn
Former Hahn Collection, Köln / Cologne
Erworben / Acquired in 1978

Niki de Saint Phalle
Tir (Schuss / Shot), 1961
Farbe, Brotschneidemaschine, Gips, Glas und
verschiedene Materialien, auf Holzplatte fixiert
Paint, bread cutter, plaster, glass and various
materials mounted on wooden board
145 x 44 x 33 cm
Ehemals Sammlung Hahn
Former Hahn Collection, Köln / Cologne
Erworben / Acquired in 1978

Adrian Schiess
Flache Arbeit (Flat Work), 1996/1997
Lack auf Kunststoffverbundplatte, Kanthölzer
Lacquer on laminated plastic board, squared
timbers
2-teilig / In two parts: Je / each 200 x 300 x 2 cm
Erworben / Acquired in 1999

Alfons Schilling
Ohne Titel (Untitled), 1962
Acryl, Pulverfarbe auf Molino
Acrylic, powder paint on molino
Ø 221,5 cm
Erworben / Acquired in 1994

Alfons Schilling
Cosmos Action Painting / Desperate Motion, 1962
8-mm-Film transferiert auf DVD, S/W, Ton /
8mm film transferred to DVD, b&w, sound,
12:00 min
Regie / Directed by Niklaus Schilling
Erworben / Acquired in 2009

Florian Schmidt
Untitled 1 (Governance), 2008
Holz, Metall, Kunststoff, Karton, Metallfolie,
Heißsiegelkleber, Nägel, Acrylmasse, Dispersion
Wood, metal, plastic, cardboard, metal foil,
hot glue, nails, acrylic filler, emulsion paint
105 x 75,2 x 5 cm
Erworben / Acquired in 2009

Florian Schmidt
Untitled 3 (Governance), 2008
Lack, Dispersion auf Holz
Lacquer, emulsion paint on wood
105 x 75,2 x 5 cm
Erworben / Acquired in 2009

Bernard Schultze
Migof-Mantel-Stilleben, 1964–1971
Öl auf Draht, Eisen, Holz, Kunststoff, Hand einer
Schaufensterpuppe und diverse Materialien
Oil on wire, iron, plastic, hand of a shop window
mannequin and various materials
180 x 140 x 120 cm
Ehemals Sammlung Hahn
Former Hahn Collection, Köln / Cologne
Erworben / Acquired in 1978

Rudolf Schwarzkogler
Ohne Titel (Sigmund-Freud-Bild)
(Untitled [Sigmund Freud Picture]), 1965
Lack, Schnur, Korkstöpsel, Rasierklinge auf
Pressspanplatte / Lacquer, string, cork stopper,
razor blade on particle board
108 x 53 x 5,5 cm
Leihgabe der Österreichischen Ludwig-Stiftung
On loan from the Austrian Ludwig Foundation,
seit / since 1984

Pierre Soulages
Peinture (Bild / Painting), 1959
Nussbeize auf Papier auf Leinwand
Nut stain on paper on canvas
76 x 56 cm
Erworben / Acquired in 1963

Daniel Spoerri
Où est la vipère – Une page d'histoire
(Wo ist die Viper – eine Seite der Geschichte /
Where Is the Viper—A Page of History), 1974
Glas, Knochen, Schmetterling, Pinsel, Farbe,
verschiedene Materialien auf Papier auf Holz
montiert / Glass, bone, butterfly, paintbrush,
paint, various materials on paper mounted
on wood
57 x 76 x 14 cm
Ehemals Sammlung Hahn
Former Hahn Collection, Köln / Cologne
Erworben / Acquired in 1978

Henryk Stażewski
Relief, 1965
Kupfer, Holzplatte, Acryl
Copper, wooden board, acrylic
45 x 37 x 2 cm
Erworben / Acquired in 1992

Frank Stella
Lipsko II, 1972
Mischtechnik / Mixed media
249 x 238,5 cm
Leihgabe der Österreichischen Ludwig-Stiftung
On loan from the Austrian Ludwig Foundation,
seit / since 1998

Christian Stock
Blaues Würfelbild (Blue Cube Painting),
Juli 1989–Mai 1990 / July 1989–May 1990
Acryl auf Leinwand / Acrylic on canvas
15 x 15 x 15 cm
Erworben / Acquired in 1990

Jessica Stockholder
Garden Seat (Gartenschaukel), 1997
Mischtechnik, Gartenschaukel, Textilien, Kabel,
Klebeband, Holz, Silikon, Lampen, Schnur,
verschiedene Materialien
Mixed media, porch swing, textiles, cable,
adhesive tape, wood, silicone, lamps, string,
various materials
176 x 404 x 294 cm
Erworben / Acquired in 2000

Jorrit Tornquist
Licht und Schatten (Light and Shadow), 1979
Acryl auf Leinwand / Acrylic on canvas
80 x 132,1 x 40 cm
Sammlung / Collection Dieter und Gertraud
Bogner im / at the MUMOK, seit / since 2007

Rosemarie Trockel
Ohne Titel (Untitled), 1991
Email auf Stahl, Herdplatten
Enamel on steel, hot plates
90 x 70 x 10 cm
Erworben / Acquired in 1998

Cy Twombly
Ohne Titel (Untitled), 1968
Wandfarbe auf Ölbasis, Wachskreide auf Leinwand
Oil-based wall paint, wax crayon on canvas
175 x 218 cm
Leihgabe der Österreichischen Ludwig-Stiftung
On loan from the Austrian Ludwig Foundation,
seit / since 1991

Walter Vopava
Ohne Titel (Untitled), 1991
Dispersion auf Leinwand
Emulsion paint on canvas
300 x 530 cm
Erworben / Acquired in 1992

Wolf Vostell
Transmigracion N. 8, 1960
Öl, decollagierte Plakatreste, Metall, Eierkarton
auf Leinwand, montiert auf Keilrahmen
Oil, decollaged poster remnants, metal,
egg boxes on canvas mounted on a stretcher
41 x 41 x 10 cm
Ehemals Sammlung Hahn
Former Hahn Collection, Köln / Cologne
Erworben / Acquired in 1978

Max Weiler
*Wie eine Landschaft, Hochmoor, neblig, sumpfig,
dunstig, nass, Gras, Kräuter, Moos. Aus dem
Werkblock „Wie eine Landschaft", großformatigen
Übersetzungen von Ausschnitten aus Probierpapieren* (Like a landscape, upland moor, foggy,
boggy, hazy, damp, grass, herbs, moss. From
the group of works "Like a Landscape", large
format transpositions of cut-out segments
from various wipe-off sheets), 1964
Eitempera auf Leinwand / Egg tempera on canvas
96 x 196 cm
Leihgabe der Artothek des Bundes / On loan
from the Artothek des Bundes, seit / since 1979

Max Weiler
Flügelbild: Große Blume
(Polyptych: Large Flower), 1968
Eitempera auf Spanplatte und Karton
Egg tempera on chipboard and cardboard
Grundfläche / Area / 50 x 150 cm, mit
geöffneten Flügeln / with opened panels:
210 x 176 cm
Leihgabe der Artothek des Bundes / On loan
from the Artothek des Bundes, seit / since 1970

Max Weiler
*Probierpapier mit Motiveingrenzung für die
Übersetzung in Gemälde* (Wipe-off sheet with
motif fields for integrating into paintings),
1960er-Jahre / 1960s
Eitempera, Bleistift auf Papier
Egg tempera, pencil on paper
29,8 x 38,9 cm
Schenkung / Donated by Yvonne Weiler, 2010

Lois Weinberger
Ohne Titel (Untitled), 1989
Kunstharzlack, Öl auf Leinwand
Acrylic lacquer, oil on canvas
129 x 100 cm
Erworben / Acquired in 1992

Otto Zitko
Ohne Titel (Untitled), 1996
Öl auf Aluminium / Oil on aluminum
300 x 440 cm
Erworben / Acquired in 1997

Leo Zogmayer
Rot (Red), 1998
Acryl auf Sperrholz / Acrylic on plywood
241 x 20 x 4 cm
Erworben / Acquired in 2000

Leihgaben / Loans

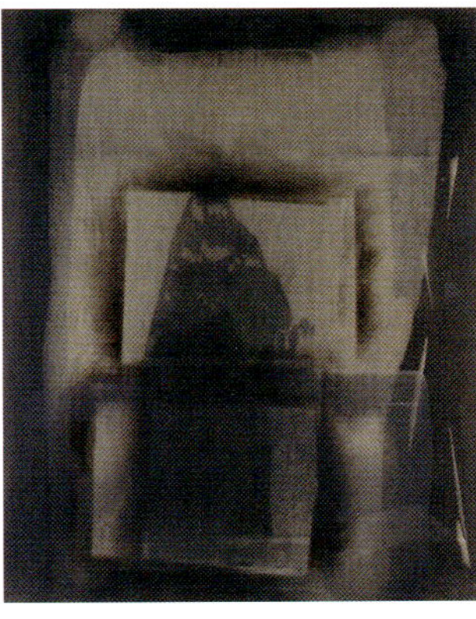

Erwin Bohatsch
Ohne Titel (Untitled), 2010
Öl, Acryl auf Leinwand / Oil, acrylic on canvas
70 x 55 cm
Leihgabe des Künstlers / On loan from the artist

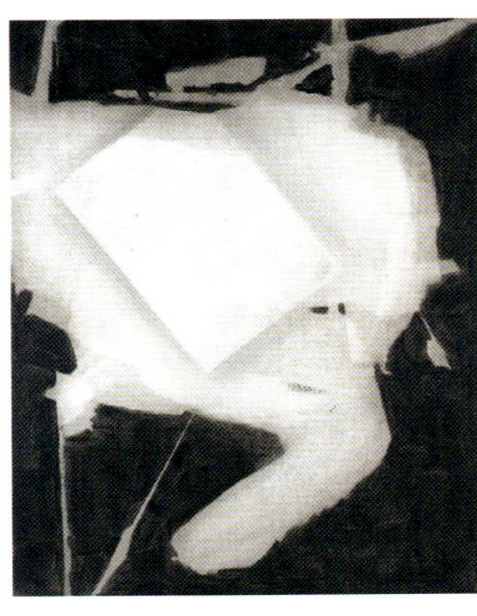

Erwin Bohatsch
Ohne Titel (Untitled), 2010
Öl, Acryl auf Leinwand / Oil, acrylic on canvas
70 x 55 cm
Leihgabe des Künstlers / On loan from the artist

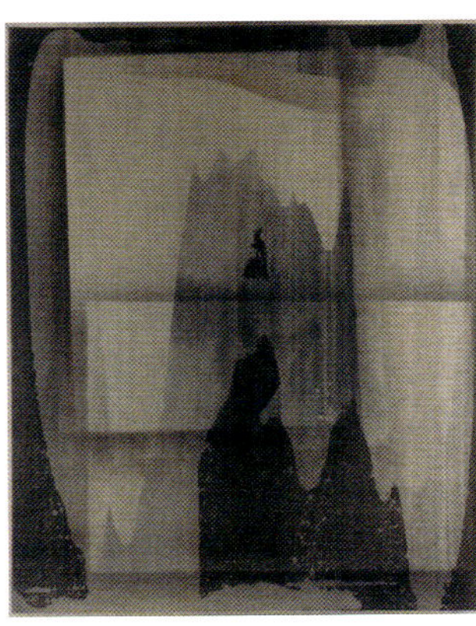

Erwin Bohatsch
Ohne Titel (Untitled), 2009
Öl, Acryl auf Leinwand / Oil, acrylic on canvas
70 x 55 cm
Leihgabe des Künstlers / On loan from the artist

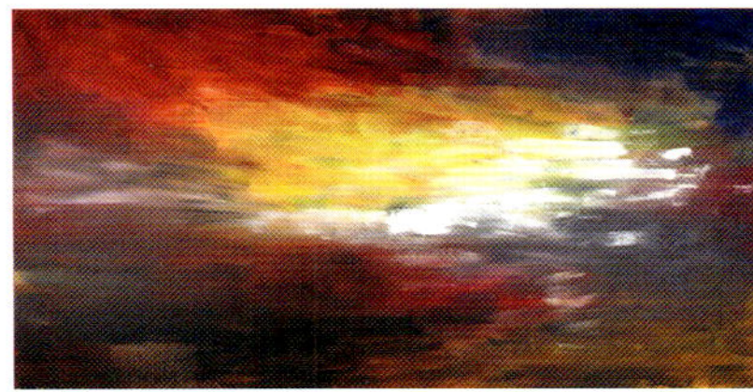

Herbert Brandl
Ohne Titel (Untitled), 2008
Öl auf Leinwand / Oil on canvas
260 x 502 cm
Sammlung / Collection Angermaier,
Wien / Vienna

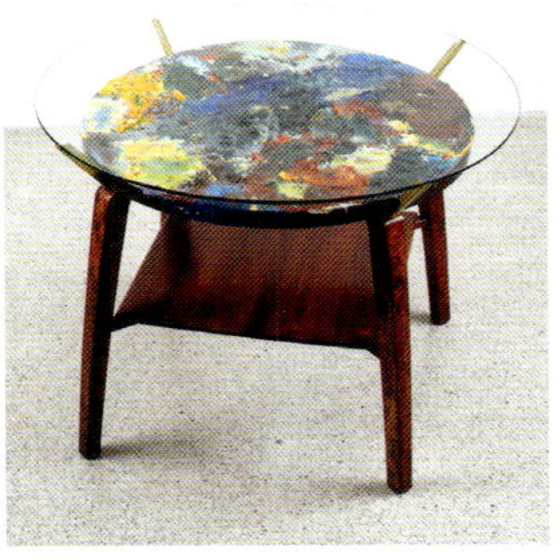

Herbert Brandl
Palettentisch (Palette table), 2010
Verschiedene Materialien / Various materials
Höhe / Height: 73 cm
Tischplatte / Table top Ø 95 cm
Sammlung / Collection Rene Schweiger

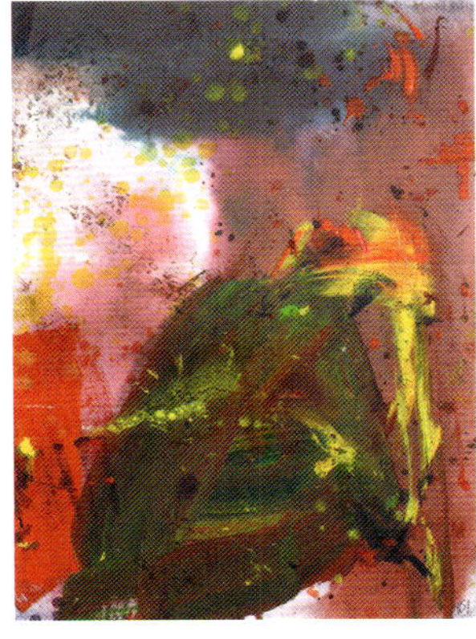

Herbert Brandl
Schmierage, 2010
Öl, Acryl auf Papier / Oil, acrylic on paper
76 x 56 cm
Courtesy Galerie nächst Sankt Stephan
Rosemarie Schwarzwälder, Wien / Vienna

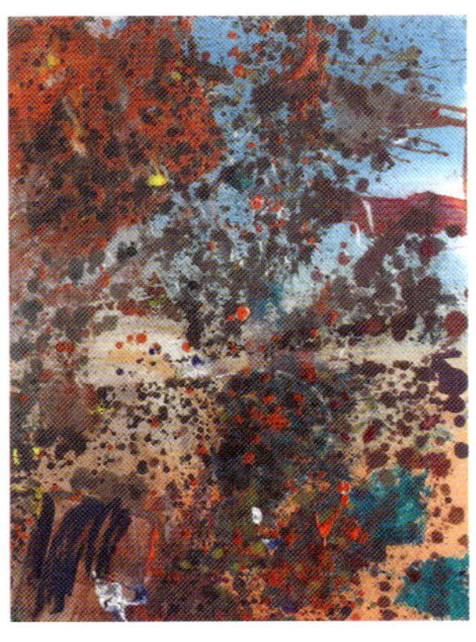

Herbert Brandl
Schmierage, 2010
Öl, Acryl auf Papier / Oil, acrylic on paper
76 x 56 cm
Courtesy Galerie nächst Sankt Stephan
Rosemarie Schwarzwälder, Wien / Vienna

Herbert Brandl
Schmierage, 2010
Öl, Acryl auf Papier / Oil, acrylic on paper
76 x 56 cm
Courtesy Galerie nächst Sankt Stephan
Rosemarie Schwarzwälder, Wien / Vienna

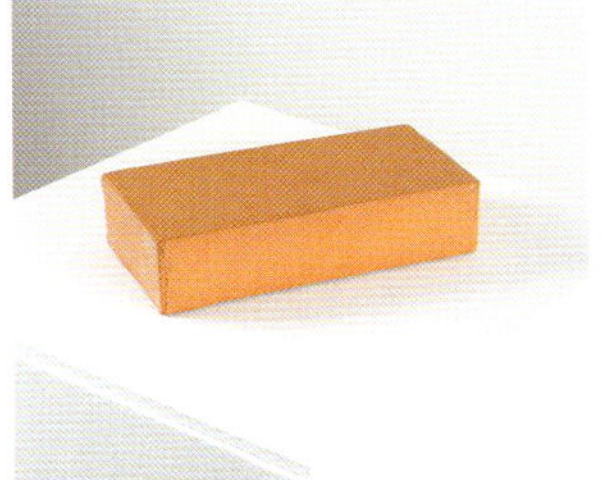

Rafał Bujnowski
Cegła (Ziegel / Brick), 2001
Ziegel / Brick
12 x 25 x 6 cm
Privatsammlung / Private collection

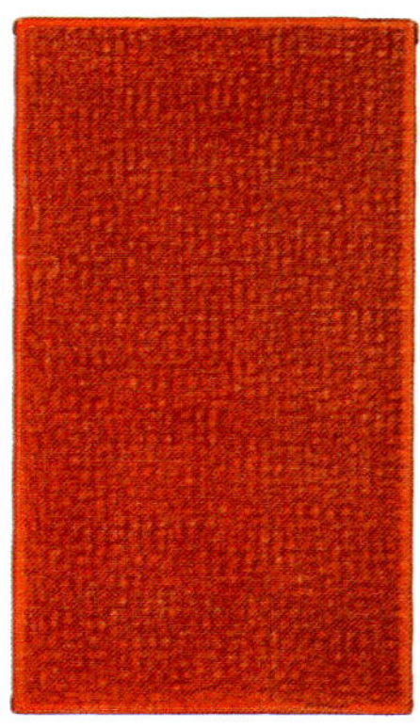

Piero Dorazio
Ferrey Rosso, 1960
Öl auf Leinwand / Oil on canvas
45 x 25 cm
Privatsammlung / Private collection

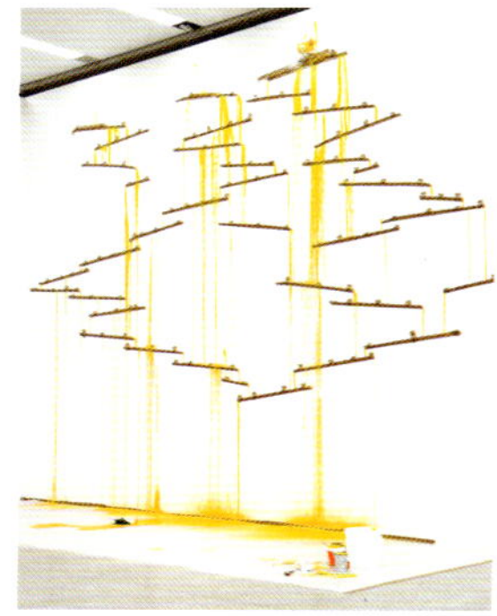

Christian Eisenberger
Ohne Titel (Untitled), 2010
Klebestreifen, Acryllack, Eimer, Hammer,
Spachtel, 3 Lackdosen mit Deckeln, Rolle Klebe-
band, 2 Zigarettenschachteln, Gießkanne, Nägel
Adhesive strips, acrylic lacquer, bucket,
hammer, palette knife, 3 paint tins with lids,
roll of adhesive tape, 2 cigarette packets,
watering can, nails
500 x 640 x 220 cm
Courtesy des Künstlers / the artist
Courtesy Galerie Konzett

Helmut Federle
Legion XXVII, 1999
Acryl auf Leinwand / Acrylic on canvas
50 x 60 cm
Sammlung Sigrid und Franz Wojda
Collection Sigrid and Franz Wojda

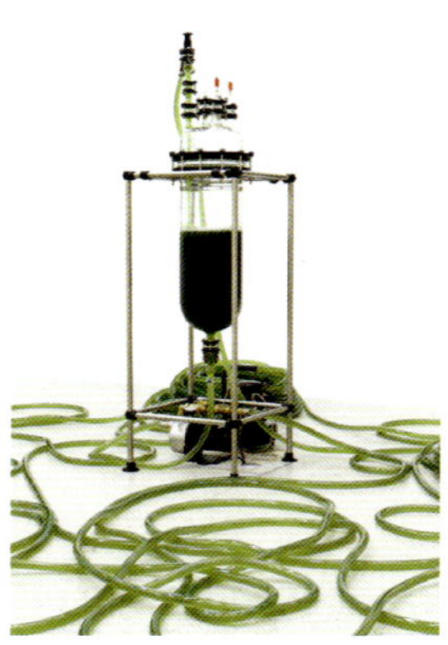

Thomas Feuerstein
Manna-Maschine IV (Manna Machine IV), 2009
Plankton, Bioreaktor, Kompressor, Pumpe,
PVC-Schläuche, Edelstahl, Glas, Wasser
Plankton, bioreactor, compressor, pump,
PVC hoses, stainless steel, glass, water
Variable Dimensionen / Variable dimensions
Courtesy Galerie Elisabeth & Klaus Thoman,
Innsbruck
Courtesy Galerie Stricker, Wien / Vienna

Thomas Feuerstein
Ernte (Harvest), 2004
Leinöl auf Holz / Linseed oil on wood
160 x 120 cm
Courtesy Galerie Elisabeth & Klaus Thoman,
Innsbruck
Courtesy Galerie Stricker, Wien / Vienna

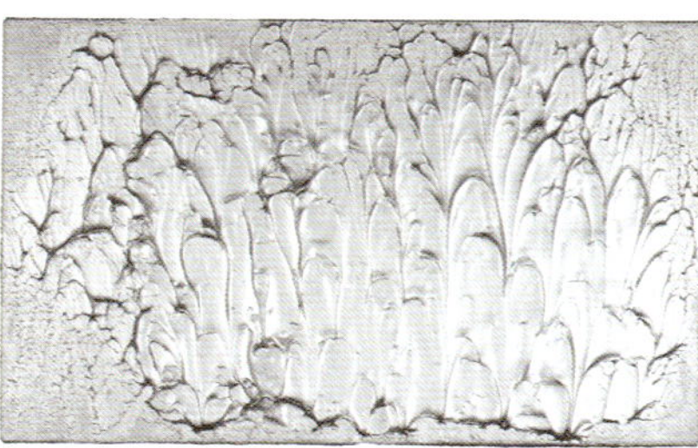

Jakob Gasteiger
Ohne Titel (Untitled), 2002
Aluminium / Aluminum
5-teilig / In five parts: Unterschiedliche Maße
Variable dimensions
Leihgabe des Künstlers / On loan from the artist

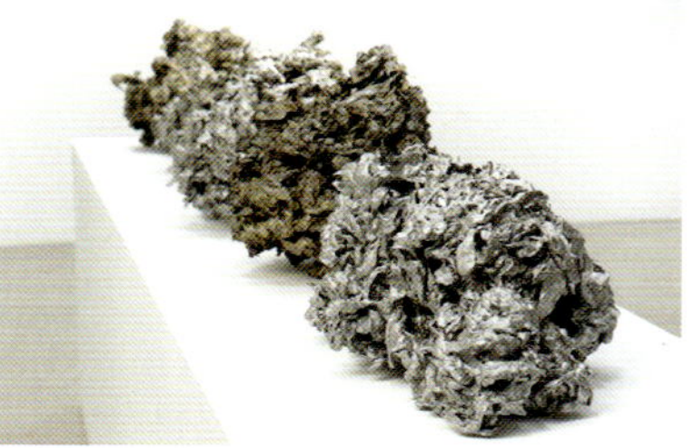

Jakob Gasteiger
Ohne Titel (Untitled), 2002
Aluminium / Aluminum
5-teilig / In five parts: Unterschiedliche Maße
Variable dimensions
Leihgabe des Künstlers / On loan from the artist

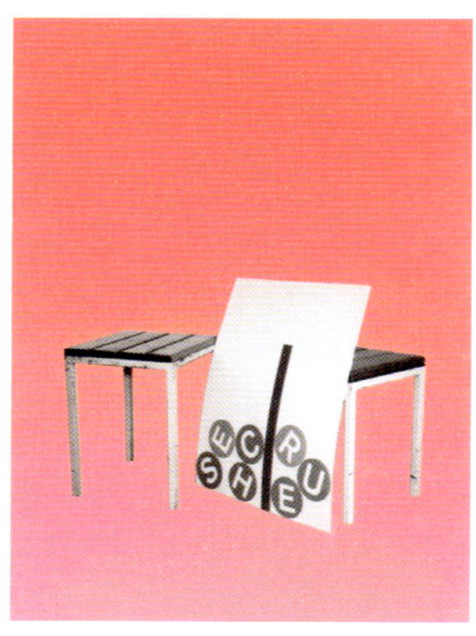

Christian Hutzinger
Ohne Titel (Untitled), 2005
C-Print, Acryl auf HDF-Platte
C-print, acrylic on HDF board
40 x 30 cm
Courtesy Galerie Martin Janda, Wien / Vienna

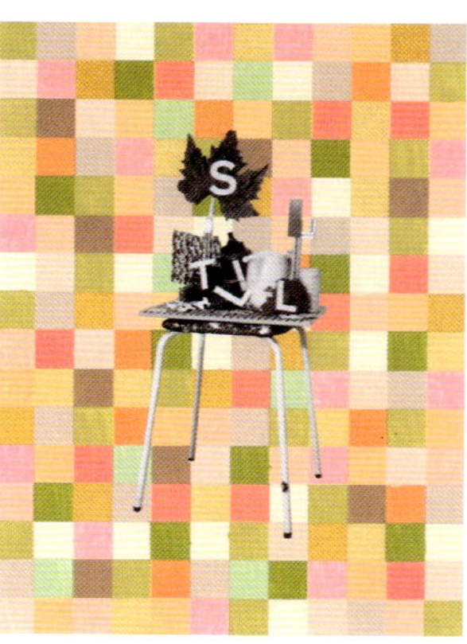

Christian Hutzinger
Ohne Titel (Untitled), 2005
C-Print, Acryl auf HDF-Platte
C-print, acrylic on HDF board
40 x 30 cm
Courtesy Galerie Martin Janda, Wien / Vienna

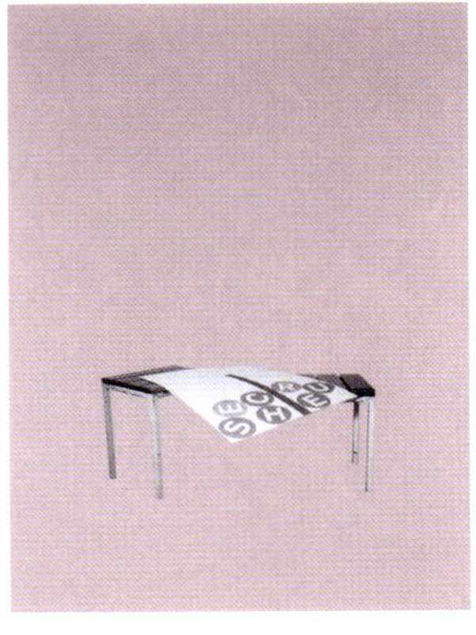

Christian Hutzinger
Ohne Titel (Untitled), 2005
C-Print, Acryl auf HDF-Platte
C-print, acrylic on HDF board
40 x 30 cm
Courtesy Galerie Martin Janda, Wien / Vienna

Thomas Jocher
Ohne Titel (Untitled), 1990
Goldenes Lamé, Schaumgummi, Holz
Golden lamé, foam, wood
43 x 61 x 7 cm
Privatsammlung / Private collection

Michael Kienzer
Ohne Titel (Untitled), 1999
Glas, Spiegelglas, Lack
Glass, mirror glass, lacquer
200 x 160 x 1,2 cm
Leihgabe des Künstlers
On loan from the artist

Ufan Lee
Dialogue (Dialog), 2008
Öl, Pigment auf Leinwand / Oil, pigment on canvas
73 x 92 cm
Courtesy Galerie nächst Sankt Stephan
Rosemarie Schwarzwälder, Wien / Vienna

Thomas Reinhold
Ariadne 1, 2007
Tempera, Öl auf Leinwand / Tempera, oil on canvas
260 x 210 cm
Leihgabe des Künstlers / On loan from the artist

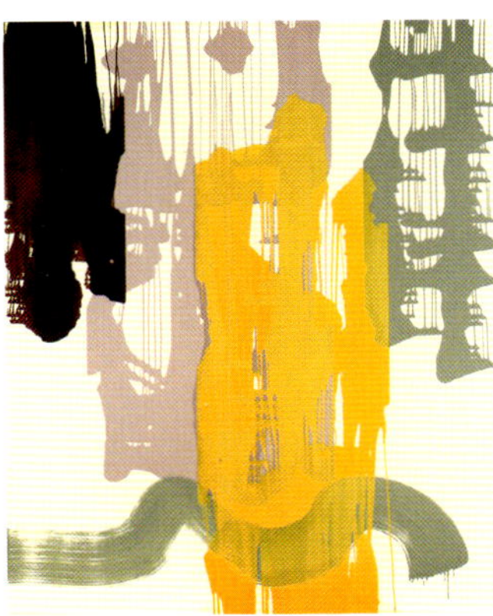

Thomas Reinhold
Ariadne 2, 2007
Tempera, Öl auf Leinwand / Tempera, oil on canvas
260 x 210 cm
Leihgabe des Künstlers / On loan from the artist

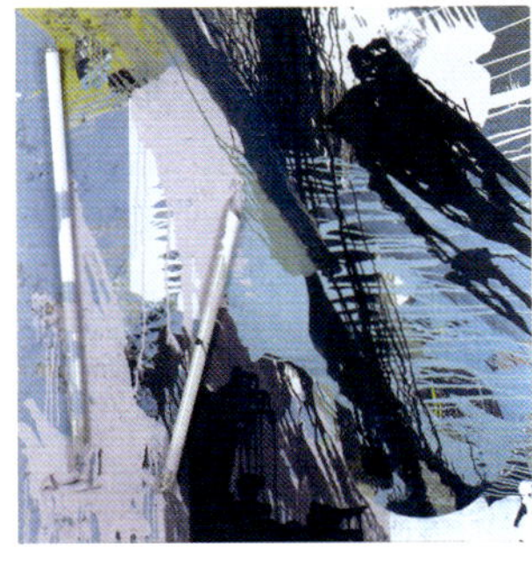

Thomas Reinhold
La Visitation, 1996/1997
Öl, Material auf Leinwand / Oil, material on canvas
157 x 147 cm
Leihgabe des Künstlers / On loan from the artist

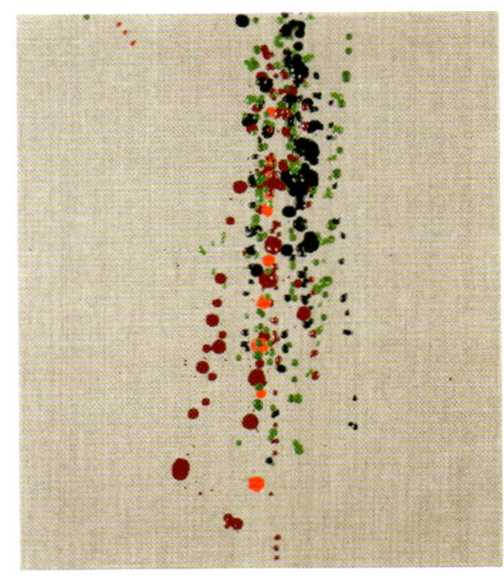

Andreas Reiter Raabe
Dripping, 2009/2010
Acryl, Lack auf Leinwand
Acrylic, lacquer on canvas
60 x 50 cm
Leihgabe des Künstlers / On loan from the artist

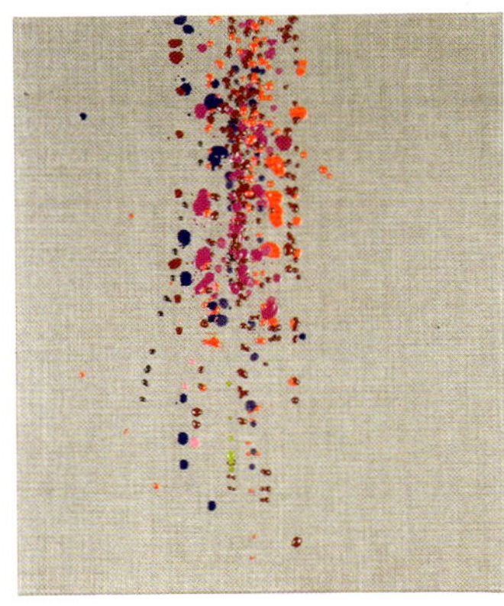

Andreas Reiter Raabe
Dripping, 2010
Acryl, Lack auf Leinwand
Acrylic, lacquer on canvas
60 x 50 cm
Leihgabe des Künstlers / On loan from the artist

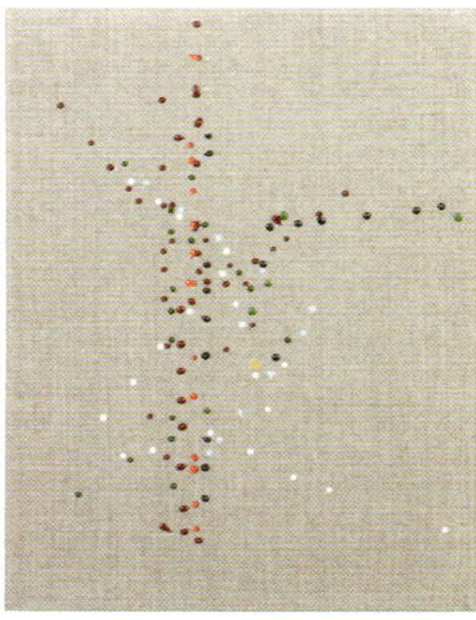

Andreas Reiter Raabe
Dripping, 2008
Acryl, Lack auf Leinwand
Acrylic, lacquer on canvas
40 x 30cm
Leihgabe des Künstlers / On loan from the artist

Karin Sander
Gebrauchsbild (Rampe) (Picture for use [Ramp]),
11.03.2005 / 11 March 2005
Baumwollgewebe auf Keilrahmen
Cotton cloth on stretched canvas
60 x 40 cm
Courtesy Galerie nächst Sankt Stephan
Rosemarie Schwarzwälder, Wien / Vienna

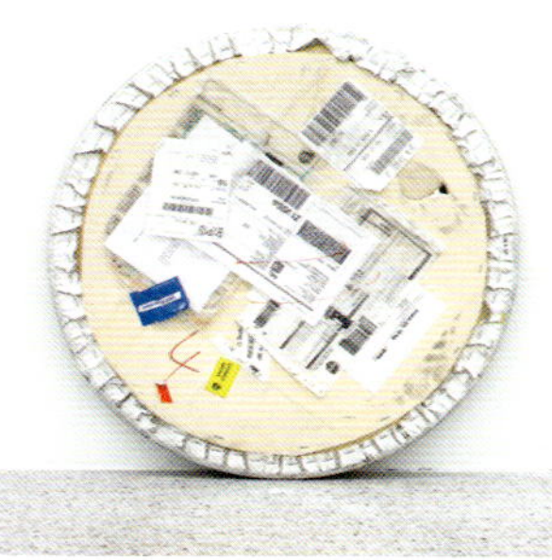

Karin Sander
Mailed Painting, Bonn–Berlin–Wien, 2007–2009
Weißgrundierte Leinwand
White primed canvas, Ø 60 cm
Courtesy Galerie nächst Sankt Stephan
Rosemarie Schwarzwälder, Wien / Vienna

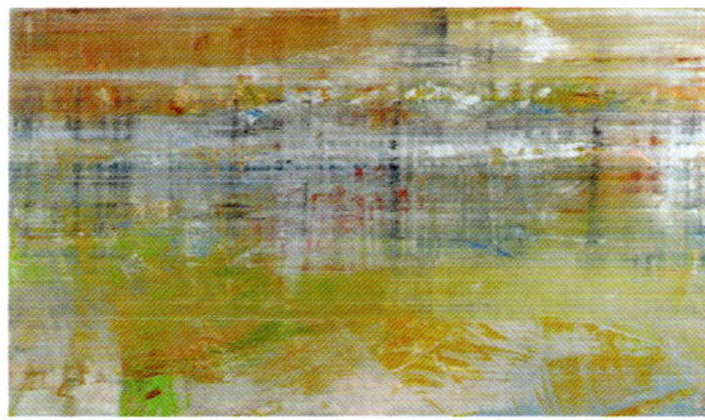

Hubert Scheibl
„... ja er reagiert so als würde er Gefühle haben"
("... yes, he reacts as if he had feelings"), 2008
Öl auf Leinwand / Oil on canvas
290 x 480 cm
Leihgabe des Künstlers / On loan from the artist

Shozo Shimamoto
Ohne Titel (Untitled), 1952
Lack auf übereinander geklebten Zeitungen
Lacquer on glued-together newspaper
47 x 40 cm
Sammlung / Collection Philipp Konzett,
Wien / Vienna

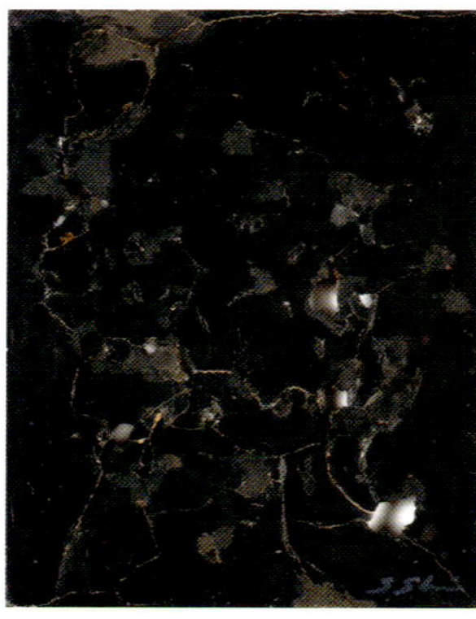

Shozo Shimamoto
Ohne Titel (Untitled), 1951
Lack auf übereinander geklebten Zeitungen
Lacquer on glued-together newspaper
42,5 x 33 cm
Sammlung / Collection Philipp Konzett,
Wien / Vienna

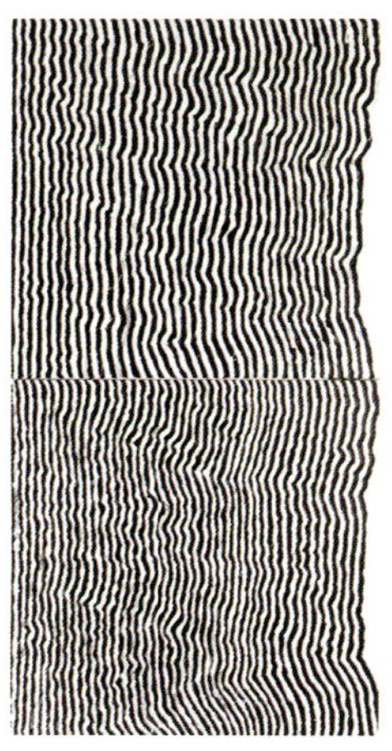

Rudi Stanzel
Ohne Titel (Untitled), 1984
Acryl auf Leinwand / Acrylic on canvas
2-teilig / In two parts: 260 x 128 cm
Courtesy Galerie Ulysses, Wien / Vienna

Rudi Stanzel
Ohne Titel (Untitled), 2008
Tusche auf Spachtelmasse auf Holz
Indian ink on filler on wood
80 x 120 cm
Courtesy Galerie Ulysses, Wien / Vienna

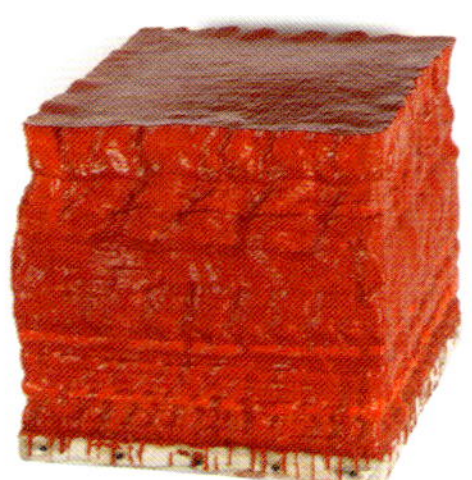

Christian Stock
Rotes Würfelbild (Red Cube Painting),
1983–1988
Acryl auf Leinwand / Acrylic on canvas
25 x 25 x 25 cm
Privatsammlung / Private collection

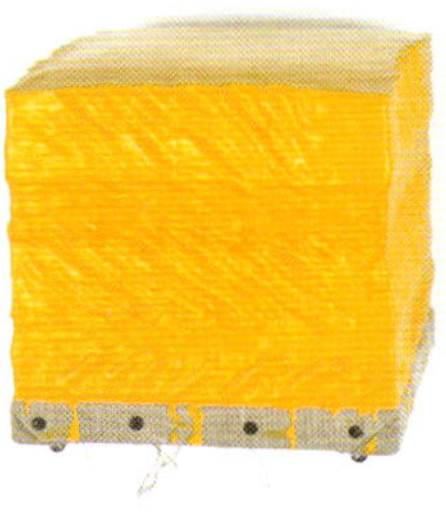

Christian Stock
Gelbes Würfelbild (Yellow Cube Painting),
1990–1992
Acryl auf Leinwand / Acrylic on canvas
18 x 18 x 18 cm
Privatsammlung / Private collection

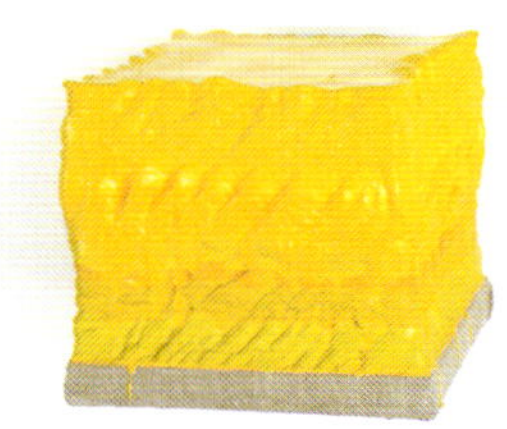

Christian Stock
Gelbes Würfelbild (Yellow Cube Painting),
1997–2010
Acryl auf Leinwand / Acrylic on canvas
18 x 18 x 18 cm
Leihgabe des Künstlers / On loan from the artist

Christian Stock
X, 1995
Acryldispersion auf Leinwand
Acrylic emulsion on canvas
100 x 100 cm
Leihgabe des Künstlers / On loan from the artist

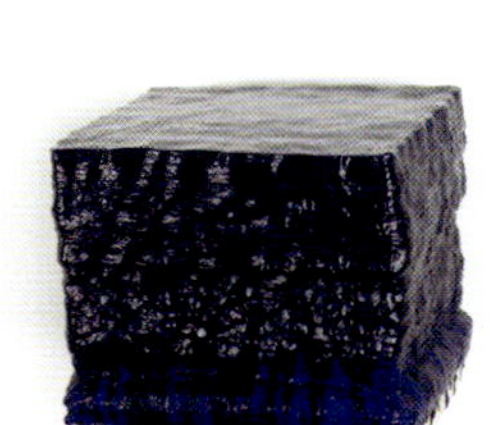

Christian Stock
Blaues Würfelbild (Blue Cube Painting),
1983–1985
Acryl auf Leinwand / Acrylic on canvas
15 x 15 x 15 cm
Leihgabe des Künstlers / On loan from the artist

Christian Stock
Unvollendete Pyramide (Uncompleted Pyramid),
1986
Acryldispersion auf Leinwand
Acrylic emulsion on canvas
23 x 23 x 4 cm
Leihgabe des Künstlers / On loan from the artist

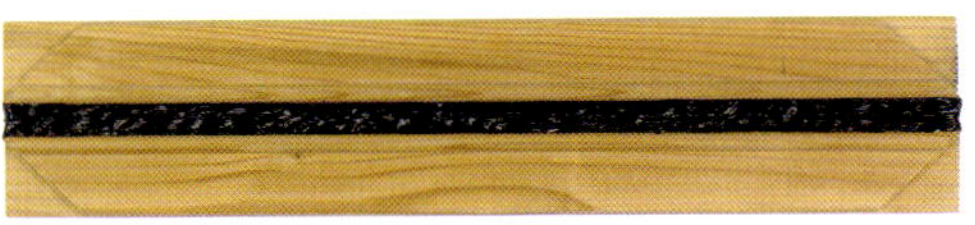

Christian Stock
DAZWISCHEN (BETWEEN), 1988
Acryl auf Keilrahmenholz
Acrylic on stretcher frame
50 x 11 cm
Leihgabe des Künstlers / On loan from the artist

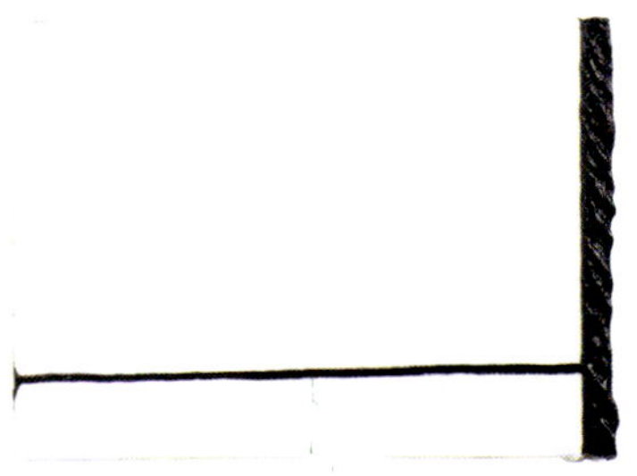

Christian Stock
DAZWISCHEN (BETWEEN), 1987
Acryl auf Leinwand / Acrylic on canvas
24 x 38 cm
Leihgabe des Künstlers / On loan from the artist

Christian Stock
Weißes Würfelbild (White Cube Painting),
1983–1985
Acrylfarbe auf Leinwand / Acrylic on canvas
18 x 18 x 18 cm
Privatsammlung / Private collection

Christian Stock
X, 1994
Acryldispersion auf Leinwand
Acrylic emulsion on canvas
60 x 60 cm
Leihgabe des Künstlers / On loan from the artist

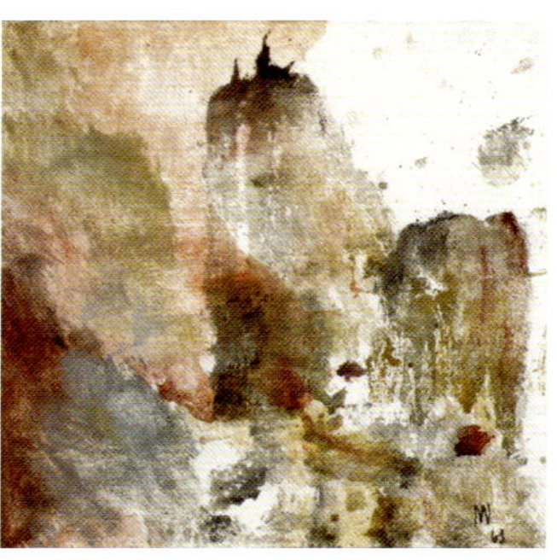

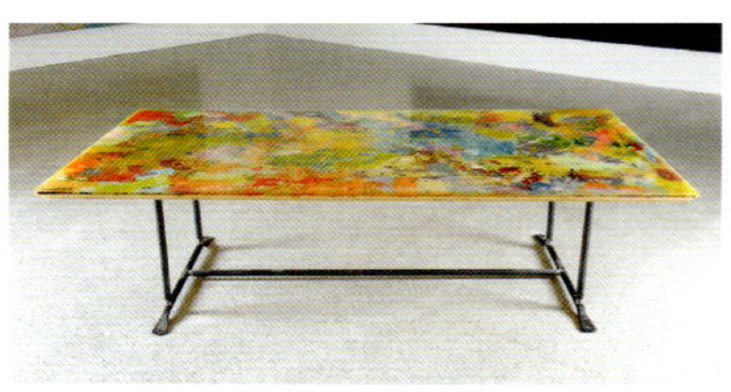

Franz West
Working table in Aspic (Arbeitstisch in Aspik),
2009
Epoxidharz, Holz, Farbe, Stahl
Epoxy resin, wood, paint, steel
252 x 133 cm, Höhe / Height 74 cm
Courtesy Almine Rech Gallery Brüssel /Brussels

Christian Stock
CANVAS CANVAS ON THE WALL, 2010
Acryldispersion auf Leinwand
Acrylic emulsion on canvas
30 x 30 cm
Leihgabe des Künstlers / On loan from the artist

Max Weiler
Wie eine Landschaft, Felsturm (nach Probierpapier)
(Like a landscape, tor [according to wipe-off
sheet]), 1963
Eitempera auf Leinwand / Egg tempera on canvas
90 x 90 cm
Privatsammlung / Private collection

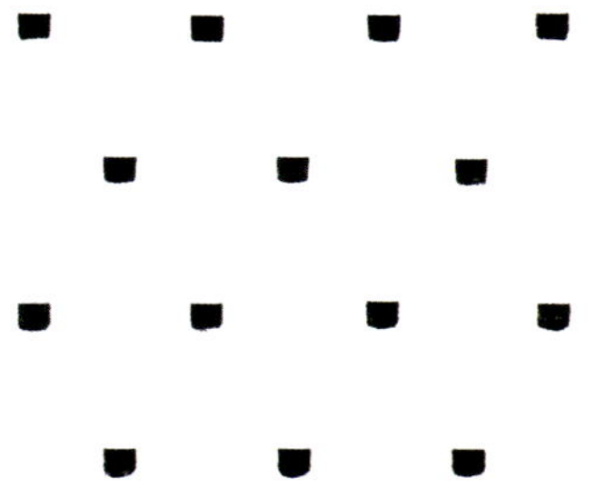

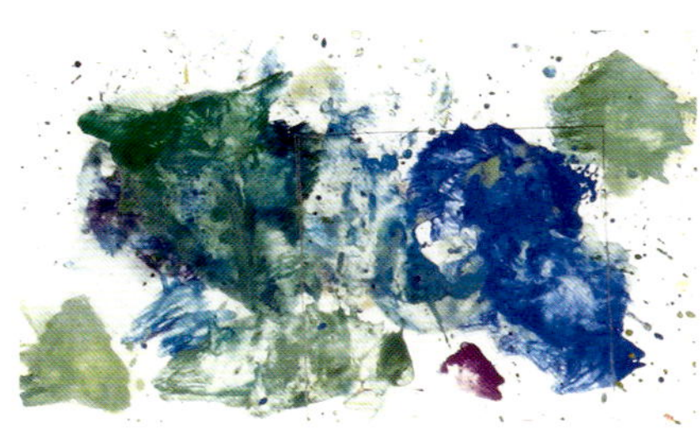

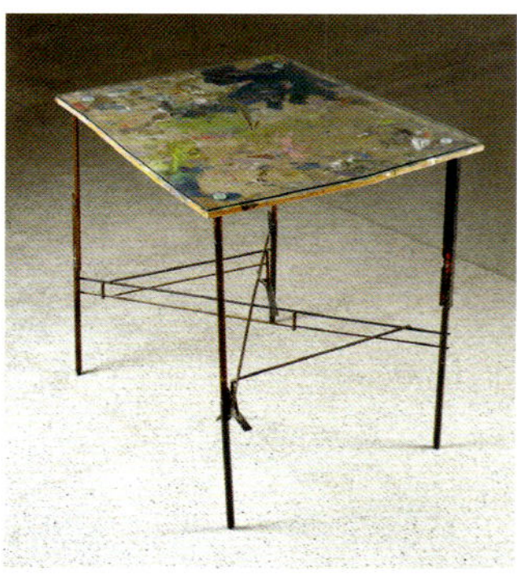

Niele Toroni
Ohne Titel (Untitled), 1988
Öl auf Leinwand / Oil on canvas
100 x 100 cm
Privatsammlung / Private collection

Max Weiler
*Probierpapier mit Motiveingrenzung für die
Übersetzung in Gemälde* (Wipe-off sheet with
motif fields for integrating into paintings)
1960er-Jahre / 1960s
Eitempera, Bleistift auf Papier
Egg tempera, pencil on paper
15,5 x 26,5 cm
Privatsammlung / Private collection

Franz West
Tisch (Table), 2000
Verschiedene Materialien, Holz, Stahl, Glas
Various materials, wood, steel, glass
104 x 84 cm, Höhe / Height 103 cm
Sammlung / Collection Philipp Konzett,
Wien / Vienna

Klaus Dieter Zimmer
dent & bend # 8, 2010
Lack auf Aluminium / Lacquer on aluminum
121 x 183 cm
Leihgabe des Künstlers / On loan from the artist

Max Weiler
*Probierpapier mit Motiveingrenzung für die
Übersetzung in Gemälde* (Wipe-off sheet with
motif fields for integrating into paintings)
1960er-Jahre / 1960s
Eitempera, Bleistift auf Papier
Egg tempera, pencil on paper
24,5 x 34,5 cm
Privatsammlung / Private collection

Günter Umberg
Ohne Titel (Untitled), 1993/94, 1994/96,
2008, 2010
Poliment, Pigment, Dammar auf Holz
Red bole, pigment, dammar on wood
4-teilig / In four parts: 3,5 x 31,5cm;
48 x 45 cm; 30 x 29 cm; 9,5 x 17cm
Sammlung Sigrid und Franz Wojda
Collection Sigrid and Franz Wojda

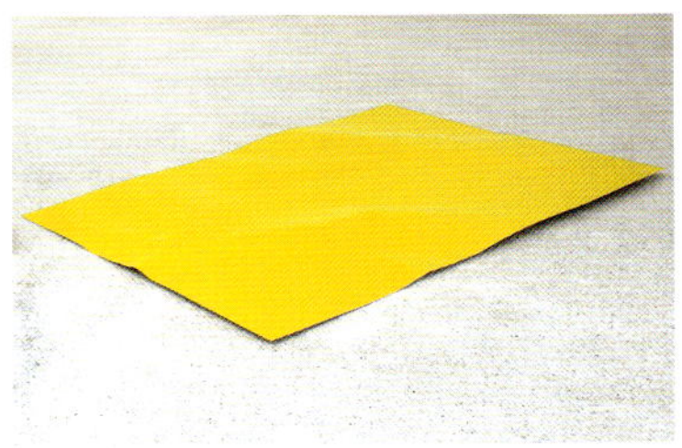

Klaus Dieter Zimmer
dent & bend # 9, 2010
Lack auf Aluminium / Lacquer on aluminum
121 x 183 cm
Leihgabe des Künstlers / On loan from the artist

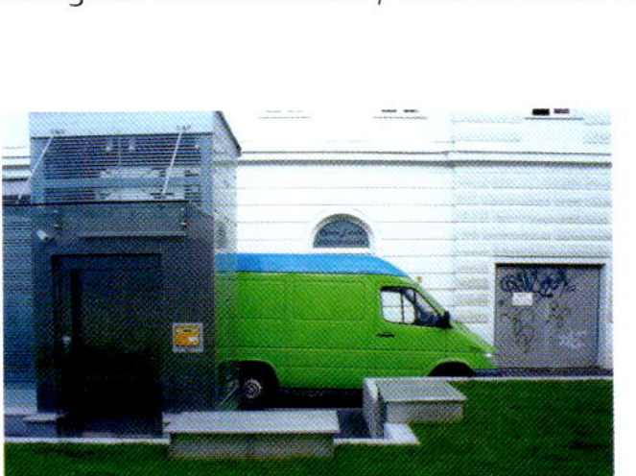

Klaus Dieter Zimmer
Aus der Serie / From the series: *auto paint*, 2007
Lambda-Print
30 x 40 cm
Leihgabe des Künstlers / On loan from the artist

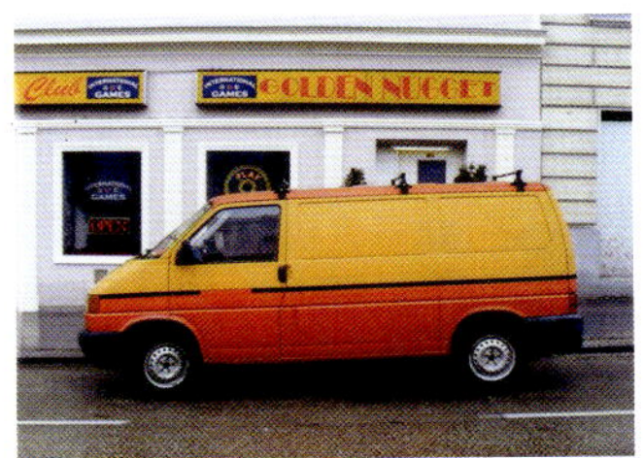

Klaus Dieter Zimmer
Aus der Serie / From the series: *auto paint*, 2010
Lambda-Print
30 x 40 cm
Leihgabe des Künstlers / On loan from the artist

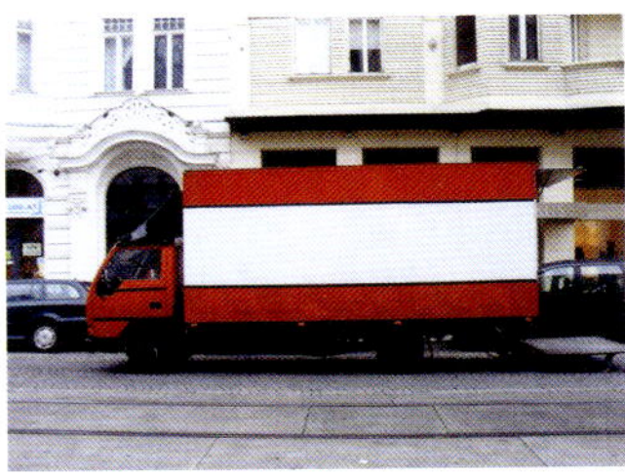

Klaus Dieter Zimmer
Aus der Serie / From the series: *auto paint*, 2009
Lambda-Print
30 x 40 cm
Leihgabe des Künstlers / On loan from the artist

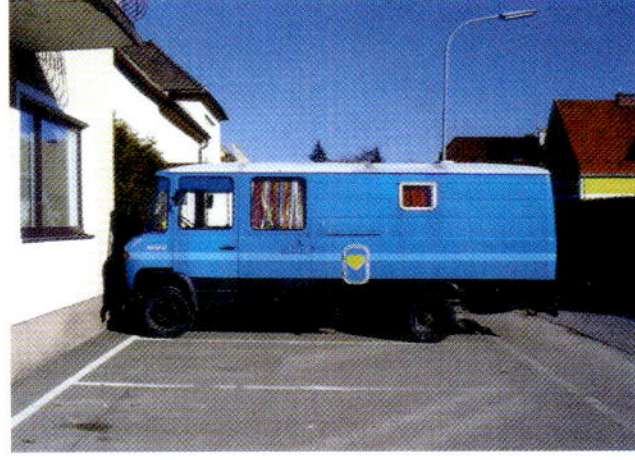

Klaus Dieter Zimmer
Aus der Serie / From the series: *auto paint*, 2008
Lambda-Print
30 x 40 cm
Leihgabe des Künstlers / On loan from the artist

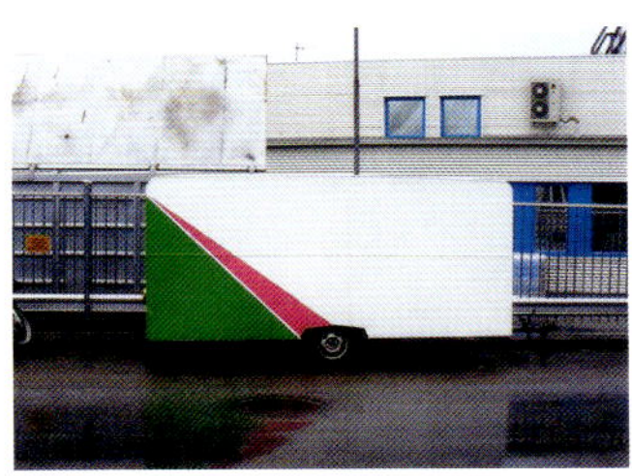

Klaus Dieter Zimmer
Aus der Serie / From the series: *auto paint*, 2009
Lambda-Print
30 x 40 cm
Leihgabe des Künstlers / On loan from the artist

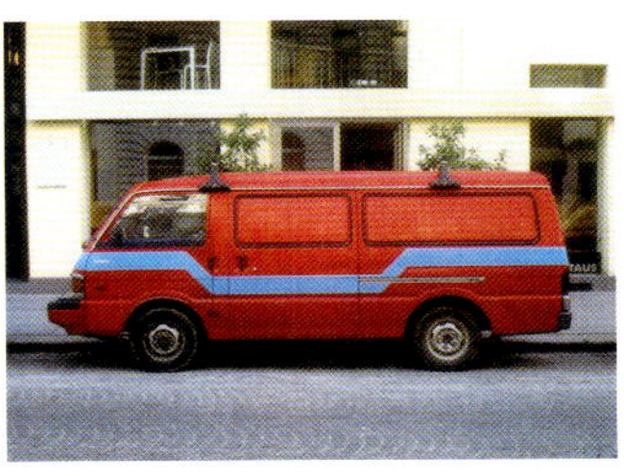

Klaus Dieter Zimmer
Aus der Serie / From the series: *No Land*, 2004
Lambda-Print
30 x 40 cm
Leihgabe des Künstlers / On loan from the artist

Heimo Zobernig
Ohne Titel (Untitled),
1989
Pressspanplatten,
bemalt mit schwarzer
Acrylfarbe
Chipboard, painted
with black acrylic
200 x 80 x 80 cm
Sammlung Generali
Foundation, Wien
Generali Foundation
Collection, Vienna

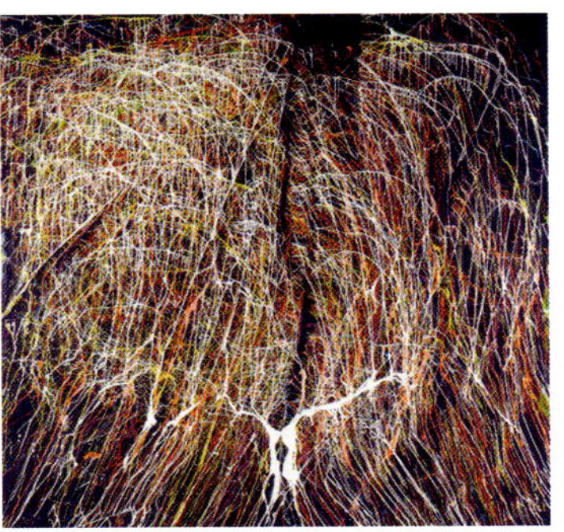

Christina Zurfluh
Strom # 3 (Stream # 3), 2009
Acryl, Lack auf Leinwand
Acrylic, lacquer on canvas
230 x 240 cm
Courtesy Galerie Mezzanin, Wien / Vienna

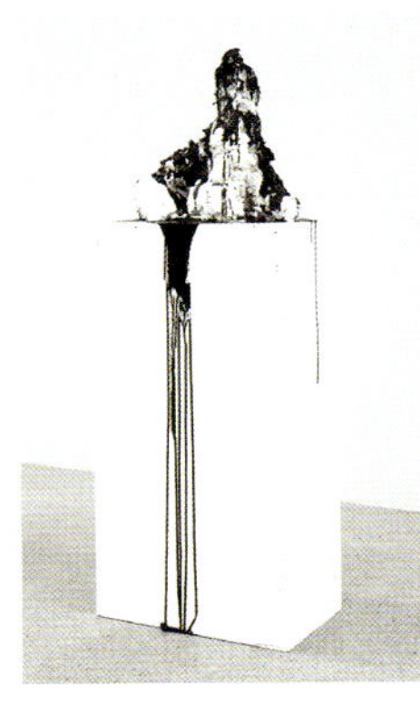

Christina Zurfluh
Aus der Serie / From the series: *Die drei Grazien:
Frohsinn* (The Three Graces: Cheerfulness), 2004
Gips, Jute, Acryl, Pressspan
Plaster, jute, acrylic, particle board
160 x 59 x 36 cm
Courtesy Galerie Mezzanin, Wien / Vienna

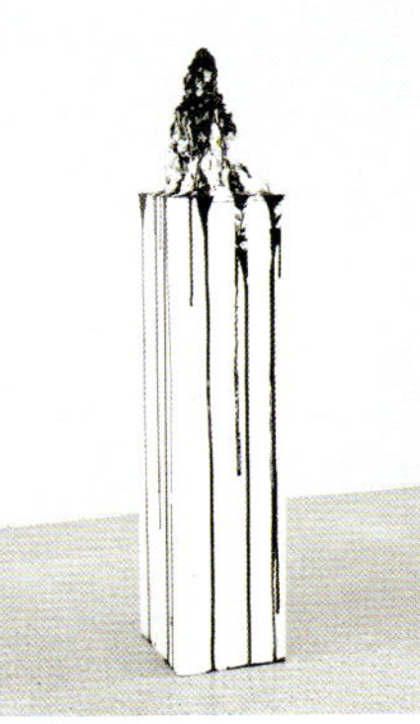

Christina Zurfluh
Aus der Serie / From the series: *Die drei Grazien:
Glanz* (The Three Graces: Brightness), 2004
Gips, Jute, Acryl, Pressspan
Plaster, jute, acrylic, particle board
150 x 35 x 25 cm
Courtesy Galerie Mezzanin, Wien / Vienna

Künstlerbiografien / Artists' Biographies

Marc Adrian 1930–2008
geboren in Wien (Österreich), lebte und arbeitete
in Wien, Hamburg (Deutschland), Cambridge,
Massachusetts (USA) und Kassel (Deutschland),
gestorben in Wien
born in Vienna (Austria), lived and worked in
Vienna, Hamburg (Germany), Cambridge, Massachusetts (USA), Kassel (Germany),
died in Vienna in 2008

John M. Armleder *1948
geboren in Genf (Schweiz), lebt und arbeitet
in Genf und New York (USA)
born in Geneva (Switzerland), lives and works
in Geneva and New York (USA)

Jo Baer *1929
geboren in Seattle, Washington (USA), lebt
und arbeitet in Amsterdam (Niederlande)
born in Seattle, Washington (USA), lives and
works in Amsterdam (Netherlands)

John Baldessari *1931
geboren in National City, Kalifornien (USA),
lebt und arbeitet in Santa Monica, Kalifornien
born in National City, California (USA), lives
and works in Santa Monica, California

Erwin Bohatsch *1951
geboren in Mürzzuschlag (Österreich), lebt und
arbeitet in Wien
born in Mürzzuschlag (Austria), lives and works
in Vienna

Hartmut Böhm *1938
geboren in Kassel (Deutschland), lebt und
arbeitet in Lünen und Berlin
born in Kassel (Germany), lives and works in
Lünen and Berlin

Herbert Brandl *1959
geboren in Graz (Österreich), lebt und arbeitet
in Wien
born in Graz (Austria), lives and works in Vienna

José Bréval *1946
geboren in Chevreuse (Frankreich), lebt und
arbeitet in Chevreuse
born in Chevreuse (France), lives and works in
Chevreuse

Günter Brus *1938
geboren in Ardning (Österreich), lebt und arbeitet
in Graz und auf den Kanarischen Inseln (Spanien)
born in Ardning (Austria), lives and works in
Graz and on the Canary Islands (Spain)

Rafał Bujnowski *1974
geboren in Wadowice (Polen), lebt und arbeitet
in Wadowice und Graboszyce
born in Wadowice (Poland), lives and works in
Wadowice and Graboszyce

Daniel Buren *1938
geboren in Boulogne-Billancourt (Frankreich),
lebt und arbeitet in Paris
born in Boulogne-Billancourt (France), lives and
works in Paris

Michael Buthe 1944–1994
geboren in Sonthofen (Deutschland), lebte und
arbeitete in Köln, Marrakesch (Marokko) und
Mallorca (Spanien), gestorben in Bad Godesberg
(Deutschland)
born in Sonthofen (Germany), lived and worked
in Cologne, Marrakesh (Morocco) and Mallorca
(Spain), died in Bad Godesberg (Germany)

Pedro Cabrita Reis *1956
geboren in Lissabon (Portugal), lebt und
arbeitet in Lissabon
born in Lisbon (Portugal), lives and works in
Lisbon

César 1921–1998
geboren in Marseille (Frankreich), lebte und
arbeitete in Paris, gestorben in Paris
born in Marseille (France), lived, worked and
died in Paris

John Chamberlain *1927
geboren in Rochester, Indiana (USA), lebt und
arbeitet in Sarasota, Florida
born in Rochester, Indiana (USA), lives and
works in Sarasota, Florida

Alan Charlton *1948
geboren in Sheffield (England), lebt und
arbeitet in London
born in Sheffield (England), lives and works
in London

Josef Danner *1955
geboren in Amstetten (Österreich), lebt und
arbeitet in Zurndorf und Wien
born in Amstetten (Austria), lives and works
in Zurndorf and Vienna

Niki de Saint Phalle 1930–2002
geboren in Neuilly-sur-Seine (Frankreich), lebte
und arbeitete in San Diego, Kalifornien (USA),
gestorben in San Diego
born in Neuilly-sur-Seine (France), lived, worked
and died in San Diego, California (USA)

Gérard Deschamps *1937
geboren in Lyon (Frankreich), lebt und arbeitet
in La Châtre
born in Lyon (France), lives and works in
La Châtre

Erik Dietman 1937–2005
geboren in Jönköping (Schweden), lebte und
arbeitete in Paris (Frankreich), gestorben in Paris
born in Jönköping (Sweden), lived and worked
in Paris (France), died in Paris

Hans Joachim Dietrich *1938
geboren in Groß-Steinberg (Deutschland), lebt
und arbeitet in Düsseldorf
born in Groß-Steinberg (Germany), lives and
works in Düsseldorf

Jim Dine *1935
geboren in Cincinnati, Ohio (USA), lebt und
arbeitet in New York
born in Cincinnati, Ohio (USA), lives and works
in New York

Noël Dolla *1945
geboren in Nizza (Frankreich), lebt und arbeitet
in Nizza
born in Nice (France), lives and works in Nice

Piero Dorazio 1927–2005
geboren in Rom (Italien), lebte und arbeitete in
Todi, gestorben in Perugia
born in Rome (Italy), lived and worked in Todi,
died in Perugia

Heinrich Dunst *1955
geboren in Hallein (Österreich), lebt und
arbeitet in Wien
born in Hallein (Austria), lives and works in Vienna

Christian Eckart *1959
geboren in Calgary (Kanada), lebt und arbeitet
in Amsterdam (Niederlande) und New York (USA)
born in Calgary (Canada), lives and works in
Amsterdam (Netherlands) and New York (USA)

Christian Eisenberger *1978
geboren in Graz (Österreich), lebt und arbeitet
in Wien
born in Graz (Austria), lives and works in Vienna

Andreas Eriksson *1975
geboren in Björsäter (Schweden), lebt und
arbeitet in Kinnekulle
born in Björsäter (Sweden), lives and works in
Kinnekulle

VALIE EXPORT *1940
geboren in Linz (Österreich), lebt und arbeitet in
Wien
born in Linz (Austria), lives and works in Vienna

Helmut Federle *1944
geboren in Solothurn (Schweiz), lebt und
arbeitet in Düsseldorf (Deutschland)
born in Solothurn (Switzerland), lives and works
in Düsseldorf (Germany)

Thomas Feuerstein *1968
geboren in Innsbruck (Österreich), lebt und
arbeitet in Wien
born in Innsbruck (Austria), lives and works in
Vienna

Dan Flavin 1933–1996
geboren in New York (USA), lebte und arbeitete
in New York, gestorben in Riverhead, New York
born in New York (USA), lived and worked in
New York, died in Riverhead, New York state

Tone Fink *1944
geboren in Schwarzenberg (Österreich), lebt
und arbeitet in Wien und Fußach
born in Schwarzenberg (Austria), lives and
works in Vienna and Fussach

Norbert Fleischmann *1951
geboren in Wien (Österreich), lebt und arbeitet
in Eisengraberamt
born in Vienna (Austria), lives and works in
Eisengraberamt

Helen Frankenthaler *1938
geboren in New York (USA), lebt und arbeitet
in New York
born in New York (USA), lives and works in
New York

Bernard Frize *1949
geboren in Saint-Mandé (Frankreich), lebt und
arbeitet in Paris
born in Saint-Mandé (France), lives and works
in Paris

Adolf Frohner 1934–2007
geboren in Großinzersdorf (Österreich), lebte
und arbeitete in Wien, gestorben in Wien
born in Großinzersdorf (Austria), lived, worked
and died in Vienna,

Jakob Gasteiger *1953
geboren in Salzburg (Österreich), lebt und
arbeitet in Wien
born in Salzburg (Austria), lives and works in
Vienna

Hermann Glöckner 1889–1987
geboren in Cotta/Dresden (Deutschland), lebte
und arbeitete in Dresden und Berlin, gestorben
in Berlin
born in Dresden (Germany), lived and worked in
Dresden and Berlin, died in Berlin

Roland Goeschl *1932
geboren in Salzburg (Österreich), lebt und
arbeitet in Wien
born in Salzburg (Austria), lives and works in
Vienna

Zbigniew Gostomski *1932
geboren in Bydgoszcz/Pomerania (Polen), lebt
und arbeitet in Warschau
born in Bydgoszcz/Pomerania (Poland), lives
and works in Warsaw

Gotthard Graubner *1930
geboren in Erlbach (Deutschland), lebt und
arbeitet in Düsseldorf, und auf der Museums-
insel Hombroich in Neuss-Holzheim
born in Erlbach (Germany), lives and works
in Düsseldorf and on the museum island
Hombroich in Neuss

Peter Halley *1953
geboren in New York (USA), lebt und arbeitet
in New York
born in New York (USA), lives and works in
New York

Geoffrey Hendricks *1931
geboren in Littleton, New Hampshire (USA),
lebt und arbeitet in New York und Cape Breton
Island, Nova Scotia (Kanada)
born in Littleton, New Hampshire (USA), lives
and works in New York and Cape Breton Island,
Nova Scotia (Canada)

Christian Hutzinger *1966
geboren in Wien (Österreich), lebt und arbeitet
in Wien
born in Vienna (Austria), lives and works in
Vienna

Thomas Jocher *1961
geboren in Saalfelden (Österreich), lebt und
arbeitet in Berlin (Deutschland)
born in Saalfelden (Austria), lives and works in
Berlin (Germany)

Jasper Johns *1930
geboren in Augusta, Georgia (USA), lebt und
arbeitet in New York und in Edisto Beach, South
Carolina
born in Augusta, Georgia (USA), lives and works
in New York and Edisto Beach, South Carolina

György Jovánovics *1939
geboren in Budapest (Ungarn), lebt und arbeitet
in Budapest
born in Budapest (Hungary), lives and works in
Budapest

Donald Judd 1928–1994
geboren in Excelsior Springs, Missouri (USA),
lebte und arbeitete in Marfa, Texas, gestorben
in New York
born in Excelsior Springs, Missouri (USA), lived
and worked in Marfa, Texas, died in New York

Thomas Kaminsky *1945
geboren in Dresden (Deutschland), lebt und
arbeitet in Wien (Österreich)
born in Dresden (Germany), lives and works in
Vienna (Austria)

Michael Kienzer *1962
geboren in Steyr (Österreich), lebt und arbeitet
in Wien
born in Steyr (Austria), lives and works in Vienna

Friedrich Kiesler 1890–1965
geboren in Czernowitz/Bukowina (Ukraine),
lebte und arbeitete in New York (USA),
gestorben 1965 in New York
born in Czernowitz/Bukovina (Ukraine), lived,
worked and died in New York (USA)

Yves Klein 1928–1962
geboren in Nizza (Frankreich), lebte und
arbeitete in Paris, gestorben in Paris
born in Nice (France), lived, worked and died
in Paris

Imi Knoebel *1940
geboren in Dessau (Deutschland), lebt und
arbeitet in Düsseldorf
born in Dessau (Germany), lives and works
in Düsseldorf

Stanislav Kolíbal *1925
geboren in Orlová (Tschechien), lebt und
arbeitet in Prag
born in Orlová (Czech Republic), lives and
works in Prague

Dezsö Korniss 1908–1984
geboren in Bistrita (Rumänien), lebte und
arbeitete in Budapest (Ungarn), gestorben
in Budapest
born in Bistrita (Romania), lived, worked and
died in Budapest (Hungary)

Jirí Kovanda *1953
geboren in Prag (Tschechien), lebt und arbeitet
in Prag
born in Prague (Czech Republic), lives and
works in Prague

Bertrand Lavier *1949
geboren in Châtillon/Seine (Frankreich), lebt
und arbeitet in Paris und Aignay-le-Duc
born in Châtillon, Seine (France), lives and
works in Paris and Aignay-le-Duc

Morris Louis 1912–1962
geboren in Baltimore, Maryland (USA), lebte und arbeitete Washington D.C., gestorben in Washington D.C.
born in Baltimore, Maryland (USA), lived, worked and died in Washington D.C.

Roy Lichtenstein *1923–1997
geboren in New York (USA), lebte und arbeitete in New York, gestorben in New York
born in New York (USA), lived, worked and died in New York

Peter Lowe *1938
geboren in London (England), lebt und arbeitet in London
born in London (England), lives and works in London

Karel Malich *1924
geboren in Holice (Tschechien), lebt und arbeitet in Prag
born in Holice (Czech Republic), lives and works in Prague

Robert Mangold *1937
geboren in North Tonawanda, New York (USA), lebt und arbeitet in New York
born in North Tonawanda, New York (USA), lives and works in New York

Brice Marden *1938
geboren in Bronxville, New York (USA), lebt und arbeitet in New York
born in Bronxville, New York (USA), lives and works in New York

Joseph Marioni *1943
geboren in Cincinnati, Ohio (USA), lebt und arbeitet in New York
born in Cincinnati, Ohio (USA), lives and works in New York

Dóra Maurer *1937
geboren in Budapest (Ungarn), lebt und arbeitet in Budapest und Wien (Österreich)
born in Budapest (Hungary), lives and works in Budapest and Vienna (Austria)

Francois Morellet *1926
geboren in Cholet (Frankreich), lebt und arbeitet in Cholet und Paris
born in Cholet (France), lives and works in Cholet and Paris

Robert Morris *1931
geboren in Kansas City, Missouri (USA), lebt und arbeitet in New York
born in Kansas City, Missouri (USA), lives and works in New York

Otto Muehl *1925
geboren in Grodnau (Österreich), lebt und arbeitet in Faro (Portugal)
born in Grodnau (Austria), lives and works in Faro (Portugal)

Hermann Nitsch *1938
geboren in Wien (Österreich), lebt und arbeitet in Prinzendorf
born in Vienna (Austria), lives and works in Prinzendorf

Kenneth Noland 1924–2010
geboren in Asheville, North Carolina (USA), lebte und arbeitete in Washington D.C., New York und Port Clyde, Maine, gestorben in Port Clyde
born in Asheville, North Carolina (USA), lived and worked in Washington D.C., New York and Port Clyde, Maine, died in Port Clyde

Oswald Oberhuber *1931
geboren in Meran (Italien), lebt und arbeitet in Wien (Österreich)
born in Meran (Italy), lives and works in Vienna (Austria)

Walter Obholzer 1953–2008
geboren in Ebbs (Österreich), lebte und arbeitete in Wien, gestorben in Wien
born in Ebbs (Austria), lived and worked in Vienna, died in Vienna

Jules Olitski 1922–2007
geboren in Gomel (Russland), lebte und arbeitete in New Hampshire (USA) und Florida, gestorben in New York
born in Gomel (Russia), lived and worked in New Hampshire (USA) and Florida, died in New York

Yoko Ono *1933
geboren in Tokio (Japan), lebt und arbeitet in New York (USA)
born in Tokyo (Japan), lives and works in New York (USA)

Claudio Parmiggiani *1943
geboren in Luzzara (Italien), lebt und arbeitet in Turin
born in Luzzara (Italy), lives and works in Turin

Pino Pascali 1935–1968
geboren in Bari (Italien), lebte und arbeitete in Rom, gestorben in Rom
born in Bari (Italy), lived, worked and died in Rome

Jackson Pollock 1912–1956
geboren in Cody, Wyoming (USA), lebte und arbeitete in New York, gestorben in East Hampton, New York
born in Cody, Wyoming (USA), lived and worked in New York, died in East Hampton, New York state

Larry Poons *1937
geboren in Ogibuko, Tokio (Japan), lebt und arbeitet in New York (USA)
born in Ogibuko, Tokyo (Japan), lives and works in New York (USA)

Arnulf Rainer *1929
geboren in Baden (Österreich), lebt und arbeitet in Wien, Enzenkirchen, Passau (Deutschland) und Teneriffa (Spanien)
born in Baden (Austria), lives and works in Vienna, Enzenkirchen, Passau (Germany) and Tenerife (Spain)

Robert Rauschenberg 1925–2008
geboren in Port Arthur, Texas (USA), lebte und arbeitete in New York und Captiva Island, Florida, gestorben in Captiva Island
born in Port Arthur, Texas (USA), lived and worked in New York and on Captiva Island, Florida, died on Captiva Island

Martial Raysse *1936
geboren in Golfe Juan (Frankreich), lebt und arbeitet in Issignac
born in Golfe Juan (France), lives and works in Issignac

David Reed *1946
geboren in San Diego, Kalifornien (USA), lebt und arbeitet in New York
born in San Diego, California (USA), lives and works in New York

Thomas Reinhold *1953
geboren in Wien (Österreich), lebt und arbeitet in Wien
born in Vienna (Austria), lives and works in Vienna

Andreas Reiter Raabe *1960
geboren in Raab (Österreich), lebt und arbeitet in Wien und Berlin (Deutschland)
born in Raab (Austria), lives and works in Vienna and Berlin (Germany)

Gerhard Richter *1932
geboren in Dresden (Deutschland), lebt und arbeitet in Köln
born in Dresden (Germany), lives and works in Cologne

Gerwald Rockenschaub *1952
geboren in Linz (Österreich), lebt und arbeitet in Berlin (Deutschland)
born in Linz (Austria), lives and works in Berlin (Germany)

Dieter Roth *1930–1998
geboren in Hannover (Deutschland), lebte und arbeitete in Basel (Schweiz), Reykjavik (Island) und Deutschland, gestorben in Basel
born in Hannover (Germany), lived and worked in Basel (Switzerland), Reykjavik (Iceland) and Germany, died in Basel

Robert Ryman *1930
geboren in Nashville, Tennessee (USA), lebt und arbeitet in New York
born in Nashville, Tennessee (USA), lives and works in New York

Karin Sander *1957
geboren in Bensberg (Deutschland), lebt und arbeitet in Stuttgart und Berlin
born in Bensberg (Germany), lives and works in Stuttgart and Berlin

Hubert Scheibl *1952
geboren in Gmunden (Österreich), lebt und arbeitet in Wien
born in Gmunden (Austria), lives and works in Vienna

Adrian Schiess *1959
geboren Zürich (Schweiz), lebt und arbeitet
in Mouans-Sartoux (Frankreich)
born in Zurich (Switzerland), lives and works
in Mouans-Sartoux (France)

Alfons Schilling *1934
geboren in Basel (Schweiz), lebt und arbeitet
in Wien (Österreich)
born in Basel (Switzerland), lives and works
in Vienna (Austria)

Florian Schmidt *1980
geboren in Raabs an der Thaya (Österreich), lebt
und arbeitet in Wien und Berlin (Deutschland)
born in Raabs an der Thaya (Austria), lives and
works in Vienna and Berlin (Germany)

Bernard Schultze 1915–2005
geboren in Schneidemühl/Westpreußen (Polen),
lebte und arbeitete in Köln (Deutschland),
gestorben in Köln
born in Schneidemühl/West Prussia (Poland),
lived, worked and died in Cologne (Germany)

Rudolf Schwarzkogler 1940–1969
geboren in Wien (Österreich), lebte und arbeitete
in Wien, gestorben in Wien
born in Vienna (Austria), lived, worked and died
in Vienna

Shozo Shimamoto *1928
geboren in Osaka (Japan), lebt und arbeitet
in Nishinomiya
born in Osaka (Japan), lives and works in
Nishinomiya

Richard Serra *1939
geboren in San Francisco (USA), lebt und arbeitet
in New York
born in San Francisco (USA), lives and works in
New York

Pierre Soulages *1919
geboren in Rodez (Frankreich), lebt und arbeitet
in Paris
born in Rodez (France), lives and works in Paris

Daniel Spoerri *1930
geboren in Galaţi (Rumänien), lebt und arbeitet
in Wien (Österreich)
born in Galaţi (Romania), lives and works in
Vienna (Austria)

Rudi Stanzel *1958
geboren in Linz (Österreich), lebt und arbeitet
in Wien
born in Linz (Austria), lives and works in Vienna

Henryk Stażewski 1894–1988
geboren in Warschau (Polen), lebte und arbeitete
in Warschau, gestorben in Warschau
born in Warsaw (Poland), lived, worked and
died in Warsaw

Frank Stella *1936
geboren in Malden, Massachusetts (USA), lebt
und arbeitet in New York
born in Malden, Massachusetts (USA), lives and
works in New York

Rudolf Stingel * 1956
geboren in Meran (Italien), lebt und arbeitet in
New York (USA)
born in Merano (Italy), lives and works in New
York (USA)

Christian Stock *1961
geboren in Tux (Österreich), lebt und arbeitet
in Wien
born in Tux (Austria), lives and works in Vienna

Esther Stocker *1974
geboren in Schlanders (Italien), lebt und
arbeitet in Wien (Österreich)
born in Schlanders (Italy), lives and works in
Vienna (Austria)

Jessica Stockholder *1959
geboren in Seattle, Washington (USA), lebt und
arbeitet in New Haven, Connecticut
born in Seattle, Washington (USA), lives and
works in New Haven, Connecticut

Jorrit Tornquist *1938
geboren in Graz (Österreich), lebt und arbeitet
in Bergamo (Italien)
born in Graz (Austria), lives and works in
Bergamo (Italy)

Niele Toroni * 1937
geboren in Muralto (Schweiz), lebt und arbeitet
in Paris (Frankreich)
born in Muralto (Switzerland), lives and works
in Paris (France)

Rosemarie Trockel *1952
geboren in Schwerte (Deutschland), lebt und
arbeitet in Köln
born in Schwerte (Germany), lives and works
in Cologne

Cy Twombly *1928
geboren in Lexington, Virginia (USA), lebt und
arbeitet in Rom (Italien)
born in Lexington, Virginia (USA), lives and
works in Rome (Italy)

Lee Ufan *1936
geboren in Kyongnam (Korea), lebt und arbeitet
in Paris (Frankreich) und Tokio (Japan)
born in Kyongnam (Korea), lives and works in
Paris (France) and Tokyo (Japan)

Günter Umberg *1942
geboren in Bonn (Deutschland), lebt und arbeitet
in Köln, Freiburg und Corberon (Frankreich)
born in Bonn (Germany), lives and works in
Cologne, Freiburg and Corberon (France)

Walter Vopava *1948
geboren in Wien (Österreich), lebt und arbeitet
in Wien und Berlin (Deutschland)
born in Vienna (Austria), lives and works in
Vienna and Berlin (Germany)

Wolf Vostell 1932–1998
geboren in Leverkusen (Deutschland), lebte
und arbeitete in Paris (Frankreich), Berlin und
Andalusien (Spanien), gestorben in Berlin
born in Leverkusen (Germany), lived and
worked in Paris (France), Berlin and Andalusia
(Spain), died in Berlin

Andy Warhol 1927–1987
geboren in Pittsburgh, Pennsylvania (USA),
lebte und arbeitete in New York, gestorben in
New York
born in Pittsburgh, Pennsylvania (USA), lived,
worked and died in New York

Max Weiler 1910–2001
geboren in Absam bei Hall (Österreich), lebte
und arbeitete in Wien und Innsbruck, gestorben
in Wien
born in Absam near Hall (Austria), lived and
worked in Vienna and Innsbruck, died in Vienna

Lois Weinberger *1947
geboren in Stams (Österreich), lebt und arbeitet
in Wien
born in Stams (Austria), lives and works in Vienna

Tom Wesselmann 1931–2004
geboren in Cincinnati, Ohio (USA), lebte und
arbeitete in New York, gestorben in New York
born in Cincinnati, Ohio (USA), lived, worked
and died in New York

Franz West * 1947
geboren in Wien (Österreich), lebt und arbeitet
in Wien
born in Vienna (Austria), lives and works in Vienna

Ryszard Winiarski *1936
geboren in Lwów (Polen), lebt und arbeitet in
Warschau
born 1936 in Lwów (Poland), lives and works in
Warsaw

Klaus Dieter Zimmer *1954
geboren in Bergneustadt (Deutschland), lebt
und arbeitet in Wien (Österreich)
born in Bergneustadt (Germany), lives and
works in Vienna (Austria)

Otto Zitko *1959
geboren in Linz (Österreich), lebt und arbeitet
in Wien
born in Linz (Austria), lives and works in Vienna

Heimo Zobernig *1958
geboren in Mauthen (Österreich), lebt und
arbeitet in Wien
born in Mauthen (Austria), lives and works in
Vienna

Leo Zogmayer *1949
geboren in Krems (Österreich), lebt und arbeitet
in Wien und Krems
born in Krems (Austria), lives and works in
Vienna and Krems

Christina Zurfluh *
geboren in Goldau (Schweiz), lebt und arbeitet
in Wien
born in Goldau (Switzerland), lives and works
in Vienna (Austria)

Künstlerverzeichnis / Index of Artists

Biografien der Autoren / Authors' Biographies

Christoph Bruckner

geboren 1975 in Amstetten (Österreich); Studium an der Akademie der bildenden Künste Wien. 2006 Förderungspreis der Stadt Wien für bildende Kunst. Veröffentlichung literarischer und kunsttheoretischer Texte in Zeitschriften und Katalogen. Lebt und arbeitet als Kunsttheoretiker, Schriftsteller und bildender Künstler in Wien.

Born in 1975 in Amstetten in Austria, he studied at the Academy of Fine Arts Vienna. In 2006 he received a fine arts award for young artists from the city of Vienna. Bruckner has published fictional work, as well as writing on art theory. He is an art theorist, writer, and fine artist, and lives and works in Vienna.

Rainer Fuchs

geboren 1959 in Judenburg (Österreich); Studium der Kunstgeschichte, Geschichte und Philosophie in Graz und Wien. Seit 1991 stellvertretender Direktor und Ausstellungsleiter des MUMOK; Ausstellungen (Auswahl): *Self Construction* (1996), *Félix González-Torres* (1998), *Lois Weinberger* (1999), *Öffentliche Rituale. Kunst/Videos aus Polen* (2003), *Christian Hutzinger* (2004), *John Baldessari* (2005), *Keren Cytter* (2007), *Mind Expanders* (2008), *Peter Kogler* (2008), *Brigitte Kowanz* (2010). Publikationen zur Moderne und Gegenwartskunst. Lebt und arbeitet in Wien.

Born in 1959 in Judenburg in Austria, he studied art history and philosophy in Graz and Vienna. Fuchs has been deputy director and head of exhibitions at MUMOK since 1991. Selected exhibitions: *Self Construction* (1996), *Félix González-Torres* (1998), *Lois Weinberger* (1999), *Public Rituals: Art/Videos from Poland* (2003), *Christian Hutzinger* (2004), *John Baldessari* (2005), *Keren Cytter* (2007), *Mind Expanders* (2008), *Peter Kogler* (2008), *Brigitte Kowanz* (2010). Fuchs has published widely on modernist and contemporary art. He lives and works in Vienna.

Ines Gebetsroither

geboren 1974 in Gmunden (Österreich); Studium der Kunstgeschichte, Germanistik sowie Kulturmanagementstudium in Wien. Bis 2008 Redakteurin beim Kunstmagazin *Spike. Art Quarterly*. Freiberufliche Autorin, Kritikerin und Lektorin. Lebt und arbeitet in Wien.

Born in 1974 in Gmunden in Austria, she studied art history, German studies and cultural management in Vienna. Gebetsroither worked on the editorial staff of the art magazine *Spike. Art Quarterly* up to 2008. She is a freelance writer, critic, and editor, and lives and works in Vienna.

Gabriel Hubmann

geboren 1987 in Braunau am Inn (Österreich); seit 2005 Studium der Kunstgeschichte und Philosophie in Wien. Texte zu moderner und zeitgenössischer Kunst sowie Rezensionen zu kunsthistorischer/-theoretischer Fachliteratur im *Journal für Kunstgeschichte. Die internationale Rezensionszeitschrift*. Mitinitiator des Projekts *Studierendengespräche* am Wiener Institut für Kunstgeschichte. Lebt und arbeitet in Wien.

Born in 1987 in Braunau am Inn in Austria, he has been studying art history and philosophy in Vienna since 2005. He has written on modern and contemporary art, as well as reviews of specialist works on art history and theory in the *Journal für Kunstgeschichte. Die internationale Rezensionszeitschrift*. Hubmann is a co-founder of the *Studierendengespräche* project at the University of Vienna's Institute for Art History. He lives and works in Vienna.

Edelbert Köb

geboren 1942 in Bregenz (Österreich); Studium der Malerei und Grafik, Kunsterziehung und Geschichte an der Akademie der bildenden Künste Wien. Von 1965 bis 1992 künstlerische Tätigkeit; Bildhauerei, Arbeiten im Grenzbereich von Kunst und Design. Von 1966 bis 1974 Assistent an der Technischen Universität Wien, Architekturfakultät. Seit 1974 Professor an der Akademie der bildenden Künste Wien; dort von 1985 bis 1995 und von 1998 bis 2000 Prorektor. Von 1982 bis 1991 Präsident der Wiener Secession. Von 1990 bis 2000 Leiter des Kunsthauses Bregenz. Seit 2002 Direktor des MUMOK. Kurator nationaler und internationaler Ausstellungen. Zahlreiche Publikationen zu Kunst und Architektur. Lebt und arbeitet in Wien.

Born in 1942 in Bregenz in Austria, he studied painting and graphic design, art education and history at the Academy of Fine Arts in Vienna. From 1965 to 1992, Köb worked in an artistic capacity, both as a sculptor and at the interface between art and design. From 1966 to 1974 he was an assistant lecturer in the architectural faculty of the Vienna University of Technology. Köb has been professor at the Academy of Fine Arts Vienna since 1974, acting as vice-president from 1985 to 1995 and 1998 to 2000. He was president of the Vienna Secession from 1982 to 1991 and headed Bregenz Kunsthaus from 1990 to 2000. In 2002, Köb became the director of MUMOK. He is the curator of national and international exhibitions and has published widely on art and architecture. Köb lives and works in Vienna.

Impressum / Colophon

Museum Moderner Kunst Stiftung Ludwig Wien
Direktor / Director: Edelbert Köb

Ausstellung / Exhibition

Kuratoren / Curators: Rainer Fuchs, Edelbert Köb
Produktionsleitung / Head of Production: Tina Lipsky
Sammlung / Collection: Sophie Haaser, Alexandra Pinter
Restauratorische Betreuung / Conservation: Brigitte Boll,
Christina Hierl, Charlotte Karl, Eva Stimm
Kunstvermittlungsprogramm / Art education program:
Claudia Ehgartner, Johanna Gudden, Jörg Wolfert & Team
Presse / Press: Eva Engelberger, Barbara Hammerschmied
Marketing + Kommunikation / Marketing + communication:
Wolfgang Schreiner, Michaela Zach
Events: Katharina Radmacher, Elisabeth Zelger
Fundraising: Christina Hardegg, Bärbel Holaus
Ausstellungsdesign / Exhibition design: Rainer Fuchs, Edelbert Köb
Ausstellungsaufbau / Exhibition installation: Olli Aigner & Team,
MUMOK-Team

Dank an alle Künstler, Leihgeber und Mitarbeiter, die zur Planung
und Realisierung der Ausstellung beigetragen haben.
Thanks to all artists, lenders and staff who have contributed to the
planning and realization of the exhibition.

Publikation / Publication

Diese Publikation erscheint anlässlich der Ausstellung *Malerei:
Prozess und Expansion. Von den 1950er-Jahren bis heute* im
Museum Moderner Kunst Stiftung Ludwig Wien (9. Juli 2010–
3. Oktober 2010) / This catalogue has been published on the
occasion of the exhibition *Painting: Process and Expansion.
From the 1950s to the Present Day* at the Museum Moderner
Kunst Stiftung Ludwig Wien (July 9th 2010–October 3rd 2010)

Herausgegeben von / Edited by
Museum Moderner Kunst Stiftung Ludwig Wien
Museumsplatz 1
A–1070 Wien
T: +43 1 52500
F: +43 1 52500 1300
I: www.mumok.at

Redaktion / Editors: Agnes Falkner, Rainer Fuchs, Sophie Haaser,
Anina Huck, Edelbert Köb
Produktionsleitung / Head of production: Agnes Falkner
Gestaltung / Graphic design: Susi Klocker, Wien / Vienna
Deutsches Lektorat / German copy editor: m∞bius
Übersetzungen und englisches Lektorat / Translations
and English copy editing: Tradukas GbR, Julie Gregson,
Eva-Raphaela Jaksch, Mark Willard
Texte / Texts: Christoph Bruckner, Rainer Fuchs,
Ines Gebetsroither, Gabriel Hubmann, Edelbert Köb
Lithografie / Lithograph: Markus Wörgötter, Wien / Vienna
Druck / Printed by: Rema*print*, Wien / Vienna
Schrift / Typeface: Minion, DTLArgo
Papier / Paper: GardaMattArt 170 g
Auflage / Print run: 2.500

Auf geschlechtsneutrale Formulierungen wurde verzichtet;
gemeint sind jedoch alle Geschlechter.

Bibliografische Information der Deutschen Nationalbibliothek
Die Deutsche Nationalbibliothek verzeichnet diese Publikation in der Deutschen Nationalbibliografie; detaillierte bibliografische Daten sind im Internet über http://dnb.ddb.de abrufbar.

Bibliographic information published by Die Deutsche Nationalbibliothek
Die Deutsche Nationalbibliothek lists this publication in the Deutsche Nationalbibliografie; detailed bibliographic data is available in the Internet at http://dnb.ddb.de

Bildnachweis / Photo credits
Cover: John Baldessari, *Six Colourful Inside Jobs*, 1977
16-mm-Film, Farbe / 16mm film, color, 32:53 min
Filmstill / Film still
© John Baldessari

Falls nicht anders angegeben / If not indicated otherwise
© 2010 MUMOK, Museum Moderner Kunst Stiftung Ludwig Wien / Lena Deinhardstein, Sophie Pölzl, Lisa Rastl, Rudolf Schmied

© 2010 VBK, Wien: Marc Adrian, Hartmut Böhm, Daniel Buren, Michael Buthe, César, John Chamberlain, Alan Charlton, Niki de Saint Phalle, Gérard Deschamps, Erik Dietman, Jim Dine, Noël Dolla, Piero Dorazio, Andreas Eriksson, VALIE EXPORT, Helmut Federle, Thomas Feuerstein, Dan Flavin, Tone Fink, Helen Frankenthaler, Bernard Frize, Jakob Gasteiger, Hermann Glöckner, Christian Hutzinger, Jasper Johns, György Jovánovics, Donald Judd, Thomas Kaminsky, Yves Klein, Imi Knoebel, Stanislav Kolíbal, Dezsö Korniss, Bertrand Lavier, Roy Karel Malich, Robert Mangold, Brice Marden, Francois Morellet, Robert Morris, Otto Muehl, Hermann Nitsch, Kenneth Noland, Jules Olitski, Jackson Pollock, Larry Poons, Robert Rauschenberg, Martial Raysse, David Reed, Gerhard Richter, Robert Ryman, Karin Sander, Bernard Schultze, Pierre Soulages, Daniel Spoerri, Frank Stella, Rosemarie Trockel, Wolf Vostell, Tom Wesselmann, Heimo Zobernig

Roy Lichtenstein © Estate of Roy Lichtenstein/VBK, Wien 2010 (167)
Andy Warhol © The Andy Warhol Foundation for the Visual Arts.Inc./VBK, Wien 2010 (34)

© Archiv Gerwald Rockenschaub, Berlin (165); Digital image © 2010, The Museum of Modern Art, New York/Scala, Florence (34)
© Geoffrey Clements / CORBIS (30); Collection of De Pont Museum of Contemporary Art (35); © Louisiana Museum of Modern Art (30)

Fotografien / Photographs
Jorit Aust: 66, 90, 98, 99, 108, 113, 116, 117, 190, 193, 200, 201, 207, 209, 210, 241, 242, 244, 247, 258, 261, 262, 263, 266, 278–299; David Brandt, Dresden-Berlin (264); © Collection Centre Pompidou, Dist. RMN / Philippe Migeat (143); Peter Cox (35); Courtesy des Künstlers und / The artist and the Foksal Gallery, Warsaw (153); Michael Herling / Aline Gwose © N.C.A.F. – Donation Niki de Saint Phalle – Sprengel Museum Hannover (42); Ludwig Hoffenreich (44, 45, 149, 183); Ugo Mulas © Ugo Mulas Heirs. All rights reserved (137); Hans Namuth, Courtesy Center for Creative Photography © Hans Namuth Estate (28); Österreichische Friedrich und Lillian Kiesler-Privatstiftung, Austrian Frederick and Lillian Kiesler Private Foundation, 2010 (142); Yves Klein Archives (142, 148); © Alfons Schilling (42)

Erschienen im / Published by
Verlag der Buchhandlung Walther König, Köln
Ehrenstr. 4, 50672 Köln
T: +49 (0) 221 20 596 53
F: +49 (0) 221 20 596 60
E: verlag@buchhandlung-walther-koenig.de

ISBN 978-3-86560-832-1
(Verlag der Buchhandlung Walther König)

ISBN 978-3-902490-62-9
(MUMOK)

Printed in Austria

Vertrieb / Distribution

Schweiz / Switzerland
AVA Verlagsauslieferungen AG
Centralweg 16, Postfach 27
CH-8910 Affoltern a.A.
T: +41 (0) 1 762 42 00
F: +41 (0) 1 762 42 10
E: buch2000@ava.ch

Großbritannien & Irland / UK & Eire
Cornerhouse Publications
70 Oxford Street
GB-Manchester M1 5NH
T: +44 (0) 161 200 15 03
F: +44 (0) 161 200 15 04
E: publications@cornerhouse.org

Außerhalb Europas / Outside Europe
D.A.P. / Distributed Art Publishers, Inc.
155 6th Avenue, 2nd Floor
New York, NY 10013
T: +1 (0) 212 627 1999
F: +1 (0) 212 627 9484
www.artbook.com